PRODUCING ANCIENT SCRIPTURE

Producing
Ancient Scripture

Joseph Smith's Translation Projects in the Development of Mormon Christianity

edited by
MICHAEL HUBBARD MACKAY,
MARK ASHURST-MCGEE,
& BRIAN M. HAUGLID

The University of Utah Press | Salt Lake City

The Defiance House Man colophon is a registered trademark of The University of Utah Press. It is based on a four-foot-tall Ancient Puebloan pictograph (late PIII) near Glen Canyon, Utah.

Library of Congress Cataloging-in-Publication Data

Names: MacKay, Michael Hubbard, editor. | Ashurst-McGee, Mark, editor. | Hauglid, Brian M., 1954– editor.
Title: Producing ancient scripture : Joseph Smith's translation projects in the development of Mormon Christianity / edited by Michael Hubbard MacKay, Mark Ashurst-McGee, Brian Hauglid.
Identifiers: LCCN 2019040629 (print) | LCCN 2019040630 (ebook) | ISBN 978-1-60781-743-7 (hardcover) | ISBN 9781607817383 (paperback) | ISBN 9781607817390 (ebook)
Subjects: LCSH: Smith, Joseph, Jr., 1805–1844. | Book of Mormon—Authorship.
Classification: LCC BX8627 (print) | LCC BX8627 (ebook) | DDC 289.3/22—dc23
LC record available at https://lccn.loc.gov/2019040629
LC ebook record available at https://lccn.loc.gov/2019040630

Errata and further information on this and other titles available online at UofUpress.com

Printed and bound in the United States of America.

CONTENTS

FIGURES

TABLES

MORMON CANON OF SCRIPTURE

The Standard Works of the Church of Jesus Christ of Latter-day Saints

THE BIBLE

The Old Testament

Genesis	2 Chronicles	Daniel
Exodus	Ezra	Hosea
Leviticus	Nehemiah	Joel
Numbers	Esther	Amos
Deuteronomy	Job	Obadiah
Joshua	Psalms	Jonah
Judges	Proverbs	Micah
Ruth	Ecclesiastes	Nahum
1 Samuel	Song of Solomon	Habakkuk
2 Samuel	Isaiah	Zephaniah
1 Kings	Jeremiah	Haggai
2 Kings	Lamentations	Zechariah
1 Chronicles	Ezekiel	Malachi

The New Testament

Matthew	Ephesians	Hebrews
Mark	Philippians	James
Luke	Colossians	1 Peter
John	1 Thessalonians	2 Peter
Acts	2 Thessalonians	1 John
Romans	1 Timothy	2 John
1 Corinthians	2 Timothy	3 John
2 Corinthians	Titus	Jude
Galatians	Philemon	Revelation

THE BOOK OF MORMON

Title Page
Testimony of Three Witnesses
Testimony of Eight Witnesses
1 Nephi
2 Nephi
Jacob
Enos
Jarom
Omni
Words of Mormon
Mosiah
Alma
Helaman
3 Nephi
4 Nephi
Mormon
Ether
Moroni

THE DOCTRINE AND COVENANTS

Sections (1–138)
Official Declarations (1–2)

THE PEARL OF GREAT PRICE

Moses
Abraham
Joseph Smith—Matthew
Joseph Smith—History
Articles of Faith

SHORT CITATIONS TO THE JOSEPH SMITH PAPERS

JSP-A1: Matthew J. Grow, Ronald K. Esplin, Mark Ashurst-McGee, Gerrit J. Dirkmaat, and Jeffrey D. Mahas, eds., *Council of Fifty, Minutes, March 1844–January 1846*, vol. 1 of the Administrative Records series of *The Joseph Smith Papers*, ed. Ronald K. Esplin, Matthew J. Grow, and Matthew C. Godfrey (Salt Lake City: Church Historian's Press, 2016).

JSP-D1: Michael Hubbard MacKay, Gerrit J. Dirkmaat, Grant Underwood, Robert J. Woodford, and William G. Hartley, eds., *Documents, Volume 1: July 1828–June 1831*, vol. 1 of the Documents series of *The Joseph Smith Papers*, ed. Dean C. Jessee, Ronald K. Esplin, Richard Lyman Bushman, and Matthew J. Grow (Salt Lake City: Church Historian's Press, 2013).

JSP-D2: Matthew C. Godfrey, Mark Ashurst-McGee, Grant Underwood, Robert J. Woodford, and William G. Hartley, eds., *Documents, Volume 2: July 1831–January 1833*, vol. 2 of the Documents series of *The Joseph Smith Papers*, ed. Dean C. Jessee, Ronald K. Esplin, Richard Lyman Bushman, and Matthew J. Grow (Salt Lake City: Church Historian's Press, 2013).

JSP-D3: Gerrit J. Dirkmaat, Brent M. Rogers, Grant Underwood, Robert J. Woodford, and William G. Hartley, eds., *Documents, Volume 3: February 1833–March 1834*, vol. 3 of the Documents series of *The Joseph Smith Papers*, ed. Ronald K. Esplin and Matthew J. Grow (Salt Lake City: Church Historian's Press, 2014).

JSP-D4: Matthew C. Godfrey, Brenden W. Rensink, Alex D. Smith, Max H Parkin, and Alexander L. Baugh, eds., *Documents, Volume 4: April 1834–September 1835*, vol. 4 of the Documents series of *The Joseph Smith Papers*, ed. Ronald K. Esplin, Matthew J. Grow, and Matthew C. Godfrey (Salt Lake City: Church Historian's Press, 2016).

JSP-D5: Brent M. Rogers, Elizabeth A. Kuehn, Christian K. Heimburger, Max H Parkin, Alexander L. Baugh, and Steven C. Harper, eds., *Documents, Volume 5: October 1835–January 1838*, vol. 5 of the Documents series of *The Joseph Smith*

Papers, ed., Ronald K. Esplin, Matthew J. Grow, and Matthew C. Godfrey (Salt Lake City: Church Historian's Press, 2017).

JSP-D6: Mark Ashurst-McGee, David W. Grua, Elizabeth A. Kuehn, Alexander L. Baugh, and Brenden W. Rensink, eds., *Documents, Volume 6: February 1838–August 1839*, vol. 6 of the Documents series of *The Joseph Smith Papers*, ed. Ronald K. Esplin, Matthew J. Grow, and Matthew C. Godfrey (Salt Lake City: Church Historian's Press, 2017).

JSP-D7: Matthew C. Godfrey, Spencer W. McBride, Alex D. Smith, and Christopher James Blythe, eds., *Documents, Volume 7: September 1839–January 1841*, vol. 7 of the Documents series of *The Joseph Smith Papers*, ed. Ronald K. Esplin, Matthew J. Grow, and Matthew C. Godfrey (Salt Lake City: Church Historian's Press, 2018).

JSP-D8: Brent M. Rogers, Mason K. Allred, Gerrit J. Dirkmaat, and Brett D. Dowdle, eds., *Documents, Volume 8: February–November 1841*, vol. 8 of the Documents series of *The Joseph Smith Papers*, ed. Ronald K. Esplin, Matthew J. Grow, Matthew C. Godfrey, and R. Eric Smith (Salt Lake City: Church Historian's Press, 2019).

JSP-D9: Alex D. Smith, Christian K. Heimburger, Christopher James Blythe, eds., *Documents, Volume 9: December 1841–April 1842*, vol. 9 of the Documents series of *The Joseph Smith Papers*, ed. Matthew C. Godfrey, R. Eric Smith, Matthew J. Grow, and Ronald K. Esplin (Salt Lake City: Church Historian's Press, 2019).

JSP-H1: Karen Lynn Davidson, David J. Whittaker, Mark Ashurst-McGee, and Richard L. Jensen, eds., *Histories, Volume 1: Joseph Smith Histories, 1832–1844*, vol. 1 of the Histories series of *The Joseph Smith Papers*, ed. Dean C. Jessee, Ronald K. Esplin, and Richard Lyman Bushman (Salt Lake City: Church Historian's Press, 2012).

JSP-H2: Karen Lynn Davidson, Richard L. Jensen, and David J. Whittaker, eds., *Histories, Volume 2: Assigned Historical Writings, 1831–1847*, vol. 2 of the Histories series of *The Joseph Smith Papers*, ed. Dean C. Jessee, Ronald K. Esplin, and Richard Lyman Bushman (Salt Lake City: Church Historian's Press, 2012).

JSP-J1: Dean C. Jessee, Mark Ashurst-McGee, and Richard L. Jensen, eds., *Journals, Volume 1: 1832–1839*, vol. 1 of the Journals series of *The Joseph Smith*

Papers, ed. Dean C. Jessee, Ronald K. Esplin, and Richard Lyman Bushman (Salt Lake City: Church Historian's Press, 2008).

JSP-J2: Andrew H. Hedges, Alex D. Smith, and Richard Lloyd Anderson, eds., *Journals, Volume 2: December 1841–April 1843*, vol. 2 of the Journals series of *The Joseph Smith Papers*, ed. Dean C. Jessee, Ronald K. Esplin, and Richard Lyman Bushman (Salt Lake City: Church Historian's Press, 2011).

JSP-J3: Andrew H. Hedges, Alex D. Smith, and Brent M. Rogers, eds., *Journals, Volume 3: May 1843–June 1844*, vol. 3 of the Journals series of *The Joseph Smith Papers*, ed. Ronald K. Esplin and Matthew J. Grow (Salt Lake City: Church Historian's Press, 2015).

JSP-R1: Robin Scott Jensen, Robert J. Woodford, and Steven C. Harper, eds., *Revelations and Translations, Volume 1: Manuscript Revelation Books*, facsimile edition, vol. 1 of the Revelations and Translations series of *The Joseph Smith Papers*, ed. Dean C. Jessee, Ronald K. Esplin, and Richard Lyman Bushman (Salt Lake City: Church Historian's Press, 2009).

JSP-R2: Robin Scott Jensen, Richard E. Turley Jr., and Riley M. Lorimer, eds., *Revelations and Translations, Volume 2: Published Revelations*, vol. 2 of the Revelations and Translations series of *The Joseph Smith Papers*, ed. Dean C. Jessee, Ronald K. Esplin, and Richard Lyman Bushman (Salt Lake City: Church Historian's Press, 2011).

JSP-R3: Royal Skousen and Robin Scott Jensen, eds., *Revelations and Translations, Volume 3: Printer's Manuscript of the Book of Mormon*, facsimile edition, vol. 3 of the Revelations and Translations series of *The Joseph Smith Papers*, ed. Ronald K. Esplin and Matthew J. Grow (Salt Lake City: Church Historian's Press, 2015).

JSP-R4: Robin Scott Jensen and Brian M. Hauglid, eds., *Revelations and Translations, Volume 4: Book of Abraham and Related Manuscripts*, vol. 4 of the Revelations and Translations series of *The Joseph Smith Papers*, ed. Ronald K. Esplin, Matthew J. Grow, Matthew C. Godfrey, and R. Eric Smith (Salt Lake City: Church Historian's Press, 2018).

The Joseph Smith Papers: Online edition of *The Joseph Smith Papers* (accessible at www.josephsmithpapers.org).

1

Introduction

MICHAEL HUBBARD MACKAY, MARK ASHURST-MCGEE,
AND BRIAN M. HAUGLID

When Joseph Smith was gunned down by vigilantes in 1844, it may not have surprised some of his early American contemporaries—due in part to his audacious and confrontational reimagining of the cultural, political, and religious landscape of his day. Smith had presented himself as a prophet, a man who claimed to speak for God as had Moses and Isaiah. Furthermore, he claimed to have recovered lost books of ancient prophetic writings, which he had "translated" by "the gift and power of God." These new works of scripture prophesied of a promised land in North America. Smith and his missionaries advocated a geographical withdrawal from worldly society, migration to a center of gathering, and joining with fellow believers to build a holy city comparable to ancient Jerusalem. Most of Smith's contemporaries considered him a false prophet or conniving imposter, or both. But thousands responded to his message, uprooted themselves from family farms and ancestral homelands, and gathered to the Mormon Zion.

Beyond being foundational to the Mormon brand of Christianity, the revelations and translations that Joseph Smith produced put forth their own prophetic critique of American society. Through scriptural creations, Smith exposed the continuum between democracy and mob violence; condemned the contentious nature of denominational proliferation, class stratification, and party formation; and critiqued various other aspects of antebellum culture. American Protestants reacted bitterly to Mormon Christianity's stinging indictments, heretical heterodoxy, and successful proselytizing. Over the course of the nineteenth century, they defined themselves in part by using

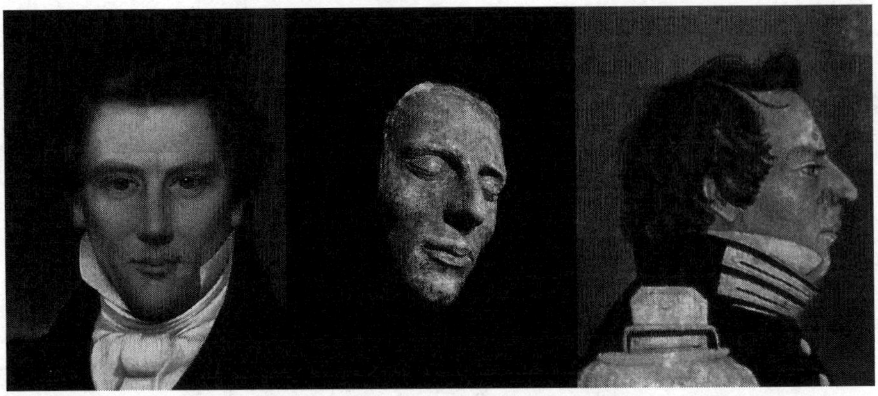

FIGURE 1.1. Joseph Smith. Three contemporaneous likenesses of Joseph Smith, founding prophet of the Church of Jesus Christ of Latter-day Saints. Left: Portrait of Joseph Smith by David Rogers, 1842. Community of Christ Archives, Independence, MO; photograph by Ronald Read. Center: Death mask of Joseph Smith. Church History Museum, Salt Lake City, UT; photograph by Alex D. Smith. Right: Profile of Joseph Smith by Sutcliffe Maudsley, circa 1842. Church History Museum, Salt Lake City; photograph by Ronald Read.

Mormonism as a foil.[1] Protestants accused Smith of popery and even associated Mormonism with a more ancient enemy, Islam. Smith was frequently branded as the American Muhammad.[2]

If Smith were the American Muhammad, the Book of Mormon was the American Qur'an.[3] Smith's church was built on the foundation of the Book of Mormon, a new book of scripture, similar in structure and style to the Bible. And his movement was guided further by other translations and revelations. His scriptural library is impressive in both volume and scope. The Book of Mormon, translated in 1829, chronicled a thousand years of sacred history regarding Christian prophets and peoples in ancient America. Smith claimed that an angel had revealed to him the location of an ancient set of gold plates, upon which a sacred record was engraved, and that the Book of Mormon was a divinely inspired translation of those plates. The church accepted it as a second book of scripture.

1. See R. Laurence Moore, "How to Become a People: The Mormon Scenario," chap. 1 in *Religious Outsiders and the Making of Americans* (Oxford and New York: Oxford University Press, 1986); J. Spencer Fluhman, *"A Peculiar People": Anti-Mormonism and the Making of Religion in Nineteenth-Century America* (Chapel Hill: University of North Carolina Press, 2012); Sarah Barringer Gordon, *The Mormon Question: Polygamy and Constitutional Conflict in Nineteenth-Century America* (Chapel Hill: University of North Carolina Press, 2002). See also Kathleen Flake, *The Politics of American Religious Identity: The Seating of Senator Reed Smoot, Mormon Apostle* (Chapel Hill: University of North Carolina Press, 2004); and W. Paul Reeve, *Religion of a Different Color: Race and the Mormon Struggle for Whiteness* (Oxford and New York: Oxford University Press, 2017).

2. Fluhman, *"A Peculiar People,"* 31–39.

3. Ibid., 34–38.

The Book of Mormon included prophecies that many "plain" and "precious" truths would be removed from the Bible between the time of Christ and the last days. Accordingly, from 1830 to 1833 Smith expanded and otherwise revised the King James Version of the Holy Bible, in what he called a "new translation."[4] He considered this project a noteworthy part of his prophetic calling.[5] In 1835, Smith purchased some Egyptian papyri from which he began translating the writings of the biblical patriarch Abraham. Most of Smith's revelations, however, were directed to fellow church members—calling them to live righteously, to travel and preach, to move their families to Zion, and to consecrate everything to the Lord. These revelations were eventually compiled and published as a third book of scripture, the Doctrine and Covenants. Later, after his death, parts of Smith's New Translation of the Bible, the Book of Abraham, and other writings were compiled and canonized as a fourth standard work of scripture called the Pearl of Great Price. Smith's new scriptural works were, and are, for millions of members of the Church of Jesus Christ of Latter-day Saints an enduring religious and historical contribution.

For Smith to produce a new scriptural text, revise the old accepted canon, and publish a book of his own new revelations in early nineteenth-century Protestant America was a cultural transgression tantamount to heresy, because religious authority was so bound to the existing Bible. America's Protestant clergy had inherited the work of their theological forebears, the great reformers of the early modern period who had championed the doctrine of *sola scriptura* in their effort to tip the scales of power away from Catholic popes and priests. Historian David F. Holland has written that "scriptural canonicity (the very idea that there must exist a definitive repository of divine truths) was a basic mental structure of the early modern era, an assumption so large and deeply rooted that all other intellectual activity had to deal with its presence."[6] In time, however, Protestantism had to learn to balance the authority of the Bible with both the populist empowerment of independent congregations and the maintenance of ministerial efficacy. Disestablishment in early national America

4. Joseph Smith occasionally used the title "new translation" to refer to his revision of the Bible. See Letter to Church Leaders in Jackson County, Missouri, 21 April 1833, in *JSP*-D3:68; Letter to Church Leaders in Jackson County, Missouri, 25 June 1833, in *JSP*-D3:154; Letter to Church Leaders in Jackson County, Missouri, 2 July 1833, in *JSP*-D3:167; Letter to Church Leaders in Jackson County, Missouri, 6 August 1833, in *JSP*-D3:233.

5. Joseph Smith, History, 1838–1856, vol. A-1, November 1831, 175 (accessible in the Histories series of the online edition of *The Joseph Smith Papers*).

6. David F. Holland, *Sacred Borders: Continuing Revelation and Canonical Restraint in Early America* (Oxford and New York: Oxford University Press, 2011), 8.

quickly led to denominational proliferation. While the Bible provided a common language enabling a kind of mainline ecumenicalism and moral establishment that held political influence over civic matters, it also fueled intense doctrinal debates among the diverse and competing churches. Denominational competition and sectarian strife depended upon proof-texted appeals to the authority of the Bible in a way that made it all the more radical to abdicate even a small fraction of its authority and cultural capital to any other book of scripture.[7]

This was one of the reasons Joseph Smith had such a difficult time finding a publisher who was willing to turn the Book of Mormon manuscript into an actual book. Jonathan Hadley, one of the many New York printers who had turned Smith down, recognized the threat that the Book of Mormon posed and denounced the work before it was even published: "The Public should not be imposed upon by this work, pronounced as it is, by its proselytes, to be superior in style, and more advantageous to mankind, than the Holy Bible!"[8] Hadley's concern represented a broad array of problems that might result if an upstart bible were to gain any cultural legitimacy. The religious authority of a new work of scripture might diminish the authority of the Bible, transfer power into the hands of unproven religious leaders, or even shift the ground of the dialogue about religious authority in the spiritual marketplace of potential proselytes.

Smith's other scriptural productions also had the potential to threaten biblical culture. An early history of Bible translations in America held that his New Translation contained "the most astonishing claims ever made in connection with the Bible, and the most peculiar alterations of any Bible in English ever published."[9] Smith turned his 1830 revelation regarding visions seen by the prophet Moses, not recorded in the Bible, into the first chapter of his revised Bible, prefixed to Genesis 1.[10] In doing so, he essentially provided a preface for the Bible, and thereby reframed the entire tome through the lens of prophets

7. For works on religious authority in early America, see Nathan O. Hatch, *The Democratization of American Christianity* (New Haven, CT: Yale University Press, 1989); David Sehat, *The Myth of American Religious Freedom* (Oxford and New York: Oxford University Press, 2011); Amanda Porterfield, *Conceived in Doubt: Religion and Politics in the New American Nation* (Chicago: University of Chicago Press, 2012); and Holland, *Sacred Borders*.

8. Jonathan A. Hadley, "Golden Bible," *Palmyra Freeman*, 11 August 1829, 3.

9. P. Marion Simms, *The Bible in America: Versions that Have Played Their Part in the Making of the Republic* (New York: Wilson-Ericson, 1936), 235, quoted in Richard L. Bushman, "Joseph Smith as Translator," in *The Prophet Puzzle: Interpretive Essays on Joseph Smith*, ed. Bryan Waterman (Salt Lake City: Signature Books, 1999), 74.

10. "Visions of Moses," in *JSP*-D1:150–56 [Moses 1]; Joseph Smith, *Joseph Smith's New Translation of the Bible*, ed. Scott H. Faulring, Kent P. Jackson, and Robert J. Matthews (Provo, UT: Religious Studies Center, Brigham Young University, 2004), 83–86.

speaking face to face with God. In historian Kathleen Flake's analysis, the revisions that Smith made to the story of Adam and Eve "radically subverted centuries of theologizing on who God is and how humans are to worship God."[11] Smith also added an extensive expansion on Genesis 5:24, regarding Enoch. This mysterious patriarch, Noah's great-grandfather, had "walked with God: and he was not; for God took him." Smith's expansion added that Enoch was the leader of a holy city, the original "Zion," that was taken up with him into heaven. The extensive description of Enoch's Zion provided a model of Christian society far surpassing the depiction of the primitive church given in Acts 2. Later, Smith's translation of the writings of the biblical patriarch Abraham provided a new narrative about the father of the faithful, and one with implications for his heirs. The "Book of Abraham" narrative also conveyed a form of polytheism and posited the premortal existence of humankind. Smith's "Gold Bible" and his other enduring scriptural works, produced between 1829 and 1844, thus challenged the canonical boundaries of antebellum America.

Joseph Smith was not America's only prophet. In the late eighteenth century, Shaker leader Ann Lee presented new revelatory texts, and the radical Quaker Jemima Wilkinson, the "Publick Universal Friend," established Jerusalem, New York. In the succeeding generation, Ellen G. White would provide the disappointed followers of Millerite millenarianism with a book of visions. Lee, Wilkinson, Smith, White, and other prophetic figures produced revelatory texts that threatened to constantly expand a Christian canon long considered closed. However, the Mormons and the Shakers were the only churches to officially canonize scriptures beyond the Bible.[12]

Paul C. Gutjahr, a professor of English who has studied the history of the Bible in America, has written that the Book of Mormon "might be considered the most important religious text ever to emerge from the United States."[13] With a growing acknowledgment of its significance, the Book of Mormon is slowly becoming part of the study of early American cultural and religious history.[14]

11. Kathleen Flake, "Translating Time: The Nature and Function of Joseph Smith's Narrative Canon," *Journal of Religion* 87, no. 4 (October 2007): 526.

12. The new Shaker scripture, dictated by Philemon Stewart, was published as *A Holy, Sacred and Divine Roll and Book; from the Lord God of Heaven, to the Inhabitants of the Earth* [...] (Canterbury, NH: United Society [of Believers in Christ's Second Appearing], 1843). See also Stephen J. Stein, *The Shaker Experience in America: A History of the United Society of Believers* (New Haven and London: Yale University Press, 1992), 177–83; Holland, *Sacred Borders*, 130–33.

13. Paul C. Gutjahr, *The Book of Mormon: A Biography* (Princeton and Oxford: Princeton University Press, 2012), 10.

14. For examples in popular history, see Hatch, *The Democratization of American Christianity*, 113–22; Daniel Walker Howe, *What Hath God Wrought: The Transformation of America, 1815–1848* (Oxford and New

Indeed, it constitutes a rare case of New World scripture. The Bible, Qur'an, Bhagavad Gita, Daodejing, and almost all scriptural texts of the world's major religions were of Eurasian origin. In recent decades, the Book of Mormon and the religion bearing its name have made great inroads in Latin America, the Pacific, and other areas of the globe. Now translated into over one hundred languages, the Book of Mormon has been used as the Mormon Church's primary proselytizing tool in most nations of the world, and the balance of those who have accepted it as scripture now reside outside of the United States.[15] The 16 million adherents of Mormon Christianity now thrive in numbers comparable to the adherents of (approximated in millions) Shintoism (3), Jainism (4), Daoism (9), Judaism (14), and Sikhism (25).[16] The Book of Mormon and Smith's other New World scriptural productions are thus becoming works of world scripture.

JOSEPH SMITH'S TRANSLATION PROJECTS

While Smith is only one of several modern prophets, he diverged from the others when he went beyond providing new revelations to recovering old ones. Historian Richard L. Bushman has recently remarked that Joseph Smith brought the idea of spiritual translation forward "as no other religious leader or seer of his time." Naming Charles Finney, Ann Lee, William Miller, Nat Turner, Alexander Campbell, Walt Whitman, Ralph Waldo Emerson, and Orestes Brownson, Bushman noted that none of them had taken up translation as Joseph Smith had. "Translation," Bushman states, "was one of the distinguishing eccentricities of Joseph Smith's prophethood."[17] Many may consider the polygamy that Smith would later introduce among his followers to be his most distinctive feature, but Jacob Cochran, John Humphrey Noyes, and others

---

York: Oxford University Press, 2009), 312–19. For examples in American literature and American theology, see Joseph Smith Jr., trans., *The Book of Mormon*, Penguin Classics series (New York: Penguin Books, 2008); Elizabeth Fenton and Jared Hickman, eds., *Americanist Approaches to* The Book of Mormon (Oxford and New York: Oxford University Press, 2019); Grant Hardy, *Understanding the Book of Mormon: A Reader's Guide* (Oxford and New York: Oxford University Press, 2010); John Christopher Thomas, *A Pentecostal Reads the Book of Mormon: A Literary and Theological Introduction* (Cleveland, TN: CPT Press, 2016).

15. *Deseret News 2013 Church News Almanac, The Church of Jesus Christ of Latter-day Saints* (Salt Lake City: Deseret News, 2012), 203–9.

16. Pew Research Center, "The Future of World Religions: Population Growth Projections, 2010–2050," 2 April 2015, 8, 124, http://www.pewforum.org/2015/04/02/religious-projections-2010-2050.

17. Richard L. Bushman, "History and Context" (paper, presented at "New Perspectives on Joseph Smith and Translation," Utah State University, Logan, UT, 27 April 2017), www.faithmatters.org/blog/2017/4/27/new-perspectives-on-joseph-smith-and-translation.

introduced similar practices.[18] The gathering was certainly a fundamental aspect of early Mormonism—perhaps its essence—but the Shakers, Harmonists, and others gathered in similar ways.[19] New scripture was certainly uncommon, but Shakers, Spiritualists, and several others embraced extrabiblical writings that came to be considered sacred within their communities.[20] However, Smith was unquestionably rare, if not unique, in his particular practice of translation.

According to the Book of Mormon, translation was the work of a seer. One passage in the book relates that the prophet-king Mosiah possessed an instrument into which he could "look" and thereby "translate all records that are of ancient date." This looking instrument was later described as "two stones which were fastened into the two rims of a bow." The stones were called "interpreters" and were "for the purpose of interpreting languages." It was further explained that "whosoever has these things is called seer." But being a seer was more than possessing the interpreters; it also meant possessing a spiritual gift of seership. This was a "high gift from God" and indeed the highest—"a gift which is greater can no man have." A seer, therefore, was "a revelator and a prophet also" and even "greater than a prophet."[21]

Smith identified himself in terms of his translating role. A revelation he dictated when he organized the church stated: "Behold there Shall a record be kept among you & in it thou shalt be called a seer & Translator & Prop[h]et an Apostle of Jesus Christ an Elder of the Church through the will of God the Father & the grace of our Lord Jesus Christ."[22] This construction split the roles of seer and translator. Smith soon appointed several more church elders and in 1835 organized a council of twelve apostles. In 1836, he said that his counselors in the church's First Presidency and the apostles were all "Prophets and Seers." In 1841, he dictated a revelation appointing his brother Hyrum as "a prophet, and a seer, and a revelator." The same revelation later affirmed Smith's role as "a Translater, a Revelator, a Seer, and Prophet."[23] Smith had designated other leaders as prophets, seers, and revelators, but never appointed anyone else to the office of translator. This title and role he reserved to himself.

18. See Raymond Lee Muncy, *Sex and Marriage in Utopian Communities: Nineteenth-Century America* (Bloomington and London: Indiana University Press, 1973).

19. Stephen J. Stein, *Communities of Dissent: A History of Alternative Religions in America* (Oxford and New York: Oxford University Press, 2000), 49–65.

20. See Laurie F. Maffly-Kipp, ed., *American Scriptures: An Anthology of Sacred Writings* (New York: Penguin Group, 2010).

21. Mosiah 8:13–18; 28:13–16.

22. Revelation, 6 April 1830, in *JSP*-D1:129 [D&C 21:1].

23. Joseph Smith, Journal, 27 March 1836, in *JSP*-J1:203–4; Revelation, 19 January 1841, in *JSP*-D7:524, 527 [D&C 124:94, 125].

The shorter revelations that Smith dictated were usually referred to as "commandments." They were primarily commandments from God through Smith as his mouthpiece, and were directed to Smith himself, other individual church members, the church in general, or the world at large. Other revelations clarified biblical doctrine or unsealed the mysteries of heaven. They occasionally foretold the future and, in a few instances, even recovered pieces of the past. The commandments, therefore, were not unlike what Smith called translations. But however much they had in common, Smith differentiated between the two. Bushman notes that Smith "presented them as 'translations,' just as the King James title page said that it was 'translated out of the original tongues' . . . even though he operated on, apparently, entirely different principles."[24] These were not simply translations from one language to another. In fact, the various translation projects did not utilize the same methodology; they appear to have had substantial differences in how they were produced and yet they all fell under Smith's role as a translator.

Aside from Smith's own categorization, there are readily apparent differences between what was presented as a translation and what was presented as a revelation. Whereas Smith dictated commandments and other "thus saith the Lord" revelations as a prophet in his own time, the spiritual gift of translation was only used to recover the writings of ancient prophets. Smith never used this gift to translate the work of foreign-tongue contemporaries. Moreover, the translations were not only presented as ancient texts, but usually associated with some kind of artifact—whether real or imagined—such as plates or parchment or papyri. Most of the revelations, in contrast, were direct transmissions given through no other medium than Smith's mind and his inherited vocabulary. Because of this, the revelations differed in narrative voice. They were delivered in the voice of the living God—often directed to specific individuals in the immediacy of present circumstances and employing familiar address. In contrast, the translations were narrated in the voice of ancient prophets and generally addressed an unknown audience of scripture readers somewhere far off in the distant future. The narrative dimension of the translations further differentiated them from the revelations. The revelations usually give commandments and teach principles in a didactic manner, whereas the translations are often autobiographical or even historical—frequently reading much like the biblical books of Kings and Chronicles.

24. Bushman, "History and Context."

In some respects, Smith's translation texts may have contested traditional Christian conceptions of authority more than his revelations. The transmission of purportedly ancient scripture opened a conduit to the prophets of the past. Through the production of ancient prophetic writings that could supplement, clarify, or even correct the Bible, Smith could bypass both the Protestant authority of a clergy trained in interpretation and the Catholic authority of church tradition. The hermeneutical authority of priests and preachers could be supplanted by a prophet recovering the sacred past directly.

Beyond the issue of religious authority, the translations seem to imply a kind of universalist theology. The Book of Mormon speaks of many books of scripture, scattered and hidden across the globe, and makes the point that God speaks to all people in all ages. In a revelation to the prophet Nephi, God explains himself: "And I do this that I may prove unto many that I am the same yesterday, today, and forever; and that I speak forth my words according to mine own pleasure. And because that I have spoken one word ye need not suppose that I cannot speak another; for my work is not yet finished; neither shall it be until the end of man."[25] The God portrayed in the Book of Mormon is constant and thus continually operating in the world for the salvation of humankind. The recovery of ancient texts through the gift of translation was a manifestation of a strange but strong breed of Christian universalism supplementing the special calling of Israel—even before the resurrection of Jesus Christ.

Smith's revision of the Bible added more sacred history to the growing collection of Mormon scriptures. Whereas the Old Testament gave a brief and patchy history of the pre-Abrahamic age, Smith's Bible revision narrated the baptism of Adam and traced an unbroken lineage of priesthood ordination extending from Adam and Seth through Enoch and Noah to Melchizedek and Abraham. Smith's biblical expansions thus functioned to replace discontinuity with continuity and with a model of dispensationalism. His Bible revisions, including the Book of Moses, transformed the biblical narrative into a dispensational history while his Book of Abraham amplified one of these dispensations from the pre-Mosaic age of the patriarchs. The translations loosely stitched all of the dispensations of Judeo-Christian religion together, ultimately culminating in Smith's own restorationism.

This dispensationalism had further eschatological implications. Smith saw himself as part of "the dispensation of the fulness of times" mentioned in the

25. 2 Nephi 29:9.

New Testament epistle to the Ephesians, when God would "gather together in one all things in Christ, both which are in heaven, and which are on earth."[26] For Smith, this gathering of all things was primarily a gathering of God's people, but it also included the collection of all the revelations he had given to the world. Richard L. Bushman notes that translation, for Smith, was "not merely a mechanical operation to facilitate the transmission of information." It was much more—"a divine calling, embedded in the providential workings of history, in which one people's prophets instruct the people of another time and place." The work of translation thus brought "people of different times and cultures together in a harmony of shared histories."[27]

A similar idea seems to have been expressed in Smith's teachings regarding the practice of baptisms for the dead. Drawing on Hebrews 11:40, he wrote to his followers regarding "principals in relation to the dead and the living that cannot be lightly passed over, as pertaining to our salvation; For their salvation is necessary and essential to our salvation ~~see~~ as Paul says concerning the fathers 'That they without us can not be made perfect'; Neither can we without our dead be made perfect." He further explained:

> the earth will be smitten with a curse, unless there is a welding link of some kind or other, between the fathers and the children, upon some subject or other. And behold, what is that subject. It is the baptism for the dead. . . . For it is necessary in the ushering in of the dispensation of the fulness of times; which dispensation is now beginning to usher in that a whole, and compleat, and perfect union, and welding together of dispensations and keys and powers and glories should take place, and be revealed from the days of Adam even to the present time.[28]

It was not enough to be saved alone, and indeed salvation consisted in being saved together. Like baptism for the dead, the restoration of lost scriptures by the gift of translation could help bridge the gap between the living and the dead and unite the family of Adam and Eve.[29] For Joseph Smith it was not enough to get revelations from heaven. He needed to gather the revelations of the past as

26. Ephesians 1:10.

27. Bushman, "History and Context."

28. Joseph Smith to "The Church of Jesus Christ of Latter Day Saints," 7 September 1842 [D&C 128:15–18] (accessible in the Documents series of the online edition of *The Joseph Smith Papers*).

29. On Smith's effort to overcome the problem of death, see Klaus J. Hansen, *Mormonism and the American Experience* (Chicago and London: University of Chicago Press, 1981), 84–112; Douglas J. Davies, *The Mormon Culture of Salvation: Force, Grace and Glory* (Aldershot, England, and Burlington, VT: Ashgate

well. More than a mere manifestation of God's past involvement in the world, the translation of ancient scripture was one of God's methods for saving it. The act of translation itself seemed to carry soteriological connotations reflecting Smith's communitarian impulse.

PRODUCING TRANSLATION

All of this translation activity began with the Book of Mormon. At the onset of his translation work, Smith was reportedly looking at the golden plates through a pair of "spectacles"—like the interpreters held by Mosiah in the Book of Mormon and later associated with the biblical "urim and thummim" worn by the high priest of ancient Israel.[30] Before long, however, Smith was instead using one or more of the "seer stones" he also had. He had previously used these stones within the context of the enduring European folk tradition of helping others find things that were missing, or even to locate buried treasure.[31] Joseph Smith's wife, friends, and others who served as his scribes or otherwise saw him while translating the record reported remarkably similar descriptions of the process. Sometimes the golden plates were on the same table at which he sat, or were nearby, but other times they were hidden, even far away from where he sat translating. Regardless, Smith would place a seer stone into the crown of his upturned hat, press his face into the brim of the hat to eclipse ambient light, and then peer at his seer stone in the darkness of the hat's interior. Those around Smith during the translation frequently witnessed him doing this.

Then, as they recount it, the words of the English translation of the characters on the plates would appear on the stone. The common ground in their descriptions of what Smith saw in his stone—given by those who could only observe the process from outside of his hat—seem to point to Smith himself as

Publishing, 2000); Samuel Morris Brown, *In Heaven as It Is on Earth: Joseph Smith and the Early Mormon Conquest of Death* (Oxford and New York: Oxford University Press, 2012), see esp. chap. 5.

30. Joseph Smith's wife, Emma Hale Smith, later recounted that "the first my <husband> translated, was translated by the use of the Urim, and Thummim, and that was the part that Martin Harris lost, after that he used a small stone, not exactly, black, but was rather a dark color," Emma [Hale Smith] Bidamon to Emma Pilgrim, 27 March 1870, in Dan Vogel, comp. and ed., *Early Mormon Documents* (Salt Lake City: Signature Books, 1996), 1:532–33. See also Joseph Smith, History, circa Summer 1832, 5, in *JSP*-H1:15; Joseph Smith, History, 1838–1856, vol. A-1, 5, in *JSP*-H1:222; compare Exodus 28:30; Leviticus 8:8; Numbers 27:21.

31. For perspectives on Joseph Smith's involvement with treasure seeking, see Ronald W. Walker, "Joseph Smith: The Palmyra Seer," *BYU Studies* 24, no. 4 (Fall 1984): 461–72; D. Michael Quinn, "Divining Rods, Treasure-Digging, and Seer Stones," chap. 2 in *Early Mormonism and the Magic World View*, 2nd ed. (Salt Lake City: Signature Books, 1998); Richard L. Bushman, *Joseph Smith: Rough Stone Rolling* (New York: Alfred Knopf, 2005), 41–52.

their origin.[32] As David Whitmer related it, Joseph Smith would peer into his seer stone "and parchment would appear . . . upon which was a line of characters from the plates, and under it, the translation in English; *at least, so Joseph said*."[33] Smith was apparently telling others what was happening inside the hat: he saw words and read them out loud to the scribes who then wrote them down. Whether or not this was what was objectively occurring, it seems to be what Smith was experiencing—or at least what he said he saw.

One of Smith's scribes, Oliver Cowdery, wanted to experience the same spiritual gift and assist with the translation. Smith dictated a revelation granting Cowdery this gift and privilege, but Cowdery somehow faltered in the attempt. Smith then dictated another revelation in which Cowdery's failure was explained:

> Behold you have not understood, you have supposed that I would give it unto you, when you took no thought, save it was to ask me; but behold I say unto you, that you must study it out in your mind; then you must ask me if it be right, and if it is right, I will cause that your bosom shall burn within you: therefore you shall feel that it is right; but if it be not right, you shall have no such feelings, but you shall have a stupor of thought, that shall cause you to forget the thing which is wrong. . . . Now if you had known this, you could have translated: nevertheless, it is not expedient that you should translate now.[34]

Cowdery apparently believed that the translation would come easily, but he was mistaken. To paraphrase, the revelation corrected his misunderstanding by describing an interior process of thought, study, and inquiry, followed by the ability either to "feel that it is right" (by some kind of spiritual or physiological burning sensation in the "bosom") or to have "no such feelings" (as well as a "stupor" of forgetfulness). This cognitive and emotional process seems at odds with the visual and almost mechanical process Smith had apparently related to others.

32. The various sources, both Mormon and non-Mormon, have been compiled in several scholarly studies. See James E. Lancaster, "The Translation of the Book of Mormon," in *The Word of God: Essays on Mormon Scripture*, ed. Dan Vogel (Salt Lake City: Signature Books, 1990), 97–112; Michael Hubbard MacKay and Nicholas J. Frederick, *Joseph Smith's Seer Stones* (Provo, UT: Religious Studies Center, Brigham Young University; Salt Lake City, UT: Deseret Book, 2016), 45–64.

33. J. L. Traughber Jr., "Testimony of David Whitmer," *Saints' Herald*, 15 November 1879, 341 (emphasis added).

34. Revelation, April 1829-D, in *JSP*-D1:50 [D&C 9:7–10].

Mormon scholars have wrestled with these somewhat contradictory clues regarding Smith's translation experience for decades. In addition to these and other *descriptions* of translation, there are the *transcriptions* of the various translation efforts—the resulting texts. Whether or not one believes Smith was really translating the Book of Mormon by the power of God, the products of his effort are now part of the religious landscape. The translation texts, which are voluminous, can be studied critically for further clues into the production process and the religious meaning of what Smith was doing. And, unless one dismisses his reported methods as sheer deception, his subjective experience is also at issue. What was Smith doing or experiencing that would come to have such a powerful effect in the lives of so many?

Since 1830, when the Book of Mormon became a basis of religious authority in the church Smith founded, many have been at least tangentially interested in the production of Smith's translations. However, an openness to the human aspects of translation by believers has been slow in coming. Similarly, the reductionist urge to simply dismiss Smith's translation experiences and texts along with his incredible claims has persisted until fairly recently. During Mormonism's first century, historical writing on the translation of the Book of Mormon and other Mormon scriptures was generally marked by deep biases from both defenders and detractors, with defenders arguing for the book's antiquity and detractors for its modernity. It was not until the late twentieth century that academic scholarship began to surmount the polemics of the past, although devotional writing from Latter-day Saints and attacks from evangelicals and skeptics persist to this day.

Whatever the original source of the Book of Mormon, Joseph Smith rendered its text in the Modern English of the last half millennium, so the book is certainly modern. And it is thus further modern because of the heavy freight of cultural baggage and even historical connotation that is unavoidably carried along by any language. The Book of Mormon is also modern in that some of its prophets foresee the contemporary age and even directly address its current readers. The question of whether the text is also ancient will not be debated in this volume.[35] Although most of the contributors to this collection

35. For classic examples of scholarly skepticism and defense, see Brent Lee Metcalfe, ed., *New Approaches to the Book of Mormon: Explorations in Critical Methodology* (Salt Lake City, UT: Signature Books, 1993); and Noel B. Reynolds, ed., *Book of Mormon Authorship Revisited: The Evidence for Ancient Origins* (Provo, UT: Foundation for Ancient Research and Mormon Studies, 1997). A closely related body of literature that assumes both ancient origins and divinely aided translation seeks to understand the mechanics of divine translation. The prime example of this literature is Brant A. Gardner, *The Gift and Power: Translating the Book of Mormon* (Salt Lake City, UT: Greg Kofford Books, 2011).

are practicing Latter-day Saints who believe that the Book of Mormon and Smith's other translation texts are both ancient and modern, this book only explores their modern aspects. Smith claimed to have translated "by the gift and power of God" while also leaving an inordinate amount of historical and textual evidence behind—with which his own role in the production of Mormon scripture can be examined.

This, then, is what is meant by the title *Producing Ancient Scripture*: the volume takes advantage of this extant evidence and epistemologically focuses on what was observed at the time of Smith's production of what was considered translation, as well as on what can be observed now regarding the nature of the resulting products. It analyzes the texts that Smith produced in terms of his personal practices and experiences, his immediate environment and circumstances, his biographical background and cultural context, and the broader contours of early American history. Investigating the modern and human dimensions of Smith's translation projects does nothing to strip them of their intrinsic religious value, their profound influence on millions of believers, or even the possibility of their genuine antiquity and divine inspiration. Though religion tends to either presuppose or demand a real and fundamental connection to the divine, it is also inevitably defined and shaped by those engaged in the pursuit of that connection. In this book, the purpose of a modernist approach is to move past the polarizing effects of belief or skepticism that Smith's translations naturally tend to provoke.

Since the 1980s, critical studies of the text of the Book of Mormon have created a foundation for understanding its production. For this and other reasons, the lion's share of scholarly analysis has gone to Smith's most extensive translation project. Until recently this depth and breadth of analysis has not extended far beyond the Book of Mormon.[36] Though there are some studies on the production of Joseph Smith's New Translation of the Bible and the Book of Abraham, they are distinctly fewer in number and more specialized than the scholarship on the Book of Mormon.[37] Moreover, Smith's translation texts are generally studied apart from one another, without a comparative methodology

36. See the *Journal of Book of Mormon Studies*, currently published by the University of Illinois Press on behalf of the Neal A. Maxwell Institute for Religious Scholarship at Brigham Young University in Provo, Utah. There is no such periodical devoted to the study of Joseph Smith's New Translation of the Bible, the Book of Abraham, or any other translation project.

37. See Robert J. Matthews, *"A Plainer Translation": Joseph Smith's Translation of the Bible; A History and Commentary* (Provo, UT: Brigham Young University Press, 1975); John Gee, *An Introduction to the Book of Abraham* (Provo, UT: Religious Studies Center, Brigham Young University; Salt Lake City: Deseret Book, 2017).

or a strong sense of commonality. This has created artificial boundaries in the scholarship, especially considering that most of the Mormon canon was produced within a relatively small geographical area (spanning less than three hundred miles) and within a relatively short period of time (a mere half-dozen years). The spatiotemporal context of one translation project is the same for the others. Furthermore, each resulting scriptural work overlapped with at least one other. The Book of Mormon was published the same year that Smith began his revision of the Bible, and he also began his work on the Book of Abraham the same year he published the Doctrine and Covenants. Many revelations later published in the Doctrine and Covenants were originally dictated as responses to questions that emerged during the translation of the Book of Mormon and the Bible.

It is also more than obvious that passages from the King James Bible appear throughout each of Smith's scriptural works. As radical and heretical as mainline Christians have viewed Smith's extracanonical scriptures, they are thoroughly biblical. The Bible seems to burn steady like a massive sun, an inescapable center of gravity around which Smith's various scriptural creations revolve in their orbits. The Bible is ever present for Smith as something that needs to be expounded, clarified, or even corrected. Though Mormon scripture is tethered to the Bible in complex ways, this connection has been largely neglected.[38] The intricate biblical intertextuality of Mormon scripture has generally been dismissed by believers, usually understood in terms of repetitious revelation or providential concurrence. Conversely, it has been hardly noticed by detractors, who have instead seen only evidence of simple plagiarism. Instead of following either reductionist urge, some of the chapters in this book investigate biblical intertextuality for the sake of achieving a deeper understanding of what Smith's translations are about and how they work. Throughout this volume, biblical passages are quoted from the King James Version. This was the version familiar to Joseph Smith, his early followers, and the early American culture of Protestant Christianity within which they thought and acted.[39]

This book examines the full range of Joseph Smith's translation projects. Several chapters probe the translation of the Book of Mormon. This was Smith's

38. For a rare example of intertextual scholarship about the Bible and the Book of Mormon, see Nicholas J. Frederick, *The Bible, Mormon Scripture, and the Rhetoric of Allusivity*, Fairleigh Dickinson University Press Mormon Studies Series (Madison and Teaneck, NJ: Fairleigh Dickinson University Press, 2016).

39. Philip L. Barlow, *Mormons and the Bible: The Place of the Latter-day Saints in American Religion*, rev. ed. (Oxford and New York: Oxford University Press, 2013), 1–79; Gordon Campbell, *Bible: The Story of the King James Version, 1611–2011* (Oxford and New York: Oxford University Press, 2010), 194–98.

most extensive translation project—yielding a book of over five hundred pages in almost any edition—and is by far his most influential product. But this volume's focus on the Book of Mormon is proportional. There are also path-breaking chapters on the New Translation of the Bible, the Book of Abraham, and other lesser known translation projects (at least one chapter in the book is devoted to each of Smith's translation efforts). And, while most chapters take one project as a focus, they also generally explore interrelationships among other projects and intertextual relationships with the Bible.

Among the various chapters, Smith's translation activity is viewed at every aperture. The scope of analysis ranges from the broadest context of Western thought to the economic constraints of early American print culture to the interpersonal dynamics between Smith and his scribes to the dark confines of the interior of an old hat. Several chapters also closely scrutinize the translation texts themselves for indications of Smith's translating process and experience.

Finally, this collection of chapters also seeks to understand Joseph Smith's translation projects by exploring them with several different methodological approaches. The chapters generally employ a traditional historical lens, but most also engage with other disciplines, theories, or methods. The book includes chapters drawing upon documentary editing, book history, historical theology, sociology, material culture, religious studies, feminist theory, narrative theory, biblical studies, and comparative religion. Each chapter is an original contribution.

The chapters are arranged in roughly chronological order and are further organized into four parts. Part 1 provides approaches to the broad cultural and religious context within which Smith donned the prophetic mantle and pursued his supernatural translation projects—as well as the commencement of his work as a translator. Part 2 approaches various aspects of the production of the Book of Mormon. Part 3 covers Smith's New Translation of the King James Bible and other closely related projects. Part 4 includes Smith's attempt to recover the pure language of Adam, his translation of the Book of Abraham, and his mistaken but telling attempt to translate the fraudulent Kinderhook plates.

PART 1: CONTEXT AND COMMENCEMENT

As noted above, Smith's translation projects have generally been examined individually and within narrow parameters, often overlooking broader cultural and intellectual trends beyond Smith's immediate environment. This sharp focus leaves much to be reconnoitered. Part 1 offers new explorations of the contours of the world in which Smith introduced himself as a translator.

When Smith claimed that he translated the Book of Mormon by "the gift and power of God," he was thus implicitly explaining the book's miraculous translation, at least in part, by using the New Testament language of spiritual gifts. In "'By the Gift and Power of God': Translation among the Gifts of the Spirit," Christopher James Blythe draws on his background in religious studies to examine the Book of Mormon and Smith's translation projects generally within the Christian tradition of spiritual gifts. He looks especially at the gifts of speaking in tongues and the interpretation of tongues, and how Smith's perception of these gifts may have influenced his understanding of translation. Blythe also demonstrates how ideas about the gift of translation paralleled ideas about other gifts of the spirit in the teachings and experiences of Smith and other early Mormons he knew. He therefore makes some sense of Smith's astounding claims to translate ancient scripture by situating the notion of a gift of translation within Smith's own primitivist restoration project and in the margins of Christian pneumatology.

Jared Hickman then proposes an overarching theory of translation for all of Smith's projects, sidestepping the traditional paradigm of linguistic translation to consider the metaphysical translation described in the Mormon canon through narratives about prophets like Enoch and Alma. In "'Bringing Forth' the Book of Mormon: Translation as the Reconfiguration of Bodies in Space-Time," Hickman starts with the lexical relationship between these two types of translation and shows how they were used in the King James Bible and in the American English of Joseph Smith's time. He further relates metaphysical translation to the movements of treasures and treasure guardians in the treasure-seeking culture that influenced young Smith. These aspects of translation in the deep background of Smith's linguistic and cultural inheritance, Hickman argues, influenced his entire religious project.

Michael Hubbard MacKay investigates Joseph Smith's earliest efforts toward translation, when he transcribed the characters on the golden plates and sent the transcript with Martin Harris, his friend and benefactor, to have it translated by scholars in New York City. In "Performing the Translation: Character Transcripts and Joseph Smith's Earliest Translating Practices," MacKay considers the practice of linguistic translation as it was understood at the time by both scholars and lay people. He demonstrates that Smith's religious production of a text that was translated took place within an intellectual context that placed demands and limits on his idea of what a translation was and could be.

Amy Easton-Flake and Rachel Cope challenge the traditional, male-centered narrative of translation in "Reconfiguring the Archive: Women and the Social Production of the Book of Mormon." Here they apply theoretical work from an intersection between gender studies and archival studies to highlight a substantial body of often overlooked documentation regarding the production of Mormonism's founding text. They show how Lucy Mack Smith, Lucy Harris Harris, Mary Musselman Whitmer, and Emma Hale Smith made Joseph Smith's translation work possible and took on the role of witnesses to the golden plates and their translation.

PART 2: TRANSLATING THE BOOK OF MORMON

From the moment the Book of Mormon was published, it almost seems as if the text has been begging for its true source to be either confirmed, exposed, or otherwise investigated and identified. The text has engaged devout defenders, orthodox opponents, and skeptical critics who have put forth explanations ranging from divine to diabolical revelation and from creative genius to audacious plagiarism. Part 2 of this book problematizes some of the traditional accountings of the book while offering new possibilities for understanding its production.

In "Seeing the Voice of God: The Book of Mormon on Its Own Translation," Samuel Morris Brown briefly surveys the broad range of models—transcendent, immanent, and mixed—that attempt to describe and explain the mechanics of the translation. Noting problems with these models, Brown offers fresh readings of the Book of Mormon, investigating the text itself for clues to the mechanism of its own translation. Brown examines accounts of translation *within* the text, as well as the exercise of related spiritual gifts in the generation of scripture. These readings challenge traditional interpretations of Smith's translation experience, demonstrate various new possibilities, and suggest the outlines of a new, often visionary model.

Instead of searching deep within the Book of Mormon, Ann Taves looks far beyond the text and its translator. Taves finds a comparative case in Helen Schucman, who dictated the text of *A Course in Miracles*—another long and complex religious text produced within a relatively short period of time. In "Joseph Smith, Helen Schucman, and the Experience of Producing a Spiritual Text: Comparing the Translating of the Book of Mormon and the Scribing of *A Course in Miracles*," Taves points out parallels between Smith's and Schucman's dictation processes and draws upon her background in the psychology of religious experience to analyze these comparisons. She identifies an interesting point of intersection and posits a new model that could account for both scriptural productions.

Richard Lyman Bushman explores the ways in which the Book of Mormon has a heightened and unusual awareness of its own construction as a *book*—and even a book of books—like the Bible. The text, both in particular passages and taken as a whole, almost presents itself as a kind of narrative treatise in book history. In "Nephi's Project: The Gold Plates as Book History," Bushman considers how the Euro-American history and culture of books and bookmaking may have influenced Smith in this and other translation projects. Bushman also suggests how a text so transparent about its construction—and in this sense quite *unlike* the Bible—may have been received and understood in Smith's time.

It was during the translation process that Joseph Smith began dictating other revelations. When the Book of Mormon was completed, the shorter revelations continued as Smith's primary vehicle of prophetic pronouncement. In "Ancient Plates and Modern Commandments: The Book of Mormon in Comparison with Joseph Smith's Other Revelations," Grant Hardy explores ways in which these new and unusual genres of scriptural production compare in some ways but differ in others. He looks particularly at the Book of Mormon's narration in terms of how that narrative might influence its own reception and interpretation. Hardy considers perspectives within the book, historical aspects of the narrative, literary aspects of the text, and correspondences with the Bible. Drawing on his expertise in Eastern philosophy and comparative scripture, he masterfully elucidates the rhetorical power of a historical narrative brought forth as the translation of an ancient religious text.

PART 3: TRANSLATING THE KING JAMES BIBLE

The Book of Mormon constituted a companion scripture to the Bible, but its relationship to the Bible was much more than that. The book included hundreds of allusions to the Bible and scores of paraphrases and quotations corresponding to biblical passages. In fact, there are entire chapters of Isaiah and Malachi that appear in the Book of Mormon. Engagement with the Bible can be found throughout Smith's scriptural productions.

One of Smith's earliest revelations, dated April 1829, is closely related to a passage in the twenty-first chapter of the Gospel of John. Smith rendered this revelation as a first-person narration by John, the "beloved" disciple of Jesus. This new account of John relates Jesus giving John power to bring souls unto salvation. In "The Tarrying of the Beloved Disciple: The Textual Formation of the Account of John," David W. Grua and William V. Smith trace the trajectory of the document's physical transmission and textual development between 1829 and 1835. Although a history-like narrative, similar to the Book of Mormon and other translations, the Account of John was filed with and copied along with Smith's revelations. Moreover, its earliest interpretive headings referred to it as a "commandment" and "revelation." In 1832, a new heading was attached to the Account of John identifying it as a translation of a "parchment" that had been "hid up" by the ancient disciple of Christ, thereby more strongly invoking parallels with the gold plates and the miraculous *translation* of the Book of Mormon into English. When preparing the Account of John for publication in the 1835 Doctrine and Covenants, Joseph Smith and a small committee substantially expanded the text by clarifying ambiguities and adding intertextual connections with the King James Bible. Grua and Smith show how the text was changed in ways much like the revelations on priesthood and church government, which were revised to reflect modifications that had occurred as Smith's institutional church grew and its ecclesiastical structure developed. Through careful historical and textual scholarship, Grua and Smith explore the porous relationship between Smith's translations and revelations and how they are occasionally indistinguishable.

In 1830, within a few months of the publication of the Book of Mormon, Smith began what he called a "new translation" of the Bible and worked on the project periodically through 1833. He dramatically expanded some passages of the Bible, especially in Genesis, but the large majority of the changes were much smaller. He ultimately made over three thousand revisions to Christianity's most sacred text. In "A Recovered Resource: The Use of Adam Clarke's Bible Commentary in Joseph Smith's Bible Translation," Thomas A. Wayment and Haley Wilson-Lemmon demonstrate that most of Smith's translation of the Bible can be more properly viewed as a revision of the King James text. They do this by showing that several of his changes were taken word for word or otherwise drawn from Methodist scriptorian Adam Clarke's influential Bible Commentary, *Holy Bible, Containing the Old and New Testaments*. Their research invites scholars to reconsider Smith's translation projects generally, investigating the possibility that he drew upon scholarly sources while also infusing his own prophetic inspiration into the resulting text.

The King James Bible that Smith was using as the base text for his New Translation included the Apocrypha, so when Smith was finishing the Old Testament, he asked God whether he should translate the Apocrypha as well. Smith then dictated a revelation declaring that the Apocrypha contained truths and errors, that Latter-day Saints could rely upon the Gift of the Holy Ghost to distinguish between the two, and that it was therefore unnecessary for Smith to translate any further. In "Lost Scripture and 'The Interpolations of Men': Joseph Smith's Revelation on the Apocrypha," historian Gerrit Dirkmaat articulates the conceptual problems for interpreting this revelation. The revelation's description of the Apocrypha as a mixture of truth and error was not unlike the rationale behind Smith's translation of the Old and New Testaments. Why, then, would the revelation conclude by ruling out a continuation of the same effort? Dirkmaat explores some possible solutions to this problem as well as their implications for understanding the Bible revision project.

Between his revelation regarding the Apocrypha and the conclusion of his New Translation, Smith dictated a theological revelation (now section 93 of the Doctrine and Covenants) with an intriguing translation text embedded within. This passage, which is closely related to the opening verses of the Gospel of John, is presented within the revelation as an excerpt from the "record of John" mentioned in John 1:19. In "Translation, Revelation, and the Hermeneutics of Theological Innovation: Joseph Smith and the Record of John," Nicholas J. Frederick applies his training in biblical studies and expertise in intertextual scholarship to the text of the translated Record of John within its context of a modern revelation. Whether or not Smith's translation from the Record of John derives from an ancient original, Frederick demonstrates that it functions much like apocryphal and pseudepigraphal literature to legitimize doctrinal innovation.

PART 4: PURE LANGUAGE, THE BOOK OF ABRAHAM, AND THE KINDERHOOK PLATES

Toward the end of the Book of Mormon, the final ancient prophet to write in the book includes an abridgment of a record that was ancient even for his time: the history of an earlier people who had left the Old World for the New when God cursed humankind at Babel. These people, the Jaredites, had preserved the original human tongue—presumably the same language that Adam had spoken when he conversed with God in the Garden of Eden. The concept of a primitive language that was pure and unconfounded, even divine, influenced Smith's subsequent translation projects.

In "'Eternal Wisdom Engraven upon the Heavens': Joseph Smith's Pure Language Project," David Golding investigates the concept of a pure language in Smith's scriptural productions. Golding places this effort to recover divine language within the broad traditions of Western esotericism and Christian mysticism—examining the beginnings of this idea in the Book of Mormon and its development in the New Translation of the Bible. Golding then closely inspects Smith's circa 1832 document, "A Sample of Pure Language," which consisted of a few words from this pure language as well as their English translations. He also explores the way in which Smith's search for the pure language of God influenced his translation of the Egyptian papyri he acquired in Kirtland, Ohio, in 1835. Finally, he explains how Smith's early endeavor to reach beyond imperfect languages ultimately became entangled in the very problem it was intended to solve.

An 1835 letter written by William W. Phelps suggests that Phelps, Smith, and perhaps others had made some further progress working on the pure language project and were still interested in it that year when a traveling mummy show arrived in Kirtland. Smith and a few others purchased four mummies along with several fragments of Egyptian papyri. At this point in time, the pure language project was apparently converted into an Egyptian language project, which ultimately resulted in a counting document, an alphabet document, and the beginnings of a grammar book. The papyri purchase was also followed by a translation of the writings of Abraham. In "'Translating an Alphabet to the Book of Abraham': Joseph Smith's Study of the Egyptian Language and His Translation of the Book of Abraham," Brian M. Hauglid examines the Egyptian language documents and the Abraham translation documents. He establishes a chronology for the creation of these documents, demonstrating the concurrence of their production and the intertextual relationships among them. Closely analyzing these relationships, Hauglid suggests that at least some parts of the Book of Abraham translation text were derived from parts of the language project documents. Hauglid thus proposes that Smith's approach to translating the Book of Abraham involved both intellectual investigation and reliance on a prophetic gift. He concludes that the Book of Abraham at least partially reflects Smith's own creative involvement in its production.

In late 1835, Joseph Smith's translation work on the Book of Abraham was evidently put on hold and he began a formal study of the Hebrew language. Years later, in 1842, Smith resumed his translation of the Book of Abraham. A few scholars have noted that Smith's 1842 translation work, unlike his 1835 efforts, includes the presence of Hebrew words, phrases, and other influences. In "Approaching Egyptian Papyri through Biblical Language: Joseph Smith's Use of Hebrew in His Translation of the Book of Abraham," Matthew J. Grey makes substantial progress on understanding this development by closely tracing the transition from Smith's 1835 translation work to his commencement of Hebrew study. Grey systematically examines Smith's incorporation of Hebrew in the text of the Book of Abraham, particularly within the context of the precise Hebrew resources to which Smith had access.

Finally, Don Bradley and Mark Ashurst-McGee investigate Smith's 1843 translation of a set of inscribed brass plates that were disinterred from an Indian mound near Kinderhook, Illinois, but were later shown to be modern forgeries planted in the mound as a prank on local Mormons. The Kinderhook plates were taken to Nauvoo later that year and shown to Joseph Smith. When he and others examined the plates, the characters on them were compared to both Egyptian and Hebrew characters and were even associated with the Jaredites—the people in the Book of Mormon who had escaped the curse of Babel and preserved the primitive tongue. In "'President Joseph has Translated a Portion': Joseph Smith and the Mistranslation of the Kinderhook Plates," Bradley and Ashurst-McGee closely investigate this curious episode. They demonstrate that Smith's translation of "a portion" of these plates was most likely conceived as a traditional translation—different from the Book of Mormon, the Book of Abraham, and other supernatural translation projects. They also draw out some of Smith's ideas regarding languages and translation as manifest in this mistaken effort.

CONCLUSION

Although these chapters collectively provide a comprehensive and concentrated examination of the Joseph Smith translation projects, they offer neither a Sunday school answer nor a scholarly Grand Unification Theory explaining everything he produced under the umbrella of the apparently capacious term "translation." Nevertheless, by closely investigating each of Smith's translation projects—and by approaching them from a variety of disciplines and scopes of context—this inclusive compilation attempts to move toward a more holistic understanding of what translation meant for Smith and those who accepted his message. This book also explores commonalities among the translation projects, with several chapters overlapping or in dialogue with one another and thereby opening new and more informed avenues of research. Smith's overarching translation project, broadly conceived, is therefore ripe with opportunity for even deeper scholarly study. Further examination holds forth the prospect of reaching a greater understanding of the human yearning to be connected or even in communion with a sacred past—that which has passed before our time and yet may still pass through us.

PART I

Context and Commencement

2

"By the Gift and Power of God"

Translation among the Gifts of the Spirit

CHRISTOPHER JAMES BLYTHE

Early Mormonism contained a prominent strain of charismatic religious practice. After being baptized, converts to the fledgling faith received the "Gift of the Holy Ghost" by the laying on of hands, and they expected, in the words of early missionary-apostle Parley Pratt, that this "would cause them to dream dreams, see visions, and prophesy, and would impart to them many gifts."[1] This practice dated back to the day the church was organized, and was explicated prior to that in the Book of Mormon. Joseph Smith's "*gift* to translate the book [of Mormon]"[2] was understood through this lens as one of numerous gifts God had bestowed on latter-day believers. Early Mormons believed these gifts of the Spirit confirmed their faith that the Church of Christ, later renamed the Church of Jesus Christ of Latter-day Saints, was indeed the latter-day restoration of the primitive church in preparation for the Millennium.[3] Smith stated that he had translated the Book of Mormon "by the *gift* and power of God."[4] By conceiving of the "translation" of scripture as akin to the Pauline "spiritual gifts"—such as visions, healing, speaking in tongues, or interpreting tongues—Smith and his followers were able to explain the extraordinary translation of

1. Parley P. Pratt, *An Answer to Mr. William Hewitt's Tract against the Latter-day Saints* (Manchester: W. R. Thomas, 1840), 12.

2. Revelation, March 1829, in *JSP*-D1:16 (emphasis added) [D&C 5:4].

3. Richard T. Hughes, "Joseph Smith as an American Restorationist," in *The Worlds of Joseph Smith: A Bicentennial Conference at the Library of Congress,* ed. John W. Welch (Provo, UT: Brigham Young University Press, 2006), 31–39.

4. The Book of Mormon: An Account Written by the Hand of Mormon, upon Plates Taken from the Plates of Nephi, trans. Joseph Smith, Junior (Palmyra, NY: E. B. Grandin, 1830), iii, also 589 [The Testimony of Three Witnesses]. See also Joseph Smith, History, 1838–1856, vol. E-1, 7 September 1843, Addenda, 8 (emphasis added) (accessible in the Histories series of the online edition of *The Joseph Smith Papers*).

the Book of Mormon by framing it within a New Testament rationale and thereby legitimating the radical act of adding to the scriptural canon.

Considering Joseph Smith's various translation projects, this chapter examines Smith's gift in its historical context as one of many spiritual gifts practiced among his early followers. By focusing on the early history of spiritual gifts within Smith's movement, the chapter compares translation with other gifts, demonstrating how it operated in accordance with early Mormonism's theology of spiritual gifts generally. A special emphasis is placed on the gifts of tongues and interpretation of tongues, which Latter-day Saints specifically linked to the gift of translation.

CHARISMATA IN SCRIPTURAL AND HISTORICAL CONTEXT

The Hebrew Bible depicts many prophetic figures with special access to Deity and with the power to foretell the future and even perform miracles. The very act of prophecy was a spiritual power given to the prophet as a heavenly gift. Prophets like Isaiah and Ezekiel saw grand visions of heaven and of future events. Moses worked miracles with the aid of a staff. Samuel heard the voice of God. The prophet Elijah, known for calling down fire from heaven, also restored a child's life. Joseph, the son of Jacob, received divine guidance through prophetic dreams in his youth and later in his life was able to interpret the dreams of others, including Pharaoh.[5] Similarly, Daniel was able to interpret the dream of King Nebuchadnezzar.

The case of Daniel is particularly relevant to Mormon ideas of the gift of translation. After his experience interpreting Nebuchadnezzar's dream, Daniel was called upon to interpret undecipherable writing that Nebuchadnezzar's son, King Belshazzar, had seen written on the wall of his palace. The king first called on astrologers and soothsayers to interpret the strange writing, but they were unsuccessful.[6] At his wife's behest, Belshazzar turned to Daniel, who had previously interpreted one of the King's dreams. Knowing that Daniel could "make interpretations," Belshazzar hoped that he could also "read the writing, and make known the interpretation thereof."[7] Daniel succeeded.[8] In this story,

5. Genesis 37:5–11, 40–41.

6. Daniel 5:7.

7. Daniel 5:16.

8. Scholars have often suggested that the diviners could not interpret the writing because it was coded in some way. Another compelling reading is that the writing was only visible to the king and that the court astrologers and wizards he first asked to interpret it simply could not see it. Michael Segal, "Rereading the Writing on the Wall (Daniel 5)," *Zeitschrift für die Alttestamentliche Wissenschaft* 125, no. 1 (2013): 166–67.

the gift of interpreting dreams was expanded to the ability to make interpretations generally, including for supernatural writing.

The prophetic tradition recorded in the Hebrew Bible influenced the reception that John the Baptist and his cousin Jesus would later receive and build upon. King Herod had John murdered, but in doing so "he feared the multitude, because they counted him [John] as a prophet."[9] John's cousin, Jesus of Nazareth, even taught that "there is not a greater prophet than John the Baptist."[10] After John's death, Jesus adopted his disciples and built upon John's mission of prophetic critique and the preaching of righteousness. Some believed that Jesus was Elijah, who had ascended from the earth in a heavenly chariot, and now returned to the earth. Others believed he was one of the other ancient prophets.[11] Still others considered him to be the prophet of whom Moses had prophesied, who would be great like unto Moses.[12] John and Jesus therefore successfully revitalized the prophetic tradition. When Jesus restored life to a dead man in Nain, the people "glorified God, saying, That a great prophet is risen up among us; and, That God hath visited his people."[13] The disciples of Jesus considered him "a prophet mighty in deed and word before God and all the people."[14]

In addition to foretelling the future and raising the dead, Jesus reportedly healed the sick and disabled, performed exorcisms for those possessed by demons, and worked astounding miracles. Before his death, he prophesied that his disciples would carry on this ministry: "Verily, verily, I say unto you, He that believeth on me, the works that I do shall he do also; and greater works than these shall he do; because I go unto my Father."[15] His apostles soon began performing exorcisms.[16] After Jesus was crucified, the apostles claimed that he appeared to them, as the resurrected Christ, and commanded them to go "into all the world, and preach the gospel to every creature." Jesus further stated that miraculous signs would attend the believers: "In my name shall they cast out devils; they shall speak with new tongues. . . . They shall lay hands on the sick, and they shall recover."[17] During the life of Jesus, there was never a need to

9. Matthew 14:5. See also Mark 11:32; and Luke 20:1.
10. Luke 7:28.
11. Mark 8:27; and Luke 9:7.
12. John 6:13, and 7:40.
13. Luke 7:16. See also John 4:19, and 9:17.
14. Luke 24:18.
15. John 14:12.
16. Matthew 17:14–21. See also Mark 9:38–39.
17. Mark 16:14–20.

speak in foreign tongues, as he and his disciples never left their homeland. But this had now changed with the commission to proselytize in "all the world."

The first miracle after the Christian church received the Holy Ghost was the mass performance of speaking in foreign tongues. At the Feast of Pentecost, shortly following Jesus's death, his disciples "were all filled with the Holy Ghost, and began to speak with other tongues, as the Spirit gave them utterance."[18] Jews from other countries who had come to Jerusalem for the feast observed this manifestation of God's spirit and each "heard them speak in his own language."[19] The apostle Peter declared the scene a fulfillment of Joel's prophecy: "And it shall come to pass in the last days, saith God, I will pour out of my Spirit upon all flesh: and your sons and your daughters shall prophesy, and your young men shall see visions, and your old men shall dream dreams: And on my servants and on my handmaidens I will pour out in those days of my Spirit; and they shall prophesy."[20] Speaking in tongues, then, was similar to the prophecies, visions, and dreams of the ancient prophets and patriarchs. All derived from the outpouring of God's spirit. A new era of spiritual blessings and gifts had been inaugurated.

The book of Acts also documented other miracles among these early believers: visions, dreams, exorcising evil spirits, angelic visitations, and even an inexplicable feat of teleportation.[21] Further manifestations of speaking in tongues also occurred.[22] The apostle Paul referred to these and other miraculous abilities as "spiritual gifts."[23] Paul's writings frequently referenced charismatic gifts. A list of these appeared in one of his epistles to the Christians in Corinth: "For to one is given by the Spirit the word of wisdom; to another the word of knowledge by the same Spirit; To another faith by the same Spirit; to another the gifts of healing by the same Spirit; To another the working of miracles; to another prophecy; to another discerning of spirits; to another divers kinds of tongues; to another the interpretation of tongues."[24]

It is clear that the performance of tongues had moved beyond the role it served at Pentecost in allowing the Christians to preach to foreigners. Instead, Christians at Corinth spoke in tongues as a form of worship and prayer. They also "sang in the spirit."[25] The gift of tongues as practiced in Corinth seems

18. Acts 2:4.
19. Acts 2:6.
20. Joel 2:28–29; as quoted in Acts 2:17–28.
21. Acts 8:26–40.
22. Acts 10:46, 19:6.
23. See 1 Corinthians 12:1, 14:1, 12.
24. 1 Corinthians 12:8–10.
25. 1 Corinthians 14:15.

FIGURE 2.1. *Pentecost* by El Greco. Oil on canvas; part of main altarpiece in church of the Augustine College of María de Aragón, Madrid, Spain; circa 1600. An expressionist depiction of the event in Acts 2:1–21, when early Christians spoke in tongues at the Hebrew celebration of Pentecost. © Photographic Archive Museo Nacional del Prado, Madrid.

to have consisted of glossolalia (supernaturally speaking in an unknown language) instead of xenoglossia (supernaturally speaking in a known language that is unfamiliar to the speaker, as had occurred earlier at Pentecost). When Paul wrote to the Corinthians, he differentiated between "the tongues of men [xenoglossia] and of angels [glossolalia]."[26] Glossolalia, while it may have been understood by the speaker, was apparently unintelligible to others except when decoded by someone with the gift of interpretation. Like Joseph and Daniel interpreting the dreams of kings, the miracle of speaking in tongues required a matching miracle of interpretation.

Paul expressed some concern with this problem of communication. He stated that while he too spoke in tongues and even "more than ye all"—referring to the believers in Corinth—"yet in the church I had rather speak five words in my understanding . . . than ten thousand words in an unknown tongue."[27] He preferred the "greater" gift of prophecy and warned the Corinthians that "He that speaketh in an unknown tongue edifieth himself; but he that prophesieth edifieth the church."[28]

Over the succeeding centuries, Christianity was divided between those who believed that spiritual gifts had ceased after the first generation of the church and those who continued to look for examples of charismatic gifts bestowed upon the faithful. While some argued the gifts were only necessary as signs to build up the infant church, most Christians continued to believe that the particularly devout could work miracles by divine grace. There was however skepticism of charismatic movements, as was the case with the heretical second-century Montanists, that promoted the gifts among the general Christian body and by implication threatened to render the authority of the ecclesiastical structure obsolete.[29]

During the Reformation, Catholic and Protestant theologians were starkly divided on the issue of spiritual gifts. The Protestant reformers insisted that the gifts of the Spirit had ceased sometime in the distant past. Catholics responded to Protestant accusations of superstition by creating hagiographies detailing the miracles and gifts performed by saints. These miracle workers had performed great feats, including levitation and telepathy.[30] Catholics continued

26. 1 Corinthians 13:1.

27. 1 Corinthians 14:18–19.

28. 1 Corinthians 14:4.

29. Terryl L. Givens, *Feeding the Flock: The Foundations of Mormon Thought; Church and Praxis* (New York and Oxford: Oxford University Press, 2017), 216.

30. Carlos M. N. Eire, *Reformations: The Early Modern World, 1450–1650* (New Haven and London: Yale University Press, 2016), 402–4.

to place faith in apparitions, visions, dreams, and even speaking in tongues. As historian Carlos M. N. Eire has explained, the Catholic hagiographers and apologists argued that "any Christian church that had no saints or miracles must be a false church."[31]

In colonial America, the Shakers embraced charismata, with adherents reporting visions, prophesying, and speaking in tongues.[32] Early American Methodists likewise experienced visions, dreams, prophecy, and although extremely rare, the gift of tongues.[33] While spiritual gifts were certainly in decline among Methodists in the early nineteenth century, there were still those who claimed them.[34] That was left to the smaller, marginalized Christianities of the Second Great Awakening, including Mormonism.

EARLY MORMONS AND SPIRITUAL GIFTS

Early Mormons, who emerged in a largely Protestant milieu but who believed spiritual gifts were essential, were not consistent in how they told the history of spiritual gifts. On one hand, an argument for the Great Apostasy held that spiritual gifts had been absent from Christianity since the first century in the Old World, with the death of the apostles, and since the fifth century in the New World, with the destruction of the Nephites. On the other hand, it was not uncommon for early Latter-day Saints to recall spiritual manifestations they had received prior to their conversions to Mormonism.[35]

Joseph Smith's own mother, Lucy Mack Smith, wrote a lengthy narrative that included several visionary dreams that she and her husband had experienced while their children were still young.[36] On one occasion, when Lucy was

31. Ibid., 403.

32. Clarke Garrett, *Origins of the Shakers: From the Old World to the New World* (Baltimore: John Hopkins University Press, 1987), 166–68.

33. Christopher C. Jones, "'We Latter-day Saints are Methodists': The Influence of Methodism on Early Mormon Religiosity" (master's thesis, Brigham Young University, 2009), 78–79, 103–4.

34. John H. Wigger, "Methodism Transformed," chap. 8 in *Taking Heaven by Storm: Methodism and the Rise of Popular Christianity in America* (New York and Oxford: Oxford University Press, 1998); Ann Taves, *Fits, Trances, and Visions: Experiencing Religion and Explaining Experience from Wesley to James* (Princeton, NJ: Princeton University Press, 1999), 113. In England, the Catholic Apostolic Church—or "Irvingites" as they were often called—also spoke in tongues and prophesied. P. E. Shaw, *The Catholic Apostolic Church: Sometimes Called Irvingite, A Historical Study* (Morningside Heights, NY: King's Crown Press, 1946), 33–35, 58.

35. Christopher C. Jones and Stephen J. Fleming, "'Except among that Portion of Mankind': Early Mormon Conceptions of the Apostasy," in *Standing Apart: Mormon Historical Consciousness and the Concept of the Apostasy*, ed. Miranda Wilcox and John D. Young (New York and Oxford: Oxford University Press, 2014), 65–71.

36. Lucy Mack Smith, *Lucy's Book: A Critical Edition of Lucy Mack Smith's Family Memoir*, ed. Lavina Fielding Anderson (Salt Lake City: Signature Books, 2001), 291–330.

deathly ill, she heard the voice of Christ and was miraculously healed.[37] Joseph Smith's father, Joseph Sr., used a divining rod for water witching and treasure seeking.[38] Like his parents, Joseph Smith was a believer in charismata. Like his father, he learned to witch for water and hunt for treasure with a dowsing rod.[39] He surpassed his father in learning to use a seer stone.[40] Whereas his parents, especially his father, had visionary dreams, young Joseph had waking visions. Like Peter on the day of Pentecost, he may have believed that he had witnessed a fulfillment of Joel's prophecy of "the last days," when God would "pour out [his] Spirit upon all flesh." Joel foretold that "old men shall dream dreams" and "young men shall see visions."[41]

Most famously, Joseph Smith saw visions of God, Jesus, and angels. He recalled that in 1829, after he and Oliver Cowdery had baptized one another, they emerged from the water with the gift of prophecy: "No sooner had I baptized Oliver Cowdery than the Holy Ghost fell upon him and he stood up and prophecied many things which should shortly come to pass." Joseph Smith, in turn, "prophecied concerning the rise of this church, and many other things connected with the Church and this generation of the children of men."[42] Smith would remain an advocate of spiritual gifts throughout his ministry.

The Book of Mormon, which Smith produced in 1829, contains many references to spiritual gifts and miracle working experienced among a group of Israelites that had departed Jerusalem around 600 BCE and sailed to the New World. The text's first prophet, Lehi, sees visions and dreams.[43] His son and successor, Nephi, shares these same gifts and others. At one point, he is able to "shock" his brothers who persecute him.[44] Other figures from the text prophesy, heal, experience visions, and have angelic visitations.

A few passages even supply lists of gifts. One of these lists names "the gift of speaking with tongues, and the gift of preaching, and the gift of the Holy

37. Smith, *Lucy's Book*, 276–78.

38. Jesse Smith, Stockholm, New York, to Hyrum Smith, Palmyra, New York, 17 June 1829, transcribed in Joseph Smith Letterbook 2, 1837–1843, 59–61, Joseph Smith Collection, Church History Library, The Church of Jesus Christ of Latter-day Saints, Salt Lake City (hereafter Church History Library). See also Mark Ashurst-McGee, "A Pathway to Prophethood: Joseph Smith Junior as Rodsman, Village Seer, and Judeo-Christian Prophet" (master's thesis, Utah State University, 2000), 75–94.

39. Ashurst-McGee, "A Pathway to Prophethood," chap. 2.

40. Ibid., 198–231, also 118–20.

41. Joel 2:28–29; as quoted in Acts 2:17–28.

42. Joseph Smith, History, 1838–1856, vol. A-1, 18 [Joseph Smith-History, 1:73] (accessible in the Histories series of the online edition of *The Joseph Smith Papers*).

43. 1 Nephi 1, and 8.

44. 1 Nephi 17:53.

Ghost, and the gift of translation."[45] This "gift of translation," unattested in the Bible, would be the very means by which Joseph Smith would bring forth the ancient record. The prophet Mormon, for whom the record was named, emphatically opposes those who accept cessationist views on spiritual gifts:

> Has the day of miracles ceased? Or have angels ceased to appear unto the children of men? Or has he [God] withheld the power of the Holy Ghost from them? Or will he, so long as time shall last, or the earth shall stand, or there shall be one man upon the face thereof to be saved? Behold I say unto you, Nay; for it is by faith that miracles are wrought; and it is by faith that angels appear and minister unto men; wherefore, if these things have ceased wo be unto the children of men, for it is because of unbelief, and all is vain.[46]

Mormon explicitly called out those who would say that there were "no revelations, nor prophecies, nor gifts, nor healing, nor speaking with tongues, and the interpretation of tongues."[47] The Book of Mormon was clear and emphatic that if miracles had ceased it was only temporarily and due to disbelief.

Many embraced the Book of Mormon and its teachings, seeing the book itself as a miracle, and were eager to practice charismata after joining the church. This was particularly the case in 1831 with a large number of converts from Kirtland, Ohio, and vicinity. A Protestant church at Kirtland had converted en masse following the arrival of Mormon missionaries, who had sought out the community's leader, Sidney Rigdon, as a potential supporter. Rigdon had been a prominent leader among the Reformed Baptists—Alexander Campbell's Christian Primitivist movement—but had become estranged from Campbell due to Campbell's rejection of spiritual gifts and his aversion to communalism.[48] The conversions of the Reformed Baptists led by Rigdon not only bolstered the fledgling Mormon movement numerically but also affected its religious practice. Spiritual gifts had been experienced among earlier converts to Mormonism, but the ecstatic performances among the Kirtland Saints dramatically exceeded them.

45. Alma 9:21.

46. Moroni 7:35–37.

47. Mormon 9:7.

48. Richard S. Van Wagoner, *Sidney Rigdon: A Portrait of Religious Excess* (Salt Lake City: Signature Books, 1994), 52–54.

Much of this radical enthusiasm seems to have developed while the Mormon missionaries were away for the winter. Parley P. Pratt recalled that when he returned to the Kirtland area "some very strange spiritual operations were manifested, which were disgusting, rather than edifying." Pratt described some examples of this odd behavior: "Some persons would seem to swoon away, and make unseemly gestures, and be drawn or disfigured in their countenances. Others would fall into ecstasies, and be drawn into contortions, cramp, fits, etc. Others would seem to have visions and revelations, which were not edifying, and which were not congenial to the doctrine and spirit of the gospel. In short, a false and lying spirit seemed to be creeping into the Church."[49] When these practices of the early Kirtland Mormons were recounted in the history Joseph Smith initiated in 1838, they were referred to as "some strange notions and false spirits [that] had crept in among them."[50] Smith and Pratt believed that the performance of spiritual gifts had grown out of control.

The gifts under question seem to have specifically related to the church's emphasis on evangelizing American Indians, whom Mormons believed were descendants of a group of Israelites who had anciently migrated to the New World. Early Mormons considered it their duty to remind Native Americans of their forgotten identity through sharing the Book of Mormon. The Book of Mormon also prophesied that when the Lamanites accepted the Book of Mormon and were restored to their identity as a remnant of the House of Israel that the Lord would revive the covenant he had made with their ancestors and restore the land of the Americas as their own sovereign territory. The Book of Mormon warned the latter-day Gentiles to whom the book would come to repent. Otherwise, they were warned, the Lamanites "shall go forth among you as a lion, and tear you in pieces, and there is none to deliver."[51] Most unusually, the faithful in Kirtland had reportedly begun to act out scenes from the Book of Mormon or impersonate their image of a Native American. One account referred to them rowing an invisible ark as if they were the founding family of the Book of Mormon making their way to the New World.[52] Jesse Moss, who

49. Parley Parker Pratt, *The Autobiography of Parley Parker Pratt* [...], ed. Parley P. Pratt [Jr.] (New York: Russell Brothers, 1874), 65.

50. Joseph Smith, History, 1838–1856, vol. A-1, 93, Church History Library (accessible in the Histories series of the online edition of *The Joseph Smith Papers*).

51. Mormon 5:24.

52. See Mark Lyman Staker, *Hearken, O Ye People: The Historical Setting for Joseph Smith's Ohio Revelations* (Salt Lake City: Greg Kofford Books, 2009), 85; also Christopher C. Smith, "Playing Lamanite: Ecstatic Performance of American Indian Roles in Early Mormon Ohio," *Journal of Mormon History* 41, no. 3 (July 2015): 131–66.

lived in the area, reported that the early Kirtland converts "went through all sorts of Indian performances, some of them not very natural. I have seen them, in pantomime tomahawk and scalp each other, and rip open the bowels and tear out the entrails."[53] Moss also noted that "they claimed to have a special mission to the Indians." Another account reported that some would preach to invisible audiences, perhaps of Indians.

This sense of mission to the Indians reportedly led to speaking in Indian tongues. John Corrill, then a non-Mormon observer, described a meeting in which spiritual gifts were performed:

> The meeting lasted all night, and such a meeting I never attended before. They administered the sacrament, and laid on hands, after which I heard them prophecy and speak in tongues unknown to me. Persons in the room, who took no part with them, declared, from the knowledge they had of the Indian languages, that the tongues spoken were regular Indian dialects, which I was also informed, on inquiry, the persons who spoke had never learned.[54]

As if they were preparing for a Native American Pentecost, the Kirtland Mormons were apparently getting ready to preach to the Indians in their native tongues.

Smith arrived in the community in February 1831 and began to actively discourage these practices—in part through the dictation of revelations that warned against "false spirits."[55] The result, according to historian Mark Staker, was that "even though some of the gifts, such as the gift of tongues identified in revelation, were understood as coming from God, all of the ecstatic gifts as they then existed in the Church in Kirtland stopped."[56] As to be expected, this had more impact on the church's center than it did the periphery in New York and Pennsylvania where charismata were still occurring regularly.[57] According to one reminiscence, when a recently converted Brigham Young spoke in tongues, some who witnessed it warned him that the experience originated "from the devil" and would receive Smith's condemnation.[58] As it turned out,

53. Quoted in Staker, *Hearken, O Ye People*, 83.

54. John Corrill, *A Brief History of the Church of Christ of Latter Day Saints* [...] (St. Louis: Printed for the Author, 1839), 9.

55. Revelation, 9 May 1831, in *JSP*-D1:306 [D&C 50:2].

56. Staker, *Hearken, O Ye People*, 161.

57. Dan Vogel and Scott C. Dunn, "'The Tongue of Angels': Glossolalia among Mormonism's Founders," *Journal of Mormon History* 19, no. 2 (Fall 1993): 7.

58. "History of Brigham Young," *Millennial Star*, 11 July 1863, 439.

when Smith heard Young pray in glossolalia in November 1832, he endorsed it, perhaps providing a catalyst for tongues to return to general practice in Mormonism.

As Young later recounted this incident, Smith identified his utterance as "the pure Adamic language."[59] Mormon reference to such a pure language originated in the Book of Mormon's Jaredite narrative, which begins when God confounded human language at the Tower of Babel. A group of the righteous—the Jaredites—were spared this curse and maintained an unconfounded tongue.[60] The concept of a primordial language was again referenced in a revelation Joseph Smith dictated as part of his "new translation" of the King James Bible.[61] A passage written on 30 November 1830 referred to "the Language of Adam" and Adam's earliest descendants—a language that was "pure & undefiled."[62] When Smith identified Young's vocalization as humankind's original tongue, it seems to have been the first time any Mormon had an actual encounter with the language. In succeeding years, Smith introduced a handful of new words in a "Sample of pure Language"—presumably the "pure & undefiled" tongue spoken by Adam.[63]

Yet, Smith continued to worry about the prevalence of tongues in the church. A letter addressed to the Saints in 1833 explained that "no prophecy spoken in tongues should be made public, for this reason:—Many who pretended to have the gift of interpretation are liable to be mistaken, and do not give the true interpretation of what is spoken; therefore, great care should be taken as respects this thing, but, if any speak in tongues a word of exhortation, or doctrine, or principles of the Gospel, etc., let it be interpreted for the edification of the Church."[64] Smith was presumably writing with reference to glossolalia. By the Nauvoo period, Smith came to generally discourage tongues as a means of obtaining revelation. Speaking in tongues was largely confined to

59. Ibid.

60. Ether 1:33–37.

61. Joseph Smith occasionally used the title "New Translation" to refer to his revision of the Bible. See Letter to Church Leaders in Jackson County, Missouri, 21 April 1833, in *JSP*-D3:68; Letter to Church Leaders in Jackson County, Missouri, 25 June 1833, in *JSP*-D3:154; Letter to Church Leaders in Jackson County, Missouri, 2 July 1833, in *JSP*-D3:167; Letter to Church Leaders in Jackson County, Missouri, 6 August 1833, in *JSP*-D3:233.

62. Old Testament Manuscript 1, 11, in Joseph Smith, *Joseph Smith's New Translation of the Bible: Original Manuscripts*, ed. Scott H. Faulring, Kent P. Jackson, and Robert J. Matthews (Provo, UT: Religious Studies Center, Brigham Young University, 2004), 96–98 [Moses 6:5–6].

63. See David Golding, "'Eternal Wisdom Engraven upon the Heavens': Joseph Smith's Pure Language Project," Chapter 14 herein.

64. Joseph Smith, History, 1838–1856, vol. B-1, 180 (accessible in the Histories series of the online edition of *The Joseph Smith Papers*).

xenoglossia. It was explicitly and solely for those who would preach the gospel in foreign tongues.[65] Oddly, in 1842, he gave his blessing for the Relief Society to use tongues in their worship, although he warned them to "not indulge too much in the gift of tongues, or the devil will take advantage of the innocent."[66]

Tongues, like all revelatory spiritual gifts, were regulated by Smith and other church leaders. They were not to be performed except during specially designated meetings. Whether tongues were identified as the pure language, like that spoken by Adam, or a foreign language, like those spoken by Native Americans, some fellow believer was expected to interpret the utterance. This meant that the gift was never just an experience of personal ecstasy or even a public performance but was always supposed to convey information. These messages could comfort, inspire, or even exhort the Saints, but they were not to be considered commandments from the Lord, nor authoritative for the church as a whole.

THE GIFT OF INTERPRETING TONGUES AND THE GIFT OF INTERPRETING LANGUAGE

Though rare, Mormonism was not the first Judeo-Christian tradition to profess miraculous translations. In the second century BCE a Jewish legend of miraculous translation became associated with the Greek translation of the Hebrew Bible. According to the more dramatic versions of this legend, seventy-two scholars were kept in different rooms while translating the manuscript, but when they finished the text was the same, thus indicating God's providence and legitimizing the accuracy of their translation.[67] In the Middle Ages, Christian legends circulated of saintly individuals blessed with the ability to read or write foreign languages. While men claimed the gift of tongues to preach to foreigners, it was largely women who professed to read and write foreign languages. Christine F. Cooper-Rompato, a scholar of medieval literature, has noted that in the later Middle Ages both male and female visionaries (but more often women) experienced "the gift of the Latin language"—the language of the church and its liturgy. This gift included "speaking, aurally comprehending,

65. Discourse, between ca. 26 June and ca. 2 July 1839, in *JSP*-D6:523; Joseph Smith, Discourse, 26 December 1841, in *JSP*-D9:46–47.

66. Nauvoo Relief Society, Minute Book, 28 April 1842, 39, in Jill Mulvay Derr, Carol Cornwall Madsen, Kate Holbrook, and Matthew J. Grow, eds., *The First Fifty Years of Relief Society: Key Documents in Latter-day Saint Women's History* (Salt Lake City: Church Historian's Press, 2016), 58.

67. Moshe Simon-Shoshan, "The Tasks of the Translators: The Rabbis, the Septuagint, and the Cultural Politics of Translation," *Prooftexts* 27, no. 1 (2007): 19.

writing, or reading Latin," and frequently functioned to "authenticate their [i.e., women's] role as receivers and bearers of the divine Word."[68]

The sixteenth-century English scholar and occult practitioner John Dee provides a case of this idea that God might empower someone to translate a foreign tongue. Dee reported that an angel had given him a special "shewstone," which could be used to obtain secret knowledge. Dee hired a "skryer" named Edward Kelly to use his gift of seeing visions when looking into a scrying stone. Dee, in his private journal, recorded Kelly's dictations of what he reported to have seen and heard while looking into the stone. His visions "would range in content from entire landscapes, individual 'spirit creatures,' fleets of ships, geographic countries, grids full of letters, etc."[69] The result was an extensive record of Kelly's visions and revelations. Among these revelations were an otherwise unknown language, alleged to be the language spoken by angels and early humankind. Kelly even revealed the divine language's written script.[70]

These examples appear to be independent manifestations of a subtle tendency to expand the gift of tongues from the realm of the oral to embrace a broader notion of language that included written texts. Precursors to Smith shared a biblical literacy suggesting the possibility that they too would have been familiar with the Old Testament story of Daniel interpreting the writing on the palace wall.

The Book of Mormon contained several references to those gifted with translation. One intriguing character in the narrative, Aminadi, is referenced only once. A descendent recalls as an aside that Aminadi had "interpreted the writing which was upon the wall of the temple, which was written by the finger of God."[71] This passage closely parallels the language of KJV Daniel 5, in which the king of Babylon was frightened by an appearance of the "fingers" of God, which wrote upon "the wall of the king's palace," and therefore Daniel the Hebrew was summoned to "read the writing unto the king, and make known to him the interpretation." The intertextuality between these two stories would have shown many readers that the miraculous interpretation of written language had a biblical precedent.[72]

68. Christine F. Cooper, "Miraculous Translation in The Book of Margery Kempe," *Studies in Philology* 101, no. 3 (Summer 2004): 273.

69. James Justin Sledge, "Between Loagaeth and Cosening: Towards an Etiology of John Dee's Spirit Diaries," *Aries* 10, no. 1 (February 2010): 5.

70. Donald C. Laycock, *The Complete Enochian Dictionary: A Dictionary of the Angelic Language as Revealed to Dr. John Dee and Edward Kelley* (Newbury Port, MA: Weiser Books, 1994, 2001), 27–29.

71. Alma 10:2.

72. For a discussion of the urim and thummim, seer stones, and translation in the Bible and the Book of Mormon, see Michael Hubbard MacKay and Nicholas J. Frederick, *Joseph Smith's Seer Stones* (Provo, UT: Religious Studies Center, Brigham Young University; Salt Lake City, UT: Desered Book, 2016), 111–22.

A comparison between a different set of texts clarified that in the Book of Mormon interpreting languages was the same as or similar to interpreting tongues. The enumeration of spiritual gifts in 1 Corinthians 12 lists "divers kinds of tongues," followed by the "interpretation of tongues."[73] The parallel enumeration in the Book of Mormon, in Moroni 10, lists "all kinds of tongues," followed by "the interpretation of languages and of divers kinds of tongues."[74] The Book of Mormon thereby expands a diversity of tongues to *all* tongues. More dramatically, it extends the interpretation of tongues to "the interpretation of languages and . . . tongues." In this construction, "tongues" apparently refers to spoken language and "languages" to written language. In this way the Book of Mormon amplifies the gift of the interpretation of tongues to the gift of interpreting language generally, including the interpretation of written language.[75]

The text of the Book of Mormon also provided a model for the gift of translation—or, as it was frequently called, the gift of interpreting languages. The narrative explicitly discussed two events in which this gift was needed. The first occurred when King Limhi's people discovered twenty-four plates that caused great curiosity because they were "filled with engravings," but in an unknown script. A new opportunity opened when Limhi's people were contacted by Ammon, a Nephite scout from Zarahemla. Limhi "inquired of him to know if he could interpret languages" and explained to him their predicament: "There is no one in the land that is able to *interpret* the language or the engravings that are on the plates. Therefore I said unto thee: Canst thou *translate*?"[76] This passage equated the word "interpret"—used four times in KJV 1 Corinthians with reference to the interpretation of tongues[77]—to the word "translate." Ammon confessed he could not, but informed Limhi of one who could: Mosiah, the king of the Nephites in Zarahemla, was "a man that can translate the records; for he has wherewith that he can look, and translate all records that are of ancient date; and it is a gift from God. And the things are called interpreters, and no man can look in them except he be commanded, lest

73. 1 Corinthians 12:10.

74. Moroni 10:15–16.

75. The gift of the interpretation of tongues is also apparently expanded in an admonition appearing near the very end of Smith's translation of the Book of Mormon: "Believe in prophesying, and in revelations, and in the ministering of angels, and in the gift of speaking with tongues, and in the gift of interpreting languages" (Omni 1:25).

76. Mosiah 8:6–11 (emphasis added). The Book of Mormon later affirms that "Mosiah had a gift from God, whereby he could interpret such engravings" (Mosiah 21:28).

77. 1 Corinthians 12:30, 14:5, 13, 27.

he should look for that he ought not and he should perish. And whosoever is commanded to look in them, the same is called seer." The passage associated the gift of translation with the corresponding gift of seership and related them both to the possession of the "interpreters."[78] Ammon went on to explain that "a seer is a revelator and a prophet also." He stated that the ability to translate was a "high gift" and indeed the greatest of all spiritual gifts, for "a gift which is greater can no man have."[79]

The interpreters are described later in the book when the plates are brought to King Mosiah, who "translated them by the means of those two stones which were fastened into the two rims of a bow."[80] The "seer" would "look in them"[81]—the pair of fastened stones. He would presumably do so with his two eyes, with each eye looking through one stone like a pair of glasses. And he would thereby *see*—presumably the translation. "Now these things were prepared from the beginning," the text explains, "for the purpose of interpreting languages."[82] The Book of Mormon refers to this pair of stones in further passages, calling them either "these interpreters" or "the interpreters."[83] Here the Book of Mormon apparently associated seership with the biblical gifts of interpretation such as the Pauline interpretation of tongues, the interpretation of dreams experienced by Joseph and Daniel, and the interpretation of writing also experienced by Daniel. The translated title page of the Book of Mormon stated that the book was intended to "come forth by the gift and power of God unto the interpretation thereof—Sealed by the hand of Moroni, and hid up unto the Lord, to come forth in due time by way of the Gentile—The interpretation thereof by the gift of God."[84] However, the word "interpretation" in the Bible was not uniformly positive. The New Testament included not only the Pauline gift of the "interpretation of tongues" but the statement attributed to Peter that "no prophecy of the scripture is of any private interpretation."[85] Mosiah's instruments were called "interpreters," possibly employing Pauline language—Paul used the word "interpreter" for the person who would interpret glossolalia[86]—but these were "wherewith that he can look, and *translate* all records that are of

78. Mosiah 8:13.
79. Mosiah 8:15–16.
80. Mosiah 28:13.
81. Mosiah 8:13.
82. Mosiah 28:14.
83. Mosiah 8:13, 19; Mosiah 28:20; Ether 4:5.
84. Title Page of the Book of Mormon.
85. 2 Peter 1:20.
86. 1 Corinthians 14:28. Similarly, Joseph, son of Jacob, was an "interpreter" of dreams (Genesis 40:8).

ancient date."[87] The "interpreters" were used to "translate." Similarly, in Smith's preface to the Book of Mormon, he did not claim that he had "interpreted" the book, but that he had "translated" it.[88]

Whereas Paul, in his first epistle to the saints in Corinth, listed several good gifts from God, he admonished them to "covet earnestly the best gifts." He warned them against excesses of glossolalia, urging them to "desire spiritual gifts, but rather that ye may prophesy" and that they even "covet to prophesy." Prophesying, he explained, was a gift far superior to speaking in tongues.[89] Whereas Paul valorized prophecy over glossolalia as perhaps the greatest of gifts, the Book of Mormon identified seership and translation—closely related to the interpretation of tongues—as the greatest of all the spiritual gifts.

That Joseph Smith's gift was meant to be understood through the lens of the Book of Mormon was clear by its inclusion of a prophecy attributed to Joseph of Egypt, who had interpreted the dreams of Pharaoh. In this prophecy, Joseph had foretold that God would send a "choice seer" in the last days who would also be named Joseph.[90] In 1827, when the angel Moroni entrusted Joseph Smith with the gold plates containing the record that would be translated as the Book of Mormon, he also gave Smith a device later identified as the "urim and thummim" and "the interpreters of languages."[91] It was through this device, and later through a "seer stone," that Smith was by some accounts able to see the Reformed Egyptian language and its English translation.[92] Referring to the device as the urim and thummim linked translation to the Old Testament tradition of divination. Calling it "the interpreter of languages" evoked the interpreters of the Book of Mormon and nodded to gifts of interpretation, most notably the interpretation of tongues and the interpretation of dreams.

When Smith organized a church in April 1830, he was appointed as its leader. In this role he dictated a revelation from God in which he was called "a seer, a translator, a prophet, an apostle of Jesus Christ, an elder of the church through the will of God the Father, and the grace of your Lord Jesus Christ."[93] Five years later, he gave instructions on priesthood and church organization,

87. Mosiah 8:13 (emphasis added).

88. *The Book of Mormon*, iii.

89. 1 Corinthians 12:31, 14:1, 39.

90. 2 Nephi 3:6.

91. Characters Copied by Oliver Cowdery, circa 1835–1836, in *JSP*-D1:365.

92. See the accounts of translation by Joseph Smith and others collected in James E. Lancaster, "The Translation of the Book of Mormon," chap. 8 in *The Word of God: Essays on Mormon Scripture*, ed. Dan Vogel (Salt Lake City: Signature Books, 1990), 97–112; and MacKay and Hubbard, *Joseph Smith's Seer Stones*, 45–64, 187–89; 222–30.

93. Revelation, 6 April 1830, in *JSP*-D1:129 [D&C 21:1].

soon canonized, in which he stated he was "a seer, a revelator, a translator, and a prophet, having *all the gifts of God* which he bestows upon the head of the church."[94]

Although "translator" was one of Smith's official church titles, it was well known among church members that he had translated the Book of Mormon *prior* to the church's organization or any formal recognition of this role. Even after Smith's death, the first generation of Saints would continue to speak of his ability to translate as a gift distinct from his hierarchical position. Brigham Young, his successor as church president, frequently noted that Smith as a young man was already a seer—long before he had been ordained to the priesthood. The priesthood had given Smith the authority to perform ordinances and govern the church, but "the gift of seeing was a natural gift. . . . There are thousands in the world who are natural born Seers."[95] While Young may have been recollecting stories of a youthful Joseph Smith using his seer stone for other purposes—like finding things that were lost or hunting for buried treasure—Smith's gift of seeing was most evident in his translation of the Book of Mormon; and in the Book of Mormon the gift of seership was most manifest in King Mosiah's ability to translate an ancient record. As Smith's successor, Young claimed to possess all the keys of the priesthood and the authority to receive revelation to direct the church, but he claimed neither the "natural" gift of seership nor the gift of translation.[96] He did not consider the priesthood keys a gift but rather an extension of his apostolic office.[97]

David Whitmer, a charter member of the church who broke ranks with Smith in 1838, shared Young's view that Smith's gift of translation was distinct from his administrative roles over the church. In contrast to Young, however, Whitmer believed that Smith was wrong to take on further leadership roles. Decades later, Whitmer wrote a tract in which he directed readers to a revelation published in 1833 in the Book of Commandments stating that Smith had "a gift to translate the book" but that was all: "I have commanded him that he shall pretend to no other gift, for I will grant him no other gift." Whitmer pointed out that when this revelation was republished in 1835, as part of

94. Instruction on Priesthood, between circa 1 March and circa 4 May 1835, in *JSP*-D4:321 (emphasis added) [D&C 107:92].

95. "Tabernacle," *Deseret News*, 26 December 1860, 337.

96. Wilford Woodruff, *Wilford Woodruff's Journal: 1833–1898 Typescript*, ed. Scott G. Kenney (Midvale, UT: Signature Books, 1984), 5:550.

97. Richard E. Bennett, "The Circumference of the Apostleship," chap. 3 in *A Firm Foundation: Church Organization and Administration*, ed. David J. Whittaker and Arnold K. Garr (Provo, UT: Religious Studies Center; Salt Lake City: Deseret Book, 2011).

the Doctrine and Covenants, this line was removed and another had been inserted referring to the gift of translation as "the *first* gift that I bestowed on you"—thereby justifying Smith's subsequent accumulation of additional honors.[98] Whitmer believed that "the first error was introduced into the Church of Christ... when Smith was recognized as Prophet, Seer, and Revelator."[99] It was because of "God giving to Joseph Smith the gift to translate the plates on which was engraven the Nephite scriptures, the people of the church put too much trust in him—in the man—and believed his words as if they were from God's own mouth."[100]

Orson Pratt, a convert of 1830 and a charter member of the church's Quorum of the Twelve Apostles, also continued to think of Smith's ability to translate as one of the gifts of the Spirit. In an 1856 pamphlet titled "Gifts of the Spirit," he explained the purpose of the gift of translation: "God has revealed many important principles to people of different languages. And that these principles may be more generally useful, he has imparted to some revelators and prophets the power to translate sacred writings from one language to another." Uninspired translators simply could not adequately render the word of God into a different language. Such a text was "not the word of God, but the word of uninspired translators."[101]

While the Book of Mormon hinted at the connection between translation and the gift of tongues, Pratt's commentary was explicit: "If an unknown tongue, spoken verbally can be interpreted by the Spirit, then an unknown tongue written can be interpreted or translated by the same Spirit."[102] In fact, Smith's new translation of the King James Bible in the early 1830s described a similar scenario. Revisions to the early chapters of Genesis related that "a book of remembrance was kept" by Adam's descendants and that it was recorded in the "language of Adam, for it was given unto as many as called upon God to write by the *spirit of inspiration*."[103] Pratt also referred to Daniel's interpretation of the God-engraven script on the wall of the Babylonian king's palace as an example of the "same gift of translation ... by the power of the Holy Ghost, he [Daniel] translated the unknown writing."[104]

98. David Whitmer, "A Witness to the Divine Authenticity of the Book of Mormon," in *An Address to All Believers in Christ* (Richmond, MO: Elder David Whitmer, 1887), 57–58 (emphasis revised).

99. Ibid., 33.

100. Ibid., 4.

101. Orson Pratt, *Spiritual Gifts* ([Liverpool, Lancashire]: [Orson Pratt], [1857]), 70–71.

102. Ibid., 71–72.

103. Moses 6:5.

104. Pratt, *Spiritual Gifts*, 71.

GIFT OF TRANSLATION

The gift of translation was understood within early Mormonism to operate by the same logic as other gifts of the Spirit. Perhaps most importantly, like other spiritual gifts, it was not confined to one Prophet, Seer, Revelator, and Translator—the title bestowed on Joseph Smith when the church was organized—but could potentially be conferred upon others. All believers did not possess the gift of translation in the same sense that all members did not possess the gift of dreams or of tongues. As one of Smith's revelations explained, "all have not every gift given unto them for there are many gifts & to evry man is given a gift by the spirit of God."[105] Among various examples provided to illustrate this doctrine, it stated: "It is given to some to speak with tongues & to another it is given the interpretation of tongues."[106]

Like other gifts of the Spirit, more than one individual could possess the gift of translation—Oliver Cowdery enjoyed this gift for a brief time. While translating the Book of Mormon, Smith dictated a revelation—given in the voice of God—directed to Cowdery, his current scribe: "I grant unto you a gift if you desire of me, to translate even as my servant Joseph." Oliver was further told that if he maintained righteous desires, he would continue to enjoy this gift: "Then shall you assist in bringing to light, with your gift, those parts of my scriptures which have been hidden because of iniquity."[107] When Cowdery faltered, Smith dictated a new revelation explaining that it was no longer "expedient" that he should exercise the gift of translation and that the "privilege" of translating had been "taken away" from him, "because that [he] did not continue as [he] had commenced." The revelation assuaged Cowdery with a more distant promise: "Behold, other records have I, that I will give unto you power that you may assist to translate."[108] Smith and Cowdery likely believed this revelation was fulfilled in 1835 when Smith purchased the Egyptian papyrus from which he would translate the writings of the biblical patriarch Abraham. Cowdery assisted in this translation effort. An 1835 revelation to Warren Parrish, Smith's personal scribe at the time, stated that he too would assist with the translation of the Book of Abraham: "He shall see much of my ancient records

105. Revelation, circa 8 March 1831-A, in *JSP*-D1:283 [D&C 46:11].

106. Revelation, circa 8 March 1831-A, in *JSP*-D1:283 [D&C 46:24–25].

107. Revelation, April 1829-A, in *JSP*-D1:36–37 [D&C 6:25–27]. Another revelation encouraged Cowdery that he could "receive, a knowledge concerning the engraveings of old Records which are ancient," called this ability a "gift," and instructed him to "apply unto it." Revelation, April 1829-B, in *JSP*-D1:46 [D&C 8:1–9].

108. Revelation, April 1829-D, in *JSP*-D1:49–50 [D&C 9:1–12].

and shall know of hid[d]en things and shall be endowed with a knowledge of hid[d]en languages."[109] Frederick G. Williams and William W. Phelps also worked on the Book of Abraham with Joseph Smith.[110] Years later, shortly after the Latter-day Saints had begun relocating in what would become Utah Territory, an exploration party led by Parley P. Pratt, William W. Phelps, and John D. Fullmer discovered some Native American petroglyphs, which were identified as "the Reformed Egyptian language, or Nephite language."[111] Phelps produced a translation of the petroglyphs, perhaps using the spiritual gift of translation.[112]

Latter-day Saints of the founding generation believed that once they received a spiritual gift, they possessed it for life unless they were deprived of the ability to use it through sin or doubt. As Elizabeth Ann Whitney, who sang in tongues, later recounted, "the Prophet Joseph promised me that I should never lose this gift if I would be wise in using it; and his words have been verified."[113] Similarly, Heber C. Kimball addressed a group of Saints in Utah Territory in 1857, declaring that he could still "speak in a good, beautiful language to this people at any time"—even though he rarely spoke in tongues. He knew this, as he explained, "because God gave me the gift, and He does not give gifts to men and then take them away again, so long as those men are doing their duty.... God gives them to men and women; and so long as they improve upon them they do not forfeit them."[114] Zina Diantha Huntington Smith Young reported being deprived of the gift of tongues when, after having

109. Revelation, 14 November 1835, in *JSP*-D5:52–53.

110. For the involvement of especially Phelps, see Samuel Brown, "The Translator and the Ghostwriter: Joseph Smith and W. W. Phelps," *Journal of Mormon History* 34, no. 1 (Winter 2008): 26–62.

111. Pratt, *The Autobiography of Parley Parker Pratt*, 408–12; William Appleby, Autobiography and Journal, 1848–1856, 276, Church History Library.

112. American explorer John Gunnison, who spent time among the Latter-day Saints in Utah, reported this discovery of petroglyphs in a travel narrative. He also stated that "those who were associated with Joseph Smith as amanuenses pretended to have acquired sufficient knowledge of similar things to be enabled to decipher their signification, and have translated enough to confirm, in the most wonderful manner, the Nephite records." Gunnison reproduced a short translation of some of the petroglyphs, as offered "by one of the Regents." John W. Gunnison, *The Mormons, or, Latter-day Saints, in the Valley of the Great Salt Lake* [...] (London: Sampson Low and Son; Philadelphia: Lippincott, Grambo, 1852), 62–63. This "regent" was William W. Phelps (Brigham D. Madsen, *Exploring the Great Salt Lake: The Stansbury Expedition of 1849–50* [Salt Lake City: University of Utah Press, 1989], 312–13). Phelps had served as an amanuensis for Smith in 1835 when Smith was translating the Book of Abraham and they were working together on a collection of Egyptian counting, alphabet, and grammar documents. See Brian M. Hauglid, "'Translating an Alphabet to the Book of Abraham': Joseph Smith's Study of the Egyptian Language and His Translation of the Book of Abraham," 365–72 herein.

113. [Elizabeth Ann Whitney], "A Leaf from an Autobiography," *Woman's Exponent*, 1 November 1878, 83. When Whitney died in 1882, it was claimed that she had "always at times exercised this gift until the time of her death." Louie Wells, "In Memoriam: Elizabeth Ann Whitney," *The Contributor*, February 1882, 158.

114. Heber C. Kimball, Discourse, 11 January 1857, in *Journal of Discourses*, 26 vols. (Liverpool and London: Latter-day Saints' Book Depot, 1857), 4:170.

received a spiritual impression to use it, she "checked its utterance." Her ability to speak in tongues only returned after she repented and promised to "never check it again, no matter where or when I felt its promptings."[115] The failure of other spiritual gifts, such as the gift of healing, was also sometimes explained as a consequence of unworthiness or a lack of faith.[116]

Similarly, while Joseph Smith was the Prophet among prophets and the Translator among translators, even he could be deprived of his ability to translate. In the summer of 1828, Smith's benefactor and scribe, Martin Harris, asked him for permission to bring the handwritten manuscript of the Book of Mormon to his home to show to his wife. Smith petitioned God requesting permission for Harris but was denied. Upon further prompting from Harris, Smith asked a second time but was again turned down. When Smith prayed a third time, he received an answer from God that granted permission for Harris to take the manuscript, but under the conditions of a covenant that he would only show it to five specifically named family members: his wife, his wife's sister, his brother, and his parents. Harris broke his covenant, showing the manuscript to not only his family but several others, thereby drawing attention to it. Soon after, the manuscript was stolen. In the aftermath of this indiscretion, the angel Moroni appeared to Smith and reclaimed the gold plates as well as the urim and thummim.[117] Smith received another revelation in which he was scolded: "You have lost them, and you also lost your gift at the same time."[118] Yet another revelation commanded him to repent or he would "become as other men & have no more gift."[119] His gift was therefore "lost" but not entirely so. More specifically, it had been temporarily suspended, and was in jeopardy of being permanently revoked. Smith repented and the suspension was lifted, allowing him to complete the translation.

As with other spiritual gifts, this could also occur on a smaller scale. David Whitmer recounted that Joseph Smith occasionally struggled to exercise the gift of translation:

> At times when Brother Joseph would attempt to translate [the Book of Mormon from the golden plates] . . . he found he was spiritually blind

115. Zina D. Young, "How I Gained My Testimony of the Truth," *Young Woman's Journal*, April 1893, 319.

116. Discourse, 30 July 1840, in *JSP*-D7:366–68.

117. Joseph Smith, History, 1838–1856, April–June 1828, 10 (accessible in the Histories series of the online edition of *The Joseph Smith Papers*).

118. Revelation, Spring 1829, in *JSP*-D1:40 [D&C 10:2].

119. Revelation, July 1828, in *JSP*-D1:8 [D&C 3:11].

> and could not translate. He told us that his mind dwelt too much on earthly things, and various causes would make him incapable of proceeding with the translation. When in this condition he would go out and pray, and when he became sufficiently humble before God, he could then proceed with the translation.[120]

A godly humility and attention to the things of the Spirit were prerequisites for exercising the gifts of the Spirit.

Even then, those who possessed spiritual gifts were potentially vulnerable to Satanic deception. Church leaders commonly warned that the devil and his angels could falsify gifts, including the gift of speaking in tongues. In 1833, Joseph Smith and his counselors in the First Presidency addressed the subject of tongues in an epistle to the Saints in Missouri, cautioning them to "be careful lest in this you be deceived.... Satan will no doubt trouble you about the gift of tongues, unless you are careful."[121] Tongues were still desired, however, and especially so on certain occasions. In 1836, when the House of the Lord in Kirtland was completed and dedicated for worship, Joseph Smith prayed that it would be for the Saints "as upon those on the day of Pentacost: let the gift of tongues be poured out upon thy people, even cloven tongues as of fire, and the interpretation thereof."[122] In 1842, Smith published in the church newspaper a short history of the church that culminated in a statement of basic church doctrines. Here Smith affirmed the spiritual gifts as an article of faith: "We believe in the gift of tongues, prophesy, revelation, visions, healing, interpretation of tongues &c."[123] And yet, a month later, the caution regarding gifts—and speaking in tongues especially—was repeated by Smith in the same paper. An editorial titled "Try the Spirits"—presumably composed by Smith—warned that the devil could cause one "to speak in another tongue, as well as their own, as they were under the control of that spirit, and the devil can tempt the Hottentot, the Turk, the Jew, or any other nation; and if these men were under the influence

120. Whitmer, *An Address to All Believers in Christ*, 30.

121. Letter to Church Leaders in Jackson County, Missouri, 2 July 1833, in *JSP*-D3:167.

122. Minutes and Prayer of Dedication, 27 March 1836, in *JSP*-D5:203 [D&C 109:36].

123. Joseph Smith, "Church History," *Times and Seasons*, 1 March 1842, 706–10 (Articles of Faith 1:7). That this list of spiritual gifts begins with tongues and ends with interpretation of tongues is noteworthy in terms of the "primacy effect" and "recency effect" of reception and memory. On the study of serial position effects in cognitive psychology, see John W. McCrary Jr. and Walter S. Hunter, "Serial Position Curves in Verbal Learning," *Science* 117, no. 3032 (6 February 1953): 131–34; Bennet B. Murdock Jr., "The Serial Position Effect of Free Recall," *Journal of Experimental Psychology* 64, no. 5 (1962): 482–88; Krystal A. Klein, Kelly M. Addis, and Michael J. Kahana, "A Comparative Analysis of Serial and Free Recall," *Memory & Cognition* 33, no. 5 (2005): 833–39.

of his spirit, they of course speak Hebrew, Latin, Greek, Italian, Dutch, or any other language that the devil knew."[124] Smith never clarified whether the devil could also speak the language of Adam and his pre-Babel progeny, and thereby imitate glossolalia. However, in his new translation of the Bible, Smith revised the stories of the beguilement of Eve and the seduction of Cain, with the serpent or Satan speaking to the first humans.

Similarly, on a few occasions Smith explained that seers might be led astray—particularly through their seer stones. In 1830, he dictated a revelation condemning the revelations dictated by early Mormon Hiram Page, one of the men who claimed to have seen the golden plates of the Book of Mormon. Page had received extensive revelations through a stone of his own. Smith's revelation, given in the voice of God, stated that Page's revelations were "not of me. . . . Satan deceiveth him."[125] According to early Mormon Emer Harris, the brother of Martin Harris, Page's stone and the written revelations derived from it were destroyed. The stone was "Broke to powder and the writing Burnt."[126] In 1837, James Collin Brewster claimed that he had been visited by the angel Moroni and charged with the duty of bringing forth further ancient records. Brewster, then a ten-year-old boy, would accomplish this with a seer stone. When the church's high council in Kirtland learned of the child's claims, they pronounced it "a trick of the devil."[127] Later, in Nauvoo, Joseph Smith reportedly identified a stone brought from Staffordshire, England, as "a Urim and Thummim as good as ever was upon the earth," except that it had been "consecrated to devils."[128]

Joseph Smith had once even feared the possibility that his own gift might be corrupted. His wife, Emma Hale Smith, recounted later in her life an incident

124. "Try the Spirits," *Times and Seasons*, 1 April 1842, 743–48.

125. Revelation, September 1830-B, in *JSP*-D1:186 [D&C 28:11].

126. Quoted in D. Michael Quinn, *Early Mormonism and the Magic World View*, 2nd ed. (Salt Lake City: Signature Books, 1998), 248.

127. Dan Vogel, "James Colin Brewster: The Boy Prophet Who Challenged Mormon Authority," in *Differing Visions: Dissenters in Mormon History*, ed. Roger D. Launius and Linda Thatcher (Urbana and Chicago: University of Illinois Press, 1994), 120–21; Ohio Minutebook, 20 November 1837, Church History Library (accessible as "Minute Book 1" in the Administrative Records series of the online edition of *The Joseph Smith Papers*). Early Mormon Priddy Meeks recounted that Joseph Smith's brother Hyrum had spoken on the issue of deception:

> It is not safe to depend on peepstone in any case where evil spirits have the power to put false appearances before them while looking in a peepstone. If evil influences will not interfere, the verdict will be as true as preaching. That is my experience in the mater; also the Patriarch, Hiram Smith, the brother of the Prophet Joseph Smith, held the same idea, but stated that our faith was not strong enough to overcome the evil influences that might interfere, but seemed to think that time would come.

"Journal of Priddy Meeks," *Utah Historical Quarterly* 10, nos. 1–4 (January, April, July, October 1942): 180.

128. Wandle Mace, Autobiography, circa 1890 [Expanded], 49, Church History Library.

that occurred while she acted as a scribe for her husband's translation of the Book of Mormon. In the process, she recalled, he "dictated each sentence, word for word," but on one occasion "he stopped suddenly, pale as a sheet, and said, 'Emma, did Jerusalem have walls around it?'" When she assured him that it did, he replied "Oh! I was afraid I had been deceived."[129] For Emma, this incident was significant in that it provided evidence for the Book of Mormon containing greater knowledge of the past than Joseph possessed, that he was not sufficiently educated to have created such a text on his own. Yet this incident also demonstrates Joseph's belief that he, like others who professed the gift of seeing, could be deceived while exercising their gift—and in this case while translating.

One possible difference between the gift of interpreting tongues and the gift of translation may be useful to examine. The interpretation of tongues rarely resulted in a written text. When minutes from a church meeting recorded the content of an interpretation, it was usually by way of mere summary or paraphrase.[130] This may in part be explained by the church's warnings that messages received through tongues should not be taken as commandments or direction to the Saints.

There was, however, a special exception to the rule that the interpretation of tongues was not to be recorded: namely, the interpreted lyrics to hymns that were initially sung in tongues. Singing in tongues, mentioned in one of the Pauline epistles, was an occasional practice among early Latter-day Saints. During a worship meeting in the Kirtland temple, Joseph Smith encouraged Elizabeth Ann Whitney to sing in tongues. Early Mormon Wilford Woodruff later recounted that Smith "told her if she would rise upon her feet (while in a meeting) she should have the pure language" and that "she done so and immediately commenced singing in that language."[131] Smith reportedly identified it as "the pure Adamic language, that which was spoken in the Garden of Eden," where Adam conversed with God.[132]

These hymns might even be recorded, as was the case with one sung by Whitney and interpreted by Parley P. Pratt and another one sung by David W. Patten and interpreted by Sidney Rigdon.[133] In these cases, the pure lan-

129. Emma Hale Bidamon, interview by Edmund Briggs, 1856, in Dan Vogel, comp. and ed., *Early Mormon Documents*, vol. 1 (Salt Lake City: Signature Books, 1996), 530.

130. In 1830, Oliver Cowdery had been forbidden to "write by way of Commandment." Revelation, September 1830–B, in *JSP*-D1:185 [D&C 28:5].

131. Woodruff, *Wilford Woodruff's Journal*, 4:245.

132. Wells, "In Memoriam," 158. Whitney's singing in tongues was considered a "rare gift."

133. [Whitney], "A Leaf from an Autobiography," 83; *Mysteries of God, as Revealed to Enoch, on the Mount Mehujah, and Sung in Tongues by Elder D. W. Patton, of the "Church of Latter Day Saints"* [. . .] (n.p.:

guage source text was apparently understood to be lyrical. Interpretation was therefore not the mere articulation of content, but rather it seemed as if there were a fixed text, apparently in verse, that the interpreter brought forth in a way that was comparable to Joseph Smith's translation of ancient records. These hymns met with no controversy as would likely have been the case with other transcripts of interpreted tongue-speaking. This was likely because the dictation was poetic, like a hymn of praise offered up by the Saints to their God, rather than a message from God given by way of commandment. Nevertheless, the versified transcription of interpreted tongue songs among the Saints suggests that they viewed the interpretation of tongues as more than conceptual—that the gift of interpreting tongues was also in this sense like the gift of translation.

CONCLUSION

The early Mormon gift of translation, most famously employed by Joseph Smith in the production of the Book of Mormon, was rooted in the belief that God had long provided believers with supernatural powers. The Old Testament's descriptions of prophets and seers and its stories of interpreters of dreams and divine inscriptions led to the New Testament's expectation that the faithful would all experience spiritual gifts. While the "gift of translation" as described in the Book of Mormon could not be directly derived from either biblical testament, the text situated the seer's spiritual power of translation within the family of Pauline gifts of the Spirit, most closely akin to the interpretation of tongues. The title of seer was passed down through Joseph Smith's successors and as a result began to be thought of as a power distinctive from other spiritual gifts. Yet even to this day it is common for Latter-day Saints to ambiguously explain how the Book of Mormon was translated by quoting Smith himself. It was done "by the gift and power of God."

It is not clear that Smith followed the same method of translation in each of his translation projects. The processes that he undertook for the Book of Mormon, the new translation of the Bible, and the Book of Abraham seem quite distinct. However, understanding the ties he and other early Latter-day Saints saw between the gift of translation and the interpretation of tongues suggests

n.p., n.d.), copy at Church History Library. When Whitney died in 1882, it was claimed that "if all the hymns and poems were written as they were interpreted at the time when she sang them, they would make a beautiful volume." Wells, "In Memoriam," 158.

that the overarching method and experience of translation was supernatural and unscientific. In the same way that interpreters of tongues did not reason through their interpretations, Smith's translations were understood to have come from above more than within.

While the gift of translation was largely confined to the first generation of Mormonism—and even then it was rare—it fit quite comfortably within the larger family of spiritual gifts: it could be bestowed on others and remain with them, but it could also be lost through sin or falsified by the devil. The gift of translation was also like other gifts in terms of its demise among the Mormon people. Even over the course of Joseph Smith's life, through the process that the sociologist Max Weber called the routinization of charisma, the gift of translation was nearly confined to the leader of the church. Brigham Young, Smith's successor, carried the titles of Prophet, Seer, and Revelator, but dropped Translator. Others who had professed the gift of translation—like William Phelps possibly attempting to use it to translate petroglyphs at the age of fifty-seven—were a dying breed.[134] In time, only schismatic prophets claimed to translate ancient records. By the turn of the twentieth century, church leaders were discouraging the use of seer stones, even for personal revelation.[135] The gift of tongues was also regulated and eventually became practiced only in the sense that missionaries believed they were aided in learning foreign languages.[136] If the gift of tongues is now rare within Mormonism, the gift of interpretation is rarer still, and the related gift of translation is now viewed mainly as a special gift that was bestowed only upon the founder.

134. Phelps was born 17 February 1792. Walter Dean Bowen, "The Versatile W. W. Phelps—Mormon Writer, Educator, and Pioneer" (master's thesis, Brigham Young University, 1958), 6. Phelps evidently translated the petroglyphs sometime between 23 November 1849 and 23 January 1850. Appleby, Autobiography and Journal, 276; Pratt, *Autobiography of Parley Parker Pratt*, 408–12; Gunnison, *The Mormons, or, Latter-day Saints*, 62–63; Madsen, *Exploring the Great Salt Lake*, 312–13.

135. Quinn, *Early Mormonism and the Magic World View*, 253–55.

136. Vogel and Dunn, "'The Tongue of Angels,'" 23.

3

"Bringing Forth" the Book of Mormon

Translation as the Reconfiguration of Bodies in Space-Time

JARED HICKMAN

While inquiries into Joseph Smith's various "translation" projects have understandably defaulted to the paradigm of *linguistic* translation, this chapter offers a thought experiment: What if these projects were systematically reconsidered in light of the *other* kind of translation with which Smith was so manifestly fascinated—the removal from earth to heaven of biblical worthies like Enoch and Elijah? This form of translation, provisionally distinguished here as *metaphysical* translation, deserves deeper consideration.[1] What would it mean to say that the Book of Mormon was translated not in any way a text is typically understood to be translated, but in the way Enoch was translated? Further,

The author wishes to thank editor Mark Ashurst-McGee for his tireless and thoughtful aid in shaping this chapter, as well as the Utah State University Religious Studies Program, the Book of Mormon Studies Association, and the Mormon Theology Seminar for providing the occasions to work out many of the ideas presented in this chapter.

1. The default to the linguistic paradigm is evident in two of the most forthright efforts to solve the problem of translation as it pertains to Smith: Robert J. Matthews, "Joseph Smith—Translator," chap. 6 in *Joseph Smith: The Prophet, The Man*, ed. Susan Easton Black and Charles D. Tate Jr. (Provo, UT: Religious Studies Center, Brigham Young University, 1993); and Richard L. Bushman, "Joseph Smith as Translator," chap. 4 in *The Prophet Puzzle: Interpretive Essays on Joseph Smith*, ed. Bryan Waterman (Salt Lake City, UT: Signature Books, 1999), essentially recapitulated in Bushman's biography, *Joseph Smith: Rough Stone Rolling* (New York: Alfred A. Knopf, 2005], 130–33. Three accounts come closer to the argumentation in this chapter: Kathleen Flake, "Translating Time: The Nature and Function of Joseph Smith's Narrative Canon," *The Journal of Religion* 87, no. 4 (October 2007): esp. 501–11; Karl C. Sandberg, "Knowing Brother Joseph Again: The Book of Abraham and Joseph Smith as Translator," chap. 15 in Waterman, *The Prophet Puzzle*; and Samuel Morris Brown's description of "seeric" translation in *In Heaven as It Is on Earth: Joseph Smith and the Early Mormon Conquest of Death* (New York: Oxford University Press, 2012), esp. 115–41. This chapter grew out of conversations with Brown under the notion of coauthoring a book. What is written here has been enriched by Brown's writings on the subject, which appear in both previously published and forthcoming work, including in this volume ("Seeing the Voice of God: The Book of Mormon on Its Own Translation," Chapter 6 herein); see also Brown's "Interplanetary Travel and the Conquest of Death: Premortem Translation in Early Mormonism" (unpublished manuscript, 2007); *In Heaven as It Is on Earth*, esp. chaps. 3–5; and *Joseph Smith's Translation: The Words and Worlds of Mormonism* (Oxford and New York: Oxford University Press, 2020).

what if all of Smith's texts were understood as having been produced in the service of an overarching project of metaphysical translation? What might be illuminated by holding these "translated" texts at this angle?

The King James Version of the Holy Bible (KJV), the text that unquestionably loomed largest in Smith's early American Protestant culture and in his own mind, actually urges in this direction. The word "translate" and its variants appear only five times in the KJV, and none of these refers to linguistic translation.[2] Three of the five instances occur in a single verse: Hebrews 11:5. This enigmatic passage, recounting the life of the antediluvian patriarch Enoch, states: "By faith Enoch was translated that he should not see death; and was not found, because God had translated him: for before his translation he had this testimony, that he pleased God." This urtext of "translation" in the metaphysical sense likely seized Smith's imagination. It can even be seen as providing the script for Smith's entire career. Having launched himself as a religious leader by publishing the Book of Mormon, Smith soon initiated a project to revise the Bible that included a dramatic expansion of the Enoch narrative (now canonized as Moses 7). In Smith's retelling, Enoch founds a city of holiness named Zion that is taken into heaven with him. Enoch's Zion provided the blueprint, as Terryl Givens has described it, for Smith's subsequent work of restoration, the ultimate objective of which was nothing more or less than to build a new city of Zion, like Enoch's, that would be translated to heaven.[3] Already then, the explanatory power of privileging metaphysical rather than linguistic translation becomes apparent for a deep consideration of Smith's religious endeavors and productions.

This chapter traces the origins of Mormonism out of the notion of metaphysical translation keyed to Hebrews 11, a chapter that historian Grant Underwood notes was one of the two most frequently cited New Testament passages

2. 2 Samuel 3:10; Colossians 1:13; Hebrews 11:5. This enumeration excludes the paratexts, which *do* speak of linguistic translation in describing how the KJV came to be (see "To the Most High and Mighty Prince James, by the Grace of God, King of Great Britain, France, and Ireland, Defender of the Faith, &c").

3. For the details of Smith's formative engagement with Enoch in their historical context, see Jed L. Woodworth, "Extra-Biblical Enoch Texts in Early American Culture," in *Archive of Restoration Culture: Summer Fellows' Papers, 1997–1999* (Provo, UT: Joseph Fielding Smith Institute for Latter-day Saint History, 2000), 185–93. On Enoch, more broadly, as model for Smith, see Bushman, *Joseph Smith*, 137–42, 155; and David J. Whittaker, "Substituted Names in the Published Revelations of Joseph Smith," *BYU Studies* 23, no. 1 (1983): 1–9, which notes Smith's taking of "Enoch" as pseudonym in his revelations. On the Prophecy of Enoch as a blueprint for Smith's restoration, see Terryl L. Givens, *The Prophecy of Enoch as Restoration Blueprint* (Logan: Utah State University Press, 2013). On the building of Zion as focus of Mormon millenarianism, see Grant Underwood, *The Millenarian World of Early Mormonism* (Urbana and Chicago: University of Illinois Press, 1993), 30–36.

FIGURE 3.1. *Enoch* by William Blake. Lithograph, 1806–1807. Blake's depiction of Enoch, the enigmatic antediluvian patriarch who "walked with God" (KJV Genesis 5:22–29). Blake surrounded Enoch with artists, angelic beings, and heavenly glory. The New Testament Epistle to the Hebrews states that "Enoch was translated that he should not see death; and was not found, because God had translated him" (11:5)—evocative language that was expansively interpreted by Joseph Smith. The Metropolitan Museum of Art, New York.

in Mormon sermons during the first decade of the movement.[4] This argument first requires a close consideration of definitions, an excursion in lexical history to justify prioritizing metaphysical over linguistic translation, all toward the end of broadly redefining translation in a way that more fully encapsulates Smith's overarching project. Next, under the aegis of this redefinition, the chapter reexamines the Book of Mormon, that particular translation project of foundational importance to understanding Smith and his movement. The "translation of the Book of Mormon" will be reconceptualized and renarrated as a process governed by the spatial concerns of the early American magical treasure quest.

Although this chapter does not address Smith's subsequent translations, such as the "New Translation" of the Bible and the Book of Abraham, its contention is that the metaphysical conception of translation as creative intervention

4. Underwood, *Millenarian World*, 163–64n4. This assessment, slightly modified from Underwood's scope of analysis, considers 1828–1838 the first decade of the movement.

in space-time is even more obviously pertinent to these projects. The comprehension of these later projects as products of linguistic translation has been shown, for various reasons, to be less sustainable than for the Book of Mormon. In short, if the Book of Mormon can be shown to be amenable to the proposed model, the door is thrown open to appreciating all of Smith's translation projects as increasingly confident and proactive exercises of transhumanist creativity that, by their very nature, contributed to the goal of collapsing the distance between earth and heaven, Enoch style.[5]

In its commitment to reconceptualizing translation in metaphysical terms, this chapter builds on previous theoretical and historical work on translation—at least in "the West"—as grounded in the *translatio imperii et studii* (in fact, the *translatio imperii et studii* was one of the principal mechanisms for constructing a notion of "the West").[6] Translatable as "transfer of rule and learning," the *translatio imperii et studii* has proven a remarkably durable historiographical trope for explaining the rise and fall of imperial civilizations across space and time. In one prominent trajectory, political and intellectual empire passes from Persia to Greece to Rome to Western Europe to Britain. In the medieval Christian uptake of this classical figure, it assumed an eschatological cast. This view found a key text in Daniel 2 (which, incidentally, would be of demonstrably special significance to the early Mormon movement).[7] Daniel 2 relates the Israelite Daniel's interpretation of the Babylonian king Nebuchadnezzar's dream of a statue composed of various materials that was broken in pieces by a stone that "was cut out of the mountain without hands." Christians came to see the different materials of the statue's makeup as corresponding to

5. See Jared Hickman, "Mormonism; or, Art All the Way Down," in *The Kimball Challenge at Fifty: Mormon Arts Center Essays*, ed. Glen Nelson (New York: Mormon Arts Center, 2017), 45–53.

6. On the classical roots and medieval Christian uptake of *translatio imperii et studii* in its relation to literary production and rhetorical performance, see Rita Copeland, *Rhetoric, Hermeneutics, and Translation in the Middle Ages: Academic Traditions and Vernacular Texts* (Cambridge: Cambridge University Press, 1991). For an argument for the trope's decline as a condition of "modernity," see J. G. A. Pocock, *Barbarism and Civilization*, vol. 3, *The Decline and Fall* (New York: Cambridge University Press, 2003), 98–152. For critiques of Pocock and the case for the currency of the trope in modern historiography, see Rebecca Comay, *Mourning Sickness: Hegel and the French Revolution* (Stanford, CA: Stanford University Press, 2011), 15–18, 85–86; Dan Edelstein, *The Enlightenment: A Genealogy* (Chicago: University of Chicago Press, 2010), 77; and Cary J. Nederman, *Lineages of European Political Thought: Explorations along the Medieval/Modern Divide from John of Salisbury to Hegel* (Washington, D.C.: Catholic University of America Press, 2009), 177–89.

7. David Whittaker, "The Book of Daniel in Early Mormon Thought," in *By Study and Also by Faith*, ed. J. Lundquist and S. Ricks (Salt Lake City, UT: Deseret Book, 1990), 1:155–201; also Jeffrey R. Chadwick, "Daniel, Prophecies of," in *Encyclopedia of Mormonism*, ed. Daniel Ludlow (New York: Macmillan, 1992), 1:355–56; Terryl L. Givens, *By the Hand of Mormon: The American Scripture That Launched a New World Religion* (New York and Oxford: Oxford University Press, 2002), 13, 62–63, 261n3.

a divinely appointed series of earthly empires that would ultimately give way to the returned Christ's kingdom on earth, figured as the demolishing stone cut without hands. In both classical and Christian versions of the *translatio imperii et studii*, a salient index of this choreographed movement of power/knowledge was the evidencing of the communicative capacity of the nominal new imperium's vernacular language—through feats of appropriating learning in other languages (such as linguistic translation) and of sense from one object to another (*metaphor* and *translatio* were often used interchangeably in rhetorical manuals).[8] But the crucial point is that in this scheme, a set of virtuosic linguistic practices going under the name of translation is but a metonymic trace of a high-stakes process of theogeopolitical restructuring that provides the bottom-line referent for translation.

Joseph Smith's work of translation affords the opportunity to place this historiographical trope of *translatio imperii et studii* in a broadly phenomenological framework and by so doing to think more strenuously about the function of language in the midst of a deeply felt desire for and lived experience of the immanence of divine power/knowledge in a particular here and now. For Smith (and many others), the new republic of the United States was just such a here and now, and indeed the potential terminus of the long westward course of the *translatio imperii et studii*.[9] What is revealed in the process is that insofar as translation (as derived from *translatio imperii et studii*) involves language, it is first and foremost in a performative sense: vernacular textual production of a certain order of magnitude is an X purporting to mark the providential spot, the hopeful force of its inscription in effect an incantation summoning providence thereto. Linguistic niceties pale beneath cosmic imperatives under these conditions. Language serves as a means of eschatological signposting, the criteria for its deployment subordinated to the question: What will move humans, angels, and gods to what is profoundly sensed to be a new sacred center, a focal point of space-time? The whole game of translation, then, might be said to be metaphysical, and no case study might better prove the point than Joseph Smith.

8. Copeland, *Rhetoric, Hermeneutics, and Translation in the Middle Ages*, 235n74.

9. On the continued westward trajectory of the *translatio imperii et studii* to the United States of America, see Eric Cheyfitz, *The Poetics of Imperialism: Translation and Colonization from "The Tempest" to "Tarzan"* (Philadelphia: University of Pennsylvania Press, 1997); Nicholas Guyatt, *Providence and the Invention of the United States, 1607–1876* (New York: Cambridge University Press, 2007), 28–29, 77–78, 81–82, 101; and Avihu Zakai, *Exile and Kingdom: History and Apocalypse in the Puritan Migration to America* (New York: Cambridge University Press, 2002), 80–83.

METAPHYSICAL (RATHER THAN LINGUISTIC) TRANSLATION AS FOUNDATION

In order to fully understand what Smith meant when he called himself a "translator,"[10] two interrelated lexical reifications have to be undone: First, the semantic narrowing of the word "translation" in English usage to signify nothing more or less than the act of linguistic translation in particular. Second, the doctrinaire fixation in theological discourse of what is here called metaphysical translation as an infinitesimal set of exceptional cases unreproducible for the purposes of the common believer's experimental faith. Together these forces have conspired to sap translation of its multivalence and have therefore artificially limited the options for sympathetically understanding Smith's work.

Semantic Narrowing of the Word "Translate"

"To translate" has in effect come tautologically to mean a linguistic operation that translators perform when they translate—the *Oxford English Dictionary* grants this linguistic sense of the word a (semi-) discrete existence as well as the distinction of "chief *current* sense."[11] As a result, the discussion of Smith's translations has more or less automatically been consigned to the domain of linguistic translation. That process, it should be noted, began quite early, with the earliest attempts by Smith's various scribes to fill the vacuum left by his reticence to divulge the mechanics of the Book of Mormon translation—a reticence holding space open for the type of radically different conceptualization of translation offered here.[12] Conversely, the lexically conditioned resort to linguistic translation runs against Smith's own trajectory. Indeed, to privilege linguistic translation is to allow the tail to wag the dog.

This is not to deny that Smith himself, in his attempt to make sense of what he had wrought, predictably gravitated at times toward the sense of translation dominant in his moment—the linguistic one. Nor is this to deny that Smith

10. See The Book of Mormon: An Account Written by the Hand of Mormon, upon Plates Taken from the Plates of Nephi, trans. Joseph Smith, Junior (Palmyra, NY: E. B. Grandin, 1830), iii; Revelation, 6 April 1830, in *JSP*-D1:129 [D&C 21:1]; Instruction on Priesthood, between circa 1 March and circa 4 May 1835, in *JSP*-D4:321 [D&C 107:92].

11. Online *Oxford English Dictionary* (New York and Oxford: Oxford University Press), s.v. "translation" (emphasis added).

12. On this point, see James E. Lancaster, "The Translation of the Book of Mormon," chap. 8 in *The Word of God: Essays on Mormon Scripture*, ed. Dan Vogel (Salt Lake City, UT: Signature Books, 1990), 97–99.

proved interested in linguistic translation: from sending Martin Harris to visit the learned classicists of the eastern seaboard (like Charles Anthon) to working with William Phelps in an attempt to produce an Egyptian grammar manual to hiring Joshua Seixas to teach him Hebrew.[13] But, instructively, these occasions typically followed more extraordinary episodes of what may be recognized as a kind of metaphysical translation and were hopefully endowed with a post facto confirmatory function. The aim here will be to recover this more profound labor of translation that drove Smith, which did not necessarily preclude in his mind the possibility that the texts he produced might meet the standards and expectations of Anthon, Phelps, and Seixas.

"Translation" did not always redound to linguistic translation alone. Although it may seem incredible, it is perfectly symptomatic that one of the stock gestures of Book of Mormon criticism has not been robustly performed in this case:[14] How does Noah Webster's 1828 *American Dictionary of the English Language* define "translate"?

> 1. To bear, carry or remove from one place to another. It is applied to the removal of a bishop from one see to another. . . .
> 2. To remove or convey to heaven, as a human being, without death. By faith Enoch was translated, that he should not see death. Heb. xvi [Hebrews 11:5].
> 3. To transfer; to convey from one to another. 2 Samuel iii [2 Samuel 3:10].
> 4. To cause to remove from one part of the body to another; as, to *translate* a disease.
> 5. To change.

13. See Michael Hubbard MacKay, "Performing the Translation: Character Transcripts and Joseph Smith's Earliest Translating Practices," Chapter 4 herein; Brian M. Hauglid, "'Translating an Alphabet to the Book of Abraham': Joseph Smith's Study of the Egyptian Language and His Translation of the Book of Abraham," Chapter 15 herein; Matthew J. Grey, "Approaching Egyptian Papyri through Biblical Language: Joseph Smith's Use of Hebrew in his Translation of the Book of Abraham," Chapter 16 herein.

14. Instructive here is the one other instance the author has tracked down in which Webster's 1828 definition of "translate" appears in full in Mormon scholarship: Kevin Christensen's polemical response to Jeremy Runnells's "Letter to a CES Director: Why I Lost My Testimony" (accessible at www.cesletter.org). There, its rhetorical function is simply to score a point about the wider margin for judging the success of a linguistic translation. See Kevin Christensen, "Eye of the Beholder, Law of the Harvest: Observations on the Inevitable Consequences of the Different Investigative Approaches of Jeremy Runnells and Jeff Lindsay," *Interpreter: A Journal of Mormon Scripture* 10 (2014): 175–238. Webster's sixth definition of "translate" also shows up in a footnote in Terryl L. Givens, *Feeding the Flock: The Foundations of Mormon Thought; Church and Praxis* (Oxford and New York: Oxford University Press, 2017), 382n31, again only in order to expand the meaning of linguistic translation.

6. To interpret; to render into another language; to express the sense of one language in the words of another.
7. To explain.[15]

Most noteworthy are three facts that can be cast in syllogistic form: (1) that metaphysical translation, keyed to Hebrews 11:5, well precedes linguistic translation among these definitions; (2) that the literal sense lurking at the bottom of the English verb "translate" is an act of dynamic movement through space; and (3) that the priority of metaphysical translation is in part related to its closeness to this literal sense of physical movement. Privileging metaphysical translation over linguistic translation would thus seem to be justified but only insofar as it foregrounds the literal sense of spatial repositioning.

The idea of physical relocation that originally attached to the lexeme that would eventuate in the English verb "translate" has been largely lost in the concept of linguistic translation. It seems safe to say that when an English speaker conceives the act of rendering one language in terms of another, a vivid image of energized transportation from here to there is not conjured. Or that when one speaks of "translating a book," one is self-evidently referring to the linguistic operation called translation, not to the carrying of that book from the library to one's office. This drift of "translate" toward the apparently autochthonous and effectively autocratic meaning of "render[ing] in another language" probably has much to do with the death of scribal culture. Etymology suggests that a switch-point between the generic, foundational sense of "change the location of" and the specialized sense of "translat[ing] (into another language)" was the act of "copy[ing] out," that is, the transcribing of words from one physical repository into another.[16] But translation can now be more readily imagined as the endeavor of a disembodied mind amid dematerialized languages.

A consequence of this devolution of the English verb "to translate" away from any sense of physical or metaphysical movement and toward the single meaning of rendering one language in another is the mystification of experiences like Enoch's. As Webster's definitions make clear, Enoch's "translation" makes sense precisely as the most ontologically spectacular removal "from one place to another"—an ascension from earth to heaven. If the original sense of the lexeme eventuating in the English verb "translate" would seem to survive,

15. Noah Webster, *An American Dictionary of the English Language* [. . .] (New York: S. Converse, 1828), s.v. "translate."

16. *Oxford Latin Dictionary*, ed. P. G. W. Glare, 2nd ed. (New York and Oxford: Oxford University Press, 2012), s.v. "transferō," definitions 2, 6, and 2d.

it would be in the notion of metaphysical if not linguistic translation. But the very necessity of making this distinction between different kinds of translation, underlines how English in particular makes it even harder to hold on to the denotative literalism of the original lexeme.

A contrast reinforces this point: in other languages descended from Latin, typically there survive two terms that are translated in English as "translate." One of those terms exclusively refers to linguistic translation, whereas the other retains the lexeme's original sense of spatiotemporal repositioning and is the term used when describing metaphysical translation. Hence, in French, linguistic translation is covered by the verb *traduire*—derived from a semantically adjacent but different Latin root, *trānsdūcō*, meaning to "lead" rather than "carry across"—whereas metaphysical translation is indicated by *translater*, from the Latin *trānslātus* that also sources the English verb.

Doctrinal Diminishing of Metaphysical Translation

By virtue not just of the sheer ascendancy of translation in the linguistic sense but the submergence of the original lexeme's sense of dynamic movement (which is precisely what defined Enoch's experience in the first place), translation in the metaphysical sense is also emptied as a signifier. Metaphysical translation, to the extent it survives in esoteric corners, is thereby reduced to a dogmatic cipher. A form of circularity parallel to that evident in the verb writ large develops: just as "to translate" comes in English usage self-referentially to mean to translate—in the eclipsing linguistic sense—so translation in the metaphysical sense becomes merely the label for whatever mysterious and marvelous thing happened to Enoch, a given term of art in a science of biblical theology. What is lost is any meaningful answer to the question of *why this particular verb* to describe what happened to Enoch—an especially egregious deficiency for a tradition whose founder defined himself as a translator.

This deadening of the sense of spatiotemporal repositioning that brings Enoch's experience to life is reflected in the focus on metaphysical translation as a change of state rather than of location, even though Hebrews 11:5, the verse at the heart of this all, makes a point of predicating the former on the latter. Biblical scholars note that the verse is largely a quotation of Genesis 5:24, as translated in the early Greek version of the Old Testament, the Septuagint. An English rendering of Genesis 5:24 in the Septuagint would be, "And Enoch pleased God and he was not found, because God translated him."[17] The verb underlying "translated" in both the Septuagint and the derivative text of Hebrews is μετατίθημι (metatithemi), which the *Brill Dictionary of Ancient Greek* defines primarily as "change of position, transposition" and "shift, transfer."[18] That the thrust of meaning here is a change of location rather than a change of state is underscored by the additions the author of Hebrews makes to the verse from Genesis. New Testament scholar Harold W. Attridge flags the author's insertion of the clause "so that he did not see death" after "by faith Enoch was translated"; that is, shifted or transferred. The author thus establishes a clear cause and effect: Enoch's person is radically altered ("he did not see death") by being supernaturally displaced (he "was translated").[19] Hence, translation refers not to Enoch's escape from death but rather to God's action of taking Enoch from earth to heaven, as in KJV Genesis 5:24. More precisely, Enoch's escape from death and whatever that may imply about his ontological status is a function of his literal removal from earth to heaven.[20]

Two other pertinent pieces of evidence highlight Enoch's translation as dynamic movement. First, in other editions of the Bible, the μετετέθη of Hebrews 11:5 (a different conjugation of μετατίθημι), is translated as "Enoch was *taken*," whether "up," "away," "from this life," or "to heaven."[21] Second, the KJV's own translation of μετατίθημι and its variants—the few times they appear elsewhere in the New Testament[22]—are rendered as "carried over," "removed," "being changed," "removing," and "turning."[23]

17. Harold W. Attridge, *The Epistle to the Hebrews: A Commentary on the Epistle to the Hebrews*, ed. Helmut Koester (Philadelphia: Fortress Press, 1989), 317–18; Pamela Michelle Eisenbaum, *The Jewish Heroes of Christian History: Hebrews 11 in Literary Context* (Atlanta: Scholars Press, 1997), 152; Craig R. Koester, *The Anchor Bible: Hebrews; A New Translation with Introduction and Commentary* (New York: Doubleday, 2001), 482.

18. Franco Montanari, Madeleine Goh, and Chad Schroeder, eds., *Brill Dictionary of Ancient Greek* (Leiden: Brill, 2015), s.v. "Μετάθεσις -εως [μετατίθημι]."

19. Attridge, *Epistle to the Hebrews*, 317.

20. In Smith's moment, Enoch was often linked with Elijah, whose chariot ride up into the sky drives home the sense of metaphysical translation as dynamic movement. See Jonathan Edwards, *A History of the Work of Redemption: Containing the Outlines of a Body of Divinity, in a Method Entirely New* (Worcester, MA: Isaac Sturtevant, 1808), 42; John Gill, *An Exposition of the Old Testament in Which Are Recorded the Origin of Mankind* [. . .] (Philadelphia: William Woodward, 1817–1819), 1:44; Henry Hunter, *Sacred Biography, or, the History of the Patriarchs* [. . .], 3rd American ed. (Philadelphia: Griggs for Richardson, 1818), 1:70.

21. Compare the English translations offered in the New Revised Standard Version, New Century Version, New International Version, New International Reader's Version, English Standard Version, and Christian Standard Bible, among other versions.

22. Acts 7:16; Galatians 1:6; Hebrews 7:12, 12:27; Jude 1:4.

23. See Frederick W, Danker, ed., *A Greek-English Lexicon of the New Testament and Other Early Christian Literature* [. . .], 3rd ed., based on Walter Bauer's *Griechisch-Deutsches Wörterbuch zu den Schriften des Neuen Testaments und der Übrigen Urchristlichen Literatur*, 6th ed., ed. Kurt Aland and Barbara Aland (Chicago and London: University of Chicago Press, 2000), 639, 642.

Theological discourse further reduced metaphysical translation to an achieved state rather than a dynamic movement by funneling the term through the mode of sacred biography. Metaphysical translation becomes a quality attached to a few extraordinary scriptural figures who constitute a kind of cabinet of curiosities to puzzle and marvel over—in the Old Testament, Enoch, maybe Moses, and Elijah;[24] in the New Testament, John the apostle, and perhaps other early disciples;[25] and in the Book of Mormon, Alma the Younger (perhaps) and three of Jesus's twelve Nephite disciples (the "Three Nephites"), with the possibility held out for Ether.[26]

In popular works of biblical narrative theology and commentary by evangelical leading lights like Isaac Watts and Jonathan Edwards, a generally conservative interpretation of Genesis 5:24 and Hebrews 11:5 led to distancing awe of Enoch as an exceptional case.[27] Even in sermons whose stated aim was to make Enoch an object lesson for practical Christianity, his translation was lost in translation, so to speak. The eighteenth-century Scottish divine Henry Hunter exhorted that it was pointless, if not dangerous, to consider "the dreams of visionaries, and the fables of impostors, respecting the manner in which God disposed of Enoch after his assumption" and stated that there was "no edification" to be found "in the bold fictions of Mahomet, or the wild conjectures of a Jewish Rabbin." Enoch's translation was "an event, so entirely out of course," and one preceded by "circumstances ... likewise singular and uncommon," that its meaning had to be resolutely attenuated and dully allegorized for the common believer. Hunter's exegesis reduced Enoch's translation to the platitude "that a life of faith and holiness is but one remove from glory." Hunter wrote that Enoch, alongside Elijah and Jesus, represented a mere "instance" occurring "in each of the three great periods of the church ... of a man taken up to heaven, body and spirit, as a support and encouragement to the hope

24. Genesis 5:24; Deuteronomy 34:5–6; 2 Kings 2:11–12. Note that in the New Testament Moses appeared with Elijah on the Mount of Transfiguration (Matthew 17:3; Mark 9:4; Luke 9:30). The Book of Mormon, apparently echoing the language regarding Enoch in Genesis 5:24, states that "the Lord took Moses unto himself" (Alma 45:19).

25. John 21:20–23. See also Matthew 16:28; Mark 9:1; Luke 9:27.

26. Alma 45:18–19; 3 Nephi 28; Ether 15:34.

27. Edwards deemed Enoch's translation "the first instance that ever was of restoring the ruins of the fall with respect to the body," which "carried on" the "work of redemption ... further than ever it had been before" and thus made Enoch "a saint of greater eminency than any ever had been before him." Edwards, *History of the Work of Redemption*, 41, 38. Isaac Watts called Enoch's translation "a peculiar favour and honour done to him." Isaac Watts, *A Short View of the Whole Scripture History* [...] (Philadelphia: Rufus Little et al., 1819), 24. Woodworth offers a useful bibliography of additional such sources, see Woodworth, "Extra-Biblical Enoch Texts," 192–93n16.

of believers, of attaining the same felicity," albeit only "at length." In the end, then, these three "can be compared only with each other."[28]

Modern Mormon theological discourse has largely followed the general trend. Hence, *The Encyclopedia of Mormonism* of the late twentieth century has no entry on "translation," per se, and its entry on "translated beings" defines them (in a rather circular fashion) as "a unique class of beings, persons whom the Lord has 'translated' or changed from a mortal state to one in which they are temporarily not subject to death, and in which they experience neither pain nor sorrow except for the sins of the world."[29] Restricted to the outstanding achievement of a few characters who have undergone a change of "state" (not place), metaphysical translation stalls out, an ironic nullification of its core sense.

Joseph Smith's Reinventing of "Translation"

Joseph Smith, however, offers a way back to the original, encompassing sense of the lexeme eventuating in the English verb "translate." Within the materialist cosmos he fashioned, in which the distinction between physical and metaphysical dissolves, Smith reunified the word's disparate, deadened meanings under a single notion of translation as *a transformative because transgressive traversal of space-time.* Translation, whether of texts or persons, is a matter of projection into unexpected positions with the intention of thereby altering the field in which positions can be taken. Translation is both means and end: by careening through the cosmos one alters its fabric and thus creates new realms in which to careen.

These transformative movements may be considered "transgressive" for two reasons. First, as is fairly apparent, they are transgressive because translation on the model of Enoch's entails especially dramatic movements taking one to places where one ordinarily ought not to be. Translation unsettles established patterns of phenomenological inhabitation. Second, this kind of translation is transgressive in a way that illuminates Smith's assumption of agency as translator and may be distinguished from other emergent models of translation.[30]

28. Hunter, *Sacred Biography*, 1:62–72.

29. Mark L. McConkie, "Translated Beings," in *Encyclopedia of Mormonism*, ed. Daniel H. Ludlow (New York: Macmillan, 1992), 4:1485.

30. See, for example, Brown, *In Heaven as It Is on Earth*, 115–41. Brown's model of what he calls "seeric" translation builds on previous models. For one of the earliest articulations of a "loose" translation model, see Sandberg, "Knowing Brother Joseph Again." Flake, "Translating Time," perhaps best encapsulates: "Smith's

If these models, in their questioning of the tight-control theory of linguistic translation, open the door to treating Smith's "translations" as "revelations," this chapter is arguing just the opposite: all Smith's "revelations" subtend an encompassing project of "translation" in the sense staked out here.

A final excursion in lexical history clinches this model of translation. The μετατίθημι (*metatithemi*) of the original Greek of Hebrews 11:5 becomes in the Latin of Jerome's Vulgate Bible, *trānslātus*, and this Latinism is preserved in the KJV as "was translated." It is important to register here that *trānslātus*, from which the English verb "to translate" so obviously derives, is actually the perfect passive participle of an irregular verb—*trānsferre* in its present active infinitive form—a word that so recognizably survives in English as the distinct verb "transfer" (the same connection also being observable in the aforementioned *translatio imperii et studii*). That is, *trānslātus* does not constitute a distinct verb stem; there is no common Latin verb whose present active infinitive form would be *trānslātare*. Rather, *trānslātus* is merely a conjugation of *trānsferre*.

Returning to Hebrews 11:5, the grammatical information encoded in the Vulgate's *trānslātus* communicates that Enoch is the object rather than subject of the astonishing spiriting away being described. Simply put, Enoch does not translate; he *is* translated, which is to say transferred, by another agent—God. To this point, if God were to offer a first-person, present-tense narration of his translation of Enoch in Latin, it would be "transferō Enoch," literally rendered in English as "I *transfer* Enoch." Built into *trānslātus*, then, is an image not of autonomously moving but of being moved by an external force.

Hence, the emergence of the English verb "translate" (as distinct from "transfer") represents a neologizing activation, as it were, of what originally was an intrinsically passive formulation. In creating the freestanding verb "translate," English speakers converted an objectified relation—a "me" who *is* transferred by someone else—into a new subject position—an "I" who does something called "translating" that is nominally different from "transferring." It is this subject position that Smith assumes with unsurpassed enthusiasm. And what does it entail? To route all this back through Hebrews 11:5, this new subject position—of the one who does something called translating—is, in effect, the position occupied by the God whose creation of and ongoing dominion over the cosmos gives him the prerogative of installing Enoch elsewhere. Apropos

use of 'translate,' for all its discursive weaknesses, conveyed his experience of creative agency before a text and, simultaneously, his sense of being bound by the text as an account of events or as history" (507–8).

Hebrews 11:5, then, the English verb "translate" is inherently transhumanist—its illustration is that of human beings propelling themselves into heaven rather than waiting to be towed up. Could one ask for a better description of Smith's audacious enterprise?

METAPHYSICAL TRANSLATION AND THE CHRISTIAN TREASURE QUEST

In light of this broad redefinition of translation, how might the translation of the Book of Mormon be reconsidered? First and foremost, the focusing of translation on maneuvers in space—specifically, the single navigable space comprising earth and heaven forged by the Enoch story—highlights the salience of the magical treasure quest for understanding the Book of Mormon. As many have suggested, Smith's treasure seeking equipped him for his religion building, even as the progression of the latter at times forced him and his associates to understate or silently omit the former.[31]

Recent scholarship on the culture and beliefs of European treasure seeking has further bridged the enduring gap between "folk magic" and "Christian religion." It is important to recognize that the Bible, as Owen Davies puts it, was the most "widely available occult repository."[32] This was something the famed sixteenth-century witch hunter Reginald Scot lamented in his miming of the scriptural arguments that magical practitioners swiftly marshaled against ecclesiastical and social elites like himself, including citation of Enoch's translation as evidence of the possibility of human flight.[33]

31. See, for example, Jan Shipps, "The Prophet Puzzle: Suggestions Leading toward a More Comprehensive Interpretation of Joseph Smith," *Journal of Mormon History* 1 (1974): 3–20; see also Shipps, *Mormonism: The Story of a New Religious Tradition* (Urbana and Chicago: University of Illinois Press, 1985; Illini Books edition, 1987), 11–21; D. Michael Quinn, *Early Mormonism and the Magic World View,* 2d ed. (Salt Lake City: Signature Books, 1998), 65; Mark Ashurst-McGee, "A Pathway to Prophethood: Joseph Smith as Rodsman, Village Seer, and Judeo-Christian Prophet" (master's thesis, Utah State University, 2000); Brown, *In Heaven as It Is on Earth,* 69–87. For useful metacommentary on these developments, see Samuel M. Brown, "The Reluctant Metaphysicians," *Mormon Studies Review* 1, no. 1 (2014): 115–31; and Eric A. Eliason, "Seer Stones, Salamanders, and Early Mormon 'Folk Magic' in the Light of Folklore Studies and Bible Scholarship," *BYU Studies Quarterly* 55, no. 1 (2016): 73–93.

32. Owen Davies, *Grimoires: A History of Magic Books* (New York: Oxford University Press, 2009), 147.

33. Ibid. The mention of Enoch in relation to the idea of magical flight appeared in Reginald Scot's popular book about witchcraft, which Davies considers the "most likely" book Smith or his associates might have come across (150). Historian D. Michael Quinn identified a 1665 edition of Scot's work as one of the sources used in the creation of one of the magical documents passed down within the Smith family. See Quinn, *Early Mormonism and the Magic World View,* 98–135. Mormon apologist William J. Hamblin has critiqued Quinn's analysis on this point in his article, "That Old Black Magic," *FARMS Review of Books* 12, no. 2 (2000): 306. Davies, in his sensible sifting of the evidence presented by both Quinn and Hamblin, confirms Quinn's identification of the 1665 edition of Scot as one of the sources behind the Smith family's

Capturing Treasure to Deliver Spirits

Historian Johannes Dillinger has documented a self-consciously Christian version of the treasure quest that understood its ultimate objective to be the deliverance of the ghost who guarded the treasure. This ghost was typically imagined as the spirit of the treasure's deceased proprietor, who could not ascend to heaven until the treasure was discovered and distributed.[34] Such a process obviously resonates with initial accounts of Smith's encounters with Moroni and the golden plates and perhaps provides a way to deconstruct the opposition between "treasure guardian" and "angel" that has plagued even the best work on the topic.[35] As Dillinger sums up the logic of this Christian treasure quest:

> The recovery of treasure was an act of piety because it resulted in the redemption of a wandering soul. Some treasure hunters saw themselves, and were seen by others, first and foremost as good Christians who delivered ghosts. We cannot understand early modern treasure hunting

magical paraphernalia (Davies, *Grimoires*, 150). Regarding Enoch, Scot wrote: "Howbeit, when I deny that Witches can ride in the Air, and the miraculous circumstance thereof; by and by it is objected to me, *That Enoch and Elias were rapt into the heavenly bodily*"; and "Conjurors carry about at this day, books entituled under the names of *Adam, Abel, Toby,* and *Enoch;* which *Enoch* they repute the most divine fellow in such matters." Reginald Scot, *The Discoverie of Witchcraft* [. . .] (London: Andrew Clark, 1665), 97, 272.

34. Johannes Dillinger, *Magical Treasure Hunting in Europe and North America: A History* (New York: Palgrave Macmillan, 2012), 72–79.

35. For examples, see Ronald W. Walker, "The Persisting Idea of American Treasure Hunting," *BYU Studies* 24, no. 4 (Fall 1984): 436–38; Ronald W. Walker, "Joseph Smith: The Palmyra Seer," *BYU Studies* 24, no. 4 (Fall 1984): 461–72; Quinn, *Early Mormonism and the Magic World View*, 139–41; Ronald V. Huggins, "From Captain Kidd's Treasure Ghost to the Angel Moroni: Changing *Dramatis Personae* in Early Mormonism," *Dialogue: A Journal of Mormon Thought* 36, no. 4 (Winter 2003): 17–42; Larry E. Morris, "'I Should Have an Eye Single to the Glory of God': Joseph Smith's Account of the Angel and the Plates," *FARMS Review* 17, no. 1 (2005): 11–81; Dan Vogel, *Joseph Smith: The Making of a Prophet* (Salt Lake City: Signature Books, 2004), 44–47. For a thorough consideration of the matter, including critiques of Huggins, Morris, and Vogel, see Mark Ashurst-McGee, "Moroni as Angel and as Treasure Guardian," *FARMS Review* 18, no. 1 (2006): 34–100. Ashurst-McGee's work also influenced a master of arts thesis, see Adam Price Hock, "'Behold an Angel of the Lord Came and Stood before Me': A Cultural Examination of Joseph Smith's 1823 Visions of Moroni" (master's thesis, Brigham Young University, 2013). The frame in which Ashurst-McGee operates, which he borrows from Walker, may be at odds with what he ultimately seems to want to argue: that Moroni could have been *both* angel and treasure guardian. It presupposes a fundamental difference between angel and treasure guardian for the historian to overcome through synthesis. But this very opposition, in light of Dillinger's findings, may be an artifact of an elite Christian demonization and compounding secular trivialization of something called "magic" that stacks the deck in favor of "angel." This tends to tilt the synthesis of the scholar who aspires to a sympathetic and serious study of Mormonism toward angel and away from treasure guardian. On the methodological liabilities of dealing with magic as a subject, see the introductions to Randall Styers, *Making Magic: Religion, Magic, and Science in the Modern World* (New York and Oxford: Oxford University Press, 2004); and Wouter J. Hanegraaff, *Esotericism and the Academy: Rejected Knowledge in Western Culture* (Cambridge: Cambridge University Press, 2012).

> if we ignore its double purpose: it was a means to make money, but it was also an act of Christian devotion that helped a poor soul to finally enter the hereafter.[36]

Treasure seeking, as historian Alan Taylor puts it, can only be understood as an activity conducted within a "supernatural economy" in which easy distinctions between matter and spirit and between immanent "magical" manipulation of space-time and "religious" revelation of transcendent truths beyond space-time do not hold.[37]

Dillinger even provides a case study that should be of the greatest interest to scholars of Mormonism—a group of Christian treasure seekers in the 1770s in what is now Germany that "virtually turned into the foundation of a new Christian community." The hunt for treasure led Anna Maria Freyin to an encounter with two spirits who were haunting her master's house, spirits she redeemed. But the story did not end there. After ascending to heaven, the two spirits returned to earth to minister to their human redeemers. Given the experience of heaven these spirits had been afforded, their "utterances were regarded as divine revelation." Freyin began recording their utterances in a book that she and others came to understand as the basis of "a new gospel," joining them, furthermore, in "a nascent priesthood." The astounding similarities to Joseph Smith and early Mormonism require no elucidation.[38] The major difference is that Freyin's movement was quashed by the established Protestant church in Württemberg, while Smith's flourished in the sectarian landscape of early America resulting from church-state separation.[39]

Treasure Magic as Translation Magic (Rather Than Transfer Magic)

The piety of Christian treasure quests such as Freyin's and Smith's was underscored by practitioners' insistence on the distinction between what they did

36. Dillinger, *Magical Treasure Hunting*, 78.

37. Alan Taylor, "The Early Republic's Supernatural Economy: Treasure Seeking in the American Northeast, 1780–1830," *American Quarterly* 38, no. 1 (Spring 1986): 19–25.

38. Religious Studies scholar Steve Fleming pointed to this parallel between Freyin and Smith in an online review of Dillinger's study at the *Juvenile Instructor* blog, see "Book Review: Johannes Dillinger, *Magical Treasure Hunting in Europe and North America*," 16 February 2012, juvenileinstructor.org. For a more desultory Mormon engagement with Dillinger, see Hock, "'Behold an Angel of the Lord Came and Stood before Me,'" 103–10.

39. Dillinger, *Magical Treasure Hunting*, 168–73. See also Grant Shreve's theorization of "American secularity" in "Fragile Belief: Lydia Maria Child's *Hobomok* and the Scene of American Secularity," *American Literature* 86, no. 4 (December 2014): 655–82.

and so-called "transfer magic"—the magical seizure of material objects for the sole purpose of personal enrichment or mischief making. "Treasure magic," by contrast, was an exercise in gaining "knowledge and power" regarding the (dis)position of entities, above all spiritual entities like the treasure guardian. These might lead, yes, to a pot of gold or a chest of silver, but their more important function was to enable participation in the work of salvation.[40] Christian treasure magic, therefore, was a form of metaphysical translation as defined above—a transformative because transgressive traversal of space-time. It is all translation, through and through—from the exotic manner in which treasure is procured to the grand ascent its discovery allows the treasure guardian—and, possibly, as instances like Freyin's and Smith's suggest, the revelatory return of the ascended to earth with heaven's secrets.

Having recast treasure magic as "translation magic," the contrast with "transfer magic" resonates all the more. "Translate," as shown, originates as a passive conjugation of the Latin verb *trānsferre* whence descends the English verb "transfer." The breakaway of *translate* from *transfer* seems to imply, at a grammatical level, a bold determination to be subject rather than object, specifically as it relates to one's place in a standing ontological assemblage. In the magical context Dillinger conjures, this distinction between *transfer* and *translate* takes on additional meanings. Whereas *transfer* redounds to selfish or malicious shuffling of material goods within the earthly realm, *translate* signifies a venture toward spatial rearrangement of much higher ambition: to comprehend and conduct the commerce between earth and heaven. The difference between *transfer* and *translate* is thus one of scope of activity as determined by the imagined scale of the space within and against which that activity is intended.[41]

40. Dillinger, *Magical Treasure Hunting*, 112–13.

41. Although this chapter focuses on other spatial concerns of the magical treasure quest, it should be registered that an astrological sense of translation also governed that quest. D. Michael Quinn has established that a key source for magical paraphernalia passed down among Smith descendants is Ebenezer Sibly's, *A New and Complete Illustration of the Occult Sciences*. D. Michael Quinn, *Early Mormonism and the Magic World View*, 105–11. Sibly, in his tome, defines translation as "when a planet separates from the body or aspect of one planet, and immediately applies to the conjunction or aspect of another." The chief effect of this movement is that "light" is "translated," or transferred, from larger to smaller planets. Ebenezer Sibly, *A New and Complete Illustration of the Occult Sciences* [. . .] (London: C. Stalker, 1790), 1:280–83). Sibly also relays instructions as to how such movements bear on treasure hunting (1:307–9). That Quinn, in his close investigation of Sibly, missed this sense of translation—even as he elsewhere performed the gesture of providing a period dictionary definition in order to make sense of the Book of Mormon's production—highlights the very blind spot this chapter means to remedy (Quinn, *Early Mormonism and the Magic World View*, 193). This astrological sense of translation resonates with certain of Smith's revelations that present the cosmos as a cascade of light from the place of God downward. See Vision, 16 February 1832, in *JSP*-D2:179–92 [D&C 76]; Revelation, 27–28 December 1832, in *JSP*-D2:334–46 [D&C 88:1–126]. It may also be detected in the early

TREASURE SEEKING AND THE TRANSLATION OF THE BOOK OF MORMON

When these insights are applied to Joseph Smith, a new view of the translation of the Book of Mormon opens up. The translation is no longer strictly delimited to the period of dictating and transcribing that yielded a manuscript text in 1829, nor is it confined to the terms of linguistic translation. Rather, the translation of the Book of Mormon comprises a much longer cycle, defined early on by the context of the treasure quest, in which dynamic *virtual* movements aided by particular material objects, such as seer stones, generate momentum toward dynamic actual movements to realize in the material world what was disclosed in virtual reality.[42] Indeed, it would be well to remember that the seer stones that eventually came to be considered "interpreters" may have first been called "directors," devices, that is, for metaphysical rather than linguistic translation.[43]

---

patriarchal blessings imagining interplanetary travel. See Brown, "Interplanetary Travel and the Conquest of Death"; Brown, *Joseph Smith's Translation*.

42. This process is nicely encapsulated in William Purple's recollection of what was the beginning of Smith's treasure seeking—the story of how he obtained his first seer stone. First, Smith described looking into his neighbor Sally Chase's "glass" and seeing "*a small stone*, a great way off . . . under the roots of a tree or shrub as large as his arm, situated about a mile up a stream that puts in on the South side of Lake Erie, not far from the New York and Pennsylvania line." This dynamic virtual movement provoked a dynamic actual movement, a 150-mile trip to dig up the stone at the virtually experienced location. This realization of the virtual in turn facilitated a further dynamic virtual movement, an even more exhilarating tear through the cosmos: upon looking into the stone he found, Smith reportedly found "that time, place and distance were annihilated; that all the intervening obstacles were removed, and that he possessed one of the attributes of Deity, an All-Seeing-Eye." William D. Purple, "Joseph Smith, the Originator of Mormonism: Historical Reminiscences of the Town of Afton," *Chenango Union* (Norwich, NY), 2 May 1877, 3. This tentative postulation of a seer stone as a kind of virtual reality technology is incited by John Durham Peters's brilliant application of media theory to Joseph Smith. John Durham Peters, "Recording beyond the Grave: Joseph Smith's Celestial Bookkeeping," *Critical Inquiry* 42, no. 2 (Summer 2016): 862. In a 21 June 2016 post on Facebook, LDS First Presidency member Dieter F. Uchtdorf offered a picture of himself holding his smartphone, comparing it to the seer stones Smith used to translate the Book of Mormon (www.facebook.com/lds.dieter.f.uchtdorf/posts/400421293461887:0). Also crucially informing this analysis is Ann Taves, "History and the Claims of Revelation: Joseph Smith and the Materialization of the Golden Plates," *Numen* 61, nos. 2–3 (2014): 182–207.

43. The first possible reference to seer stones as "directors" is in the July 1828 revelation regarding the loss of the original manuscript pages. The revelation scolded Smith for having "suffered . . . the council of thy directors to be trampeled upon," Revelation, July 1828, in *JSP*-D1:9 [D&C 3:15]. The phrase "council of thy directors" follows shortly after the phrase "Councils of God" [D&C 3:13], and, notably, in later versions of the revelation, "directors" is singularized and even paratextually referred to God as an antecedent. *The Doctrine and Covenants of the Church of the Latter Day Saints* [. . .] (Kirtland, OH: F. G. Williams, 1835), pt. 2, 30:5. John Whitmer's history, speaking of the three witnesses, states they were shown "the Plates, the ball, the directers, &c." John Whitmer, History, 1831–circa 1847, 25, in *JSP*-H2:37. This leaves some ambiguity as to whether "directers" is a redundancy or apposition following "the ball" (clearly, Lehi's Liahona, which is elsewhere referred to as a "director" [Alma 37:45]); or a synonym for a different object from Moroni's treasure hoard included in some inventories of what the witnesses attested, namely, the "interpreters" (Mosiah 8:13, 19, 28:20; Alma 37:21, 24; Ether 4:5); or "spectacles" (Joseph Smith, History, circa Summer 1832, 5,

Such a cycle began when Smith experienced an encounter with the anxious guardian of what may have been initially regarded as an Indian treasure, one of the distinctive objects of the American magical treasure quest.[44] In this case, the treasure guardian sought a particular form of deliverance requiring the acquisition of a particular form of treasure. Evidence suggests that, as he had done before, Smith likely engaged in a dynamic virtual movement through a seer stone in order to locate the hoard of which Moroni spoke.[45] He then undertook a dynamic actual movement to realize what he had experienced in that virtual movement, digging in what would come to be known as the Hill Cumorah. But Smith found himself blocked from realization, a familiar motif of the treasure quest in which the tiniest violation of magical decorum could result in the treasure moving away or sinking deeper into the earth, thereby suggesting its existence was only ever virtual. This phenomenon was a source of goading frustration for treasure seekers and derisive amusement for their critics.[46]

Smith may have been initially blocked from realization because he had misidentified the treasure whose capture would deliver Moroni. The set of golden plates that Smith viewed virtually in the seer stone was not the object of realization. Rather, it was the ancient American past virtually projected by Moroni's appearance and allusions. The ascent that Moroni sought was "out of the dust" by means of the publication of his "voice" and the voices of his

---

in *JSP*-H1:15); and, eventually, "the Urim and Thummim" (Joseph Smith, History, 1838–1856, vol. A-1, 5, in *JSP*-H1:222). Importantly, the revelation that seems to definitively align "directors" with the "ball" rather than the "spectacles" is plagued by source questions. See Historical Introduction to Revelation, June 1829-E, in *JSP*-D1:82–85 [D&C 17].

44. Gerard T. Hurley, "Buried Treasure Tales in America," *Western Folklore* 10, no. 3 (July 1951): 197–216; Taylor, "The Early Republic's Supernatural Economy," 9–10; Walker, "The Persisting Idea of American Treasure Hunting," 436, 443; Brown, *In Heaven as It Is on Earth*, 72–110. Martin Harris reportedly stated that Joseph Smith was part of a group of local treasure seekers "who were digging for money supposed to have been hidden by the ancients." "Mormonism—No. II," *Tiffany's Monthly* (New York, NY), June 1859, 165. Jonathan Thompson, who had dug for a "chest of money" with Smith, reportedly stated that Smith looked into his seer stone and saw "the two Indians who buried the trunk." "A Document Discovered," *Utah Christian Advocate* (Salt Lake City), January 1886, 1. See also Emily C. Blackman, *History of Susquehanna County, Pennsylvania* [...] (Philadelphia: Claxton, Remsen & Haffelfinger, 1873), 579–80; "W. R. Hine's statement," *Naked Truths about Mormonism* (Oakland, CA), January 1888, 2.

45. Richard Van Wagoner and Steve Walker compiled Mormon and non-Mormon testimony stating that Smith claimed to have found the golden plates by means of a seer stone. Van Wagoner and Walker, "Joseph Smith: 'The Gift of Seeing,'" *Dialogue: A Journal of Mormon Thought* 15, no. 2 (Summer 1982): 57–64. See also Quinn, *Early Mormonism and the Magic World View*, 145–46; and Ashurst-McGee, "A Pathway to Prophethood," 288–94.

46. On the phenomenon of "riches" and "treasures" that "become slippery," as the Book of Mormon describes (Helaman 13:31, 33, 36; Mormon 1:18), see Walker, "The Persisting Idea of American Treasure Hunting," 444–45; and Dillinger, *Magical Treasure Hunting*, 58–61.

ancestors.[47] The treasure whose securing would permit the redemption the guardian desired in this case was not the golden plates themselves but the ancient history of America they represented. The quest with which Smith was entrusted was, as the historical sources repeatedly affirm, to "bring forth" the subterranean voices of the American past onto the ground of the American present.[48] Contrary to contemporary Mormon parlance, the Book of Mormon would not "come forth" of its own accord. But by now it is clear that such "bring[ing] forth" does not necessarily mean linguistic translation of a historical artifact. With the talents honed by the treasure quest, such voices of the past might be translated by another means—a means much closer to the literal sense of "bringing forth."

Indeed, in a passage like what is now 2 Nephi 3:15, the book's own procurement, production, publication, and the Parousia anticipated as a consequence thereof are all conceptualized in terms of "bringing forth." Lehi, who began the Book of Mormon story by bringing his family to the New World, quotes an otherwise unattested prophecy of Joseph, the favored son of Israel, regarding a future "seer" who would be "called after me [Joseph]" and would "write the writing of the fruit of thy [Lehi's] loins." And, in so doing, "the thing [the Book of Mormon], which the Lord shall *bring forth* by his hand [the hand of the future "seer" named "Joseph"], by the power of the Lord shall *bring* my people unto salvation."[49] The grammatical ambiguity and density around the phrasal verb "bring forth" suggestively confuse the vectors of agency here but ultimately can be parsed as tracing a relay of metaphysical translation.

47. For the American "voices . . . from the dust" trope, see 2 Nephi 3:19–20, 27:9; Mormon 8:23; Ether 8:24; and Moroni 10:27, 31.

48. 2 Nephi 3:15; Ether 5:2–3; Revelation, April 1829-A, in *JSP*-D1:34–37 [D&C 6]; David Patten's July 1838 epistle (quoting 2 Nephi 3:15), in Smith, History, 1838–1856, vol. B-1, 810 (accessible in the Histories series of the online edition of *The Joseph Smith Papers*). The use of the phrase in the Lucy Mack Smith history is a fascinating study in the fluctuating meanings of "translation." The history first describes Moroni as telling Joseph that the purpose of the plates is to "bring forth that light and intelligence which has been long lost in the Earth." Lucy Mack Smith, History, 1844–1845, 3:11. The history then states, but later strikes through, "the time has now come when the record should be brought forth" (5:5). Later, in an anecdote of personal testimony, the history declares that God had "raised up" Joseph Smith "to bring forth a book which was written for the salvation of the souls of people . . . a book which we know has be[en] brought forth by the gift of the Holy Ghost" (10:3). Only after all these instances does the history begin to make a distinction between "bringing forth" and "translating," thereby potentially differentiating a (meta)physical transfer and a linguistic operation. The history uses the phrases "brought forth the work and translated the book of Mormon" and "brought forth by the power of God and translated by the Same power" (11:9; 12:1). (All quotations accessible under "Other Histories" in the Histories series of the online edition of *The Joseph Smith Papers*).

49. Emphasis added. Later editions of the Book of Mormon interpose a comma after "power of the Lord," thus making the phrase a redundant apposite to the nature of the work done "by Smith's hand." But none of the editions produced in Smith's lifetime has such punctuation, which lends itself to the chiastic reformulation suggested here.

"Bring[ing] [forth]" here has two explicit grammatical subjects—"the Lord" and "the power of the Lord"—which introduces a curious distinction between divine person and divine agency. The distinction is stressed in that these two acts of "bring[ing] [forth]" have two different objects. While "the Lord" brings forth "the thing" (the Book of Mormon), it is "the power of the Lord" that brings forth the Lord's "people" (the clear referent of which in this context is the surviving descendants of Father Lehi identified as contemporary Native Americans).

This construction implies the need for a point of transfer between these distinct but parallel acts of metaphysical translation, of divinity "bring[ing] forth" sacred texts and saved bodies. And the verse supplies this mediator by the implication of a third grammatical subject of "bring[ing] [forth]"—Smith himself. If it is "by [Smith's] hand" that "the Lord shall bring forth" the Book of Mormon, then it is—most immediately—Smith who "shall bring forth" the Book of Mormon. Smith's agency is highlighted by the fact that the figure of "the hand" is attached to him rather than "the Lord." This is all the more striking because "the hand" is precisely the conventional synecdoche in Judeo-Christian scripture and tradition by which the distinction between divine person and agency is bridged.[50] The implicit metaphor uniting "the Lord" and "the power of the Lord"—"the hand of the Lord"—is conspicuously displaced in 2 Nephi 3:15 by the explicit attachment of the figure of "the hand" to Smith rather than the Lord. Hence, Smith is not simply functioning as "the hand of the Lord" under a familiar notion of human instrumentality to divine intention. Rather, it is *Smith's* hand by which the divine person and agency are united. The distinction comes into view through the plausible chiastic reformulation of 2 Nephi 3:15 as:

A_1 the hand of the Lord
  B_1 brings forth
    C the Book of Mormon
  B_2 by
A_2 the hand of Smith.

For all intents and purposes, "the hand of Smith" renders "the hand of the Lord" redundant at least so far as the "bring[ing] forth" of the Book of Mormon is concerned. Smith occupies the divine position of the translator, which is to say the

50. See Exodus 15:6.

actor who transfers bodies through space-time. With a "hand" trained in practices of metaphysical translation, as has been established, Smith was prepared to "bring forth" ancient American voices "from the dust." 2 Nephi 3:15 thus offers us a neat encapsulation of the Book of Mormon as the product of a metaphysical translation that emphasizes Smith's creative intervention in space-time rather than a linguistic translation that diminishes his substantive contribution.

Quite remarkably, this attribution seems to be amplified in the verses that follow in ways that crucially clarify the vexed politics of the Book of Mormon's claims to voice indigenous history. The "seer" (Smith), it is specified, will "write . . . *the words which are expedient* in my [the Lord's] wisdom should go forth unto the fruit of thy [Lehi's] loins . . . and it shall be *as if* the fruit of thy loins had cried unto them from the dust."[51] The foregrounding of expediency and the qualifying phrase "as if" arguably open a gap between the Book of Mormon text and indigenous voices, emphasizing Smith's role, for better and worse, as an activist; that is, someone acting on behalf of Native peoples as a "spokesman" (to use another word from the same prophecy), rather than as an actual medium of Native peoples.[52]

Following the Book of Mormon's self-description as the work of Smith's "hand," it is exactly *not* a transparent linguistic translation of indigenous voices. The curious distinction in 2 Nephi 3:15 between two "bring[ings] [forth]"—of the Book of Mormon and then of Native peoples—can now be reread as marking two phases of metaphysical translation. First, Smith's "bring[ing] forth" of the Book of Mormon; and second, the Lord's "bring[ing]" of Native peoples "to salvation." The specification of an additional intervention of "the power of the Lord" to "bring" Native peoples "to salvation" suggests that the power of the text brought forth by Smith is only potential and has to be activated by some further agency. One possible gloss would be that the Book of Mormon is an essentially original settler-colonial mediation of indigenous claims to land and world-historical significance that must be *re*-mediated in multiple senses in order to enable the metaphysical translation that it itself ultimately envisions: the winding-up of history in an *American* New Jerusalem built by Native peoples.[53] In order for the text to accomplish its stated purpose, the Book of Mormon has to be ceded to indigenous peoples and made to serve their fruition, as determined by them.

51. 2 Nephi 3:19–20 (emphasis added).
52. 2 Nephi 3:18.
53. See Ether 13:1–12.

The virtue of such an interpretation is that it enables readers both to problematize all the ways the Book of Mormon preempts modern indigenous peoples' own stories about themselves and to appreciate all the ways the Book of Mormon has already been and may yet be made by indigenous readers and their allies to serve the project of decolonization toward which it arguably points.[54] One might even take the position that the book's fulfillment of its own eschatological mandate may be predicated on acknowledging the text as, to some real extent, a product of Smith's immanent and do-it-yourself style of metaphysical translation: a virtual projection of the vitality of indigenous lives and legacies, the realization of which is in turn predicated on the text's consecration by and to ongoing indigenous lives. Following a verse like 2 Nephi 3:15 in its turn from linguistic to metaphysical translation authorizes and even encourages its readers to decouple the Book of Mormon's historical authenticity from what might be called its prophetic force.

The standard Mormon way of narrating the four-year interim between Smith's report of discovering the plates in 1823 and obtaining them in 1827 is that Smith was spiritually and intellectually maturing toward the point of undertaking a linguistic translation of a historical artifact. But another way of narrating the same period now becomes possible. Smith simply had to fully appreciate and cultivate the practices of metaphysical translation, of "bringing forth," in which he was already skilled but in relation to the proper object. This proper object was the "treasure" of indigenous history, the attainment of which was neatly identical with the form of deliverance Moroni demanded—his voicing "out of the dust." This alternative narrative begins with a rereading of the famous disclosure of Smith's mother, Lucy Mack Smith, that following his first encounter with Moroni and failure to obtain the plates in September 1823, Joseph would share things, presumably things he had seen in his seer stone, during the family's "evening conversations." According to Lucy's history, Joseph would give "some of the most ammusing recitals which could be immagined he would de[s]cribe the ancient inhabitants of this continent their dress thier maner of traveling the animals which they rode The cities that were built by them the structure of their buildings with every particular of their mode of

54. For a consideration of the Book of Mormon as a text that has indeed been meaningfully indigenized but, by the same token, is deeply problematic to privilege as actual indigenous history, see Gina Colvin, "Me and the Book of Mormon: It's Complicated," *KiwiMormon: Mormon Reflections from the Antipodes* (blog), http://www.patheos.com/blogs/kiwimormon/2017/03/book-mormon-complicated/. See also P. Jane Hafen, "Afterword," in *Decolonizing Mormonism: Approaching a Postcolonial Zion*, ed. Gina Colvin and Joanna Brooks (Salt Lake City: University of Utah Press, 2018), 263–73.

warfare their religious worship as particularly as though he had Spent his life with them."[55]

What might now be detected in Lucy's recollection is that Smith immediately set himself on an alternative trajectory to realization through a different sort of translation that he had been engaged in for quite some time, the sort that had facilitated the encounter with Moroni in the first place. In his sincere eagerness to release Moroni out of obscurity and into the bright light of unfolding salvation history, Smith may have used his seer stones for increasingly ambitious virtual expeditions, seeking out Moroni and the world for which he spoke. Perhaps at this early point he was already obtaining something like the "panoramic visions" Samuel Morris Brown posits as a mechanism for the production of the dictated English text of the Book of Mormon.[56] Smith, the most devout of all Christian treasure seekers, launched himself again and again through space and time in pursuit of the treasure that he increasingly came to understand Moroni was specifying—not the golden plates of a local hill but the lived history of ancient America that the plates represented. From the beginning, then, Smith was learning to translate himself into the ancient American world through the virtual reality technology of the seer stone and then translate that world back into his own through the virtual reality technology of oral storytelling.[57]

What Smith's Christian treasure quest was already enabling by the end of 1823, well before any plates were in hand, was both the theological justification and mechanical means of producing the narrative of ancient America that Moroni revealed was the treasure upon which his deliverance depended. By "bringing forth" the ancient American past into the present in a way that moved people, Smith was already obtaining that treasure and thereby exalting Moroni. One might go so far as to say that Smith's storytelling functioned in a sense as a seer stone for his family, affording them a dynamic virtual movement. This is where "the translation of the Book of Mormon" begins: in practices of *metaphysical* translation that reconfigure space-time in consequential

55. Lucy Mack Smith, History, 1844–1845, 4:1–2.

56. Brown, "Seeing the Voice of God," Chapter 6 herein.

57. On nineteenth-century narrative fiction, particularly forms like the romance, as the precursor to virtual reality, see Michael Saler, *As If: Modern Enchantment and the Literary Prehistory of Virtual Reality* (Oxford and New York: Oxford University Press, 2012). "Not satisfied with the Bible, as a complete revelation from God," wrote one early reviewer of the Book of Mormon, "the 'Latter-day Saints' have adopted a *romance* written in America, as a fresh revelation." Quoted in Smith, History, 1838–1856, volume C-1, [addenda], 22 (emphasis added). The orality of both Smith's "ammusing recitals" in late 1823 and his serious-minded dictation in mid-1829 is significant in that storytelling in this mode arguably highlights its virtual reality effects: to speak directly of past events at a certain locality within that locality or of past persons who clearly resemble persons in the room is to make those events and persons "come alive" in powerfully palpable ways.

ways—specifically, altering the way Euro-Christian settlers inhabit the indigenous cosmos they find themselves in.[58]

EPILOGUE: TOWARD A THEORY OF THE BOOK OF MORMON'S OWN THEORY OF (ITS OWN) TRANSLATION

It is beyond the scope of this chapter to detail how the Book of Mormon text itself further supports this conceptual shift from linguistic to metaphysical translation when theorizing and historicizing Joseph Smith's projects, textual and otherwise. Hence, a provocative gesture by way of epilogue. The Book of Mormon contains a metaliterary microcosm—Mosiah 8 to Ether 15—that arguably illuminates its distinctive process of translation. The argument for the formal integrity of this unit rests on the fact that its composition likely corresponds closely with the first, fevered arc of Smith's collaboration with Oliver Cowdery—from Cowdery's arrival in Harmony, Pennsylvania, in early April 1829 to their movement to Fayette, New York, in late May.[59] Mosiah 8 to Ether 15, considered first and foremost as a bewildering speech-event transacted between two men previously unknown to each other who suddenly find themselves engaged in a marvelous undertaking they scarcely understand, emerges as the main thrust of an ongoing attempt to theorize the process

58. On the Book of Mormon as a text that is primarily concerned with the destiny of indigenous peoples, see Jared Hickman, "The Book of Mormon as Amerindian Apocalypse," *American Literature* 86, no. 3 (September 2014): 429–61; Jared Hickman, "The Perverse Core of Mormonism: The Book of Mormon, Genetic Secularity, and Messianic Decoloniality," in *To Be Learned is Good: Essays on Faith and Scholarship in Honor of Richard Lyman Bushman*, ed. J. Spencer Fluhman, Kathleen Flake, and Jed Woodworth (Provo, UT: Neal A. Maxwell Institute for Religious Scholarship, Brigham Young University, 2017), 131–45; Jared Hickman, "600 BCE–1830 CE: The Book of Mormon and the Lived Eschatology of Settler Colonialism," in *Timelines of American Literature*, ed. Cody Marrs and Christopher Hager (Baltimore, MD: Johns Hopkins University Press, 2019), 67–84.

59. On Mosiah priority, see Brent Lee Metcalfe, "The Priority of Mosiah: A Prelude to Book of Mormon Exegesis," chap. 10 in *New Approaches to the Book of Mormon: Explorations in Critical Methodology*, ed. Brent Lee Metcalfe (Salt Lake City: Signature Books, 1993); and Susan Staker, "Secret Things, Hidden Things: The Seer Story in the Imaginative Economy of Joseph Smith," chap. 7 in *American Apocrypha: Essays on the Book of Mormon*, ed. Dan Vogel and Brent Lee Metcalfe (Salt Lake City: Signature Books, 2002). Other revelations and encounters networked to the speech-event of Mosiah 8 to Ether 15 would be the revelations of April and May 1829. See Revelation, April 1829-A, in *JSP*-D1:34–37 [D&C 6]; Revelation, Spring 1829, in *JSP*-D1:37–44 [D&C 10]; Revelation, April 1829-B, in *JSP*-D1:44–47 [D&C 8]; Account of John, April 1829-C, in *JSP*-D1:47–48 [D&C 7]; Revelation, April 1829-D, in *JSP*-D1:48–50 [D&C 9]; Revelation, May 1829-A, in *JSP*-D1:50–55 [D&C 11]; Revelation, May 1829-B, in *JSP*-D1:55–57 [D&C 12]. Four of these revelations deal with the mechanics of Book of Mormon translation (Revelation, April 1829-A [D&C 6], Revelation, April 1829-B [D&C 8], Revelation, April 1829-D [D&C 9], Revelation, Spring 1829 [D&C 10]) and one of which purports to be some sort of "translation" (Account of John, April 1829-C [D&C 7:headnote]; see also David W. Grua and William V. Smith, "The Tarrying of the Beloved Disciple: The Textual Formation of the Account of John," Chapter 10 herein).

under which the Book of Mormon was being produced even as it was being produced—to theorize, in a word, "translation."

Notably, this metaliterary microcosm opens with the discovery of an ancient record inscribed on golden plates left behind by an even earlier civilization (the Jaredites) and the intention to produce a linguistic translation through a pair of stones (the plan is to take the Jaredite record to a "seer" who can make known "what otherwise could not be made known").[60] This metaliterary microcosm then ends with the publication, as it were, of a translation of the Jaredite record in the form of the book of Ether.

However, quite strikingly, the book of Ether adduces not one but two sets of its own stones, both of which explicitly facilitate (meta)physical rather than linguistic translation. First, there are the sixteen stones (eight pairs) that "the brother of Jared" has God illuminate with his finger so the Jaredites will have light in their eight submarine-like barges during their migration from the Old World to the New.[61] In the course of persuading God to illuminate these stones, the brother of Jared sees "the finger of the Lord" and, consequently, cannot be withheld from being "brought back into [God's] presence" and "show[n] . . . all the inhabitants of the earth which had been, and also all that would be."[62] The brother of Jared is afforded a metaphysical translation and instructed to encode this experience in a record that, he is told, will only be accessible through "two stones" that "shall magnify to the eyes of men these things which ye shall write."[63] Significantly, as the novel use of the verb "magnify" (first time in a Mosiah-priority reading) here suggests, these two stones are characterized as an augmented or virtual reality technology that provides something like a re-creation or parallel realization of the brother of Jared's metaphysical translation for their user.[64] When describing the two instances that this record was opened, Moroni writes that "the very things which the brother of Jared saw" were "made manifest."[65] Hence, this second set of stones, rather than facilitating a linguistic translation and thus a textual mediation of the brother of Jared's experience, seems to promise the user's own metaphysical translation, virtual or actual. In short, the conceptual arc of the Book of Mormon's metaliterary microcosm seems to be from linguistic to metaphysical translation.

60. Mosiah 8:17. See also Mosiah 28:11–18.
61. See Ether 3:1–5, 6:1–8.
62. Ether 3:6, 13, 25–26.
63. Ether 3:21–24.
64. Ether 3:24.
65. See Ether 4:2–4.

That the Book of Mormon is practically crying out that it is a metaphysical rather than linguistic translation is perhaps indicated in the final verse of its metaliterary microcosm, which contains the Book of Mormon's single use of "translation" in the metaphysical sense of Hebrews 11:5: "Now the last words which are written by Ether are these, Whether the Lord will that I be translated, or that I suffer the will of the Lord in the flesh, it mattereth not, if it so be that I am saved in the kingdom of God."[66] Ether's musing became Smith's own and that of many who followed him. The question driving each movement of early Mormons toward or into "the borders of the Lamanites"[67] (to Ohio, Missouri, Illinois, Utah) was: Will we be translated—this time in this place?

If Smith could afford to be as blasé as Ether on this point, perhaps it was because he was in the very process of finalizing a metaphysical translation by impudently transposing all of sacred history to his America in the form of the Book of Mormon, the culminating *translatio imperii et studii*. Notably, this project of translation is arguably completed at Ether 12–13, which audaciously Americanizes the sacred past catalogued in Hebrews 11 (Smith's urtext of metaphysical translation) as well as the eschatological future limned in Hebrews 12 (which defines the millennial transformation in terms of metatithemi). If at Mosiah 8 (the commencement of the arc), a "seer" who translates ancient texts appears as the "great[est]" possible model for what Smith was doing; by Ether 15 (the conclusion of the arc), a "translator" who creatively (re)constructs cosmic space is arguably revealed as even greater than a seeric translator of texts and thus the true measure of Smith's accomplishment and aspiration.[68]

Smith was now on his way to completing the Book of Mormon and beginning a new translation of the Bible that featured a dramatic expansion of Genesis 5:24 explaining why and how Enoch and his city, called "Zion," were taken into heaven.[69] Soon thereafter Smith was building a Zion of his own, self-consciously emulating Enoch, whose name he adopted as a signature for many of his subsequent revelations regarding the establishment and translation of his latter-day Zion. From start to finish, the historical record plausibly suggests, Smith was above all a translator—albeit a metaphysical one.

66. Ether 15:34.

67. Revelation, 10 June 1831, in *JSP*-D1:336 [D&C 54:8].

68. For further development of this line of inquiry, see Jared Hickman, *The Romance of The Book of Mormon* (work in progress).

69. See *Joseph Smith's New Translation of the Bible: Original Manuscripts*, ed. Scott H. Faulring, Kent P. Jackson, and Robert J. Matthews (Provo, UT: Religious Studies Center, 2004), 103–10 [Moses 7].

4

Performing the Translation

Character Transcripts and Joseph Smith's Earliest Translating Practices

MICHAEL HUBBARD MACKAY

By 1828, Joseph Smith began dictating complex narratives that his family and friends inscribed on paper and considered scripture. Smith claimed that an angel had led him to a set of metal plates buried in a nearby hill and that his oral dictation to scribes was the miraculous translation of an ancient book of scripture like the Bible. Those who witnessed and recounted his dictation of the Book of Mormon related that he had read English words from a seer stone held in the bottom of his upturned hat.[1] The words of the Book of Mormon reportedly appeared on the stone as he read them out to his scribes. While the bulk of this volume examines what Smith meant by "translation"—for the Book of Mormon and subsequent scriptural productions—this chapter examines the brief but formative period between December 1827, when he "commenced copying the characters of ~~all~~ the plates," and February 1828, when Martin Harris took a transcript of the characters in search of a scholar to examine them.[2] During this period, Smith produced almost no translation, even though he was attempting to find a way to decipher a text from the plates. The process that he undertook demonstrates his exploratory intentions just as he was on the verge of beginning his magnum opus, the Book of Mormon.

This chapter therefore examines the very beginning of Joseph Smith's life-long translation effort by focusing on his lived experience as he approached the first and most important of his several translation projects—the Book of Mormon. Smith constituted each of his translations in real practices. They were

1. According to David Whitmer, Smith would look into his seer stone and see "a line of characters from the plates, and under it, the translation in English; at least, so Joseph said." J. L. Traughber Jr., "Testimony of David Whitmer," *Saints' Herald*, 15 November 1879, 341.

2. Joseph Smith, History, 1838–1856, vol. A-1, 9, in *JSP*-H1:238–40.

religious experiences that produced manuscripts and books. These episodes demonstrated that religion happens within material culture. In fact, many of Smith's experiences were historical, analyzable practices in which he put the material world to work. One useful way to analyze Smith's translations is through the product of that translation, the resulting text. Yet the artifacts, practices, and experiences involved in translation manifest meanings that are as resounding as the text itself. This chapter employs an epistemology that captures a brief glimpse at Joseph Smith's negotiations with the established social structures defining the idea of translation through his bodily experiences.

To develop the experiential aspect of his translations, this chapter examines the earliest practices that led Smith to his production of the Book of Mormon. It will expand his translation process from the moment the text was dictated and written down to the larger process that began with the recovery of the golden plates and ended with the established text of the Book of Mormon. Utilizing this broad conception of translation, the chapter will ask and attempt to answer two specific questions: First, why would Smith produce copies of the characters inscribed on the gold plates at the very beginning of his translation process? Second, why would he send Martin Harris with a transcript of the characters to be examined by language specialists? Examining these questions will lead to a more comprehensive assessment of what constitutes Joseph Smith's translations. Both questions will be considered within a materialist framework recognizing translation as an embodied practice.

TRANSLATION AS EMBODIED PRACTICE

The scope of what is meant by translation needs to be expanded to include practice as well as product. In order to do this, some theoretical considerations are in order. Most scholars have approached Smith's translations as metaphysical, spiritual, or ethereal phenomena—or even as the work of a religious genius—as if his translations are transcendent and beyond the materiality of the world in which humans live. However, some scholars within the field of religious studies have devoted their efforts to the study of the material artifacts that instantiate and constitute religion. Colleen McDannell, in the introduction to her study of material Christianity, notes that "significant theoretical and practical research has been directed toward understanding what it means to live in a world made up not only of ideas but of things."[3] She is part of a group

3. Colleen McDannell, *Material Christianity: Religion and Popular Culture in America* (New Haven and London: Yale University Press, 1995), 2.

of scholars like J. Z. Smith, Peter Brown, David Morgan, and Caroline Walker Bynum who study religion through the examination of ritual objects, devotional art, sacred architecture, built environments, and artificial landscapes. The artifacts and places that people create and the things that they do with and within them are like a symbolic language representing religion and its meaning. One leading theorist, Manuel A. Vasquez, calls this a "materialist" methodology "because it approaches religion as it is lived by human beings."[4] It is materialist because it focuses on material things and embodied practices.

The actions exhibited through embodied practices transform the world we live in, and do so within a dialectic of individual experiences and social structures. As Pierre Bourdieu argues, embodied historical agents are structured and embedded in socially defined situations that maintain certain power relations. It is within those situations that needs and interests are conditioned, limiting or producing specific actions or practices.[5] A materialist approach to religion must therefore incorporate the study of practice. Bruce Lincoln, a professor of history of religions, explained that to study religion, especially historically, is to "insist on discussing the temporal, contextual, situated, interested, human and material dimensions of those discourses, practices, and institutions that characteristically represent themselves as eternal, transcendent, spiritual, and divine."[6] Historically, the study of religion has focused on sacred texts and canonized scripture, instead of recognizing the association of those texts to the diverse network of other agents or practices that negotiate those relationships. Though texts do say something about something, they are still always the result of the actions that produced them and one can define them by the experiences people have through reading them. Human bodies are shaped by their environments, which include cultural artifacts that affect the way in which humans perceive their environments and even transform them. In fact, according to philosophers George Lakoff and Mark Johnson, "our sensory organs, our ability to move and manipulate objects, the detailed structure of our brain, our culture, and our interactions in our environment" are all factors

4. Manuel A. Vasquez, *More than Belief: A Materialist Theory of Religion* (Oxford: Oxford University Press, 2011), 5.

5. Pierre Bourdieu, *The Logic of Practice* (Stanford: Stanford University Press, 1990), 53.

6. Bruce Lincoln, "Theses on Method," *Method and Theory in the Study of Religion* 8, no. 3 (Winter 1996): 225–27. Closely related, but perhaps leaning too far toward the phenomenology of religion, the lived religion school is a praxis-oriented approach developing within American religious history. Robert Orsi explained that this kind of methodology—examining lived religion—was "concerned with what people do with religious practice, what they make with it of themselves and their worlds." Robert Orsi, "Everyday Miracles: The Study of Lived Religion," in *Lived Religion in America: Toward a History of Practice*, ed. David Hall (Princeton, NJ: Princeton University Press, 1997), 7.

for how we construct what we perceive to be true, which actually "depends on our embodied understanding of the situation, which in turn is shaped by all these factors."[7]

Like texts and artifacts, practices congeal into meaningful events, often preserved in one medium or another, which can be effective in symbolically conveying significant meaning. The text itself is less meaningful without the experience of a reader. Once the text is embodied as part of the production process, it is enlivened and its symbolic value may now be recognized and even interpreted.[8] In Joseph Smith's translations, broadly defined, the text cannot be separated from religious objects or the experience of producing and consuming text. One might suspend the association of the Book of Mormon with the golden plates from which they were allegedly derived, yet the text itself is *self-aware* of its material relationship with the plates and to take the text seriously one must place some kind of value on the plates—even if only in Smith's imagination.

In all of Smith's translations, he anchored the text to some kind of material artifact or physical experience. Whereas some of the other revelations he claimed to have received were presented as direct communications from God, the productions of the translated texts were always described in terms of some earthly artifact. In 1829, Smith used a seer stone to translate a document that he claimed was material, though not present, which the apostle John had inscribed on "parchment, written and hid up by himself."[9] In 1835, Smith produced a translation of the writings of the biblical patriarch Abraham after purchasing and analyzing Egyptian papyri that he believed contained Abraham's writings. In 1843, he translated a portion of a set of metal plates that were "discovered" at Kinderhook, Illinois, and brought to him (and later shown to be forgeries). Each of these artifacts was situated within a particular and complex social structure and was inseparable from Smith's embodied translation practices. In fact, it would be difficult to separate the production of the text from the artifacts that allowed him to appropriate, perceive, and accommodate the social structures within which he existed. In this way, his embodied experiences were the translation. He was *performing* translation.

7. George Lakoff and Mark Johnson, *Philosophy in the Flesh: The Embodied Mind and its Challenge to Western Thought* (New York: Basic Books, 1999), 102. Karen Barad goes as far as arguing that even theorizing is "a material practice." Karen Barad, "Posthumanist Performativity: Toward an Understanding of How Matter Comes to Matter," in *Material Feminisms*, ed. Stacy Alaimo and Susan Hekman (Bloomington: Indiana University Press, 2008), 55.

8. See Vasquez, *More than Belief*, 255–57.

9. *JSP*-D1:44–50.

COPYING CHARACTERS AND THE PERFORMANCE OF TRANSLATION

Why would Smith approach the translation process by making copies of the characters on the golden plates? For a skeptic, the answer may seem easy: there were no actual plates and no engravings to show anyone and therefore the characters had to be drawn on paper. However, this explanation fails to thoroughly answer the question because copying the characters was only the first step in the larger process of translation. Though there is no evidence that Smith ever produced a traditional translation of the characters on the plates, he originally proceeded as an academic might—as if he could discover their meaning in a scholarly fashion—and participated in a network of social practices that would support his claims.[10] Between December 1827 and February 1828, within a few months of recovering the plates, he copied "a considerable number" of their engraven characters onto paper.[11] By doing so, he claimed to have reproduced a portion of the plates, not as a translation strictly defined, but in terms of producing a facsimile and perhaps as a preliminary step in the translation process. The production of facsimiles uncovers the initial practices Smith undertook to secure himself within a broader culture of translation and lays the groundwork for how he might be convincing to local networks of people in upstate New York. This can be demonstrated in two ways: (1) examining how his practices functioned to validate and legitimize his translation, and (2) looking at Smith's scholarly (or traditional) practices of translation.

Legitimizing Translation

The reproduction of characters from the set of metal plates acted as a kind of social apparatus that validated the plates and Smith's translation process. This first point can be demonstrated by its association with public practices within both religious and scientific mentalities, in which performers convinced the public of some kind of scientific or religious principle. Beginning in the seventeenth century, the public performance of scientific experiments convinced

10. Michael Hubbard MacKay, "'Git Them Translated': Joseph Smith and a Secular Translation of the Characters on the Gold Plates," in *Joseph Smith and the Ancient World*, ed. Lincoln H. Blumell, Matthew J. Grey, and Andrew H. Hedges (Provo: Religious Studies Center, Brigham Young University, 2013), 79–112.

11. Joseph Smith, History, 1838–1856, vol. A-1, 8–9, in *JSP*-H1:237–40; Joseph Smith, History, ca. Summer 1832, 5, in *JSP*-H1:15. Smith's earlier history states: "So we proceeded to coppy some of them and he took his Journy to the Eastern Cittys and to the Learned."

audiences of the "facts" of the natural world. Watching demonstrations of experiments such as Faraday's magnetic induction ring and Boyle's air pump convinced onlookers even though most of the experiments were too complex for ordinary people to reproduce. The public believed regardless of their ability to understand the physics or interpret the observed results.[12] These kinds of performances were not limited to scientific demonstrations. Empirical observation had certainly become the discipline of science, but popular religious and spiritual practices had also placed a premium on performance observation and sensorial experience.[13] One example of this was the noisy environment of early American revivalism and antebellum America's propensity for communal experiences of ecstatic religion (and their resulting soundscapes).[14] Revival grounds and meetinghouses became a place to observe performance, practice religion, experience conversion, and discover God.

Coming into close proximity or contact with the plates, whether uncovered or not, could function similarly. While the testimonies of the witnesses who later claimed they had seen the plates are relatively well known,[15] Smith had initiated such practices from the time he first saw the plates in vision. On 22 September 1823, the day after Smith's initial vision of the gold plates, he told his father that the plates were in a nearby hill and that he had seen them in vision. His father believed him and sent him to the hill to recover them.[16] At the hill, Joseph uncovered the plates and saw and touched them, but the angel appeared again and forbid him from taking them. Though he returned home empty handed, when he told his family all that happened, they believed him.[17] On 22 September 1828, Joseph Smith went back to the hill with his wife, Emma Hale Smith, who waited for him in the wagon at the foot of

12. On the emergence of this kind of public display in the history of science, see Steven Shapin and Simon Schaffer, *Leviathan and the Air-Pump: Hobbes, Boyle, and the Experimental Life* (Princeton, NJ: Princeton University Press, 2011).

13. See Robert Jutte, *A History of the Senses: From Antiquity to Cyberspace* (Cambridge: Polity, 2005). Religious revivals and sensory experiences had been around for centuries already. However, nineteenth-century religious experience was uniquely affected by the post-Enlightenment ideas surrounding the formulation of professional scientific practices and the way they were communicated to the public at large. For an example of the development of this relationship, see Sarah Rivett, *The Science of the Soul in Colonial New England* (Chapel Hill: North Carolina University Press, 2011), 5–22.

14. See Leigh Eric Schmidt, *Hearing Things: Religion, Illusion, and the American Enlightenment* (Cambridge, MA, and London: Harvard University Press, 2000).

15. See *JSP*-D1, appendixes 4–5.

16. Joseph Smith, History, 1838–1856, vol. A-1, 5–7, in *JSP*-H1:220–34.

17. Joseph Smith, History, 1838–1856, vol. A-1, 7, in *JSP*-H1:232–234; Oliver Cowdery, "Letter VIII," *Latter Day Saints' Messenger and Advocate*, October 1835, 197–98; Lucy Mack Smith, *Lucy's Book: A Critical Edition of Lucy Mack Smith's Family Memoir*, ed. Lavina Fielding Anderson (Salt Lake City: Signature Books, 2001), 340–45.

the hill. After several hours, Smith returned to the wagon and told her that he had recovered the plates from where they lay buried on the hill but had hidden them in a hollow log. She believed him. Smith's witnesses of seeing and touching and moving the plates had a convincing verisimilitude.

In private and semipublic settings, Smith soon placed the plates in the hands of friends, family, and associates, though he kept them wrapped in a cloth or secured in a box. This kind of performance had the potential to reveal the miraculous, an ancient gold bible, in a very material way. This first occurred when Smith brought the plates to his home and handed them through the window to his friend Josiah Stowell. According to Stowell, the covering in which Smith had wrapped the set of plates presumably pulled away from the corner thereby allowing him to see a part of it.[18] Though many would doubt that Smith ever had any plates, many others were initially convinced by Smith and others who had held them (covered or not) that they existed.[19] In fall 1827, there were at least three different attempts to steal the set of plates from Smith.[20] However, they never obtained them or even saw them. Aside from Smith himself, only Stowell had seen the artifact and only by accident, since Smith claimed that the angel charged him to keep the plates from the view of others.[21] Smith's wife, Emma, later recounted that he kept them covered but he often left them on the table, requiring her to move and handle them without uncovering them. She stated that "they seemed to be pliable like thick paper, and would rustle with a metalic sound when the edges were moved by the thumb, as one does sometimes thumb the edges of a book."[22] Smith also allowed Martin Harris and others to view the transcripts of the characters he had copied from the plates.[23]

18. On this incident and its broader setting, see Michael Hubbard MacKay and Gerrit J. Dirkmaat, "Retrieving the Plates," chap. 1 in *From Darkness unto Light: The Translation and Publication of the Book of Mormon* (Provo, UT: Religious Studies Center, Brigham Young University; Salt Lake City, UT: Deseret Book, 2015).

19. Ann Taves, "History and the Claims of Revelation: Joseph Smith and the Materialization of the Golden Plates," *Numen* 61, nos. 2–3 (2014): 182–207.

20. See Lucy Mack Smith, History, 5:1–2, Church History Library, The Church of Jesus Christ of Latter-day Saints, Salt Lake City (accessible under "Other Histories" in the Histories series of the online edition of *The Joseph Smith Papers*). In some cases, those who wanted to see the plates also spent time pressuring Smith to share them in hopes of generating wealth from the metal, such as local Palmyra Township residents Willard Chase and Samuel Lawrence. See E. D. Howe, *Mormonism Unvailed* [. . .] (Painesville, OH: self-published, 1834), 240–48. See also William H. Kelley, "Interview with Lorenzo Saunders," 17 September 1884, 10, Community of Christ Library and Archives, Community of Christ, Independence, MO; Lorenzo Saunders to Thomas Gregg, 28 January 1885, transcribed in Charles A. Shook, *The True Origin of the Book of Mormon* (Cincinnati, OH: Standard Publishing, 1914), 135.

21. Joseph Smith, History, 1838–1856, vol. A-1, 5, in *JSP*-H1:226 (draft 2). See also *JSP*-D1:353–54.

22. Joseph Smith [III], "Last Testimony of Sister Emma," *The Saints' Herald*, 1 October 1879, 289–90.

23. For a discussion of these sources and their place within the context of the translation in early 1828, see MacKay and Dirkmaat, *From Darkness unto Light*, chap. 4.

Like the public who watched the natural philosopher's experiments, Harris and others may have been unequipped to interpret the performance critically, but it was convincing nonetheless.

The performance of translation went even further and it began to expand Smith's social network and involve others. His translation process, extraordinary as it was, began to be validated through social apparatus. His mother, Lucy Mack Smith, later recounted that God directed her son "to make a facsimile of some of the characters . . . and to send them to some of the most learned men that he could find and ask them for the translation of the same."[24] Over the course of two months, he reportedly worked at one time or another with his wife, Emma Hale Smith, her brother Reuben Hale, and early believer Martin Harris to produce copies of the characters. Smith sat behind a sheet, draped from the ceiling, examining the characters on the sacred plates and copying them onto paper. Emma, Reuben, and Martin—who were all positioned on the other side of the sheet—received the slips of paper from Joseph. They then copied the characters on leaves of paper, perhaps transcribing them in uniform size or arranging them in rows or columns.[25] This process may also have functioned, whether consciously or unconsciously, as a kind of validating performance. Smith involved others with him in the practice of facsimile production. Even if they only assisted him in copying the characters, and never laid eyes on the actual engravings themselves, they were involved in a systematic process of producing the characters for further examination.[26]

Copying and even printing the characters was a performance of validation, a sign of the truth claims that Mormonism was proclaiming on the antebellum American stage. How might the religiously charged environment of the Burned Over District experience Smith's translation? Was it possible to offer a glimpse of the plates without showing them? As Victor Turner argued, when

24. Lucy Mack Smith, History, 6:3. Similarly, Edward Stevenson wrote that he had interviewed Martin Harris and that Harris had told him "it was manifested to the Prophet that a facsimile of characters must be copied and sent to the most learned professors of the country, and that Martin Harris should be the bearer of them." Edward Stevenson, *Reminiscences of Joseph, the Prophet, and the Coming Forth of the Book of Mormon* (Salt Lake City: self-published, 1893), 28–29.

25. See *JSP*-D1:354–55.

26. Emma Hale Smith admitted that she had never seen the plates, but Joseph Knight Sr. explained that she helped her husband make copies of the characters. Dean Jessee, "Joseph Knight's Recollection of Early Mormon History," *BYU Studies* 17, no. 1 (Autumn 1976): 3. The history Smith initiated in 1838 also describes more than one document that Martin Harris took with him to New York City. Joseph Smith, History, vol. A-1, 8–9, in *JSP*-H1:237–40. Emily Blackman apparently interviewed a local resident of Susquehanna County, Pennsylvania, who stated that Reuben Hale "assisted Joe Smith to fix up some characters such as Smith pretended were engraven on his book of plates." Emily Blackman, *History of Susquehanna County, Pennsylvania* (Philadelphia: Claxton, Remsen & Haffelfinger, 1873), 104.

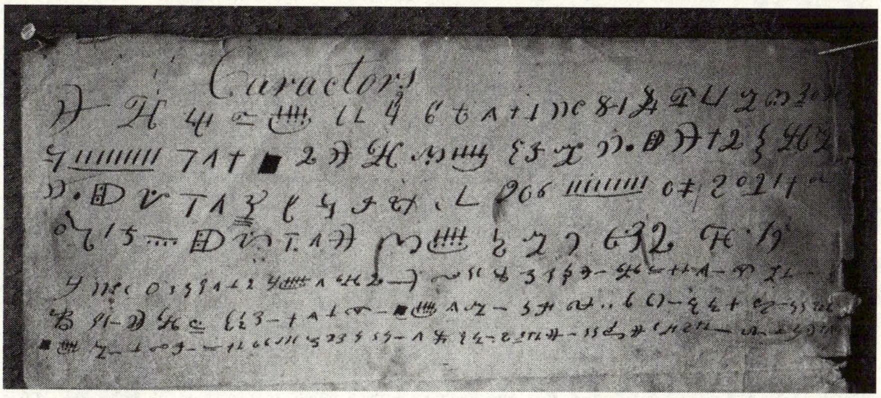

FIGURE 4.1. Characters from the gold plates. Copies of characters understood to have been transcribed from the gold plates by Joseph Smith. Photograph by Jacob Hicks, 1886. The Clay County Museum and Historical Society, Clay County, MO.

someone acts out a "play" in a social drama of everyday life, "something new may be generated" and create "hitherto unprecedented insights and even generate new symbols and meanings, which may be incorporated into subsequent performances."[27] Harris showed the characters to Episcopalian preacher John Clark, as if it would help Clark understand his interest in Smith's gold bible and generate new meaning in the anticipated translation.[28]

In fact, copies of the characters were used in missionary work and as evidence of the Book of Mormon throughout Smith's life (see Figures 4.1 and 4.2).[29] In 1835, Smith showed Michael Chandler copies of the characters when Chandler came to Kirtland with his traveling mummy show and sold Smith his Egyptiana.[30] In 1842, he presented copies of the characters to the Unitarian reverend George Moore to examine.[31] The characters were even featured on a placard that was printed in Smith's honor when he died.[32] They were part of

27. Victor Turner, *From Ritual to Theatre: The Human Seriousness of Play* (New York: PAJ Publications, 1982), 79.

28. John A. Clark, *Gleanings by the Way* (Philadelphia: W. J. & J. K. Simon; New York: Robert Carter, 1842), 217, 222–31.

29. Stanley B. Kimball, "The Anthon Transcript: People, Primary Sources, and Problems," *BYU Studies* 10, no. 3 (Spring 1970): 341–47.

30. *Latter Day Saints' Messenger and Advocate*, December 1835, 235. See also Joseph Smith, Journal, 1 October 1835 and 17 November 1835, in *JSP*-J1:67, 105.

31. Donald Q. Cannon, "Reverend George Moore Comments on Nauvoo, the Mormons, and Joseph Smith," *Western Illinois Regional Studies* 5, no. 1 (Spring 1982): 11.

32. Michael Hubbard MacKay, Gerrit J. Dirkmaat, and Robin Scott Jensen, "The 'Caractors' Document: New Light on an Early Transcription of the Book of Mormon Characters," *Mormon Historical Studies* 14, no. 1 (Spring 2013): 152, Appendix A: "Speculative Filial Chart."

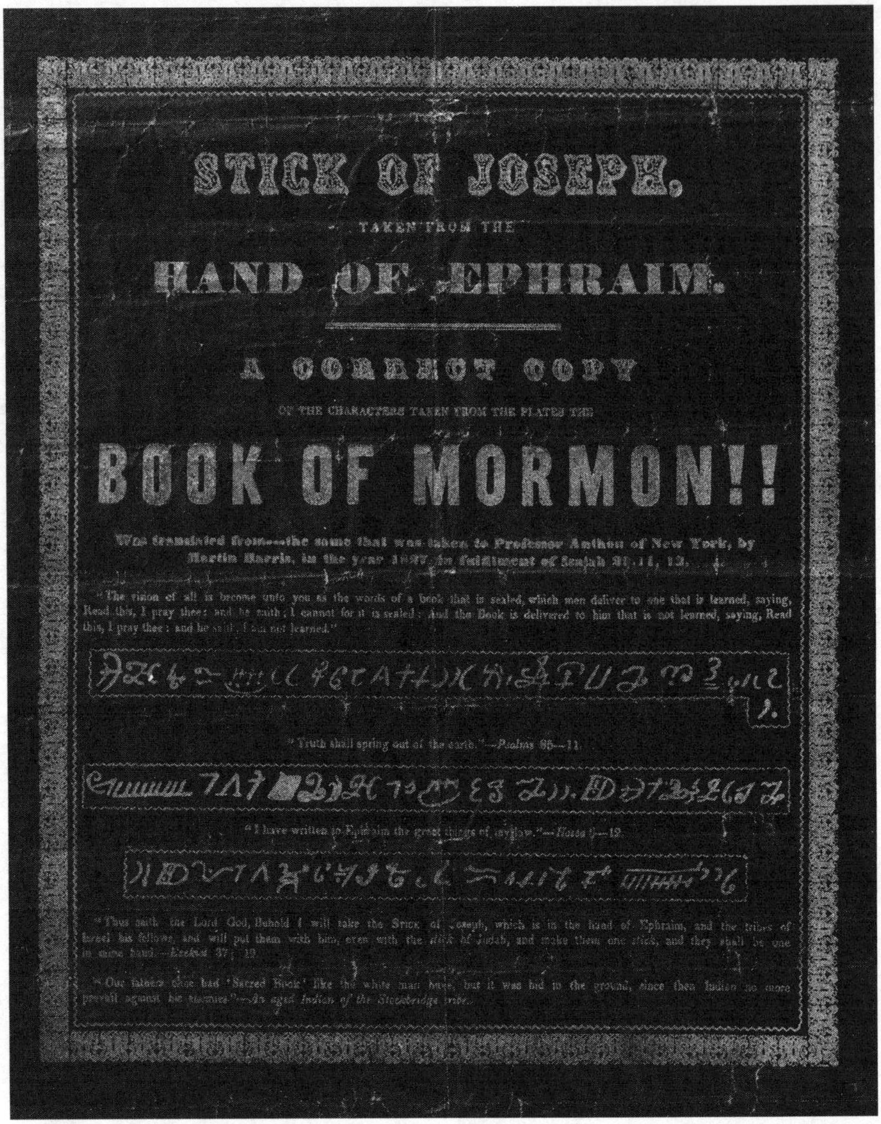

FIGURE 4.2. Broadside with characters from the gold plates. Published in 1844, upon Joseph Smith's death, by a church newspaper in New York City. Church History Library, Salt Lake City; photograph by Welden C. Andersen.

the performance that validated Smith's translation—at the very least in the mind of Martin Harris. This performance and Harris's experience of holding the characters documents in his hands offered him a sense of the reality of the translation. Moreover, because of the miraculous way in which the plates were recovered, Harris may have also opened his mind to the tangible reality of an alternative kind of translation.

Performing Traditional Practices

By Smith's day, traditional translation was already a fairly well-defined practice established by social structures of academic culture that determined the behaviors and processes of a translator. The negotiation between the translator and the language is not absolutely determined, but very constrained within systems of consensus and tradition. Translators perform their translations within those structures of constraint with varying senses of autonomy. A typical translation process, converting something written in a source language to a target language, would ordinarily include at least a few predetermined activities. Translation was a comparative process by nature. In many situations, translators would use one language to access another language before it was rendered into the target language (usually the native tongue of the translator). Jean-Francois Champollion, for example, undertook an academic study of Egyptian believing that Hebrew and Egyptian were related. Finally, the Rosetta Stone enabled an understanding of Egyptian by juxtaposing comparative panels of Egyptian and Greek script.[33] The recovery of ancient languages was an important element of higher education, which was built on a foundation of classical instruction including the study of Latin and Greek. The academic process of translation involved the production of facsimiles, alphabets, lexicons, and grammars of ancient languages.

Smith, likely unaware of the details of linguistic translation practice, endeavored to breach the boundaries of his own world and reach out to those who did understand the process. Years later, such practices were an obvious part of his efforts, such as his interpretation of the Egyptian papyri in 1835 and his formal study of Hebrew in 1836. However, the emergence of similar kinds of translation practices started in 1827.[34] The most simple of tasks, like transcribing characters from the plates, offer a window into Smith's awareness of the scholarly methods of linguistic translation and a set of practices associated with the translation of ancient languages into English—at least enough of an awareness to begin by making facsimiles and to seek out further help from real scholars.

Though Smith was unfamiliar with the academic culture of translation, he had some notion that there was such a thing and what its processes might be. There is evidence that he was trying to create some kind of systematic list of

33. Henry Wheaton, "Egyptian Antiquities," *North American Review* 29 (1829): 361–88; and Edward Everett, "Hieroglyphics," *North American Review* 32 (1831): 95–127.

34. See David E. Sloan, "The Anthon Transcripts and the Translation of the Book of Mormon: Studying It Out in the Mind of Joseph Smith," *Journal of Book of Mormon Studies* 5, no. 2 (1996): 57–81.

the known characters on the plates, indicating an attempt to follow traditional translation practices. Lucy Mack Smith and Joseph Knight Sr. both suggest that he was trying to create an alphabet or register of the various characters on the plates in order to have a lexicon created by someone else. According to Lucy, her son had been instructed in a revelation from God "to take off a facsimile of the alphabet composing the characters Alphabetically and send them to all the learned men that he could find and ask them for the translation of the same."[35] Less explicitly, Knight wrote that Smith "now Began to be anxious to git them translated" and "therefore with his wife Drew of[f] the Caricters exactley like the ancient and sent Martin Harris to see if he Could git them Translated."[36] Smith's early history indicates that he was attempting to copy "all" the characters, possibly affirming that his original purpose was to produce a comprehensive register of the various characters he found on the plates. However, the word "all" was crossed out. Charles Anthon, a prominent classicist at Columbia College, would describe the transcript of characters that Martin Harris showed to him in February 1828, as a document organized in columns, which apparently reflects some kind of conscientious arrangement and could possibly represent a list of characters (like an alphabet).[37]

Smith's history goes on to explain that at some point between December 1827 and February 1828 he abandoned his linguistic approach and began using the spectacles found with the plates to translate the characters into English.[38] As Joseph turned to his seer stones for answers about the translation, creating an alphabet or complete register of characters was rendered less important. Nevertheless, consulting with scholars about the characters apparently remained purposeful for some reason. Though Joseph would eventually rely mainly upon a religious practice—supernatural vision—to produce the book, it was inevitably tethered to and even validated by traditional practices of translation.

Though the alphabet or possible future lexicon would provide another kind of validation, it also grounded Smith's translation in the world of Enlightenment rationalism by following the kinds of practices one might perform as part of a scholarly translation of unknown characters. This was the beginning of

35. Lucy Mack Smith, History, 6:7.

36. Jessee, "Joseph Knight's Recollection of Early Mormon History," 3.

37. In 1834, Anthon wrote that the transcript he was shown "consisted of all kinds of crooked characters disposed in columns," and in 1841 he wrote that the characters "were arranged in columns." Charles Anthon to E. D. Howe, 17 February 1834, quoted in Howe, *Mormonism Unvailed*, 270–72; Charles Anthon to Rev. Thomas Winthrop Coit, 3 April 1841, quoted in *Church Record*, 17 April 1841, 231–32. Both letters reproduced from their published sources in Erin B. Jennings, "Charles Anthon—The Man behind the Letters," *John Whitmer Historical Association Journal* 32, no. 2 (Fall/Winter 2012):178.

38. Joseph Smith, History, ca. Summer 1832, 5, in *JSP*-H1:15.

Smith using traditional translation practices in an attempt to produce the Book of Mormon. These processes quickly reached their limits in terms of actual scholarly translation, but the production of the text still followed, embodied within the person of Joseph Smith as he vocalized the words of the Book of Mormon, and within his scribes as they recorded them by hand in analyzable practices of speech and writing. Those who observed this process described a scene in which Smith held an upturned hat with a rock in its crown and dictated the translation as he dipped his head in and out of the hat as if the text were inside, waiting to be scooped out.

Smith's subsequent translation projects were also defined in part by scholarly performance. They involved folk divination practices that were rarely if ever affixed to scholarly endeavors in post-Enlightenment culture and yet were curiously mixed with traditional translation practices. In the case of the "new translation" of the Bible, Smith's major translation project between 1830 and 1833, he reviewed the text with Sidney Rigdon—who had been an accomplished minister in the movement of biblical primitivism led by restorationist Alexander Campbell. Smith and Rigdon studied a Bible commentary by Methodist theologian and Bible scholar Adam Clarke to better understand the text before offering a new translation or revision of the text.[39] Between 1832 and 1835, when Smith and others made efforts to recover utterances of the "pure language" spoken by Adam, words, translations, and even characters were approached systematically, and even in rows and columns like one would see in a lexicon.[40] In 1835, when Smith began his translation of the Book of Abraham, he and others also worked with actual Egyptian papyri and characters, producing facsimiles, an alphabet, a lexicon, and rules of grammar, concurrent with his production of an English text of the Book of Abraham. In 1842, he resumed translating the Book of Abraham and drew from a Hebrew instruction manual to help with some of the words and concepts.[41] In 1843, when the Kinderhook plates were brought to him, he used a Hebrew lexicon and his own lexicon of Egyptian in an attempt to translate from the plates.[42] Glimpses of

39. Thomas A. Wayment and Haley Wilson-Lemmon, "A Recovered Resource: The Use of Adam Clarke's Bible Commentary in Joseph Smith's Bible Translation," Chapter 11 herein.

40. See David Golding, "'Eternal Wisdom Engraven upon the Heavens': Joseph Smith's Pure Language Project," 344–61 herein.

41. Matthew J. Grey, "Approaching Egyptian Papyri through Biblical Language: Joseph Smith's Use of Hebrew in His Translation of the Book of Abraham," Chapter 16 herein.

42. See Don Bradley and Mark Ashurst-McGee, "'President Joseph Has Translated a Portion': Joseph Smith and the Mistranslation of the Kinderhook Plates," Chapter 17 herein.

scholarly attempts appear alongside the claims and performance of prophetic translation.

INTERPRETING THE CHARACTERS

After the characters from the gold plates were copied, Joseph Smith willingly allowed or even asked Martin Harris to take a transcript of the characters so that scholars could examine them. Why would Smith send Harris with the characters seeking scholarly examination? Some of Smith's followers came to view this entire episode of transcribing the characters and sending them (via Harris) to the young nation's great linguists as nothing more than the providential fulfillment of prophecy. The book of Isaiah included a prophecy regarding a "sealed book" that the "learned" could not read.[43] Several scholars—both Mormon and non-Mormon—have even presented the entire effort as a *premeditated* adventure to fulfil the prophecy.[44] Smith, in his circa Summer 1832 history, recounted the episode in terms of prophecy fulfillment.[45] Oliver Cowdery, who would later become Smith's primary scribe for the Book of Mormon, wrote in 1834 that the angel had told Smith "the scripture must be fulfilled before it is translated, which says that the words of a book, which were sealed were presented to the learned for thus has God determined to leave man without excuse."[46] However, Cowdery may have been reading the Bible back into the 1828 encounter between Harris and Anthon. The earliest sources emphasize the visit to Samuel Mitchill, who was the more prominent scholar. The diminishing emphasis on Mitchill that occurred over the next decade corresponds with an increasing emphasis on Anthon and a presentation of the event that casts it as a fulfillment of prophecy.[47] As in historical investigation generally, it is important to focus on early and eyewitness accounts in attempting to determine how an incident or episode was originally understood, free from later interpretations.

43. Isaiah 29:11–12.

44. See Kimball, "The Anthon Transcript," 340–41. Orson Pratt claimed that Harris had not been aware of the Isaiah passage before he left for New York City and had not contemplated fulfilling any prophesy. Orson Pratt, Discourse, 7 January 1855, in *Journal of Discourses*, 26 vols. (Liverpool: Daniel H. Wells; London: Latter-day Saints' Book Depot, 1886), 2:288.

45. Joseph Smith, History, circa Summer 1832, 5, in *JSP*-H1:15.

46. Oliver Cowdery, "Letter IV," *Latter Day Saints' Messenger and Advocate*, February 1835, 78.

47. MacKay, "'Git Them Translated,'" 79–112.

With facsimiles in hand, Harris set out in search of a scholar who could interpret them.[48] He reached out more broadly in terms of both geography and familiar social orbits for specialists who could help in the process of translation. By sending Harris with the characters, Smith expanded the network of involved individuals and thereby broadened the scope of information that could influence his own understanding of the ensuing translation. Harris's errand shifted the network of relationships shaping Smith's understanding of the translation process. This daring adventure apparently had at least three purposes: (1) to bolster Harris's confidence in financially supporting the production of the Book of Mormon, (2) to find a scholar who could translate the characters, and (3) to verify the accuracy of at least some of the characters that Smith had translated.

Reinforcing Harris's Commitment to the Translation

Martin Harris had to be convinced before financially supporting Smith during the translation period and financing the publication of the Book of Mormon. In fall 1827, when Harris first heard of Smith's claims to have discovered the golden plates, he discounted the idea. Smith had called on Harris through his mother, Lucy Mack Smith, to solicit his help. Harris, though a friend of the family, responded cautiously. His wife and daughter visited the Smith home first and were allowed to heft the plates in a box. When they returned home, Harris queried them. Later, when he arrived at the Smith home to discuss the matter, he took Joseph's wife and family members aside individually and questioned them privately about the discovery of the plates. Though he was interested in Joseph's claims, and did not discount them out of hand, he was also cautiously skeptical, and was attempting to assess the consistency of their stories. When he had talked to everyone, he found that their stories agreed.

Nevertheless, when Joseph arrived Martin took him aside to see if Joseph's own story agreed with what he had already heard from the other Smiths. Joseph rehearsed the matter and also told Martin that the angel had revealed to him that he would receive assistance from Martin. Again, Martin responded with skepticism and caution. Joseph also let Martin heft the plates in a box. Martin then went home and prayed about the truthfulness of Joseph's claims.

48. For previous treatments of this episode, see Kimball, "The Anthon Transcript," 325–52; and Richard Bennett, "'Read This I Pray Thee': Martin Harris and the Three Wise Men of the East," *Journal of Mormon History* 36, no. 1 (Winter 2010): 178–216.

He reportedly experienced an answer to his prayers, "by the still small voice spoken in the soul," that it was indeed "the Lord's work."[49] Though Harris became invested in the project, offered Smith some support, and helped him create the facsimiles, he still travelled to New York City—at least in part—in hopes of confirming the authenticity of the characters (and, by extension, the plates). Before heading east, Harris also exhibited the transcript of the characters to family, friends, and acquaintances in Palmyra Township—as if they were evidence of the authenticity of the plates.[50]

Later, when Harris had returned from New York City and the translation had begun in earnest, he was also skeptical about Smith's method of translating with a seer stone—or at least he was concerned with how it would be accepted by others. Harris would test Smith's ability by asking him to use his stone to find a toothpick in a pile of wood shavings and to run a footrace through the trees with his seer stone bound to an eye within a blindfold.[51] He would surreptitiously replace Smith's seer stone with a stone of similar appearance, to test whether Smith was really using his special stone for the translation.[52] After scores of pages had been translated, Harris would exhibit the manuscript as evidence of the work's scriptural quality and therefore its authenticity.[53] Finally, when the translation was completed, Harris implored Smith to let him be one of the few who would get to see the plates and append their testimony to the published Book of Mormon.[54] Harris was continually trying to test or affirm Smith's claims.

In early 1828, on his way to New York City to find a scholar who could translate the characters, Harris stopped in Albany and visited Luther Bradish, an educated and successful politician. Bradish had once lived in and still had relatives in Palmyra, so apparently this is where Harris began networking. Perhaps Harris thought Bradish could offer valuable advice about who could assess the authenticity of the characters and provide him with the necessary introductions.[55]

49. Quoted in Joel Tiffany, "Mormonism," *Tiffany's Monthly*, May 1859, 166–70.

50. MacKay and Dirkmaat, *From Darkness unto Light*, chap. 4.

51. "Mormonism—No. II," *Tiffany's Monthly*, June 1859, 164.

52. Edward Stevenson, "The Three Witnesses to the Book of Mormon. No. III," *Latter-day Saints' Millennial Star*, 21 June 1886, 390.

53. See Lucy Mack Smith, History, 9:3.

54. See History Drafts, 1838–circa 1841, in *JSP*-H1:314–15. See also "Testimony of Three Witnesses, Late June 1829," in *JSP*-D1:378–84.

55. Bennett, "'Read This I Pray Thee,'" 185–86. See also Jennings, "Charles Anthon—the Man behind the Letters," 170–72.

Afterwards, Harris continued his search for other scholars who could translate the characters in New York City.[56] One such scholar was Dr. Samuel Mitchill, who had spent three decades researching the languages of the world that were currently known in Western scholarship. Mitchill was also particularly interested in Native American languages and cultures. He was invested in the work of Alexander Von Humboldt, having used language systems to develop many of his theories of Amerindian origins. In the past, Mitchill had also indulged visitors by translating manuscripts of unknown origin or language that they had brought to him.[57] When approached by Harris, Mitchill reportedly "looked at his engravings—made a learned dissertation on them—compared them with the hieroglyphics discovered by Champollion in Europe, and set them down as a language of a people formerly in existence in the East, but now no more."[58] He then sent Harris to Charles Anthon at Columbia College. Anthon reportedly validated the authenticity of the characters and even Smith's translation of some of them, but then rescinded his assessment when Harris told him the plates were delivered to Smith by an angel.[59] In fact, Anthon was vitriolic in his response to the characters' backstory. However, after Harris had visited with other academics from New York and elsewhere, he returned home to Palmyra convinced that the characters were genuine and that Smith had the ability to translate them.

Harris's trip was instrumental for the production of the Book of Mormon. Though he may have been offered countless warnings from local preachers or family members, it was his conversations with scholars that solidified his commitment to help Smith. Before Harris left, he had apparently had a dream in which God commanded him to help Smith; yet he still placed this visionary experience on hold, anxious to hear from academic scholars whether the characters were genuine.[60] He left Smith to seek after secular validation. This process, even if religiously motivated, was hardly religious in nature. In fact, the scholars he visited were convinced by the academic study of language rather than embracing any possibility of a miraculous revelation of an ancient record. Within that academic environment, as soon as Harris related that an

56. MacKay, "'Git Them Translated,'" 93–95.

57. Kimball, "The Anthon Transcript," 332–34; MacKay, "'Git Them Translated,'" 91–92; Bennett, "'Read This I Pray Thee'"; Richard E. Bennett, "'A Nation Now Extinct': Samuel L. Mitchill, Martin Harris, and the New York Theory," *Journal of the Book of Mormon and Other Restoration Scripture* 20, no. 1 (2011): 30–51.

58. James Gordon Bennett, "Mormon Religion—Clerical Ambition—Western New York—The Mormonites Gone to Ohio," *Morning Courier & New York Enquirer* (New York, NY), 1 September 1831, 1.

59. Joseph Smith, History, 1838–1856, vol. A-1, 9; in *JSP*-H1:240–44.

60. Joel Tiffany, "Mormonism—No. II," *Tiffany's Monthly*, August 1859, 169. See also Ronald W. Walker, "Martin Harris: Mormonism's Early Convert," *Dialogue: A Journal of Mormon Thought* 19, no. 4 (Winter 1986): 39–41.

angel was involved, the idea of a newly revealed scripture was rejected. Nevertheless, the final result of Harris's travels and inquiries was his decision to support the work of translation as a financier and a scribe, and to pay for the resulting text's publication. Harris had tapped into a naturalistic network of information that ironically empowered Smith to move forward and produce his supernatural translation.

Trying to Get the Characters Translated

However, the trip to the east was not just about Harris's confidence, since Smith provided him with a large enough sample of the characters that the sought-after scholars could actually provide a translation. At the most basic level, Smith and Harris probably hoped that an eminent scholar would pronounce the characters genuine. Beyond this, identifying the language of the plates was a significant part of any translation process. There is very little evidence that Smith could identify the language of the characters, even if he had access to scholarly literature. It seems that he and Harris were eager to get an identification of the language of the characters and that Harris was requesting as much. When Harris arrived in Albany with the characters in hand and showed them to Luther Bradish, the statesman approached them in a somewhat scholarly fashion by bringing out an Ottoman passport to compare the characters from the plates with the Turkish characters on his passport.[61] In New York, Mitchill reportedly "made a learned dissertation on them," which presumably included comments on the authenticity of the characters and comparable scripts.[62]

Ultimately, Smith and Harris were hoping for much more than mere confirmation of the characters' authenticity or even an identification of the language they represented. Pomeroy Tucker of Palmyra, later recounted that Harris showed him the characters and that he was hoping to meet scholars who could offer not only "bibliological scrutiny" but also "interpretation."[63] According to Joseph Knight Sr., it was right after Smith had claimed possession of the plates that he stated, "they are written in Caracters and I want them translated." Martin Harris's son later reported that his father had gone "by the request of the Prophet Joseph Smith to the city of New York, and presented a transcript of

61. Fayette Lapham, "Interview with the Father of Joseph Smith, the Mormon Prophet, Forty Years Ago. His Account of the Finding of the Sacred Plates," *Historical Magazine*, May 1879, 305–9.

62. Bennett, "Mormon Religion—Clerical Ambition—Western New York—The Mormonites Gone to Ohio," 1.

63. Pomeroy Tucker, *Origin, Rise, and Progress of Mormonism* (New York: D. Appleton, 1867), 42.

the records of the Book of Mormon to Professor Anthon and Dr. Mitchell *and ask them to translate it*. He also presented the same transcript to many other learned men at the different schools of learning in Geneva, Ithica, and Albany *with the same request*."[64]

This networking is a significant yet neglected aspect of Smith's translations. He was not just assuming that there would be a spiritual outpouring of translation from God; rather, he reached out to others, like Harris, for help. And, through Harris, he even approached a community of scholars in an effort to understand the characters. As noted by Harris's son, his father had visited with academics in Geneva, Ithaca, Albany, and New York City. He seems to have also met with scholars in Philadelphia.[65] Harris never journeyed to Boston, London, or Paris, but his travels and appointments in eastern New York represent an impressive effort on behalf of the western farmer. This practice of offering others a role in the larger process of translation requires a broader concept of translation. The translation of the Book of Mormon should not be seen as a singular prophetic act. Smith had to negotiate his own personal religious notions and social sensibilities with those of the wider culture. He continued the process by seeking after a secular translation from an academic scholar. This act may not have produced the text of the Book of Mormon, but it certainly positioned Smith within a particular frame of mind in which it was possible for someone else to translate the plates.

It is difficult, if not impossible, to know exactly what Smith hoped for at the outset. But in terms of the outcome, an interest in obtaining some kind of scholarly approval is present in the contemporaneous historical record. Local printer Jonathan Hadley wrote in 1829 that Smith had emphasized Mitchill's inspection of the characters as an important part of his narrative for how he translated and produced the Book of Mormon.[66] Even though Mitchill had not provided Harris with any translation of the characters, their mere inspection by this eminent scholar—and his opinion that they were genuine—was part of Smith's story of the translation.

Social expectations framed his approach and severed the possibility that his prophetic act of translation took place in isolation. His practices had been

64. "Martin Harris, Jr., Reports Death and Testimony of His Father," *Adventure* 1, no. 4, quoted in Simon Smith, "Correspondence," *Saints' Herald*, 1 February 1881, 43 (emphasis added).

65. Knight wrote that Harris "went to Albeny and to Philadelpha and to new york and he fond men that Could Translate some of the Carictors in all those places." Jessee, "Joseph Knight's Recollection of Early Mormon History," 34.

66. Jonathan Hadley, "The Gold Bible," *Palmyra Freeman* (Palmyra, NY), 11 August 1829, 3.

shaped by society, while his own particular perspective on what it meant to translate and perhaps even his objectives were being reshaped. The outcome of such an endeavor inevitably informed his understanding of the contemporaneous academic culture of translation. Most important, Harris's mission to get the characters inspected and translated by a secular authority demonstrates a dependence on social networks and ideas that is generally not associated with the translation of the Book of Mormon. From Harris's report of his travels and appointments, Smith likely acquired a sense of the contours and configuration of academic translation, which may have informed his understanding of the translation of the Book of Mormon that followed.

Verifying Smith's Translation

In addition to having the characters translated, Smith reportedly sent Harris to verify his own translation of at least a few characters. In the history Smith initiated in 1838, he recounted that though he had yet to begin translating the Book of Mormon in earnest—which would not take place before February 1828—he had nonetheless made facsimiles of the characters *and* had translated "some of them" by the means of the "urim and thummin."[67] Why would Smith begin translating some of the characters with this blessed instrument and then send Harris to get the characters translated by a scholar? This perplexing aspect of the 1838 account is perhaps easily explained in terms of mistaken memory. But it must also be considered and analyzed at face value as a possible complexity in the story. The situation could be read to mean that Smith had looked into the spectacles or one of his seer stones and saw words but did not know quite what to make of them.[68] He may have lacked confidence that the words were in fact the English translation of engravings on the gold plates and therefore sought some kind of authoritative confirmation. Whereas his earlier history, written circa 1832, had explained that once Harris returned from his trip (a few months later) he learned that "the Lord had prepared spectacles for [him] to read the Book[,] therefore I commenced translating the characters

67. Sometime between Harris's departure in February 1828 and his return in the spring, Joseph Smith began translating the Book of Mormon with his wife, Emma, as scribe. See MacKay and Dirkmaat, *From Darkness unto Light*, chap. 5."

68. Seer stones were used to see missing or stolen items, buried treasure, distant loved ones, the future, who one would marry, and to see other people and *things*. Seer stones were rarely if ever used to see *text*. See Michael Hubbard MacKay and Nicholas J. Frederick, *Joseph Smith's Seer Stones* (Provo, UT: Religious Studies Center, Brigham Young University; Salt Lake City, UT: Deseret Book, 2016), 55–56.

[with the spectacles]."[69] His later history, begun in 1838, suggests that though he may have already supernaturally seen words in the stones before Harris left, he was unsure of their meaning, or at least had some kind of hesitation.

Regardless, if the 1838 account of preliminary translation is accurate, it demonstrates the inevitable overlap in the natural and supernatural processes of translation. The dialectic between social forces that were both religious and academic were at work in Smith's actions. In terms of translation, specifically, Smith faced competing social realities. On the one hand, his actions were probably determined, at least in part, by an awareness of how languages and their translation worked. And, on the other hand, he was inevitably drawn and influenced by the discourses of supernaturalism in religion—particularly the Old Testament accounts of prophets and seers and the New Testament "spiritual gifts."[70]

As for Smith's preliminary translation, Anthon reportedly opined that the "translation was correct, more so than any he had before seen translated from the Egyptian."[71] Yet once Harris told Anthon that the characters he had just examined were derived from a record delivered by an angel, Anthon rescinded any support he had previously given. Even though Anthon rejected the idea of a record delivered by an angel, Harris interpreted Anthon's original participation in the practices of linguistic examination and interpretation as a validation of the authenticity of the characters he had transcribed with Smith. Harris reportedly left Anthon "and went to Dr Mitchel [Mitchill] who sanctioned what Professor Anthony [Anthon] had said respecting both the Characters and the translation."[72]

Apparently, Smith was not differentiating—or at least not segregating—his experience as a translator and the sought-after scholarly outcome of verifying the preliminary translation. He seems to have treated both modes of translation as processes that could produce the same results. Even though his seer stones were objects that embodied the supernatural aspect of his translation, he still sent Harris on his errand to the scholars of New York City and believed the worlds of the scholarly and the spiritual could seamlessly overlap—an idea that Smith perpetuated through his subsequent translation projects.[73]

The scholarly approval of the translation, at least as it was perceived and interpreted by Harris and Smith, may have confirmed to Smith that the words he envisioned in his seer stone were indeed the translation of the characters

69. Joseph Smith, History, 1838–1856, Vol. A-1, 9, in *JSP*-H1:240.
70. 1 Corinthians 12.
71. Joseph Smith, History, 1838–1839, vol. A-1, 9, in *JSP*-H1:240.
72. Joseph Smith, History, 1838–1839, vol. A-1, 9, in *JSP*-H1:244.
73. MacKay and Frederick, *Joseph Smith's Seer Stones*, 45–64.

on the plates. This academic affirmation then propelled Smith into his visionary translation of the sacred record inscribed on the plates. The translation, published in 1830 as the Book of Mormon, became the foundation of a new religious movement.

CONCLUSION

Examining why Smith produced copies of the characters inscribed on the gold plates and why he sent Martin Harris with a transcript of the characters to be examined by language specialists demonstrates that Joseph Smith was negotiating his own understanding of translation within a broader culture—a culture including academic knowledge. Harris's mission to the wise men of the east was—contrary to previous and primarily religious narratives of this episode—a predominantly intellectual pursuit in which Harris encountered strangers, like Anthon, and in which the interaction was defined by material objects, like gold plates (at least in experience and in the telling) and characters (inscribed with ink on paper). This was a translation narrative that was historicized and materialized within a complex social network of overlapping and sometimes conflicting ideas and cultures.

Western culture's proclivities for dualism and the valorization of the mind over the body have influenced Mormon culture's overwhelming desire to define the translation process as primarily metaphysical or cognitive. Perhaps this pervasive influence has been operating on Smith's followers from the beginning, and even influenced Smith himself. As his theology developed, however, he moved more radically toward materialism, rejecting the idea of an immaterial spirit that represented humankind's actual ontology. The mind or spirit in dualism reaches for a disembodied self, one that can exist beyond the physical body in a metaphysical realm. Smith acknowledged that "the spirit[,] by man[,] is thought to be immaterial, without substance," but disagreed with this common belief: "We should beg leave to differ and state that spirit is a substance; that it is material."[74] In Smith's later years he declared that there was "no such thing as immaterial matter," that "all spirit is matter." He assured his audience: "When our bodies are purified we shall see that it is all matter."[75] Smith's ideas may have derived from his later revelations and religious experiences, but even

74. "Try the Spirits," *Times and Seasons*, 1 April 1842, 745.

75. Joseph Smith, History, 1838–1856, vol. D-1, 1552 [D&C 131:7–8] (accessible in the Histories series of the online edition of *The Joseph Smith Papers*).

the theological outcome makes some sense considering his earliest experiences translating the Book of Mormon. Smith's religious experience thus recovers practice, embodiment, environment, and historicity.

The study of material religion is often defined by things and places, but it always and inevitably returns to the most common site of analysis, the body. Embodied actions and practices are in many ways like language, in their ability to communicate a shared understanding of their meaning. Theorists of practice understand the body as the site of subjectivity, contemplating how it might react to social structures and culture. The practices that defined Smith's Book of Mormon translation process, demonstrate that the process was conditioned by social structures, as if he were not completely in control of the direction it may have gone, and limited him in his own range of options in producing a credible translation. Historical dispositions helped define the behaviors of a translator; they perpetuated practices that communicated to people convincingly. Those social structures also overlapped with Smith's religious beliefs, which also limited his options in terms of producing a strictly academic translation. From such a perspective, his actions were dynamic expressions for how the translation was produced.

Smith's translations are inseparable from the embodied experiences and material processes that produced the text.[76] Though one may attempt to explain the process psychologically or spiritually (within a dualistic paradigm), the practices Smith acted out were the performance of the translation. As a social being, Smith's practices were expressions of his internalization of the existing social order, while they also reflected the dynamic relationship between him and that order as he struggled to make sense of translation within his local community and beyond, even reaching into the high-brow academic culture of translation as it then existed in the halls of his home state's finest educational institutions. Over time, the translation of the Book of Mormon was more obviously an embodied act—made tangible by its association not only with specific places and built environments, but tangible artifacts: a hefty set of metal plates (whether ancient gold or modern tin) and a rock that functioned as a seer stone. This very term "seer stone" fuses supernatural vision and a natural conglomeration of earthy matter.

76. Parley P. Pratt, who became one of the apostles in the church that Smith later organized, wrote that "God the Father is material, Jesus Christ is material. Angels are material, Spirits are material. Men are material." Parley P. Pratt, "Materiality," *The Prophet* (New York, NY), 24 May 1845, 1. See also Benjamin E. Park and Jordan T. Watkins, "The Riches of Mormon Materialism: Parley P. Pratt's 'Materiality' and Early Mormon Theology," *Mormon Historical Studies* 11, no. 2 (Fall 2010): 159–72.

Additionally, the text of the Book of Mormon emerged as part of a methodical and time-intensive process of bodily practices: Smith's head placed into a hat with the felt pressed closely around his face, his eyes peering into the darkness of the hat, his mouth speaking the words of the translated text, Harris's ears hearing the muffled words amid the noises of the household and farmland soundscape, his hand moving the quill pen, the nib of the pen transferring ink to the paper. The metaphysical translation was enacted within the physical world of sensorial bodies and inscription materials and had all began with metal plates and rocks dug out of the ground.

To diminish Joseph Smith's translations to only the end product of the resulting text is a form of reductionism that has the potential to strip away the true meaning of his scriptural works. One can discover the richness of his translations in numerous symbolic expressions including scholarly networks, physical settings, material artifacts, embodied experiences, and the inscribed documents that were thereby produced. Such a materialist methodology and experience-centered approach is far more holistic, better representing the dynamic life of an organism rather than its dissected component parts, examined separately. It avoids the natural tendency to reduce the translation to a single cause, event, or outcome. This approach also offers the possibility of avoiding the inevitable tendency to assert what is ultimately unknowable about Smith's translations.

5

Reconfiguring the Archive

Women and the Social Production of the Book of Mormon

AMY EASTON-FLAKE AND RACHEL COPE

Reflecting back on the translation of the Book of Mormon, Lucy Mack Smith recalled a "work" that had "been the object which *we as a family* had pursued so eagerly."[1] As this statement indicates, Lucy's memory of the translation as a family effort challenges and has the potential to enrich the traditional narrative—a narrative that highlights the efforts of Joseph Smith Jr. and the male witnesses and scribes that worked with him, but overlooks the many ways in which women made the translation possible. Because accounts written by Lucy and other women have been forgotten, dismissed, or gleaned for details that recount the experiences of men, the women have been written out of rather than woven into early Mormon history. Such omissions not only illustrate the subjective nature of history, but also challenge the common assumption that archives are a neutral space.[2]

In their perceptive introduction to *Contesting Archives: Finding Women in the Sources*, editors Nupur Chaudhuri, Sherry J. Katz, and Mary Elizabeth Perry point out that archivists necessarily make decisions about "what to keep, what to discard, how to organize what is kept, and for what purpose."[3] Such decisions invariably influence the creation and perpetuation of historical memory.

1. Lucy Mack Smith, History, 1844–1845, book 9:7 (emphasis added), Church History Library, The Church of Jesus Christ of Latter-day Saints, Salt Lake City (hereafter Church History Library). Images of the manuscript are also accessible under "Other Histories" in the Histories series of the online edition of *The Joseph Smith Papers*.

2. For an acknowledgment of the cultural shaping of archives from within the field of archival studies, see Randall C. Jimerson, "Embracing the Power of Archives," *American Archivist* 69, no. 1 (Spring/Summer 2006): 19–32.

3. Nupur Chaudhuri, Sherry J. Katz, and Mary Elizabeth Perry, eds., *Contesting Archives: Finding Women in the Sources* (Urbana: University of Illinois Press, 2010), xiv.

Indeed, as historian Antoinette Burton notes, "all archives come into being in and as history as a result of specific political, cultural, and socioeconomic pressures—pressures which leave traces and which render archives themselves artifacts of history."[4] The "archive" of sources used when researching the translation of the Book of Mormon was shaped by the constraints of the patriarchal culture of nineteenth-century America in which it was constructed, as well as the historiography that naturally followed. In order to expand the archive and the stories it may tell, it is important to include sources that have typically been deemed unimportant and to ask new questions of the more familiar documents in the archive. This chapter seeks to reread sources in the archive—and the individuals who produced them—unencumbered by the narrative it is generally assumed they tell or embody, and to therefore allow a new weaving together of various layers of context and information to reveal nuance and complexity.

Using this approach as a model, this chapter will consider a variety of sources reflecting the roles that Lucy Mack Smith, Lucy Harris Harris, Mary Musselman Whitmer, and Emma Hale Smith played in the translation effort. Fortunately, recent publications such as *The Joseph Smith Papers* and Dan Vogel's five-volume edition of *Early Mormon Documents* have made the archive of relevant sources on the production of the Book of Mormon more accessible.[5] However, there is still much that needs to be done in terms of expanding the scope of the archive as it is *imagined* by historians who work in the founding period and in the *received* archive of actual Mormon history production and social memory. When sources about these four women are acknowledged and read in new ways, they demonstrate the need to reconceptualize the documents and the archive. Adding forgotten voices to the narrative of the translation of the golden plates and the production of the Book of Mormon reveals the social context of scriptural production and expands the group of those who should be considered part of the creation of Mormonism's founding scripture.

LUCY MACK SMITH

The possibilities and limits of the archival sources are captured in Lucy Mack Smith's memoir, which she created shortly after the deaths of her sons Hyrum,

4. Antoinette Burton, *Archive Stories: Facts, Fictions, and the Writing of History* (Durham, NC: Duke University Press, 2005), 6.

5. *The Joseph Smith Papers* (Salt Lake City: Church Historian's Press, 2008–); Dan Vogel, comp. and ed., *Early Mormon Documents* (Salt Lake City: Signature Books, 1996–2003). See also John W. Welch, *Opening the Heavens: Accounts of Divine Manifestations, 1820–1844,* 2nd ed. (Provo, UT: Brigham Young University Press; Salt Lake City: Deseret Book, 2017), 126–227.

Joseph, and Samuel in 1844. Her history was about her *family*, not just the son that became a prophet. In her narrative, Lucy preserved the multiplicity of ways women and men witnessed and participated in the translation and publication of the Book of Mormon and other events tied to the founding of the Church of Christ (later to be known as the Church of Jesus Christ of Latter-day Saints).[6] And yet, the inclusive nature of her memoir has been obscured and overlooked by reading practices and expectations that privilege stories about men. Because the text has been received as a biography of Joseph Smith rather than as the family history Lucy intended it to be, its reception history demonstrates some of the complexities—what we preserve, stress, remember, and how we read—inherent in female-authored sources and their preservation (or disappearance).[7] Therefore, it is important to embark upon alternative readings of Lucy's manuscript—making attempts to read it "against the grain"—so that readers can discover the layers of witnessing she wove into *her* story, while simultaneously challenging social memory and reconceptualizing the cultural archive.

When considering Lucy's memoir within this context, it is significant to recognize that she, along with another woman, Martha Jane Knowlton Coray, made the initial effort to record her history and thereby archive her memory. Recognizing the value of the elderly matriarch's experiences, Coray became, as she recounted, Lucy's "amanuensis at the time the Book was written."[8] Later, Martha's husband, Howard, became involved and helped produce approximately half of the rough draft of the manuscript.[9] Upon completing this draft, Martha and Howard produced two fair copies. Eventually, one of these copies was given to Lucy and one to the church.[10] Hoping to publish the revised draft, Lucy

6. For a consideration of Lucy Mack Smith, Lucy Harris Harris, Mary Musselman Whitmer, and Emma Hale Smith as witnesses of the golden plates and their translation, see Amy Easton-Flake and Rachel Cope, "A Multiplicity of Witnesses: Women and the Translation Process," chap. 8 in *The Coming Forth of the Book of Mormon: A Marvelous Work and a Wonder,* ed. Dennis L. Largey et al. (Provo, UT: Religious Studies Center, Brigham Young University; Salt Lake City, UT: Deseret Book, 2015).

7. For further discussion, see Jan Shipps, *Mormonism: The Story of a New Religious Tradition* (Urbana: University of Illinois, 1987), 90–95; Lavina Fielding Anderson, ed., *Lucy's Book: A Critical Edition of Lucy Mack Smith's Family Memoir* (Salt Lake City, UT: Signature Books, 2001), 11–12; Rachel Cope, "Composing Radical Lives: Women as Autonomous Religious Seekers and Nineteenth-Century Memoirs," in *Nineteenth-Century American Women Write Religion*, ed. Mary McCartin Wearn (Burlington, VT: Ashgate Publishing, 2014), 45–58.

8. Martha Jane Knowlton Coray to Brigham Young, 13 June 1865, Brigham Young Office Files, Church History Library.

9. Sharalyn D. Howcroft, "A Textual and Archival Reexamination of Lucy Mack Smith's History," in *Foundational Texts of Mormonism,* ed. Mark Ashurst-McGee, Robin Scott Jensen, and Sharalyn D. Howcroft (Oxford and New York: Oxford University Press, 2018), 308–10, 312–13, 334.

10. Coray to Young, 13 June 1865.

FIGURE 5.1. Lucy Smith. Painting by Sutcliffe Maudsley, gouache on paper. Joseph Smith's mother, Lucy Mack Smith (1776–1855), holding the Book of Mormon. Smith had supported her son during the translation of the book. Church History Museum, Salt Lake City.

obtained a copyright for her manuscript in July 1845, titling the work "The History of Lucy Smith, Wife of Joseph Smith, the first patriarch of [the Church of] Jesus Christ of Latter Day Saints, who was the father of Joseph Smith, Prophet, Seer, and Revelator; containing an account of the many persecutions, trials and afflictions which I and my family have endured in bringing forth the Book of Mormon and establishing the church of Jesus Christ of Latter Day Saints."[11] This title accurately captures Lucy's perceptions of her role in the beginnings of Mormonism and her purpose for creating her memoir. Brigham Young, who succeeded her son as the church's leader, discussed the possibility of purchasing Lucy's copyright with other church leaders.[12] No extant records indicate whether they actually approached her about selling it, but by March 1853 church apostle Orson Pratt had taken Lucy's copy of the manuscript to Washington, D.C. At this point, the vision and efforts of the women who produced the memoir were "obscured"—as Lavina Fielding Anderson states—by the "men who took over the project" shortly following the manuscript's completion.[13]

During the summer of 1853, Pratt printed Lucy's memoir in Liverpool, England, as *Biographical Sketches of Joseph Smith, the Prophet, and His Progenitors for Many Generations.* The title he chose shifted the emphasis from female autobiography to male biography. Prior to its publication, Jan Shipps notes, the manuscript had already undergone three previous title changes.[14] As indicated by these changes, the significance of the manuscript as a female-authored record that highlighted the importance of shared responsibility in establishing the church was lost during the publication process. Lucy's voice was subsumed by a title that shifted the framing of the work to Joseph's story.

11. Copyright for Lucy Mack Smith, "The History of Lucy Smith," 18 July 1845, Robert Harris, Copyright Registry Records for Works Concerning the Mormons to 1870, Church History Library.

12. Joseph Smith et al., *History of the Church of Jesus Christ of Latter-day Saints*, ed. B. H. Roberts, 7 vol. (Salt Lake City, UT: Deseret Book, 1980), 7:519.

13. Smith, *Lucy's Book*, 67. Anderson's assessment, while largely accurate, does require some qualification. The original history was not entirely the work of Lucy and Martha, and it began with advice from men as well. Lucy wrote that she undertook the history due to counsel from the Quorum of the Twelve Apostles. Lucy Mack Smith to William Smith, 23 January 1845, 2, Church History Library. Moreover, both Martha and her husband Howard worked on the rough draft, with Howard apparently helping to produce roughly half of the draft. Howcroft, "A Textual and Archival Reexamination of Lucy Mack Smith's History." Furthermore, as early as January 1845, Lucy characterized the work in somewhat patriarchal terms as "a history of the family that is my Fathers Family and my own" and asked her son William to help her raise funds to purchase the paper. Lucy Mack Smith to William Smith, 23 January 1845, 2–3. In April of that year, Brigham Young and the all-male Council of Fifty considered how they could fulfill her desire to have the history printed. Council of Fifty, Minutes, 11 April 1845, in *JSP*-A1:412.

14. Shipps, *Mormonism*, 104–5. Martha and Howard Coray's fair copy, completed in 1845, was simply titled "History of Lucy Smith, Mother of the Prophet," and a secondary title page for the 1853 edition was "History of Mother Smith, by Herself." Smith, *Lucy's Book*, 2.

Institutional responses to the publication of Lucy's memoir placed further limitations on its reception as her account of her family's history. During the nineteenth century, Lucy's memoir was not widely read by Latter-day Saints and likely remained unknown to others. This can be explained in part by the controversy concerning prophetic succession that followed its initial publication.[15] Some members of the Smith family—most of whom had not traveled west under Brigham Young's leadership—established rival claims to succession by Joseph Smith's progeny.[16] Fearful that Lucy's Smith family story could divide the faithful and concerned that it would challenge the apostles' role as prophetic successors, Young ordered the destruction of printed copies of the text just twelve years after its publication, under the contention that it contained too many historical errors.[17] Although Young assigned George A. Smith and Elias Smith—members of the Smith family who did follow him to Utah[18]—to revise the text so it could be "reissued in a correct edition," the project was not completed during his lifetime.[19]

When the church-authorized edition was finally published in Salt Lake City, it had become a history of Joseph Smith. The *Improvement Era*, a church periodical, published the edited version of the memoir serially from 1901 to 1903 under the title "History of the Prophet Joseph Smith."[20] When published in book form in 1902, it bore the title *History of the Prophet Joseph by His Mother Lucy Smith as Revised by George A. Smith and Elias Smith.*[21] Adding the names of her male redactors in the title further shifted the emphasis away from Lucy as both author and subject. Since then, several popular editions of this memoir—the version with the revisions made by male church leaders—have

15. Shipps, *Mormonism*, 91; and Smith, *Lucy's Book*, 68. For details on the succession crisis following Joseph Smith's murder, see D. Michael Quinn, "The Mormon Succession Crisis of 1844," *BYU Studies* 16, no. 2 (Winter 1976): 187–233; Ronald K. Esplin, "Joseph, Brigham and the Twelve: A Succession of Continuity," *BYU Studies* 21, no. 3 (Summer 1981): 301–41; Andrew F. Ehat, "Joseph Smith's Introduction of Temple Ordinances and the 1844 Mormon Succession Question," (master's thesis, Brigham Young University, 1982); D. Michael Quinn, *The Mormon Hierarchy: Origins of Power* (Salt Lake City: Signature Books, 1994), 142–262.

16. Leonard J. Arrington noted that Brigham Young had denounced Lucy's memoir "primarily because of the favorable references and space devoted to William." Shipps, *Mormonism*, 91.

17. Ibid., 106.

18. George A. Smith was Joseph Smith's cousin—the son of the brother of Joseph's father—and was also serving at the time as both an apostle and the church historian. Howard C. Searle, "Church Historians," in *Encyclopedia of Mormonism* (New York: Macmillan, 1992), 1:590. Elias Smith, a former printer, was another of Joseph Smith's cousins. Elias Smith, Journal, 10 May 1843, Church History Library; "Death of Judge Elias Smith," *Deseret News*, 4 July 1888, 390; "Joseph Smith Pedigree Chart" (accessible under "Charts" in the "Media" tab at the online edition of *The Joseph Smith Papers*).

19. Wilford Woodruff, Journal, 22 April 1866, Church History Library.

20. Smith, *Lucy's Book*, 8.

21. *History of the Prophet Joseph by His Mother Lucy Smith as Revised by George A. Smith and Elias Smith* (Salt Lake City, UT: Improvement Era, 1902).

been published. Moreover, these editions have been published with the same or similar titles, thereby further defining Lucy's memoir as a history of Joseph Smith.[22] Consequently, despite its preservation and publication, Lucy's purpose in recording her narrative—and the complexity and nuance her memoir has the potential to add to Mormon historiography—have largely been neglected. Readers, preconditioned by the title, have, as Lavina Fielding Anderson argues, read it simply for what it says about Joseph Smith rather than what it reveals about all the individuals who participated in laying the foundations of the Church of Jesus Christ of Latter-day Saints.[23]

Most recently, the manuscript version of Lucy's memoir has been digitized as a part of *The Joseph Smith Papers* online archive. Although its inclusion has increased accessibility, many of the questions asked of the document still hinge on what female-authored sources can tell us about men rather than letting female authors speak on their own terms. Scholars working on the Joseph Smith Papers conclude: "Though there are errors in the dating of some events and occasionally in place and individual names, overall her account is of inestimable value, providing a rarely heard woman's voice as it traces JS's life from beginning to end."[24] While this statement expands the reading of Lucy's memoir in some respects, it also continues to limit it by suggesting that the purpose of the manuscript is what it reveals about her son's life. In fact, this is precisely the reason for this rare inclusion of a non-Joseph Smith document on the Joseph Smith Papers website. However, a closer and more careful reading of Lucy's memoir on its own terms reveals a rich and complex narrative about devout though flawed believers who willingly made sacrifices to help bring forth a new book of scripture and create a lasting religious community.

Looking specifically at what Lucy's narrative reveals about the translation of the Book of Mormon, one may see her providing an enlarged understanding of the many ways that individuals witnessed the plates and participated in the translation effort. She introduces various ways in which the translation was facilitated that include an entire community of people who contributed to the

22. See Preston Nibley, *History of Joseph Smith, by His Mother, Lucy Mack Smith* (Salt Lake City, UT: Bookcraft, 1956); Scot Facer Proctor and Maurine Jensen Proctor, *The Revised and Enhanced History of Joseph Smith by His Mother* (Salt Lake City, UT: Bookcraft, 1996); Susan Easton Black, *The History of Joseph Smith by His Mother Lucy Mack Smith* (Springville, UT: Cedar Fort, 2016). Although scholarly use of the text generally followed this interest in Joseph Smith, some scholars began to consider the narrative more broadly. See Shipps, *Mormonism*, chap. 5.

23. Two historians of Mormonism have provided a reception history of Lucy's memoir. See Shipps, *Mormonism*, 91–107; and Smith, *Lucy's Book*, 66–163.

24. See Historical Introduction to Lucy Mack Smith, History, 1844–1845.

translation and publication of this foundational text of Mormon Christianity. While Lucy's history captures details about the production of the Book of Mormon that can be found in other accounts, her propensity to include her family in the story often captured events differently. Her written account, therefore, expands the scope of the narrative through its preservation of forgotten details that reveal how lesser-known historical actors helped enable the translation. Details about Lucy Harris Harris, Mary Musselman Whitmer, and Emma Hale Smith each figure in her account.

Lucy's narrative also highlights her own significant role in the work of translation as she details her intimate involvement with each step that prepared the Book of Mormon for publication. Her manuscript reveals that she was among the first to whom her son confided that he had been visited by an angelic messenger directing him to the location of the golden plates. During the years Joseph reportedly met with the angel Moroni, Lucy and her family heard his fireside stories and descriptions of the people whose history was recorded on the plates. She felt a spiritual witness that it was a divinely influenced work and anxiously awaited the plates' acquisition. It was Lucy who encouraged Joseph and Emma to take Joseph Knight Sr.'s horse and wagon to the hill where the plates were hidden, and it was she who covered for them in the early morning when Knight wondered where his horse was. She prayed for her son when he traveled to the hill in which the ancient record was buried, and once he obtained the plates, she helped hide them in her home. She became one of the first witnesses of the materiality of the plates as she handled them covered with a cloth and observed the outline of their shape. She also handled, through a cloth, the instrument her son had discovered with the plates and that he initially used to translate them.

Lucy's involvement continued. She approached Lucy and Martin Harris about financing the translation project. She watched the members of her family, as well as friends—old and new—experience the plates in sensory and spiritual ways, and she willingly invested her time and interest in the protection of the record and the effort of its translation. She shared in her son's devastation when, early on, the scores of inscribed pages bearing his translation up to that time were lost. She saw the stress that resulted from the project. She knew about the three witnesses who saw the plates with her son in vision; and about the eight witnesses, including her husband and two of her other sons, who saw and handled the plates in an ordinary manner. She received word as soon as the translation was completed. She saw the work it took to get it published. She bore witness of it to enemies, friends, and family members. And then she wrote a memoir that captured important elements of its history in an inclusive way. Together, Lucy's memoir suggests, her family members and friends became witnesses of the gold plates and enablers of their translation. Though Lucy was not present to experience the entire translation and its related events, she claimed to be quite aware of what happened along the way. Her persistence in making her history inclusive of family members, friends, and associates led her to capture the role of women more fully than any other account, if we will read her memoir for what it is.

LUCY HARRIS HARRIS

One of the most intriguing stories found within the pages of Lucy Mack Smith's memoir is that of Lucy Harris Harris's paradoxical relationship to the gold plates and the translation effort. Smith subtly disparages Harris for her alleged involvement in losing the initial translation from the golden plates and primarily depicts her as a villain or as a foil to her husband, Martin Harris, who financed the printing of the Book of Mormon. Yet Smith also incorporates details into her narrative that reflect Lucy Harris's early interest in and willingness to provide financial support for the translation of the gold plates.[25] The details that Lucy Smith preserved both foster and challenge the views of Lucy Harris that have been presented by historians, hagiographers, and apologists, and by extension, encourage contemplation about the way primary sources are read and interpreted.[26] By asking new questions of Lucy Smith's history and weaving together layers of context and information, a much more complex version of Lucy Harris appears. Indeed, readers of Lucy Mack Smith's memoir must ask, was Lucy Harris the villain that she has been made out to be?

Lucy Smith's disdain for Lucy Harris is palpable. She describes her as a "peculiar" and very difficult woman—"habitually of a very jealous temperament" and often "suspicious of some secret being in agitation that was designedly kept from her hearing."[27] Harris was, in fact, hard of hearing—a condition that probably contributed to her suspicions that others were talking past her.[28] When Joseph asked his mother to speak to the wealthy farmer Martin Harris

25. Smith, *Lucy's Book*, 395.

26. Lucy Mack Smith, History, book 6:3–12, and book 7:1, 5–8; Rhett S. James, "Lucy Harris: Toward a Compassionate Reinterpretation," *Nauvoo Journal* 9, no. 1 (1997): 49–57; Fawn Brodie, *No Man Knows My History: The Life of Joseph Smith* (New York: Alfred A. Knopf, 1945), 54.

27. Lucy Mack Smith, History, book 6:3–5.

28. See James, "Lucy Harris."

about the possibility of providing some financial backing for the translation project, Lucy Smith decided to first approach his wife in order to avoid potential problems with her later. After Smith described the purpose for her visit—detailing particulars about the record her son Joseph had obtained—Lucy Harris immediately offered to donate "a considerable amount of money" that she kept in her own "private purse."[29] Smith, in her memoir, recalls responding to the generous offer with suspicion, forcefully declaring that she "did not want her money" and that "Joseph would attend to his own affairs."[30] Lucy Smith then approached Martin Harris—she did need money, after all—about providing financial assistance. In contrast to the immediate enthusiasm and generosity offered by Lucy Harris, Martin Harris initially brushed off Lucy Smith's request, and only later agreed to speak with her son.[31]

Given Lucy Harris's initial interest in the plates and offer of support, coupled with her husband's seeming skepticism and caution, it is compelling that Lucy Smith depicts her as petty and selfish and her husband as kind and generous. Such contradictions suggest that there are alternative ways to read the story, and thus call for careful questions to be drawn from and about the source material provided by Smith and the Corays. When reading this anecdote in Smith's memoir, historians should grapple with the fact that she is recalling this experience nearly twenty years after the fact, and shortly after losing her sons as martyrs. Therefore, a reader might ask, did those same suspicions of Lucy Harris exist at the time of enquiry, or were subsequent developments influencing her recollection of the event? Since Smith associated Lucy Harris with the loss of the earliest portions of the translation, was Smith creating a narrative that foreshadowed what was to come, vilifying Harris from the beginning to implicitly suggest that she could not be trusted? Alternatively, was Smith affected by the socioeconomic differences that separated her from Harris? Was Smith uncomfortable taking Harris's money because she did not trust her, or was she uncomfortable asking for charity from her social and economic superior? Might Lucy Smith's refusal to accept financial assistance from Lucy Harris reveal her own status anxiety?

Some of the details woven throughout the subsequent stories Lucy Smith narrated about Lucy Harris likewise suggest that there are other angles from which Harris's story can be interpreted—even though the known information

29. Lucy Mack Smith, History, book 6:4.
30. Ibid.
31. Ibid., 3–5.

FIGURE 5.2. Lucy Harris home. Martin Harris and Lucy Harris Harris lived in this well-to-do home in Palmyra Township, Wayne County, New York. Though Lucy came to distrust Joseph Smith, she had initially supported him as he was beginning his translation of the Book of Mormon. The comfortable Harris home indicates the wealth with which she offered to help Smith during the translation. Church and Smith family historic sites, 1907, Church History Library, Salt Lake City; photograph by George Albert Smith.

is derived from Smith's own portrayal. Often overlooked by readers are the stories in Smith's memoir that reveal Lucy Harris's support of the project, her willingness to make financial sacrifices on its behalf, and the physical and spiritual witnesses she received of the plates. Shortly after learning about the gold plates, Lucy Harris and her daughter visited the Smith home. Before committing to provide financial support for the project, Harris hoped to see the golden plates. Joseph, however, explained that he could not show them to her because the angel who had placed them in his care said he could only show them to those whom God called as witnesses. According to Lucy Smith, Lucy Harris was displeased with this response and declared, "Now Joseph . . . I will tell [you] what I will do If I can get a witness that you do speak the truth I will beleive it."[32] She then informed the young man that she would provide financial support regardless, after which she retired (she was staying in the Smith home for the night).

That night, Lucy Smith later recalled, Lucy Harris had "a very remarkable dream."[33] In the morning, she shared her dream with the Smith family—

32. Ibid., 5–6.
33. Ibid.

a common practice in the nineteenth century.[34] She reported that a "personage" had appeared and chastised her for disputing "the servant of the Lord."[35] However, he then showed her the plates. From this visionary dream, Lucy Harris was able to describe the gold plates to Joseph in vivid detail, and she insisted on giving him money to help with the project.[36] Impressed by her experience, Joseph allowed Lucy Harris and her daughter to heft the box containing the plates. When they returned home, Martin questioned them. He later recounted that his wife said the plates "were very heavy" with his daughter adding the detail that they "were about as much as she could lift."[37] The experience of hefting the plates, albeit in a box, added a tangible witness to the vision Harris had already received. While some may discount Lucy Harris's experiences due to her later antagonism, it is important to remember that each of the official "Three Witnesses"—including her husband Martin—and three of the official "Eight Witnesses" would themselves, over the years, become antagonistic toward Joseph Smith and the church. Should readers allow Lucy Smith's later doubts about and dislike for Lucy Harris—which are also laced through her recollection of this particular story—to overshadow the witnessing experiences that Harris had and the support that she and her husband therefore gave to Joseph Smith at the very beginning of the translation?

As Lucy Smith's narrative progresses, her comments about Lucy Harris's growing doubts about the plates, her contempt for her husband's involvement and investment in the work of translation, and the loss of the early manuscript pages become a central thread in the story. While one could easily use Smith's account to label Harris as faithless and fickle, and to make her an antagonist who was always attempting to hinder the translation's progress, it is again important to contextualize the story, and to question why Harris responded to events in the way Smith suggests she did. Smith notes that Harris was extremely upset when her husband traveled to New York City to show a transcript of some of the characters engraved on the plates to language specialists.[38] Although Smith criticized Harris for reacting negatively to the situation, a careful reading of the account reveals that Harris actually seems to have

34. See Mechal Sobel, *Teach Me Dreams: The Search for Self in the Revolutionary Era* (Princeton: Princeton University Press, 2002); and Phyllis Mack, *Heart Religion in the British Enlightenment: Gender and Emotion in Early Methodism* (New York: Cambridge University Press, 2008), 219–60.

35. Lucy Mack Smith, History, book 6:5–6.

36. Ibid. Lucy wanted to give Joseph twenty-eight dollars.

37. "Interview with Martin Harris," *Tiffany's Monthly,* August 1859, 168.

38. Richard Bennett, "'Read This I Pray Thee': Martin Harris and the Three Wise Men of the East," *Journal of Mormon History* 36, no. 1 (2010): 180.

been upset because her husband had not informed her of the trip. Harris, one might conclude, was initially supportive of the project, and had tangible and spiritual witnesses of the reality of the plates but grew suspicious and frustrated as her husband made commitments without consulting or informing her. Was it the plates themselves, or the secrecy surrounding them that bothered her? Was her real issue Joseph Smith's astounding supernatural claim, or was it a question regarding her husband's trustworthiness based on their interactions? Although Lucy Smith connected Lucy Harris's actions to unbelief and a lack of support for the translation, an alternative reading suggests that Harris was merely protecting herself and her property[39]—perhaps fearful that she could lose everything.

Although the loss of the early manuscript pages is primarily a story about Joseph Smith and Martin Harris, Lucy Smith framed it in such a way that Lucy Harris also becomes a primary figure. The story begins with Martin repeatedly asking Joseph for permission to show manuscript pages of the English translation, part of which he had transcribed, to his wife. After repeatedly praying about the situation, Joseph reluctantly agreed to let Martin take the manuscript home, under the promise that he would only show it to his wife and a few other specified individuals. Pleased that Martin had finally shared the manuscript with her, Lucy allowed him to lock it in a set of bureau drawers she had—to which he normally lacked access—for its protection. The couple then went to visit relatives. When Martin decided to return home, Lucy opted to remain behind for a longer visit. Upon his return, Martin agreed to show the manuscript to a curious friend, thus breaking the promise he had made to Joseph Smith. Because he could not find the key to Lucy's bureau, he picked the lock and damaged it in the process.[40] Martin then placed the manuscript in his own set of drawers, and subsequently showed it to anyone who expressed an interest. Given the social decorum and culture of early nineteenth-century America, it would have been men, not women, with whom he shared the manuscript. According to Lucy Smith, when Lucy Harris returned home she "beheld the marred and injured state of her beaureau her irr acible temper

39. Lucy Smith's account seems to reveal marital tensions between Martin and Lucy Harris. When Martin returned from his trip to New York, "his wifes anger kindled afresh at her husbands presence so much so that she prepared a bed and room for him alone which she refused to enter." Lucy Mack Smith, History, book 6:8. Later, Lucy Harris "carried away her furniture her linen and bedding and other movable articles till she well nigh divested the premises of everything which could conduce to comfort or conveiniance These things She deposited with her friends where She reposed suficient confidence to assure her of ~~this~~ ~~their~~ the safety of her property." Lucy Mack Smith, History, book 6:10.

40. Lucy Mack Smith, History, book 7:8.

knew no bounds and an intolerable storm ensued throughout the house which descended with greatest force upon the head of the devoted husband."[41] Shortly thereafter, Martin discovered that the manuscript was missing. Although he blamed Lucy for its disappearance, she insisted that she knew nothing of its whereabouts.

According to several accounts of this episode, Lucy Harris had stolen the manuscript.[42] Although Lucy Smith never explicitly blames her for doing so, the tone Smith uses when recounting stories about her certainly encourages the assumption that Harris played a role in the manuscript's disappearance. One must question, however, whether Harris was just upset about her marred furniture or distressed that the work she and her husband had sacrificed so much for had been lost. Was she angry with Martin for breaking his promise to Joseph? She had, after all, seemed satisfied by the privilege to see the manuscript and had provided a safe place to keep it. Is the reading that she was being manipulative accurate, or was she offering protection for a project for which she felt a sense of interest and commitment?

When details drawn from Lucy Smith's memoir are read in relation to other historical documents, such as Joseph Smith's revelations, a rather different picture emerges. Indeed, in the revelations Joseph dictated following the loss of the translated pages, God chastised him for being influenced by the "persuasions of men" and specifically referred to Martin as a "wicked man." The revelations also refer to the role that "wicked men" played in stealing the manuscript.[43] Since Latter-day Saints give greater credence to revelation than to historical memory, it is noteworthy that the latter accounts have had a stronger influence in shaping the narrative than the former. Perhaps the scapegoating of Lucy Harris is simply evidence that it is easier for historians and hagiographers alike to place blame on an "antagonistic" woman over a prophet and an official witness—both men. Even though she was oppositional in the end, it is important to recognize that Lucy as well as Martin provided the personal support and financial backing to begin the work of translation. This was a manifestation of her commitment, at least early on, to what would become an immense and collective undertaking. Her doubts and struggles should not negate the support she offered. Nor should her story be reduced, in the end,

41. Ibid.

42. See Frederic G. Mather, "Early Days of Mormonism," *Lippincott's Magazine*, August 1880, 198–211; Pomeroy Tucker, *Origin, Rise and Progress of Mormonism: Biography of Its Founders and History of Its Church* [. . .] (New York: Appleton, 1867), 46.

43. Revelation, July 1828, in *JSP*-D1:6–9 [D&C 3]; and Revelation, Spring 1829, in *JSP*-D1:37–44 [D&C 10].

to a caricature. Though she later turned on her husband and his friend Joseph Smith, she had been one of Smith's earliest supporters and had helped the work of translation begin.

MARY MUSSELMAN WHITMER

Like Lucy Mack Smith and Lucy Harris Harris, Mary Musselman Whitmer helped support the translation effort.[44] Moreover, she became the first known individual to see the plates besides Joseph Smith, and the only person to see them without Joseph present.[45] And yet, her witnessing experience and the important role she played in the translation effort have been largely neglected in the historical record and institutional memory of the mainstream church.[46] Fortunately, an account of her story has been preserved through the statements of two family members: her son David Whitmer and her grandson John C. Whitmer. Reflecting on the disuse of documents recounting her visual witness in relation to those of the official male witnesses indicates much about the ways in which nineteenth-century culture shaped the church's archive and memory, while also highlighting some of the consequences that stem from legitimizing and canonizing certain source types over others. By carefully contextualizing these accounts and asking new questions of them, and of Mary Whitmer's experience, it becomes possible to gain a fuller understanding of the vital labor she and others gave to enable the translation of the plates.

Mary Whitmer's role in the translation effort began in June 1829 when she and her husband, Peter Whitmer, opened their home in Fayette, New York, to Joseph Smith and Oliver Cowdery—and later Emma Hale Smith—to complete the translation of the Book of Mormon. The Whitmers had learned of

44. Mary Whitmer was born Mary Musselman in Germany on 27 August 1778. She immigrated to Pennsylvania and married Peter Whitmer (Sr.), who was also of German descent. They moved to Fayette, New York, in 1809. Andrew Jenson, *Latter-day Saint Biographical Encyclopedia*, vol. 1 (Salt Lake City: Andrew Jenson History, 1901), 283.

45. Others may have accidently seen the plates. Josiah Stowell claimed that when Joseph brought the plates home and handed them to him through a window, a corner of their covering slipped off and he caught a glimpse of the artifact. "Mormonism," *New England Christian Herald* (Boston, MA), 7 November 1832; see also Michael Hubbard MacKay and Gerrit Dirkmaat, *From Darkness unto Light: Joseph Smith's Translation and Publication of the Book of Mormon* (Provo, UT: Religious Studies Center, Brigham Young University; Salt Lake City: Deseret Book, 2015), 13.

46. Since the authors originally wrote this chapter and presented it at a conference on Joseph Smith and translation in 2014, Whitmer's story has become more mainstream. We highlighted her experience as a witness of the Book of Mormon in our article "A Multiplicity of Witnesses." More significantly, Whitmer's story is told in *Saints*, the new church history produced by the Church of Jesus Christ of Latter-day Saints. *Saints: The Story of the Church of Jesus Christ in the Latter Days*, vol. 1, *The Standard of Truth, 1815–1846* (Salt Lake City, UT: Church of Jesus Christ of Latter-day Saints, 2018), 70–71.

Joseph and the gold plates through their son David. On a visit to Palmyra, New York, where Joseph Smith's family lived, David Whitmer had become acquainted with Oliver Cowdery. There, the two men heard about the gold plates and became determined to learn more. Oliver told David he would let him know what he learned after meeting Joseph. Subsequently, he wrote David three letters relating his experience as Joseph's scribe and sharing his testimony that the book being translated was the word of God. In the third letter, Oliver asked if the translation could be finished at David's home.[47] Since David still resided under his father's roof this decision was not his alone to make. Peter Whitmer Sr. may have made the decision with his wife Mary. In any case, David later recounted that his father told him he should not travel to Pennsylvania to bring the Smiths and Oliver to the farm unless he received "a witness from God that it is very necessary." When miraculous events allowed David to accomplish two days' worth of work in one, the family believed the translation work to be of God, and David left the following day to bring Joseph and Oliver to his family's farm.[48]

Mary felt keenly the burden of boarding three additional individuals at her home. As David later recounted: "My father and mother had a large family of their own, the addition to it therefore of Joseph, his wife Emma and Oliver very greatly increased the toil and anxiety of my mother. And although she had never complained she had sometimes felt that her labor was too much, or at least she was perhaps beginning to feel so."[49] A farmer's wife in early nineteenth-century New York was typically responsible for milking, butter churning, gathering eggs, and caring for livestock; planting, weeding, and harvesting the kitchen garden; shearing sheep, turning wool into yarn, and sewing garments; cooking, cleaning, laundry, and other chores.[50] Much of the additional labor of cooking, cleaning, and caring for the visitors would have fallen upon Mary—a woman who was likely already overworked. Encapsulated in

47. "Mormonism," *Kansas City Daily Journal,* 5 June 1881, 1.

48. Lucy Mack Smith, History, book 8:8–10. See also David Whitmer, interviewed by Joseph F. Smith and Orson Pratt, reported in *The Latter-day Saints' Millennial Star,* 9 December 1878, 772. For more information, see Richard Lloyd Anderson, *Investigating the Book of Mormon Witnesses* (Salt Lake City: Deseret Book, 1981), 67.

49. David Whitmer, *Deseret Evening News,* 16 November 1878, 1, reproduced in Vogel, *Early Mormon Documents,* 5:51–52.

50. For more information on the work of early American farming women, see Sally Ann McMurry, *Families and Farmhouses in Nineteenth-Century America: Vernacular Design and Social Change* (New York: Oxford University Press, 1988), 59–61; Catherine Clinton and Christine Lunardini, eds., *The Columbia Guide to American Women in the Nineteenth Century* (New York: Columbia University Press, 2000), 35–36; Nancy Grey Osterud, *Bonds of Community: The Lives of Farm Women in Nineteenth-Century New York* (Ithaca, NY: Cornell University Press, 1991), 156–58.

David's statement is an important reminder of the labor and goods that Mary, along with many other individuals, provided so that Joseph, a poor farmer dependent on the work of his own hands, might devote his time and energy to the translation. It also summarizes how nineteenth-century farm wives were expected to behave—they were to work tirelessly without complaint.

Since her essential contributions to the translation effort fell under the purview of expected domestic labor, they have been largely unheralded and overlooked by historians and hagiographers in their retellings of the story. Significantly, Mary's descendants have not done the same. Her labor and witness mattered to them, so they recorded and preserved it. John C. Whitmer, her grandson, related her experience as follows:

> One evening, when (after having done her usual day's work in the house) she went to the barn to milk the cows, she met a stranger carrying something on his back that looked like a knapsack.... He then untied his knapsack and showed her a bundle of plates, which in size and appearance corresponded with the description subsequently given by the witnesses to the Book of Mormon. This strange person turned the leaves of the book of plates over, leaf after leaf, and also showed her the engravings upon them; after which he told her to be patient and faithful in bearing her burden a little longer, promising that if she would do so, she should be blessed; and her reward would be sure, if she proved faithful to the end. The personage then suddenly vanished with the plates, and where he went, she could not tell.[51]

Mary's son David additionally reported the words the messenger spoke to her: "You have been very faithful and diligent in your labors, but you are tired because of the increase of your toil; it is proper therefore that you should receive a witness that your faith may be strengthened."[52]

That the emphasis in both accounts is on Mary Whitmer's physical labor and God's recognition of her sacrifices indicates that Whitmer and her family saw her experience with the plates as divine recognition of her work and role in enabling the translation. Because of the messenger's encouragement, Whitmer and her family seem to have received spiritual validation that their

51. Statement of John C. Whitmer, quoted in Andrew Jenson, *The Historical Record* 7, nos. 8–10 (October 1888): 621.

52. David Whitmer, interviewed by Orson Pratt and Joseph F. Smith, 7–8 September 1878, quoted in "Report of Elders Orson Pratt and Joseph F. Smith," *Deseret Evening News*, 16 November 1878, 1.

efforts enabled the work of translation—a validation that also challenged cultural assumptions about what type of work was important.[53] Whitmer's indispensable domestic labor reportedly merited a miraculous manifestation so that she would have the assurance she needed to continue her role in making the translation possible.

Within the month, Mary Whitmer would no longer be the only person other than Joseph Smith who had seen the plates. Smith chose all of the male members of her family, besides her husband, to be shown the plates and become public witnesses of their physical reality. Six of the eleven public witnesses of the Book of Mormon were Whitmers by blood or marriage.[54] Given women's legal status and public stature in early nineteenth-century America, Smith's choice of all male witnesses is unsurprising. Due to the English legal doctrine of coverture—which still applied in New York[55]—married women were generally unable to hold property, make contracts, devise wills, participate in other legal transactions, or control any wages they might earn individually. In this environment, the testimonies of men held more credence than those of women. Consequently, when Joseph chose others to share the responsibility of testifying to the reality of the plates, he assuredly looked to men in good standing in the community. Smith had lived in the Whitmer home and knew the Whitmer men were both honorable and supportive of his mission to translate the plates. It is also possible that he looked to the Whitmer brothers, at least in part, because they were sons of a previous witness. Nine of the eleven witnesses were related to either Joseph Smith or Mary Whitmer—the two people who had already seen the plates.

A significant purpose of the public witnesses was to relieve Joseph's burden of testifying alone of the reality of the golden plates.[56] Recognizing this makes it

53. Although women's contributions to the farm were valued, both men and women seem to have viewed fieldwork as more crucial than household tasks. Women were expected to work in the field whenever their assistance was required. See Osterud, *Bonds of Community,* 162–65.

54. Mary Musselman Whitmer raised seven children to adulthood. Five of her sons became witnesses of the golden plates, as did her son-in-law, Hiram Page, who had married her daughter Catherine Whitmer in 1825. Testimony of Three Witnesses, late June 1829, in *JSP*-D1:378–82 [Testimony of Three Witnesses]; and Testimony of Eight Witnesses, late June 1829, in *JSP*-D1:385–87 [Testimony of Eight Witnesses]; "Page, Hiram," in Jenson, *LDS Biographical Encyclopedia,* 1:277–78. Later, in 1832, Oliver Cowdery (another one of the witnesses) would marry her daughter Elizabeth. Jackson Co., MO, Marriage Records, 1827–1917, vol. 1, 20, microfilm 1,019,759, U.S. and Canada Record Collection, Family History Library, The Church of Jesus Christ of Latter-day Saints, Salt Lake City.

55. For more information, see Hendrik Hartog, *Man and Wife in America: A History* (Cambridge, MA: Harvard University Press, 2000), 119–21.

56. As Joseph reportedly stated to his father, mother, and Mary Whitmer:

> You do not know how happy I am The Lord has caused the plates to be shown to 3 more besides me who have also seen an angel and will have to testify to the thuth [truth] of what I have said for they know for themselves that I do not go about to deceive the people and I do feel as though I was relieved of a

more understandable why the statements of the three and eight witnesses were canonized and became a part of the archive, while Mary Whitmer's experience has been largely overlooked. Her experience was a personal encounter that could not be corroborated. In contrast, the male witnesses provided objectivity, physical evidence, and, perhaps most important, collective experience. The testimony of the eight witnesses, written in the language of an affidavit, focuses solely on the tangible reality of the plates and employs legalistic language to seemingly distance the witnesses from personal bias:[57] "We bear record with words of soberness, that the said Smith has shown unto us [the plates], for we have seen and hefted, and know of a surety that the said Smith has got the plates of which we have spoken."[58] While the testimony of the three witnesses includes the appearance of an angel, and thereby provides corroboration for Smith's own accounts of seeing the heavenly messenger, it still carries validity as a collective experience of three men who were unrelated to him.

A more intriguing issue than its original status, then, is the continued neglect of Whitmer's experience and the consequences of it remaining outside the traditional narrative of the translation. As a private witness, Mary's experience has remained a part of family history rather than church history, and, therefore, has been somewhat suspect even among believing church members. One Mormon apologist wrote, "If the history of their family is correct, we must add an eighth member of the family who saw the plates—their mother, Mary Musselman Whitmer."[59] In contrast, he states as fact that each of the men "saw the gold plates." The equivocation he places around Whitmer's private experience, but not on the witnesses that were made public, is common and illustrates both the power of archives to legitimate sources and the lesser status often accorded to family documents in relation to institutional ones. Historians specializing in women's history have long recognized that the depreciation of family histories, memoirs, and oral histories is problematic as it leads to a privileging of sources in which men, rather than women, are at the center—thus

---

> dreadful burden which was almost too much for me to endure, but they will now have to bear a part and it does rejoice my soul that I am not any longer to be entirely alone in the world.

Lucy Mack Smith, History, book 8:11. Likewise, in the revelation appointing the three witnesses, which Smith dictated in the voice of Deity, God commanded the witnesses to "testify of [the reality of the plates], by the power of God; and this you shall do that my servant Joseph Smith, Jun., may not be destroyed." Revelation, June 1829-E, in *JSP*-D1:82–85 [D&C 17:3–4].

57. MacKay and Dirkmaat, *From Darkness unto Light*, 155.

58. The Book of Mormon: An Account Written by the Hand of Mormon, upon Plates Taken from the Plates of Nephi, trans. Joseph Smith, Junior (Palmyra, NY: E. B. Grandin, 1830), 590.

59. Keith Perkins, "True to the Book of Mormon—The Whitmers," *Ensign*, February 1989, 34–42.

perpetuating the neglect of the significant roles and experiences women have had. Without altering fundamental views of what sources should be archived and valued, historians will continue to write histories that reinforce gender divides, experiences such as Whitmer's will be depreciated and dismissed, and generations will wonder why women were not an integral part of events—when in reality they were.[60]

Investigating material culture, as many historians now do, is another way to incorporate women into historical narratives as their contributions are often recorded in the artifacts they produced, rather than the documents they wrote. Such is the case with Mary Whitmer. When her son David exhibited the manuscript copy of the Book of Mormon that had been used by the printer for typesetting, he pointed out the "woolen yarn" with which the leaves were sewn together and stated that the yarn was "his mother's."[61] Before the industrial revolution, women commonly made yarn and fabric from flax, wool, cotton, and other materials. The leaves of the original manuscript of the Book of Mormon were sewn together with yarn as well, which may also have been made by Whitmer, or by her daughters.[62] Whitmer may even have sewn the manuscripts herself. In any case, her involvement in the production of the Book of Mormon extended beyond providing free room and board to Smith as he continued the translation.

Like Whitmer's witness experience, the yarn with which the leaves of the translation manuscript were bound together should be accepted as a text in its own right and admitted to the archive of sources used to understand the production of the Book of Mormon. A similar argument could be made for

60. The question of legitimate sources continues to be at the center of understanding Mary Musselman Whitmer's experience. A new oral history recounting a story passed down originally from a distant relative and now through many generations offers additional insight into why Whitmer was given this witness. According to this newly emerged source, first documented by Royal Skousen, Whitmer was not only burdened by the additional household work, but was actually quite irritated by Smith and Cowdery: "She thought they might just as well carry her a bucket of water or chop a bit of wood as to skate rocks on a pond. She was about to order them out of her home." This account places both Smith and Cowdery, as well as Whitmer, in a more negative light and changes the perceived motive behind the angel's visit to Whitmer. No longer is the visit primarily about recognizing and valuing Whitmer's labor and strengthening her for the trials ahead. Instead, it is a necessary sign so that Smith and Cowdery would not have to find a new home in which to complete the translation. While the new source is of questionable validity—having been orally transmitted over many generations and open to any number of alterations—it does recall the accounts offered by Whitmer's son and grandson. For more information on this new source, see Royal Skousen, "Another Account of Mary Whitmer's Viewing of the Golden Plates," *Interpreter: A Journal of Mormon Scripture* 10 (2014): 35–44.

61. George Q. Cannon, "Topics of the Times," *Juvenile Instructor,* 1 April 1884, 107.

62. Robin Scott Jensen, "A Bit of Old String: Mary Whitmer's Unheralded Contributions," *Treasures of the Collection* (Salt Lake City, UT: Church History Department, 25 April 2013), https://history.lds.org/article/mary-whitmer-book-of-mormon?lang=eng.

FIGURE 5.3. Whitmer family yarn. Likely twined by Mary Musselman Whitmer. The yarn was used to sew the gatherings of the original manuscript of the Book of Mormon, possibly by Whitmer. She and other women supported Joseph Smith during his translation of the Book of Mormon, making its production possible, and may have participated in its material production. Book of Mormon manuscript twine, circa 1829, Church History Library, Salt Lake City.

the foolscap paper upon which the translation was written, for the brown ink in which the words were inscribed, and for the quill pens by which the scribes put ink to paper. But Whitmer's contribution of the yarn is more significant than these because her involvement in the material production of the Book of Mormon was tied more intimately to the translation both chronologically and geographically, as well as literally. Her yarn stands as reminder of the goods and services through which she and her family contributed to the work of translation.

EMMA HALE SMITH

Common representations of Emma Hale Smith by historians and hagiographers illustrate how official histories may at times obscure reality. Although Emma was arguably more intimately involved in the translation of the gold plates than any individual besides Joseph Smith and Oliver Cowdery, her role in the process and the witness she bore have been historically marginalized in church publications. Initially this was largely because of her rift with Brigham Young after her husband's death and her decision to remain in Illinois rather than follow Young to Alta California. Viewed as an apostate and referred to by Young as "one of the dam[ne]dest liars,"[63] Emma was, to a great extent, written out of the canonized version of church history.[64] An article about Emma that Linda King Newell and Valeen Tippetts Avery coauthored for a church magazine in 1979 was the first serious treatment of her life to appear in any official church publication in over a century.[65] Newell and Avery expanded their research and produced the first scholarly biography of Emma Smith. *Mormon Enigma*, published in 1984, has led to a general reappraisal of Emma and a greater recognition of the role she played in early Mormon history.[66] Still, when Emma's part in Mormon history is acknowledged, hagiographers and historians have largely undercut her actions and callings in the early church by attributing them to her relationship to Joseph Smith rather than her own qualifications.[67]

That such a reading of Emma is incomplete is suggested by her significant involvement in Mormon origins prior to and throughout the translation effort. According to Joseph Knight, one of the first early Mormon converts, Joseph Smith was first told by the angel Moroni that he must bring his oldest brother Alvin with him to retrieve the plates. After Alvin's death, the angel directed Joseph to bring Emma Hale.[68] At the time, Joseph and Emma were not married,

63. Brigham Young, "Remarks, by President Brigham Young, at the Semi-Annual Conference G. S. L. City, Oct 7th, 1866," 14, in Historian's Office Reports of Speeches, Church History Library. Likewise, Young stated that "more hell was never wrap[p]ed up in any human being, than there is in her." Brigham Young, "Remarks By President Brigham Young, G. S. L. City, Bowery, Oct. 7, 1863," 4, in Historian's Office Reports of Speeches, Church History Library.

64. See Smith et al., *History of The Church of Jesus Christ of Latter-day Saints*, 1:18–31; *Our Heritage: A Brief History of the Church of Jesus Christ of Latter-day Saints* (Salt Lake City, UT: Church of Jesus Christ of Latter-day Saints, 1996), 5–19; *Church History in the Fulness of Times* (Salt Lake City, UT: Church of Jesus Christ of Latter-day Saints, 2003), 52–66.

65. Valeen Tippetts Avery and Linda King Newell, "The Elect Lady: Emma Hale Smith," *Ensign*, September 1979, 64–67. See also Linda King Newell, "The Emma Smith Lore Reconsidered," *Dialogue: A Journal of Mormon Thought* 17, no. 3 (Autumn 1984): 87–100.

66. For more information, see Max Perry Mueller, "Changing Portraits of the Elect Lady: Emma Smith in Non-Mormon, RLDS, and LDS Historiography, 1933–2005," *Journal of Mormon History* 37, no. 2 (Spring 2011): 212–13.

67. See John Henry Evans, *Joseph Smith: An American Prophet* (Salt Lake City, UT: Deseret Book, 1989); Francis M. Gibbons, *Joseph Smith: Martyr, Prophet of God* (Salt Lake City, UT: Deseret Book, 1977); Donna Hill, *Joseph Smith: The First Mormon* (Salt Lake City, UT: Signature Books, 1999); Norma J. Fischer, *Portrait of a Prophet's Wife: Emma Hale Smith* (Salt Lake City, UT: Silver Leaf Press, 1992); Roy Arthur Cheville, *Joseph and Emma Smith, Companions for Seventeen and a Half Years, 1827–1844* (Independence, MO: Herald Publishing House, 1977); Gracia N. Jones, *Emma and Joseph: Their Divine Mission* (American Fork, UT: Covenant Communications, 1999).

68. Knight recalled: "Joseph says, 'who is the right Person?' The answer was you will know. Then he looked in his glass and found it was Emma Hale, Daughter of old Mr Hail of Pensylvany, a girl that he had seen Before, for he had Bin Down there Before with me." Dean C. Jessee, "Joseph Knight's Recollection of Early Mormon History," *BYU Studies* 17, no. 1 (Autumn 1976): 31.

FIGURE 5.4. Emma Smith. Contemporaneous images of Joseph Smith's wife, Emma Hale Smith, who served as one of the principal scribes during the translation of the Book of Mormon. Left: 1842 painting, oil on canvas by David Rogers. Courtesy Community of Christ Archives, Independence, MO. Right: circa 1845 daguerreotype. Courtesy Community of Christ Archives, Independence, MO.

so if Joseph was directed to bring Emma, he was not simply being advised to involve his wife but rather to recruit an individual who possessed skills and attributes that would aid the work of translation.

Primary documents long ignored within Mormon historiography, although now generally recognized and accepted, suggest that Emma proved herself to be an apt companion for Joseph in protecting the plates and producing their translation. She placed her confidence in Joseph Smith when she decided to marry him and eloped. She was with Joseph when he recovered the plates. She rode with him at midnight to the hill where he said they lay buried, and she waited with the horse and carriage on the road through the early morning hours until he retrieved the plates from the hill.[69] When persecution in the Palmyra-Manchester area immediately ensued, Emma assisted in guarding the plates. Lucy Smith recounted that on one occasion Emma mounted a horse and traveled to a neighboring township to alert Joseph to the fact that men were searching for the plates in the woods where he had hidden them.[70] She had helped her husband recover the plates from the hill and now she was his

69. Lucy Mack Smith, History, book 5:6.
70. Ibid., 9–10.

companion in keeping them secure. She may also have aided Joseph in acquiring Martin Harris's invaluable support of the translation project. As Harris recalled, he spoke with Joseph's family members separately, "his wife, brothers, sister, his father and mother" to make sure their "stories agreed." Their matching accounts along with the witness Harris reported receiving from the Lord secured his financial and scribal support.[71] Perhaps most notably, Emma's educational background and time teaching school in Harmony gave her the necessary skills to act as Joseph's scribe for much of the lost book of Lehi.[72] For two years, Joseph's and Emma's lives revolved around protecting and translating the plates.

Emma's disappearance from the history of the translation sadly began with her husband. In both the short history Joseph Smith wrote circa summer 1832 and the longer history he initiated in 1838, he mentioned Martin Harris and Oliver Cowdery as scribes for the Book of Mormon translation, but not Emma. She was therefore not mentioned as a Book of Mormon scribe in the church's serialized publication of Smith's 1838–1856 history nor in the compiled version thereof: the official *History of the Church of Jesus Christ of Latter-day Saints,* edited by B. H. Roberts and first published in 1902 as a seven-volume series. The official history had a tremendous influence on public memory in the church. While other accounts—both those produced by the church and by historians and hagiographers—have briefly mentioned Emma's time as scribe, such publications clearly align Martin Harris and Oliver Cowdery with the scribal role, while implicitly suggesting that Emma, as Joseph's wife, simply filled in as a substitute scribe until a more apt candidate could be found. Even works directly focused on Emma impart the same narrative. In *Emma and Joseph: Their Divine Mission*, her contribution is described in a single line: "Emma served as scribe for Joseph, although her time was limited because of her household work,"[73] whereupon the focus shifts to Harris and Cowdery. This oversimplification is particularly noteworthy given the work's title *Emma and Joseph: Their Divine Mission*. This example illustrates how the traditional narrative continues to strongly influence other interpretations, including works seeking to illuminate Emma.

71. Joel Tiffany, "Mormonism," *Tiffany's Monthly*, May 1859, 167–70.

72. For more information on Emma's schooling and educational background, see Linda King Newell and Valeen Tippetts Avery, *Mormon Enigma: Emma Hale Smith* (Urbana: University of Illinois Press, 1994), 3–4, 6.

73. Jones, *Emma and Joseph*, 25. See also Erwin E. Wirkus, *Judge Me, Dear Reader: Emma's Story* (Springville, UT: Cedar Fort, 2008), 7.

In contrast to this traditional and dominant narrative, several primary sources present Emma acting as a vital scribe for her husband. According to Joseph Knight, when Joseph Smith recovered the plates he was "anxious to git them Translated he therefore with his wife Drew of[f] the Caricters exactly like the ancient." Emma never saw the plates or their engravings, so apparently Joseph copied the characters from the plates and Emma made a fair copy that Harris could take to scholars in New York City.[74] She also may have inscribed the majority of Joseph's translation for the lost book of Lehi, as Harris remembered that he wrote "about one third of the first part of the translation of the plates as [Joseph] interpreted them by the Urim and Thummim."[75] Harris's time as scribe was relatively brief, lasting for only two months (mid-April to mid-June 1828).[76] Notably, these were the two months prior to the birth of Emma's first child—a coincidence that opens up the possibility that Harris may have assisted Joseph only when Emma's health made it more difficult for her to continue to fulfill this role. This interpretation would contrast with Joseph Knight's perspective—which has come to be the dominant interpretation—that Emma only scribed for Joseph until he could find someone else to write for him.[77] While it is uncertain how long, how much, or precisely why Emma scribed for Joseph, if Harris's statement is accurate, it indicates that she recorded roughly two-thirds of the lost book of Lehi and was Joseph's most prolific scribe besides Oliver Cowdery. Emma's own recollection of the translation also indicates that she spent an extensive amount of time transcribing for Joseph: "I frequently wrote day after day, often sitting at the table close by him . . . and [he] dictating hour after hour with nothing between us."[78] Though the sources describing this period of the translation leave room for ambiguity, there is still a distinct discrepancy between what the primary sources reveal about Emma's role in

74. Quoted in Jessee, "Joseph Knight's Recollection of Early Mormon History," 34.

75. Quoted in *Saints' Herald,* 24 May 1884, 324. Possibly contradicting this point, Harris reportedly claimed on one occasion that he "wrote a great deal of the Book of Mormon . . . as Joseph Smith translated or spelled the words out in English." Anthony Metcalfe, *Ten Years before the Mast* (Malad City, ID: Research Publications, 1888), 70–71.

76. Richard Lyman Bushman, *Joseph Smith: Rough Stone Rolling* (New York: Alfred A. Knopf, 2005), 66.

77. Knight also recollected that Emma Hale Smith's brother, likely Reuben Hale, occasionally scribed for Joseph: "Now when he Began to translate he was poor and was put to it for provisions and had no one to write for him But his wife and his wifes Brother would sometimes write a little for him through the winter. . . . The next Spring Came Martin Harris Down to pennsylvany to write for him." Jessee, "Joseph Knight's Recollection of Early Mormon History," 35. Emma later stated that her brother Reuben had scribed for the Book of Mormon. Emma Hale Smith Bidamon, interviewed by Joseph Smith III, February 1879, Miscellany, RLDS Church Library-Archives (now Community of Christ Library and Archives), Independence, MO (hereafter CCLA), reproduced in Vogel, *Early Mormon Documents,* 1:537. See also Emily C. Blackman, *History of Susquehanna County, Pennsylvania* (Philadelphia: Claxton, Remsen & Haffelfinger, 1873), 104.

78. Bidamon, interviewed by Smith, reproduced in Vogel, *Early Mormon Documents,* 1:539.

the translation process and the narratives that continue to be written about her. This signals that the principal problem in recovering Emma's scribal role is not a lack of historical sources,[79] but rather preconceptions of Emma and the translation based on previous narratives of the event.

Emma's reminiscences also provide some of the best source information available on the plates and the process of translating them. Emma emphasized the tangible reality of the plates. She recounted that she would "lift and move them when she swept and dusted the room and furniture."[80] The eight witnesses of the plates stated that they had seen and "handled" the plates and that they bore every appearance of being ancient and authentic. While Emma never viewed the plates uncovered, and only felt them through a cloth, she left a much more specific account of their tangibility. She stated that "they seemed to be pliable like thick paper, and would rustle with a metalic sound when the edges were moved by the thumb, as one does sometimes thumb the edges of a book."[81] In addition to providing this specific evidence of the physical plates, Emma added a report of *hearing* the plates to the testimonies of those who saw and touched them.

In terms of the translation, she remembered Joseph "sitting with his face buried in his hat, with the stone in it . . . he had neither manuscript nor book to read from."[82] Her explanation of the process has been used by Mormon scholars to argue for a tightly controlled translation process.[83] As she reportedly recounted: "When my husband was translating the Book of Mormon, I wrote a part of it, as he dictated each sentence, word for word, and when he came to proper names he could not pronounce, or long words, he spelled them out, and while I was writing them, if I made any mistake in spelling, he would stop me and correct my spelling, although it was impossible for him to see how I was writing them down at the time."[84] Few have considered, however, the role Emma would have played in developing a translation process for the Book of Mormon. The scribes were an intricately interwoven part of the process as apparently Joseph could not see more of the translation—could not of himself

79. This is not to imply that the primary sources on Emma are plentiful. They are not. This is probably, at least in part, because her personal correspondence was not recognized as worth preserving.

80. Joseph Smith III to Mrs. E. Horton, 7 March 1900, Miscellany, CCLA, reproduced in Vogel, *Early Mormon Documents*, 1:546–47.

81. Bidamon, interviewed by Smith, in Vogel, *Early Mormon Documents*, 1:539.

82. Ibid., 1:539, 663.

83. Royal Skousen, "How Joseph Smith Translated the Book of Mormon: Evidence from the Original Manuscript," *Journal of Book of Mormon Studies* 7, no. 1 (1998): 25.

84. Quoted in Edmund C. Briggs, "A Visit to Nauvoo in 1856," *Journal of History* 9 (January 1916): 454, reproduced in Vogel, *Early Mormon Documents*, 1:530–31.

translate any further—until the scribe had written it down correctly and perhaps had read it back. Describing the translation process, Martin Harris related that by the "aid of the seer stone, sentences would appear and were read by the Prophet and written by [Martin], and when finished he would say, 'Written,' and if correctly written, that sentence would disappear and another appear in its place, but if not written correctly it remained until corrected."[85] As the first of Joseph's primary scribes, Emma likely helped him develop the dynamic patterns of interaction that he would continue with later scribes.

The continued marginalization of Emma's role as scribe can be attributed in part to changes made to the recorded text of a revelation received in her behalf through Joseph Smith, shortly following the publication of the Book of Mormon. Notably, in this revelation, Emma was once again called as scribe: "Thou shalt go with [Joseph] at the time of his going [to the churches] & be unto him a Scribe that I may send Oliver whithersoever I will."[86] While the revelation casts Emma as a substitute for Oliver, it also assigned her two more important roles within the early church. She was called to "make a selection of Sacred Hymns" and to be "ordained under [Joseph's] hand to expound Scriptures & exhort the Church according as it shall be given thee by my spirit."[87] Throughout Joseph's ministry, his scribes were his most valued colleagues and the calling of scribe was even initially associated with his counselors in the church's First Presidency. And although scribes were used commonly during that time—most often employed by politicians and other prominent figures—Emma's appointment to this role was surprising as scribing was a decidedly male occupation.[88] Similarly, creating hymnals was generally the task of the male clergy, and Emma's calling to "expound" and "exhort" scripture sounded like the role and duty of the (male) Methodist itinerant preachers in antebellum America.[89] Consequently, Emma and others reading the revelation may

85. "One of the Three Witnesses: Incidents in the Life of Martin Harris," *Deseret Evening News*, 13 December 1881, 4.

86. Revelation, July 1830-C, in *JSP*-D1:161–64.

87. Ibid.

88. For a more extensive discussion of scribes as members of a predominantly male profession in nineteenth-century America, see William E. Henning, *An Elegant Hand: The Golden Age of American Penmanship and Calligraphy* (New Castle, DE: Oak Knoll Press, 2002), 1–2.

89. Men, primarily ministers, were responsible for the creation of hymn books—in large part because of the doctrinal value associated with hymns. Consequently, through this calling, Emma was given the rare if not unique opportunity, as a woman, to select which doctrines her church would highlight. Likewise, her call in 1830 to "expound Scriptures & exhort the Church" was highly irregular. A woman would not be ordained a minister in America until 1851, and in the 1830s women's public speaking was highly controversial. Mary De Jong, "'Theirs the Sweetest Songs': Women Hymn Writers in the Nineteenth-Century United States," in *A Mighty Baptism: Race, Gender, and the Creation of American Protestantism*, ed. Susan Juster and

have seen her assignment to each of these exclusively male functions as an indication that God did not abide by nineteenth-century gender prescriptions. Emma, this revelation makes clear, is not merely an appendage to Joseph but rather an important actor in her own right.

The revelation for Emma, however, has not been generally understood to mean that she was made an essential actor in God's work. Rather, because of significant alterations in the 1835 version of the revelation, which was canonized, readers have inherited a text that has been generally interpreted as presenting Emma in a less favorable light.[90] The 1835 addition of the clause "while there is no one to scribe for him"[91] to Emma's original calling seems to portray her appointment as scribe as only temporary, a position she would fill until someone more suitable could be found. The canonical form of the text thus reinforces the traditional narrative of Emma as a supportive wife, filling in as scribe only until a qualified male could be found. Here again, canonization and preconceived ideas about women are profoundly influential in obscuring a portrait of a more capable and trusted Emma from view.

Events surrounding the lost book of Lehi reinforce the noncanonical characterization of Emma as competent and fully invested in the work. The day after Martin left with the translation manuscript, Emma gave birth to her first son who died within an hour.[92] Having undergone an extremely difficult labor, Emma's life was in danger for a couple of weeks. As her health improved, she became concerned about the manuscript and, as related by Lucy, expressed her anxiety to her husband: "I feel so uneasy . . . that I cannot rest and shall not be at ease untill I know something about what Mr Harris is doing with it do you not think it would be advisable for you to go and enquire into the reason of his not writing or sending any word back to you since he left us."[93] Emma's insistence that Joseph leave her to seek news of the manuscript says much about her own commitment to the work, especially in the face of her own precarious health and the devastating loss of her first child.

Lisa MacFarlane (Ithaca, NY: Cornell University Press, 1996), 146–47; Nancy A. Hardesty, *Women Called to Witness: Evangelical Feminism in the Nineteenth Century*, 2d ed. (Knoxville: University of Tennessee Press, 1999), 72–73.

90. To quote one representative example of such interpretation, "the inference from this revelation is that Emma was a proud, fearful, murmuring woman, and later events corroborated this analysis to a large extent." Gibbons, *Joseph Smith*, 90.

91. Revelation, July 1830-C, in *JSP*-D1:161–64 [D&C 25:6].

92. For more information, see Mark L. Staker, "'A Comfort unto My Servant, Joseph': Emma Hale Smith (1804–1879)," in *Women of Faith in the Latter Days: Volume One: 1775–1820*, ed. Richard E. Turley Jr. and Brittany A. Chapman (Salt Lake City: Deseret Book, 2011), 357.

93. Lucy Mack Smith, History, book 7:2.

Although some scholars have attributed Emma's professed concern to worry over Joseph's increasing despondency,[94] such a move discounts Emma's own labor in inscribing much of the lost book of Lehi—perhaps two-thirds of the text—and the great sacrifice she had made to aid the translation. Joseph's response to Martin when he learned that he had lost the manuscript reinforces this portrait of Emma as intricately involved in the translation project: "Then must I . . . return to my wife with such a tale as this I dare not do it least I should kill her at once."[95] Given Emma's fragile health, Joseph's words may record his actual concern that her health may not have been able to withstand the additional loss of their collective labor.

Although scholars have begun to appreciate Emma's explanations for what they relay about Joseph, the plates, and the translation process, they still fail to describe what Emma's writings reveal about Emma. Consequently, her reminiscences and testimonies have come to play a similar role in Mormon scholarship to that of Lucy Smith's history, and thus follow the larger trend of all sources from women connected to famous men—they are read for what they may reveal about a notable man rather than the woman herself.

Emma believed in Joseph, joined him in recovering the plates, and helped to transcribe their characters. And as a scribe she helped him develop the translation process and transcribed a significant portion of the original text. Her statement, made at the end of her life, that she "was an active participant in the scenes that transpired, and was present during the translation of the plates, and had cognizance of things as they transpired," is certainly borne out by a close investigation of the available historical evidence.[96] However, the magnitude of what she experienced and made possible may only be understood by returning to primary sources free of received preconceptions. With a fresh lens and new questions, we find a more complete, capable, and involved Emma.

CONCLUSION

Although an archive is often understood as a "repository of information," the source material relating to Lucy Mack Smith, Lucy Harris Harris, Mary Musselman Whitmer, and Emma Hale Smith makes it clear that each of these women is actually—as Nupur Chaudhuri, Sherri J. Katz, and Mary Elizabeth Perry put

94. See Newell and Avery, *Mormon Enigma*, 28; Jones, *Emma and Joseph*, 27; Bushman, *Joseph Smith*, 67.
95. Lucy Mack Smith, History, book 7:6.
96. Bidamon, interviewed by Smith, in Vogel, *Early Mormon Documents*, 1:539.

it—a "site for the production of knowledge."[97] As the production, transmission, and reception history of their extant accounts demonstrates, archivists, researchers, writers, editors, and readers are always making decisions, even if unwittingly, about the way history is remembered. And, because sources about these women have continued to be examined selectively through the lens of a received tradition, the narratives that have resulted overlook important details that enrich and expand perceptions of the past. However, by returning to the sources, both canonized and neglected—and by asking new questions of these sources, unencumbered by preconceived notions—a much more inclusive and nuanced view of the various ways individual women witnessed, enabled, and participated in the translation effort can come into focus.

Furthermore, as this chapter illustrates, the archive does have the power, as Antoinette Burton states, "to shape all of the narratives which are to be found there."[98] Consequently, it is important for scholars to continue to question the space and purpose of preservation as much as the documents themselves and the questions asked of them. Indeed, it is essential to remember that because archives are never fully formed, the possibilities of inclusion, expansion, and reinterpretation are ever possible. The archive is, after all, a space where knowledge can be reproduced. Equally important is the fresh perspective that scholars may bring to the archive in asking new questions and reading against the grain. By adding the experiences of women to the archive of knowledge regarding the translation of the golden plates and to our historical memory, it becomes possible to reconfigure the archive in a gender-inclusive way that will facilitate future investigation and enable a reconstruction of the historical narrative. In this reconstructed narrative, we see that a small community of people around the prophet—both men and women—helped him produce the foundational text of a new religious tradition.

97. Chaudhuri, Katz, and Perry, *Contesting Archives,* xiii.
98. Burton, *Archive Stories,* 6.

PART II

Translating the Book of Mormon

6

Seeing the Voice of God

The Book of Mormon on Its Own Translation

SAMUEL MORRIS BROWN

In 1834, half a decade after serving as the primary scribe for Joseph Smith's translation of the Book of Mormon, Oliver Cowdery wrote a letter for publication in the church newspaper describing his early experiences as Smith's amanuensis. "These were days never to be forgotten," Cowdery recalled, "to sit under the sound of a voice dictated by the *inspiration* of heaven, awakened the utmost gratitude of this bosom! Day after day I continued, uninterrupted, to write from his mouth, as he translated, with the *Urim* and *Thummim*, or, as the Nephites would have said, 'Interpreters,' the history, or record, called 'The book of Mormon.'"[1]

This exuberant account frames longstanding debates about what was happening as Smith spoke and Cowdery (and others) wrote. The Book of Mormon remains a focus of curiosity and controversy nearly two centuries after its publication. With increased academic interest and a shifting intellectual landscape has come greater scholarly attention to the ways in which the English-language Mormon scripture came into being.

To phrase the relevant question simply: What, exactly, was Smith experiencing when he dictated the text of the Book of Mormon? Scholars, believers, and critics have elaborated various models of the mechanics of Book of Mormon translation over the years. None is entirely compatible with all others; some are mutually exclusive. The models divide into broadly theistic and nontheistic camps. Within these camps some of the specific models overlap heavily, while others are more discrete. The usual models have been explored

1. Oliver Cowdery to William W. Phelps, 7 September 1834, in *Latter Day Saints' Messenger and Advocate*, October 1834, 14 (emphasis in original).

at length in multiple venues. This chapter advances an alternative approach that hews closely to the text itself rather than to late reminiscences, reasoning from doctrinal assumptions, stylometry, or tenuous connections to ostensibly plagiarized texts.[2]

This chapter thus begins the work of extending the range of interpretive approaches to the nature of scriptural translation in early Mormonism by focusing on the church's first scripture. As both complement and contrast to the literary-critical approach to translation proposed by Jared Hickman in this volume,[3] this chapter considers possible mechanisms of translation that derive from the Book of Mormon itself and remain open to a metaphysics of translation that fits within the worldviews of Smith and his disciples. Traditional understandings of Book of Mormon translation have downplayed the role of oral language and the translator's agency. The argument of this chapter, moving across multiple lines of textual evidence, is that the translation of the Book of Mormon should likely be seen as an oral and revelatory project. Recognizing the fundamentally oral nature of the scriptural text opens a window onto a robust and previously misunderstood metaphysics of translation. While the work of elaborating this metaphysics is a much larger project, this chapter proposes readings of the Book of Mormon foundational to that work.[4]

As for Smith's behavior during the translation, the documentary evidence is consistent. After a brief initial phase in which he copied characters for consultations with Eastern academics and to provide followers a glimpse at the glyphs, Smith sat at a table—often, but not always, near the shrouded plates—with an amanuensis. Sometimes, perhaps when the plates themselves were not directly covered, he was separated from the amanuensis by a curtain. Smith placed a special stone—an "interpreter" or a "seer stone"[5]—into the bottom of a hat, positioned his face in the brim of the hat (probably to exclude ambient light), and dictated to his scribe. The scribe was initially his wife, Emma

2. Brant A. Gardner reviews the proposed models for Book of Mormon translation. Brant A. Gardner, *The Gift and Power: Translating the Book of Mormon* (Salt Lake City: Greg Kofford Books, 2011), 147–56. The most recent comparative attempt to understand the subjective experience of translation is offered by Ann Taves, "Joseph Smith, Helen Schucman, and the Experience of Producing a Spiritual Text: Comparing the Translating of the Book of Mormon and the Scribing of *A Course in Miracles*," Chapter 7 herein.

3. Jared Hickman, "'Bringing Forth' the Book of Mormon: Translation as the Reconfiguration of Bodies in Space-Time," Chapter 3 herein.

4. The larger project is presented in Samuel Morris Brown, *Joseph Smith's Translation: The Words and Worlds of Mormonism* (New York and Oxford: Oxford University Press, 2020).

5. The stones have been labeled many things. Over time, the identification of traditional seer stones with the ancient Hebrew *Urim and Thummim* (associated with the breastplate worn by the high priest in ancient Israel and used for divining) came to predominate, as it did in Cowdery's letter.

Hale Smith, then a handful of others (most famously Cowdery). While some imposture theories assume that Smith or his scribes simply plagiarized some other text to produce the Book of Mormon, those accounts lack credibility.[6] Whatever was happening to Smith subjectively, objectively he was dictating a text while looking into a hat containing a special stone.[7]

The text Smith dictated is a fascinating one. Whatever mechanistic model ultimately appears adequate, readers may struggle to make sense of the complex, sometimes strikingly multivocal text issuing from an unschooled, albeit visionary, migrant agricultural worker. While Latter-day Saint authors have at times hyperbolized his limited education, it is nevertheless remarkable that Smith produced the Book of Mormon, a complex document with braided strands of narrative and an intricate, multi-layered biblical exegetical project.[8] Even if one is not trying to advocate for miraculous origins, this particular juxtaposition of author and text is perplexing. Clues to the nature of this juxtaposition may be found in the text itself, particularly as it reflects on its own production. This chapter begins with a consideration of formal clues in the pattern of words and sentences of the text, and then considers what the English language text may have to say about how it came to be.

FORMAL CLUES TO TRANSLATION MECHANISM

The text of the Book of Mormon offers up several hints regarding translation mechanism. Some of the clues are by now familiar, others less well-known. Together, these indications within the text itself point toward a Book of Mormon that is primarily an oral production captured in English text by scribes. This model differs from several prior proposals. Some scholars have argued that certain formal, linguistic clues support a specific translation mechanism, what is here called the "visual-verbal" model because according to this model

6. See Lester E. Bush Jr., "The Spalding Theory Then and Now," *Dialogue: A Journal of Mormon Thought* 10, no. 4 (Autumn 1977): 40–69.

7. See Michael Hubbard MacKay and Nicholas J. Frederick *Joseph Smith's Seer Stones* (Provo, UT: Religious Studies Center, Brigham Young University; Salt Lake City: Deseret Book, 2016), 45–64; and John W. Welch, "The Miraculous Timing of the Translation of the Book of Mormon," in *Opening the Heavens: Accounts of Divine Manifestations, 1820–1844*, ed. John W. Welch, 2nd ed. (Provo, UT: Brigham Young University Press; Salt Lake City: Deseret Book, 2017), 79–227.

8. While various Mormon authors have put forward arguments that the English Book of Mormon could not possibly have come from Smith except through supernatural means—arguments that skeptics find unpersuasive—Grant Hardy and others have contended that the text is more than one would expect from a young farmhand in terms of its narrative structure, formal variability, internal textual interdependence, and, possibly, aspects of the text that feel antique. See Grant Hardy, *Understanding the Book of Mormon* (New York: Oxford University Press, 2010).

Joseph Smith *saw English words*. Given the traditional status of the visual-verbal model, this section begins with the observations often adduced in favor of that model, reinterprets them, and then considers other formal aspects of the text that likely tell a different mechanistic story.

Linguistic Markers and Dictation Blocks

According to the visual-verbal model, Smith saw English words in or through his seer stones (much like a modern teleprompter) and then read those visible words aloud to his clerks, who transcribed them into the Book of Mormon manuscript. Based primarily on late reminiscences from some who observed the translation, the visual-verbal model has dominated much writing about Book of Mormon translation mechanics. This model suggests a limited agency for the translator, as Smith's only role was to read aloud the words that God showed him with the stones.

Royal Skousen, a linguist who has performed the most extensive study of the prepublication manuscripts of the Book of Mormon, has demonstrated that the original manuscript was orally dictated rather than visually copied from a written source text. Whatever Smith might or might not have seen, his scribes did not see an English text. Skousen's linguistic evidence focuses primarily on instances in which scribes made errors that are more likely when the scribe mishears a text that is read aloud than when a scribe misreads a text he or she is personally viewing.[9] This evidence does not indicate whether Smith himself was reading what he was speaking.

As part of his account, Skousen argues that Smith dictated in blocks of text, what could be called "dictation blocks," of around twenty to thirty words and then waited for his scribe to confirm the correct transcription before moving on to the next block. Skousen identifies two instances, at Alma 56:41 and 2 Nephi 25:6, of what he calls "scribal anticipation," a term of art from textual criticism, in support of these dictation blocks. In scribal anticipation, the writer places phrases too early in the text, skipping over words, sentences, or lines in the source text. In the case of the original Book of Mormon manuscript, the amanuensis taking dictation may have occasionally placed phrases too early in

9. Skousen lays out his argument at length et passim in his multivolume *Analysis of Textual Variants of the Book of Mormon* (Provo, UT: FARMS, 2004). He summarizes the main arguments for a popular audience in his "How Joseph Smith Translated the Book of Mormon: Evidence from the Original Manuscript," *Journal of Book of Mormon Studies* 7, no. 1 (1998): 23–31. See also Stanford Carmack, "Joseph Smith Read the Words," *Interpreter: A Journal of Mormon Scripture* 18 (2016): 41–64.

the text, skipping over words, sentences, or lines in the flow of Smith's spoken words. From a few cases of apparent anticipation and a single instance in which Smith took over writing from Cowdery for a couple of clauses in Alma 45:22, Skousen infers that Smith *saw* a block of about twenty to thirty words, spoke them, and reviewed the dictation before those words passed from his vision.[10]

Skousen's observations indeed suggest that, at least occasionally, Smith dictated in blocks. A similar method is attested by William McLellin in his 1849 description of Smith's dictation of contemporaneous revelations (texts for which no one has ever proposed a visual-verbal model of revelation).[11] This proposed connection to the visual-verbal model is equivocal. Skousen's implicit claim that Smith could not possibly have held twenty words in memory without having the words depicted visually in the stone in the hat is unpersuasive, even within a strongly theistic worldview. A God who could show a prophet English words through seer stones could easily enhance that same prophet's memory. From a purely naturalistic perspective, whatever Smith's lack of formal education, he had a prodigious textual memory that may have been enhanced by the mental focus that surely attended his translation task.

The scribal anticipations on which Skousen relies do indicate that: (a) Smith at least occasionally spoke faster than his scribes could take dictation (as expected, since no shorthand was used); and (b) at least once when that happened someone (either Smith or his scribe) corrected the erroneous transcription. Smith's correction of such errors no more suggests that he was reading words he saw in the stone in his hat than any other mechanism of textual production. These rare scribal anticipations have been a mainstay of the visual-verbal model, which otherwise relies on late reminiscence and conjectures about the spelling of some proper nouns.[12] This analytic tradition must be interpreted alongside textual evidence suggesting that Smith was not reading words in the darkness of his hat.

10. See Skousen, *Analysis of Textual Variants*, 4:808–9; and Skousen, "How Joseph Smith Translated the Book of Mormon," 22–31. Skousen's other examples of anticipation are less persuasive, both as examples of anticipation and as evidence of larger dictation blocks. See Skousen, *Analysis of Textual Variants*, 4:658, 1351.

11. Quoted in *JSP*-D2:122.

12. Skousen offers evidence in favor of the occasional correction of misspelled proper names. Royal Skousen, "Translating the Book of Mormon: Evidence from the Original Manuscript," in *Book of Mormon Authorship Revisited: The Evidence for Ancient Origins*, ed. Noel B. Reynolds (Provo, UT: FARMS, 1997), 75–82. Nevertheless, this evidence does not necessarily favor any one translation mechanism over any other. One can spell words without seeing them visually, although it is probably more common to first learn the spelling of a word from reading it or hearing it spelled. The spellings to which Smith corrected his scribe need not have been the original spellings, just the spellings that Smith favored as translator. See also Gardner, *The Gift and Power*, 157–58.

Skousen has clearly demonstrated that the scribes were not reading a source text. He has missed, however, evidence suggesting that *no one* was reading a source text for the Book of Mormon. A handful of verbal false starts and missteps, along with their associated corrections, suggest that the Book of Mormon was primarily an oral production. These missteps and corrections sound most like the explanatory emendations and revisions that are ubiquitous in spoken language but should be rare in primarily written works. In simple terms, these missteps sound more like errors of speaking than errors of reading. They suggest that neither the scribes *nor Smith* was reading the English text of the Book of Mormon.[13]

Examples of this phenomenon abound. In Mosiah 7:8, a small group of prisoners are "permitted, or rather commanded" to speak to the king. Read in context, the plain sense is the latter. In a reading of a written text, one would expect simply "commanded," whereas in oral language the verbal misstep may well stand alongside its immediate correction.[14] In Alma 2:34, "the ground" is emended to "the bank," as if in dictation Smith realized that he had spoken too generically of land adjacent to a body of water. Such missteps are not generally of the kind that one would associate with misreading a written text: "permitted" doesn't look like "commanded," and the "ground" cannot be mistaken for the "bank." In the account of the Ammonite pacifists, these Christian converts "would suffer even unto death, rather than to commit sin; and thus we see, that they buried the weapons of peace," a misstep immediately revised to "or they buried the weapons of war, for peace."[15] In Alma 54:5, the "war which ye have waged" is expanded to "thy brother hath waged ... and ... ye are still determined to carry on." And in Alma 37:21, "their secret works" was clarified to "the secret works of those people which have been destroyed." In 3 Nephi 7:7, a parenthetical emendation of this sort obscures the meaning of the passage by creating an incomplete sentence, one that wasn't corrected in the church-published

13. For early forays into the examinations of missteps, see Edgar C. Snow Jr., "Reformed Egyptian Druthers," *Sunstone* 19, no. 1 (March 1996): 16–17; and Brent Lee Metcalfe, "Hypertextual Book of Mormon Study," *Dialogue: A Journal of Mormon Thought* 29, no. 4 (Winter 1996): 202–4.

14. A similar odd phrasing occurs in Alma 30:9 and several other passages with the same straightforward interpretation. See Alma 13:16, 14:11, 15:17, 13:37, 24:19, 39:16, 43:16, 43:19, 45:13. The story in Alma 18:9 seems to suddenly realize that a mention of horses is non sequitur and a clarification is required. A longer version seems possible in Alma 49:2–3, in which the recently razed city of Ammonihah is described as if it is populated, with a two-staged acknowledgment that it has been at least partially rebuilt by the Nephites.

15. Alma 24:19.

editions until 1905.[16] Similarly, Mosiah 2:31 immediately corrects an accidental arrogation of authority: "If ye shall keep the commandments of my son or the commandments of God which shall be delivered unto you by him." If these were examples of Smith misreading the English text displayed in the stone, one might expect that he would have simply corrected them with his scribe—that is a core assumption of the scribal anticipation argument.

While it may be possible to read some of these missteps as odd-sounding Hebrew couplets, contextually that seems unlikely. Many of the verbal missteps are identified by the use of the conjunction "or rather." The words "or rather" only appear once in the King James Bible, at Galatians 4:9, as a translation of *mallon de* after *nun de.* There the words serve a clear rhetorical purpose of distinguishing or clarifying a prior statement—"that ye have known God, or rather are known of God."[17] Such an explanatory conjunction sheds light on some of the "or rather" formations in the Book of Mormon. In Alma 36:14, "murdered" is emended to "led them away unto destruction," an acknowledgment of the moral culpability of causing spiritual death even when physical homicide has not been committed. In Alma 17:18, a reference to Ammon being "the chief" is emended to indicate that he "did administer unto them," to emphasize that this leader served his people rather than ruling over them. In 3 Nephi 6:20, the "resurrection of Christ" defines the "redemption which the Lord would make for his people." These clarifying uses of "or rather" appear distinct from the verbal missteps. Therefore, one cannot assume that all instances of "or rather" indicate a verbal misstep.

Conversely, not every verbal misstep is signaled by "or rather." In Helaman 3:33, Moroni recalls that life was good in Nephite civilization, "save it were the pride which began to enter into the church—not into the church of God, but into the hearts of the people who professed to belong to the church of God." This correction disambiguates the church itself—always pure—from its members, who were prone to episodes of sinful pride. In another example, in a sermon on the afterlife risks of iniquity, the Lamanite prophet Samuel warned the wicked Nephites, "ye can do good and be restored unto that which is good, or have that which is good restored unto you; or ye can do evil and have that which is evil restored unto you."[18] The lack of the extra "be restored unto" in

16. Skousen, *Analysis of Textual Variants*, 5:3295–96. Skousen notes this specific misstep but attributes it to Mormon rather than Smith.

17. The phrase "or rather" appears eleven times in the Book of Mormon (Mosiah 7:8; Alma 1:15, 2:34, 17:18, 30:9, 32:16, 36:14, 39:16, 50:32, 53:10, 54:5; see also Mosiah 8:17).

18. Helaman 14:31.

the second clause suggests that the first instance—"be restored unto that which is good"—was an error that was corrected on the fly, with the first instance of the conjunction "or" signaling this emendation.

Sometimes the Book of Mormon text adds clauses that specify a particular group or qualify a claim. When enumerating the societies at war in 3 Nephi 3:14, the narrator introduces "armies both of the Nephites and of the Lamanites" but then immediately adds a clarification—"or of all them which were numbered among the Nephites."[19] Later, in explaining a reference to Jews, Nephi elaborates in 2 Nephi 33:8—"I say Jew because I mean them from whence I came."

Another possible misstep, in 1 Nephi, employs different language. After claiming that the wicked "trample" God "under their feet," the narrator clarifies, "I say trample under their feet, but I would speak in other words: they do set him at naught."[20] While it may be that the New Testament formula of "which is, being interpreted" is gently echoed here, the most straightforward explanation is that Smith corrected his language extemporaneously. Similarly, at 3 Nephi 27:30–31, the text speaks of the current generation and asserts that "none of them are lost," but then clarifies: "I mean them who are now alive of this generation" (acknowledging the massive deaths that occurred immediately before Christ's coming to America). It seems implausible to attribute these impromptu emendations to a process other than the derivation of the transcribed English text from Smith's primarily oral utterance.

The evidence is occasionally harder to classify. One particular misstep implies substantial knowledge of the overall structure of the book. Early in the Book of Helaman, the narrator indicates that he will return to the topic of Gadianton robbers at the end of "this book," then immediately clarifies: "Behold I do not mean the end of the book of Helaman, but I mean the end of the book of Nephi, from which I have taken all the account which I have written."[21] The prediction is correct, as the promised material is later covered, starting in 4 Nephi 1:42. This appears to be a case of a verbal misstep that is corrected with a specific view to the ultimate structure of the final product, the kind of scope that an ancient editor presumably would have had but a view that Smith did not elsewhere exhibit.[22]

19. Consider also 3 Nephi 9:9, where "unto me" and "any more" trade places in a repeated phrase.

20. 1 Nephi 19:7.

21. Helaman 2:12–15.

22. Skousen does not engage the relationship between Helaman 2:12–14 and 4 Nephi 1:42 in his critical edition. See Skousen, *Analysis of Textual Variants*, 5:2899; 6:3576.

Some have wondered whether something about the nature of Reformed Egyptian or of engraving text in metal plates could account for the verbal missteps in the English Book of Mormon.[23] Perhaps, in other words, the verbal missteps come compliments of Mormon rather than Joseph Smith. Since nothing substantial is known of Reformed Egyptian as a script, a truly rigorous argument is impossible. Still, text-internal clues provide useful insights. The Book of Mormon authors saw Hebrew as their oral language and their coded Egyptian script as much more economical than Hebrew: it was, in fact, marvelously concise.[24] In 1835, when Smith purchased papyrus scrolls containing typical Egyptian hieroglyphs that reminded many in his inner circle of the Book of Mormon glyphs, he again endorsed the remarkable—even mystical—concision of Egyptian glyphs.[25] Such pictographically concise hieroglyphs are unlikely to be the source of missteps and corrections tied so closely to specific words or phrases in the English text. It seems implausible that any hieroglyphic syntax could so perfectly mimic the flow of English, particularly when the hieroglyphs are themselves a pictographically concise encoding. The Book of Mormon's obsession with economizing space on the plates also argues against the writers refusing to fix obvious errors. Furthermore, Smith's similar practice in his own dictated revelations argues against another source (such as the engravings on the plates) for the missteps and corrections. One of Smith's early revelations, which he dictated while speaking in the voice of God, indicates that it is difficult for Smith to "judge the righteous"—an ambiguous phrase: Are the righteous to be judged for residual sinfulness or to be distinguished from the wicked? After the conjunction "or," the revelation advances the latter interpretation: God would "tell the wicked from the righteous."[26]

Similar apparently extemporaneous revisions are present in other revelations dictated by Smith.[27] These differ from Smith's general use of "or, in other words" in his revelations, which do sound like an explanatory expansion rather than a correction per se.[28] Seven years after the initial publication of the Book

23. See Snow Jr., "Reformed Egyptian Druthers," 16–17. Brent Lee Metcalfe has noted, however, that engravings on metal plates could be cancelled by strike-through or cross-out engraving. Metcalfe, "Hypertextual Book of Mormon Study," 202n9.

24. On hieroglyphic concision, see 1 Nephi 1:2 and Mormon 9:32–34.

25. Samuel Morris Brown, "Joseph (Smith) in Egypt: Babel, Hieroglyphs, and the Pure Language of Eden," *Church History* 78, no. 1 (March 2009): 26–65, esp. 41–42, 59–61.

26. Revelation, Spring 1829, in *JSP*-D1:37–43 [D&C 10:37]. A similar "or" passage in Smith's revelation of 26 April 1832 is harder to classify. See Revelation, 26 April 1832, in *JSP*-D2:233–36 [D&C 82:17].

27. See Revelation, 10 March 1831, in *JSP*-D1:287–88 [D&C 48:5]; Revelation, 1 August 1831, in *JSP*-D2:15 [58:20]; Revelation, 12 August 1831, in *JSP*-D2:42 [61:29]; and Revelation, 11 September 1831, in *JSP*-D2:65–66 [64:27].

28. A possible exception to this rule may be Revelation, 6 May 1833, in *JSP*-D3:90 [D&C 93:45].

of Mormon, when Smith returned to the text to prepare it for a new edition, he introduced such an emendation to the Isaiah 48 material in 1 Nephi 20.[29] The same pattern of verbal missteps and emendations exists in both Smith's dictated revelations and the Book of Mormon. While no single argument is definitive, taken together these formal indications within the text suggest that the Book of Mormon is primarily oral.

TEXTUAL AND NARRATIVE CLUES TO TRANSLATION MECHANISM

Specific aspects of the English Book of Mormon narratives tend to corroborate the formal/linguistic evidence. While the Book of Mormon does not explicitly describe its own translation mechanism, it nevertheless provides several potential clues. This section explores statements or narratives within the Book of Mormon that provide potential insights into the mechanisms at play in Joseph Smith's translation. In particular, this section considers spiritual gifts, inspired words, special objects, and panoramic visions as potentially relevant to translation. Together these lines of evidence, context, and precedent suggest something of the non-ordinary nature of Smith's translation experience. Whereas the prior section considered the Book of Mormon as primarily oral, this section considers potential mechanisms by which the concepts rendered into English might have entered Smith's awareness. This section begins with a necessary detour into the story of another set of plates because the Book of Mormon itself positions those plates as an interpretive key, and the relationship between the two sets of plates confirms the deeply typological nature of the Book of Mormon.

The Plates within the Plates

The nested narrative of the Jaredite gold plates, presented with extensive editorializing by Moroni as the book of Ether, illuminates the broader Book of Mormon. It is, to borrow the language of the Book of Mormon's obsession with typology,[30] a "type" for the complete set of gold plates compiled by Mormon

29. Joseph M. Spencer, *The Vision of All: Twenty-Five Lectures on Isaiah in Nephi's Record* (Salt Lake City: Greg Kofford Books, 2016), 96. The phrase was fixed in the 1840 edition of the Book of Mormon. The Book of Mormon, trans. Joseph Smith, 3rd ed. (Nauvoo, IL: Robinson and Smith, 1840), 52–53 [1 Nephi 20:1].

30. The Book of Mormon regularly uses the language of typology to describe itself. See 2 Nephi 11:4; Ether 3:17–18, 13:6–7. For a close investigation, see Joseph M. Spencer, *An Other Testament: On Typology* (Provo, UT: Neal A. Maxwell Institute for Religious Scholarship, Brigham Young University, 2015).

and his son Moroni. The story of the Jaredite plates and their translation is told several times in the Book of Mormon, including highlights in the title page. In brief, Jared and his brother, Moriancumer,[31] led their tribe from Babylon to America perhaps two millennia BCE in a prefiguring of the Lehite migration circa 600 BCE. Rather than fleeing the Babylonian exile as the Lehites did, the Jaredites fled the multiplication of languages associated with the curse of the Tower of Babel. Both Lehites and Jaredites were led by God from the Old World across the ocean to a new promised land, a land "choice above all the earth,"[32] and preserved as a righteous remnant when the Old World was in apostasy. Both peoples would, in the central tragedy of the book, betray the covenant of their promised land and collapse in iniquity and war. Intensifying the parallels between the Jaredite and Lehite stories, both peoples preserved their identity and their scripture on gold plates in sacred languages no longer accessible to their peers. The Jaredites inscribed their records in their native tongue, apparently the pure language that was confounded at Babel, while the Lehites inscribed theirs in Reformed Egyptian.[33]

The Jaredites, fleeing the tumult of Babel, received a blessing from God that their language would not be "confounded" as was the case for the rest of humankind. Their record, therefore, was inscribed in humankind's original mother tongue. When they were found centuries later, the Jaredite plates necessitated the same solution that Mormon's plates had required in the 1820s: a seer to "translate and cause to be written" their sacred text. According to the title page, the Jaredite narrative would allow moderns to know the "covenants of the Lord," a framing that is elsewhere a description of the goals of the entire Book of Mormon.[34] After arriving in America, the Jaredites, corrupted by their own affluence, succumb to America's curse: the extinction of those who betray its covenant. The Jaredites' priestly record is stored on gold plates that come to rest on a battleground named Ramah. This is apparently the same battleground,

31. The book of Ether in the Book of Mormon refers to this man as "the brother of Jared." The name "Moriancumer" is used as a Jaredite place name in Ether 2:13. Oliver Cowdery, Smith's principal scribe, later identified the brother of Jared as the eponym for that place name. Oliver Cowdery, "Letter VI," *Latter Day Saints' Messenger and Advocate*, April 1835, 112. A later tradition, attributed to Joseph Smith, maintains that Jared's brother was named "Mahonri Moriancumer." "The Jaredites," *Juvenile Instructor*, 1 May 1892, 282. Given the later date of this tradition, *Moriancumer* alone is used here.

32. See Ether 1:38.

33. Ether 3:22–24; Mormon 9:32.

34. On the usage of "translate" and "cause to be written," see Samuel Morris Brown, "'To Read the Round of Eternity': Speech, Text, and Scripture in the Book of Mormon," in *Americanist Approaches to the Book of Mormon*, ed. Elizabeth Fenton and Jared Hickman (New York and Oxford: Oxford University Press, 2019), 159–83. See also Smith's telling characterization of the work of his scribes in Smith, History, circa Summer 1832, in *JSP*-H1:15–16.

then named Cumorah, on which Mormon's plates were found[35]—another close parallel between the Lehite and Jaredite peoples—where it is discovered by a small group of Nephites.

Once these plates make their way to the main people of Book of Mormon history, they present the same problem posed by Mormon's plates in the nineteenth century. Ancient sacred history is hidden within an unknown language. The solution to this problem may hold insights into Book of Mormon translation mechanics. King Limhi, head of a smaller group of Nephites, turns to Ammon, the leader of an exploratory expedition from the main group, and asks "if he could interpret languages."[36] Ammon responds that the king of the main group of Nephites possesses special stones that make him a seer—"he hath wherewith that he can look, and translate all records that are of an ancient date"—and that the plates should be brought to this king, Mosiah, for interpretation. Mosiah's capacity to interpret comes because he is a "seer," a status that derives at least in part from his possession of the translation stones. In Ammon's phrase, "whosoever is commanded to look in them [the stones], the same is called seer."[37] In several other cases, the seer is the one with custody of these special stones.[38]

Using the same framing employed for Book of Mormon translation, Mormon reports in Omni 1:20–21, 25 that Mosiah "did interpret the engravings by the gift and power of God," a schema reiterated in Mosiah 21:28. Beyond this general gesture, the story of Mosiah and the Jaredite plates remains silent about the details of translation mechanics. The reader is only informed that translation happened "by the means of those two stones . . . which were prepared from the beginning . . . for the purpose of interpreting languages."[39] In Mosiah 28, a narrative lacuna between 28:16 and 28:17 typifies other gaps in the record. In 28:16, Mosiah is identified as a seer capable of interpreting a mysterious record. With no transition at all, 28:17 reports that the translation has been completed. Ultimately, the text refuses to disclose in any detail the method by which it came to be. It does, however, take some time to describe the office of

35. Samuel Morris Brown, *In Heaven as It Is on Earth: Joseph Smith and the Early Mormon Conquest of Death* (New York: Oxford University Press, 2012), 77–80.

36. Mosiah 8:6.

37. Mosiah 8:13. The book revisits Mosiah's translation in Alma 37:9, 21–22. See also Mosiah 8:16 and 1 Nephi 13:35.

38. See Mosiah 28:13–16 and Smith's testimony on the book's original title page: "Use of these stones were what constituted 'seers' in ancient or former times" [Title Page]. Compare Revelation, 6 April 1830, in *JSP*-D1:129 [D&C 21:1].

39. Mosiah 28:13–15.

seerhood. Seers would see visions, make prophecies, translate lost records, and provide methods to connect the past, present, and future.

The story of the Jaredite gold plates within Mormon's gold plates sets the tone for the Book of Mormon perspective on scriptural translation. Special objects—interpreter stones—are required for translation; those special objects and the capacity to employ them are a gift from God. Translations must be accomplished by a specialist, called a seer, who knows how to wield the interpreter stones properly. These objects simultaneously tether the translation process to the physical world and to a field of power that is not merely physical. This juxtaposition foregrounds the relevance of the text's account of and Smith's use of such objects to understanding the metaphysics of Smith's translation.[40]

Special Objects

The stones that made Mosiah a seer had a history as ancient as the plates they helped to translate. The interpreter stones apparently began life in parallel to supernatural lanterns for Jaredite submersibles in the book of Ether.[41] Moriancumer, the seeric brother of Jared, the tribal leader, needed a way to light the closed ships in which the Jaredites would recapitulate Noah's voyage in his ark.[42] Moriancumer therefore forged "out of rock sixteen small stones; and they were white and clear, even as transparent glass,"[43] language strongly reminiscent of the apocalyptic phrases of Revelation 2:17 and 21:21.[44] Moriancumer asked God: "Touch these stones, O Lord, with thy finger and prepare them that they may shine forth in darkness."[45] He then saw the finger of Jesus, a miracle by which Moriancumer was drawn from earthly time and into God's physical presence.[46] After a discussion between Jesus and Moriancumer about the nature of faith and divine embodiment, two parallel stones are introduced into the narrative almost as a non sequitur. The sacred stones are intended to translate the scriptural text that Moriancumer will write. In this event and subsequent commentary on it, *Gazelem* becomes a name for both the stones

40. See also Samuel M. Brown, "Minds, Bodies, and Objects," *Mormon Studies Review* 5 (2018): 26–32.

41. The text does not make clear precisely how the two interpreter stones and the sixteen lantern stones are related, but they appear in the same context and with parallel roles. Their intertwined stories begin in Ether 3, especially verses 1–6, 23–28. See also Revelation, June 1829—E, in *JSP*-D1:84 [D&C 17:1].

42. See Ether 6:7, where the division of languages mimics the annihilating flood.

43. Ether 3:1.

44. Smith later employed the former scripture as the basis for a theory of seer stones. See William Clayton, Journal, 2 April 1843, in *JSP*-J2:404 [D&C 130:10–11]).

45. Ether 3:4.

46. Ether 3:1–20.

FIGURE 6.1. Joseph Smith's seer stone. About 2 inches long; dark brown with brown stripes. Smith used this seer stone during his translation of the Book of Mormon. Office of the First Presidency, the Church of Jesus Christ of Latter-day Saints. Church History Library, Salt Lake City; photograph by Welden C. Andersen and Richard E. Turley Jr.

and the seer who wields them, implying a kind of unity between the seer and the implements of seership.[47]

As special objects, pregnant with divine power, the stones could pose substantial peril for the user. The risks of unauthorized use could be on a par with unmediated contact with God. In the introduction to Mosiah's ownership of the stones, it is explained that "no man can look in them, except he be commanded, lest he should look for that he had not ought and he should perish."[48] A similar injunction would apply to the "interpreters" and Mormon's gold plates once Smith acquired them.[49]

While the lantern stones and interpreter stones are apparently distinct in the account in early Ether, the lantern stones appear to explain in part the significance of the interpreter stones, with the Book of Mormon occasionally failing to maintain a distinction even as it ultimately suggests that the lantern

47. On *Gazelem*, see Alma 37:23 and the early printed version of Smith's 1 March 1832 revelation, where Smith's code name is Gazelam. *The Doctrine and Covenants of the Church of the Latter Day Saints* [...] (Kirtland, OH: F. G. Williams, 1835), 204 [2:75:2] [D&C 78:9].

48. Mosiah 8:13.

49. See Welch, "The Miraculous Timing of the Translation of the Book of Mormon," documents 57 (an 1888 interview with Martin Harris); 71 (an 1841 interview with Oliver Cowdery); 157 (an 1833 letter from Jesse Townsend); and 163 (an 1834 letter from Jesse Townsend), on pages 152, 158, 206, 209 respectively.

stones are siblings of, rather than identical to, the seer stones. Thus Alma 37:23 indicates that God prepared "a stone, which shall shine forth in darkness unto light, that I may discover unto my people who serve me, that I may discover unto them the works of their brethren, yea, their secret works, their works of darkness, and their wickedness and abominations."[50] Such interpreter stones are used, more than anything, to cast a light on antiquity, uncovering lost history and providing a vision of what came before.

The connection of light and navigation with the objects of seerhood appears in related narratives in the Book of Mormon. The "Liahona," a supernatural compass, is an antitype (albeit introduced earlier in the flow of the final text) of both kinds of Jaredite stones, as well as a parallel to the brass plates of Lehi's proto-bible. The Liahona is implicitly compared to the lantern stones and vice versa.[51] The Liahona "director" guides Lehi's family across Arabia as a compass but also provides intermittent written messages from God. It is brass like the plates on which the proto-bible is written,[52] has a spindle like a compass, produces divine script like the glyphs engraved in metal plates, and is described as an antitype of Christ's word, a guide through the wilderness.[53]

The Book of Mormon uses the term "director" as one of a few titles for the Liahona compass.[54] Such a use of the term makes sense as a reference to a supernatural compass. The original text employs the plural form of the same word explicitly to refer to the interpreter stones,[55] a reading that was corrected almost a century later to "interpreters."[56] In a fraught application of the same term, Smith apparently referred to his seer stones as "directors" that provided "counsel."[57] The use of this term points to the connection between seer stones and guidance: the seer and the Jaredite sailors were both navigating a long distance, through darkness.

Without a seer to give utterance to the words of their ancient scripture, moderns would have no knowledge of the "great things the Lord hath done for their fathers." In the words of God relayed to Moriancumer in the book of

50. Regarding the lantern stones, the text states that "the Lord caused stones to shine in darkness" (Ether 6:3).

51. Alma 37:23–25, 38; Ether 2:19.

52. See 2 Nephi 5:12, where the two brass objects are both held to provide access to the word of God.

53. See Alma 37:44.

54. Alma 37:38, 45; Mosiah 1:16.

55. Alma 37:21, 24.

56. Royal Skousen, ed., *The Printer's Manuscript of the Book of Mormon: Typographical Facsimile of the Entire Text in Two Parts* (Provo, UT: Foundation for Ancient Research and Mormon Studies, Brigham Young University, 2001), 579; compare Alma 37:21, 24.

57. Revelation, July 1828, in *JSP*-D1:9 [D&C 3:15].

Ether, "the language which ye shall write I have confounded; wherefore I will cause in my own due time that these stones shall magnify to the eyes of men these things which ye shall write."[58] The term *magnify* appears to frame seer stones as magnifying glasses—bestowing the ability to see across expanses of scale—and that imagery fits with the small-to-large themes of the Book of Mormon overall.[59] Distant, inscrutable, sealed things are opened to view; they become comprehensible and near. In context, these stones were intended to exhume ancient truth from the grave of scripture written in a long-dead script. Speaking of the Book of Mormon as a whole, Moroni editorialized near the end of the book, "the Lord knoweth the things which we have written, and also that none other people knoweth our language; and because that none other people knoweth our language, therefore he hath prepared a means for the interpretation thereof."[60] But what did the stones do? What did the see-er *see* that was hidden from ordinary eyes? If they were like the seer stones of early modern Atlantic folk culture, then the seer saw events, locations, and objects rather than words.[61]

Spiritual Gifts

In addition to including seers and their special implements, the Book of Mormon clearly endorses God's close participation in the process of translation. Frequently, God's involvement in the process is expressed in terms of the gifts of the Spirit. The title page of the Book of Mormon describes the book as having been "written by the Spirit of Prophesy and of Revelation," an allusion to the spiritual gifts tradition that is crucial context for understanding Smith's overall religious project. The early church positively brims with spiritual gifts. They are described ubiquitously in the Book of Mormon and other early Latter-day Saint scripture, in articles published in church periodicals, and in sermons. Part and parcel of Latter-day Saint anticessationism, spiritual gifts emphasized God's consistency over time and his ongoing active presence among humankind.[62]

58. Ether 3:13–15, 23–24.

59. The Book of Mormon occasionally employs a small-to-large motif. See Mark Thomas, *Digging in Cumorah: Reclaiming Book of Mormon Narratives* (Salt Lake City: Signature Books, 1999), 36, 64.

60. Mormon 9:34.

61. Mark Ashurst-McGee, "Pathway to Prophethood: Joseph Smith Junior as Rodsman, Village Seer, and Judeo-Christian Prophet" (master's thesis, Utah State University, 2000), 109–11, 157, 161–62, 168, 184, 242, 262. See also MacKay and Frederick, *Joseph Smith's Seer Stones*, 55–56.

62. See Samuel Morris Brown, "The Language of Heaven: Prolegomenon to the Study of Smithian Translation," *Journal of Mormon History* 38, no. 3 (Summer 2012): 51–71. The miracles literature is relevant context here. See Jane Shaw, *Miracles in Enlightenment England* (New Haven: Yale University Press, 2008);

The Book of Mormon itself contains an anticessationist manifesto.[63] Nephi's prophetic vision of Smith's America (seerhood now reversing its usual temporal polarity to function more as prophecy) denounces the iniquity of antebellum Protestantism for its failure to honor spiritual gifts.[64] When the people no longer accept miracles, this prophecy maintains, the nation is in peril.[65]

Smith's scriptural texts reuse the Pauline litany of spiritual gifts in both the Book of Mormon and the Doctrine and Covenants.[66] A brief nod in Alma 9:21 (including, notably, translation as one of the gifts) precedes a much longer recapitulation near the end of the Book of Mormon. In the midst of miscellaneous addenda from Moroni—who was by then the unexpected proprietor of the edited record of his father, Mormon—the litany of gifts recurs at the very end of the Book of Mormon. A strong anticessationist pronouncement in Moroni 10:7 introduces the Pauline material, arguing that readers should look to the past to understand the present. Then begins a reworking of the New Testament text that incorporates several subtle additions connecting it to Smith's work on the Book of Mormon. There, in Moroni 10:13, "prophecy" expands to "prophesy concerning all things," a gentle nod toward the all-encompassing, panoramic visions of history described below. In 10:16, "interpretation of tongues" opens up slightly into "interpretation of languages and of divers kinds of tongues." In 10:14, Moroni's list also includes "the beholding of angels and ministering spirits"—a possible foreshadowing of Moroni's appearances to Joseph Smith. The Book of Mormon's modified list of spiritual gifts suggests the ways that spiritual gifts will figure in the self-representation of the Book of Mormon. Figures from the past and future commingle, a meeting made possible by the obliteration of linguistic distance.[67]

and Robert Bruce Mullin, *Miracles and the Modern Religious Imagination* (New Haven: Yale University Press, 1996). On Mormonism, see Craig James Hazen, *The Village Enlightenment in America: Popular Religion and Science in the Nineteenth Century* (Urbana: University of Illinois Press, 2000). See also Female Relief Society of Nauvoo, Minutes, 28 April 1842, in *The First Fifty Years of Relief Society: Key Documents in Latter-day Saint Women's History*, ed. Jill Mulvay Derr et al. (Salt Lake City: Church Historian's Press, 2016), 54–59.

63. See Mormon 9:7–8.

64. 1 Nephi 13:37, 14:1.

65. See also 2 Nephi 28:26; Mormon 1:14.

66. The first known discussion of spiritual gifts in the Christian canon is Paul's enumeration in 1 Corinthians 12. Contextually, Paul was trying to control charismatic schismatics in order to maintain the integrity of the Corinthian church. Acknowledging the diversity of supernatural gifts practiced among early Christians, he then issues a moving call for unity in diversity framed as a metaphor of the church as Christ's body, with each group representing a body part ("member" in the influential language of the King James Version). Paul describes a handful of gifts available to the Christian believer, including "prophecy" and "the interpretation of tongues," the gifts most relevant to Smith's translation projects.

67. This theme is pursued at length in Brown, *Joseph Smith's Translation*, chapter 7.

Spiritual gifts involving language are often characterized in terms of glossolalia and xenoglossia. Glossolalia, an ecstatic revelation in an otherworldly tongue, requires the paired gift of "interpretation of tongues," a rendering of a revelatory experience into a destination language. Xenoglossia, by contrast, is a direct rendering from an earthly language that the speaker has not learned or studied to one the hearer understands. The visual-verbal model of Book of Mormon translation represents one particularly simplistic version of xenoglossia. On the other hand, several translation mechanisms could integrate well with what could be described as a glossolalic understanding of translation.[68] The precedent of spiritual gifts was readily available to Smith and something he appropriated comfortably. But even the most relevant of the gifts, the gift of tongues, is itself ambiguous, as either a xenoglossic or glossolalic model is compatible with the known facts and contexts of Book of Mormon translation. The reliance on spiritual gifts does, however, demonstrate how thoroughly the Book of Mormon saw itself as refuting the Protestant accommodation of cessationism. In its very translation, the Book of Mormon was no cheap gimmick or treasure-digger's fancy; it was a miracle to prove that God would always work miracles.

Inspired Words

Perhaps in support of a primarily revelatory dynamic at play in Smith's translations, several threads in Latter-day Saint scripture describe the possibility that God inspires special individuals to say certain things. Such a mechanism lacks the visionary eyewitness element of the panoramic vision described below, while nevertheless foregrounding the translator's agency. An "inspired words" model would be difficult to distinguish from revelation as it is understood outside translation contexts. Such a model would therefore have the advantage of integrating Smith's Book of Mormon work with the other scriptures that followed.

This model is present from the beginning of the Book of Mormon. Nephi, during a prolonged verbal attack on his resentful brothers, announces that he has been possessed by God, that he is so "full of the spirit" that he is physically weak.[69] Shortly thereafter, he states that "by the Spirit are all things made known unto the prophets."[70] This spirit may, implicitly, have told Nephi (and perhaps also Smith) what words to say out loud. In a telling sequence that

68. Brown, "The Language of Heaven," 51–71. See also Christopher James Blythe, "'By the Gift and Power of God': Translation among the Gifts of the Spirit," Chapter 2 herein.

69. 1 Nephi 17:47.

70. 1 Nephi 22:2.

occurs many years later, the prophet Alma seeks inspiration from God about how to manage a threat to believers and in answer receives an elaborate set of explicit instructions. At the conclusion of the encounter, Alma creates written scripture: "And it came to pass when Alma had heard these words [from God] he wrote them down that he might have them, and that he might judge the people of that church according to the commandments of God."[71]

The book of Helaman includes examples of inspired words as the mechanism by which revelation is received. It tells of two Nephite preachers who "were filled as if with fire, and they could speak forth marvelous words."[72] In the introduction to the Samuel the Lamanite sequence of Helaman 13–15, the narrator indicates in 13:3 that the "voice of the Lord" came to Samuel, telling him to "Prophesy unto the people whatsoever things should come into his heart." Shortly thereafter, at Helaman 13:5, the text clarifies the source of those inspired things: Samuel reports that he was to "speak the words of the Lord which he doth put into my heart."

Inspired words are also a source of speech that is especially persuasive. When Helaman's sons Nephi and Lehi headed out on their preaching mission, they "had what they should speak given unto them" and could therefore "speak unto the great astonishment of the Lamanites, to the convincing of them."[73] While Smith doesn't explicitly indicate that the spirit or an angel told him which specific words to dictate to his assistants, such stories provide another perspective on spiritual gifts as Smith may have understood them in his translation work.

Smith's other scriptural productions exhibit the same model of inspired words. The 1830 revelatory account of Enoch makes a general statement about the nature of scripture: "As many as called upon God" were enabled "to write [by the spirit] of inspiration."[74] Enoch reports shortly thereafter that he himself is "slow of speech"[75]—an echo of Moses's complaint in Exodus 4:10—and God therefore commands Enoch: "Open thy mouth and it shall be filled I will give thee utterance for all flesh is in my hands and I will do as seemeth me good."[76]

71. Mosiah 26:33.

72. Helaman 5:45.

73. Helaman 5:18–19. Shortly before that, the report of holy men is that "it was given unto them what they should pray" (3 Nephi 19:24).

74. Old Testament Manuscript 1, 11, in Scott H. Faulring, Kent P. Jackson, and Robert J. Matthews, eds., *Joseph Smith's New Translation of the Bible: Original Manuscripts* (Provo, UT: Religious Studies Center, Brigham Young University, 2004), 97 [Moses 6:5].

75. Old Testament Manuscript 1, 12, in *Joseph Smith's New Translation of the Bible*, 99 [Moses 6:31].

76. Old Testament Manuscript 1, 12, in *Joseph Smith's New Translation of the Bible*, 99 [Moses 6:32]. In a similar vein, God communicates to his prophet, "my spirit is upon you wherefore all thy words will I justify" (99 [6:34]).

Panoramic Visions of History

A complementary spiritual gift provides yet another possible approach to understanding what the Book of Mormon has to say about Smith's subjective experience of translation: seeing visions. This as yet unexplored explanation of the seer's work involves a particular nontextual visionary experience that could be called a panoramic vision. Ubiquitously the source of primary scripture in the Book of Mormon, such visions of human history are circumstantially associated with translation in several places. Such a mechanism accords with ideas about seerhood and the nature of translation in Mosiah 8 as well as Smith's apparent sense of what he was doing as a prophetic figure. While not definitive, this mechanism may be productive for contextualization and explanation. Smith's revelations and translations, especially but not exclusively the Book of Mormon, include descriptions of prophetic visions of the grand arc of human history. In the Book of Mormon's visions, prophets—generally in the company of God or the angel of God's presence—witness large segments, if not the entirety, of human history.

In Oliver Cowdery's 1834 account of the 1829 translation of the Book of Mormon, he emphasized the intimate association between that book and the future of the American Indian. Cowdery and other early Latter-day Saints believed that American Indians, as descendants of the Lamanite peoples of the Book of Mormon, were essential players in the restoration of Israel prophesied by the Hebrew and Christian Bibles.[77] He began by sketching out the details of Smith's initial encounter with the angel Moroni, who introduced the Book of Mormon to Smith. In setting up the comparison between the Book of Mormon and the restoration of the Lamanites, Cowdery maintained that Isaiah had a panoramic vision of the Lost Ten Tribes of Israel—from their captivity in Assyria to their ultimate restoration in the last days.[78] Cowdery indicated that this vision was the source of the excerpt from the beginning of Isaiah that he then read into evidence for the restoration of the last heirs of Lehi.[79] Concluding his account of Smith's encounter with Moroni, Cowdery described the complexity of reducing a visionary encounter, infused with the spirit, into written language.

77. Jared Hickman, "The Book of Mormon as Amerindian Apocalypse," *American Literature* 86, no. 3 (2014): 429–61.

78. Oliver Cowdery, "Letter VI," 109–10.

79. Isaiah 1–2.

> You will understand, then, by this, that while those glorious things were being rehearsed, the vision was also opened so that our brother [Joseph Smith] was permitted to see and understand much more fully and perfectly than I am able to communicate in writing. I know much may be conveyed to the understanding in writing and many marvelous truths set forth by the pen, but after all, it is but a shadow compared to an open vision of *seeing, hearing, and realizing* eternal things.[80]

While he was using a specific angelic encounter to ruminate on the nature of visionary experiences generally, Cowdery's insights seem relevant to the broader question of revelation and, perhaps, translation.

Accounts of panoramic visions saturate the Book of Mormon narrative. According to Nephi's report,[81] Lehi has a taste of such a vision mediated by a bible that Christ delivers from the future[82]—providing a focused vision of Jerusalemites under siege and taken into exile by the Babylonians.[83] Lehi's son Nephi then asks for a repeat of his father's vision of Jerusalem's near future. Nephi's subsequent panoramic vision was ostensibly an interpretation of Lehi's dream, but the vision was rather more detailed and intricate than the original. Nephi's vision focuses on Book of Mormon instead of Bible narrative, albeit with biblical-Christological narratives as its foundation.[84] Using language that elsewhere describes the gift of translation, Nephi requests his panoramic vision "by the power of the Holy Ghost, which is the gift of God."[85] He is then transported from thoughtful prayer to a mythically high mountain where he sees a vision of a "Tree of Life" and the coming of Christ, the same figure who had visited Lehi as his guide. The angel then shows Nephi something like the Lucan nativity narrative followed by a précis of the Synoptic Gospels. Nephi is *watching* the New Testament in his vision and then writes what he has seen. While the third-person historical narrative of the Book of Mormon is different from Nephi's first-person account of what he saw, it opens up the possibility that Smith was similarly *watching* the Book of Mormon before putting it into words.

80. Oliver Cowdery, "Letter VI," 112 (emphasis added).

81. 1 Nephi 1.

82. On this future bible, see Brown, "'To Read the Round of Eternity.'"

83. See 1 Nephi 13.

84. 1 Nephi 11–14.

85. 1 Nephi 10:17; compare The Book of Mormon: An Account Written by the Hand of Mormon, upon Plates Taken from the Plates of Nephi, trans. Joseph Smith, Junior (Palmyra, NY: E. B. Grandin, 1830), iii, also 589 [The Testimony of Three Witnesses]. See also Joseph Smith, History, 1838–1856, vol. E-1, 7 September 1843, Addenda, 8 (accessible in the Histories series of the online edition of *The Joseph Smith Papers*).

By chapters 12–13, Nephi has transitioned to witnessing the grand arc of Nephite history, including the denouement of Lamanite civilization after the destruction of his own descendants, the Nephites. The substance of the panoramic vision comes in chapter 12. In Nephi's words, "I saw the multitudes of the earth gathered together . . . I beheld, and saw the people of the seed of my brethren that they had overcome my seed; and they went forth in multitudes upon the face of the land. . . . I beheld, after they had dwindled in unbelief they became a dark, and loathsome, and a filthy people." In these spare sentences, Nephi reports that he has seen the Book of Mormon narrative from the beginning to the bitter end. The panoramic visions of father and son are only the first of many such chronicled in the Book of Mormon narratives. On Lehi's deathbed, he reports to his son Joseph that Joseph of Egypt had a vision like Nephi's, in which he witnessed ancient American history as well as a flash-forward through the Egyptian captivity and the liberation of the Hebrews from slavery in Egypt.[86]

Moroni reports that Ether experienced a panoramic vision of not only Nephite history but, apparently, New Testament Israel, seeing "the days of Christ" in perhaps both America and the Old World.[87] Moroni himself reports something like a panoramic vision of his antebellum American readers: "I speak unto you as if ye were present—and yet ye are not—but behold Jesus Christ hath shewn you unto me, and I know your doing."[88] Nephi, in explaining the coming of Jesus after the great apostasy of his descendants, reports: "Notwithstanding the pains of my soul, I have seen it; wherefore I know that it shall come to pass."[89] In an editorial endorsement of Nephi's seeric power,[90] the narrator describes Nephi as "having been visited by angels and also by the voice of the Lord, therefore having seen angels and being eyewitness, and having had power given unto him that he might know concerning the ministry of Christ." Several possible mechanisms simmer together in this account, potentially including panoramic visions.

Panoramic visions have an apocalyptic feel to them. They represent both mechanism and content, where the content is generally the secrets of the world's future. Apocalyptic meditations are common in the Book of Mormon, especially through reinterpretations of Isaiah and of John's Apocalypse. In the

86. 2 Nephi 3:5.
87. Ether 13:4.
88. Mormon 8:35.
89. 2 Nephi 26:10.
90. 3 Nephi 7:15.

rumination on and revision of Isaiah 29, Isaiah's mysterious book (strongly identified with the Book of Mormon) contains secret words that "reveal all things from the foundation of the world unto the end thereof."[91] While that clause is pregnant with esotericism and apocalypticism, it also recalls the panoramic vision of history. Prophets were obligated to see and report *all* the secret places of human history.

In the encounter between King Limhi and Ammon in early Mosiah,[92] a seer is associated with an apparent allusion to panoramic visions. After describing the power to translate records, Ammon reports that these translating seers "can know of things which are past, and also of things which are to come, and by them shall all things be revealed, or, rather, shall secret things be made manifest, and hidden things shall come to light, and things which are not known shall be made known by them, and also things shall be made known by them which otherwise could not be known." While the language is imprecise, it nevertheless suggests that seers can view the human story in all its phases: past, present, and future.

The matter is particularly clear in early Ether, the Jaredite book that held the key to the entire Book of Mormon. When Moriancumer received the stones necessary to unlock the Book of Mormon from its coded hieroglyphs, God told him to write the secrets in his scripture. Those secrets came via a panoramic vision:

> He [God] showed unto the brother of Jared [Moriancumer] all the inhabitants of the earth which had been, and also all that would be; and he withheld them not from his sight, even unto the ends of the earth. For he had said unto him in times before, that if he would believe in him that he could show unto him all things—it should be shown unto him; therefore the Lord could not withhold anything from him, for he knew that the Lord could show him all things. And the Lord said unto him: Write these things and seal them up; and I will show them in mine own due time unto the children of men.[93]

This Ether material depicts the original receipt of revelation through a panoramic vision, which is then inscribed in the uncorrupted language. Since that

91. 2 Nephi 27:10 (phrase not present in Isaiah 29).
92. Mosiah 8:17.
93. Ether 3:25–26.

language was unknown to any other people, this scripture was encoded and would need one day to be decoded by the just-revealed seer stones. While the text does not explicitly indicate anything other than that seer stones would be required to recover the secrets, the conjunction of stones and panoramic vision is noteworthy. Shortly thereafter, Moroni indicates that Euro-Americans ("Gentiles") will themselves have Moriancumer's panoramic visions once they "become sanctified" in Christ,[94] a process that the Book of Mormon consistently prophesies will occur as the Book of Mormon is revealed and disseminated. In this case, the prophecy promises: "Then will I manifest unto them the things which the brother of Jared saw, even to the unfolding unto them all my revelations." The things the brother of Jared saw are precisely panoramic visions, thus promised to all.

When Christ comes to America shortly after his death and resurrection, he appears to expound a panoramic vision, and its description is explicitly intended to acquaint his New World audience with Old World scriptures not available in the Americas.[95] As the narrator recounts, "he did expound all things, even from the beginning until the time that he should come in his glory—yea, even all things which should come upon the face of the earth—even until the elements should melt with fervent heat and the earth should be wrapped together as a scroll and the heavens and the earth should pass away, and even unto the great and last day."[96] In this he introduced the missing elements of the Bible as part of a merger of past, present, and future in himself. And he did so in self-consciously apocalyptic terms.

Smith and the narrators of the Book of Mormon see scriptures as reaching out across temporal divides: they are designed to "be given unto future generations."[97] Panoramic visions represent temporal disruption—they do not reveal just a contemporary panorama, but often many successive panoramas—sometimes as a subset of the fundamental act of interhuman connection. Several times the editor-narrator addresses his readers through a variant of the panoramic visions. In one instance, Mormon's son Moroni addresses Joseph Smith directly, much as he would address Smith in person some fourteen hundred years later.[98] It is not much of a stretch to imagine a window through time, through which Smith saw these ancient individuals in the same collapse of temporal distance.

94. Ether 4:7.
95. 3 Nephi 26:2.
96. 3 Nephi 26:2–4.
97. 3 Nephi 26:2.
98. Ether 5.

The Book of Mormon also describes encounters with truths that cannot be spoken or written, evading the grasp of human language. The obsession of this written scripture with the inherent inability of written scripture to capture all truth is arresting and important.[99] Such apophatic mysticism integrates well with panoramic visions. Prophets and seers constantly walk the edge between what can and cannot be expressed in human language. What they are trying to convey is more than language, as are the contents of their immersive, panoramic visions.

Panoramic visions persisted in Smith's other scriptural works. Joseph Smith's "new translation" of the Bible includes two more examples of a comprehensive vision of human history. In June 1830, about a year after Smith completed the Book of Mormon translation, he dictated what he apparently called the "Visions of Moses," a text that serves as a new, primordial preface to the Bible while fulfilling a prophecy in Ether.[100] In that vision, God reports that "all things are present with me," and then imparts to Moses a vision of every single living person: Moses "beheld the world & the ends thereof, & all the Children of men."[101] This claim is reiterated shortly thereafter: "There was not a soul" that Moses did not behold "& he discerned them by the Spirit of God."[102]

In 1830 Smith also produced a dramatic expansion of Genesis 5:24 (his "Extract from the Prophecy of Enoch"), filling in a lacuna suggested by Jude 1:14. In this scriptural text, Enoch anoints his own eyes with clay (echoing Christ's miraculous bestowal of sight on a blind man in John 9:6–7). Endowed thereby with supernatural sight, Enoch views things "not visible to the natural eye," becoming a seer who "beheld the spirits that God had created." Contextually, his vision was of the "host of men [that God] brought in upon the face" of the earth.[103] Where Jude had suggested that the "saints" would come to condemn the wicked at the last day, in Smith's Prophecy of Enoch the special souls come instead to provide a heavenly example of righteous communal life, in the form of his City of Zion. In Smith's story of Enoch, the clay substitutes

99. See Brown, "'To Read the Round of Eternity.'"

100. Ether 1:1–5.

101. Old Testament Manuscript 1, 1, in *Joseph Smith's New Translation of the Bible*, 83 [Moses 1:8].

102. Old Testament Manuscript 1, 2, in *Joseph Smith's New Translation of the Bible*, 85 [Moses 1:27–28]. This use may contain a complex echo of Deuteronomy 34:1, a connection noticed by Greg Sorensen (personal communication to author). Incidentally, this preface thereby solves a famous problem with the Pentateuch: that it describes the death of Moses, its traditional author. In point of fact, Smith may be suggesting, Moses had seen it all himself, in panoramic vision, long before he died.

103. Old Testament Manuscript 1, 13, in *Joseph Smith's New Translation of the Bible*, 100 [Moses 6:44].

for the seer's stones. But whatever their specific equipment, seers experience panoramic visions.

In his Egyptian project of 1835–1842, Smith reported a panoramic vision attributed to the biblical patriarch Abraham. There, a dramatic vision is explicitly tied to the devices of seerhood. Possibly dictated in 1842 (although it draws on material Smith was preaching as early as 1839), this text reflects a meditation on seerhood, the nature of space-time, and the application of panoramic visions. The chapter begins by advertising Abraham's ownership of "the Urim and Thummim" (special objects so closely identified with the Book of Mormon interpreters and Smith's own seer stones that they are often difficult to distinguish) and then launches into a spectacular merger of astronomy, the nature of temporality, the macrocosm/microcosm of space-time, and sacerdotal genealogy.[104] Then comes a typical panoramic vision. Abraham possesses the device(s) of seership and employs them to gain the vision, along the way meditating on the nature of time and the interdependence of cosmic and human history.[105]

In that panoramic vision, Abraham witnesses a backward extension of the visions to the time before mortal time—what could be called, without distortion, a theogony. There Abraham learned that God "came down in the beginning in the midst of all the intelligences"—human spirits before their mortal birth—that he had seen. Then follows a parenthetical comment to explain the reference to a vision of intelligences "that were organized before the world was." God tells Abraham that his story started at that assembly of the best of the premortal human spirits. As happens often with theogony, the scene devolves rapidly into a cosmic war among the gods. Jesus Christ is introduced much like his presentation as part of Moriancumer's panoramic vision in Ether, as is his brother, a Lucifer similar to Milton's Satan. This cosmic war initiated the sequence of events that would be witnessed in panoramic visions.

Panoramic visions of history thus figure in all of Smith's scriptural works. While there is no definitive proof, the evidence for an association between such visions and translation is suggestive. Nephi, Moriancumer, and Moroni repeatedly connect panoramic visions to scripture and the emblems of seeric translation, and the pattern of panoramic visions persisted in Smith's later revelations, when he used a seer stone much less often.

104. On sacerdotal genealogy, see Brown, *In Heaven as It Is on Earth*, 204–8.
105. "The Book of Abraham," *Times and Seasons*, 15 March 1842, 719 [Abraham 3].

Seers are translators. Seers see panoramic visions. Are these parallel methods to puncture the wall of time, or could they be facets of the same activity? Why use "seer" to describe the sacred translator and then discuss seers' panoramic visions unless to suggest that such activities were relevant to the Book of Mormon's production? Contextually, these activities overlap substantially. The relevance of panoramic visions to translation mechanics may raise a few concerns, however, that merit evaluation.

Panoramic Visions and Translation Mechanism

How might the panoramic visions of seers relate to translation mechanics? Much of the Book of Mormon is written from the first-person perspective, in the voice of its narrators. While long sections read as if the narrator is an external observer who utilizes secondhand reports, substantial sections report the inner mental life of participants. Readers occasionally hear the narrators' voices directly. If panoramic visions account at least in part for translation mechanics, how is it that the book is written as if Smith were himself taking dictation from Nephi or Mormon? Relevant precedents from Mormon scriptures that use the voice of God may illuminate this question.

Both the Book of Mormon authors and Smith in his own revelations periodically speak in the first person on behalf of Christ.[106] While the proposal of this chapter opens another series of questions about the mechanics of religious experience, Smith may have understood himself as seeing with Christ's eyes in those situations, and thereby speaking from Christ's perspective. On this model, first-person narratives arise from a kind of seeing and then speaking on behalf of the individual whose vision has been shared. Indeed, the panoramic visions themselves generally involve a guide who shares the perception of the vision. Whatever experience or authority allowed Smith to speak in the first-person voice of Jesus could allow Smith to speak similarly on behalf of Nephi, Jacob, Alma, Mormon, and Moroni.

The famous Book of Mormon opener, "I, Nephi," could be read differently in light of panoramic visions and first-person vicarious revelation. One could imagine Smith seeing Nephite history through Nephi's eyes and reporting what he saw using Nephi's voice. A vision of Nephi's story plus the capacity to speak in the name of Nephi could account for the text as it exists today. Such

106. See Revelation, 13 August 1831, in *JSP*-D2:44–55 [D&C 62]; Revelation, 11 September 1831, in *JSP*-D2:61–67 [D&C 64]; 2 Nephi 10; and Jacob 2.

an explanation would have the benefit of contextualizing Smith's work on the Book of Mormon within his other religious texts while mirroring several key narratives within the Book of Mormon—especially those relating to seerhood.[107]

A passage late in Alma may provide support for this idea. In a report of a letter from the army general Helaman to the senior commander Moroni, Helaman suddenly and transiently changes from the first person to the third person before reverting back to the first person.[108] The momentary lapse of first-person narration occurs again in 3 Nephi 21:11, where the phrase "which am Jesus Christ" is inserted almost parenthetically. The occasional instability of narrative voice—while it could hypothetically represent an intentional editorial practice—might reflect Smith's fluctuating from his own voice to the voice of the individual for whom he was speaking. Some of the apparent stylistic differences underlying stylometric disputes in the Book of Mormon could represent Smith's resonance with the personality of the individual for whom he was writing (or, in a strictly naturalistic reading, the personality of the character he was imagining).

A story in the Book of Alma provides a possible mechanism whereby such a vision could incorporate the mental lives of the people whose lives are on display. When the Lamanite King Lamoni first encounters the Nephite evangelist Ammon, this Ammon performs a wonder—"being filled with the Spirit of God," therefore Ammon "perceived the thoughts" of Lamoni. This causes the king to wonder whether Ammon were a divine being, but Ammon explains that his capacity to read minds comes because "a portion of [the Holy] Spirit dwelleth in me, which giveth me knowledge." Tying this telepathy to panoramic visions, Ammon explains to Lamoni that God "looketh down upon all the children of men; and he knows all the thoughts and intents of the heart; for by his hand were they all created from the beginning."[109] Other examples of telepathy appear in the encounter between Alma and Korihor in Alma and again in 3 Nephi.[110] Shortly before Christ's visit to America, onlookers describe a later prophet named Nephi as being godlike in his special abilities, including the fact that "he has told us the thoughts of our hearts."[111]

107. This might also explain how Nephi can speak in the first person for his father's deathbed sermon in 2 Nephi 3.

108. Alma 56:52.

109. Alma 18:16–32.

110. Alma 30:42, 52–53; 3 Nephi 28:6.

111. Helaman 9:41.

Outside the Book of Mormon text, a panoramic vision model of translation makes sense of two reports of Smith's exposures to ancient America that are otherwise obscure. In his 1842 history of the church, Smith reported that as a result of his encounter with the angel Moroni, he was "also informed concerning the aboriginal inhabitants of this country, and shown who they were, and from whence they came." Moreover, he was given "a brief sketch of their origin, progress, civilization, laws, governments, of their righteousness and iniquity, and the blessings of God being finally withdrawn from them as a people." This, he reported, "was made known unto me."[112] Smith did not define what he meant precisely by "shown" and "made known," but the former verb suggests something like a panoramic vision of history.

Shortly after Smith's death, his mother, Lucy Mack Smith, remembered changes in their family life subsequent to Joseph Jr.'s encounter with Moroni. In her later account, she reported:

> During our evening conversations, Joseph would occasionally give us some of the most amusing recitals that could be imagined: he would describe the ancient inhabitants of this continent; their dress, mode of travelling, and the animals upon which they rode; their cities, and their buildings, with every particular; he would describe their mode of warfare, as also their religious worship. This he would do with as much ease, seemingly, as if he had spent his whole life with them.[113]

Lucy Mack Smith's chronology may or may not be reliable, but it seems reasonable to believe that Joseph Jr. reported to his family, probably independent of the dictation of the Book of Mormon, events from ancient American history. Such details might have been available to him from panoramic visions of that history, the same sort of visions that the Book of Mormon repeatedly described. If Lucy is a reliable witness on fact if not chronology, then her son apparently claimed, at least implicitly, to have had visions of ancient American history in general terms, even if he did not formally associate them with translation mechanics.

112. Joseph Smith, "Church History," *Times and Seasons*, 1 March 1842, 707. The quoted section remained unchanged in a revised version made for inclusion in a contemporaneous survey of American churches. See I. Daniel Rupp, ed., *An Original History of the Religious Denominations at Present Existing in the United States* (Philadelphia: J. Y. Humphreys, 1844), 410.

113. Lucy Mack Smith, History, 1845, 87, handwriting of Howard Coray and Martha Jane Knowlton Coray, Church History Library, The Church of Jesus Christ of Latter-day Saints, Salt Lake City.

A late, hostile reminiscence of an 1826 legal hearing in which Smith was accused, roughly, of being a confidence man, purported to describe Smith's experience of seerhood. While there is a high risk of inaccuracy in such late and critical accounts, this observer reported Smith as indicating that he "discovered that time, place and distance were annihilated" when he was seeing through his seer stones, the instruments on which he primarily relied for the Book of Mormon translation.[114] Friendly reminiscences—also late and biased—have tended to endorse similar models of Smith as a seer of panoramic visions. One, typically, maintains that Smith reported seeing the "grand panorama" of at least Genesis and perhaps the whole of Bible history.[115] In an 1843 sermon, Smith described what he had "seen in vision," including his family rising from their tombs at the time of the general resurrection.[116] Reflecting generally on the nature of his prophetic revelations, Smith then described his desire to have his followers understand the visions that, in his own words, "roll like an overflowing surge before my mind."[117]

Later in his career, Smith gave some indication of his experience of revelation generally, of which translation appears to be a specific subset. In characterizing revelation around 1839, Smith indicated, according to a contemporaneous account, that when a believer becomes pure and filled with faith, "the visions of the heavens will be opened unto him & the Lord will teach him face to face & he may have a perfect knowledge of the mysteries of the kingdom of God. & this is the state & place where the ancient Saints arived at when they had such glorious visions. Isaiah[,] Ezekiel, John upon the Isle of Patmos, St Paul in the third heavens."[118] Isaiah and John of Patmos were key figures in the Book of Mormon's apocalyptic tradition, commonly associated with panoramic visions. It seems likely that Joseph Smith was describing the chance that his followers could experience what he himself had.

A panoramic theory of translation must grapple with various problems, including the fact that the Book of Mormon does not explicitly invoke

114. William D. Purple, "Joseph Smith, the Originator of Mormonism: Historical Reminiscences of the Town of Afton," *Chenango Union*, 2 May 1877, 3.

115. According to a late reminiscence, Joseph Smith once stated: "After I got through translating the Book of Mormon, I took up the Bible to read with the Urim and Thummim. I read the first Chapter of Genesis and I saw the things as they were done. I turned over the next and the whole passed before me like a grand panorama and so on chapter after chapter until I read the whole of it. I saw it all!" Lorenzo Brown, statement, 1880, quoted in Robert J. Matthews, *"A Plainer Translation": Joseph Smith's Translation of the Bible; A History and Commentary* (Provo, UT: Brigham Young University, 1975), 25.

116. Joseph Smith, Journal, 21 January 1835, in *JSP*-J1:167–68 [D&C 137].

117. Joseph Smith, Journal, 16 April 1843, in *JSP*-J2:360.

118. Joseph Smith, Discourse, between circa 26 June and circa 2 July 1839, in *JSP*-D6:525.

panoramic visions as the mechanism of its own translation. However, the lack of explicit endorsement of the panoramic vision model is the same as for all other models of translation mechanics. One could reason that if a seer can see anything, he or she can see text. And yet the Book of Mormon reports no such textual visions. Neither Smith nor his scriptures ever explicitly described the specifics of the translation process. All attempts to account for the subjective experience of translation will require suggestive rather than definitive evidence. Models will have to be judged at some level on how well they comport with what is known about overlapping elements of early Latter-day Saint thought and culture and whether they account for other aspects of Smith's work. In this model of a prophetic God's-eye-view of human history that creates scripture, the Book of Mormon text may illuminate at least part of its own production. Whatever translation mechanism is ultimately adopted, it will need to engage the visions that are ubiquitous within Smith's scriptures and closely tied to the seer's powers and obligations.

CONCLUSION

No available evidence can definitively settle the question of Smith's subjective experience as he spoke aloud the English words that became the Book of Mormon. Text-internal clues from the scriptures Smith was responsible for strongly suggest that he was, in general, not reading from a seer stone or from any other source text. Whatever else was happening, if this evidence is correct, Smith was speaking but not reading. How specifically he obtained the words he spoke cannot be conclusively demonstrated on the basis of current evidence, although some hints do exist.

Whatever the mechanism, Smith considered translation to be among the spiritual gifts that were central to his anticessationist gospel. The closest models of Smith's subjective experience, at least on the basis of text-internal evidence, are probably either direct inspiration or something like panoramic visions. While the plates and the stones were the core special objects for a seer, at once antique echoes and mystical conduits of supra-individual power, Smith's contact with them does not appear to have been in support of a visual-verbal model.

These observations about the possible nature of Smith's translations point toward a key theme: Smith's translations are deeply metaphysical and concerned fundamentally with human transformation and interconnection. There are linguistic elements in these translations to be sure, but liberating these documents from the requirement that they be linguistic in the flat, secular sense appears truer to the documents at hand. The mechanistic insights identified in this chapter—the primacy of orality, the relevance of panoramic visions, Smith's transformative agency—are part and parcel of a broader metaphysics of translation that place Smith and his followers in a strenuous contest with key aspects of modern secularity. This contest has important implications for Latter-day Saints and their observers.

7

Joseph Smith, Helen Schucman, and the Experience of Producing a Spiritual Text

Comparing the Translating of the Book of Mormon and the Scribing of A Course in Miracles

ANN TAVES

When Mormon historian Steven C. Harper responded to my presentation on the "materialization" of the golden plates at the 2013 conference of the Mormon History Association, he asked how I would explain the relatively rapid production of the Book of Mormon, if there were no ancient golden plates.[1] Harper's question was premised on a feature of the process that many Mormon apologists have used to defend the validity of the Book of Mormon. I responded by saying that this question should be approached by comparing the process of producing the Book of Mormon with the production of other complex texts that the authors attribute to otherworldly sources.

Although a number of scholars have suggested the idea,[2] Scott Dunn offered the first sustained comparison of this sort. Dunn, the managing editor of *Sunstone* magazine—a periodical dedicated to Mormon theology, history, and cultural studies—wrote an article for the magazine on "spirit writing," in which

1. This paper was later published: Ann Taves, "History and the Claims of Revelation: Joseph Smith and the Materialization of the Golden Plates," *Numen* 61, no. 1–2 (2014): 182–207. See also Ann Taves, "History and the Claims of Revelation: Joseph Smith and the Materialization of the Golden Plates," chap. 7 in *The Expanded Canon: Perspectives on Mormonism & Sacred Texts*, ed. Blair G. Van Dyke, Brian D. Birch, and Boyd J. Petersen, UVU Comparative Mormon Studies (Salt Lake City: Greg Kofford Books, 2018). The author compared the religious experiences and activities of Joseph Smith, Helen Schucman, and Bill Wilson in her book *Revelatory Events: Three Case Studies of the Emergence of New Spiritual Paths* (Princeton and Oxford: Princeton University Press, 2016). This chapter focuses on the close comparison between Smith's production of the Book of Mormon and Schucman's production of *A Course in Miracles*, especially considering how Schucman's production experience may shed light on Smith's production experience.

The author expresses gratitude to Steven C. Harper, Stephen J. Fleming, Kathleen Flake, and participants in the Translation Seminar for comments and feedback on earlier versions; to Michael MacKay and Mark Ashurst-McGee for their detailed editorial suggestions; and to Judith Skutch Whitson for permission to quote from the Schucman DVD.

2. See, for example, Lawrence Foster, "New Paradigms for Understanding Mormonism and Mormon History," *Dialogue: A Journal of Mormon Thought* 29, no. 3 (Fall 1996): 62.

he concluded that "Smith's translation experience fits comfortably within the larger world of scrying, channeling, and automatic writing," and helps to illuminate a number of issues that are otherwise difficult to explain.[3] Mormon scholars have largely dismissed Dunn's comparative approach, though Robert A. Rees—a Mormon humanities professor—offered a thoughtful critique, and religious studies scholars have failed to elaborate on it.[4] This chapter builds on Dunn's work, refining and clarifying issues of method and offering a specific comparison—Helen Schucman and her dictation of *A Course of Miracles*—that may advance our understanding of what Smith experienced while engaged in the "translation" of the Book of Mormon.

ISSUES OF METHOD IN COMPARATIVE STUDIES

All comparisons begin with a perceived point of similarity, which then allows a consideration of both similarities and differences between the phenomena being compared.[5] Religious studies scholars often use a single term or short phrase to identify this point of comparison. These words and phrases are often loaded with presuppositions that bias the comparison in one way or another. In this case, the terms used to refer to the production of texts—such as writing, translating, scribing, channeling, scrying, copying, forging, and so on—embed claims regarding the original source of the text and its current mode of production or transmission. When Joseph Smith and his followers refer to "translating" the Book of Mormon, they presuppose the recovery of an ancient text in an archaic language—which requires translation. When Helen Schucman and her followers refer to scribing *A Course in Miracles,* they presuppose the presence of a voice dictating the text—which needs to be transcribed. Comparisons can be made more evenhandedly by avoiding the application of labels that those being compared would not apply to themselves and by specifying the point of similarity that interests us in terms that would be acceptable to those with a stake in the phenomena being compared.

When Dunn referred to "automaticity" in the title of his article on the Book of Mormon, he was alluding to the literature on "automatic writing"—a term

3. Scott C. Dunn, "Automaticity and the Dictation of the Book of Mormon," in *American Apocrypha: Essays on the Book of Mormon*, ed. Dan Vogel and Brent Lee Metcalfe (Salt Lake City: Signature Books, 2002), 33; Scott C. Dunn, "Spirit Writing: Another Look at the Book of Mormon," *Sunstone*, June 1985, 17–26.

4. Robert A. Rees, "The Book of Mormon and Automatic Writing," *Journal of Book of Mormon Studies* 15, no. 1 (2006): 4–17.

5. Jonathan Z. Smith, *Drudgery Divine: On the Comparison of Early Christianities and the Religions of Late Antiquity* (Chicago: University of Chicago Press, 1990), 51.

that is sometimes used to distinguish the methods used in "channeling and scrying" texts from ordinary writing methods. Dunn compared Joseph Smith with Pearl Curran, who published poetry and fiction in the early twentieth century that she claimed was authored by a "discarnate entity" and communicated to her by means of a Ouija board. In setting up his comparison between Smith and Curran, Dunn adapted Ian Stevenson's definition of automatic writing. Stevenson, a professor of psychiatry and an investigator of the paranormal, defined automatic writing as: "Writing that is done without the writer being conscious of what he is writing . . . Perhaps I should say [Stevenson adds] 'fully conscious' because automatic writers may have some awareness of why they are writing as they write. The activity seems to occur, however, without the subject's ordinary voluntary control and for this reason is called automatic."[6] Dunn adapted this definition to apply to texts that were written or dictated "in a relatively rapid, seemingly effortless and fluent manner with no sense of control over the content. Indeed, except for sometimes knowing a word or two moments in advance of writing or speaking, the individual is typically not consciously aware of what the content of the writing will be."[7] In revising Stevenson's definition, Dunn made two important moves: he included dictating as well as writing, and he did not specify whether the individual was in an ordinary state of waking consciousness or an altered state of some sort, such as a trance. His focus was thus on the production of words, either written or dictated, in a "seemingly effortless and fluent manner with no sense of control over the content."

Although Rees acknowledged some similarities between Smith and "producers of some automatically written texts,"[8] as well as some key differences, Dunn's point of analogy is problematic, because it focuses too much on alleged features of "automatic writing." In overemphasizing the "rapid, seemingly effortless and fluent manner" in which the text is dictated and the ostensible lack of control over the content, it misses the more crucial underlying feature: the speakers' sense that the words they are dictating are not their own. The crucial point of analogy is the subjects' ability to produce a complex text through a process of speaking or writing words that they (presumably sincerely) feel are not their own, and the rapid, fluid pace of the text's production that leads them and (at least some) others to conclude that the words come from sources beyond themselves.

6. Quoted in Dunn, "Automaticity and the Dictation of the Book of Mormon," 37n5.
7. Ibid., 18.
8. Rees, "The Book of Mormon and Automatic Writing," 10.

JOSEPH SMITH'S EXPERIENCE OF TRANSLATING THE GOLDEN PLATES

Before speculating on what Smith might have experienced when he was translating, it is important to distinguish between *descriptions* that those involved in the process offered of what Smith was doing, *inferences* that they drew from his actions, and explicit *claims* made by Smith and his followers about those actions. We can start with the last point: the claim that Smith translated ancient gold plates. Because historians—both Latter-day Saints and otherwise—agree that Smith did not look at the plates when translating, this claim about what he was doing does not directly affect the effort to piece together what he experienced while doing so. Rather, as Terryl Givens argues, the presence of this material object grounded the Book of Mormon in "artifactual reality."[9] Although Smith did not look at the plates while dictating the text, the presence of this concealed object bolstered the insider *explanation* of what was taking place by establishing that there was something to translate. In doing so, it created an ostensibly firm boundary between the Book of Mormon as a translated work of scripture and a channeled or fictional work. It has also led to much speculation by Smith's contemporaries and by later Mormon scholars on the relationship between the process and the ancient plates.

Sidestepping that issue for the moment, we can begin with the evidence derived from the observations of eyewitnesses and the manuscript version of the Book of Mormon.[10] Based on this evidence, Mormon historian and apologist Daniel C. Peterson offers a list of facts that should not be overlooked in offering explanations of the production of the Book of Mormon. For instance, Smith orally dictated a lengthy and complex book to his scribes in a short period of time. The scribes could see Smith and reported that he did not make use of books or manuscripts or even the golden plates, which were obscured, but that he looked at a stone buried in the bottom of a hat, with the hat drawn

9. Terryl L. Givens, *By the Hand of Mormon: The American Scripture that Launched a New World Religion* (Oxford and New York: Oxford University Press, 2002), 12, 42, 177–78; Kathleen Flake, "Translating Time: The Nature and Function of Joseph Smith's Narrative Canon," *Journal of Religion* 87, no. 4 (October 2007): 501.

10. Daniel C. Peterson, "A Response: What the Manuscripts and Eyewitnesses Tell Us about the Translation of the Book of Mormon," in *Uncovering the Original Text of the Book of Mormon: History and Findings of the Critical Text Project*, ed. M. Gerald Bradford and Alison V. P. Coutts (Salt Lake City: Neal A. Maxwell Institute, 2002); Daniel C. Peterson, "Editor's Introduction—Not So Easily Dismissed: Some Facts for Which Counter Explanations of the Book of Mormon Will Need to Account," *FARMS Review* 17, no. 2 (2005): xi–xlix; Royal Skousen, "How Joseph Smith Translated the Book of Mormon: Evidence from the Original Manuscript," *Journal of Book of Mormon Studies* 7, no. 1 (1998): 22–31.

around his face to block out exterior light. Also, according to David Whitmer, who was one of the scribes, Smith could not translate if he had unresolved emotional issues, such as conflict between himself and his wife, Emma Hale Smith. Martin Harris, another scribe, recounted that he could not translate with a similar stone that Harris slipped into the hat. Smith could apparently see and orally spelled out names of people and places. And, there were parts of the text he did not understand and words he could not pronounce. Additionally, Emma Smith and others said they did not believe Joseph Smith was intellectually capable of dictating the Book of Mormon off the top of his head.[11] On one occasion, Emma anecdotally illustrated this point:

> When he stopped for any purpose at any time he would, when he commenced again, begin where he left off without any hesitation, and one time while he was translating he stopped suddenly, pale as a sheet, and said, "Emma, did Jerusalem have walls around it?" When I answered, "Yes," he replied "Oh! I was afraid I had been deceived." He had such a limited knowledge of history at that time that he did not even know that Jerusalem was surrounded by walls.[12]

In addition to portraying Joseph's limited historical knowledge, Emma's reminiscence shows that Smith was aware of what he was dictating and was able to pause to comment on words that presumably did not seem to be his own.

Based on corrections in the original text, Royal Skousen, a Mormon professor of linguistics at Brigham Young University, found evidence to support the claim that it was dictated orally and that the scribes had difficulty keeping up with Smith.[13] The speed at which the translation occurred is also attested by the relatively short period (three months) in which the bulk of the text was produced. Skousen also found indications that Smith could recognize breaks between units in the text but could not tell in advance whether any particular break signaled a new chapter or a new book, from which Skousen infers that Smith did not know what the text was going to say or how it would be organized.[14]

11. Dan Vogel, comp. and ed., *Early Mormon Documents* (Salt Lake City: Signature Books, 1996–2002), 1:542; Peterson, "Editor's Introduction," xv.

12. Emma Smith Bidamon, interview with Edmund C. Briggs, 1856, in Vogel, *Early Mormon Documents*, 1:530–31.

13. Skousen, "How Joseph Smith Translated the Book of Mormon," 25.

14. Ibid., 27–28.

While many sources attest to these points, a few who were close to, but not actually involved in, the translation process offer more details. Joseph Knight Sr. explained that when looking in the hat, "a sentence would apper in Brite Roman Letters then he would tell the writer [i.e., the scribe] and he would write it then that would go away the next sentance would Come and so on But if it was not Spelt rite it would not go way till it was rite."[15] According to David Whitmer, however, "the [spiritual] light and characters appeared in the hat together with the interpretation which he uttered and was written by the scribe." In an interview a few years later, Whitmer said that when looking in the hat, "he [Smith] would see, not the stone, but what appeared like an oblong piece of parchment on which the hieroglyphics would appear, and also the translation in the English language, all appearing in bright luminous letters."[16]

There are several problems with taking these accounts at face value. First, although the sources agree that Smith saw things when looking in the hat, they disagree about what he saw. In one case he saw sentences in bright roman letters and in the other he saw individual characters, each interpreted in English. Second, both go well beyond what an external observer could have seen in terms of describing what Smith perceived, something that Smith did not indicate directly. Third, these are late reports that could have been based on what Smith told them, but, given the differences, it seems more likely that they made inferences about what he perceived from what they observed and what they believed. Thus, the best extant eyewitness evidence conveys the fact that Smith dictated words to a scribe while looking at a stone in a hat, but reveals little about what Smith perceived while doing so. As MacKay and Dirkmaat indicate, the eyewitness evidence does not establish *how* the words he dictated came to him, including "whether the words actually appeared on the stone or were only in his head."[17]

Nonetheless, in grappling with the relationship between Smith's dictation and the claim that he was translating ancient plates, Mormon scholars have speculated about what Smith perceived. Royal Skousen argues that Smith saw specific words written out in English and read them off to the scribes.[18] Daniel C. Peterson adopts a similar position, arguing that "Smith seems to have

15. Vogel, *Early Mormon Documents*, 4:17–18.

16. Ibid., 5:82, 104.

17. Michael Hubbard MacKay and Gerrit J. Dirkmaat, *From Darkness unto Light: Joseph Smith's Translation and Publication of the Book of Mormon* (Provo, UT: Religious Studies Center, Brigham Young University, 2015).

18. Skousen, "How Joseph Smith Translated the Book of Mormon," 23.

been reading from something . . . that was new and strange to him, and . . . that required a certain emotional or mental focus before it could be read."[19] This theory, while faithful to the scribes' descriptions, makes Smith a reader of the text rather than a translator, which some LDS scholars find problematic. To get around this, others have argued for a two-step process in which Smith received ideas, impressions, or images, which he then translated by putting them into his own words. Stephen D. Ricks, D. Michael Quinn, and Kathleen Flake all rely on Smith's revelation dictated to Oliver Cowdery in which Cowdery was told "you must study it out in your mind" to support their view.[20] Quinn and Ricks do not dismiss the evidence that Smith saw words, but argue that the English words appeared after he formulated a translation of the ideas or impressions he received. Brant Gardner, a Latter-day Saint who has studied Mesoamerican history, offers a recent version of this theory. Drawing from research in psychology and neuroscience, he proposes that Smith received revelation in the form of pre-language, which then appeared as "eidetic images." This experience allowed Smith "to 'see' the words in English that he read to his scribes."[21]

Scott Dunn questions the use of this revelation to understand Smith's experience, as does Dan Vogel. Both note that the revelation was addressed to Oliver Cowdery, who was told in a previous revelation that he had two gifts, the gift of "revelation" and "the gift of working with the rod."[22] Dunn and Vogel suggest that Cowdery translated using his divining rod rather than Smith's seer stone.[23] Unlike seer stones, which were used by those seeking supernatural vision, divining rods were used for their movement, which were often interpreted as yes or no responses. This interpretation suggests a more interactive process in which Cowdery was expected to "study it out in [his] mind" and then check what he came up with by means of his divining rod—or by an internal, spiritual, experience that nevertheless mirrored the binary model of rod divination.[24] Whether or not this was the case, one should not simply

19. Peterson, "A Response," 70.

20. *JSP*-D1:48–50; D. Michael Quinn, ed. and trans., "The First Months of Mormonism: A Contemporary View by Rev. Diedrich Willers," *New York History* 54, no. 3 (1973): 320–21; Stephen D. Ricks, "Notes and Communications: Translation of the Book of Mormon; Interpreting the Evidence," *Journal of Book of Mormon Studies* 2, no. 2 (1993): 201–6; Kathleen Flake, "Translating Time," 497–527.

21. Brant A. Gardner, *The Gift and Power: Translating the Book of Mormon* (Salt Lake City: Greg Kofford Books, 2012), 319.

22. Revelation, April 1829-B, in *JSP*-D1:44–47 [D&C 8].

23. Dunn, "Automaticity and the Dictation of the Book of Mormon," 31; Dan Vogel, *Joseph Smith: The Making of a Prophet* (Salt Lake City: Signature Books, 2004), 172–73. See also Gardner, *The Gift and Power*, 310–15.

24. Cowdery was told: "You must study it out in your mind; then you must ask me if it be right, and if it is right, I will cause that your bosom shall burn within you: therefore, you shall feel that it is right; but if

assume from this revelation to Cowdery that Smith himself was studying the translation out in his mind in this manner. The translation method employed by Smith, based on his experience with seer stones, may have been different from the translation method employed by Cowdery, based on his experience with a divining rod or instructions he received from Smith.

Vogel also draws attention to the earlier revelation in a way that is rarely cited in discussions of what Smith perceived. In the earlier revelation, also dictated to Cowdery in April 1829, Cowdery was told:

> I say unto you that as Shuredly as the Lord liveth . . . shall ye receive a knowledge of whatsoever things ye shall ask with an honest heart believeing that you Shall receive, a knowledge concerning the engraveings of old Records which are ancient which contain those parts of my Scriptures of which hath been spoken by the manifestation of my Spirit yea Behold I will tell you in your mind & in your heart by the Holy Ghost which Shall come upon you & which shall dwell in your heart now Behold this is the spirit of Revelation . . . this is thy gift . . . this is thy gift now this is not all for thou hast another gift which is the gift of working with the sprout [later published as "the gift of working with the rod" and even later as "the gift of Aaron"].[25]

This revelation, delivered in the first person by an unnamed source, does not say anything about the observable mechanics of the process, but rather offers an internal description of how knowledge was conveyed to those who ask with "an honest heart believeing that you Shall receive." It specifically refers to receiving "knowledge concerning the engraveings of old Records," but associates this with both the gift of revelation and the gift of translation. Indeed, the original heading supplied by John Whitmer reads: "A Revelation to Oliver he being desirous to know whether the Lord would grant him the gift of ~~Revelation & th~~ Translation."[26] This early revelation, given shortly after Cowdery arrived to help with the translation, is a contemporaneous text that predates all of the accounts given by eyewitnesses to the translation process. It suggests (1) that Smith, in giving voice to this revelation, was not making a clear

it be not right, you shall have no such feelings, but you shall have a stupor of thought, that shall cause you to forget the thing which is wrong." Revelation, April 1829-D, in *JSP*-D1:50 [D&C 9:8–9].

25. Revelation, April 1829-B, in *JSP*-D1:46 [D&C 8:1–6].

26. Revelation, April 1829-B, in *JSP*-D1:45.

distinction between the gift of revelation and the gift of translation; and (2) that the Holy Ghost was involved in the process.

The role of the Holy Ghost in this 1829 description of the translation-revelation process parallels the account offered by the Whitmer family's former pastor, Diedrich Willers, in June 1830.[27] As translated from the German by Neal Chandler, it reads: "The Lord had appointed him to translate the same [golden plates] from ancient languages into English. . . . And that through the use of these spectacles he (Smith) was enabled to read these languages which he had never studied and that the Holy Ghost would give him the translation in English."[28] In this formulation, while the spectacles enabled Smith to read languages he had never studied, it was nonetheless the Holy Ghost that actually gave him the English translation.

OBSERVATIONS ON SMITH'S TRANSLATION EXPERIENCE

Three observations can be drawn from the foregoing analysis:

1. The two-stage theory, which distinguishes between reading and translating, is premised on the belief that there was an original text in an ancient language. This theory also relies heavily on the directive to "study it out in [his] mind," which was addressed to Cowdery, and may or may not have reflected Smith's experience.
2. The one-stage theory and the second stage of most two-stage theories build on the descriptions provided by the scribes and other witnesses. That he engaged in spelling out names is the best evidence that Smith visually saw words. Although the scribes provide first hand *observations* of Smith's outward behavior, they did not have direct access to his subjective experience. Because the scribes were observers, they made inferences about what Smith was experiencing based on what they saw, what they learned from discussions with Smith, what they believed, or some combination thereof. Evidence that Smith *sometimes* spelled words does not mean that he *always* saw words.
3. Except for Quinn, neither theory reflects on the role of the Holy Ghost in the process as mentioned in the revelation about Cowdery's gifts and the Willers letter. Although the earlier revelation regarding

27. Quinn, "The First Months of Mormonism," 320–21, 323.
28. Vogel, *Early Mormon Documents*, 5:272–73.

Cowdery's gifts, like the later revelation about studying out a translation in one's mind, was addressed to Cowdery, the description of the role of the Holy Ghost seems to be a general statement about the subjective experience of receiving revelation, which is specified as knowledge of the engravings on the ancient records. The Willers letter, written about a year later, corroborates the role of the Holy Ghost in the translation process. The contemporaneous revelations, coming directly from the Lord via Smith (or from the recesses of Smith's mind) at the time when Smith and Cowdery were in the midst of producing the Book of Mormon, are the closest thing we have to a real-time, subjective report of Smith's experience. When the revelation states, "I will tell you in your mind & in your heart by the Holy Ghost," it suggests a process of "telling" in which "the Holy Ghost [put knowledge in the form of words] in [Smith's] mind & in [his] heart."

COMPARING JOSEPH SMITH AND HELEN SCHUCMAN

An understanding of what Smith perceived can be advanced by comparing the indirect evidence that is available for Smith with the more detailed information provided by Helen Schucman, who produced *A Course in Miracles*. Schucman, a psychologist at Columbia University, claimed that she "scribed" *A Course in Miracles* by writing down the words dictated by the "voice of Jesus" in shorthand. She then read the words aloud to her colleague, psychologist William Thetford, who transcribed them (see Figure 7.1).

On the surface, translating an ancient record by the gift and power of God sounds rather different from scribing the voice of Jesus. Whereas Smith is generally believed to have *seen* things in his seer stone, Schucman usually referred to *hearing* an internal voice. Smith dictated what he saw to scribes; Schucman scribed what she heard in shorthand and then dictated the shorthand to a colleague, who typed it. Both, nonetheless, produced a complex text through a process of speaking or writing words that they felt were not their own; moreover, they produced the text in a fashion that led them and others to conclude that the words originated from sources beyond themselves.

Both texts—the Book of Mormon and *A Course in Miracles*—are lengthy and complex, although they reflect very different genres. The 1830 edition of the Book of Mormon was 588 pages long; *A Course in Miracles* includes the main text (669 pages), a workbook (448 pages), a manual for teachers (92 pages),

FIGURE 7.1. Helen Schucman with William Thetford. Between 1965 and 1972, Helen Schucman "scribed" *A Course in Miracles* in shorthand as the words came to her from an inner Voice. She read the shorthand to William Thetford, who served as her typist. Foundation for Inner Peace, Mill Valley, CA.

and two supplements (46 pages). The Book of Mormon was transcribed intermittently over the course of eleven months, with most of the transcription taking place between April and June of 1829. Schucman transcribed the three main texts of *A Course in Miracles* over the course of seven years—beginning in October 1965 and ending in September 1972—with a break of about seven months between the text and the workbook and about a year between the workbook and the manual. In terms of genre, the Book of Mormon reflects the composite structure of the Hebrew Bible, with its multiple books, authors, and points of view. As stated by Grant Hardy, a professor of history and a Book of Mormon scholar, the Book of Mormon "is first and foremost a narrative, offered to us by specific, named narrators. The heterogeneous materials in the Book of Mormon ... are all represented as the work of the three primary editor/historians."[29] It reflects the language and cadence of the King James Version of the Bible and makes use of chiasmus, a rhetorical device found in portions of

29. Grant Hardy, *Understanding the Book of Mormon: A Reader's Guide* (Oxford and New York: Oxford University Press, 2010), xv.

the Bible, in which clauses are inverted to create a parallel structure. *A Course in Miracles*, by way of contrast, is a complex, philosophically-oriented teaching text with a workbook for students and a manual for teachers. In terms of genre, it is didactic, rather than narrative, although much of it is composed in blank verse and iambic pentameter and thus quite poetic.[30]

Although both books were edited, most of the original transcript of the Book of Mormon is extant and so is the entire set of Schucman's shorthand notebooks, as well as numerous subsequent versions of each. Beyond the first five chapters of the published *Course*, the original dictated text, like the Book of Mormon, was only lightly revised.[31] The unedited versions of both texts have features, such as the lack of punctuation, that are characteristic of oral composition or stream of consciousness writing.

Like Smith, Schucman did not feel like the words of the text were her own. The words came quickly, and she could not anticipate them ahead of time. As she wrote in her autobiography: "I would feel it coming on almost daily, and sometimes more than once a day. . . . I wrote in shorthand in a notebook that I soon began to carry around with me, just in case."[32] Moreover, she continued: "I never knew when I started a sentence how it would end, and the ideas came so rapidly that I had trouble keeping up with them even in the system of shorthand symbols and abbreviations I had developed during many years of taking class notes and recording therapy sessions."[33] In light of the evidence Skousen presented regarding the difficulty Smith's scribes had keeping up with him, it appears they too might have been aided by knowledge of shorthand. Moreover, if Skousen is correct in his inference that Smith did not know in advance what the text was going to say or how it would be organized, then he like Schucman may not have known at the outset how a sentence would end.

Followers of both Smith and Schucman argue that the texts are too complex for them to have invented them, given their individual limitations. Smith's followers stress his ignorance. His wife, Emma Smith, later reminisced that he "could neither write nor dictate a coherent and well worded letter, let alone . . . a book like the Book of M[ormon]."[34] In the wake of Martin Harris's visit to the

30. Kenneth Wapnick, "The History of the Manuscripts of *A Course in Miracles*," 9, www.facimoutreach.org/qa/questions/ACIM_Manuscript_History.pdf.

31. Kenneth Wapnick, *Absence from Felicity: The Story of Helen Schucman and Her Scribing of* A Course in Miracles, 2nd ed. (Temecula, CA: Foundation for *A Course in Miracles*, 1999), 180.

32. Ibid., 182.

33. Ibid.

34. Emma Smith Bidamon, interview with Joseph Smith III, February 1879, in Vogel, *Early Mormon Documents*, 1:539.

linguists, Harris interpreted the experts' inability to recognize the characters as evidence that the Lord was making use of the "foolish"—in the language of 1 Corinthians 1:27—"to confound the wise." According to Eber Howe, a contemporary critic, "The extreme ignorance and apparent stupidity of this modern prophet, were, by his early followers, looked upon as his greatest merit, and as furnishing the most incontestable proof of his divine mission."[35] Given her doctorate and academic career, Schucman's followers did not stress her ignorance, but rather her intense skepticism and her inability to embrace the teachings of the *Course*. Judith Skutch, an early supporter, stressed the importance of Schucman's and Thetford's lack of preparation in a 1977 interview. "It was important for me," she stated, "that neither of these two people had the background or interest in spiritual literature or psychical experiences that might have prepared them for this."[36] Looking back, Thetford wrote: "As I read the material, I recognized that Helen's ego self in no way could have written what I was reading. It was totally alien to her background, to her interests, and to her mode of conceptualizing abstract ideas. There was simply no way that the ego part of Helen could have done this."[37] Kenneth Wapnick, Schucman's biographer and a teacher of the *Course*, paints a more complex picture, stressing that "the form of the Course is from Helen," though in his view the content was not. In terms of form, Wapnick gave Schucman credit for its idiomatic American English; its poetic, Elizabethan manner of speech; its underlying Platonic philosophy and Freudian ego psychology; its logical structure; and its curricular format.[38]

Both Smith and Schucman were immersed in the genres of their respective texts. Smith was steeped in the King James Version of the Bible; Schucman was a philosophy major in college who loved Plato and Shakespeare.[39] Schucman also knew the Bible very well, quoting from it "almost as readily as she could from Shakespeare."[40] She was a psychologist, trained in Freudian psychology, who did research on ego development. She was also an educator. According to Kenneth Wapnick, she had "one of the most logical minds I have ever seen."[41] At the same time, insider accounts acknowledge factors about both writers that they do not

35. Eber D. Howe Account, 1834, in Ibid., 3:303.

36. Judith Skutch, "A *New Realities* Interview with Judith R. Skutch," conducted by James Bolen, in *New Realities Magazine*, April 1977, http://acim-archives.org/Media/Interviews?Judy-Interview.html.

37. William Thetford, *Life Story* (Mill Valley, CA: Foundation for Inner Peace, 1983, 2009), 19.

38. Wapnick, "The History of the Manuscripts of *A Course in Miracles*," 9.

39. Wapnick, *Absence from Felicity*, 33–34.

40. Ibid., 407.

41. Wapnick, "The History of the Manuscripts of *A Course in Miracles*," 9.

stress, such as Smith's storytelling abilities and Schucman's lifelong attraction to Catholicism and her exposure to the American metaphysical tradition, including Christian Science.[42] Moreover, insiders intimately bound up in the process recount details that prepared Smith to translate and Schucman to scribe. Thus, Smith's mother, Lucy Mack Smith, related that Joseph had (or believed he had) experienced several conversations with an angelic personage who recounted what was written on the plates before the translation began; and Kenneth Wapnick pointed out how much Schucman sounded at times like the Voice in letters she wrote to Thetford months before it instructed her to "take notes."[43]

Finally, while both Smith and Schucman were reluctant to discuss what the process of translating and scribing was like, Schucman participated in a taped interview with David Hammond, the associate editor of *New Reality Magazine*, in 1976 on the condition that it would not be published or circulated. The tape was turned over to James Bolen, the publisher of *New Reality* and a friend of Schucman. In 2006, it was released on DVD by the Foundation for Inner Peace with the understanding that Schucman's conditions applied only during her lifetime. Due to the probing questions of the interviewer, the interview is more revealing than any other surviving description of what Schucman was experiencing as the process unfolded.

SCHUCMAN'S EXPERIENCE OF SCRIBING *A COURSE IN MIRACLES*

Excerpts from the interview are provided in this section, with reformatted paragraphing and questions by the interviewer in italics.

> *Regarding the voice you heard in scribing* A Course in Miracles, *did it come from outside or from within?*
>
> There's nothing that I would call ordinary audition about this at all. It doesn't really . . . it's a curious thing that would be very difficult to explain. Somebody asked whether it was as though your hand was just moving. No, I wrote perfectly voluntarily in response to. . . . I call it "a voice," but a voice has sounds . . . or sounds as though it has something to do with hearing. And I didn't hear anything. I think it's a sort

42. Lucy Smith history, in Vogel, *Early Mormon Documents*, 1:295–96; Wapnick, *Absence from Felicity*, 32, 61 (on Christian Science), 28, 406–7 (on Catholicism).

43. Lucy Smith history, in Vogel, *Early Mormon Documents*, 1:295–96; Wapnick, *Absence from Felicity*, 150, 176–77.

of hearing that you can't really describe. It doesn't have anything to do with ears, or waves hitting a drum or anything on that order. I don't really know. I think maybe I'm using the wrong word when I say "hear." I sort of recognized it. It was very rapid, I couldn't . . . if I didn't catch a phrase, I could sort of say, "Would you mind doing that again?"

This was in your mind?

This was strictly mental. . . .

Is it comparable to anything in terms of how we hear ourselves talk, or like you talk to yourself?

It wasn't my voice. It couldn't have been because it talked about a whole area with which I am entirely unfamiliar.

What about sub-vocalizing? When you're sub-vocalizing, you're hearing the words, you're actually hearing them.

Oh, there's no sub-vocalization. It's a process I really would find impossible to explain. It's never happened to me before. . . .

You could hear the words clearly in your mind even though you didn't hear a sound?

I knew that that was the word . . . I think "knew" may be a better word than "heard." I did not know consciously at the beginning of the sentence how it was going to end. And that puts me under a further handicap in terms of ordinary language. Because ordinarily, I think if you are going to say a sentence you know what it's going to be, you sort of get the Gestalt immediately. But I didn't. And it came very easily, very rapidly, very smoothly. I guess even painlessly, except that it annoyed me to death, but that's irrelevant. I guess "hear" isn't the right word. I could stop anything or pick it up anytime, and I did it in cabs and subways and anywhere, or sort of between phone calls. But you're raising a question I don't think I can answer.

So a certain mechanism went on there, because you heard something you translated into the shorthand style . . .

Yes, but I'm used to shorthand. I use it for group therapy sessions, so shorthand is quite familiar to me. It's really a matter of speed. I couldn't have kept up with it in ordinary writing . . .

Oh, you couldn't . . .

Oh no, it was very rapid. I needed the shorthand.

What about automatic writing, a thing when pen takes over and writes for the person? The person doesn't have any control. Is that similar to what you are describing?

> No, that didn't happen at all. I could have stopped it at any time, and I frequently did. And I was very frequently interrupted, so that I would have to stop . . . I didn't lose awareness of where I was or what I was doing. . . .

At a later point in the interview, Hammond asked Schucman about her desire to change words as she scribed the text. She said that she very quickly learned that doing so interfered with the internal consistency of the text, so she and Thetford went back and replaced the revised words with the original words. Hammond then asked her whether she could remember the original words, in order to restore them, or whether she had to ask for them anew. Schucman responded that she usually remembered, but that there were a few exceptions.

> . . . sometimes—I wouldn't say more than two or three times—I didn't know. But I was aware that there was a goof-off in through there [a change introduced in the text], and I would feel the goof-off more than the right answer. And then, I would sort of look at a blackboard in my head and see it written, the word it should have been. And I would ask, "Can I see it on the blackboard?"
>
> *You would ask and also see it? . . .*
>
> Then I would be reading it. Because on the blackboard I would see it in letters.
>
> *Then it was a very visual thing in your mind.*
>
> Then it was visual. Ordinarily it wasn't. But I think that modality had to come in where I had kind of lost my way and then I really didn't know what the word should be.[44]

AN ALTERNATIVE HYPOTHESIS FOR SMITH'S TRANSLATION METHOD

Comparing Joseph Smith and Helen Schucman allows for several hypotheses. First, although Schucman's experiences are typically characterized more in terms of "hearing" and Smith's in terms of "seeing," the differences are less pronounced upon a closer examination of the details. As Schucman explained, she believed that the term "knew" described the encounter more accurately

44. "A Rare Interview in which Dr. Helen Schucman Describes the 'Voice' that Dictated *A Course in Miracles* (includes the Transcript)" (Foundation for Inner Peace (www.acim.org), 1976, 2006), DVD.

than "heard." Schucman's experience of "knowing" may be a plausible description of what it might have been like if, as suggested, "the Holy Ghost [put knowledge in the form of words] in [Smith's] mind & in [his] heart." Schucman's description was not quite hearing or seeing words, but it was more than receiving impressions or images. Schucman's use of "know" and the revelation's use of "tell" might both infer a flow of words that are consciously recognized (known), while at the same time experienced as arising outside of consciousness as if "told to" the consciously aware self. To clarify, Smith and Schucman might have had a sense of meaning so immediate as to feel as if it were a word.

Second, like Schucman, Smith may have had a great deal of control over the flow of words. According to those involved in the process, Smith was able to stop and start the flow at will, picking up where he left off without prompts from the scribes, as long as he could maintain a certain emotional state. This may have allowed him to pace his delivery to his scribes' ability to write, which was most likely slower than Schucman's shorthand. Schucman said that scribing was not like automatic writing, if that meant "the person doesn't have any control." Her experience, she explained, was that she could have stopped at any time, and often did, either by choice or because she was interrupted.

Third, neither Schucman nor Smith seems to have felt they were in a noticeably altered state of consciousness. As Schucman specifically stated, she did not lose awareness of her surroundings or her own activity. Similarly, Smith's ability to question the accuracy of his own dictation suggests that he was aware of—and at least to some extent able to reflect on—the flow of words as they emerged. Both Schucman and Smith may have been in a state of highly focused awareness.

Finally, Smith, like Schucman, may have been able to shift from a "flow of words" modality into a visual modality in which he was able to see words spelled out. Ordinarily, Schucman said, the process was not visual; it was a matter of "knowing" the words. She switched modes when she sensed she had made a mistake in scribing the text; at which point she was able to envision it as if written on a blackboard and thereby correct any errors. Smith evidently spelled out some proper names, but like Schucman, he may have had the ability to shift into a visual, blackboard-like mode when necessary in order to "see" the spelling, when he was uncertain of what the word should be.

CONCLUSION

Based on similarities in the methods that Smith and Schucman used to produce complex texts that they attributed to a source other than themselves, this chapter has used Helen Schucman's detailed description of what it was like to "scribe" *A Course in Miracles* to suggest an alternative interpretation of the surviving evidence of what it was like for Joseph Smith to "translate" the Book of Mormon. The alternative interpretation brackets the plates as physical artifacts, since Smith did not look at them while dictating, and attempts instead to reconstruct Smith's experience based on what the scribes observed, the evidence embedded in the original transcription, and the revelation that seems to offer the best real-time evidence of what the revelation-translation process was like. This approach suggests that Smith had a highly focused awareness, a strong and immediate sense of meaning (experienced as a flow of words), a considerable degree of control over the experience, and even the ability (as needed) to shift into a visual modality in which he was able to see words spelled out.

8

Nephi's Project
The Gold Plates as Book History

RICHARD LYMAN BUSHMAN

Joseph Smith was not particularly forthcoming about how he translated ancient scripture. In the original preface to the Book of Mormon, he said only that it was done "by the gift and power of God."[1] The few glimpses of the translating process do not describe him looking at the plates. Much of the time, they were wrapped in a cloth lying on the table or hidden away. Smith stared into the interpreters or his seer stone, and spoke the words of the translation. He apparently did not know or even claim to know the language on the plates. Moroni, the final author of the Book of Mormon, called the inscription language "reformed Egyptian."[2] Smith copied some of the script but did not create a lexicon to explain the meaning of the characters.[3] The various accounts depict him sitting day after day looking into the seer stone, shaded from the light by his hat, and pronouncing the words that Oliver Cowdery or another scribe wrote down.[4]

These few clues are of little help in understanding the translation. How did Joseph Smith come by the tens of thousands of words that Latter-day Saints now accept as words from God? Did they come from the engravings on the plates? Did Smith see them in the seer stone? Did they come out of his imagination? Did divine power insert them into his mind as he mouthed them?

1. The Book of Mormon: An Account Written by the Hand of Mormon, upon Plates Taken from the Plates of Nephi, trans. Joseph Smith, Junior (Palmyra, NY: E. B. Grandin, 1830), iii, also 589 [The Testimony of Three Witnesses]. See also Joseph Smith, History, 1838–1856, vol. E-1, 7 September 1843, Addenda, 8 (emphasis added) (accessible in the Histories series of the online edition of *The Joseph Smith Papers*).

2. Mormon 9:32.

3. See Michael Hubbard MacKay, "Performing the Translation: Character Transcripts and Joseph Smith's Earliest Translating Practices," Chapter 4 herein.

4. See John W. Welch, ed., *Opening the Heavens: Accounts of Divine Manifestations, 1820–1844*, 2nd ed. (Provo, UT: Brigham Young University Press; Salt Lake City, UT: Deseret Book, 2017), 126–227.

FIGURE 8.1. First edition of the Book of Mormon. Translated by Joseph Smith, published by E. B. Grandin of Palmyra, New York, in 1830. Publishing Services Department, The Church of Jesus Christ of Latter-day Saints, Salt Lake City; photograph by Welden C. Andersen.

While Joseph Smith's translation process is largely conjectural, there is a great deal written about the process of scripture making within the Book of Mormon. The book reveals its own editorial processes with unusual candor. The reception of inspiration, the delivery of prophecy, and the writing down of the words; forming them into sermons, treatises, and histories; collecting, editing and abridging—all these are remarkably clear. Scholars do not have to tease out how texts were blended and editors intervened as students of the Bible do. Smith's book freely confesses itself to be the product of editors working over old texts for their own purposes. The book discusses at length how it was made: its motivating purposes and political intentions, its physical construction and laborious inscription, its editing and abridgement, its intergenerational transmission and future publication, and its anticipated readership and expected reception. The book provides a transparent account of how scripture emerged from a prophetic society. The Book of Mormon begs to be read as book history and, more particularly, as scriptural book history.

This revelation of editorial process does not clarify exactly how Joseph Smith translated the Book of Mormon: Was it pure inspiration or partly the work of his own imagination? Still, reading the text as book history does have bearing. Understanding how the Book of Mormon was made permits its readers to see translation as part of an ongoing process originating within the book itself. Joseph was one more scripture-maker in a long line of makers beginning with Nephi. Seen in that light translation takes on a new guise. It appears as more a collaboration between God and man than an entirely miraculous intervention.

METAL PLATES AND RECORD KEEPING

The attention to plates on the first page signals the text's intention to focus on book production. The word "plates" appears twice in the title. Texts do not ordinarily announce immediately that they were inscribed on parchment or printed on paper or cut in stone. The Book of Mormon title twice tells readers that the book comes from plates ("An Account Written by the Hand of Mormon upon Plates Taken from the Plates of Nephi"). In the first instance, the words "Written by the Hand of Mormon upon Plates" echo the phrase in 2 Thessalonians 2:17, "the salutation of Paul with mine own hand," attesting to the authenticity of the writing. From the start, readers are given an idea of how the book was put together. In the second instance, the phrase "Taken from the Plates of Nephi" identifies the major source of Mormon's narrative: the collection of plates gathered under the name of Nephi. It is as if a writer explained that she located most of her material in *The Papers of Thomas Jefferson* or the *Acts and Resolves of Massachusetts Bay*.

This opening statement begins the series of references to plates scattered through the book. They are mentioned well over a hundred times. After the title page, they turn up next in the first chapter of the narrative. Lehi, the prophet and father of the migrating family of ancient Israelites, keeps a journal as his family leaves Jerusalem, and his son Nephi assures his readers that he has written an abridgement of his father's account "upon plates which I have made with mine own hands."[5] Then, to his surprise, a decade later Nephi is commanded to make more plates: "I, Nephi, had kept the records upon my plates, which I had made, of my people thus far. And it came to pass that the Lord God said unto me: Make other plates; and thou shalt engraven many things upon them which are good in my sight."[6] The presence of a second record complicates the story, requiring still more comments about plates. The first set was devoted to "the wars and contentions and destructions of my people"—the political history—while the second set was for prophecies and spiritual experiences. All that is explained on several occasions.[7]

5. 1 Nephi 1:17.
6. 2 Nephi 5:29–30.
7. See, for example, 1 Nephi 19:4.

The plates receive further mention as they are transmitted from writer to writer. Nephi intended his plates to inaugurate a tradition. He commanded that they should be handed down from "one generation to another, or from one prophet to another, until further commandments of the Lord."[8] In ten centuries of Nephite history, the plates passed from one record keeper to another twenty-one times. The transmission was usually noted and the possessor at any given moment is always made explicit in the text. For instance, when Nephi, the son of Helaman, left the land of Zarahemla, he did not do so without "giving charge unto his son Nephi, who was his eldest son, concerning the plates of brass, and all the records which had been kept, and all those things which had been kept sacred from the departure of Lehi out of Jerusalem."[9] With the transfer of plates from one generation to another went the charge "that ye keep a record of this people, according as I have done, upon the plates of Nephi, and keep all these things sacred which I have kept, even as I have kept them."[10]

The book notes the transmission of the plates down through the ages, until the early fifth century CE, when Mormon handed them to his son Moroni, the last Nephite prophet.[11] His civilization having collapsed and his people destroyed, Moroni had no successor to carry on the tradition. He buried the plates and, after a long recess, appeared to Joseph Smith in 1823 to inform him of their location.[12] Though far removed chronologically from the Nephite prophets, Smith's retrieval of the plates in 1827 was the twenty-second transmission. He translated the contents, carrying the plates' story to its conclusion in the publication of the Book of Mormon.[13] Given the centrality of the plates in this long narration, the first newspaper notice of Smith's visionary proceedings appropriately headlined the story the "gold bible," after the plates' supposed appearance.[14]

As the term "gold bible" implied, the Book of Mormon was clearly linked to the Bible. It offers itself as a holy text for the New World. Yet the Bible itself says almost nothing about the medium on which it was inscribed and is far less self-conscious about its own composition. Various inscription media are

8. Ibid.

9. 3 Nephi 1:2.

10. Alma 37:2.

11. John W. Welch, *Charting the Book of Mormon: Visual Aids for Personal Study and Teaching* (Provo, UT: Foundation for Ancient Research and Mormon Studies, 1999), charts 16 and 17.

12. Mormon 8:4; Moroni 10:2.

13. Richard L. Bushman, "The Book of Mormon in Early Mormon History," in *New Views of Mormon History: A Collection of Essays in Honor of Leonard J. Arrington*, ed. Davis Bitton and Maureen Ursenbach Beecher (Salt Lake City: University of Utah Press, 1987), 3–18.

14. "The Book of Mormon," *Wayne Sentinel* (Palmyra, NY), 26 June 1829, 3.

mentioned, but on rare occasions. The Ten Commandments were written on tablets of stone.[15] Job pled that his words be "graven with an iron pen and lead in the rock forever!"[16] The word "parchment" occurs once in the Bible, in 2 Timothy 4:13. References to "rolls," implying parchment or papyrus scrolls, occur more frequently. "Take thee a roll of a book, and write therein all the words that I have spoken unto thee," God tells Jeremiah.[17] Slight references like these are the only hints about the materiality of the original source.

Brass plates appear in the Bible, but as part of the ten lavers in the first temple, not as books; the plates were part of the bases holding up great vats of water.[18] Exodus mentions a few sacred words inscribed on a small gold plate: "They made the plate of the holy crown *of* pure gold, and wrote upon it a writing, *like to* the engravings of a signet, HOLINESS TO THE LORD."[19] Aaron was to wear this plate on his miter when he came into the tabernacle in the wilderness. None of these references suggests that the Bible was written on plates.

Nineteenth-century Bible dictionaries offer little more help. They spoke of a variety of possible writing media. *The Dictionary of the Holy Bible*, a book found in Smith's Nauvoo library, speculated about writing materials in terms found in many other reference books: "Men used anciently to write upon tables of stone, copper, wood, wax, bark, or leaves."[20] No hint was given as to which predominated. Later research has shown that writing on plates was not unknown in the centuries around 600 BCE, but none of the extant examples consisted of long historical records comparable to the Book of Mormon.[21]

15. Exodus 24:12.

16. Job 19:24.

17. Jeremiah 36:2; compare Jeremiah 36:14–28; Ezra 6:2; Zechariah 5:1, 2.

18. 1 Kings 7:30; John Barton and John Muddiman, eds., *The Oxford Bible Commentary* (Oxford: Oxford University Press, 2001), 238.

19. Exodus 39:30.

20. "Book" in John Brown, *A Dictionary of the Holy Bible* (London: Thomas Trigg, 1824), 110. The list of books in the Nauvoo library gives only the title. The author may be James Wood, who wrote a book by the same name, but the descriptions of books were almost the same in both volumes. See Michael Reed, "The Notion of Metal Records in Joseph Smith's Day," 2011 summer seminar, Neal A. Maxwell Institute for Religious Scholarship (Provo, UT: Brigham Young University, 2011), 12n11. Other writers listed brass among the materials from which books were made in antiquity, but on a long list: leaves of trees, bark of trees, a table of wood, linen, papyrus, parchment, tables of lead, tables of brass, stones or rocks, tiles, and sand. John Jahn, a Viennese scholar whose works on biblical culture were translated into English and published in many editions, judged that "*Books*, (which are described as well known in the time of Job . . .) were first written on skins, linen, cotton cloth, or the papyrus; and subsequently on parchment." He did, however, leave room for harder materials: "Such books as were engraved on tables of wood, lead, brass, or ivory, were connected together by rings at the back, through which a rod was passed, and served as a hand to carry them by." John Jahn, *Archaeologia Biblica: A Manual of Biblical Antiquities*, trans. T. C. Upham, 3rd ed. (Oxford: D. A. Talboys, 1836), 86–89.

21. William J. Hamblin, "Sacred Writing on Metal Plates in the Ancient Mediterranean," *FARMS Review* 19, no. 1 (2007): 37–54.

The Book of Mormon world was exceptional in the proliferation of plates. At the beginning of the story, Lehi's family takes from Jerusalem a set of brass plates, which becomes the model for the first set of plates created by Lehi's son Nephi. Later in the history, a small colonizing party that left the main body of Nephites kept a history on plates, which they proudly brought out when their colony was rediscovered.[22] Mormon spoke of a trove of plates from which he abridged his history, as if many segments of the population wrote on plates. He said he hid up "all the records which had been entrusted to me by the hand of the Lord, save it were these few plates which I gave unto my son Moroni."[23] The plates he passed on to Moroni were a slim fraction of the whole.

All of these, along with the brass plates of Laban and Nephi's and Ether's plates, makes the keeping of a detailed history on metal plates look like a cultural tradition in Nephite society. Nothing in nineteenth-century speculation about ancient writing prompted the insertion of so many plates into the story. Plates in this quantity and of such extensive use are a Book of Mormon invention.

TEXTUAL SELF-AWARENESS

In the Book of Mormon world, the plates have one preeminent purpose: to carry the record of the Nephite people. As Nephi said, "I did make plates of ore that I might engraven upon them the record of my people."[24] The aim, as his brother Jacob said, was "to write a few words upon plates, which will give our children, and also our beloved brethren, a small degree of knowledge concerning us, or concerning their fathers."[25]

The book offers only one reason for the use of metal plates: durability. Metal would keep the record intact. Otherwise, they were hard to deal with. Nephi's brother Jacob complained of the physical challenge of engraving the plates. "I cannot write but a little of my words," he wrote, "because of the difficulty of engraving our words upon plates." But he persisted because, as he explained, "we know that the things which we write upon plates must remain." Nothing else would serve as well: "Whatsoever things we write upon anything save it be upon plates must perish and vanish away." And so, he wrote, "we labor

22. Mosiah 8:5.

23. Words of Mormon 1:3, 10; Mormon 6:6.

24. 1 Nephi 19:1.

25. Jacob 4:2. The Book of Mormon authors use the word "engraven" repeatedly as if to highlight the act connecting words from a mind with the metal of the plates. For a few examples, see 1 Nephi 3:3, 12, 24, 4:16, 24, 5:10.

diligently to engraven these words upon plates, hoping that our beloved brethren and our children will receive them with thankful hearts."[26] The point of the plates, from the book's perspective, was to preserve the story so that the message would get through. In the Book of Mormon, the plates are not a mystical object, a relic, a treasure, or a sign, but a durable record.[27]

What is to be made of the singular interest in book construction in the Book of Mormon? What is the internal logic of plates? One possibility is that the authors consider the history they are writing so important that readers should know how the record came to be. In the authors' eyes, the writings on the plates of Nephi will change the course of history when they emerge in the last days. Other books, coming from other peoples, will serve a similar purpose. One might even say that the Book of Mormon is a book about the importance of books. Perhaps Book of Mormon authors look at book history for the same reason modern scholars do: because they believe books matter.[28]

Only a few pages into the story, Lehi charges his sons to return to Jerusalem to acquire brass plates containing "the record of the Jews" from a local leader named Laban.[29] To obtain the plates, Nephi and his brothers sacrifice all of their father's considerable property, and ultimately kill Laban.[30] Nephi, though questioning his right to take Laban's life, reasons that his people could not keep God's commandments unless they had the law, and he knew "the law was engraven upon the plates of brass."[31] Then the spirit of God spoke to him, explaining that it was "better that one man should perish than that a nation should dwindle and perish in unbelief."[32] A book with the power to preserve a nation justified murder.

Not far into the Book of Mormon, the narrative underscores the accuracy of Nephi's decision. Another group of refugees from Jerusalem, who arrived in

26. Jacob 4:1–3. The prophet Alma said the virtue of the plates was that they "must retain their brightness" (Alma 37:5).

27. Lehi attributed supernatural qualities to the brass plates when he prophesied that they "should never perish; neither should they be dimmed any more by time" (1 Nephi 5:19).

28. Among many works on book history, see David Pearson, *Books as History: The Importance of Books beyond Their Texts* (New Castle, DE: Oak Knoll Press, 2012); David D. Hall, *Cultures of Print: Essays in the History of the Book* (Amherst: University of Massachusetts Press, 1996); David D. Hall, *On Native Ground: From the History of Printing to the History of the Book* (Worcester, MA: American Antiquarian Society, 1984); Hugh Amory and David D. Hall, eds., *A History of the Book in America*, vol. 1, *The Colonial Book in the Atlantic World* (Cambridge, UK: Cambridge University Press, 1999); Robert Darnton, *The Great Cat Massacre and other Episodes in French Cultural History* (New York: Basic Books, 1985); and *The Literary Underground of the Old Regime* (Cambridge, MA: Harvard University Press, 1982).

29. I Nephi 5:12.

30. 1 Nephi 3:24.

31. 1 Nephi 4:16.

32. 1 Nephi 4:13.

the New World at about the same time as Lehi's band, came without records. When the two groups met a few centuries later, the culture of the second group had decayed. "Their language had become corrupted; and they had brought no records with them; and they denied the being of their Creator; and Mosiah, nor the people of Mosiah, could not understand them."[33] Without records, the whole culture deteriorated. A later monarch, King Benjamin, taught his sons to read the Egyptian on the brass plates in the belief that without those writings their forefathers "would have dwindled in unbelief." How could faith be sustained without written scriptures? How else to "understand of his mysteries and have his commandments always before our eyes?"[34]

To drive home the importance of the plates, the book tells about yet another civilization, a much earlier one, which followed the same pattern of record keeping as the Nephites. A party of Nephites stumbled upon the ruins of this vanished people while on an exploratory expedition, and while rummaging amid some artifacts discovered a set of twenty-four gold plates. This record, later translated by one of the Nephite kings, told of a nation that had fallen away from God and destroyed itself through devastating wars, foreshadowing the Nephites' own demise. The people who discovered these plates were intensely curious to know what they contained: "They were desirous beyond measure to know concerning those people who had been destroyed."[35] Their curiosity proved to be well-founded. When the record was translated and read to them, its tragic tale "did cause the people of Mosiah to mourn exceedingly … nevertheless, it gave them much knowledge in the which they did rejoice."[36] This kind of illumination, so the record says, was meant for everyone: "It is expedient that all people should know the things which are written in this account."[37] Plates carried critical information from one civilization to another.

In fact, in a vision given to Nephi, he learned that his plates were part of a vast record-keeping operation going on everywhere. "I command all men," God declared, "both in the east and in the west, and in the north, and in the south, and in the islands of the sea, that they shall write the words which I speak unto them." All the various contingents of the House of Israel—the Jews in Jerusalem, the Nephites in the New World, and all "the other tribes of the house of

33. Omni 17.
34. Mosiah 1:5.
35. Mosiah 28:12.
36. Mosiah 28:18.
37. Mosiah 28:19.

Israel" would keep records.[38] In the end, at the culmination of history as Nephi foresaw it, all these various records would come together: "The Jews shall have the words of the Nephites, and the Nephites shall have the words of the Jews; and the Nephites and the Jews shall have the words of the lost tribes of Israel."[39] Nephi's plates would be his people's entry into this great congress of records.

Focus on its own making sets the Book of Mormon apart from its prototype, the Bible, and from most if not all other books in nineteenth-century America. Perhaps the book's insistence on its own importance underlies its belabored effort to explain how it came to be. It writes itself as book history because it thinks so highly of books, its self-awareness motivated by its own pretensions as a cultural force in the day when it is brought to light.

PRODUCING THE PLATES

As the Book of Mormon tells its own story, the record was kept by society's cultural elite. The engravers of the plates were not plain men with a message or lone prophets emerging from the wilderness. The first Nephi was the son of the family's patriarch and eventually elected king. For a long stretch, the records were kept by monarchs, and then passed to chief judges and high priests. Alma, who was the high priest but not the ruler, tried to transfer the plates to Nephihah, the chief judge, and only when refused conferred them on his son Helaman.[40] Mormon was the general of the Nephite army and his son Moroni a commander of ten thousand troops.[41] The plate keepers who did not occupy high office were familiar with the nation's political and military chieftains. The story line in the book never strays far from the court and the centers of power. The plates were engraven at the upper echelons of Nephite society.

The plate keepers were further set off by their learning. The brass plates, which were written in Egyptian, were not accessible to everyone. Lehi could read them "for he having been taught in the language of the Egyptians therefore he could read these engravings, and teach them to his children, that thereby they could teach them to their children, and so fulfilling the commandments of God."[42] From then on, the plates of Nephi were written in the language of Lehi, which consisted of "the learning of the Jews and the language of the

38. 2 Nephi 29:11–12.
39. 2 Nephi 29:13.
40. Alma 50:38.
41. Mormon 6:12.
42. Mosiah 1:4.

Egyptians."[43] Keepers of the plates had to be inducted into this learning before they could assume their duties. The sons of King Benjamin had to be "taught in all the language of his fathers, that thereby they might become men of understanding; and that they might know concerning the prophecies which had been spoken by the mouths of their fathers."[44] By Mormon's day, a half millennium later, the plates were still written "in the characters which are called . . . the reformed Egyptian," which had been "handed down and altered by us, according to our manner of speech."[45] By that time, the plates' language was unrecognizable outside this small coterie: "None other people knoweth our language."[46] These bilingual elites not only spoke the creole Hebrew of the Nephites, but could read and write in "reformed Egyptian." Esoteric language erected a barrier around the plates that restricted plate keeping to the learned.

These eminent men felt no shame in doing the hard work of manufacturing and engraving plates. Nephi, the forefather of the Nephite race, began this tradition.[47] At the end of the epic saga, Mormon rather proudly said, "I do make the record on plates which I have made with mine own hands."[48] It was not viewed as the hot and dirty work of early American metalsmithing. Rather, working on plates was honorific, like eighteenth-century ladies pouring tea from a silver pot. The grace of the object reflected favorably on the activities associated with its use.[49] For the plate makers, the esoteric language, the metal, the divine purpose, and the high calling of prophet elevated everything associated with plates. "And I engraved that which is pleasing unto God," Nephi assured his readers. "And if my people are pleased with the things of God they will be pleased with mine engravings which are upon these plates."[50]

TRANSFERRING CUSTODY

For most of their thousand-year history, the collection of plates was in the possession of two families: the descendants of Lehi and the descendants of Alma. Nephi, the first plate maker, was the son of Lehi, the presiding patriarch

43. 1 Nephi 1:2.
44. Mosiah 1:2.
45. Mormon 9:32.
46. Mormon 9:34.
47. 2 Nephi 5:31.
48. 3 Nephi 5:11.
49. On tea service in early America, see Richard L. Bushman, *The Refinement of America: Persons, Houses, Cities* (New York: Vintage Books, 1992), 184–85.
50. 2 Nephi 5:32. Nephi also wrote: "The Lord God said unto me: Make other plates; and thou shalt engraven many things upon them which are good in my sight, for the profit of thy people" (2 Nephi 5:30).

of the clan; from Nephi, the plates went to his younger brother Jacob. For over four centuries, the plates were in the hands of nine caretakers from the Lehite clan. Finally, "having no seed," the last of these stewards turned the plates over to King Benjamin, believing him "to be a just man."[51] The plates remained in Benjamin's family for only two generations. Then his son, King Mosiah, abdicated the throne and relinquished them to Alma, the son of a prophet also named Alma who had formed a church in one of the Nephite colonies. The junior Alma had risen to prominence in Zarahemla, the capital city of Mosiah's kingdom, where he was eventually appointed high priest and elected chief judge. King Mosiah conferred "the plates of brass" and "all the records, and also the interpreters," on Alma. This transfer of the plates included a charge for Alma to "keep a record of the people, handing them down from one generation to another, even as they had been handed down from the time that Lehi had left Jerusalem."[52]

Alma and his descendants kept the records through eleven generations to Ammaron, the last of Alma's line. In a time of growing wickedness, Ammaron hid "all the sacred records which had been handed down from generation to generation," and looked around for another caretaker.[53] Departing from precedent, he selected Mormon, a ten-year-old boy with no known relationship to Alma's lineage. Mormon later wrote that at this time he "began to be learned somewhat after the manner of learning of my people," a prerequisite for carrying on the record.[54] Ammaron told Mormon: "Take the plates of Nephi unto yourself, and the remainder shall ye leave in the place where they are; and ye shall engrave on the plates of Nephi all the things that ye have observed concerning this people."[55] Mormon was the most influential of all the record keepers. He not only engraved his portion of Nephite history on the plates but went back to the cache of plates and wrote an entire history of Lehi's clan from their departure from Jerusalem about 600 BCE to their imminent destruction in 385 CE when he turned the plates over to his son Moroni. Then Mormon led the remaining Nephites into battle, and annihilation. Moroni completed the story and buried the plates for their long rest in the ground.

As the Book of Mormon imagines the construction of a sacred record, the collection of revelations was not an afterthought. Revelations did not prompt

51. Omni 1:25.
52. Mosiah 28:20.
53. 4 Nephi 48.
54. Mormon 1:2.
55. Mormon 1:4.

people to think of compiling a collection. People were charged in advance to prepare the book and collect revelations as they came along. Someone was always watching for inspiration from God. One caretaker named Abinadom added only four sentences to the plates. He "saw much war and contention" but he knew of "no revelation save that which has been written."[56] That relieved him of the responsibility to write; in dry periods, nothing was recorded. But someone in the great families was always there to record the story.

The plates gave this charge concrete form. The previous curator not only passed along an admonition to keep a record but also handed over the physical plates, adding weight to the record-keeping commission. The plates called out for something to be entered on them. Omni confessed: "I of myself am a wicked man, and I have not kept the statutes and the commandments of the Lord as I ought to have done." But he had to write something. His father, Jarom, had commanded that he "should write somewhat upon these plates to preserve our genealogy," and so he did, rather perfunctorily noting, "we had many seasons of peace; and we had many seasons of serious war and bloodshed." Omni, satisfied that he had "kept the plates according to the commandments of my fathers," conferred them upon his son with a good conscience.[57]

The momentum imparted by plates kept the history going through the dry seasons. Most of the time, the caretakers found plenty to write about. They told of changes in government, missionary journeys, encounters with heretics, expeditions to new lands, wars with the Lamanites, natural disasters, moral decay, and seasons of righteousness. The caretakers included accounts of sermons, visions, and prophecies. Knowing they must write, they gathered material.

REPORTERS AND EDITORS

The Book of Mormon sheds a little light on one crucial step in the process. How were the long sermons and prophecies recorded? Some of them go on for pages. How does the book imagine these statements being transferred to the plates? The transition from oral to written text comes up in many ancient documents. Pericles's great funeral oration to the Athenians after the first battles in the Peloponnesian War is a well-known example. Is the speech really that of Pericles, or should it be attributed to Thucydides, the historian who wrote it

56. Omni 1:11.
57. Omni 1:1–3.

for his history? In the Book of Mormon, were invisible scribes taking notes as orations were given? King Benjamin's closing oration fills several pages; who wrote it down? The text suggests the presence of scribes. When the gathered people could not hear him from his tower, Benjamin "caused that the words which he spake should be written and sent forth among those that were not under the sound of his voice."[58] Likewise, after hearing a sermon of Jacob's, Nephi "caused to be written" the parts he liked best.[59] Did he, by this time in his reign, have engravers working for him? In other places, believers had copies of the scriptures other than the brass plates and the plates in the prophets' care. The persecutors of one group seized "their records which contained the holy scriptures, and cast them into the fire."[60] A little later, "all those engravings which were in the possession of Helaman were written and sent forth among the children of men throughout all the land," almost like the King James Bible in 1611.[61] These incidents imply written language, scribes who could write, and something other than plates to write on.

Nephi's charge to his brother Jacob, as he passed along the plates to him, may have suggested enough to make the process intelligible to nineteenth-century readers. Jacob was instructed: "If there were preaching which was sacred, or revelation which was great, or prophesying, that I should engraven the heads of them upon these plates, and touch upon them as much as it were possible, for Christ's sake, and for the sake of our people."[62] Nephi presumes active reporters on the scene, always on the lookout for inspired words, summarizing the "heads" of the discourses on the plates with members of the great families overseeing the operation and usually writing it themselves.

Nephi's great project faltered at first. His enthusiasm for record keeping did not last among his descendants. Nephi wrote two dense books (somewhat comparable to 1 and 2 Samuel). Jacob added his own prophecies after Nephi's death, in one shorter book (somewhat comparable to Ezra or Amos). Then over the next three centuries, record keeping progressively thinned out. Jacob's son Enos recorded a short but memorable account of his personal religious experience, and the next six caretakers wrote only fitfully. They were charged to write a report on the "small" plates, which Nephi conceived as a spiritual history of his people. Political history was left to the royal line, which had its

58. Mosiah 2:8.
59. 2 Nephi 11:1.
60. Alma 14:8.
61. Alma 63:12.
62. Jacob 1:4.

own set of plates. Jacob's descendants had little to say about religion, referring instead—somewhat wistfully—to the record of the kings where all the action lay: "And I, Jarom, do not write more, for the plates are small. But behold, my brethren, ye can go to the other plates of Nephi; for behold, upon them the records of our wars are engraven, according to the writings of the kings, or those which they caused to be written."[63] Eventually the small plates filled up, and this experiment in a divided history came to an end.[64] The subsequent plates mingled both religious and political history, and the story line flourished again. By then the culture of record keeping had diffused through Nephite society. Alma's family took up where Lehi's left off, piling up more and more plates. In the end, Mormon had ample material to work with when he compiled his comprehensive history.

Indeed, most authors suffered from the opposite problem. Author after author complained of how much they were forced to omit. Mormon bemoaned the fact that he could not include a fraction of all that had happened:

> But behold, a hundredth part of the proceedings of this people, yea, the account of the Lamanites and of the Nephites, and their wars, and contentions, and dissensions, and their preaching, and their prophecies, and their shipping and their building of ships, and their building of temples, and of synagogues and their sanctuaries, and their righteousness, and their wickedness, and their murders, and their robbings, and their plundering, and all manner of abominations and whoredoms, cannot be contained in this work.[65]

Jacob used the same phrase: "And a hundredth part of the proceedings of this people, which now began to be numerous, cannot be written upon these plates." Many others lamented their omissions.[66]

The laments imply the writers worried that they were leaving out stories and sermons that deserved inclusion. What if critical matters had been omitted? In one peculiar exchange, the visiting post-resurrection Christ asked about a prophecy of people rising from the graves. To their dismay, the Nephite historians found they had neglected to include the incident and had to hurriedly amend

63. Jarom 1:14.

64. Omni 1:30.

65. Helaman 3:14.

66. Jacob 3:13. Compare 2 Nephi 31:1, 33:1; Words of Mormon 1:5; Alma 8:1, 13:31; Mosiah 8:1; 1 Nephi 6:3, 17:6; Jacob 4:1; 3 Nephi 5:8, 7:17, 17:15, 19:34, 26:6; Helaman 8:3, 14:1; Moroni 9:19; Ether 12:25, 15:33.

the record.[67] In one way or another, a number of the record keepers expressed concern about the selection process. Nephi said he tried to avoid errors: "I do not write anything upon plates save it be that I think it be sacred." And yet he knew he could make mistakes and tied himself in knots explaining why. "If I do err, even did they err of old; not that I would excuse myself because of other men, but because of the weakness which is in me, according to the flesh." After all, it was not entirely his fault. "The things which some men esteem to be of great worth . . . others set at naught."[68] The problem could not be easily resolved.

All the record keepers faced difficult choices. Some editorial mistakes, however, were not innocent. Nephi prophetically commented on the editing of the Bible after its composition, accusing the editors of malicious excisions. In his vision of future events, Nephi foresaw the Bible coming forth initially as a true revelation: "Thou hast beheld that the book proceeded forth from the mouth of a Jew; and when it proceeded forth from the mouth of a Jew it contained the fulness of the gospel of the Lord, of whom the twelve apostles bear record; and they bear record according to the truth which is in the Lamb of God."[69] But when these writings fell into the hands of subsequent editors, significant parts were removed. A great and awful church took control of the texts and defaced them: "They have taken away from the gospel of the Lamb many parts which are plain and most precious; and also many covenants of the Lord have they taken away. And all this have they done that they might pervert the right ways of the Lord, that they might blind the eyes and harden the hearts of the children of men."[70] Nephi gave no explanation of why the excisions were made, but the consequences were fatal. From a book of truth, the Bible became a marred, partial account. The omission of the plain and precious truths from the Bible led its readers to lose their way: "Because of these things which are taken away out of the gospel of the Lamb, an exceedingly great many do stumble, yea, insomuch that Satan hath great power over them."[71] Abandoning any thought of scriptural infallibility, Book of Mormon writers assume the Bible was an edited volume, and with dire results. Malevolent editing yielded a flawed holy book and a faulty religion. Behind it all, Nephi saw the hand of Satan, thwarting God's purposes. The devil's method was to corrupt the process of book making. His agents were editors who censored the text.

67. 3 Nephi 23:7–13.
68. 1 Nephi 19:6–7.
69. 1 Nephi 13:24; compare 1 Nephi 13:25.
70. 1 Nephi 13:26–27.
71. 1 Nephi 13:29.

THE HUMANITY OF SCRIPTURES

The Book of Mormon took the mystery of out of scripture making. It implicitly lifted the veil on how the Bible came to be. In the book's internal world, religious figures forged plates and their hands grew weary incising the metal. The words ran through human minds and passed through human hands before they landed on the pages that became scripture.

The content of the Book of Mormon, moreover, came largely from ordinary experiences. Much of the book consists of letters, discourses, and personal accounts—the sort of thing religious people produced in fulfilling their duties. Most of the book is history: stories of group migration, political conflicts, destructive wars, missionary labors, and efforts to regulate the affairs of the church. Revelations, dreams, and miracles occur regularly but they are blended into stories of particular lives and grow out of everyday struggles such as trying to recover from a broken bow or preventing rustlers from stealing cattle. The Book of Mormon is the story of a people and a civilization; it is human history moved by divine aspirations.

That view of scripture took some of the steam out of biblical infallibility. Joseph Smith's candor about the creation of the Book of Mormon resembled the method of the higher criticism in that both returned the scriptures to history. The essence of the critical approach was to imagine Bible authors as writers based in concrete cultural and historical circumstances. The higher critics read the Bible as they would any historical document, discerning the influences of the times on its production. They imagined the prophets and apostles as historical figures writing holy words, but under human influence. Book history in the Book of Mormon followed in the same vein. In the book's pages, the scriptures are a human production: minds writing under heavenly influence but in particular historical circumstances. Scripture making takes place within history.

The exception to this mundane setting could be translation. The power to translate seems removed from the course of ordinary history in the Book of Mormon. Ammon, a scout from the Nephite capital, called the ability to translate "a high gift from God." He explained this to the leader of a Nephite colony who had come across ancient plates with writing on them and wanted them translated. Ammon said that King Mosiah had a gift: "He has wherewith that he can look, and translate all records that are of ancient date."[72] Translation for

72. Mosiah 8:13–14.

Ammon was out of this world, anything but ordinary: "A gift which is greater can no man have, except he should possess the power of God."[73]

That exalted view of translation carried over to Joseph Smith. His revelations spoke of translation as a gift that he could lose if his obedience faltered. God had given him the "right to translate," one revelation said. But, unless he repented, he would "become as other men & have no more gift."[74] In Smith's earliest revelations, it seemed like translation required something special, something far from the ordinary run of quotidian existence. Translation for Joseph Smith, as for King Mosiah, required a high gift.

But that exalted sense of translation does not hold true throughout the Book of Mormon. By the end of the book, translation as a "high gift" fades. The last record keeper, Moroni, undertook to give an account of the Jaredites, the ancient inhabitants of the northern country. It is possible that he relied upon King Mosiah's previous translation of the Jaredite plates, but this is not stated or implied. Moroni wrote: "I take my account from the twenty and four plates which were found by the people of Limhi"—as if it were a direct translation of his own. Strangely, he undertakes this task without mentioning a high gift. He does explain how the Lord gave the Jaredite prophet Ether two stones to be sealed up with his writings. The stones, the Lord said, "shall magnify to the eyes of men these things which ye shall write."[75] The word for translation was "magnify." There is no mention of special powers. Moroni went ahead with no further explanation of how translation occurred, as if it had become routine, requiring no comment. By Moroni's time, translation had sunk back into the regular sequence of affairs as a necessary step in the natural course of writing the history of another people.

Joseph Smith's gift of translation evolved in the same direction. He feared losing his precious gift after the initial pages of translation were lost. But gradually the gift became routine. By the time Oliver Cowdery joined him as a scribe, Joseph Smith seemed to feel that translation was something others could do. A revelation said that the gift to "translate even as my servant Joseph" was available to Oliver too.[76] Cowdery failed in the attempt, but only because he did not quite get the knack of it: "You must study it out in your own mind," he was told, "then you must ask me if it be right, and if it is right, I will cause that your

73. Mosiah 8:16.

74. Revelation, July 1828, in *JSP*-D1:8 [D&C 3:11–12]. The word "right" rather than "sight" appeared in the earliest version of this revelation.

75. Ether 3:23–24.

76. Revelation, April 1829-A, in *JSP*-D1:36 [D&C 6:25].

bosom shall burn within you."[77] Cowdery did not need more divine power, more high gift. He only had to focus his thought and ask for confirmation.

Translation did require special powers; it was a gift. But that did not prevent translation from being absorbed into Smith's daily routine. For months, he worked long hours every day. Instead of going to the fields like other farmers, he went to the table where the plates lay. His wife, Emma Hale Smith, and the Whitmer family that hosted Joseph Smith and Oliver Cowdery during the translation looked in on Smith as he dictated to Cowdery. Sometimes Smith tired and had to take a break. If translation was a miracle, it was one that occurred day after day, all day long, for months. Like the rest of scripture making in the Book of Mormon, translation became routine. It is no surprise that almost immediately after publishing the Book of Mormon, Smith went on to the Bible and translated the Book of Moses. Translation had become his work.[78]

The Book of Mormon shows scripture flowing from the ordinary lives of people, their teachers, and their leaders. Words that began as admonition and instruction became the Word of God. A people's day by day struggles between sin and righteousness became a holy narrative. The book shows its readers a world where humans and God collaborated continuously in the production of holy writing. Even the high gift of translation was routinized. The Book of Mormon and Smith's subsequent translation texts prepared the Mormon people to believe, as one of his revelations put it, that whatever good men spoke "when moved upon by the Holy Ghost shall be Scripture."[79]

77. Revelation, April 1829-D, in *JSP*-D1:50 [D&C 9:8].

78. An early revelation said that one of Smith's standard designations was "Translater." Revelation, 6 April 1830, in *JSP*-D1:129 [D&C 21:1].

79. Revelation, 1 November 1831-A, in *JSP*-D2:101 [D&C 68:4].

9

Ancient History and Modern Commandments

The Book of Mormon in Comparison with Joseph Smith's Other Revelations

GRANT HARDY

The first edition of the Book of Mormon, published in 1830, opened with a brief preface by Joseph Smith and concluded with the testimonies of several men who claimed to have seen the gold plates from which the book had been translated. Both of these items alluded to Smith's miraculous translation from the plates. In this way, notices of its supernatural origins sandwiched the text. From the very beginning, the book was presented to the world as a divinely preserved ancient record that had been translated "by the gift and power of God."[1] It was an unusual claim. The history of religion is filled with accounts and transcripts of revelations, most of which take a direct, personal form along the lines of "the Lord said to me . . ." or "the heavens opened and I saw . . ." or "caught up in God, I experienced a sensation like . . ." or "while in meditation, I became enlightened and understood that. . . ."[2] Joseph Smith professed these sorts of revelatory experiences even before the publication of the Book of Mormon, with visitations from God and angels as early as 1820, and written transcripts of messages received from Deity beginning in July 1828. But the

1. The title page of the first edition also included the attribution "By Joseph Smith, Junior, author and proprietor," but this was done for copyright purposes. The same page referred to ancient plates and "the interpretation thereof by the gift of God." The first public notice that the book was available for purchase came in a 26 June 1829 article in the *Wayne Sentinel*, which quoted the recently filed copyright application and offered the standard story of "a pretended discovery, through superhuman means, of an ancient record, of a religious and a divine nature and origin, written in ancient characters, impossible to be interpreted by any to whom the special gift has not been imparted by inspiration." "The Book of Mormon," *Wayne Sentinel* (Palmyra, NY), 26 March 1830, 3.

2. See Keith Ward, *Religion and Revelation: A Theology of Revelation in the World's Religions* (Oxford and New York: Oxford University Press, 1994), 87–110. For examples closer to Joseph Smith's time, see Susan Juster, *Doomsayers: Anglo-American Prophecy in the Age of Revolution* (Philadelphia: University of Pennsylvania Press, 2003); and David F. Holland, *Sacred Borders: Continuing Revelation and Canonical Restraint in Early America* (Oxford and New York: Oxford University Press, 2011).

Book of Mormon was different. Its claim to religious authority was connected to Smith, to be sure, yet also to prophets from an otherwise unknown Christian civilization in the pre-Columbian Americas in a way that highlights concepts of literacy, bookishness, and canon. The Book of Mormon's self-identification as an ancient text that was "translated"—as opposed to a collection of direct revelations—has significant implications for its reception and interpretation.

Smith could have learned about the history of this civilization, the "Nephites," from his experience of angelic visitations, or visions, or even spiritual impressions; and then conveyed the information communicated in those events in his own words, much as his mother remembered him doing in family gatherings when he was a teenager:

> During our evening conversations, Joseph would occasionally give us some of the most amusing recitals that could be imagined. He would describe the ancient inhabitants of this continent, their dress, mode of travelings, and the animals upon which they rode; their cities, their buildings, with every particular; their mode of warfare; and also their religious worship. This he would do with as much ease, seemingly, as if he had spent his whole life among them.[3]

A book of stories about the Nephites, perhaps including Smith's own comments and interpretations, could have been given scriptural status in the church he founded and then could have guided the development of its distinctive doctrines and practices. But that is not the Book of Mormon.

Alternatively, Smith could have produced a transcript of his conversations with the spirits of Nephite prophets of old coming to visit him as angels, giving their answers to his questions, much as in early Judeo-Christian apocalypses or the writings of Emanuel Swedenborg. Or he might have channeled the voice of Mormon, the penultimate Nephite prophet for whom the book is named, recounting the lamentable history of his people. Such a practice goes back to the biblical medium of Endor, summoning the ghost of Samuel. And it continues into the modern era, with people like John Ballou Newbrough and the spirit of Jehovih in Newbrough's *Oahspe* (1882), or J. Z. Knight and Ramtha in Knight's *Ramtha: The White Book* (1999). None of these would have required the transmission of a text or a miraculous translation.

3. Lucy Mack Smith, *Lucy's Book: A Critical Edition of Lucy Mack Smith's Family Memoir*, ed. Lavina Fielding Anderson (Salt Lake City: Signature Books, 2001), 344.

The Book of Mormon, however, was not put forward as a record of Joseph Smith's experiences with Nephite spirits, or God's direct revelations to him, or visions of episodes from ancient American history. It is, rather, a tightly organized text, purportedly written and edited by historical individuals who were working within a scriptural tradition (the Brass Plates) and who realized that their own writings would someday have scriptural status. The Book of Mormon is built on a carefully worked-out system of primary sources that were utilized by the three major narrators, and the narrative moves forward within a coherent, consistent, chronological framework. This allows for the insertion of verbatim transcripts of documents, the inclusion of contemporaneous subplots or flashbacks, and regular allusions to both past events and future developments (in the form of prophecies and fulfillments or of editorial promises that are later brought to fruition). In addition, some of the embedded literary units are themselves carefully crafted, as can be seen in the Psalm of Nephi,[4] which follows the classic form of a Psalm of Individual Lament;[5] or in Abinadi's defense speech,[6] which quotes a series of biblical passages in order to answer the initial question of the priests who accused him; or in the extended chiasmus of Alma chapter 36;[7] or in the way the Jaredite king-list of Ether 1 is reversed and expanded in chapters 7–11 (and interspersed with editorial comment sections written by Moroni). The Book of Mormon is a remarkably *bookish* sort of scripture, which is almost obsessively concerned with its internal sources, organization, editing, and transmission.[8]

There are other scriptures that claim to be incarnations of earlier texts. One such parallel might be Levi Dowling's *Aquarian Gospel of Jesus Christ* (1908), said to have been "transcribed from the Book of God's Remembrances, known as the Akashic Records," which are "wholly in the domain of Supreme Intelligence, or Universal Mind" (though Mormon's gold plates seem to have been more stubbornly materialistic). Dowling's translation apparently involved

4. 2 Nephi 4:16–35.

5. Matthew Nickerson, "Nephi's Psalm: 2 Nephi 4:16–35 in the Light of Form-Critical Analysis," *Journal of Book of Mormon Studies* 6, no. 2 (1997): 26–42.

6. Mosiah 12–16.

7. John W. Welch, "A Masterpiece: Alma 36," in *Rediscovering the Book of Mormon*, ed. John L. Sorenson and Melvin J. Thorne (Salt Lake City: Deseret Book; Provo, UT: Foundation for Ancient Research and Mormon Studies, 1991), 114–131.

8. The current official edition, which retains the seventeenth-century formatting of the King James Version (double columns and separate verses) tends to obscure poetic passages, intertextual allusions, embedded documents, and narrative structures—all of which can be more easily perceived in the reader's edition of the book edited by the author. See Grant Hardy, *The Book of Mormon: A Reader's Edition* (Urbana: University of Illinois Press, 2003).

receiving impressions and then putting them into his own words: "When the mind of man is in exact accord with the Universal Mind[,] man enters into a conscious recognition of these Akashic impressions, and may collect them and translate them into any language of earth with which he is familiar."[9] More significant, but further afield religiously, are dozens of major Mahayana sutras that began to emerge in the first century BCE, which were said to have been hidden away safely in heaven or in earthly caves or in the underwater palaces of dragon spirits, or were heard and preserved by celestial bodhisattvas who were now revealing them.[10] There are somewhat later examples of Daoist transcripts of heavenly books, perhaps most famously the Shangqing revelations dictated by immortal Celestial Masters to Yang Xi in the fourth century.[11] (Chinese civilization has traditionally cared a great deal about books and literacy, and that cultural predisposition is reflected in their scriptures.) The Qur'an is similarly considered by most Muslims to be the transcript of a heavenly, eternally existing book, the "Preserved Tablet."[12]

Yet the Book of Mormon is not a heavenly book. It claims to have been composed by divinely directed but human authors in specific historical circumstances. Smith told his followers that he had found physical plates that had been engraved by the editor/narrators themselves—not an ordinary manuscript, but an autograph document nonetheless. Unfortunately for modern scholars, Smith explained that when he finished translating the gold plates, he returned them to the angel who had first told him of their existence and whereabouts. The pattern of recovered ancient documents fits other scriptures as well: the book of Deuteronomy discovered during the reign of Josiah, much of the pseudepigrapha of Second Temple Judaism, the Zohar, and the apocryphal gospels, acts, epistles, and apocalypses of early Christianity. However, these texts were usually written in the language of their putative discoverers,

9. Levi H. Dowling, *The Aquarian Gospel of Jesus Christ* (1908; repr., Los Angeles: E. S. Dowling, 1911), 2, 11, 12. The translation of an absent text, perhaps in the spiritual realm, also occurs in one of Joseph Smith's 1829 revelations, see Revelation, April 1829-C, in *JSP*-D1:47–48 [D&C 7]. See also David W. Grua and William V. Smith, "The Tarrying of the Beloved Disciple: The Textual Formation of the Account of John," Chapter 10 herein. For some interpretations of Smith's Book of Abraham, see Michael D. Rhodes, "Why Doesn't the Translation of the Egyptian Papyri Found in 1967 Match the Text of the Book of Abraham in the Pearl of Great Price?," *Ensign*, July 1988, 51–53; John Gee, "The Relationship of the Book of Abraham Text to the Papyri," chap. 7 in *An Introduction to the Book of Abraham* (Provo, UT: Religious Studies Center, Brigham Young University; Salt Lake City: Deseret Book, 2017).

10. See Paul Williams, *Mahayana Buddhism: The Doctrinal Foundations* (London: Routledge, 1989).

11. See Stephen R. Bokenkamp, *Early Daoist Scriptures* (Berkeley: University of California Press, 1997); and Kristofer Schipper and Franciscus Verellen, eds., *The Taoist Canon: A Historical Companion to the Daozang* (Chicago: University of Chicago Press, 2004).

12. Qur'an 85:22.

and thus did not require translation (and they generally did not consist of lengthy, integrated narrative histories).[13]

By contrast, Smith asserted that the Book of Mormon was inscribed in the lost language of Reformed Egyptian, and thus could only be read with divine assistance. He employed seer stones to do this, which were themselves quite material—several people saw or handled these objects, and the stone that Smith most frequently used to translate the Book of Mormon is still in the possession of the leaders of the church he founded.[14] The translation happened in a miraculous way: Smith looked at a seer stone placed in his hat and then dictated the text of the Book of Mormon to scribes at a fairly rapid pace, with very few later revisions aside from stylistic or grammatical corrections.[15]

Joseph Smith never gave any details about the translation process—at least, nothing he wrote about it is extant—and surviving evidence from the original manuscript and eyewitness accounts is inconclusive. Some Mormon scholars believe that the seer stone helped provide mental impressions, which Smith then put into his own words (perhaps something like his reception of most of the revelations in the Doctrine and Covenants or, from an outsider's point of view, like Levi Dowling's transcription of the Akashic Records). This mode of translation might account for the irregular grammar, the anachronisms, and the phrases borrowed from the King James Bible (KJV), as well as Smith's willingness to modify the wording of later editions. Other Mormon scholars, however, think that Smith saw the text in the seer stone and read it aloud—which better explains the precision of the language, the intricacies of the narrative, the internal allusions, and the immediate corrections that appear regularly in the original manuscript when scribes got a word wrong or misspelled a proper noun.[16] In this case, Smith would have been using the seer

13. More suspect still are stories of modern travelers who publish recovered texts for which the original manuscripts and the helpful, local translators have all disappeared, as with William Mahan's "Archko Volume" (1884), and Nicolas Notovitch's *Unknown Life of Jesus Christ* (1894). Nevertheless, the Tibetan "Book of the Dead" (1927) was an obscure text that was indeed found and publicized by an American adventurer, Walter Evans-Wentz, with the assistance of a Tibetan translator. William D. Mahan, *Archaeological Writings of the Sanhedrin and Talmuds of the Jews Taken from the Ancient Parchments and Scrolls at Constantinople and the Vatican at Rome* (St. Louis: Perrin & Smith, 1884); Nicolas Notovitch, *La Vie Inconnue de Jésus-Christ* (Paris: Paul Ollendorff, 1894); Walter Y. Evans-Wentz, *The Tibetan Book of the Dead* (London: Oxford University Press, 1927).

14. Photographs of this seer stone are available in Figure 6.1 herein; and *JSP*-R3:1:xx–xxi.

15. *JSP*-D1:xxix–xxiii. The editors note that "after 1830, however, Joseph Smith apparently dictated revelations without the use of an external instrument" (that is, without any seer stones).

16. In a single chapter (Alma 30) the original manuscript shows Oliver Cowdery immediately correcting "number" to "numbers" (v. 2), "these" to "this" (v. 10), "traditions" to "tradition" (v. 16), "there" to "these" (v. 24), "hath never" to "never hath" (v. 28), "by" to "in" (v. 31), "causes" to "causeth" (v. 35), "was" to "is" (v. 53), and adding a missed "also" (v. 41). These corrections seem to have taken place as Cowdery read

stone to gain access to a previously existing translation, perhaps one done by God or by angels. Either way, the Book of Mormon is nearly the opposite of the standard Christian conception of the Bible—which Joseph Smith shared. The Bible was God-breathed in its original writing but then subject to human influences in its transmission and translation. Inversely, the Book of Mormon presents itself as mostly human in its origins, and then this quite human (though inspired) record was preserved and translated through divine providence and intervention.

The Book of Mormon is, as the early LDS apostle Parley P. Pratt once noted, "a very strange book," and few other world scriptures are comparable in their modes of creation, canonization, and narrative.[17] It is much easier to find sacred texts that are closer to Smith's other scriptural productions. The texts in the "thus saith the Lord" genre of revelations that appear in the Doctrine and Covenants read somewhat like the direct revelations of the nineteenth-century Bahá'í prophet Bahá'u'lláh (though the latter are much more voluminous).[18] The Book of Moses and Book of Abraham expand upon Genesis in a manner reminiscent of Jewish midrash and targum, particularly the book of Jubilees. And Joseph Smith's "new translation" of the Bible is a prophetic revision of the Bible that would be matched a couple of decades later by the Chinese visionary rebel Hong Xiuquan.[19]

---

a line of dictation back to Smith. And although there are several variant spellings for names in the original manuscript, the first appearance of a name is often marked by very deliberate spelling (as with "Coriantumr" at Helaman 1:15). It appears that the two men were working hard to get the words exactly right. See Royal Skousen's multivolume *Analysis of Textual Variants of the Book of Mormon* (Provo, UT: Foundation for Ancient Research and Mormon Studies, 2004–2006). One of Smith's contemporaneous revelations suggests that he himself was greatly involved in the process of "translation," which required him to "study it out in [his] mind" and then have the words confirmed by a spiritual feeling. See Revelation, April 1829-D, in *JSP*-D1:50 [D&C 9:7–8]. However, the revelation, which was directed toward Oliver Cowdery, may have been specific to him, without direct application to Smith. By contrast, a passage in the Book of Mormon itself implies that Smith was actually reading a text. Nephi prophesies that the Lord will speak to the future translator and explain, "I am able to do my own work; wherefore thou shalt read the words which I shall give unto thee" (2 Nephi 27:19). These issues are grappled with in Samuel Morris Brown, "Seeing the Voice of God: The Book of Mormon on Its Own Translation," Chapter 6 herein; and Ann Taves, "Joseph Smith, Helen Schucman, and the Experience of Producing a Spiritual Text: Comparing the Translating of the Book of Mormon and the Scribing of *A Course in Miracles*," Chapter 7 herein.

17. Parley P. Pratt, *The Autobiography of Parley Parker Pratt* [. . .], ed. Parley P. Pratt [Jr.] (New York: Russell Brothers, 1874), 37.

18. Interestingly, some of Bahá'u'lláh's revelations were apparently dictated quite rapidly. The hundred-page *Kitáb-i-Íqán [Book of Certitude]* (1861) was said to have been produced in just two days and two nights, and eventually Bahá'u'lláh's scribes developed a type of shorthand they called "revelation writing" to keep up with the flow of his words. Adib Taherzadeh, *The Revelation of Bahá'u'lláh*, rev. ed. (Oxford, UK: George Ronald, 1976), 1:21–29, 34–37, 110, 157–58.

19. See Jonathan D. Spence, *God's Chinese Son: The Taiping Heavenly Kingdom of Hong Xiuquan* (New York: W. W. Norton, 1996), 254–61. Joseph Smith's revised version of the Bible was canonized by

Given the remarkable claims and contents of the Book of Mormon, it is worth asking what, if anything, would be lost if Joseph Smith had instead dictated, by divine inspiration, a work of systematic theology such as the contemporary church's *Gospel Principles* manual.[20] Or if he had produced a history of the Nephites in his own voice, based on visions or conversations with angels? Or what if his scriptural output consisted solely of direct revelations like those compiled in the Doctrine and Covenants? Producing revelatory texts that were not translations still would have supported Smith's claims to prophethood and allowed him to organize a church and establish its basic doctrines. Certainly, other founders of Christian denominations managed to be successful without producing supernatural translations. So, what difference did the Book of Mormon make? What benefits did it have to offer?

Some of the analysis that follows considers the Book of Mormon from a traditional Mormon perspective as a translation of a previously existing narrative written and edited by historical individuals. It is possible to read the book as a work of myth, or as religious fiction written by Joseph Smith, or even as fiction written by God and revealed to Joseph Smith—all of which may be hypotheses worth exploring—but in trying to understand the implications of reading the book as a translation, at least from the view of those who have been converted by it, it has to be imagined as an extensive, multigenerational production of ancient record keepers writing in a distant language and culture. From this perspective the question may be posed again, in a slightly different way: What does the Book of Mormon do that the Doctrine and Covenants cannot? Potential

the Missouri-based Reorganized Church of Jesus Christ of Latter Day Saints (now Community of Christ) as the "Inspired Version." *The Holy Scriptures: Inspired Version, Containing the Old and New Testaments; An Inspired Revision of the Authorized Version, by Joseph Smith, Jr., Reorganized Church of Jesus Christ of Latter Day Saints* (Independence, MO: Herald Publishing House, 1974, 1987). Smith's Bible revision has generally been referred to within the Utah-based Church of Jesus Christ of Latter-day Saints as the "Joseph Smith Translation" (or "JST") since 1979, when parts of it were incorporated into the church's official edition of the King James Bible. *The Holy Bible, Containing the Old and New Testaments, Translated out of the Original Tongues* [...] (Salt Lake City: The Church of Jesus Christ of Latter-day Saints, 1979). Although Smith himself called the project a "translation," the term was (and is still) easily misunderstood because he was not working with any Hebrew or Greek text. Perhaps this is an indication of his rather expansive view of the term translation. In the author's opinion it would be better to use the older title "Inspired Version," or even the title "Joseph Smith Revision," suggested by David P. Wright, particularly when writing for non-Mormon audiences. David P. Wright, "'In Plain Terms that We May Understand': Joseph Smith's Transformation of Hebrews in Alma 12–13," in *New Approaches to the Book of Mormon: Explorations in Critical Methodology*, ed. Brent Lee Metcalfe (Salt Lake City: Signature Books, 1993), 165–229. The Joseph Smith Papers presents and refers to the relevant documents as "Bible Revision Manuscripts" (accessible in the Revelations and Translations series of the online edition of The Joseph Smith Papers).

20. *Gospel Principles* (Salt Lake City: The Church of Jesus Christ of Latter-day Saints, 1978, 2009).

answers may be organized into at least four categories: internal perspectives, historical implications, literary considerations, and biblical comparisons.

INTERNAL PERSPECTIVES

The Book of Mormon is a remarkably self-aware book. Its narrators speak regularly about their own writing and editorial processes, their qualifications for such work, their ambitions, and the divine guidance they have received. They often address future readers directly, and they conceptualize the book they are producing as a record of a branch of the house of Israel—a record that will someday be recovered and distributed throughout the world with the help of the Gentiles. Indeed, the Book of Mormon may be the most self-referential of major world scriptures, after the Qur'an.[21] Yet these self-aware, self-revealing narrators do not simply declare eternal truths; they tell stories. And one of the advantages of scriptural narrative is that religious principles can be demonstrated through (presumed) historical events rather than simply asserted.

For instance, the discovery and translation of the gold plates by Joseph Smith is prefigured in the Book of Mormon itself by an episode in which the people of Limhi found twenty-four Jaredite gold plates written in an unknown language. These plates were translated with the help of physical but spiritually operated devices called "interpreters" (which appear to have been seer stones of some sort), and the account on the plates was preserved by a series of Nephite record keepers until it eventually was edited by Moroni as the book of Ether.[22] There is also a brief reference to a miraculous translation of cryptic inscriptions on a Jaredite stele and to the "interpreters" that would later allow Joseph Smith to translate the Book of Mormon.[23] The fascination with written texts, scripture, canon, scriptural interpretation, record keeping, transmission, and translation—all worked out in multiple overlapping narratives, localities, and time frames—is characteristic of the Book of Mormon. The story of the Jaredite plates may offer a sense of how the Book of Mormon might see itself, as a parallel case. What does it mean for the Mormon scripture to be implicated in this economy of sacred text production, particularly when Joseph Smith, like King Mosiah, "interpret[ed] the engravings by the gift and power of God"?[24]

21. See Stefan Wild, ed., *Self-Referentiality in the Qur'an* (Wiesbaden, Germany: Harrassowitz Verlag, 2006).

22. Mosiah 8:5–21, 28:10–20; Alma 37:21–31; Ether 1:1–2.

23. Omni 1:20–22; Ether 4:4–5.

24. Omni 1:20.

A Translation Can Solve a Historical Mystery

From the time that Europeans first came to America, they wondered about the Indians—who they were, where they had come from, what had happened to them, and what their connection was to the artifacts and earthen structures that the new settlers had encountered.[25] (There is a parallel mystery as well with attempts to decipher Egyptian hieroglyphs from the seventeenth to early nineteenth centuries.[26]) The Book of Mormon offered answers to similar questions that occurred within its narrative framework. King Limhi told Ammon how his men had discovered the Jaredite plates in "a land which was covered with bones of men, and of beasts, and was also covered with ruins of buildings of every kind."[27] Limhi thought the plates might "give us a knowledge of a remnant of the people who have been destroyed . . . or perhaps they will give us a knowledge of this very people who have been destroyed," and he concluded, "Doubtless a great mystery is contained within these plates."[28]

A Translation Can Provoke Curiosity

Many people are interested in broad religious topics about the nature of God, what he might say to humans, and what he wants from them—subjects that are often addressed in revelatory texts. Yet the heightened focus on materiality, history, and specificity involved in a translation of an actual record may make its information seem more urgent. The possibility that some people in the past had greater access to the divine or to surpassing wisdom, and that their insights are worth the laborious (or miraculous) work of rendering them into another language, can be tantalizing. In addition, translations are nearly always based on some precious physical object (a manuscript, an inscription, engraved plates, etc.) that has been passed down from person to person, or hidden away and later recovered. When Mosiah's people learned of Jaredite plates, "they were desirous beyond measure to know concerning those people who had been destroyed."[29]

25. See Robert Silverberg, *Mound Builders of Ancient America: The Archaeology of a Myth* (Athens: Ohio University Press, 1986); and Lorett Treese, *A Serpent's Tale: Discovering America's Ancient Mound Builders* (Yardley, PA: Westholme, 2016).

26. Matthew J. Grey, "Approaching Egyptian Papyri through Biblical Language: Joseph Smith's Use of Hebrew in His Translation of the Book of Abraham," 396–98 herein.

27. Mosiah 8:8.

28. Mosiah 8:12, 19.

29. Mosiah 28:12.

A Translation Can Serve as Evidence for an Implausible Story

Religious experiences are notoriously difficult to authenticate, which may be why early Mormon missionaries talked much more about the Book of Mormon than about Smith's first vision of Deity. Many people in early nineteenth-century America claimed to dream dreams, see visions, or hear heavenly voices; at some point believers simply have to take these accounts on faith. A translation, however, holds out the possibility of independent verification; there may be internal or external evidences to back up the narrative. King Limhi recounted to Ammon a wild tale of how his men stumbled onto the remnants of a lost civilization and then continued, "For a testimony that the things that they had said are true, they have brought twenty-four plates which are filled with engravings."[30]

Joseph Smith's stories of gold plates, angels, and ancient American Christians were certainly incredible, but the sheer existence of a lengthy, complex text, with attestations of witnesses who claimed to have seen the plates, might forestall easy dismissals, at least for some. By contrast, the "Testimony of the Twelve Apostles to the Truth of the Book of Doctrine and Covenants" is less persuasive since it doesn't quite jump from the spiritual to the material realm: "We, therefore, feel willing to bear testimony . . . that the Lord has borne record to our souls, through the Holy Ghost . . . that these commandments were given by inspiration of God."[31] In addition, according to the Book of Mormon, seers who can use "interpreters" stand in the ranks of prophets and are worthy of great respect.[32]

A Translation Can Reveal Patterns of Human Evil and Divine Justice

A translated history can reveal human works of darkness and God's justice in a series of precedents, patterns, and fulfilled prophecies. At least, this seems to be the main lesson to be drawn from the prophet Alma's description of the contents of the twenty-four Jaredite plates. The occasion was the transfer of the plates from Alma to his son Helaman. Recounting the outline of the book of

30. Mosiah 8:9.

31. *The Doctrine and Covenants of the Church of Jesus Christ of Latter-day Saints* [. . .] (Salt Lake City: The Church of Jesus Christ of Latter-day Saints, 1981), iv–v. This testimony was included in the first edition of the Doctrine and Covenants, see *The Doctrine and Covenants of the Church of the Latter Day Saints* [. . .] (Kirtland, OH: F. G. Williams, 1835), 256.

32. Mosiah 8:15–18.

Ether (before it was dictated by Smith), Alma noted the wickedness of the Jaredites, the prophecies they had received that "if they did not repent they should be destroyed from off the face of the earth," and a warning that their "secret works" would be made known to those who came after them. Alma continues, "And now, my son, we see that they did not repent; therefore they have been destroyed, and thus far the word of God has been fulfilled; yea, their secret abominations have been brought out of darkness and made known unto us."[33] Coming at the end of the Book of Mormon, the book of Ether suggests that what happened to the Nephites was not a strange anomaly in world history; the Lord generally sends prophets to guide people, and if they are rejected and the people turn to wickedness, God then sends destruction and, especially in the case of the New World, other people will eventually be allowed to inherit the land. Indeed, by including the story of the Jaredites, Moroni—as an editor—imparts a typological quality to the tale of the Nephites, with an implicit warning to Gentile inhabitants of the Americas in the last days.[34]

The Jaredite plates narrate a complete cycle of the pattern, wherein prophecies can be matched up with their fulfillments. The Nephites are themselves in a subsequent cycle; Alma worries that his own people might "fall into darkness also and be destroyed." (Oddly enough, at this point in the book first-time readers will know little of the fate that awaits the Nephites and almost nothing of the Jaredites.) Alma concludes with what appears to be a timeless pattern: "Cursed be the land forever and ever unto those workers of darkness and secret combinations, even unto destruction, except they repent before they are fully ripe." Modern American readers might well see themselves as being in yet a third iteration of the cycle, with prophecies from the Book of Mormon serving as a divine message warning them of impending destruction.[35]

A Translation Can Forge an Emotional Connection to People and Events

Readers of direct revelations may feel a connection to the recipient of those divine communications (think of Muhammad, Hildegard, St. Francis, Swedenborg, Bahá'u'lláh, or Nakayama Miki), and the stories of how specific

33. Alma 37:21–31.

34. See Ether 2:9–12.

35. Nevertheless, the relationship between the Jaredites and the Nephites is not exactly parallel to that between the Nephites and modern readers. The existence of the Jaredites was never doubted by the Nephites, while the historicity of the Nephites is very much in question for many of those who read the Book of Mormon today.

revelations came at particular times in the life of a prophet or an early faith community may be compelling. But knowledge of historical context is something that readers themselves have to bring to these sacred writings (perhaps with the help of later editors, such as those who wrote the introductions to each revelation in the Doctrine and Covenants), and the focus of empathy remains fairly narrow. By contrast, a translated narrative such as the Book of Mormon includes several major narrator/editors, a dozen writers, and more than two hundred named individuals. There are stories upon stories—and often stories within stories—in which readers can feel admiration for the good, repulsion for the wicked, and sympathy for those caught in between. The reader can identify with and respond to ordinary people, not just prophets and seers. Our situation as readers is similar to what is seen at the end of the book of Mosiah, when the translated account of the destruction of the Jaredites "did cause the people of Mosiah to mourn exceedingly, yea, they were filled with sorrow."[36] Narratives matter, and translations of histories provide access to many more stories.

HISTORICAL IMPLICATIONS

The Book of Mormon's alleged status as a miraculous translation of an ancient document, even one that is no longer extant, is not without precedent among recent world scriptures. However, its claim to be the history of an otherwise unknown civilization is striking.[37] The historical presentation of the narrative is almost relentless, often in the form of a yearly chronicle and frequently narrated with the phrase "and it came to pass" (see Figure 9.1). The relationship between revealed scripture and assumed historicity has several implications, in addition to the obvious message that there is indeed a God who has a plan for humanity operating throughout history.

36. Mosiah 28:18.

37. The closest parallels may be with the terma (*gter-ma*) texts of Tibetan Buddhism—a genre that includes *The Tibetan Book of the Dead*. These were "treasure texts" that were hidden around the landscape of Tibet by enlightened Buddhist masters from the seventh to ninth centuries CE, to be rediscovered hundreds of years later at times when they would have particular spiritual value. Some of these treasures were physical objects secreted in caves, mountains, lakes, and valleys, while others were "mind treasures" hidden in the minds of future treasure revealers. See Janet Gyatso, "Signs, Memory and History: A Tantric Buddhist Theory of Scriptural Transmission," *Journal of the International Association of Buddhist Studies* 9, no. 2 (1986): 7–35; Tulku Thondup Rinpoche, *Hidden Teachings of Tibet: An Explanation of the Terma Tradition of Tibetan Buddhism*, ed. Harold Talbott (Boston: Wisdom Publications, 1997); and Andreas Doctor, *Tibetan Treasure Literature: Revelation, Tradition, and Accomplishment in Visionary Buddhism* (Ithaca, NY: Snow Lion, 2005). A significant difference, however, is that Joseph Smith was not writing within a well-established religious tradition of recovered esoteric texts.

FIGURE 9.1. Original manuscript of the Book of Mormon. The first few lines of the first extant page of the original manuscript of the Book of Mormon (now 1 Nephi 2:2–23). The narrative style of the Book of Mormon—including its ubiquitous use of the phrase "and it came to pass"—is seen in these opening lines of the text. The narrative begins with the prophet Lehi and his family leaving Jerusalem, traveling across the Arabian Peninsula to the Indian Ocean, sailing to the Americas, and settling in a new "promised land." Faded manuscript photographed with multi-spectral imaging. Church History Library, Salt Lake City.

A Translated Narrative Can Be Corroborated by External Sources

Many early Latter-day Saints expected that archaeological discoveries would provide evidence for the Book of Mormon, and indeed Joseph Smith believed that the work of John Lloyd Stephens, the Mesoamerican explorer, "corresponds with & supports the testimony of the Book of Mormon."[38] Lengthy excerpts from Stephens's *Incidents of Travel in Central America* were published in the church newspaper from February to October 1842. The potential for independent confirmation is matched by a possibility of disconfirmation as well, and this has caused distress for some Latter-day Saints as the history of the ancient Americas has turned out to be more complex than one might imagine from simply reading the Book of Mormon. Still, Mormon scholar Hugh Nibley and others have sought parallels with the better-known cultures of the Ancient Near East, always asking how much of this Smith could have known in 1829. Many Latter-day Saints today still believe that decisive historical evidence may someday be unearthed in the jungles of Central America.

A Translated Narrative Can Allow for Inaccuracies and Anachronisms

Because the Book of Mormon's original text was said to have been written by human authors, inspired though they might have been, it is possible that

38. Letter to John M. Bernhisel, 16 November 1841, in *JSP*-D8:296.

they misunderstood a few details, or were misled by their sources, or simply made mistakes—a possibility that they freely acknowledged. As the last prophet wrote in his final words: "If there are faults they are the mistakes of men; wherefore, condemn not the things of God."[39] And a *translation* of ancient inscriptions puts another level of distance between readers and the historical events narrated by the text. By contrast, direct revelations might be thought of as exact transcriptions of God's words or as a prophet's interpretation of a revelatory experience. Both of these modes of divine communication might seem more reliable than a miraculous translation, but they may also be held to an impossibly high standard—any errors could undermine the credibility of the revelation. Translations, on the other hand, may be literal, idiomatic, or anything in between.

A Translated Narrative Can Be Viewed as an Impressive Achievement

Even without much external corroboration, and even while allowing room for error, the Book of Mormon is in itself a remarkable work. It is certainly possible to extemporize long, stream-of-consciousness exhortations, or theological expositions, or episodic stories, but the Book of Mormon consists of over five hundred pages in almost any edition of tightly constructed, coherent, integrated narrative—with almost one hundred different place names and more than two hundred named individuals. There are multiple narrators and editors who are writing within carefully worked out parameters of plates and records, genealogical relationships, kingship lists, scriptural exegesis, internal citations, and literary units that include contemporaneous subplots, parallel narratives, embedded documents, and flashbacks. As Richard L. Bushman has noted:

> In [Mormon's] narrative, derived from the available source materials, he quotes other prophets and sometimes quotes them quoting still others. Moroni injects a letter from his father, and Nephi inserts lengthy passages from previous scriptures. Mormon moves in and out of the narrative, pointing up a crucial conclusion or addressing readers with a sermon of his own. Almost always two minds are present, and sometimes three, all kept account of in the flow of words.[40]

39. Title page. See also 1 Nephi 19:6; 2 Nephi 33:4, 11; Ether 12:23–25.

40. Richard L. Bushman, *Joseph Smith and the Beginnings of Mormonism* (Urbana and Chicago: University of Illinois Press, 1984), 119.

In addition, theological and political understandings develop over the course of the book. Some forms of complexity may be in the eye of the reader, but at least a few are quite objective, including the ticking chronology of the years of the judges (with some years getting just a sentence or two and others spanning several chapters). Indeed, all this is handled virtually without contradiction or errors of consistency. The fact that Joseph Smith dictated the whole of the Book of Mormon to scribes over a three-month period, one time through, while looking at a seer stone in his hat, makes the book even more of a marvel. By now it should be obvious that the Book of Mormon wants things both ways. It presents itself as an ancient document that was laboriously and carefully written by many different authors and editors over the course of a millennium, yet at the same time it also claims to be the product of an extraordinary revelatory experience as it was dictated rapidly by a nineteenth-century American prophet over the course of a few months.

LITERARY CONSIDERATIONS

Since direct archeological evidence has not been forthcoming, the Book of Mormon today stands as a relatively closed, complete literary unit. There are no other Nephite texts for comparison, no ancient sources that explicitly mention Nephites, no identifiable Nephite artifacts or known settlements to pin down a geographical setting, and no information about Nephite culture other than what is contained in the scripture. Yet the text itself is open to literary analysis. When faced with a translated narrative, one can ask how it works and whether it is done well or poorly. There is some overlap here with how the text might be read as fiction, but a translated text can be read as both history and fiction. Whether the narrators were actual people or figments of the author's imagination, a reader can nevertheless analyze what they are doing with their sources within the framework of the text. Revelations given in God's own voice—such as Joseph Smith's "thus saith the Lord" revelations in the Doctrine and Covenants—seem less susceptible to sophisticated literary interpretation.

A Translated Narrative Can Have Integrated Parts that Work Together

The Book of Mormon contains a number of different genres—sermons, memoirs, history, prophecy, scriptural interpretation, an apocalypse, letters, and poetry—all supposedly written by different authors over the course of a thousand years, yet each takes a deliberate place within the overarching scheme of the "small" and the "large" sets of plates, edited by Nephi, Mormon, and Moroni. There are structures within the narrative—the original chapter divisions, multichapter blocks, parallel stories, chiasmus, and so forth—and there may be meaning in these literary units. That is to say, the editors (or author) may have intended readers to interpret certain events or characters in light of each other. For instance, the fact that Alma's confrontation with the Antichrist Korihor originally appeared in the same chapter as his sermon to the Zoramites on faith (the current edition now places these events in Alma 30 and 32) might indicate that readers were intended to weigh them against each other.[41]

A Translated Narrative Can Be Self-Authenticating

Because the Book of Mormon primarily takes the form of a history-like narrative, it can be seen that prophecies given early in the record are fulfilled in later chapters. This may not be persuasive to skeptics, but for believers, the prophecy-fulfillment pattern suggests that prophecies that have yet to materialize, whose fulfillment may lie in the latter days beyond the chronological parameters of the book, are nevertheless reliable. The many details and specifics of a lengthy translated history, even apart from the possibility of external corroboration or falsification, are nevertheless subject to tests of internal coherence and consistency—tests that the Book of Mormon passes remarkably well.[42] In addition, the incongruity between the form of the Book of Mormon (as a complex, multivocal, interconnected narrative) and the circumstances of its production (by rapid oral dictation, apparently by someone unaware of its overall contours) means that the book itself provides evidence of some extraordinary, if not supernatural, process of composition.[43]

41. See Heather Hardy, "Alma's Experiment in Faith: A Broader Context," *Dialogue: A Journal of Mormon Thought* 44, no. 3 (Fall 2011): 67–91.

42. There are apparently only two geographical mistakes in the Book of Mormon, that is, instances for which location information does not fit with information found elsewhere in the text. The first occurs at Alma 51:25–26, where the city of Nephihah is mentioned in passing as one of the captured cities on the coast. The second occurs at Alma 53:6, which places the city of Melek in the land of Nephi. Both contradictions, however, may be due to scribal errors. See Skousen, *Analysis of Textual Variants*, 4:2647–49, 2676–78.

43. As he was dictating, Joseph Smith apparently did not know when a new (internal) book was beginning, or how long any given book might be. And even though the Book of Mormon went through two more editions during Smith's lifetime—each of which included numerous grammatical and stylistic revisions by Smith himself—he never seemed to realize that the "Amalekites" in the middle of the book of Alma (chaps. 21–24, 27, and 43) were the same people as the "Amlicites" appearing in the beginning of the book of Alma (chaps. 2–3), a misspelling that makes a considerable difference in the narrative. See Royal Skousen, "Translating the Book of Mormon: Evidence from the Original Manuscript," in *Book of Mormon*

A Translated Narrative Can Illustrate Theology in Action

It is one thing to talk about religious principles such as repentance, forgiveness, courage, or faithfulness in the abstract; it is another to see them enacted by specific individuals in specific circumstances. The Book of Mormon is full of dysfunctional families, political malfeasance, ethnic conflict, religious corruption, social collapse, and faith crises. It can be instructive to watch people work through such challenges. As illustration—the missionary tales of the sons of King Mosiah are probably more engaging and inspiring than the simple, oft-repeated refrain that the gospel must go forth to "every nation, kindred, tongue, and people."[44]

A Translated Narrative Can Present Multiple Points of View

It is worth noting that Joseph Smith's voice is never explicitly or directly presented in the Book of Mormon (other than in the preface to the 1830 edition). He never shows up in the narrative as an external, nineteenth-century editor or commentator. Rather, everything in the book is seen through the eyes of its own characters, who interpret events and comment on actions through dialogue, formal speeches, and writing. The major narrators have a privileged point of view, but even they exhibit somewhat different agendas or editorial strategies, and individual understandings and opinions may develop over time. It is also possible to critically evaluate their efforts, or to look for the story behind the story. As argued in *Understanding the Book of Mormon*, Nephi describes his older brothers in ways that intentionally alienate readers from their point of view, Mormon's over-the-top praise for Captain Moroni seems at odds with the stories he chooses to tell, and Moroni's writings include three separate attempts to find a satisfactory ending for his father's history—all of which make the narrators interesting characters.[45] The variety of opinions and perspectives—from Nephi to Jacob, Alma to Helaman, or Mormon to Moroni—offers readers diverse examples of contact with divinity. It appears that God can interact with people, even faithful people, in very different ways.

Authorship Revisited: The Evidence for Ancient Origins, ed. Noel B. Reynolds (Provo, UT: Foundation for Ancient Research and Mormon Studies, 1997), 61–93; and Skousen, *Analysis of Textual Variants*, 3:1605–9.

44. See Mosiah 15:28.

45. Grant Hardy, *Understanding the Book of Mormon: A Reader's Guide* (Oxford and New York: Oxford University Press, 2010), 33–44, 109–10, 263–65.

A Translated Narrative Can Be Open to Interpretation

Individual readers can find different yet equally valid lessons in the same stories, in accordance with their own needs, experiences, or understanding. Indeed, it is quite possible for a single person to read the Book of Mormon at various times in his or her life and gain new insights. Latter-day Saints currently read the racial elements in the Book of Mormon in ways that diverge sharply from Latter-day Saints' views in the nineteenth or early twentieth centuries.[46] Sometimes these interpretations become more accurate over time, but it is also true that no single reading exhausts the meaning of a story, unlike works of propositional theology that attempt to be as precise and unequivocal as possible. The multivalency of narrative means that religious texts can continue to speak to readers in new circumstances, generation after generation.

A Translated Narrative Can Enable a Relationship with Its Narrators

The narrators in the Book of Mormon are fairly open about their concerns, intentions, and editorial decisions, and it is possible for readers to recognize their characteristic styles in shaping stories and interacting with source materials. From the other side, the narrators are consciously writing for a future readership, which they claim to know through prophetic insight. The narrators are hardly perfect—there are gaps in what they present, and at times they misjudge the needs of their audience (as in the nearly total exclusion of female voices and characters)—yet readers can learn to appreciate their narrators' quirks and their goodness, and even come to admire them. Quite unusually, both Nephi and Moroni assert that a virtual relationship with readers will someday become personal and face to face.[47] A person's connection to characters in the Book of Mormon can be somewhat separate from his or her impressions of Joseph Smith; it might be possible to feel a great deal of affection for Nephi, Alma, or Mormon, while still having reservations about Smith's financial judgment, management style, or social skills. Smith's other revelations, by contrast, seem much more entangled with his abilities and personality than the Book of Mormon.

46. Armand L. Mauss, *All Abraham's Children: Changing Mormon Conceptions of Race and Lineage* (Urbana and Chicago: University of Illinois Press, 2003), 114–57.

47. 2 Nephi 33:11; Moroni 10:34.

BIBLICAL COMPARISONS

In trying to expand the long-closed canon of Christianity, a new scripture that is similar to the Bible has some decided advantages. It can be seen as reassuringly familiar, and many investigators will want to compare the two books closely, looking for commonalities and contradictions. Early converts to Mormonism sometimes reported that they found the two books entirely compatible.[48]

A Translation Can Seem Like the Bible

Not only does the Book of Mormon sound roughly biblical, with its Elizabethan grammar and King James idioms, but the contents are generally similar: a series of books named for ancient prophets or kings, which relate the history of a chosen people—in this case, a branch of the house of Israel in the New World—interspersed with lengthy sermons and prophecies. Although there is little in the Nephite scripture that corresponds to biblical law codes, collections of psalms, or wisdom literature, there are nevertheless long excerpts from Isaiah, and the narrative is reminiscent of the historical sections of the Bible.

A Translation Can Be a Sequel to the Bible

The main story of the Book of Mormon begins just about the time that the Old Testament's central narrative comes to an end. The sequence of events from Moses leading the children of Israel to the promised land, and then from the reign of judges through the united monarchy and the eventual conquest of both Israel and Judah covers a span of about six hundred years. The Book of Mormon fits into the biblical story just before the Babylonian conquest, and then follows an offshoot of the house of Israel through another thousand years as it expands the story of God's relationship with his chosen people into new lands and new generations. Those centuries of additional history give the Book of Mormon a scriptural gravitas that matches the sweep and scope of the Bible

48. Examples include Warren Foote, John Young, William Miller, Joel Hills Johnson, and David Pettegrew. Susan Easton Black, ed., *Stories from the Early Saints: Converted by the Book of Mormon* (Salt Lake City: Bookcraft, 1992), 11, 20, 24, 51, 59). See also Janiece Johnson, "Becoming a People of the Books: Toward an Understanding of Early Mormon Converts and the New Word of the Lord," *Journal of Book of Mormon Studies* 27 (2018): 1–43.

itself. A few revelations to a single prophet at one particular point in history will not have the same claim to standing alongside the Bible as a companion volume. Indeed, the Book of Mormon speaks only rarely and somewhat obliquely about Joseph Smith and nineteenth-century America (generally in the form of Nephite prophecies). It tells its own story, full of unique characters, geographic settings, plot twists, interconnections, and extended development.

A Translation into the Language of the KJV Can Facilitate Intertextuality

Readers of the Book of Mormon encounter not just King James-style English, but also the pervasive use of phrases borrowed from the Old and New Testaments. At times, the comparison of contexts helps the reader see events in the Book of Mormon in particular ways, or biblical expressions may be modified or expanded so as to reinterpret the original. For instance, at 1 Nephi 13:37 there is a conflation of Isaiah 52:7 ("How beautiful upon the mountains are the feet of him . . . that publishes peace: that bringeth good tidings of good") with Luke 2:10 ("good tidings of great joy"), which gives readers familiar with the KJV a better sense of the messianic or Christological implications of Isaiah's prophecy.

A second example occurs at the end of First Nephi, when Nephi alludes to another prophecy of Isaiah. In Isaiah 49:22–23, the Lord God declares, "Behold, I will lift up mine hand to the Gentiles, and set up my standard to the people . . . and kings shall be thy nursing fathers, and their queens thy nursing mothers." In contrast, in 1 Nephi 22:6, Nephi states that scattered Israel "shall be nursed by the Gentiles," explaining that "the Lord has lifted up his hand upon the Gentiles and set them up for a standard." It is notable that in Nephi's version, it is the Gentiles themselves who will serve as a standard.

A third instance can be seen at Mosiah 6:1, where King Benjamin decides to make a register of "the names of all those who had entered into a covenant with God to keep his commandments." Similar language is found in 2 Kings 23:3 and 2 Chronicles 34:31, when King Josiah "made a covenant before the Lord . . . to keep his commandments." Perhaps readers are meant to see a parallel between Josiah's and Benjamin's reform efforts (though it is interesting that the responsibility is put on the people in the Book of Mormon, rather than on the monarch). Dozens of similar examples are available, including a good number provided by the resurrected Christ himself during his three-day visit to the Nephites. Joseph Smith's revelations in the Doctrine and Covenants also regularly employ biblical phrases, but the intertextuality between the Book of Mormon and the Bible is more complex and, arguably, more interesting.

A Translation Can Engage the Bible on Its Own Terms

The Book of Mormon fills in gaps and clarifies ambiguities in the Bible, yet it does so not as a commentary but as a sacred narrative in its own right. In fact, the Mormon scripture is presented in ways that seem to improve on the Bible—or at least answer the concerns of some readers in the nineteenth century. Rather than a collection of short, independent writings collected, revised, and canonized over centuries by unknown hands, the Book of Mormon is a coherent whole, organized for the most part by a single prophetic editor in the fourth century. It is as if the Old Testament had been put together in its entirety by Ezra, or as if Paul had written the book of Acts and then combined it with the gospels and a handful of letters before sending it out into the world with explanations as to why he had chosen these texts and not others. In Joseph Smith's day, skeptics and Deists took delight in pointing out the many contradictions in the Bible, which were indeed a problem for those committed to the principle of *sola scriptura*, but the Book of Mormon, as a thoroughly edited text, seems to be much more consistent and harmonious in its parts.

Nephi, Mormon, and Moroni were not just chroniclers but prophets with a sense of their audience in the distant future, and they were aware that their words would someday become scripture. In addition, the narrators all report revelations from God in which they were commanded to include or omit specific details.[49] While the Book of Mormon gives the impression of a Bible-like collection of heterogeneous writings, there is an overarching narrative framework by which readers are assured that these materials were selected and edited by prophets, with Jesus himself essentially playing the role of the general editor (since he was the one giving them explicit instructions concerning content). It is as if the Book of Mormon took the authority claimed for the Bible and then squared it. And this applies not just to the original writing and subsequent editing, but also to the text's transmission and translation. In contrast to the English Bible, Joseph Smith was working with autographs rather than manuscript copies of copies; there is a single authorized version; and that translation was divinely assisted, rather than being grounded in scholarly, human expertise.

49. See 1 Nephi 14:18–30; 2 Nephi 28:1, 32:7; 3 Nephi 26:6–12, 30:1–2; Ether 12:22–41.

CONCLUSION

The fact that the Book of Mormon is presented as a translation of an ancient record rather than simply a direct revelation to Joseph Smith is one of its most salient features, which profoundly impacts its claims, its reception, and the sorts of analytical approaches that it invites.[50] Eber D. Howe, an early critic of the Book of Mormon, provided a detailed synopsis in his *Mormonism Unvailed* (1834), but it is obvious that he did not really grasp what the text was trying to do as a translated narrative. He complained about its archaic language, and then expressed puzzlement about its contents:

> If God chose to reveal himself, it would be reasonable to expect that it would be done definitely, and in such language as could be easily understood by all; and why this long circumlocution of history? It has nothing to do with salvation. Christ, nor the inspired writers of the New Testament, furnish no such example; the bare facts of the plan of redemption is set before us, and a few self-evident rules to govern our moral conduct.[51]

Nevertheless, when read on its own terms, the "long circumlocution of history" has everything to do with the book's message of salvation.

The Book of Mormon, as a translation, seems more impressive, more motivating, and more interesting than the shorter revelations (of the kind compiled in the Doctrine and Covenants). This is an arguable position and may ultimately depend on the reader, but the genre of scripture consisting of a lengthy, integrated, historical narrative translated miraculously from an ancient record is certainly much rarer. Muslims believe that the Qur'an was Muhammad's greatest miracle. The same might be said of the Book of Mormon and Joseph Smith. Certainly, Smith never produced anything like it again. The Doctrine

50. Some of the observations made above have limited application to Joseph Smith's other translation projects, particularly the Book of Moses and the Book of Abraham. Both texts involve a great deal of intertextuality with the Bible, revise conventions of biblical narration by giving voice to first-person narrators, and give increased attention to literary sources. See Old Testament Manuscript 2, in Joseph Smith, *Joseph Smith's New Translation of the Bible: Original Manuscripts*, ed. Scott H. Faulring, Kent P. Jackson, and Robert J. Matthews (Provo, UT: Religious Studies Center, 2004), 86 [Moses 2:1, 6:5–22]; *JSP*-R4:308–11 [Abraham 1:14, 28, 31]; Terryl Givens with Brian M. Hauglid, *The Pearl of Greatest Price: Mormonism's Most Controversial Scripture* (Oxford and New York: Oxford University Press, 2019). But in general, these other translations are too brief and too closely tied to specific biblical passages to offer the sort of striking contrasts with Smith's other revelations that the Book of Mormon can provide.

51. E. D. Howe, *Mormonism Unvailed* [...] (Painesville, OH: published by the author, 1834), 24.

and Covenants, primarily concerned with doctrine, church organization, and instructions to individuals, consists of short, distinct revelations given over about twenty-five years, which were then collected, edited, and substantially revised throughout Smith's life and beyond. The Joseph Smith Translation, including the Book of Moses and Joseph Smith—Matthew (both in the Pearl of Great Price), was actually more of an inspired revision and explication of the King James Bible than a fresh translation. In the five brief chapters of the Book of Abraham, the first three offer only a few new stories about an already familiar biblical patriarch while the last two chapters simply rework Genesis 1–2. None of these subsequent revelatory projects even comes close to the scope, inventiveness, narrative complexity, structural sophistication, and literary exuberance of the Book of Mormon. Indeed, without the Book of Mormon, nothing that Joseph Smith later produced would matter much at all.

PART III

Translating the King James Bible

10

The Tarrying of the Beloved Disciple

The Textual Formation of the Account of John

DAVID W. GRUA AND WILLIAM V. SMITH

Joseph Smith and Oliver Cowdery had been translating the Book of Mormon for only a matter of days or weeks in April 1829 when they debated the fate of Jesus's apostle, John the son of Zebedee. For eighteen hundred years, Christian interpreters had scrutinized the meaning of an ambiguous passage in the final chapter of the Gospel of John that suggested that Jesus's Beloved Disciple—commonly identified in the nineteenth century as John the Apostle—would tarry until Christ's second coming. Rather than further debate the interpretive possibilities of the passage, Smith and Cowdery decided to seek an answer through the "Urim and Thummim," a revelatory instrument that Smith had been using to "translate" the Book of Mormon. In response to the question regarding the Beloved Disciple's fate, Smith dictated a brief firsthand narration—referred to in this chapter as the Account of John—that described the resurrected Christ informing John, the "beloved," that he would tarry until the second coming in order to fulfill his desire to bring souls to salvation.[1]

The resulting text would be revised over the course of the next six years before reaching its final form as what is now known as Section 7 of the Doctrine and Covenants, a compilation of Smith's revelations that constitutes one

1. When Joseph Smith later recounted this incident in his documentary history, he stated that the revelation had resolved his "difference of opinion" with Oliver Cowdery "about the account of John the Apostle." Joseph Smith History, 1838–1856, A-1, 15, in *JSP*-H1:284. Although Smith's history used the phrase "account of John" to refer to John 21, the editors of the *Joseph Smith Papers* re-appropriated this phrase to refer to the revelatory text Smith produced in April 1829. Account of John, April 1829-C, in *JSP*-D1:47–48 [D&C 7]. This chapter follows the usage of the *Joseph Smith Papers*. On Smith's use of the "Urim and Thummim" spectacles and other seer stones, see Michael Hubbard MacKay and Nicholas J. Frederick, *Joseph Smith's Seer Stones* (Provo, UT: Religious Studies Center, Brigham Young University; Salt Lake City, UT: Deseret Book, 2016).

of the four standard works of Latter-day Saint scripture.[2] From 1829 to 1835, the Account of John would be in a state of flux, both interpretively and textually. Interpretively, the early church custodians of the text evidently vacillated between classifying the Account of John as either a *translation* or a *revelation*, the two main genres of Smith's scriptural productions. Smith's translations are history-like narratives, generally presented (and understood) to be English-language versions of ancient records that have been literally translated, although through a supernatural gift rather than by scholarly linguistics. Revelations are communications in the voice of Deity directed to Smith and his early followers, and make no claim to have an ancient source text.[3] Textually, the Account of John was expanded by more than one hundred words between its 1829 dictation and its 1835 publication, expansions that harmonized the 1829 text with subsequent doctrinal and ecclesiastical developments in the fledgling church. When the Account of John reached its final form in the 1835 Doctrine and Covenants, it settled the genre question by presenting the text as a "translation." Unlike other Christian thinkers who sought to use reason or tradition to unravel the mysteries of John 21 in biblical commentaries and similar works, Smith intervened in the long reception history of the passage by claiming to produce the translation of an extrabiblical scripture, written by the apostle John himself, which resolved the question of the Beloved Disciple's (im)mortality.[4]

JOHN 21 AND ITS RECEPTION HISTORY

The Account of John cannot be fully understood except in relation to the final verses of the concluding chapter of the Gospel of John—the fourth and final

2. See Clyde J. Williams, "Standard Works," in *Encyclopedia of Mormonism: The History, Scripture, Doctrine, and Procedure of The Church of Jesus Christ of Latter-day Saints*, ed. Daniel H. Ludlow (New York: Macmillan, 1992), 3:1415–16.

3. See "Joseph Smith as Revelator and Translator," in *JSP*-R1:xix. On "history-like narratives" and the application of this term to the Book of Mormon, see Hans W. Frei, *The Eclipse of Biblical Narrative: A Study of Eighteenth and Nineteenth-Century Hermeneutics* (New Haven: Yale University Press, 1974); and Grant Hardy, *Understanding the Book of Mormon: A Reader's Guide* (Oxford and New York: Oxford University Press, 2010), 26.

4. Perhaps due to its small size, scholars have largely neglected the Account of John. For two of the better treatments, see Frank F. Judd Jr. and Terry L. Szink, "John the Beloved in Latter-day Scripture (D&C 7)," in *The Doctrine and Covenants: Revelations in Context*, ed. Andrew H. Hedges, J. Spencer Fluhman, and Alonzo L. Gaskill (Provo, UT: Religious Studies Center, Brigham Young University; Salt Lake City: Deseret Book, 2008), 90–107; and Nicholas J. Frederick, "Of 'Life Eternal' and 'Eternal Lives': Joseph Smith's Engagement with the Gospel of John," in *Approaching Antiquity: Joseph Smith and the Ancient World*, ed. Lincoln H. Blumell, Mathew J. Grey, and Andrew H. Hedges (Provo, UT: Religious Studies Center, Brigham Young University; Salt Lake City: Deseret Book, 2015), 194–98. This chapter's approach to textual formation is influenced by David M. Carr, *The Formation of the Hebrew Bible: A New Reconstruction* (Oxford and New York: Oxford University Press, 2011).

canonical account of the life of Jesus. And these final verses ended in ambiguity. John 21 describes a post-resurrection appearance of Jesus to his disciples, explicitly including Peter and "that disciple whom Jesus loved." The relevant passage, comprised of verses 18–23,[5] begins with a conversation in which Jesus prophesies Peter's martyrdom. Peter then asks in regard to the Beloved Disciple, "What *shall* this man *do?*" In response, Jesus asks, "If I will that he tarry till I come, what *is that* to thee?" The passage then transitions to a description of how the "saying went abroad among the brethren that that disciple should not die." However, the text then clarifies that "Jesus said not unto him, He shall not die; but [rather], If I will that he tarry till I come, what is that to thee?"

The first interpretive problem posed in these verses is determining the identity of the elusive Beloved Disciple, and by implication, the author of the book. For reasons that remain unclear, the author of the Gospel of John opted for anonymity—apparently as an intentional literary strategy—leaving only obscure, third-person references to the Beloved Disciple as possible clues to his identity. The Beloved Disciple first appears in chapter 13 "leaning on Jesus' bosom" during the Lord's Last Supper.[6] This Disciple is likely the unnamed individual in John 19:35 who witnessed Jesus's death on the cross and bore record of it. Lastly, John 21:24 claims that the Beloved Disciple was the same individual who "testifieth of these things, and wrote these things." Despite the ambiguity in the text, by the late second century early Christian commentators—likely due to oral tradition and a desire to ascribe apostolic authorship to the text—were identifying John the son of Zebedee as the author of the gospel.[7] It was apparently around this time that the words "According to John" were added to the title of the book to distinguish it from the other written accounts of Jesus's life.[8] Beginning in the late eighteenth century, biblical scholars began to question the traditional designation, suggesting alternative candidates for the Beloved Disciple.[9] These suggestions included another John (the "Elder"), Lazarus, and even Thomas.[10] While the traditional designation still has some

5. Italics in the following quotations are original to the King James Version.

6. John 13:23–26.

7. For a detailed examination of early Christian reception of the gospel, see Ernst Haenchen, *A Commentary on the Gospel of John*, trans. Robert W. Funk, 2 vols. in *Hermeneia: A Critical and Historical Commentary on the Bible*, ed. Robert W. Funk with Ulrich Busse (Philadelphia: Fortress Press, 1984), 1:6–18.

8. Jean Zumstein, "Intratextuality and Intertextuality in the Gospel of John," trans. Mike Gray, in *Anatomies of Narrative Criticism: The Past, Present, and Futures of the Fourth Gospel*, ed. Tom Thatcher and Stephen D. Moore (Atlanta, GA: Society of Biblical Literature, 2008), 128–29.

9. See R. Alan Culpepper, *John, the Son of Zebedee: The Life of a Legend* (Columbia: University of South Carolina Press, 1994), 280–81; Haenchen, *A Commentary on the Gospel of John*, 1: chap. 2.

10. Craig S. Keener, *The Gospel of John: A Commentary* (Grand Rapids, MI: Baker Academic, 2003), 1:86–87, 95–98.

defenders,[11] scholarship on the gospel generally posits an anonymous author with ties to a late first-century, Jewish-Christian community.[12]

Another interpretive challenge is the question of what Jesus meant in John 21:22—"If I will that he tarry till I come, what *is that* to thee?" Verse 23 indicates that the statement circulated among some early Christians who interpreted it to mean "that that disciple should not die." The author of the text appears to challenge this interpretation by emphasizing that Jesus did *not* state, "He shall not die." However, the next verse merely repeats exactly what Jesus reportedly *did* say. It does not foreclose the early understanding or offer an alternative interpretation of Jesus's words. Some biblical scholars today believe that the Beloved Disciple—whoever he was—may have had a longer than normal lifespan and that the saying of Jesus was used to explain his longevity.[13] Apparently, however, the Beloved Disciple eventually died or was at least presumed to have died, requiring early Christians to rethink the meaning of Jesus's words. This effort is preserved in John 21:23—"yet Jesus said not unto him, He shall not die; but, If I will that he tarry till I come, what is that to thee?" Many modern scholars conclude that verse 23, and likely the whole of chapter 21, represents a later addition to the text of the gospel, which appears to have ended originally at John 20:21. These scholars propose that the final chapter was added to the text by the Beloved Disciple's followers, drawing upon oral traditions and perhaps written materials preserved within their community.[14]

Although John 21:23 may have been written in order to disabuse early Christians of the idea that the Beloved Disciple would not die, interpretation of the verse among subsequent commenters would vary considerably. Many likely agreed with the early church father Tertullian when he wrote that John was

11. Keener, *The Gospel of John*, 1:83–91.

12. John M. Court, Ruth Edwards, and Barnabas Lindars, *The Johannine Literature* (Sheffield, UK: Sheffield Academic Press, 2000), 30–79; Raymond F. Collins, "John (Disciple)," in *The Anchor Bible Dictionary*, ed. David Noel Freedman (New York: Doubleday, 1992), 3:885.

13. See Raymond E. Brown, *An Introduction to the Gospel of John*, ed. by Francis J. Moloney (New York: Doubleday, 2003), 214.

14. See Haenchen, *A Commentary on the Gospel of John*, 2:229–34; George R. Beasley-Murray, *John*, vol. 36, *Word Biblical Commentary*, ed. Bruce M. Metzger et al., rev. ed. (Grand Rapids, MI: Zondervan, 1999), 392–418; and Francis J. Moloney, "John 21 and the Johannine Story," in *Anatomies of Narrative Criticism*, 237–51. Other scholars have presented textual evidence suggesting that some ancient versions of the fourth gospel circulated without chapter 21. See Gesa Schenke, "Das Erscheinen Jesu vor den Jüngern und der Ungläubige Thomas: Johannes 20:19–31," in *Coptica, Gnostica, Manichaica: Mélanges Offerts À Wolf-Peter Funk*, ed. Louis Painchaud and Paul-Hubert Poinier [Laval, France: University of Laval Press, 2006], 893–904; and Brent Nongbri, "P.Bodmer 2 as Possible Evidence for the Circulation of the Gospel According to John without Chapter 21," *Early Christianity* 9, no. 3 [2018]: 345–60.

dead.[15] However, the belief nevertheless persisted among others that he was still alive. In the fourth century, Bishop Hilary of Poitiers wrote: "Let John speak to us, while he is waiting, just as he is, for the coming of the Lord; John, who was left behind and appointed to a destiny hidden in the counsel of God, for he is not told that he shall not die, but only that he shall tarry. Let him speak to us in his own familiar voice."[16] There were efforts to reconcile the interpretation that the Beloved Disciple would not die with a tradition that John the Apostle had been buried at Ephesus. Augustine reported that in the fourth century there was also a tradition that although John had been buried, he was merely sleeping. As evidence for this view, Augustine cited reports that the ground around the tomb would expand and contract as if it were breathing. While the bishop of Hippo was skeptical that John still lived, he was unwilling to dismiss the possibility, based on the "not altogether unreliable witnesses" who reported the ground tremors.[17]

In the eighth century, Bede the Venerable wrote that he was drawing on "reliable" sources for his teachings regarding the death of John the Apostle, who "let himself down into the place that had been hallowed out for his burial, and when he had made his prayer he was gathered to his fathers, as free from the sorrow of death as he was a stranger to the corruption of the flesh." Bede added his own interpretation of John 21:22, that the statement of Jesus "I wish him to remain thus until I come" suggested "the state of contemplative virtue, which is not to be ended through death . . . but after death is to be more perfectly completed."[18] Whereas Bede followed a tradition that John had died, this tradition and his own exegesis of John 21:22 nevertheless show that he was wrestling with the interpretation of this provocative passage of scripture.

In the thirteenth century, Thomas Aquinas drew on Augustine and others, taking a conservative position in favor of John being yet alive, although he found difficulties with the idea. Aquinas reported opinions ranging from John being taken to heaven with Enoch and Elias, to John living until 70 CE (see below). Aquinas described statements of preachers who claimed that John entered his tomb in Ephesus while alive and was then transported to heaven,

15. See Joel C. Elowsky, *Ancient Christian Commentary on Scripture IVb, John 11–21* (Downers Grove, IL: InterVarsity Press, 2007), 389.

16. Hilary de Poitiers, *On the Trinity*, Book VI, trans. Stephen McKenna (Washington, D.C.: Catholic University of America Press, 1968), 209.

17. See St. Augustine, *Tractates on the Gospel of John, 112–124; Tractates on the First Epistle of John*, trans. John W. Rettig (Washington, D.C.: Catholic University of America Press, 2013), 82–96.

18. Bede the Venerable, *Homilies on the Gospels*, trans. Lawrence T. Martin and David Hurst (Kalamazoo, MI: Cistercian Publications, 1991), 2:218–19.

while others thought he remained alive in the tomb or had died but was immediately resurrected.[19]

In the sixteenth century, the chief architects of the Protestant Reformation could only articulate the passage's ambiguity. Martin Luther wrote:

> The Evangelist shows clearly enough that Christ did not wish to let us know, therefore we should not pry into the matter. He says: Jesus did not say he should not die, neither does he say that he should die. He thus lets it hang in doubt. If Christ had said: I will that he tarry till I come, it might have been understood that he would die on the last day. But that he says, "If I will, that he tarry", it is still much more in the dark, in that he does not say right out whether he will or will not.[20]

While Luther did not take a position on the issue, he did relay at least one contemporaneous idea: that the Beloved Disciple was not truly immortal but would live until Christ's second coming and then die. Like Luther, Calvin showed an ambivalence on the meaning of Christ's words to Peter.[21]

This Protestant uncertainty persisted in the Church of England and its sectarian offshoots. In the mid-seventeenth century, Puritan thinker George Hutcheson maintained that John might indeed still be alive but admitted that the text of John rendered the proposition uncertain.[22] A century later, John Wesley—the founder of Methodism—wrote that John "certainly . . . did tarry, till Christ came to destroy Jerusalem [in 70 CE]. And who can tell, when or how he died."[23] The first major Baptist theologian, John Gill, argued in the early eighteenth century that John 21:22 meant that:

> It was [Christ's] pleasure that he should live, not till his second coming to judge the quick and dead at the last day, but till he should come in his power and take vengeance on the Jewish nation, in the destruction of their city and temple by the Romans, and in dispersing them through

19. St. Thomas Aquinas, *Commentary on the Gospel of John*, trans. Fabian R. Larcher (New York: Magi Books, 1998), Lecture 5:2644–51. Jerome believed that John lived on because he remained a virgin. F. P. Badham, "The Martyrdom of John the Apostle," *American Journal of Theology* 8, no. 3 (July 1904): 552.

20. John Nicholas Lenker, *Sermons of Martin Luther* (Grand Rapids, MI: Baker Book House, 1989), 231.

21. John Calvin, *Commentary on the Gospel According to John*, trans. William Pringle (Edinburgh: Calvin Translation Society, 1847), 2:297–98.

22. George Hutcheson, *The Gospel According to John* (London: Printed for Ralph Smith, 1657), 437–38.

23. John Wesley, *Explanatory Notes upon the New Testament* (New York: Carlton & Porter, 1754), 273.

the nations of the world; till which time John did live, and many years after; and was the only one of the disciples that lived till that time.[24]

This bewilderment regarding the meaning of John 21:22–23 persisted into the nineteenth century. In his influential New Testament commentary first published in 1817, Methodist scholar Adam Clarke summarized four proposals that had been offered by commentators. The dominant position, that Jesus meant that "John should *never die*," was held by "many eminent men, *ancients*, and *moderns*." Others held that Jesus intended to say that "John should live till Christ came to judge and destroy Jerusalem," which was fulfilled in 70 CE when John was the only apostle to survive the carnage. Still others believed that Jesus meant that John would be the only apostle to die a natural death rather than suffer martyrdom. Finally, Clarke explained, many preferred to read Jesus's words as referring simply to John spatially tarrying apart from Jesus and Peter for the moment while they concluded their current conversation. Clarke's solution may have reflected post-Enlightenment efforts by Christian theologians such as himself to supply rational explanations for seemingly impossible Bible stories. Nevertheless, Clarke concluded his commentary on this passage with a humble acknowledgment of its ambiguity: "For nearly eighteen hundred years, the greatest men in the world have been puzzled with this passage. It would appear intolerable in me to attempt to *decide* where so many eminent doctors have disagreed, and do still disagree."[25]

THE PRODUCTION OF THE ACCOUNT OF JOHN

In April 1829, Joseph Smith and Oliver Cowdery entered into this longstanding debate. Cowdery, a schoolteacher by profession, arrived on 5 April at Smith's residence in Harmony, Pennsylvania, offering his talents as a scribe to Smith, whose work on the Book of Mormon translation had ground to a halt the previous year. Scholars believe that Smith commenced his dictation to Cowdery with what is now the book of Mosiah—more or less where Smith had left off

24. John Gill, *An Exposition of the New Testament* (London: Printed for the Author, 1746), s.v. "John 21:22."

25. Adam Clarke, *The New Testament of Our Lord and Saviour Jesus Christ* (New York: N. Bangs and J. Emory, 1825), 1:631 (emphasis in original). On "evidential Christianity," see E. Brooks Holifield, *Theology in America: Christian Thought from the Age of the Puritans to the Civil War* (New Haven: Yale University Press, 2003), chap. 8.

in 1828.[26] Early in the narrative, King Mosiah II was described as a *seer* who possessed a "high gift from God" to "translate all records that are of ancient date." In addition, the text defined a seer as "a revelator and a prophet also," with power to reveal "secret things" from the past and the future: "Things shall be made known by them which otherwise could not be known."[27] When acting as a revelator and as a translator, Mosiah II used *interpreters*—"two stones" that had been "prepared from the beginning . . . for the purpose of interpreting languages."[28] The description of Mosiah II as a translator and as a revelator foreshadowed Smith's own adoption of these titles[29] as well as his use of stones variously known as "spectacles," "interpreters," and "Urim and Thummim," both to translate the Book of Mormon and to dictate revelations.[30]

During April 1829, apart from the Book of Mormon, Smith dictated four additional texts to Cowdery: three revelations and the Account of John. The revelations spoke of "great and marvelous . . . mysteries" that would soon be revealed[31] and of "ancient Records which have been hid up which are Sacred" that would soon be translated.[32] Although Cowdery hoped to participate in translating these records, he evidently "feared" and was unable to translate. Instead, he was directed to "continue" writing for Smith until they had "finished this record," meaning the Book of Mormon.[33]

It was in this context of Smith translating the recently revealed ancient record and dictating revelations to Cowdery regarding other hidden scriptures that the two men discussed the fate of John the Apostle and the meaning of John 21. While there is no surviving evidence that either individual had by that time read Clarke's commentary or anything else written on the matter,[34] the two men were sufficiently aware of the issue to ask, according to Smith's later

26. Joseph Smith, History, 1834–1836, in *JSP*-H1:41; "The Printer's Manuscript of the Book of Mormon," in *JSP*-R3:xvii–xxv; Brent Lee Metcalfe, "The Priority of Mosiah: A Prelude to Book of Mormon Exegesis," chap. 10 in *New Approaches to the Book of Mormon*, ed. Brent Lee Metcalfe (Salt Lake City: Signature Books, 1993).

27. Mosiah 8:13–17.

28. Mosiah 8:13, 28:13–14.

29. Revelation, 6 April 1830, in *JSP*-D1:129 [D&C 21:1]; and Visions of Moses, June 1830, in *JSP*-D1:152 [Moses 1].

30. See MacKay and Frederick, *Joseph Smith's Seer Stones*, 49–55; Robin Scott Jensen, "'Rely upon the Things Which Are Written': Text, Context, and the Creation of Mormon Revelatory Records," (master's thesis, University of Wisconsin-Milwaukee, 2009), chaps. 3–4.

31. Revelation, April 1829-A, in *JSP*-D1:36 [D&C 6:11].

32. Revelation, April 1829-B, in *JSP*-D1:46 [D&C 8:11].

33. Revelation, April 1829-D, in *JSP*-D1:49–50 [D&C 9:1, 11].

34. Within a few years, Smith would extensively utilize Clarke's commentary in his revision of the Bible. Thomas A. Wayment and Haley Wilson-Lemmon, "A Recovered Resource: The Use of Adam Clarke's Bible Commentary in Joseph Smith's Bible Translation," Chapter 11 herein.

history, which he initiated in 1838, "whether he [the Beloved Disciple] died, or whether he continued."[35] The question may have been prompted by a passage in the Book of Mormon in which an ancient prophet, Alma, had "departed out of the land" and "was never heard of more." The narrative further stated that "the saying went abroad in the church that he was taken up by the Spirit, or buried by the hand of the Lord, even as Moses."[36] This language paralleled John 21:23, which recounted that the "saying went abroad among the brethren" that the Beloved Disciple would not die. The similarity in language may have prompted the discussion between Smith and Cowdery regarding the Beloved Disciple.[37]

Smith also recounted in his 1838 history that he and Cowdery "agreed to settle" their difference of opinion via the Urim and Thummim, the interpretive device Smith had been using to translate the Book of Mormon.[38] David Whitmer, who witnessed parts of this process, later reminisced that Smith would place the stone "in the crown of a hat" and seal the brim of the hat around his face "so as to exclude the external light." In the darkness of the hat, Whitmer explained, "a spiritual light would shine forth, and parchment would appear before Joseph, upon which was a line of characters from the plates, and under it, the translation in English."[39] Presumably, a similar process was used when

35. Joseph Smith, History, 1838–1856, vol. A-1, 15, in *JSP*-H1:284.

36. Alma 45:19.

37. Frank Judd and Terry Szink first proposed Alma 45:18–19 as a possible catalyst for the dictation of the Account of John. See Judd and Szink, "John the Beloved in Latter-day Saint Scripture," 93–95. This proposal has merit since Smith and Cowdery may have reached Alma 45 in the Book of Mormon translation by late April 1829, see Smith, History, 1834–1836, in *JSP*-H1:42. Judd and Szink also proposed that 3 Nephi 28—a Book of Mormon passage describing how Jesus granted three Nephite disciples the power to "tarry" in a similar fashion to John—may have prompted the dictation of the Account of John. Pointing to linguistic similarities between the two texts, Judd and Szink favored 3 Nephi 28 (over Alma 45:18–19) as the passage most likely to have provoked the conversation between Smith and Cowdery leading to the Account of John, see Judd and Szink, "John the Beloved in Latter-day Saint Scripture," 95–96. However, their proposal most likely requires redating the Account of John from April, the traditional month of its dictation, to early or mid-May 1829, when Smith likely dictated 3 Nephi 28. See Smith, History, 1834–1836, in *JSP*-H1:42; Smith, History Drafts, 1838–ca. 1841, in *JSP*-H1:294; Brian Q. Cannon, "Priesthood Restoration Documents," *BYU Studies* 35, no. 4 (1995–1996): 182. The earliest evidence for dating the revelation in April is Cowdery's assignment of that month to the revelation when he inserted dates in the BCR, see Account of John, April 1829, in *JSP*-R1:17–19. This likely occurred sometime in 1831, when Cowdery and others began preparing the revelations for publication, and certainly occurred by December 1832, when the dated revelation was printed in the first gathering of the Book of Commandments. See Historical Introduction to Revelation Book 1, in *JSP*-R1:6; and Historical Introduction to Book of Commandments, in *JSP*-R2:9. In addition, when the Account of John was inscribed in the BCR it was grouped with other April revelations, rather than with the May revelations. Revelation Book 1, 11–14, 207, in *JSP*-R1:12–19, 384–85. In contrast, there is no historical evidence for a May date.

38. Joseph Smith, History, 1838–1856, vol. A-1, 15, in *JSP*-H1:284.

39. David Whitmer, quoted in "Documents of the Translation of the Book of Mormon," in *Opening the Heavens: Accounts of Divine Manifestations, 1820–1844*, ed. John W. Welch, 2nd ed. (Provo, UT: Brigham

Smith dictated the Account of John. Cowdery almost certainly acted as the scribe for the text as Smith dictated it.

The resulting Account of John—a brief text that numbered a mere 139 words—answered many of the questions that had plagued readers of John 21 over the centuries. The account was related from the first-person perspective of a narrator named "John," whom Jesus called "my beloved." John recounted that Jesus asked what he desired. John, in reply, asked for "power" to "bring souls" unto Jesus, with Jesus granting John's request: "thou shalt tarry until I come in my glory." The text reproduced verbatim the canonical version of this conversation in the King James Version of the Bible (hereafter KJV) translation of John 21:22, with Jesus putting a question to Peter: "If I will that he tarry until I come what is that to thee"?[40] Jesus then explained that John's desire to "tarry" was a "greater work" than Peter's desire to "come unto [Christ] in [his] kingdom," although both desires were good and would be rewarded. The Account of John was copied in 1831 into the "Book of Commandments and Revelations" (hereafter BCR), a blank book used to record Smith's early revelations.[41]

The Account of John made explicit what had previously been only implicit, as "John [the] beloved" replaced the mysterious Beloved Disciple. As noted above, it was generally assumed in 1829 that John the Apostle *was* the Beloved Disciple, despite the absence of clear textual evidence for that interpretation. The Account of John therefore represented a striking shift in voice from the Gospel of John. While the vast majority of nineteenth-century readers could—and did—read the canonical gospel as being the work of John the Apostle, this

---

Young University Press; Salt Lake City: Deseret Book, 2017), 164, item 83. See also Don Bradley, "Written by the Finger of God? Claims and Controversies of Book of Mormon Translation, Part 1: History," *Sunstone*, December 2010, 23–27. Smith himself was apparently reluctant to provide any details of his translation method, see Minutes, 25–26 October 1831, in *JSP*-D2:84. On the stone spectacles found with the gold plates, Smith's other seer stones, and the developing use of the term "Urim and Thummim," see Richard Van Wagoner and Steve Walker, "Joseph Smith: 'The Gift of Seeing,'" *Dialogue: A Journal of Mormon Thought* 15, no. 2 (Summer 1982): 49–68.

40. The Account of John reproduced the phrase from John 21:22 verbatim, including the italicized words "is that." The translators of the KJV italicized the words in their translation that were used to round out the meaning that was implicit in the original language, though it had no direct correspondence in terms of the individual Hebrew or Greek words of the text. Thomas A. Wayment and Tyson J. Yost, "The Joseph Smith Translation and Italicized Words in the King James Version," *Religious Educator* 6, no. 1 (2005): 51–64.

41. See Account of John, April 1829, in *JSP*-R1:17–19. There is another manuscript copy of the Account of John in the handwriting of early Latter-day Saint Frederick G. Williams. Amounting to 140 words, the Williams version is nearly identical to the version in the BCR. Analysis of the textual variations between the two versions suggests that the Williams copy reflects edits made to the text in the anticipation of its being published in the Book of Commandments (in 1833). However, as will be explored in more detail below, the heading attached to the Williams copy may represent an early form of the heading that appeared in the BCR in 1831. Frederick G. Williams, manuscript, Revelations Collection, Church History Library, The Church of Jesus Christ of Latter-day Saints, Salt Lake City, Utah (hereafter Church History Library).

TABLE 10.1. John 21 and the Account of John

John 21:18–23 (KJV)	Account of John (BCR)
18 Verily, verily, I say unto thee, When thou [Peter] wast young, thou girdedst thyself, and walkedst whither thou wouldest: but when thou shalt be old, thou shalt stretch forth thy hands, and another shall gird thee, and carry *thee* whither thou wouldest not. 19 This spake he, signifying by what death he should glorify God. And when he had spoken this, he saith unto him, Follow me. 20 Then Peter, turning about, seeth the disciple whom Jesus loved following; which also leaned on his breast at supper, and said, Lord, which is he that betrayeth thee? 21 Peter seeing him saith to Jesus, Lord, and what *shall* this man *do*?	And the Lord said unto me. John my Beloved what desiredst thou & I said Lord give unto me power that I may bring souls unto thee & the Lord said unto me Veriley Verily I say unto thee because thou desiredst this thou shalt tarry until I come in my glory
22 Jesus saith unto him, If I will that he tarry till I come, what is that to thee? follow thou me.	& for this cause the Lord said unto Peter if I will that he tarry till I come what is that to thee For he desiredst of me that he might bring souls unto me but thou desiredst that thou mightest come unto me in my kingdom I say unto thee Peter this was a good desire but my beloved hath undertaken a greater work Verily I say unto you ye shall both have according to your desires for ye both Joy in that which ye desired
23 Then went this saying abroad among the brethren, that that disciple should not die: yet Jesus said not unto him, He shall not die; but, If I will that he tarry till I come, what is that to thee?	

tradition was built on drawing connections and scrutinizing clues scattered throughout the book. The Account of John, in contrast, required no such interpretive maneuvers or inherited tradition, with "John [the] beloved" explicitly identified as the text's narrator.

By framing the divergent fates of Peter and the Beloved Disciple as being in accordance with the "desires" of both men, the Account of John differed from John 21. The biblical text was silent as to the desires of the two men, instead presenting Jesus's remarks concerning his disciples as prophecies of their futures based on his own foreknowledge. In contrast, the Account of John emphasized the agency of Peter and John in the expressions of their personal desires and was therefore reminiscent of another conversation, reported in

Mark 10:35–40, between Jesus and two disciples regarding their fates: "And James and John, the sons of Zebedee, come unto him, saying, Master, we would that thou shouldest do for us whatsoever we shall desire." When Jesus asked James and John what they sought, they responded, "Grant unto us that we may sit, one on thy right hand, and the other on thy left hand, in thy glory." Jesus then stated that the brothers would be required to follow him in his impending suffering and death, not unlike what Jesus told Peter in John 21:18–19. Despite many differences between the Account of John and Mark 10, both texts shared an emphasis on the *desires* of the disciples, a theme absent from John 21.

The Account of John also cut through the Gordian knot surrounding Jesus's statement that the Beloved Disciple would "tarry till I come." The text defined the tarrying of the Beloved Disciple as an outgrowth of John's desire to "bring souls unto" Jesus, presumably with the Disciple enjoying a prolonged life. Furthermore, the Account of John added "in my glory" to Jesus's statement, possibly borrowing from Mark 10:37, quoted above, or Matthew 25:31, in which Jesus prophesied of the time when "the Son of Man shall come in his glory." As shown above, various interpreters had debated the meaning of the phrase "till I come," offering solutions that ranged from the termination of the immediate conversation between Jesus and Peter, to the Roman destruction of Jerusalem in 70 CE, to John's reported longevity in the late first century, to Christ's triumphal second coming at the end of days. By adding "in my glory" to Jesus's statement, the Account of John overtly took a position on this unresolved issue by signaling that the apostle had lived not only until seventy or into the nineties but into the present and would remain alive until Christ's glorious second coming.

The resulting text presumably settled the question for Smith and Cowdery, who thereafter resumed the rapid dictation and transcription of the Book of Mormon. One of the two men likely filed the original manuscript of the Account of John in their papers. Although the original is not extant, evidence suggests that it probably contained only the text of the Account of John and therefore lacked additional information regarding the context of the dictation, such as the date, location, and circumstances that prompted Smith and Cowdery to ask the question in the first place.[42] The original likely offered no clues on the manuscript itself, and neither Smith nor Cowdery made a contemporary record such as a journal entry or a note to illuminate whether

42. See Robin Scott Jensen, "Contextualizing Revelations: Changing Attitudes towards Sacred Texts in the Church of Christ, 1829–1831," *Journal of Mormon History* 46, no. 1 (January 2020): 26–52.

they classified the document as a translation, implying an ancient text; or as a revelation, requiring no such implication. Based on genre and context, there is reason to believe that the pair viewed the text as a translation. As a firsthand narration, the Account of John was closer in style to the Book of Mormon, which was clearly understood as a translation, than to the extant revelations from the same period that were presented in the voice of Deity. In addition, as noted above, Smith's April 1829 revelations referenced hidden ancient scriptures, suggesting that he and Cowdery may have viewed the Account of John as a translation of one of those ancient records.

Yet there are limits to relying on genre and context to reconstruct the earliest view of the Account of John. Notably, the document lacked the self-awareness as a *written text* that was so characteristic of the Book of Mormon,[43] such as internal references to John making a record. Instead, it presented itself as an oral recounting of the conversation with Jesus.[44] Furthermore, the Book of Mormon and the April 1829 revelations both spoke of revealing new knowledge that was not previously known, raising the possibility that Smith and Cowdery may have viewed the Account of John as a revelation. This ambiguity regarding how the document was understood by Smith and Cowdery in 1829 would have significant implications for subsequent interpretations of the text.

INTERPRETIVE HEADINGS AND THE ACCOUNT OF JOHN

Over the next four years, the Account of John was preserved, transmitted, and then prepared for publication. A widening circle of Smith's associates would play key roles in this process—most notably John Whitmer and William W. Phelps—illustrating what historian David D. Hall calls "social authorship," a phrase that captures the contributions of people "who intervened to bring a book into being" through copying, editing, and typesetting. For Hall, "the making of printed texts" is "a process of collaboration," involving not only the primary author of a text but also the intermediaries that bring it to publication.[45] Both Whitmer and Phelps, presumably with the input of Smith and

43. On the Book of Mormon's self-awareness of being based on written texts, see Richard Lyman Bushman, "Nephi's Project: The Gold Plates as Book History," Chapter 8 herein; and Grant Hardy, "Ancient Plates and Modern Commandments: The Book of Mormon in Comparison with Joseph Smith's Other Revelations," Chapter 9 herein.

44. Revelation, April 1829-B, in *JSP*-D1:46 [D&C 8:1, 11]; see also Revelation, April 1829-B, in *JSP*-D1:26 [D&C 6:26]; and Revelation, April 1829-D, in *JSP*-D1:49 [D&C 9:2].

45. David D. Hall, *Ways of Writing: The Practice and Politics of Text-Making in Seventeenth-Century New England* (Philadelphia: University of Pennsylvania Press, 2008), 82.

Cowdery, were instrumental in the creation of the earliest headings attached to the Account of John, first in manuscript and then in print. Interpretive headings often textualize oral traditions and accurately preserve the context of the original dictation. In other instances, headings capture later developments and impose them anachronistically, albeit creatively, onto the original dictation setting. In any case, interpretive headings provide an important window into ways that Smith's early followers viewed the Account of John and how that understanding may have changed over time. Although separate and distinct from the text that Smith had dictated in 1829, these headings would have a profound impact on ways that subsequent readers would understand the Account of John.[46]

John Whitmer was one of the earliest converts to Smith's new movement, and had performed various scribal tasks for Smith in 1829 and 1830.[47] In March 1831, Smith dictated a revelation that appointed Whitmer to assist "in Transcribing," or copying, Smith's revelations and "to Keep the Church Record & History." The revelation further stated that it would be given to Whitmer "by th[e] comforter," meaning the Holy Ghost, "to write these things."[48] This language suggested the importance placed on Whitmer's duties, as the scribe was promised revelatory assistance while performing his tasks. Not long after accepting this appointment, Whitmer began copying Smith's revelations into the BCR, possibly from the original manuscripts or loose-leaf copies.[49]

Whitmer inscribed the Account of John on pages 11 and 12 of the BCR between two of the revelations directed to Cowdery in April 1829, suggesting that these documents had been grouped together previously.[50] The inclusion of the Account of John in a book designated for revelations was indicative of how Smith's early disciples saw the text.[51] Early in his copying process, Whit-

46. Literary scholar Gérard Genette used the term "paratext" to describe headings and other elements added to a book that framed the main text. Gérard Genette, *Paratexts: Thresholds of Interpretations,* ed. and trans. Jane E. Lewin (Cambridge: Cambridge University Press, 1997). Historian Robin Scott Jensen has applied the term to the headings attached to manuscript copies of Smith's early revelations. Jensen, "Revelations, Scribal Contextualization, and Changing Attitudes towards Sacred Texts".

47. Ronald E. Romig, *Eighth Witness: The Biography of John Whitmer* (Independence, MO: John Whitmer Books, 2014); "Printer's Manuscript of the Book of Mormon," in *JSP*-R3:xxiv; Kent P. Jackson, ed., *The Book of Moses and the Joseph Smith Translation Manuscripts* (Provo, UT: Religious Studies Center, Brigham Young University, 2005), 3–17; Joseph Smith, 1839 draft history, 22, in *JSP*-H1:424.

48. Revelation, ca. 8 March 1831-B, in *JSP*-D1:286 [D&C 47:3–4].

49. Historical Introduction to Revelation Book 1, in *JSP*-R1:4–5.

50. Revelation, April 1829-B, in *JSP*-R1:15 [D&C 8]; and Revelation, April 1829-D, in *JSP*-R1:19 [D&C 9].

51. Alternatively, had the Account of John been understood in 1831 to be a translation connected with the Bible, the manuscript might have been included with the papers associated with Joseph Smith's revision of the New Testament, a project that was designated as "A Translation of the New Testament translated by the power of God." Smith began his work on the New Testament in March 1831 concurrently with Whitmer's

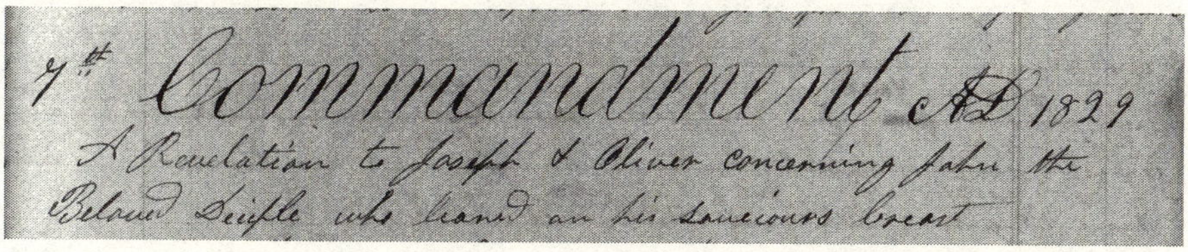
7th Commandment AD 1829
A Revelation to Joseph & Oliver concerning John the
Beloved Deciple who leaned on his Saveiours breast

FIGURE 10.1. Manuscript heading for Account of John. The Account of John (now D&C 7) appeared as the seventh "Commandment" copied into "A Book of Commandments & Revelations," the church's earliest copybook of Joseph Smith's revelations. Church History Library, Salt Lake City.

mer began a simple classification system, creating a heading that numbered each copied document, apparently in chronological order of dictation as he understood it.[52] He then labeled each text a *commandment*, a word often used by early church members interchangeably with *revelation*,[53] and inscribed "AD" and the year. Inserting the Account of John into this schema, Whitmer wrote "7th. Commandment AD 1829" above the copied text (see Figure 10.1). Calling the text a "commandment" further suggests that they understood the Account of John more as a revelation than as a translation. Alternatively, Whitmer may have applied the label "commandment" in line with the formatting practice that he had already established in his work, as he compiled this short revelatory text along with the other commandments that he uniformly labeled as such.

Following this classificatory label, or title of sorts, Whitmer inscribed a more detailed heading contextualizing the original dictation. He had developed a formula for these more detailed headings, first designating the text "A Revelation," followed by identifying the name or names of the document's recipients, providing a very brief synopsis of its contents, and specifying the geographical location and more specific date of the dictation (if known). For the Account of John, Whitmer wrote: "A Revelation to Joseph & Oliver concerning John the Beloved Deciple who leaned on his Saveiours breast given

---

copying work in the BCR. See New Testament Revision 1, 1, in Joseph Smith, *Joseph Smith's New Translation of the Bible: Original Manuscripts*, ed. Scott H. Faulring, Kent P. Jackson, and Robert J. Matthews (Provo, UT: Religious Studies Center, Brigham Young University, 2004), 159. Smith's June 1830 dictation of a text called the "Visions of Moses"—which presented itself as extrabiblical scripture and was identified as a "revelation given to Joseph the Revelator"—provides a comparative case. As the Bible revision project developed further, the Visions of Moses text was grouped with the Bible revision manuscripts (rather than with the revelation manuscripts). See Historical Introduction to Visions of Moses, June 1830, in *JSP*-D1:150–56 [Moses 1].

52. The first and second revelations copied into the BCR lacked this classification system, see Revelation Book 1, 1–2, in *JSP*-R1:8–11 [D&C 3–4]. This suggests that Whitmer developed his process after he began copying. The next several pages of the BCR are no longer in the book and apparently not extant. See *JSP*-R1:10–13. However, the revelation immediately preceding the Account of John was labeled "6th Commandment AD 1829." Revelation Book 1, in *JSP*-R1:15–16 [D&C 8].

53. See Jensen, "Rely upon the Things Which Are Written," 16–21.

in Harmony Susquehannah County Pennsylvania."[54] Whitmer's more detailed heading signaled that he and likely other early church members, viewed the document as a revelation, similar in kind to other revelations dictated by Smith. Whitmer's synopsis interestingly only loosely summarized the content of the Account of John, instead alluding to John 21:20, thereby reinforcing the association between the final chapter of the Gospel of John and Smith's dictated text. It is also noteworthy that the heading mentioned nothing about the document being a translation of an ancient text. It remains uncertain how much Whitmer consulted with Smith or Cowdery when composing this heading, although Cowdery subsequently added the month and year, "April 1829," strongly implying that he had reviewed, and likely approved, the heading's contents.[55]

In July 1831, Smith dictated a revelation that called William W. Phelps, a recent convert and newspaper editor, to be "a Printer unto the Church."[56] Phelps, along with John Whitmer and Oliver Cowdery, was appointed in April 1832 to review the revelations and "select for printing such as shall be deemed by them proper, as dictated by the spirit & make all necessary verbal corrections."[57] Given that the church's printing office was located in Independence, Missouri—more than eight hundred miles away from Smith's primary residence in Ohio—this authorization of Phelps, Whitmer, and Cowdery to select, prepare, and publish Smith's revelations demonstrated the trust that was placed in these men to frame and present the revelations to the public.

Over the next several months, Phelps, Whitmer, and Cowdery worked together to accomplish these tasks in the church's printing office in Independence, Missouri. They reviewed the Book of Commandments and Revelations and selected revelations for publication, first in the church's newspaper, the *Evening and the Morning Star*, and then in a compilation called the *Book of*

54. The Frederick G. Williams copy of the Account of John contains this heading: "A revelation concerning John the beloved deciple" (Williams, manuscript [D&C 7]). The similarities between the Williams and Whitmer headings strongly suggest a textual relationship, although the nature of the relationship remains unclear. As historian Robin Jensen has argued, headings were likely introduced—paratextually prefixed to the revelations—in 1830 in order to contextualize the revelations. Jensen, "Revelations, Scribal Contextualization, and Changing Attitudes towards Sacred Texts." Two 1830 headings followed this schema: "Commandment to [recipient name] [Year]" ("Commandment to the Church AD 1830" [D&C 27] and "Commandment to Ezra Northrop, Oct. 1830" [D&C 33] [both in Partridge Copies of Revelations, Church History Library]). It was apparently not until the following year that church clerks realized the inefficiency of using recipients' names to organize the revelations, and began adding synopses to the headings. The Williams heading was a synopsis.

55. See Account of John, April 1829, in *JSP*-R1:17–19 [D&C 7].

56. Revelation, 20 July 1831, in *JSP*-D2:11–12 [D&C 57:11–13].

57. Minutes, 30 April 1832, in *JSP*-D2:239.

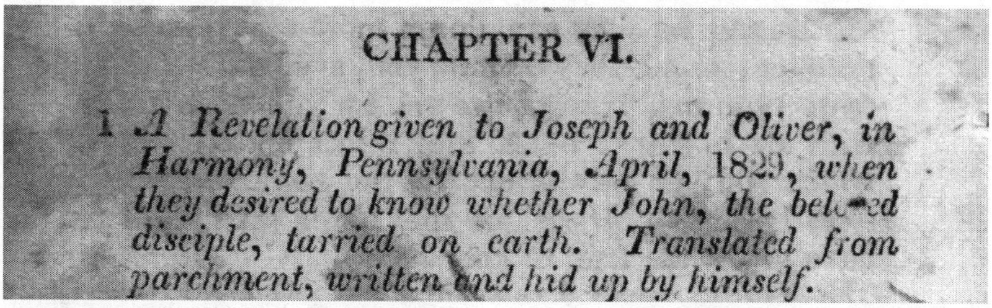

CHAPTER VI.

1 *A Revelation given to Joseph and Oliver, in Harmony, Pennsylvania, April, 1829, when they desired to know whether John, the beloved disciple, tarried on earth. Translated from parchment, written and hid up by himself.*

FIGURE 10.2. Printed heading for Account of John. A revised version of the Account of John (now D&C 7) appeared as the sixth chapter in *A Book of Commandments*, the first published collection of Joseph Smith's revelations. Church History Library, Salt Lake City.

Commandments (hereafter BoC).[58] Many of the revelations were copyedited prior to publication. On the main, the revisions were minor, involving punctuation, spelling, and grammar. In some cases, however, the revelations were updated to reflect ecclesiastical changes.[59] In July 1832, Smith wrote to Phelps instructing him "to be careful not to alter the sense" of the revelations, suggesting that while conservative copyedits and proofreading were permissible in Smith's view, more substantive revisions were not.[60] As evidenced by the changes made to the Account of John for the BoC, this counsel was followed. Aside from adding punctuation and versification, the revisions made were minimal, increasing the total word count from 139 words to 141.[61]

As part of this process, Phelps, Whitmer, and Cowdery also prepared new interpretive headings for the revelations. The first part of the new heading for the Account of John showed some continuities with the BCR heading: "A Revelation given to Joseph and Oliver, in Harmony, Pennsylvania, April, 1829" (see Figure 10.2). Thus far, the new heading retained the BCR heading's schema of identifying the text as "a revelation," then naming the recipients, the location of dictation, and the date. Whereas the BCR's heading summarized the contents by stating that it was a revelation "concerning John the beloved deciple" and then alluding to John 21, the new heading added more context for the original dictation: "When they [Smith and Cowdery] desired to know whether John,

58. See Historical Introduction to BoC, in *JSP*-R2:3–11; and Historical Introduction to Revelations Printed in the *Evening and the Morning Star*, in *JSP*-R2:195–201.

59. Historical Introduction to Book of Commandments, in *JSP*-R2:7.

60. Letter to William W. Phelps, 31 July 1832, in *JSP*-D2:266.

61. The editors revised "until" to "till," modernized "hath" to "has," and inserted "have" within "that which ye <have> desired." The most significant change improved awkward language, revising "but thou desiredst that thou mightest come unto me" to "but thou desiredst that thou might speedily come unto me."

the beloved disciple, tarried on earth." But it was the final sentence that represented the most dramatic departure from the BCR and prior documented understandings of the Account of John: "Translated from parchment, written and hid up by himself," indicating that John the Apostle had been materially involved in a process of documentary production.[62]

The new interpretive heading thereby provided a sacred origin story for the Account of John that resonated with several themes from the Book of Mormon and Smith's 1829 revelations. First, and perhaps most significantly, the Account of John was said to have been "written" by John the Apostle himself. Whereas the text lacked the self-awareness so prominent in Smith's other translations, the new heading explicitly claimed that the apostle had inscribed it himself. Second, the physical medium of John's writing was identified as "parchment," a word that appeared in 2 Timothy 4:13 as an ancient writing medium.[63] Third, like the golden plates of the Book of Mormon, which had been buried with the expectation that they would come forth providentially at some later date, the parchment of John was represented as being an actual and material document that had been "hidden up" to be recovered at some later time. Lastly, the Account of John was said to have been "translated," presumably in the same manner as the Book of Mormon, through the miraculous Urim and Thummim spectacles or a single seer stone.

Whether this sentence simply textualized an otherwise unattested oral tradition about the Account of John or articulated a new understanding remains uncertain. Cowdery, as one of the recipients of the dictated text, may have provided some continuity of understanding between the 1829 dictation and the 1832 heading. Phelps, who was known among his early coreligionists as a self-taught savant and a master of languages, was fascinated with ancient languages and texts and the idea of divinely inspired translation. He may also have contributed to the language of the new heading.[64] Yet the new heading also retained an important element from Whitmer's 1831 heading by calling the Account of John a "revelation." When the Account of John first appeared in print in the Book of Commandments, it was therefore presented as a revelation, but with

62. Heading to Chapter VI in BoC, 18, in *JSP*-R2:30 [D&C 7: heading].

63. One possibility is that the idea of parchment as the writing medium was somehow associated with Joseph Smith's experience in translating the Book of Mormon. According to David Whitmer, Smith would peer into his seer stone "and *parchment* would appear before Joseph, upon which was a line of characters from the plates, and under it, the translation in English; at least, so Joseph said." J. L. Traughber Jr., "Testimony of David Whitmer," *Saints' Herald,* 15 November 1879, 341 (emphasis added).

64. See Samuel M. Brown, "The Translator and the Ghost Writer: Joseph Smith and W. W. Phelps," *Journal of Mormon History* 34, no. 1 (Winter 2008): 26–62.

a distinction: the revelation was more specifically a supernatural translation of a text written on parchment and hidden up by the apostle John himself.

CULTURAL RECEPTION OF THE ACCOUNT OF JOHN

Even as interpretations of the Account of John remained unstable in the early 1830s, the text of the document remained relatively stable. The 1829 Account of John, however, anticipated several doctrinal and ecclesiastical developments, manifesting the influence of the document on church thought and culture in the early 1830s. Doctrinally, its dictation previewed a passage in the Book of Mormon in which the resurrected Jesus granted power to three New World disciples to tarry on the earth as John had. In addition, Smith began teaching publicly by 1831 that John the Beloved was yet alive and was ministering among the Lost Tribes of Israel. Lastly, as the ecclesiastical organization of the church became more hierarchical, with a presidency comprised of Smith and two counselors, the Mormon prophet began to teach that anciently, Peter had similarly presided over the church with the assistance of two counselors. These developments provided the background and context to the changes that would be made to the Account of John in 1835.

In May 1829, about a month after the Account of John was inscribed, Smith dictated a passage in the Book of Mormon, now known as 3 Nephi 28, that was strongly reminiscent of the Account of John. The passage described a scene in which Jesus Christ visited a group of people known as Nephites in the Americas following his resurrection. During the visit, Christ selected twelve disciples and on one occasion asked them: "What is it that ye desire of me, after that I am gone to the Father?" Nine of the twelve expressed a desire to join Jesus in his heavenly kingdom, paralleling Peter's desire in the Account of John. The remaining three, referred to colloquially in Latter-day Saint literature as "the Three Nephites," remained silent.[65] Then Jesus stated: "Behold, I know your thoughts, and ye have desired the thing which John, my beloved, who was with me in my ministry, before that I was lifted up by the Jews, desired of me." Like John, who chose a "greater work" than Peter, the Three Nephites would be "more blessed" than the other nine. As Jesus explained, "ye shall live . . . until all

65. See Oliver Boardman Huntington, "History of the Life of Oliver B. Huntington, 1878–1900," 5, L. Tom Perry Special Collections, Harold B. Lee Library, Brigham Young University, Provo, Utah. See also, "Sunday School Lesson for Theological Department," *Latter-day Saints' Millennial Star*, 18 April 1912, 256. Hector Lee, *The Three Nephites: The Substance and Significance of the Legend in Folklore* (Albuquerque: University of New Mexico Press, 1949).

things shall be fulfilled according to the will of the Father, when I shall come in my glory." These were "the three who were to tarry," remaining on the earth until the end times. Like John, Jesus said, the Three Nephites would "bring the souls of men unto me, while the world shall stand."[66]

Expanding beyond the explanation given in the Account of John for the apostle's longevity, 3 Nephi 28 drew upon language from various biblical texts to explain the change that the Three Nephites experienced that permitted them to tarry like John. Jesus in 3 Nephi 28:7 indicated that the three disciples would "never taste of death," paralleling language from John 8:52.[67] In another example, at 3 Nephi 28:13, the Three Nephites were "caught up into heaven"—using the vocabulary of 2 Corinthians 12:2—where they "saw and heard unspeakable things." This, according to 3 Nephi 28:15, "did seem unto them like a transfiguration of them, that they were changed from this body of flesh into an immortal state, that they could behold the things of God." The word "transfiguration" was the same used to describe the glorification of Jesus on the Mount of Transfiguration before Peter, James, and John in Mark 9:1–2 and Matthew 17:2–3; although in the Book of Mormon the language was used to describe the change experienced by the three disciples rather than by Jesus.[68] Finally, 3 Nephi 28:30 stated that the three disciples were "as the angels of God," which gave them power to either reveal themselves to or conceal themselves from ordinary humans.

In 3 Nephi 28, the Nephite prophet and historian Mormon retrospectively recounted the extended lives of the Three Nephites in the years following their transfiguration. They ministered, preached to, and baptized believers into the "church of Christ."[69] Enemies of the three disciples attempted to imprison them, as had been the lot of Joseph in the Old Testament, Peter in the New Testament, and several other figures in the Bible and the Book of Mormon; trap them in a pit, like Joseph before he was sold into bondage; incinerate them, like Shadrach, Meshach, and Abed-nego in the fiery furnace; and feed them to wild beasts, like Daniel in the lion's den. Yet they always emerged unscathed. Beyond perpetual longevity, the Three Nephites had power over mortal danger.

66. 3 Nephi 28:6–12.

67. See also Mark 9:1; Matthew 16:8; Luke 9:27.

68. In 1839, Smith would apply this same idea when teaching that Peter, James, and John were transfigured with Jesus on the Mount of Transfiguration. Discourse, between ca. 26 June and ca. Aug. 1839-A, in *JSP*-D6:543–44.

69. 3 Nephi 28:18, 23.

Verse 29 indicated that the three men would "minister unto all the scattered tribes of Israel, and unto all nations, kindreds, tongues, and people." This language paralleled Revelation 14:6, in which John the Revelator saw an angel preaching the "everlasting gospel . . . to every nation, and kindred, and tongue, and people." The men were to linger on the earth until Christ's glorious return, at which time they would "be changed in the twinkling of an eye from mortality to immortality," a phrase that paralleled 1 Corinthians 15:52, after which they would dwell with Christ and the Father. The Three Nephites of the Book of Mormon therefore joined John the Beloved in the church's early eschatology as immortalized humans who had tarried on the earth from the time of Christ's first coming and would continue their ministry until Christ's second coming. Several more details were added in 3 Nephi 28 that explained the change that the men experienced that granted them extended longevity and power over death. Like John, they were to spend their days preaching the gospel and seeking to bring souls to Christ.

In public venues, Smith also taught about and elaborated on John's ongoing ministry. John Whitmer, as the church's appointed historian, wrote that in June 1831 Smith "prophecied that John the Revelator was then among the ten tribes of israel who had been lead away by Salmaneser King of israel, to prepare them for their return, from their Long dispersion, to again posses the land of their father's."[70] Similarly, in March 1832, Smith dictated a statement interpreting Revelation 10, in which John the Revelator saw an angel holding a little book and "took the little book out of the angel's hand, and ate it up."[71] Smith expounded this passage, explaining that the book was "a Mission and an ordinance for him to gather the tribes of Israel."[72] Smith's public teachings popularized the ideas—first articulated in the Account of John and then elaborated in 3 Nephi 28—that John was still alive, remaining among mortals, and that, like the Three Nephites, he was undertaking a great work among the scattered House of Israel.

As Smith's church grew and expanded geographically in the early 1830s, so did the ecclesiastical structure of the organization. In late 1831, Smith dictated a revelation regarding the appointment of a "president of the high Priesthood," with the responsibility "to preside over the whole church & to be like unto Moses." This president was also "to be a Seer a revelator a translator &

70. John Whitmer, History, 27, in *JSP*-H2:39.
71. Revelation 10:10. For context, see all of Revelation 10.
72. Answers to Questions, between ca. 4 and ca. 20 March 1832, in *JSP*-D2:213 [D&C 77:14].

a prophet having all the gifts of God which he bestoweth upon the head of the church." In early 1832, Smith was appointed to this position and selected two counselors who joined him in a three-man "presidency." In 1833, he dictated a revelation stating that all three would hold the "keys of the kingdom," meaning the authority to preside over the church.[73] In early 1834, Smith taught that the apostle Peter similarly presided over the ancient Christian church and that the apostle "held the Keys of the Kingdom of God." Peter was also assisted by two counselors, with whom he held "the keys of [Christ's] kingdom."[74] Smith did not explicitly identify Peter's counselors on that occasion, but given the chief apostle's biblical association with the brothers James and John—especially as witnesses of Christ's transfiguration—Smith could plausibly have understood in 1834 that the two apostles were the counselors in Peter's ancient church presidency.[75]

Finally, in late 1834, Smith added his father, Joseph Smith Sr., to the First Presidency as an "Assistant President" and at the same time ordained him the church's "patriarch," a new ecclesiastical office patterned after the biblical patriarchs who gave special blessings to their posterity by the laying on of hands.[76] Over the next half decade, Joseph Smith Sr. gave hundreds of such blessings to Latter-day Saints.[77] These blessings provide a fascinating window into ways that the church patriarch—and presumably many of those whom he blessed—made sense of the miraculous and the divine in everyday life. One of Smith Sr.'s recurrent themes was the prediction that individuals, if they so desired, could "tarry" until Christ's return in glory. Latter-day Saint apostle Orson Pratt was told in 1835 that through his preaching, he would "bring many souls to the knowledge of the truth, and tarry till the Savior comes."[78] The same year, Smith Sr. told another church member, Calvin Beebe, "Thou hast asked thy God to let thee tarry till the Son of Man comes: and if thou art faithful, and keep all the commandments

73. Note, 8 March 1832, in *JSP*-D2:201–4; Revelation, 15 March 1832, in *JSP*-D2:207–8 [D&C 81]. On the church's developing ecclesiastical structure and related textual expansions in Smith's revelations, see William V. Smith, "Early Mormon Priesthood Revelations: Text, Impact, and Evolution," *Dialogue: A Journal of Mormon Thought* 46, no. 4 (2013): 1–84.

74. Minutes, 17 February 1834, in *JSP*-D3:437.

75. In 1839, Smith taught that Peter, James, and John received the "Keys" when they were transfigured with Jesus on the Mount of Transfiguration. Discourse, between ca. 26 June and ca. August 1839-A, in *JSP*-D6:543–44). On "keys" in early church thought, see Smith, "Early Mormon Priesthood Revelations."

76. Smith, History, 1834–1836, 17–20, in *JSP*-H1:37–38; Patriarchal Blessings, 1:9, Church History Library.

77. See Historical Introduction to Blessing from Joseph Smith Sr., 9 December 1834, in *JSP*-D4:200.

78. Joseph Smith Sr., Patriarchal Blessing for Orson Pratt, 29 April 1835, Patriarchal Blessings, 1:21, transcribed in *Early Patriarchal Blessings of The Church of Jesus Christ of Latter-day Saints*, comp. H. Michael Marquardt (Salt Lake City: Smith-Pettit Foundation, 2007), 26–27.

of the Lord thou shalt have thy desire."[79] This language was clearly reminiscent of the Account of John and demonstrates that the ideas in the document were shaping the Mormon religious imagination by the mid-1830s.

Smith Sr.'s patriarchal blessings also consider "tarrying" like the Beloved Disciple until Christ's second coming as just one of three options for righteous believers. Elijah Fordham was told that he would "have the desire of thy heart, whether to sleep in the dust, be translated, or tarry till the Savior comes."[80] In the nineteenth century, the word "translated" had a broad range of connotations. The first definition in Noah Webster's 1828 *American Dictionary* was "the act of removing or conveying from one place or another," citing as an example "the removal of a bishop from one see [or jurisdiction] to another." Webster's next defined *translation* as "the removal of a person to heaven without subjecting him to death," offering the biblical example of Enoch. Genesis 5:24 indicated that "Enoch walked with God: and he was not; for God took him." Hebrews 11:5 interpreted this to mean that "Enoch was translated that he should not see death." The idea was that Enoch "was not" on the earth because God had transported him to heaven before he died.[81] Whereas Enoch was translated away from the earth, John and the Three Nephites remained on the earth, tarrying among mortals and ministering to them. Smith Sr. built on this eschatology, juxtaposing "translation" and "tarrying" as related yet distinct paths for the faithful who had been granted power over death.[82]

Taken together, these examples demonstrate how strongly the tarrying of the Beloved Disciple, as first described in the Account of John, resonated in the early church. It was echoed in the account of the Three Nephites in the Book of Mormon and apparently influenced Smith's teachings on John's latter-day ministry, the development of the church's ecclesiastical structure, and the promises given to the Saints in patriarchal blessings. Through scripture, preaching, organization, and practice, the Account of John was making its mark on Latter-day Saint thought and culture. When the document was prepared for publication in 1835, it would be revised and expanded in ways that encompassed these developments.

79. Joseph Smith Sr., Patriarchal Blessing for Calvin Beebe, 4 May 1835, Patriarchal Blessings, 1:26, transcribed in *Early Patriarchal Blessings of The Church of Jesus Christ of Latter-day Saints*, 29–30.

80. Joseph Smith Sr., Patriarchal Blessing for Elijah Fordham, undated, Patriarchal Blessings, 1:87, transcribed in *Early Patriarchal Blessings of The Church of Jesus Christ of Latter-day Saints*, 119–20.

81. See Noah Webster, *An American Dictionary of the English Language* (New York: S. Converse, 1828), s.v. "translate."

82. For similar formulations, see the 1835 blessings for Elisha H. Groves and Jesse Hitchcock in *Early Patriarchal Blessings of The Church of Jesus Christ of Latter-day Saints*, 40 and 56.

REVISING THE ACCOUNT OF JOHN

While the earliest interpretation of the Account of John was fluid, the text itself remained essentially unchanged from early 1829 through late 1832, with only minor changes being made in anticipation of its publication in the Book of Commandments. This would change conspicuously in 1835, when the Account of John was prepared for publication in the Doctrine and Covenants (hereafter D&C), a compilation that combined theological lectures and Smith's revelations. When the Account of John appeared as Section 33 of the D&C, it had been expanded from 141 words to 252 words—an increase of 79 percent. These changes further developed points made only implicitly in the 1829 text and harmonized the Account of John with subsequent doctrinal and ecclesiastical developments.[83]

Despite church leaders' plans to publish the BoC, a mob attacked the church's Missouri print shop on 20 July 1833, destroying the printing office prior to completion of the work. Although dozens of proof sheets were recovered from the building and subsequently bound, circulation of the incomplete book was limited. In 1834 and 1835, a committee composed of Smith, Cowdery, Sidney Rigdon, and Frederick G. Williams worked to prepare a new edition of Smith's revelations in Kirtland, Ohio.[84] Smith's direct involvement in the committee remains unclear, although textual evidence suggests he participated in the editing of at least some of his revelations.[85] Like the BoC, the production of the D&C was a collaborative project, as Smith shared the responsibility of preparing his revelations for publication with his most-trusted associates. Cowdery provided continuity between the D&C committee and the group that prepared the BoC, although Phelps would join the D&C project team in May 1835, prior to the typesetting of the Account of John.[86]

Only one public statement was made regarding the D&C committee's editorial approach. Cowdery noted that they had sought to ensure that the revelations were printed accurately, although he confessed that the printed versions

83. Scholars have argued that Joseph Smith's Bible revision project was, in part, an effort to harmonize the Bible both internally and with Smith's revelations. The revisions made to Smith's own revelations as published in the D&C in 1835 seem to have reflected a similar objective. See Philip L. Barlow, "Joseph Smith's Revision of the Bible: Fraudulent, Pathologic, or Prophetic?," *Harvard Theological Review* 83, no. 1 (January 1990): 56; Thomas A. Wayment, "Intertextuality and the Purpose of Joseph Smith's New Translation of the Bible," chap. 4 in *Foundational Texts of Mormonism*, ed. Mark Ashurst-McGee, Robin Scott Jensen, and Sharalyn D. Howcroft (Oxford and New York: Oxford University Press, 2018).

84. Minutes, 24 September 1834, in *JSP*-D4:175.

85. Historical Introduction to Doctrine and Covenants, 1835, in *JSP*-R2:305.

86. Historical Introduction to Doctrine and Covenants, 1835, in *JSP*-R2:305–6.

might not correspond with the revelation manuscripts "in every word." Echoing Smith's 1832 directive to Phelps that the "sense" of the revelations not be altered, Cowdery explained that the revelations, as printed in 1835, would be accurate "in principle."[87] Cowdery's statement only partially captured the committee's editorial approach to the revelations. While many of the revisions focused on word choice and grammar to make the revelations read more clearly, other changes were far more substantial, as several of the revelations were expanded significantly. Some of these expansions amalgamated texts that had initially been dictated as separate revelations.[88] Others contained new material that was integrated seamlessly into the revelations.[89] Smith was presumably consulted regarding the more significant changes made to his revelations and likely even directed those changes—especially the more substantial expansions and revisions that altered the sense of the text. However, as noted, evidence confirming his involvement is limited.

The text of the Account of John was revisited in 1835, along with the texts of the revelations, and significantly revised. It was presumably believed by either Smith on his own as revelator and translator or the committee as a whole (or possibly both) that the expansions then made to the Account of John were consistent with the principles of the original text, at least as those principles were understood in 1835. The committee relied on the version of the Account of John that had been printed in the BoC, rather than the manuscript version in the BCR, as evidenced by the fact that the D&C retained the handful of changes that first appeared in the BoC. Accounting for the textual revisions that did occur between 1829 and late 1832, Table 10.2 below will refer to the pre-1835 text as the "early" Account of John.[90]

It is noteworthy that despite the substantial expansions, the early text of the Account of John was largely preserved in the revised edition. Biblical scholar David M. Carr has shown that ancient scribes copying the Hebrew scriptures combined their duty to replicate and conserve with the impulse to add. "In cases of expansion," Carr has observed, "the bulk of the tradition was preserved, but enriched through additional exclusively oral traditions, theological updates, or other elements perceived as enhancements to the sacred

87. *Evening and the Morning Star*, June 1832 (reprinted January 1835), 16.

88. See Smith, "Early Mormon Priesthood Revelations."

89. See Revelation, ca. June 1835, in *JSP*-D4:354–59 [D&C 68]; Revelation, ca. August 1835, in *JSP*-D4:408–12 [D&C 27].

90. In the BoC, verse 1 included the interpretive heading. BoC 6:1 (18); Book of Commandments, in *JSP*-R2:30 [D&C 7: heading].

TABLE 10.2. 1835 Textual Expansions

Early Account of John Book of Commandments	Revised Account of John Doctrine and Covenants
1 AND the Lord said unto me, John my beloved, what desirest thou?	1 And the Lord said unto me, John, my beloved, what desirest thou? For if ye shall ask, what you will, it shall be granted unto you.
and I said Lord, give unto me power that I may bring souls unto thee.—	And I said unto him, Lord, give unto me power over death, that I may live and bring souls unto thee.
And the Lord said unto me: Verily, verily I say unto thee, because thou desiredst this, thou shalt tarry till I come in my glory:	And the Lord said unto me, Verily, verily, I say unto thee, because thou desiredst this thou shalt tarry until I come in my glory, and shall prophesy before nations, kindreds, tongues and people.
2 And for this cause, the Lord said unto Peter:—If I will that he tarry till I come, what is that to thee? for he desiredst of me that he might bring souls unto me: but thou desiredst that thou might speedily come unto me in my kingdom: I say unto thee, Peter, this was a good desire, but my beloved has undertaken a greater work.	2 And for this cause the Lord said unto Peter, If I will that he tarry till I come, what is that to thee? For he desiredst of me that he might bring souls unto me; but thou desiredst that thou might speedily come unto me in my kingdom. I say unto thee, Peter, this was a good desire, but my beloved has desired that he might do more, or a greater work, yet among men than what he has before done;
	yea, he has undertaken a greater work; therefore, I will make him as flaming fire and a ministering angel: he shall minister for those who shall be heirs of salvation who dwell on the earth; and I will make thee to minister for him and for thy brother James: and unto you three I will give this power and the keys of this ministry until I come.
3 Verily I say unto you, ye shall both have according to your desires, for ye both joy in that which ye have desired.	3 Verily I say unto you, ye shall both have according to your desires, for ye both joy in that which ye have desired.

deposit of more ancient material."[91] The D&C committee likely approved of the revised Account of John and other expanded revelations in similar terms.

In general, the committee's expansions increased the Account of John's intertextual relationship with the Bible. In the early text, only one phrase—"if I

91. Carr, *Formation of the Hebrew Bible*, 100.

will that he tarry until I come what is that to thee"—was clearly a quotation from the KJV. As noted above, adding "in my glory" after "till I come" may have been intended to allude to Matthew 25:31, and the emphasis on the "desires" of Peter and John may have had an implicit parallel with Mark 10:35. The 1835 expansions to the Account of John paralleled language in at least five other biblical passages—in Psalms, Matthew, John, Hebrews, and Revelation—which were used to clarify and further develop the meaning of the text. The added language built upon the early text's answers to the interpretive difficulties of John 21, extending and clarifying specific points regarding the identity of the Beloved Disciple and his fate. The 1835 editors drew on scriptural language from a variety of texts to reveal a continuity between the ancient and antebellum worlds. That is, their expansion of the Account of John with biblical phrasing elaborated it as a manifestation of the foundational theme that Mormon Christianity was a restoration of lost ancient truth. The expanded Account of John reiterated to early church members that the ecclesiastical structure of the restored church was patterned after the structure of the primitive church.

As noted above, the Account of John differed from John 21 in that the early text imputed agency to the Beloved Disciple, with Jesus asking the Disciple what he desired. The 1835 expansion augmented the section by having Jesus state, "For if ye shall ask, what ye will, it shall be granted unto you." This language closely paralleled John 15:7, "If ye shall abide in me, and my words abide in you, *ye shall ask what ye will*, and *it shall be* done *unto you*" (emphasis added). The 1835 expansion further developed the nature of John's desire, making explicit a point that was ambiguous in the early text. Initially, John stated his desire thus, "give unto me power that I may bring souls unto thee." The 1835 text clarified that John requested "power *over death*, that I may *live and* bring souls unto thee" (emphasis added).

The D&C committee attempted to harmonize the Account of John with elements of 3 Nephi 28. With John's power over death, the expanded text clarified that the apostle would "prophesy before nations, kindreds, tongues, and people," alluding to Revelation 14:6, in which John the Revelator saw an angel preaching the "everlasting gospel . . . to every nation, and kindred, and tongue, and people." As noted above, the description of the Three Nephites likewise alluded to Revelation 14:6; it was therefore a logical intertextual expansion in the 1835 Account of John.

This coordination with 3 Nephi 28 was also apparent in another significant expansion to the 1835 text, in which Jesus made John the "Beloved" the angel who would take the gospel to all nations: "Therefore I [Jesus] will make him

TABLE 10.3. Biblical Intertextuality

Psalm 104:4	Hebrews 1:7, 14	1835 Account of John
Who maketh his angels spirits; his ministers a flaming fire	7 And of the angels he saith, Who maketh his angels spirits, and his ministers a flame of fire.	I will make him as flaming fire and a ministering angel:
	14 Are they [the angels] not all ministering spirits, sent forth to minister for them who shall be heirs of salvation?	he shall minister for those who shall be heirs of salvation who dwell on the earth

[John] as a flaming fire and a ministering angel; he shall minister for those who shall be heirs of salvation who dwell on the earth." This passage elaborated the story of John's post-biblical life as an angel by combining biblical phraseology from Psalm 104 and Hebrews 1. Psalm 104 is a hymn of praise acclaiming Yahweh for creating the world and celebrating his glory and grandeur. Verse 4 depicts God making "angels spirits" and "his ministers a flaming fire." Hebrews 1 presents an argument for Jesus having divine status, holding authority over the angels, with verses 7 and 14 elaborating on Psalm 104:4.[92] The 1835 Account of John synthesized these biblical verses and applied them to John, simultaneously identifying the change that permitted the Beloved Disciple to tarry and his proselytizing mission among the "heirs of salvation" on the earth. Who precisely were the "heirs of salvation" was left unstated, although 3 Nephi 28 and Smith's teachings in the early 1830s suggested that the term may have included remnants of the House of Israel.

It is noteworthy that Smith and his associates did not identify John as a *translated being,* like Enoch, in the 1835 expansions. Beings who were either "translated" or "tarried" were later conflated in Latter-day Saint thought—both in scholarly and popular literature—rendering John a translated being.[93]

92. By 1835, the new scripture produced by Joseph Smith had alluded to Hebrews 1:14 on at least three occasions: in mid-1829, near the very end of the translation of the Book of Mormon; on 16 February 1832, in the vision of the afterlife written by Joseph Smith and Sidney Rigdon; and later in early 1832, in the revision of Hebrews 1:7 in the "new translation" of the Bible. See Moroni 10:14; Vision, 16 February 1832, in *JSP*-D2:190 [D&C 76:85–86, 88]; New Testament Manuscript 2, Folio 4, 138 (second numbering), in Smith, *Joseph Smith's New Translation of the Bible*, 535. These earlier allusions anticipated some of the wording in the 1835 version of the Account of John.

93. For popular treatments, see Bruce R. McConkie, *Mormon Doctrine*, 2nd ed. (Salt Lake City: Bookcraft, 1979), s.v. "Translated Beings"; and *Encyclopedia of Mormonism,* s.v., "Translated Beings." For recent treatments by Mormon scholars of John the Beloved as a translated being, see John A. Tvedtnes, "Translated

The Account of John, however, did not use that term, although the concept may have been implied when the Lord made John a ministering angel, suggesting a change in bodily state. As surveyed above, Joseph Smith Sr.'s patriarchal blessings seemed to treat "tarrying" on the earth and "translation" to heaven as related and yet separate and distinct options for the faithful, perhaps reflecting broader usage in the early church. This may explain why the 1835 Account of John did not adopt the latter designation.[94]

The D&C committee also harmonized the 1835 Account of John with the emergence of Smith's presidency in the early 1830s. The revised text had Jesus instructing Peter: "I will make thee to minister for him [John] and for thy brother James: and to you three I will give this power and the keys of this ministry until I come."[95] Although the early Account of John confined its comments on Peter to his desire to "come unto me [Jesus] in my kingdom," the revised account indicated that Peter, along with John and his brother James, would hold "the keys of this ministry" until Christ's coming.[96]

Taken together, these 1835 revisions to the Account of John reflected the interests of Smith and his associates in clarifying and expanding the early text's initial interactions with John 21. The changes also augmented the Account of John's intertextual relationship with the KJV. While the early text was almost entirely preserved in the 1835 revisions, the expansions sought to enrich, update, and harmonize the Account of John with Smith's subsequent scriptures and teachings. The expanded Account followed 3 Nephi 28 in transforming the

---

Beings: Access to the Ancients," *Meridian Magazine*, http://ldsmag.com/article-1-200/; and Judd and Szink, "John the Beloved in Latter-day Scripture."

94. For references to other translated beings, see Hebrews 11:5; Smith's Genesis expansion regarding Enoch (Old Testament Manuscript 2, 21, 25, in Smith, *Joseph Smith's New Translation of the Bible*, 617–23 [Moses 7:21–69]); and the Joseph Smith insertion following Genesis 14:24 (Old Testament Manuscript 2, in Smith, *Joseph Smith's New Translation of the Bible*, 641–42). See also Ether 15:34.

95. This expansion includes some interesting problems with pronoun antecedents. At the beginning of the expansion Jesus is talking to Peter, clearly speaking to him about John's mission as a ministering angel. However, in the words that follow—"I will make thee to minister for him and for thy brother James"—the object becomes unclear as the referent of "thee" is apparently no longer Peter but John (since James was the brother of John). However, it is also possible that Jesus is referring to James as Peter's "brother" in the family of Christ. The meaning of the text remains uncertain.

96. This expansion anticipated substantial changes made to another revelation in the D&C addressing this same ecclesiastical development. Section 50 (now 27) included new language in which "the voice of Jesus Christ, your Lord" stated that he had "committed the keys of my kingdom" to Peter, James, and John. And, according to this expansion, the Lord had recommitted the keys in the last days. As the voice of the Lord recounted, Smith had been visited by the three apostles, "by whom I have ordained you and confirmed you to be apostles and especial witnesses of my name, and bear the keys of your ministry." Revelation, ca. August 1835, in *JSP*-D4:411 [D&C 27:12–13]. For other accounts of the visitation of Peter, James, and John, and their conferral of divine authority on Smith and Cowdery, see Brian Q. Cannon, "The Earliest Accounts of the Restoration of the Priesthood."

Beloved Disciple into a ministering angel who would preach unto all nations, kindreds, tongues, and people. In addition, the 1835 text was coordinated with ecclesiastical developments by indicating that John, along with Peter and James, held the keys of the ministry and administration of Christ's kingdom on earth.

The D&C committee made one final decision as the revised Account of John was prepared for typesetting. They retained the BoC's interpretive heading, thereby framing the expanded Account of John as a translation of a text written by the apostle John on parchment and hidden up in anticipation of providential recovery in the Lord's due time.[97] This heading, a version of which remained attached to the text in all subsequent editions of the Doctrine and Covenants, continues to frame how contemporary Latter-day Saints approach the Account of John.

CONCLUSION

What began as a question by Joseph Smith and Oliver Cowdery regarding the meaning of an obscure passage at the end of the Gospel of John resulted in a text that explained, from John the Apostle's first-person perspective, what Jesus had meant when he said that the Beloved Disciple would "tarry" until Christ's coming. The resulting text dictated by Joseph Smith in 1829 was only the first step in a six-year process of textual formation for the Account of John. While it remains unclear how Smith and Cowdery viewed the document in 1829—as either a revelation or a translation—in 1831 John Whitmer clearly classified it as a commandment and a revelation. The 1832 BoC heading retained the revelation designation, while also presenting the text as a translation of a document written by the apostle.

The Account of John also anticipated doctrinal and ecclesiastical developments that the D&C committee incorporated by expanding the text by more than one hundred words in 1835. Scriptural, ecclesiastical, and doctrinal

97. Although beyond the scope of this chapter, the 1835 revisions also raise questions regarding how Smith viewed the relative plasticity of his translations. While it remains unclear whether Smith understood the Account of John to be a translation in 1829, by 1835 he almost certainly was aware of the BoC heading that designated the document as a "translation" and was presumably involved in the decision to retain the heading in the D&C. Smith's best-known translation, the Book of Mormon, also underwent substantial editing in his lifetime, although the changes were primarily grammatical in nature with some diction revisions. In contrast, the original grammar and word choice of the Account of John were left largely untouched, with expansions providing the bulk of the textual revisions. On the textual history of the Book of Mormon, see Royal Skousen, "Changes in the Book of Mormon," *Interpreter: A Journal of Mormon Scripture* 11 (2014): 161–76.

developments—the Three Nephites in the Book of Mormon, John's sojourn among the Lost Tribes, the emergence of ecclesiastical "keys" and their association with the First Presidency, and patriarchal blessings—informed how the D&C committee went about revising the Account of John in 1835. In its final form, John himself reported that he had been granted power over death, had been made as a "ministering angel" to the "heirs of salvation," and had been given the keys of the Kingdom, elements that were absent in the early text but that were, nevertheless, integral components to how the Account of John engaged with John 21.

The Account of John therefore represents a unique intervention in the long reception history of the final chapter of the Gospel of John. For eighteen hundred years, John 21 had baffled readers. A long line of Christian theologians had reported disparate interpretations of Jesus's words regarding the tarrying of the Beloved Disciple and frequently weighed in on the question themselves. Indicative of Joseph Smith's audacious claims to prophetic authority, his Account of John was not presented as a mere commentary on the meaning of John 21, but instead as a revealed first-person narration by the apostle John himself. Furthermore, when the text reached its final form in 1835, it was presented as translation of a parchment, written and hidden up by the ancient apostle, and recently brought forth providentially to explain, at long last, the tarrying of the Beloved Disciple.

11

A Recovered Resource

The Use of Adam Clarke's Bible Commentary in Joseph Smith's Bible Translation

THOMAS A. WAYMENT AND HALEY WILSON-LEMMON

The revised text of the Bible that Joseph Smith called his "new translation" has attracted significant attention in recent decades, drawing the interest of a wide variety of academics and those who affirm its nearly canonical status as a sacred text of the Church of Jesus Christ of Latter-day Saints.[1] Research into the origins of Smith's Bible translation, presented here, has uncovered evidence that Smith and his scribes used a readily available Bible commentary while working on the new translation—or more properly revision—of the King James Version of the Holy Bible (hereafter KJV). The commentary, Adam

1. Joseph Smith occasionally used the title "New Translation" to refer to his revision of the Bible. See Letter to Church Leaders in Jackson County, Missouri, 21 April 1833, in *JSP*-D3:68; Letter to Church Leaders in Jackson County, Missouri, 25 June 1833, in *JSP*-D3:147–58; Letter to Church Leaders in Jackson County, Missouri, 2 July 1833, in *JSP*-D3:167; Letter to Church Leaders in Jackson County, Missouri, 6 August 1833, in *JSP*-D3:233. For a recent treatment of the Joseph Smith Bible translation, see Seth Perry, "The Many Bibles of Joseph Smith: Textual, Prophetic, and Scholarly Authority in Early-National Bible Culture," *Journal of the American Academy of Religion* 84, no. 3 (October 2015): 1–26. See also Philip L. Barlow, "Joseph Smith's Revision of the Bible: Fraudulent, Pathologic, or Prophetic?," *Harvard Theological Review* 83, no. 1 (January 1990): 45–64. Barlow treated the subject again in *Mormons and the Bible: The Place of the Latter-day Saints in American Religion*, rev. ed. (Oxford and New York: Oxford University Press, 2013), 49–67. The subject of Smith's Bible translation has been of immense interest to Latter-day Saints, in part because of the lingering question of whether the revised biblical text has canonical implications. See Robert J. Matthews, "The Role of the Joseph Smith Translation in the Restoration," in *Plain and Precious Truths Restored: The Doctrinal and Historical Significance of the Joseph Smith Translation*, ed. Robert L. Millet and Robert J. Matthews (Salt Lake City: Deseret Book, 1995), 42; Robert J. Matthews, *"A Plainer Translation": Joseph Smith's Translation of the Bible; A History and Commentary* (Provo, UT: Brigham Young University, 1975), 12. Others who have directly addressed the question of the canonicity of the text include Robert L. Millet, "Hard Questions about the Joseph Smith Translation," in *Plain and Precious Truths Restored*, 147–62. Millet describes the translation as "a beacon of light to which we would do well to give heed as we seek to gain the more sure knowledge of the word of prophecy" (161). See also Kent P. Jackson, "New Discoveries in the Joseph Smith Translation of the Bible," in *By Study and by Faith: Selections from the Religious Educator*, ed. Richard Neitzel Holzapfel and Kent P. Jackson (Provo, UT: Religious Studies Center, 2009), 169–79. Jackson states that Smith's Bible revision "is a miracle—a divine act of God" (178).

Clarke's famous *Holy Bible, Containing the Old and New Testaments*, was a mainstay for Methodist theologians and biblical scholars alike, and was one of the most widely available commentaries in America during the mid-1820s and 1830s.[2] Joseph Smith's use of this source in his translation efforts has only recently been suggested, and only in two instances.[3] Based on a recent comparison of Clarke's commentary on the Bible and Smith's translation of the Bible, the fundamental question of what Smith meant by the term *translation* with respect to his efforts to rework the biblical text can now be broadened to include an academic interest in improving the English text of the Bible. This new evidence effectively forces a reconsideration of Smith's translation projects, particularly his Bible revision, and how he used a scholarly source while simultaneously melding his own prophetic inspiration into the resulting text.

This chapter begins by presenting the evidence for Joseph Smith's reliance upon Adam Clarke's Bible Commentary and showing the nature of his usage of Clarke. The chapter then investigates how Smith approached the question of the quality of the KJV translation that he was using in 1830 and what the term "translation" meant to him and his close associates. Finally, a suggestion is offered as to how Smith came to use Clarke, and the overall question of what these findings imply about Smith's other translation projects is assessed.

JOSEPH SMITH'S "NEW TRANSLATION" OF THE BIBLE

Beginning in June 1830, Joseph Smith began an ambitious project to retranslate or revise the KJV Bible without the aid of a dictionary, lexica, or language training in Hebrew or Greek. With the help of scribes, Smith began the revision by dictating a substantially altered version of Genesis that generally followed the text of the Bible but expanded the story in dramatic ways and also engaged in rewording, rearranging, and otherwise altering the KJV text. Smith may have been encouraged in his efforts to revise the Bible through passages in the Book of Mormon that spoke of the removal of truths from the Bible. The Book of Mormon also taught that doctrinal disagreements and the proliferation of sects

2. Adam Clarke, *The Holy Bible Containing the Old and New Testaments* (London: Butterworth, 1815; Nashville: Abingdon, 1977). On the commentary's influence, see Thomas Jackson, *Memoirs of the Life and Writings of the Reverend Richard Watson: Late Secretary to the Wesleyan Missionary Society* (New York: B. Waugh and T. Mason, 1834), 174; Abel Stevens, *Life and Times of Nathan Bangs* (New York: Carlton and Porter, 1868), 189–90.

3. See Ronald V. Huggins, "'Without a Cause' and 'Ships of Tarshish': A Possible Contemporary Source for Two Unexplained Readings from Joseph Smith," *Dialogue: A Journal of Mormon Thought* 36, no. 1 (Spring 2003): 157–79.

was "because of the most plain and precious parts of the gospel of the Lamb which have been kept back by that abominable church."[4]

Working with John Whitmer as his scribe, Smith's revision of Genesis 1:1–6:13 resulted in the production of seven new chapters of scripture that loosely follow the storyline of Genesis 1–6. Excerpts of the translation were published in early church newspapers.[5] In 1851, the Church of Jesus Christ of Latter-day Saints republished the Bible revision for the early chapters of Genesis as the "Book of Moses." This was one of various texts published in a pamphlet under the title *The Pearl of Great Price*.[6] In 1880, the Pearl of Great Price was canonized as the fourth of the four standard works of the Church of Jesus Christ of Latter-day Saints.[7] Other selected passages of Smith's revision of the Bible have been placed in footnotes and a section of back matter of church editions of the KJV. In 1867, the Reorganized Church of Jesus Christ of Latter Day Saints (now the Community of Christ) published a complete edition of Smith's revised Bible.[8]

In December 1830, while Smith was still revising Genesis, Sidney Rigdon began acting as scribe. Then, in March 1831, Smith dictated a revelation wherein he was directed to suspend his work on the Old Testament and begin translating the New Testament.[9] Once Smith and Rigdon had finished revising the New Testament, they returned to the Old Testament and finished revising it in July 1833. Smith and his associates spoke very little about the Bible translation and how it was carried out, leaving a historical puzzle for historians and other scholars to attempt to understand.

ADAM CLARKE'S BIBLE COMMENTARY

Adam Clarke's massive commentary on the entire Bible was published in London in six volumes between 1810 and 1825, and was available for purchase in America at least by 1824.[10] The commentary was immensely popular—

4. 1 Nephi 13:34.

5. See *Evening and the Morning Star*, August 1832, 2–3; March 1833, 1; April 1833, 1–2; *Times and Seasons*, January 1843, 71–73.

6. Franklin D. Richards, ed., The Pearl of Great Price (Liverpool: R. James, 1851).

7. Kent P. Jackson, *The Book of Moses and the Joseph Smith Translation Manuscripts* (Provo, UT: Religious Studies Center, 2005), 36.

8. *The Holy Scriptures Translated and Corrected by the Spirit of Revelation, by Joseph Smith Jr., the Seer* (Plano, IL: [Reorganized] Church of Jesus Christ of Latter-Day Saints, 1867).

9. Revelation, 7 March 1831, in *JSP*-D1:279 [D&C 45:60].

10. Stevens, *Life and Times of Nathan Bangs*, 189–90. In December 1829, an anonymous review of Clarke's commentary lamented that the volumes were overly expensive for the commentary's intended users. "Review of Adam Clark's Discourses," *Quarterly Christian Spectator* 1, no. 4 (December 1829): 553–85.

FIGURE 11.1. Adam Clarke. Methodist theologian Adam Clarke (circa 1761–1832) authored an influential Bible commentary that was used by Joseph Smith during his "new translation" of the Bible. Artist unknown, Welsh Portrait Collection, Llyfrgell Genedlaethol Cymru—National Library of Wales, Aberystwyth, Wales.

as indicated through widespread quotation and citation—because of its sheer breadth of discussion and strong academic foundation.[11] Clarke himself (see Figure 11.1) was a renowned Methodist minister who devoted his life to producing a singularly broad commentary that detailed historical, theological, and textual matters with scholarly acumen. Theologically speaking, he held peculiar views about the incarnation of Jesus Christ that drew the ire of some of his contemporaries, but his biblical commentary was otherwise considered unassailable within the English-speaking world of transatlantic Protestantism.[12] Joseph Smith, who later stated that in his youth he had been "somewhat partial to the Methodist sect," may have first heard Clarke's commentary quoted or cited in the popular religious services he attended in upstate New York as often

11. Stevens, *Life and Times of Nathan Bangs*, 189–90.

12. Richard Watson, *Remarks on the Eternal Sonship of Christ; and the Use of Reason in Matters of Revelation* (London: T. Cordeux, 1818).

"as occasion would permit."[13] As indicated by the evidence presented below, he apparently acquired a copy of the commentary or perhaps gained access to one through another individual, such as Sidney Rigdon, his principal scribe for the Bible revision.

Efforts to locate a copy either owned or used by Smith have so far proven unsuccessful. There is some possibility that Smith had a copy of Clarke's commentary near the beginning of the Bible translation process. Nathaniel Lewis, the uncle of Joseph Smith's wife, Emma Hale Smith, claimed this was the case. In an account published several years after the events, Lewis reportedly stated:

> And when the story came out about the "gold plates," and the great spectacles, he (Lewis) asked Joe if anyone but himself could translate other languages into English by the aid of his miraculous spectacles? On being answered in the affirmative, he proposed to Joe to let him make the experiment upon some of the strange languages he found in Clarke's Commentary, and stated to him if it was even so, and the experiment proved successful, he would then believe the story about the gold plates. But at this proposition Joe was much offended, and never undertook to convert "Uncle Lewis" afterward.

The story is retold in several later accounts, some of which report that Lewis pulled Clarke's commentary from his own bookshelf and then questioned Smith, or even that Lewis said "I've got Clarke's commentary."[14]

There are certainly concerns about taking the report at face value, but the fact that Lewis, a Methodist deacon,[15] would call attention to foreign languages found in Clarke is credible enough. Also, the actual ownership of the commentary may be questioned. Lewis may have owned it but brought it to Smith intending to test him, and left it with him. Emma Hale Smith's family, being devout Methodists, may have already owned a copy—to which Nathanael Lewis could have had access if this confrontation occurred while Smith was

13. Joseph Smith, History, 1838–1856, volume A-1, 210, Church History Library, The Church of Jesus Christ of Latter-day Saints, Salt Lake City, Utah (accessible in the Histories series of the online edition of *The Joseph Smith Papers*).

14. The earliest account of the interchange appears to be George Peck, "Mormonism and the Mormons," *Methodist Quarterly Review* 3 (January 1843): 113. See also George Peck, *Early Methodism within the Bounds of the Old Genesee Conference from 1788 to 1828* (New York: Carlton and Porter, 1860), 332–33, quoted in Dan Vogel, comp. and ed., *Early Mormon Documents* (Salt Lake City: Signature Books, 1996–2003), 4:333.

15. Records of the Methodist Episcopal Church, Lanesboro, Pennsylvania, 1812–1912, 9, cited in Larry C. Porter, "Reverend George Lane—Good 'Gifts,' Much 'Grace,' and Marked 'Usefulness,'" *BYU Studies* 9, no. 3 (1969): 332.

living on the Hale farm. If the Hale family had the commentary, Smith would also have had access to it.

RELIANCE ON CLARKE'S BIBLE COMMENTARY IN SMITH'S BIBLE TRANSLATION

However Smith may have obtained it, it is evident that he did. The direct parallels between Adam Clarke's commentary on the Bible and Joseph Smith's revision of the Bible are simply too numerous and too close to explain as mere coincidence or happenstance.[16] Parallels between the two texts number into the hundreds, an amount that is well beyond the limits of this chapter's ability to analyze. Several, however, demonstrate quite clearly Smith's reliance upon Clarke and show that he was inclined to depend on Clarke's commentary for matters of history, textual questions, clarification of wording, and theological nuance. In assembling the evidence, this chapter presents a broad categorization of the types of changes that Smith made when he used Clarke as a source. While Smith's revision of the Bible may also have been influenced by other scholarly sources, none have been identified.[17]

Among the more compelling parallels are the omission of entire biblical verses or the rearrangement of parts of biblical verses. One modification concerned Colossians 2:20–22:

> (20) Wherefore if ye be dead with Christ from the rudiments of the world, why, as though living in the world, are ye subject to ordinances,
> (21) (Touch not; taste not; handle not;
> (22) Which all are to perish with the using;) after the commandments and doctrines of men?

Smith rearranged the order of the words as they appear in the KJV so that a revised clause from verse 22—"which are after the doctrines and commandments

16. In doing research for this chapter, the authors also encountered numerous theological parallels to Charles Buck's *Theological Dictionary* (London: Knight and Compton, 1802). The parallels to Buck's dictionary, however, are inherently different from those identified in Clarke's commentary. They are broadly conceptual and lack the close wording of the Clarke parallels.

17. The authors have consulted the commentaries of John Gill, *An Exposition of the Old Testament* (Philadelphia: William W. Woodward, 1817–1819); Matthew Henry, *An Exposition of the Old and New Testaments* [...] (London: Joseph Ogle Robinson, 1828); Matthew Poole, *Annotations upon the Holy Bible* (London: Thomas Parkhurst et al., 1696–1698); and Thomas Scott, *The Holy Bible: Stereotyped Edition from the Fifth London Edition* (Boston: Samuel T. Armstrong, 1827).

of men"—is appended directly to the end of verse 20, a verse that ends with a comma in the KJV. This change directly follows Adam Clarke's statement regarding it: "*After the commandments and doctrines of men?* These words should follow the 20th verse, of which they form a part; and it appears from them that the apostle is here speaking of the tradition of the elders."[18] The change does little to smooth out the flow of the English translation, and nothing to clarify the meaning. It seems beyond coincidence that Clarke and Smith both removed the same words from one verse and then both moved those words to the end of the same earlier verse.

An example of an omission of text occurs at Luke 19:25, a parenthetical aside: "(And they said unto him, Lord, he hath ten pounds)." Clarke's commentary reports: "This whole verse is omitted by the *Codex Bezae*, a few others, and some copies of the Itala. It is probably an observation that some person made while our Lord was delivering the parable, with a design to correct him in the distribution."[19] Smith's translation omits the verse in its entirety. In this instance, however, Smith or Rigdon may have misread Clarke's intent, who noted that the omission was attested in inferior manuscripts such as Bezae (now commonly referred to as D) and some Latin manuscripts (Clarke's "Itala"). Clark did not explicitly spell out the implicit conclusion that the parenthetical aside of Luke 19:25 *was* included in the more reliable manuscripts.

Another example that demonstrates fairly direct borrowing from Clarke is found in Isaiah 34:7 where the KJV uses the word *unicorns*: "And the unicorns shall come down with them." Smith, in this instance, changed "unicorns" to "Re-em," which is readily recognizable as a transliteration of the Hebrew word translated into English as "unicorns." Smith's revised translation of the passage reads "And the Re-em shall come down with them." Given that Smith would not formally study Hebrew for more than two years after he completed his Bible translation, it is likely that information regarding the Hebrew was acquired from an outside source.[20] Clarke appears to have been the source of this revision. Referencing the Hebrew, Clarke notes: "ראמים reemim, translated

18. Clarke, *Clarke's Commentary: Matthew–Revelation*, 525.

19. Ibid., 478.

20. Robert J. Matthews suggested that this revision was added later, as a result of Smith's Hebrew study. Matthews, *Joseph Smith's Translation of the Bible*, 213. However, Smith's revisions have no other direct transliterations of Hebrew words or any other revisions bearing any indication that they were made after 1833. Moreover, the Hebrew manuals that Smith acquired in 1835 transliterate the word differently. Joshua Seixas's guidelines would render the word as *rameem* and Moses Stuart's transliteration guidelines would render the word *rêmim*. See Joshua Seixas, *A Manual Hebrew Grammar for the Use of Beginners* (Andover: Gould & Newman, 1834), 6; Moses Stuart, *A Grammar of the Hebrew Language* (Andover: Gould & Newman, 1835), 11.

wild goats by Bishop Lowth. The ראם reem Bochart thinks to be a species of wild goat in the deserts of Arabia. It seems generally to mean the rhinoceros."[21] Furthermore, whereas Clarke's "reemim" as a plural of "reem" is readily recognizable as a Hebrew transliteration for the word in question, most sources would render the transliteration "rəʾēmêm"—further pointing to Clarke's commentary as the source for Smith's revision.[22]

Borrowing Where Smith Accepted Clarke's Scholarly Arguments

Some of Smith's changes that are grammatically nuanced and imply a careful reading of the English text may rely on Clarke's commentary. To illustrate, in Luke 23:32, the KJV phraseology could be misinterpreted to mean that Jesus was a malefactor like the men who were crucified on either side of him: "And there were also two other, malefactors, led with him to be put to death." Clarke's commentary points this out, noting: "It should certainly be translated two others [plural], malefactors, as in the Bibles published by the King's printer, Edinburgh. As it now stands in the text, it seems to intimate that our blessed Lord was also a malefactor."[23] Apparently in deference to Clarke, Smith rendered the problematic line in precisely the same way, "there were also two other<s>, malefactors" (hereafter, angle brackets signify insertion and a strikethrough bar signifies cancellation).

Similarly, Smith was apparently persuaded when Clarke argued quite forcefully against the usual translation of 2 Timothy 3:16—"All scripture is given by inspiration of God, and is profitable for doctrine, for reproof, for correction, for instruction in righteousness":

> This sentence is not well translated; the original πασα γραφη θεοπνευστος υφελιμος προς διδασκαλιαν, κ. τ. λ. should be rendered: Every writing Divinely inspired is profitable for doctrine, etc. The particle και, and, is omitted by almost all the versions and many of the fathers, and certainly does not agree well with the text. The apostle is here, beyond all controversy, speaking of the writings of the Old Testament, which, because they came by Divine inspiration, he terms the Holy Scriptures.[24]

21. Clarke, *Clarke's Commentary: Job–Malachi*, 143.

22. A modern transliteration of the word "unicorns" would render it rəʾēmêm. See *The SBL Handbook of Style*, 2nd ed. (Atlanta: SBL Press, 2014), 56–57.

23. Clarke, *Clarke's Commentary: Matthew–Revelation*, 496.

24. Ibid., 635 (Clarke did not use accents or diacritics in his Greek or Hebrew).

In Smith's new translation, the beginning of the verse reads, "<And> all scripture ~~is~~given by inspiration of God, ~~and~~is profitable for doctrine."[25] Apparently persuaded by Clarke's reading of the verse, Smith removed the "and" (Greek "και") following "God." He then repositioned the "and" at the beginning of the verse, although the retention of the KJV comma following "God" was then grammatically incorrect.

Smith also implemented Clarke's changes in Hebrews 9:15–17, which the KJV rendered as:

> (15) And for this cause he is the mediator of the new testament, that by means of death, for the redemption of the transgressions that were under the first testament, they which are called might receive the promise of eternal inheritance.
> (16) For where a testament is, there must also of necessity be the death of the testator.
> (17) For a testament is of force after men are dead: otherwise it is of no strength at all while the testator liveth.

In these verses, the KJV translators had used the English word *testament* to translate the Greek word διαθήκες. This choice of the more technical Latin-derived word had the advantage of connoting a legally binding document. In contrast, Clarke's commentary argued for the word *covenant*, which in the early nineteenth century better reflected the sense of the original Greek term. Clarke contended, "There was no proper reason why our translators should render διαθηκη by testament here, when in almost every other case they render it covenant, which is its proper ecclesiastical meaning, as answering to the Hebrew ברית berith, which see largely explained, Genesis 15:10, and in other places of the Pentateuch." Smith changed the KJV wording of "testament" to "covenant" six times within Hebrews 9:15–20, apparently emulating Clarke's revision of each of the six instances.[26]

Smith was also likely influenced by Clarke to reject the Song of Solomon *in toto*. Clarke's commentary provided an unusually lengthy examination of the Song of Solomon that situated the book within the genre of erotic love

25. Smith did add the word "and" to the beginning of the verse, an addition that is not mentioned by Clarke. It appears that the addition was an attempt to smooth out the flow between verses 15 and 16.

26. At the end of this passage, Clarke remarked: "Very few persons are satisfied with the translation of the following verses to the 20th, particularly the 16th and 17th; at all events the word covenant must be retained." Clarke, *Clarke's Commentary: Matthew–Revelation*, 747–48.

poetry. In his concluding comments, Clarke solemnly declared that "this inimitably fine elegant Hebrew ode" included "nothing of *Christ* and *his Church*." He therefore advised ministers to "avoid preaching" from the text.[27] Given the presence of its overt sexual content and the absence of some genuine connection to Christ and his church (or even Hebrew religion), Clarke was unable to accept the book as authoritatively scriptural. For Smith, this apparently translated into a dismissal of the book as uninspired. The form of the note recording Smith's rejection of the book may also hint at Clarke's influence. Whereas the Bible Smith was using in conjunction with his revisions titled the book "Song of Solomon,"[28] the chapter on the book in Clarke's commentary was entitled "Canticles, or Song of Solomon." In the examination that followed, several places referred to "odes" or "songs," in grammatical agreement with the plural title "Canticles" rather than with the singular title "Song of Solomon."[29] Thus readers of Clarke's commentary could understandably come to conceive of this biblical text not as a single song but as a collection of songs—like the collections of psalms and proverbs that preceded it.[30] The note recording Smith's revision employed this plural interpretation in its statement that "the Songs of Solomon are not inspired writings."[31] Smith was apparently willing to follow Clarke so far as to reject an entire book of scripture.

Occasionally, Smith was also willing to follow Clarke's commentary on even the smallest of matters. In Romans 11:2, in which Elias "maketh intercession to God against Israel," Smith changed the word "intercession" to "complaint"—a suggestion that was made by Clarke.[32] And in Smith's translation, the word "Christ" inexplicably appears in 1 John 3:16 in the place of "God": "Hereby perceive we the love of ~~God~~ <Christ>." The change is intended to clarify the identity of "God" as referring to either God the Father or his Son Jesus Christ. Clarke's commentary rightly noted that the verse was itself interpreting John 3:16 and thus refers to the Son. Clarke also pointed out that some

27. Clarke, *Clarke's Commentary: Job—Malachi*, 844, 849 (italics in original).

28. Joseph Smith's copy of *The Holy Bible, Containing the Old and New Testaments* [. . .] (Cooperstown, NY: H. & E. Phinney, 1828), 422, copy at Community of Christ Library and Archives, Community of Christ, Independence, MO.

29. Clarke, *Clarke's Commentary: Job—Malachi*, 841–49. Dana Pike rejects Clarke as a source of influence for Smith's statements on the Song of Solomon. Dana M. Pike, "Reading the Song of Solomon as a Latter-day Saint," *Religious Educator* 15, no. 2 (2014): 92–95, esp. 107n18.

30. Smith may also have taken the title Ecclesiastes—with its terminal "es"—as a plural form.

31. Joseph Smith, Old Testament Manuscript 2, 97, in Joseph Smith, *Joseph Smith's New Translation of the Bible: Original Manuscripts*, ed. Scott H. Faulring, Kent P. Jackson, and Robert J. Matthews (Provo, UT: Religious Studies Center, 2004), 785.

32. Clarke, *Clarke's Commentary: Matthew–Revelation*, 126.

Arabic and Syriac texts contain the clarification that God in 1 John 3:16 is really Christ.[33]

There were other small changes. In Jude 1:11 ("they have gone in the way of Cain, and ran greedily after the error of Balaam for reward, and perished in the gainsaying of Core"), Smith changed the past tense "perished" to a future tense "shall perish"—a change that is directly noted by Clarke.[34] And in a similar vein, Clarke reasoned that in Matthew 20:21, the passage about the exalted role of the sons of Zebedee, the possessive pronoun "thy" had been mistakenly rendered by a "the" in the KJV translation: "The one on thy right hand and the other on the left, in thy kingdom." Clarke restated the passage: "*One on thy right hand, and the other on (Thy) left,*" explaining that he had "added the pronoun in the latter clause on the authority of almost every MS. and version of repute." Smith, apparently reflecting Clarke, changed the verse in the same manner: "The one on thy right hand and the other on ~~the~~ <thy> left, in thy kingdom."[35] Smith seems to have become increasingly confident in Clarke's linguistic abilities. This appears obvious in Smith's revision as the later changes in the New Testament tend to engage Clarke's emendations that were based on manuscript evidence and grammatical notes.

Borrowing to Harmonize the Scriptures?

While many of Smith's revisions have been interpreted as part of an attempt to harmonize the texts of the four gospels, some of those supposed harmonizations may be explained by Smith following Clarke, who had the same textual agenda. Smith revised the end of Mark 8:29 to read, "Thou art the Christ <, the son of the living God>." Initially, one could suspect that Smith was harmonizing this verse with Matthew 16:16, where his addition to Mark appears in the same form.[36] Given that Smith was often adopting Clarke's commentary, he may have been following Clarke's statement regarding Mark 8:29: "Three

33. Ibid., 916.
34. Ibid., 953.
35. Ibid., 147.
36. Kent P. Jackson has observed that some changes in Smith's Bible revision "probably edit the text to bring it into harmony with truth found in other revelations or elsewhere in the Bible." Jackson, "New Discoveries in the Joseph Smith Translation of the Bible," 173. Similarly, Faulring, Jackson, and Matthews assert that "where a passage was inconsistent with information elsewhere in the Bible, a change was often made." Scott H. Faulring, Kent P. Jackson, and Robert J. Matthews, "Joseph Smith's New Translation of the Bible," in Smith, *Joseph Smith's New Translation of the Bible*, 9. See also Thomas A. Wayment, "Intertextuality and the Purpose of Joseph Smith's New Translation of the Bible," chap. 4 in *Foundational Texts of Mormonism*, ed. Mark Ashurst-McGee, Robin Jensen, and Sharalyn Howcroft (Oxford and New York: Oxford University Press, 2017).

MSS. and some versions add, the Son of the living God."[37] In this example, the Greek text of Mark has apparently been harmonized with Matthew by an early Christian editor. Despite the weak manuscript support for the change to Matthew, it appears that Smith's revision was heeding a suggestion made by Clarke.

A second example that has appeared to harmonize with another gospel source is found in Matthew 27:37. Smith added an extensive explanation about the *titulus crucis* at the beginning of the verse: "<And Pilate wrote a title, and put it on the cross, and the writing was, Jesus of Nazareth, the King of the Jews, in letters of Greek, and Latin, and Hebrew. And the chief priest said unto Pilate, it should be written> and set up over his head his accusation, ~~written~~ This is <he that said, he was> JESUS THE KING OF THE JEWS." Smith's revisions may well have been an effort to harmonize Matthew 27:37 with John 19:20 and Luke 23:38. However, Smith's changes may also be explained in terms of him imitating Clarke's commentary on this verse, which addresses the languages of the sign fastened to the cross: "Both Luke, Luke 23:38, and John, John 19:20, say that this accusation was written in Greek, Latin, and Hebrew. In those three languages, we may conceive the label to stand thus, according to the account given by St. John; the Hebrew being the mixed dialect then spoken."

Overall, it seems that what scholars have classified as "harmonizations" were heavily influenced by other sources such as Clarke and therefore may not necessarily represent any original motivating interest or scope of intention on Smith's part in reconciling the gospel accounts to one another. In a situation where Smith would have had the Bible in front of him along with Clarke's commentary, it is not absolutely certain that he would have always relied on Clarke instead of utilizing the Bible alone, or vice versa. This entire category of changes, therefore, warrants closer investigation.

Borrowing with Theological Consequences

While the above revisions made little difference to the meaning of the text, other alterations had a potentially significant theological impact. Smith's revision of Romans 14:23 may have influenced later Mormon thought regarding the doctrine of the judgment of the wicked. The KJV text reads, "And he that doubteth is damned if he eat, because he eateth not of faith: for whatsoever is not of faith is sin." Smith revised the first part of this to "And he that doubteth is ~~damned~~ <condemned>." Clarke's commentary argues for this same minor

37. Clarke, *Clarke's Commentary: Matthew–Revelation*, 315.

change of wording: "This verse is a necessary part of the preceding, and should be read thus: *But he that doubteth is condemned if he eat, because* he eateth *not of faith*."[38] Smith's revision seems to indicate his acceptance of the quality of Clarke's scholarship even in instances that might entail doctrinal implications.

Such trust can be seen in a number of other examples as well. In Titus 2:11, Smith revised the text to read, "For the grace of God ~~that~~ <, which> bringeth salvation <to all men>, hath appeared ~~to all men~~." Clarke's commentary offers a different rendering of the verse, which he presented as a literal translation of the Greek: "Literally translated, the words stand thus: For the grace of God, that which saves, hath shone forth upon all men. Or, as it is expressed in the margin of our authorized version: The grace of God, that bringeth salvation to all men, hath appeared."[39] The Bible that Smith marked up for his new translation did not include the marginalium referenced by Clarke. However, given two options—Clarke's own translation or the marginalium following the KJV language—Smith chose the more familiar KJV marginal rendering, which he apparently learned by reading Clarke.[40]

Some of the revisions made by Smith appear to have larger theological implications, such as the one that occurs at Matthew 22:14—"For many *are* called, but few are chosen." In that verse, Smith added an explanatory comment to the end of the verse so that the concept of being chosen by God would be denoted by the possession of a "wedding garment": "For many are called, but few ~~*are*~~ Chosen <, wherefore all do not have on the wedding garment>." Clarke's commentary, after addressing the textual quality of the verse, interprets it as follows: "Many are called by the preaching of the Gospel into the outward communion of the Church of Christ; but few, comparatively, are chosen to dwell with God in glory, because they do not come to the master of the feast for a marriage garment—for that holiness without which none can see the Lord." It seems implausible that both Clarke and Smith would independently interpret verse 14 using the word "garment," associate this garment with a wedding costume, and imply that possession of a marriage garment signified a person being permitted into a wedding feast that symbolized divine communion.

38. Ibid., 154 (emphasis in original).

39. Ibid., 653.

40. Smith used an 1828 copy of the KJV Bible published by the H&E Phinney Company of Cooperstown, New York. See Kent P. Jackson, "Joseph Smith's Cooperstown Bible: The Historical Context of the Bible Used in the Joseph Smith Translation," *BYU Studies* 40, no. 1 (2001): 41–45. It remains possible that Smith or one of his associates had access to a KJV Bible that contained marginalia, including the marginalium mentioned by Clarke, but the authors have been unable to find any evidence for such a Bible in Smith's social context.

It appears that Smith also used Clarke several times to clarify subtleties in the text that required a knowledge of the original language to resolve.[41] An example can be found in John 2:24, for which Smith revised the familiar yet odd phrase "because he knew all men" to "because he knew all things." Clarke's commentary revised this verse in precisely the same language: "Instead of παντας all men, EGH, and about thirty others [i.e., early manuscript copies of John], read παντα, every man, or all things; and this I am inclined to believe is the true reading. Jesus knew all things; and why? Because he made all things and because he was the all-wise God."[42] Clarke's altered reading, which is based on poor manuscript evidence, has implications for the theological issue of Jesus's omniscience in the Gospel of John.[43] From this review of various revisions Smith made in the new translation, it is fairly clear that he had some confidence in Clarke's scholarly arguments and that he was willing to follow Clarke's revisions, even in cases where there were theological consequences.

SMITH'S SKEPTICISM OF BIBLE TRANSLATIONS

Given this evidence that Smith utilized Clarke's commentary in his revision of the Bible, it is worth considering what Smith intended to achieve in revising the Bible and how he envisioned the resulting work to be received by his followers. To do so, it is necessary to describe briefly the chronology of the translation and the resulting documents. This process of revising the Old and New Testaments took approximately three years, beginning in June 1830 and ending in July 1833.[44] Recent work on the surviving manuscripts associated with the translation—a marked-up Bible and the accompanying manuscripts—has

41. In contrast, Ronald Huggins has asserted:

> That Smith was not interested in correcting the [Bible] in light of the best available manuscript evidence of his day is demonstrated on a larger scale at those points where the JST . . . adopts readings from the [King James Bible] which were even then widely recognized as inferior. This becomes immediately apparent, for example, in reference to the most familiar disputed texts: the longer ending of Mark 16:9–20, the woman taken in adultery (John 8:1–11), the replacement of "tree" with "book" (Rev. 22:19), and—by far the most debated biblical verse in Smith's day—1 John 5:7, the so-called *comma Johanneum*. All of these were known to Smith's contemporaries.

Ronald V. Huggins, "Joseph Smith's 'Inspired Translation' of Romans 7," *Dialogue: A Journal of Mormon Thought* 26, no. 4 (1993): 169–70.

42. Clarke, *Clarke's Commentary: Matthew–Revelation*, 529.

43. The manuscripts E, G, and H date to the eighth and ninth centuries, and scholars generally consider them as weak witnesses to the early text of the New Testament. See Kurt Aland and Barbara Aland, *The Text of the New Testament*, trans. Erroll F. Rhodes, 2nd ed. (Grand Rapids: Eerdmans, 1987), 110.

44. The marked-up Bible used by Smith includes a notation at the end of Malachi: "Finished on the 2d day of July 1833." Smith, *Joseph Smith's New Translation of the Bible*, 851.

resulted in a much clearer picture of how Smith and his associates carried out the translation. In broad strokes, the translation process began when Smith and his associates used an 1828 edition of the King James Bible, which they copied out entirely on paper while also deleting KJV punctuation, versification, and modern textual divisions apart from some commas, periods, and apostrophes.[45] This process of copying the Bible lasted through Genesis 1:1–24:41, at which point Smith and his associates turned their attention to the New Testament, where they again copied out the text of the Bible up through John 5:47. Beginning at John 6:1, a new system was employed whereby one of Smith's scribes would write only the text that was to be changed, and then make an accompanying mark in the Bible to indicate where the insertion or deletion would take place.[46] After completing the New Testament, Smith and his scribes returned to Genesis 24:42, where they used the new system employed at John 6:1 and completed the translation through the end of the Old Testament.[47] As a result of these two processes, there are manuscript pages for Genesis 1:1–24:41 and Matthew 1:1–John 5:47 that function as a complete text and do not require comparison with the marked-up Bible. For the remaining portions of the new translation, the marked Bible is necessary to understand the location and wording of the revisions.

Smith's exact method of revising is less clear, but the surviving documents provide some clues. The manuscript pages contain numerous strikethroughs of words and phrases, interlinear insertions, and omissions—some of which were certainly scribal errors. At the same time, there are many instances in which significantly revised passages were not inserted above the line or by means of crossing out words after one of Smith's scribes had copied out the KJV text. Instead, the changed text was written out as though it were dictated to a scribe in complete sentences. It seems therefore that when Smith dictated some of the new translation text, he was reading out of the KJV Bible and occasionally making significant changes to the text. What is not certain is whether Smith dictated an already revised text, or whether he read the Bible and extemporaneously revised the text while having his scribes wait until he had articulated a revision

45. The presence of punctuation in the translation manuscripts is rather haphazard, suggesting that Smith and his associates did not attempt to copy the KJV's punctuation with any precision.

46. The relationship of the various manuscripts is discussed in Smith, *Joseph Smith's New Translation of the Bible*, 60–81; Richard P. Howard, *Restoration Scriptures: A Study of Their Textual Development*, rev. (Independence, MO: Herald House, 1995), 63; and the introduction by Faulring, Jackson, and Matthews in Smith, *Joseph Smith's New Translation of the Bible*, 3–7.

47. Smith did not provide a new translation for the Apocrypha, though it was included in the Bible he was using. See Gerrit Dirkmaat, "Lost Scripture and 'the Interpolations of Men': Joseph Smith's Revelation on the Apocrypha," Chapter 12 herein.

of the passage under consideration. By the time Smith started revising the New Testament, the revisions were quite short and tended to focus on textual issues. Smith's shift in focus to textual issues, about the time he began translating the New Testament, may reflect the influence of Clarke's commentary. The shift to shorter revisions in the New Testament has important consequences when placed alongside a radically revised Old Testament. The Old Testament and New Testament revisions may demonstrate prophetic and textual interests being joined side-by-side in the production of the Bible revision.[48]

One of the discernable features of the marked Bible is that Smith, or one of his associates, struck through many of the italicized words. In some sections of the Bible there are a few italicized words that have been stricken, whereas other sections have a considerable number of such deletions. Smith offered no explanation for striking italicized words, or even whether he was interested in those italicized words because they potentially indicated that the KJV Bible translation was inaccurate.

However, there are clues that Smith was operating with the understanding that the italicized words had been added to the text later by translators and could not be trusted. In January 1833, half a year before Smith completed the Bible revision, the church newspaper printed an editorial that may have reflected his thinking: "The book of Mormon, as a revelation from God, possesses some advantage over the old scripture: it has not been tinctured by the wisdom of man, with here and there an Italic word to supply deficiencies."[49] About seven months later, the church newspaper again impugned the italicized words in the Bible: "The old and new testaments are filled with errors, obscurities, italics and contradictions, which must be the work of men."[50] Approximately one decade after that, the church newspaper sarcastically condemned the italicized words in language that implied it was common knowledge that they were of dubious origins:

> Much has been said about the bad translations of the Bible.... Every school boy seems to know that when either of the sectarian translators

48. Seth Perry has addressed the question of intent in the Bible translation. See Perry, "The Many Bibles of Joseph Smith," 16–18.

49. [No author], "The Book of Mormon," *Evening and the Morning Star*, January 1833, 2. The *Evening and the Morning Star* was published in Independence, Missouri, by W. W. Phelps & Co. At the time of this editorial Smith was in Kirtland. The statement, probably written by Phelps, appears to reflect a sentiment that was popular among church members in 1833, at a time when Smith and his associates were completing the translation of the Bible.

50. [No author], "Errors of the Bible," *Evening and the Morning Star*, July 1833, 106.

> failed in making the two ends of a sentence meet, he filled up the vacuity with *italic*, by which means God has been greatly helped towards expressing himself so as to be understood by the learned world.... if their thoughts should not happen to be God's thoughts, it is a matter of fact that the mother of harlots holds in her hands *a golden cup full of the filthiness of her abominations.*[51]

This skepticism found expression in Smith's translation through his revision of about half of the italicized words in the Bible.[52]

Aside from mere cancellations, the revisions associated with italicized words were typically shorter additions and rearrangements of words and phrases. Conversely, Smith's substantial expansions of the biblical text seldom begin with italicized words. The mere omissions of italicized words may be classified as modifications of the biblical text based on an underlying suspicion of the quality of the KJV translation. They do not appear to have the same revelatory intent of the longer insertions, like those in Smith's revision of Genesis 1–6.[53]

THE EVOLUTION OF SMITH'S BIBLE REVISION

A careful analysis of the revisions made throughout the Bible confirm a genuine difference between the changes to Genesis 1:1–24:41 and the remainder of the Bible revision. This difference may be explained by a change in the mechanics of the translation process. In short, it may have shifted from a more revelatory mode to a more secular mode.

In a statement recorded decades later, Lorenzo Brown recounted that Smith had related the following to him regarding his Bible translation: "After I got through translating the Book of Mormon, I took up the Bible to read with the Urim and Thummim, I read the first chapter of Genesis, and I saw the things

51. "Not the Prophet, S. T. P.," to the Editor of the Times and Seasons [John Taylor], *Times and Seasons*, 1 September 1843, 318.

52. Thomas A. Wayment and Tyson Yost, "The Joseph Smith Translation and Italicized Words in the King James Version," *Religious Educator* 6, no. 1 (2005): 51–64.

53. Smith's translation of Genesis 1:1–6:13 was so substantial that it was eventually canonized as a new book of scripture, the Book of Moses, consisting of eight distinct chapters. See Jackson, *The Book of Moses and the Joseph Smith Translation Manuscripts* (Moses). The majority of the other changes to the Bible are much shorter additions, deletions, and alterations. Only Matthew 24 in the New Testament was changed as substantially as the early chapters of Genesis. Other major additions to the biblical text occur at Genesis 14:25–40, 48:5–11, and 50:24–38. Old Testament Manuscript 2, 39, 63, 64–65, in Smith, *Joseph Smith's New Translation of the Bible*, 641–42, 676–79, 680–85.

as they were done. I turned over the next and the next, and the whole passed before me like a grand panorama; and so on chapter after chapter until I read the whole of it. I saw it all!"[54] Brown's recollection is remarkable because it contradicts the long-standing opinion among scholars that Smith used neither the Urim and Thummim spectacles nor his seer stones for the new translation. Indeed, this is the only known source suggesting he used either device in the Bible revision. More important, however, is the fact that Smith reportedly claimed that while revising Genesis he experienced a vision or at least some form of revelation.

Earlier commentators who have looked at this question have tended to favor apostle Orson Pratt's statement that Smith did not use the Urim and Thummim or the seer stones. Pratt explained, "the translation of the book of Mormon by the use of the Urim and Thummim had rendered him so well acquainted with the Spirit of Revelation and Prophecy, that in the translating of the New Testament he did not need the aid that was necessary in the 1st instance."[55] It may be that both Pratt and Brown were correct, with Brown accurately describing the stronger prophetic interest during the revision of Genesis and Pratt accurately describing the remainder of the Bible revision.

"TRANSLATION" IN SMITH'S VOCABULARY AND EXPERIENCE

Smith employed the terminology of translation to various efforts during his lifetime—especially to the production of the Book of Mormon between 1827 and 1829, his work on the Bible between 1830 and 1833, and his efforts in 1835 and 1842 concerning some Egyptian papyri that resulted in the Book of Abraham. The evidence presented in this chapter suggests that a major reconsideration of Smith's understanding of *translation* is in order. Because questions regarding the intent and impact of Smith's translation projects have tended to focus on the meaning of the word *translation* as Smith and his associates understood it, it is necessary to briefly review some of the historiographical positions.[56]

Richard P. Howard has observed that for the budding prophet "'translation' did not involve fluency in language other than Smith's own tongue."[57] However,

54. Quoted in Matthews, *Joseph Smith's Translation of the Bible*, 25.

55. Ibid., 40.

56. See *JSP*-J3:xvii–xxviii.

57. Richard P. Howard, "Latter Day Saint Scriptures and the Doctrine of Propositional Revelation," in *The Word of God: Essays on Mormon Scripture*, ed. Dan Vogel (Salt Lake City: Signature Books, 1990), 12–13.

with respect to the production of the Bible revision and the Book of Abraham, Smith's translation efforts involved not only the experience of a supernatural gift, but a natural engagement with ancient languages, including the realization that he was augmenting his own meager language skills by probing the work of established scholars.[58] All of Smith's translation efforts included some aspect of naturalistic interest in ancient language—specifically in identifying a scholar or academic resource that could facilitate ordinary translation efforts.[59] For the Book of Mormon, Smith sent Martin Harris, his benefactor and scribe, to consult with the likes of Luther Bradish (an amateur archaeologist), Samuel Mitchill (a polymath and renowned educator at Rutgers Medical College), and Charles Anthon (a classicist at Columbia).[60] For the Bible, Smith and Rigdon studied Adam Clarke's commentary. For the Egyptian papyri, Smith and some associates consulted Joshua Seixas (a Hebraist at Oberlin) and his manuals, and perhaps other Hebrew reference works.[61] For the Kinderhook plates, they examined the "Grammar and Alphabet of the Egyptian Language" produced in connection with the Book of Abraham, a Hebrew lexicon, and perhaps other sources.[62] In some sense, then, Smith's translations involved scholarly inquiry, with a recognition that traditional translation skills were part of, or at least related to, the process.

It also seems that Smith viewed these efforts as a facet of his calling as a prophet, perhaps suggesting that he felt compelled to translate despite his academic limitations. His history recounts, "After Oliver Cowdery and John Whitmer had departed for Jackson county, Missouri, I resumed the translation

58. Joseph Smith studied Hebrew under Joshua Seixas while in Kirtland, Ohio. Seixas arrived in Kirtland to teach Hebrew to the Latter-day Saints in late January 1836. He then stayed through that summer, but no exact date for his departure from Kirtland is known. See Matthew J. Grey, "'The Word of the Lord in the Original': Joseph Smith's Study of Hebrew in Kirtland," in *Approaching Antiquity: Joseph Smith and the Ancient World*, ed. Lincoln H. Blumell, Matthew J. Grey, and Andrew H. Hedges (Provo, UT: Religious Studies Center, Brigham Young University; Salt Lake City: Deseret Book, 2015), 262–72.

59. For a discussion of Smith's quest to have American academics identify the language of the Book of Mormon and perhaps assist in the translation, see Michael H. MacKay and Gerrit J. Dirkmaat, *From Darkness unto Light: Joseph Smith's Translation and Publication of the Book of Mormon* (Provo, UT: Religious Studies Center, 2015), 37–53. Compare the statement attributed to Joseph Smith's younger brother William Smith that Joseph "brought them [the golden plates of the Book of Mormon] home, but was unable to read them" and "afterwards made a facsimile of some parts of the inscription, and sent it to professor Anthon of New York City." See James Murdock, "The Mormons and Their Prophet," *Congregational Observer* (Hartford, CT), 3 July 1841, 1.

60. See Michael Hubbard MacKay, "'Git Them Translated': Translating the Characters on the Gold Plates," chap. 4 in *Approaching Antiquity*.

61. See Matthew J. Grey, "Approaching Egyptian Papyri through Biblical Language: Joseph Smith's Use of Hebrew in His Translation of the Book of Abraham," Chapter 16 herein.

62. See Don Bradley and Mark Ashurst-McGee, "'President Joseph Has Translated a Portion': Joseph Smith and the Mistranslation of the Kinderhook Plates," Chapter 17 herein.

of the Scriptures and continued to labor in this branch of my calling with elder Sidney Rigdon as my scribe."[63] Similarly, Smith dictated a revelation in early 1831 including a commandment that he was to continue translating as part of his calling: "& now behold I say unto you it shall not be given unto you to know any farther then this until the New Testament be translated & ~~it~~ in it all things shall be made known."[64]

Kathleen Flake has characterized Smith's unique translation process emphasizing the prophetic activity rather than the academic interests emphasized in this chapter. According to Flake, the word *translate* "expressed Smith's experience of 'study[ing] it out in [his] mind' or his sense of agency in front of the text. Smith did not think of himself as God's stenographer. Rather, he was an interpreting reader, and God the confirming authority. He did not experience revelation 'as dictated, as something whispered in someone's ear.'"[65] Drawing on the Oxford English Dictionary, she offers another meaning for *translation* that was circulating in Smith's time. In 1815, there was a published reference to a cobbler's shop that would "translate old shoes into new ones." Flake remarked: "It is doubtful that one could properly 'renovate, turn, or cut down . . . or make new [Bibles] from the remains of (old ones).' This was unthinkable at best, heresy at worst, and certainly not 'translation.'"[66] For some nineteenth-century Americans, the concept of translation also entailed a fundamental reworking, a renovation, where the old was redeveloped.

Philip L. Barlow is more critical of Smith's new translation of the Bible, in many instances referring to it as "no more than a 'common sense' commentary on the Authorized Version and a reconciliation of apparent internal

63. Smith, History, 1838–1856, volume A-1, 175 (punctuation standardized). Richard Bushman writes: "Joseph's prophethood was based on a gift peculiarly his own. In an 1830 revelation, Joseph was called 'a seer, a translator, a prophet, an apostle of Jesus Christ, an elder of the church.' The series of titles implied that prophethood was connected to translation. Though unusual for one of his education and social status, 'translator' became his permanent role." Richard Lyman Bushman, *Joseph Smith: Rough Stone Rolling* (New York: Alfred A. Knopf, 2005), 130.

64. Revelation, circa 7 March 1831, in *JSP*-D1:274–80 [D&C 45:60]. For other revelations relating directly or indirectly to Smith's translation of the Bible, see Revelation, 30 December 1830, in *JSP*-D1:226–27 [D&C 37]; Revelation, 10 January 1832, in *JSP*-D2:154–57 [D&C 73]; Vision, 16 February 1832, in *JSP*-D2:179–92 [D&C 76]; Answers to Questions, between circa 4 and circa 20 March 1832, in *JSP*-D2:208–13 [D&C 77]; Revelation, 6 December 1832, in *JSP*-D2:324–27 [D&C 86]; Revelation, 9 March 1833, in *JSP*-D3:32–35 [D&C 91]; and possibly Revelation, 12 July 1843 [D&C 132] (accessible in the Documents series of the online edition of *The Joseph Smith Papers*).

65. Kathleen Flake, "Translating Time: The Nature and Function of Joseph Smith's Narrative Canon," *The Journal of Religion* 87, no. 4 (October 2007): 507.

66. Ibid., 505. Flake continues: "Because religious diversity made heresy an elusive concept in early nineteenth-century America, most of his contemporaries had to settle for labeling Smith a fraud. Sensitive as he was to these charges and no doubt knowing the difference between shoes and Bibles, Smith's stubbornly persistent use of 'translation' to describe the process by which he created his texts invites analysis."

conflicts."[67] Barlow's work also views the Bible revision as exploratory, willing to creatively delve into the meaning of the text through a process described as translation.[68] These trends in Smith's translation are discernable, and should now be broadened to include Smith's academic interest and reliance upon contemporaneous scholarly sources that were sensitive to traditional faith as was Clarke's commentary.

The echoes of one of Smith's earliest revelations—in which the voice of Lord admonished Oliver Cowdery to "study it out" as part of the translation process—are now much more obvious in Smith's Bible translation process.[69] This encouragement to "study it out" could mean more than simple mental exertion, it was an informed mental engagement with all available resources within and without the mind, and one that eventually relied upon actual "study" in available published resources. He leaned into the logic of the revelation, and carried it out to its logical consequence: the informed intellect was a productive seed bed for inspiration.

SMITH'S SELECTIVE USE OF CLARKE'S COMMENTARY

In assessing the viability of the theory presented here, one might wonder why some of the major textual issues of the Bible were not addressed or noted by Smith. It is strange that clearly redacted verses were not removed from Smith's translation, with the most egregious example being 1 John 5:7—"For there are three that bear record in heaven, the Father, the Word, and the Holy Ghost: and these three are one." Of this verse, Clarke's commentary solemnly declared, "In short, it stands on no authority sufficient to authenticate any part of a revelation professing to have come from God."[70] At other times, Smith was quite

67. Barlow has contended that Smith believed "common sense" was made uncommon by inspiration. Barlow, "Joseph Smith's Revision of the Bible," 48. Barlow has also noted that whereas "Smith offered interpretive expansions," the difference was that "Smith claimed to do his work by inspiration and common-sense logic, not by scholarship, and he actually interpolated the text rather than placing his additions in marginal notes" (57). H. Michael Marquardt has similarly noted that "Joseph Smith's work is a revision rather than a translation, since church members knew that Joseph Smith had not studied Hebrew or Greek to produce his manuscript." H. Michael Marquardt, *The Rise of Mormonism, 1816–1844* (Maitland, FL: Xulon Press, 2005), 326. Mark Lyman Staker has similarly characterized Smith's "new translation" of the Bible as one of "ideas rather than language." Mark Lyman Staker, *Hearken, O Ye People: The Historical Setting of Joseph Smith's Ohio Revelations* (Salt Lake City: Greg Kofford Books, 2009), 313.

68. Philip Barlow, "Why the King James Version? From the Common to the Official Bible of Mormonism," *Dialogue: A Journal of Mormon Thought* 22, no. 2 (Summer 1989): 19.

69. Revelation, April 1829-D, in *JSP*-D1:50 [D&C 9:8].

70. This verse was the subject of intense scholarly debate in the early nineteenth century, and Clarke's commentary engaged the academics of his day. See Clarke, *Clarke's Commentary: Matthew–Revelation*, 923–33.

willing to change the text in rather nuanced and subtle ways that did little to alter the meaning of the KJV text. While the data presented herein accounts for a significant advance in understanding the origins of Smith's Bible translation, it is still unclear how he determined which verses were to be revised and which were to be left unaltered. Moving forward, we encourage scholars to examine whether there is a unified purpose in the choice of verses that were changed. Our preliminary impression is that Smith was especially inclined to follow Clarke's commentary in instances where Clarke drew upon manuscript evidence or language expertise.

CONCLUSIONS

In analyzing Smith's larger project of revising the Bible, Philip L. Barlow has argued that Smith's revisions can be sorted into five different categories.[71] While this chapter has only dealt with some of Barlow's proposed categories, it is helpful in conclusion to see the larger constellation of changes made to the Bible:

1. Long insertions that interrupt the biblical narrative and have no obvious textual source;
2. Theological corrections;
3. Interpretive additions that seek to clarify the text;
4. Harmonizations, particularly among the Synoptic gospels;[72] and
5. Grammatical changes, including technical clarifications and the modernization of terms.

Given the evidence presented in this chapter, it would seem prudent to recognize that Barlow's first category belongs overwhelmingly to Smith's early prophetic expansions of Genesis and that his third, fourth, and fifth categories appear to be frequently influenced by Clarke's commentary. In fact, it is arguable that Clarke is the primary source Smith drew upon in making these types of revisions. However, while Smith apparently turned to Clarke's commentary to provide grammatical, linguistic, and historical assistance as he carried out his work, the commentary was not a source for the content in Smith's significant expansions. Therefore, it can be argued that it was less a

71. Barlow, "Joseph Smith's Revision of the Bible," 55–57.

72. Barlow utilizes the example of the revision of Matthew 27:3–8, which narrates the death of Judas Iscariot and seems at variance with the rendition of Judas's death in Acts 1:18–19. Smith combined the two accounts and eliminated the discrepancy. See Barlow, "Joseph Smith's Revision of the Bible," 56.

theological source than a practical resource. Smith somehow became familiar with the commentary—perhaps at the urging of Sidney Rigdon—and utilized it at varying levels of engagement throughout the remainder of the translation process.[73]

73. The suggestion that Rigdon influenced Smith's thought has been made by others. David Whitmer would eventually accuse Rigdon of introducing errors into church doctrine and ecclesiology. See David Whitmer, *An Address to All Believers in Christ: By a Witness to the Divine Authenticity of The Book of Mormon* (Richmond, MO: David Whitmer, 1887), 35. Compare John Wickcliffe Rigdon, "I Never Knew a Time When I Did Not Know Joseph Smith: A Son's Record of the Life and Testimony of Sidney Rigdon," ed. Karl Keller, *Dialogue: A Journal of Mormon Thought* 1, no. 4 (Winter 1966): 19–20.

12

Lost Scripture and "the Interpolations of Men"

Joseph Smith's Revelation on the Apocrypha

GERRIT DIRKMAAT

On 25 June 1833, Joseph Smith wrote from Ohio to the members of the Church of Christ, often referred to as Mormons, living at the church's far-flung outpost nearly a thousand miles away at Independence, Missouri. Since his dictation of a revelation declaring that this was indeed the place where the long-prophesied City of Zion and its accompanying temple(s) were to be built, a steady stream of letters between Ohio and Missouri made the arduous, weeks-long transit between the two locales, bringing vital, though painfully delayed, communications. In this particular missive, he responded to the church members in Missouri who had inquired about various topics and attempted to address their concerns.

"Brethren," Smith wrote, "we have received your last containing a number of questions which you desire us to answer, this we do the more readily as we desire with all our hearts the prosperity of Zion and the peace of her inhabitents."[1] He first responded to practical questions about the ongoing effort to print the Book of Commandments in Missouri, then answered a technical inquiry about the allocation of some copies of the Book of Mormon. What followed, however, responded to a specific question about the possible recovery of new scripture. Smith wrote, "We have not found the book of Jasher nor any of the other lost books mentioned in the bible as yet nor will we obtain them at present[2]—respecting the Apochraphy the Lord said to us that there

1. Joseph Smith, Sidney Rigdon, Frederick G. Williams, and Martin Harris, Kirtland, OH, to "Brethren," Independence, MO, 25 June 1833, Joseph Smith Collection, Church History Library, The Church of Jesus Christ of Latter-day Saints, Salt Lake City, Utah (hereafter Church History Library).

2. It is not clear to what extent early church members were interested in the book of Jasher, beyond what is offered in this letter. Two passages in the Old Testament refer to "the book of Jasher" (Joshua 10:13;

were many things in it which were true and there were many things in it which were not true and to those who desired, it should be given by the spirit to know true from the false." For all of the practical difficulties encountered by church members living in Missouri—which would become manifest in the form of organized mob violence only days after this letter was sent—they were keenly interested in the possibility of new scripture being discovered or revealed, in particular the book of Jasher mentioned in the Old Testament and the Apocrypha.[3]

Smith's declaration that he would not attempt a "translation" of the Apocrypha like he had with the Bible remains inscrutable to historians. Given the affinity and interest of newly believing followers of his nascent church in lost doctrines, teachings, and scriptures—and their willingness to accept as authoritative any translation Joseph Smith produced involving actual or alleged ancient texts—Smith might have readily supplied exactly what his parishioners were searching for by translating the Apocrypha anew: newly recovered teachings of scripture that had the authority of ancient origin but specifically responded to the theological concerns of his early nineteenth-century followers. This chapter examines the context of Smith's decision to set the Apocrypha aside as a translation project and explores questions about the consistency with which Smith approached his various translation projects.[4]

PASSING OVER THE APOCRYPHA

The interest of the Missouri Mormons in the discovery of new "lost" books of scripture was not unique to those living on the American frontier, but was the result of their abandonment of the almost universally accepted Christian

2 Samuel 1:18). The book was first translated into English by Moses Samuel, a Jewish scholar residing in Liverpool, England. Samuel's translation was published in New York in 1840. See Moses Samuel, *Sefer ha-yashar, or, the Book of Jasher: Referred to in Joshua and Second Samuel* (New York: Mordecai M. Noah & A. S. Gould, 1840). Church members, however, first showed interest in the lost books of the Bible from very early in the church's history. See Joseph Smith, History, 1838–1856, vol. A-1, 80, Church History Library (accessible in the Histories series of the online edition of *The Joseph Smith Papers*). The personal copy of the Book of Mormon owned by Frederick G. Williams provides another example of early Mormon interest in lost books. On the inside of the back cover, Williams inscribed the names of several nonbiblical books mentioned in the Bible—including the "Book of Jasher" and "Enoch's Prophecy." Frederick G. Williams copy of Book of Mormon, David O. McKay Library, Brigham Young University—Idaho, Rexburg, Idaho. For more on early Mormon views of lost and apocryphal books of the Bible, see Edward J. Brandt, "The Book of Jasher and the Latter-day Saints," in *Apocryphal Writings and the Latter-day Saints*, ed. C. Wilfred Griggs (Provo, UT: Religious Studies Center, Brigham Young University, 1986), 297–318.

3. See Revelation, 9 March 1833, in *JSP*-D3:32–35 [D&C 91].

4. The author would like to thank Mark Ashurst-McGee and Jana Riess, who provided not only insightful and helpful edits but substantive ideas and direction to some of the research presented here.

belief that the scriptural canon was forever closed and had been for nearly two millennia. Indeed, their very acceptance of the radical faith required Mormon devotees to embrace the Book of Mormon as an entirely new book of scripture. Early Mormons accepted the book's claims that it had been written by several generations of prophets among a colony of ancient Israelites living in the Americas; and that this prophetic record, written in an unknown language, was then miraculously translated by Joseph Smith. In addition to accepting an expansion of the traditional canon by thousands of words and hundreds of pages, early church members also looked to Joseph Smith to receive revelations from God that were to be regarded with the same reverence as scripture. This early reliance on new revelation—comingled as it was with an attempt to recreate the primitive Christian church—naturally led followers of Smith to look to him to bring forth more "new" ancient scripture.[5]

The Book of Mormon itself made reference to several ancient American records that were not included among the gold plates that Smith had recovered, but that were deemed scripture by the prophets who wrote about them on the plates in his possession. The twenty-four gold plates of the Jaredites, the plates of brass, and the large plates of Nephi were all cited by the Book of Mormon text but not fully transcribed within its pages.[6] Book of Mormon prophets referenced the teachings of predecessor prophets named Zenock, Neum, and Zenos, whose writings were apparently part of the plates of brass brought to the new world, though unattested in the Bible.[7] Further, the first book of Nephi, which opened the Book of Mormon, declared on nearly a dozen occasions that many "plain and precious" parts of the Bible had been lost due to deliberate excisions from the text by the "great and abominable church."[8]

But even while translating the Book of Mormon, Smith claimed a revelatory experience that produced a lost manuscript of the ancient apostle John. Smith and his principal scribe, Oliver Cowdery, had apparently been discussing John 21:22–23:

5. Levi Hancock reported that in 1831 this impulse to recover more primitive religion had led to "preaching in Kirtland . . . against the use of Pork." Hancock even confronted Joseph Smith about his raising of pigs, only to have Smith disabuse him of the idea that it was sinful to eat pork. Hancock recorded that after this conversation he was "left to this conclusion there are sometimes extremes in Preaching." Levi Hancock, Autobiography, Church History Library, 22.

6. On the twenty-four gold plates of the Jaredites, see Mosiah 8:9 and Alma 37:21. On the plates of brass, see 1 Nephi 3–5. On the large plates of Nephi, see 1 Nephi 9:2–4 and Words of Mormon 1:3. See also Omni 1:20–22 regarding the discovery of an engraved Jaredite stone.

7. 1 Nephi 19:10.

8. See 1 Nephi 13:26–40; 1 Nephi 14:23.

> Jesus saith unto him [Peter], "If I will that he [John] tarry till I come, what is that to thee? follow thou me." Then went this saying abroad among the brethren, that that disciple should not die: yet Jesus said not unto him, "He shall not die; but, If I will that he tarry till I come, what is that to thee?"[9]

Following a disagreement over whether John had died or was yet living, Smith dictated a revelation—rendered in first-person narrative in the voice of John—which answered affirmatively that Jesus had granted a request made by John for "power over death."[10] Unlike Smith's other revelations up to this date, which were spoken in the first-person voice of God, the words of this revelation were presented as a text that had been "translated from parchment, written and hid up" by John himself.[11] While the Book of Mormon text purportedly came as a translation of gold plates that Smith had in his possession, this revelation regarding John claimed to be a translation of a parchment document that remained undiscovered and far removed from Smith's ownership.[12]

Following these initial efforts to recover lost prophetic writings, Smith undertook his most substantive translation effort beyond the Book of Mormon: his "new translation" of the Old and New Testaments. Initiated following a revelation that expanded greatly the creation account in Genesis, Smith, for whatever reason, did not attempt to translate the Bible in the same manner as he had the Book of Mormon. While nearly all eyewitness accounts of the production of the Book of Mormon describe Smith's use of a seer stone to dictate the English text that was translated from the engravings on the gold plates, Smith apparently did not employ a similar method of textual creation when retranslating the Bible. Neither did he revisit the original Hebrew or Greek texts in order to perform a scholarly translation. Instead, he began going through the King James Version of the Bible and dictated changes to various verses as he felt so inspired.

It remains an open question why Smith employed this new method of translation to recover lost ancient text. With the gold plates of Mormon and the parchment of John, Smith had relied upon seer stones for the translation or re-creation of the lost writings. This is especially curious given the fact that while Smith was apparently using the seer stones less and less in his revelations

9. Punctuation modernized.

10. Account of John, April 1829, in *JSP*-D1:47–48 [D&C 7:3].

11. *A Book of Commandments, for the Government of the Church of Christ, Organized according to Law, on the 6th of April, 1830* (Zion [Independence, MO]: W. W. Phelps, 1833), VI:1 (18).

12. See David W. Grua and William V. Smith, "The Tarrying of the Beloved Disciple: The Textual Formation of the Account of John," Chapter 10 herein.

by mid to late 1830 he was still using a seer stone to receive at least some revelations as late as September of that year.[13] Additionally, Smith's revision of the Bible seemed to follow very little discernable pattern. He expanded the accounts of Genesis by thousands of words, changed phrases, included new stories, and more. Yet he passed over entire books in the Old Testament without making any changes to them at all.

Whatever his method, this revision of the Bible occupied much of Smith's time for three years—between mid-1830 and mid-1833. Mormonism had already challenged the suzerainty of the Bible as *sola scriptura* by asserting the Book of Mormon to be an equal, if not superior, scripture. Now Joseph Smith began making insertions, deletions, and other revisions to the long-accepted and sacrosanct text of the Holy Bible itself.[14] Plans to publish the new edition of the Bible were well-known and highly anticipated by Missouri members. A small excerpt from the Bible revision had already been published in August 1832 in the *Evening and the Morning Star* (the church newspaper published in Missouri).[15] However, by early April 1833, Smith wrote Missouri leaders that "it is not the will of the Lord to print any of the new translation in the Star but when it is published it will all go to the world together in a volume by itself, and the new Testament and the book of Mormon will be printed together."[16]

By February 1833 Joseph Smith and Frederick G. Williams had completed the revisions to the New Testament. As Williams noted, they had "completed the translation and the reviewing of the New testament and sealed [it] up no more to be broken till it goes to Zion."[17] Yet much of the latter half of the Old Testament still remained for Smith to revise. Already compelled to complete the years-long project so it could be printed along with a proposed new edition of the Book of Mormon and the forthcoming Book of Commandments, Smith received further motivation to quicken his pace in a revelation he dictated on 8 March 1833. This revelation informed Smith that some of his duties in the church were contingent upon his completion of the Bible revision: "Now verely I say unto you I give unto you a commandment that you continue in this ministry and presedency and when you have finished the translation of

13. See Revelation, 4 November 1830, in *JSP*-D1:208–11 [D&C 34], see esp. 208.

14. The earliest published account of Joseph Smith finding the gold plates and translating the Book of Mormon was quick to attack his followers for pronouncing the Book of Mormon "superior in style, and more advantageous to mankind, than the Holy Bible!" "Golden Bible," *Palmyra Freeman* (Palmyra, NY), 11 August 1829, 2.

15. "Extract from the Prophecy of Enoch," *Evening and the Morning Star,* August 1832, 2–3.

16. Letter to Church Leaders in Jackson County, Missouri, 21 April 1833, in *JSP*-D3:68.

17. Minute Book 1, 2 February 1833, Church History Library (accessible under Minute Books in the Administrative Records series of the online edition of *The Joseph Smith Papers*).

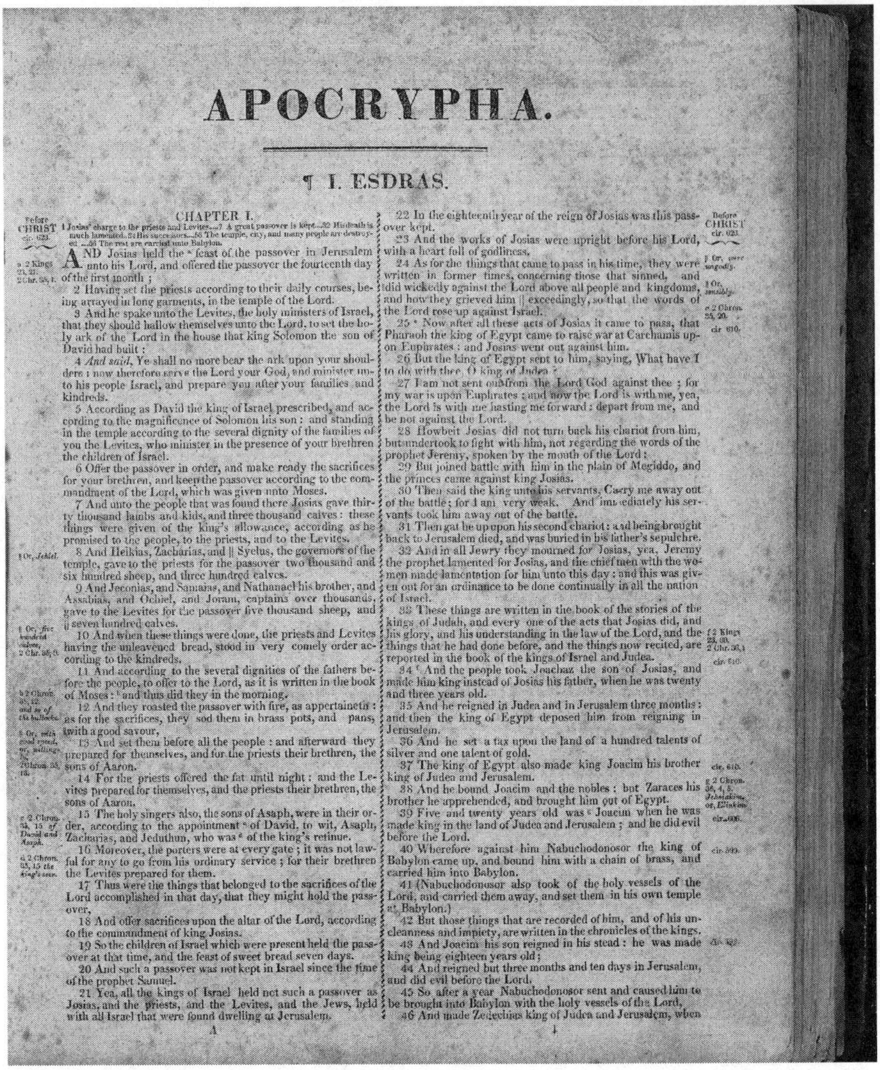
APOCRYPHA.

¶ I. ESDRAS.

CHAPTER I.

FIGURE 12.1. The Apocrypha in Joseph Smith's Bible. The Bible that Joseph Smith worked from while engaged in his "new translation" of the Bible included the Apocrypha. Personal copy of Joseph Smith. Courtesy Community of Christ Archives, Independence, MO.

the prophets you shall from thence forth preside over the affairs of the Church and the School."[18] He was further promised that after the completion of his translation of the Bible he would "receive revelations to unfold the mysteries of the kingdom."[19] Emphasizing the importance of completing his scriptural revisions, this declaration may have led Smith to wonder whether the "translation

18. Revelation, 8 March 1833, in *JSP*-D3:24–32 [D&C 90:12–13].
19. Revelation, 8 March 1833, in *JSP*-D3:24–32 [D&C 90:14].

of the prophets" he was commanded to complete also included the books of the Apocrypha that had been combined together at the end of the Old Testament in the Bible he was using for his translation (see Figure 12.1). The revelation he dictated the next day, answering his question about whether to translate the Apocrypha, apparently reflected a question in Smith's own mind that arose from the Protestant world he lived in.

THE APOCRYPHA IN PROTESTANT AMERICA

The word *Apocrypha* transliterates a Greek term meaning "hidden" or "concealed."[20] Protestants used the term to denote the dozen or so books not found in the Hebrew canon but that were included in the Greek version of the Old Testament known as the Septuagint. Because the Septuagint was the basis for early Latin translations of the Old Testament, the Apocrypha was integrated into early Christian Bibles. The Catholic scholar Jerome hesitated to include the books along with his translation of the Hebrew canon in the fourth century, but they eventually came to be widely regarded as scriptural in medieval Christianity. Martin Luther, in his 1534 translation of the Bible, included most of the books of the Apocrypha from the western tradition of Christianity. He placed them at the end of the Old Testament and explained that they were "not held equal to the Holy Scriptures, and yet are profitable and good to read."[21] Throughout the Reformation, subsequent editions of the Bible also placed these books in a separate section labeled Apocrypha. The Catholic Church responded in 1546, at the Council of Trent, by affirming the canonical status of all but three of the books; thus, acceptance or rejection of the authority of the Apocrypha was at times related to larger Reformation era disputes in both Europe and America.[22]

Shortly before Smith began his translation of the Book of Mormon, a widely publicized and acrimonious debate took place within the British and Foreign Bible Society over the inclusion of the apocryphal books within the Bibles it distributed. Some members of the society accused their leaders of "adulterating

20. According to the late biblical scholar Bruce M. Metzger: "From the point of view of those who approved of these books, they were 'hidden' or withdrawn from common use because they were regarded as containing mysterious or esoteric lore, too profound to be communicated to any except the initiated. From another point of view, however, it was held that such books deserved to be 'hidden' because they were spurious or heretical." Bruce M. Metzger, *An Introduction to the Apocrypha* (New York and Oxford: Oxford University Press, 1957), 5.

21. Metzger, *An Introduction to the Apocrypha*, 183.

22. "Introduction to the Apocryphal/Deuterocanonical Books," in *New Oxford Annotated Bible* (New York and Oxford: Oxford University Press, 1962), 3–6.

the Scriptures, by circulating the lies and fables of the *Apocrypha* along with the words of eternal life."[23] After multiple schisms, the Society finally relented and in 1827 adopted a resolution banning the distribution of Bibles that included the Apocrypha.[24] The American Bible Society, witnessing the fallout caused by arguments within its British counterpart, made the same decision in 1828.[25] In the United States an insurgent animosity toward the Apocrypha was manifested by an 1826 publication on the biblical canon by Archibald Alexander, a professor at Princeton Theological Seminary. Alexander railed against the idea that there were any lost books of scripture, including even books mentioned in the Bible, such as Jasher. He categorically dismissed the books of the Apocrypha as illegitimate and noncanonical, arguing that "the Bible is complete, containing all things necessary to guide the faith and practice of every sincere Christian." He added that there was "no other revelation, but what is recorded in these sacred books." For Alexander, the Apocrypha represented the way in which Catholics had corrupted the true canon.[26]

Public disputes about the Apocrypha continued in the United States. In 1832, an Ohio newspaper denounced the Apocrypha in an article designed to prove the veracity of the accepted canonical books of the Old and New Testaments, writing that "the claims of the Apocrypha must be despatched in few words" and that the authors of it could not "comport with a claim to a divine origin."[27] In his widely published 1833 letters against Catholicism, Calvinist theologian William Craig Brownlee specifically denounced those who would "decorate the apocrypha with the honors of inspiration."[28]

EARLY MORMONS AND THE APOCRYPHA BEFORE THE REVELATION

Despite this general movement of American Protestants away from the Apocrypha in the early nineteenth century, Mormons did not seem to view the

23. "News Item," *Kent and Essex Mercury,* 19 September 1826, 4.

24. Reverend George Browne, *History of the British and Foreign Bible Society, from Its Institution in 1804, to the Close of Its Jubilee in 1854* (London: British and Foreign Bible Society, 1859), 2:360–65.

25. "American Bible Society," *Vermont Chronicle*, 23 May 1828, 81.

26. Archibald Alexander, *The Canon of the Old and New Testaments Ascertained, or the Bible Complete without the Apocrypha and Unwritten Traditions* (New York: Princeton Press, 1826), v–vi. For more on Alexander's quest to defend and define the biblical canon, see David Holland, *Sacred Borders: Continuing Revelation and Canonical Restraint in Early America* (Oxford and New York: Oxford University Press, 2011), 114–22.

27. "Evidences of Divine Revelation," *Observer and Telegraph* (Hudson, OH), 26 April 1832, 3.

28. William Craig Brownlee, New York City, NY, to "Doctors Power, Varela, and Levins," 18 February 1833, in William Craig Brownlee, *Letters in the Roman Catholic Controversy* (New York: Published for the Author, 1834), 11.

Apocrypha with the same disdain. Perhaps this was due to the foundational belief of church members in the existence of scriptural books outside of the Old and New Testaments, such as the Book of Mormon.[29] Joseph Smith dictated a revelation in April 1829 that explained, in the voice of God, that there were "records which contain much of my gospel, which have been kept back because of the wickedness of the people" and that "parts of my scriptures . . . have been hidden because of iniquity."[30] Early members of the church regularly discussed the notion that teachings were missing from the canon. Joseph Smith's history, for instance, related the concern for missing biblical books as the background for his lengthy dictation in December 1830 termed the "Prophecy of Enoch," which provided additional information about Enoch and other figures from early Genesis:

> Much conjecture and conversation frequently occurred among the saints, concerning the books mentioned and referred to, in various places in the old and new testaments, which were now no where to be found. The common remark was, they are "lost books"; but it seems the apostolic churches had some of these writings, as Jude mentions or quotes the prophecy of Enoch the seventh from Adam. To the joy of the little flock, which in all, from Colesville to Canandaigua, numbered about seventy members, did the Lord reveal the following doings of olden time from the prophecy of Enoch.[31]

While Protestants were busy culling noncanonical books from the canon, early Mormons were anxiously anticipating more.

This acceptance of the notion of additional scripture apparently extended to the Apocrypha in the minds of many early church members. In July 1832, the church newspaper quoted from 2 Maccabees and derided the treatment of the Apocrypha as noncanonical, explaining that it was "the wisdom of man" that "has seen fit to call [it] Apocrypha."[32] In January 1833, the same newspaper

29. The Book of Mormon frequently employs language from both the Old and New Testaments, and possibly employs some language from the Apocrypha as well. See Thomas A. Wayment, "Joseph Smith's Developing Relationship with the Apocrypha," in *Approaching Antiquity: Joseph Smith and the Ancient World*, ed. Lincoln H. Blumell, Matthew J. Grey, and Andrew H. Hedges (Provo, UT: Religious Studies Center, Brigham Young University; Salt Lake City: Deseret Book, 2015), 331–36, 337–40, 346–49.

30. Revelation, April 1829-A, in *JSP*-D1:34–37 [D&C 6:26–27].

31. Smith, History, 1838–1856, vol. A-1, 80–81; see also Joseph Smith, Old Testament Revision 1, 13–19 [Moses 7] (accessible in the Revelations and Translations series of the online edition of *The Joseph Smith Papers*).

32. "Hosea Chapter III," *Evening and the Morning Star,* July 1832, 6.

again disparaged negative attitudes toward Apocryphal works when it published an excerpt from the Apocrypha's addition to the book of Esther, "which the ancient men of the world, put down as doubtful."[33]

Perhaps the greatest evidence of the early incorporation of Apocryphal teachings into Mormon theology is the very dedication of the land of Zion itself. In a special conference held there in August 1831, Sidney Rigdon made an "Exhortation to obedience to the requisition of Heaven by delivering a charge in the name of the Lord Christ to the Bishop, Rulers & members of the Church planted in their inheritances in the land of Zion."[34] John Whitmer explained that Rigdon's "exhortation to obedience" took this form:

> Brother Sidney Rigdon stood up and asked saying: Do you receive this land for the land of your inheritanc[e] with thankful hearts from the Lord? answer from all we do, Do you pledge yourselves to keep the laws of God on this land which you have never have kept in your own land? we do. Do you pledge yourselves to see that others of your brethren, who shall come hither do keep the laws of God? We do. After prayer he arose and said, I now pronounce this land consecrated and dedicated to the Lord for a possession and inheritanc[e] for the Saints, (in the name of Jesus Christ having authority from him.) And for all the faithful Servants of the Lord to the remotest ages of time. Aamen.[35]

Rigdon took the text of the pledge he asked of the assembled members of the church directly from 2 Esdras in the Apocrypha. There Esdras recounts how the lost ten tribes of Israel, after having been carried away captive into Assyria, "took this counsel among themselves, that they would leave the multitude of the heathen, and go forth into a further country, where never mankind dwelt, That they might there keep their statutes, which they never kept in their own land." Using the very language of the Apocrypha, Rigdon admonished these modern-day Israelites to go out from Assyria to their promised land of Zion and there serve God as they never had before.[36]

33. "The Book of Esther," *Evening and the Morning Star,* January 1833, 6. Years later, an article published in the church newspaper would recommend that Latter-day Saints read the apocryphal writings of Esdras, see "The Beauty of the Writings of the Prophet Esdras," *Times and Seasons,* 1 July 1841, 464–66.

34. Minute Book 2, 4 August 1831, 5, Church History Library (accessible under Minute Books in the Administrative Records series of the online edition of *The Joseph Smith Papers*).

35. John Whitmer, History, 1831–circa 1847, 31–32, in *JSP*-H2:44.

36. 2 Esdras 13:42–43. Rigdon may have already had an affinity for the Apocrypha from years of association with the Christian primitivist movement led by Alexander Campbell. Campbell did not consider

THE REVELATION ON THE APOCRYPHA

Faced with what he considered to be a divine admonition to quickly complete the Biblical translation and move on to other pressing duties, the desire among his followers to find and recover more lost truths from the Bible, and the public and complete Protestant rejection of the Apocrypha as scripture, Smith apparently made the matter a subject of prayerful inquiry. Smith dictated this 9 March 1833 revelation in response:

> Verely thus saith the Lord unto you concerning the Apocrypha there are many things contained therein that are true and it is mostly translated correct—there are many things contained therein that are not true which are interpelations by the hands of men varely I say unto you that it is not needful that the Apocrypha should be translated therefore whoso readeth it let him understand for the spirit manifesteth truth and and whoso is enlightened by the spirit shall obtain benifit therefrom and whoso receiveth not the spirit cannot be benefited; Therefore it is not needful that it should be translated. Amen.[37]

This revelation did not prohibit Smith from undertaking a translation of the Apocrypha, but neither did it command him to do so and it stated flatly that such a project was unnecessary.

Smith himself apparently understood the revelation to mean that the Apocrypha *should not* be translated. This was the position he took when he responded to inquiries about lost and ancient scripture in his 25 June 1833 reply to church members in Missouri. Smith informed them that God had told him that "there were many things in it which were true and there were many things in it which were not true and to those who desired, it should be given by the spirit to know true from the false."[38]

The text of Smith's revelation and his subsequent letter to Missouri perhaps raise as many questions as answers. Unlike William Brownlee, Alexander

---

the Apocrypha scripture; he specifically declared that he "rejected" it. See *A Debate on the Roman Catholic Religion between Alexander Campbell and the Right Reverend John B. Purcell* (Cincinnati, OH: J. A. James, 1837), 257. Nevertheless, his newspaper, the *Millennial Harbinger*, for years carried an unattributed, modified quotation on its masthead from 1 Esdras: "Great is the truth, and mighty above all things, and will prevail." The quotation appears to combine parts of 1 Esdras 1:35 ("great is the truth, and stronger than all things") and 1:41 ("Great is Truth, and mighty above all things").

37. Joseph Smith, Revelation, Kirtland Township, Geauga County, OH, 9 March 1833, in Ohio Revelation Book, 55, Revelations Collection, Church History Library; see also *JSP*-D3:32–35 [D&C 91].

38. Joseph Smith et al., to "Brethren," 25 June 1833.

Archibald, and other Protestant theologians who completely rejected the Apocrypha as an unauthorized Catholic expansion to the canon, Smith's revelation began first by affirming the opposite of prevailing opinion. It declared that the Apocrypha contained "many things . . . that are true and it is mostly translated correct." This declaration—that individual church members could encounter a text laden with spurious content and spiritually discern truth from error—was unique among Smith's revelatory instructions about ancient texts. Smith seemed to affirm this position when he visited the home of Edward Stevenson and examined the family Bible, which included the Apocrypha. Decades later, Stevenson recounted that Smith had "remarked that much of the Apochraphy was true as well as the bible," although it "required much of the Spirit of God to select from those things correctly."[39] Rather than accept the Apocrypha as scripture and undertake to correct its errors as he had the Bible, or completely reject the Apocrypha as had most of the Protestant world, Smith's revelation took the unique position of affirming that there were many truths in the book and yet that it was still somehow different than the other flawed biblical texts. One might wonder then how the Apocrypha differed from the Bible itself in Smith's mind. His view of the problems existing in the King James Bible seem very similar if not just the same. Moreover, if the Apocrypha contained truths that could be discerned by those "enlightened by the spirit," why then could the existing truths in the Bible not be detected in the same way without the years of effort put into the translation project?

THE RECEPTION OF THE REVELATION

It is unclear how members in Missouri and elsewhere in the church responded to the revelation, as there is essentially no known discussion of it by members and church leaders for the remainder of Smith's life. Most Bibles published in America after 1827 no longer contained the Apocrypha.[40] Therefore, as time progressed, it became all the more apocryphal to Mormons, who only encountered the books when they made a specific effort to seek out the text. Additionally, the outbreak of violence and mob resistance to Mormon settlement only a few months later halted the production on the Book of Commandments, the new edition of the Book of Mormon, and the inspired version of the Bible. Smith

39. Edward Stevenson, Autobiography, circa 1891–1893, 22, Edward Stevenson Collection, 1849–1922, Church History Library.

40. David Norton, *A Textual History of the King James Bible* (Cambridge: Cambridge University Press, 2005), 119.

was unable to publish even a book of his own revelations until 1835. A new translation of the Apocrypha was probably not the most urgent project in his mind, nor the church publication most needed or desired by church members.

Nevertheless, anecdotal evidence suggests that Joseph Smith still considered the Apocrypha to be an essential part of the Bible. According to one eyewitness account made years later by Samuel Miles, Smith's affinity for the Apocrypha actually influenced the cornerstone ceremony of the Nauvoo temple in September 1841. Amidst a crowd of hundreds, Smith ceremoniously placed several sacred writings and some other artifacts of significance into the temple's southeast cornerstone. When it came time to place a copy of the Bible into the stone, Joseph balked, because the one on hand did not contain the Apocrypha. He reportedly explained that he thought it necessary that the Bible "should be complete—containing the Apocrypha." Miles continued: "As there seemed to be none within reach, except large, high-prized family Bibles, Brother Reynolds Cahoon volunteered to go to his home, which was nearby and cut out the Apocrypha from his large family Bible, which was accepted and the Bible thus made complete."[41] While this account may be as apocryphal as the books themselves, the particularity of this seemingly odd remembrance suggests that there was some discussion or at least mention of the Apocrypha at the ceremony. Apparently, despite Smith's growing tendency to regard the Apocrypha as separate from the Biblical canon, he still saw the Bible as incomplete without the Apocrypha's inclusion.

It seems likely, then, that Smith would have included the Apocrypha in the version of the Bible he intended to publish. Since at least a month before his revelation on the Apocrypha, Smith had been planning to finish his new translation of the Bible and send it to the church printers in Jackson County, Missouri, to have it published.[42] These plans were foiled later that year by the anti-Mormon mob who razed the church's printing shop, damaged its press, scattered its type, and ultimately evicted the Saints from the county. Smith, nevertheless, hoped he would someday publish the New Translation.[43] And,

41. Samuel Price, quoted in "Recollections of the Prophet Joseph Smith," *The Juvenile Instructor*, 15 March 1892, 175. It is possible that Price was recalling the more well-known cornerstone deposit ceremony of the Nauvoo House, which occurred only a week later, but William Clayton affirmed in his record of the temple construction that "a deposit was made in the south-east corner stone of the temple." William Clayton, "An Interesting Journal," *The Juvenile Instructor*, 15 February 1886, 4, 60.

42. Minute Book 1, 2 February 1833 [first of two entries]. See also Letter to Church Leaders in Jackson County, Missouri, 21 April 1833, in *JSP*-D3:68; Joseph Smith et al., to "Brethren," 25 June 1833.

43. The intention and effort to publish the New Translation continued, but was not accomplished during Joseph Smith's life. See Revelation, 2 August 1833-B, in *JSP*-D3:206 [D&C 94:10]; see also Robert J.

presumably it would have been printed with the Apocrypha included between the testaments in the same way it had been printed since the original King James translation—thus providing Latter-day Saints with their own version of a "complete" Bible. However, such an inclusion would pose a problem since Smith had performed his new translation for both the Old and New Testaments but not for the Apocrypha in-between them. Perhaps he would have added a headnote to the Apocrypha making reference to the revelation on the Apocrypha and explain why it was included but was not "translated." The mob that destroyed the printing establishment and forced the Saints from the county effectively reduced what may have been included in Smith's anticipated version of the Bible to conjecture and speculation.

Despite Smith's 1833 decision to pass by the Apocrypha without revision, the attractiveness of the Apocryphal books as possibly authoritative scripture was not lost upon all of Smith's followers. Indeed, the idea of more hidden scripture tied to the Apocrypha became the source of a fairly substantial schismatic breakaway from Smith's larger Mormon movement. In 1837, church members Zephaniah and Jane Brewster began to claim that their ten-year-old son James had the gifts of revelation and prophecy. James had begun using a seer stone to produce revelation in a manner similar to Smith's production of the Book of Mormon and other early revelations. Furthermore, according to Mormon sources dismissive of their claims, James was also using his stone to search for buried treasure—a venture reminiscent of Smith's early employment to help a group of treasure seekers dig for a cache of money.[44] Foremost among Brewster's revelations was what he called the "lost books" of Esdras, purportedly a translation of books by one of the authors of the Apocrypha. Brewster claimed that his revelation was one of the 204 books Esdras had written after receiving forty straight days of revelation from God. Brewster also contended that Esdras was expressly forbidden to discuss seventy of those books publicly as they could only be delivered to "such as be wise among the people."[45]

In 1841, Zephaniah Brewster attempted to convince Smith of the validity of his son's Apocrypha-inspired revelations prior to their publication. Smith

---

Matthews, *"A Plainer Translation": Joseph Smith's Translation of the Bible; A History and Commentary* (Provo, UT: Brigham Young University, 1975), 41–53.

44. For more on Joseph Smith's use of a seer stone to receive revelations and translate the Book of Mormon, see Michael Hubbard MacKay and Gerrit J. Dirkmaat, *From Darkness unto Light: Joseph Smith's Translation and Publication of the Book of Mormon* (Provo, UT: Religious Studies Center, Brigham Young University, 2015), 61–139.

45. James C. Brewster, *The Words of Righteousness to All Men: Written from One of the Books of Esdras* [...] (Springfield, IL: Ballard & Roberts, 1842); 2 Esdras 14:44–46.

examined Brewster's writings and prayed about them. Then, as noted in his journal, "the Lord told me the book was not true—it was not of him[.]" This entry continued: "If God ever cal[l]ed me. or spoke by my mouth. or gave me a revelation he never gave revelations to that Brewster Boy or any of the Brewster race."[46]

Despite Smith's repudiation of Brewster's revelations, their purported ancient content and miraculous reception convinced dozens of church members to abandon Smith and plan an emigration to Alta California to settle with Brewster as their prophet and leader. That writings purporting to relate to the Apocrypha from schismatic Mormons had the ability to convince dozens of Latter-day Saints in the 1840s and early 1850s to abandon Smith and his successors in favor of a new prophet and new revelations demonstrates how keen some Mormons were to embrace the Apocrypha as containing lost revelatory information. These Mormons believed that the Apocrypha, like the Book of Mormon, had been wrongfully rejected by a blind and sinful Protestant America. Smith's decision to forgo a revelatory examination of the Apocrypha despite his followers' interest in it opened the door for someone like Brewster to use his own Apocrypha-associated revelatory text to challenge Smith's authority to receive revelation for the church.

Further obfuscating the rationale behind Smith's decision to set aside a revelatory translation of the Apocrypha is that this decision came in the midst of other projects whereby he continued to produce scriptural texts that he claimed had ancient origins. Although Smith declined to perform his revision work on the Apocrypha, it did not stop his other efforts to reclaim lost ancient texts. Just two months later, in May 1833, he was still laboring to finish the Old Testament revision when he dictated a revelation that not only significantly expanded upon the biblical text of the first chapter of John but contested some of the most fundamental assumptions of Protestant and Catholic Christianity. The revelation challenged the prevailing Christian understanding of the human and divine nature of Christ that had been ostensibly settled at the Council of Chalcedon, asserted the premortal and co-eternal existence of humankind with God, and even refuted the concept of God's unfettered omnipotence.[47] Only two years later, Smith would come into possession of a few Egyptian mummies and papyrus scrolls and declare that from the scrolls

46. Joseph Smith, Journal, 31 December 1842, in *JSP*-J2:205–6.

47. Revelation, 6 May 1833, in *JSP*-D3:83–91 [D&C 93]. See also Nicholas J. Frederick, "Translation, Revelation, and the Hermeneutics of Theological Innovation: Joseph Smith and the Record of John," Chapter 13 herein.

he had restored more "ancient" scripture: a translation of the writings of the Old Testament patriarch Abraham. Clearly, Smith's willingness to translate, produce new scripture related to the Bible, and proclaim new, radical doctrines continued after his decision to pass by the Apocrypha.

Church members accepted revelations dictated by Smith as being from God and embraced the idea that the canon was not only *not* closed but should have been much larger if all of the world's hidden prophetic writings were revealed, recovered, and translated. Given the manifest desire Smith's followers had for more revealed scripture and Smith's obvious willingness to flaunt Christendom's generally accepted canonical and doctrinal limitations, it is difficult to assign a motive for his reluctance to engage with the Apocrypha. A new translation of the Apocrypha could have been another useful vehicle to provide church members with his view of the Christian gospel, stamped with the authenticity of texts that had existed for two millennia. If Smith were simply avoiding engagement with the Apocrypha due to the hostility of the Protestant world that surrounded him, he quickly and resoundingly abandoned this position with his May 1833 revelation. The doctrine of this revelation, on Christology and the co-eternality of God and humankind, thoroughly rejected foundational Protestant views. Given the decisiveness of this theological refutation, any commentary on the Apocrypha probably would have paled in comparison.

For his part, Smith claimed that the decision to let the Apocrypha go without an inspired revision came as the result of a revelation from God, who informed him that he need not translate the Apocrypha and also explained why. Yet the reason—that there existed both errors and truths in the text—was what Smith maintained of the Bible generally. If the revelation had maintained there were no truth in the Apocrypha at all, it would have created a much more readily acceptable and defensible position. To the Protestant American culture that surrounded Smith and increasingly detested the Apocrypha, a singular refutation of the Apocrypha would have signaled that the Mormons had gotten at least one thing right: the categorical rejection of these noncanonical books.

Moreover, a clear statement that the Apocrypha was false would have given Smith clear justification for avoiding it altogether and would have closed the door—at least to some extent—on the kind of schismatic possibilities illustrated by the Brewsterite movement. Brewster's claims were allowed to flourish for a time because Smith's revelation largely endorsed the text but then failed to engage in it. Smith had earlier taken precisely this course of action when dismissing the often scandalous language and content of the Song of Solomon in the Old Testament. Rather than heralding the good and either deleting or fixing the "interpolations," Smith's Bible manuscript simply remarked that "the Songs of Solomon are not Inspired writings." This middle ground occupied by Smith in relation to the Apocrypha would have neither satisfied Mormons hungry for new scripture of ancient origin nor made any inroads with the Protestants who rejected anything and everything outside of their old and new testaments.

POSSIBLE REASONS FOR NOT TRANSLATING THE APOCRYPHA

In the end, one can only speculate upon the reasons for Smith's decision to treat the Apocrypha differently from the rest of the King James Bible. By early 1833, Smith had been working on the Bible revision project in fits and starts for nearly three years and evidence indicates that he thought he would have the project completed before that time. As he unfolded his plans for building a Mormon stronghold in Kirtland and anticipated a still more grandiose construction of the city of Zion in Jackson County, Missouri, Smith may well have wished to move on from the translation. He certainly hoped the project would be completed soon enough to be put to press along with the other Mormon scriptures he intended to be published later that year in Jackson County. Indeed, as he neared the end of his translation of the Bible, Smith's changes no longer resembled the extensive revisions he made when examining Matthew, to say nothing of the thousands of additional words he had added to Genesis at the very beginning of the project.[48] He passed over entire books in the latter half of the Old Testament without making any changes, at one point pronouncing the books of the minor prophets Micah, Nahum, Habakkuk, Zephaniah, and Haggai "Correct" in quick succession.[49] Still, if such brisk and apparently cursory approval of these latter books was an indication of fatigue, Smith could have easily done the same thing for the individual books of the Apocrypha—or even for the Apocrypha as a whole—and thereby endorse members' already

48. See Joseph Smith, *The Complete Joseph Smith Translation of the New Testament: A Side-by-Side Comparison with the King James Version*, ed. Thomas A. Wayment (Salt Lake City: Deseret Book, 2005), 67–74 [Joseph Smith—Matthew]; Joseph Smith, *The Complete Joseph Smith Translation of the Old Testament: A Side-by-Side Comparison with the King James Version*, ed. Thomas A. Wayment (Salt Lake City: Deseret Book, 2009), 1–47 [Moses].

49. Old Testament Revision 2, 118, Community of Christ Library and Archives (images accessible under Bible Revision Manuscripts in the Revelations and Translations series of the online edition of *The Joseph Smith Papers*).

latent belief in its truthfulness. Conversely, he could have easily declared the Apocrypha uninspired and conformed with Protestant America. If attrition were the primary cause of his decision to pass on the Apocrypha, a simple pronouncement of "correct" or "not inspired" as he had done with other biblical books could have just as easily ended a comprehensive review of the Bible and freed up his time.

Whatever Smith's reason(s) for choosing to bypass the Apocrypha, the revelation that he dictated establishing the church's scriptural position on its utility actually hearkened back to the earliest Protestant interactions with the text. Martin Luther had been troubled by these extracanonical works that had been included in the Catholic bible for a millennium, but did not deem them forgeries nor remove them from his version of the Bible. Luther recognized them as less than scripture, but still "profitable and good to read." Similarly, Smith apparently regarded the Bible as incomplete without these texts but also saw them as somehow different from the rest of the canon in that they were (somewhat contradictorily) both inspired and flawed. Like Luther, Smith affirmed that someone reading the books with the Spirit would "obtain benefit therefrom." Unlike the Father of the Reformation, Smith specifically declared that there was "truth" to be found in the books of the Apocrypha. It was not to be excised and discarded, but neither was it to be held in the same regard as holy writ. As radical as Smith's other claims and teachings were, when it came to the Apocrypha, it was the Protestant world around Smith that had become more iconoclastic three centuries after Luther.

Joseph Smith's various translation projects resulted in hundreds of pages of content that he claimed to have derived from various methods of divine translation. While the question of how Smith produced these various translations is essential to understanding his theology, a close examination of his interaction with the Apocrypha demonstrates that there is no easily discernable or formulaic way to categorize his course of action (or inaction). Smith chose to deliver sweeping translations of some texts while ignoring others. At times, his dictated revelations directly responded to current social and theological concerns, and on other occasions, the translated or otherwise revealed texts that he produced seemed to ignore rather than react to such issues. In the case of the Apocrypha, the contemporaneous controversy surrounding the books, and the desire of church members for more revealed scripture, likely provoked Smith's question about whether to include the writings in his Bible revision project. Yet rather than issuing a definitive answer—one that would settle the matter for Mormon theology and canon—he instead dictated a revelation extolling the virtues of the text while also highlighting its many errors. In relation to the Apocrypha, Joseph Smith may have acted upon, or at least in concert with, a previously dictated revelation: "And as all have not faith, seek ye diligently, and teach one another, words of wisdom, yea seek ye out of the best books, words of wisdom, seek Learning even by study, and also, by faith."[50] The books of the Apocrypha appear to have been among the first of these "best books" by which readers of faith could seek out extracanonical truth.

50. Revelation, 27–28 December 1832, in *JSP*-D2:334–46 [D&C 88:1–126].

13

Translation, Revelation, and the Hermeneutics of Theological Innovation

Joseph Smith and the Record of John

NICHOLAS J. FREDERICK

Joseph Smith was a radical in his own theological innovations, yet his ideas found supporters and his religion gathered thousands who were willing to accept new ideas about God. Central to his success was his production, as the prophet and seer of his church, of three volumes of new scripture. Smith's scripture wove together the already accepted biblical text with new ways of thinking about God, the church, and eschatology. Though the Book of Mormon, his "new translation" of the Bible, and the Book of Abraham are well-known examples of presenting revelations that he claimed were translations of ancient text into modern English, he also dictated lengthy individual modern "revelations"—often explicitly in "the voice of the Lord"—to direct the governance and teachings of his church. A revelation dictated on 6 May 1833 is considered by many Mormon intellectuals to be one of Smith's most theologically profound.[1] This doctrinally rich revelation sheds light on the production of both his revelations and his translations due to the presence of a translated text embedded within a larger revelation—a rare occurrence in Mormon scripture.

The circumstances behind the reception of Smith's 6 May 1833 revelation remain largely shrouded.[2] The revelation promises in the "voice of the Lord"

1. See Blake T. Ostler, *Exploring Mormon Thought: Of God and Gods* (Salt Lake City: Greg Kofford Books, 2008), 366–69; and Terryl L. Givens, *Wrestling the Angel: The Foundations of Mormon Thought* (Oxford and New York: Oxford University Press, 2014), 120.

2. Joseph Smith's documentary history only states that "On the 6th [of May] I received the following." Joseph Smith, History, 1838–1856, vol. A-1, 291 (accessible in the Histories series of the online edition of *The Joseph Smith Papers*). Early Mormon bishop Newel K. Whitney gave his own summary of the revelation's contents, noting that it dealt with "chastisement" and was "relative to the Father & Son" (quoted in *JSP*-D3:83). Whitney's comment, although outside the scope of this paper, indicates that the primary purpose of this revelation was chastisement, with the material relating to Jesus, the Father, intelligence, the premortal life, and other doctrinal subjects all being secondary. Fully one-third of the revelation is directed at certain

that all those who "keepeth all my commandments" will "see my face and know that I am."[3] The Lord declares that He is both Father and Son and that He will condescend into the world. Then, abruptly, the voice of the Lord introduces "John," who was apparently John the Evangelist of the New Testament, and states that a previously unknown record, produced by this John, offers textual support and an additional witness to his "glory" and "fullness." The voice of the Lord further states that "the fulness of John's record" has yet to be "revealed." Having offered this tantalizing information, the voice of the Lord then recites several passages from this unknown "record of John," apparently translated by the Lord into English and offered up to Joseph Smith by revelation (see Figure 13.1). Following the conclusion of the embedded translation of the "record of John," the voice of the Lord relays the remainder of the revelation to Joseph Smith.

It is significant that the information contained in this revelation encapsulated the revolutionary nature of much of Joseph Smith's theological innovation. According to editors of the *Joseph Smith Papers*, the revelation "directly challenged several of the prevailing Christian beliefs at the time, including doctrines regarding the nature of Jesus Christ, especially his humanity and divinity, that most Christians believed had been settled by the 451 CE Council of Chalcedon."[4] Throughout the May 1833 revelation, Smith provided solutions to thorny theological issues such as *creatio ex nihilo* and the nature of humanity. This was accomplished largely through the creation of a "vocabulary of exaltation," employing terms such as "intelligence," "light," and "truth," in ways that were previously unfamiliar or unexplored. Through arguments both ontological and teleological, Smith arrived at the conclusion that "exaltation" was achieved through the accumulation of "intelligence." But this intelligence, while it may have included "knowledge" in the sense of facts or data, was beyond the natural and empirical; it also embraced the metaphysical and the supernatural.[5]

---

male church members, including Joseph Smith, and relates to their roles as fathers. However, these verses are often ignored in favor of the more grandiose topics presented in the first two-thirds of the revelation. Whitney's statement suggests that the more prominent features of the revelation are intended to be viewed within the context of parenting, as if the Lord is explicating why Smith and others needed to be better parents by laying out for them the nature of the premortal existence and the higher purposes of mortality. God's own spirit children were entrusted to mortal parents, and the expectation was that these mortal parents would work to ensure the exaltation of his spirit children that were born into their mortal families.

3. Revelation, 6 May 1833, in *JSP*-D3:83–91 [D&C 93:1].

4. Historical Introduction to Revelation, 6 May 1833, in *JSP*-D3:84 [D&C 93].

5. This "intelligence," in historian Richard Lyman Bushman's reading, was a "capacity for comprehension and insight, accounting for past, present, and future, grasping the moral and spiritual meaning of things, and radiating power . . . That capacity for seeing and comprehending supernaturally—with a spiritual mind,

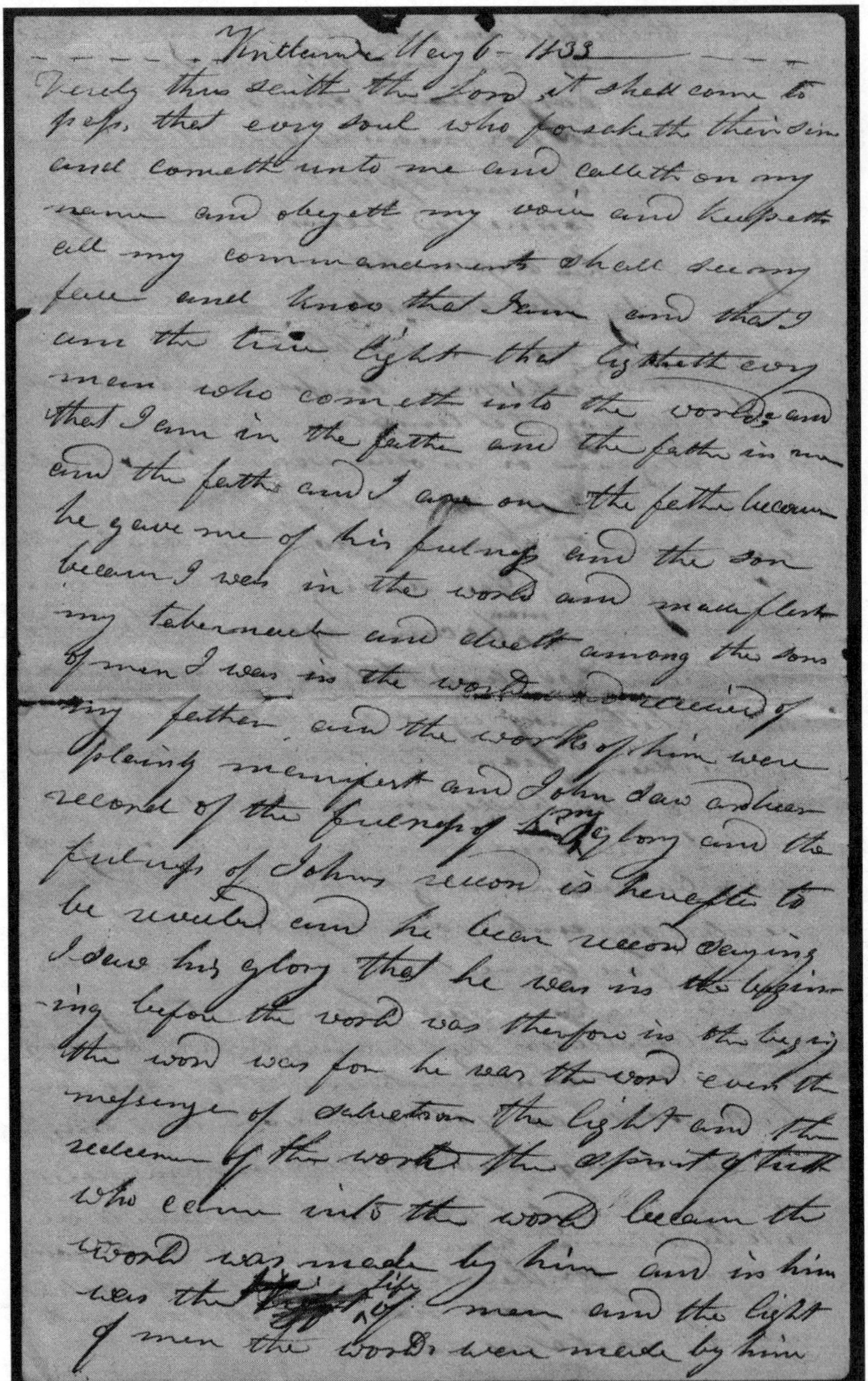

FIGURE 13.1. The "record of John" from an early manuscript copy—possibly the original dictation transcript—of Joseph Smith's 6 May 1833 revelation (now D&C 93). Copy in handwriting of Frederick G. Williams. Newel K. Whitney Papers, L. Tom Perry Special Collections, Harold B. Lee Library, Brigham Young University, Provo, UT.

This chapter argues that the primary purpose of the translation of the record of John embedded into the May 1833 revelation was to provide authoritative and hermeneutical support for the theological innovations presented throughout this revelation.[6] The claim that Smith had access to an unknown record of John supplied evidence for a nineteenth-century audience who saw in the convergence between Smith's revelations and the established biblical text the "infallible proofs" of Smith's authority.[7] Furthermore, the additional witness of a renowned biblical figure such as John to the innovations introduced by Smith in this revelation demonstrated that Smith's interpretations were sound and reliable.

In relying upon the voice of an established biblical author to provide authoritative support for the May 1833 revelation, Smith availed himself of a popular technique that has been generally referred to in an unflattering way as pseudepigraphy—although perceptions of the corpus have recently begun to change. According to Old Testament scholar Moshe J. Bernstein, "Originally, 'pseudepigrapha' was used to describe texts falsely ascribed to an author (usually of great antiquity) in order to enhance their authority and validity. Gradually, the connotation of this word was expanded to include a collection of Jewish and Christian writings dating from the last centuries BCE to the first centuries CE which did not become part of the canon in either religion."[8]

as he called it—was to him the zenith of human experience." Richard Bushman, *Joseph Smith: Rough Stone Rolling* (New York: Knopf, 2005), 208.

6. Earlier, in the Book of Mormon, quotations and allusions to the Prologue of the Gospel of John appear throughout. This is particularly notable in 3 Nephi 9:15–18, where the voice of Jesus Christ announces his appearance with a statement composed largely of phrases from John 1:1–18. See Nicholas J. Frederick, *The Bible, Mormon Scripture, and the Rhetoric of Allusivity* (Madison, NJ: Fairleigh Dickinson University Press and The Rowman and Littlefield Publishing Group, 2016), 1–7.

7. For a discussion of how the Book of Mormon provided "infallible proofs" for a nineteenth-century audience, see Steven C. Harper, "Infallible Proofs, Both Human and Divine: The Persuasiveness of Mormonism for Early Converts," *Religion and American Culture* 10, no. 1 (Winter 2000): 99–118. Additionally, it is important to distinguish between Joseph Smith's "authorial motives" and his "communicative intentions." According to theologian Stephen Fowl, the former could be defined as "a desire for fame and fortune, hopes of acquiring tenure, a deep psychological need for self-expression, and so forth." (Dan Vogel's biography of Joseph Smith is an example of a work seeking to explore "authorial motives." Dan Vogel, *Joseph Smith: The Making of a Prophet* [Salt Lake City, UT: Signature Books, 2004]). More important for this work is the concept of "communicative intentions," which "requires attention to matters of semantics, of linguistic conventions operative at the time, and of implication and inference, among other factors . . . attention to these matters is inescapably historical." Stephen Fowl, "The Use of Scripture in Philippians," in *Paul and Scripture: Extending the Conversation*, ed. Christopher D. Stanley (Atlanta: Society of Biblical Literature, 2012), 163–84. This chapter is not intended to take us further inside the mind of Joseph Smith, but to explore how Smith's use of an embedded translation found expression and relevance in nineteenth-century America.

8. Moshe J. Bernstein, "Pseudepigraphy in the Qumran Scrolls: Categories and Functions," in *Pseudepigraphic Perspectives: The Apocrypha and Pseudepigrapha in Light of the Dead Sea Scrolls*, ed. Esther G. Chazon and Michael Stone (Leiden: Brill, 1999), 1.

Exclusion from the Jewish or Christian canon ought not, however, to diminish the value of many of these texts, especially when their contextual and literary links with similar texts that were canonized as scripture are considered.

Furthermore, the biblical text provided a rich vocabulary and a powerful paradigmatic force from which to draw upon, one that would evoke powerful images and meaning in the minds of readers. By alluding to the language and verbiage of the biblical texts, later authors could intentionally link themselves to earlier authors. Reasons for this may vary, but, as Isaiah scholar Benjamin D. Sommer writes: "By acknowledging a predecessor, an author may seek to gain entry into a canon; through allusion the poet avows, 'This work is worth reading, just as its predecessors were.' In such a case, allusion represents an attempt to bolster the authority of the work."[9] In the case of a text such as Jubilees, which presents a different account (one delivered by an angel to Moses) of the events in Genesis and Exodus with a hypersensitivity to legal concerns, John J. Collins writes that "verbal echoes of the older scriptures would probably have facilitated acceptance of *Jubilees* as a credible account of Sinaitic revelation."[10] In this case, the allusions to the Hebrew Bible provide the foundation of textual authority for Jubilees. However, while allusion may serve to tether two texts together, it also paradoxically "can distance the new work from the old, since it is precisely when one juxtaposes two works (as one is forced to do by allusion) that one notices their differences." This, explains Sommer, allows "the new text to achieve a distinct identity in opposition to the older work."[11] Thus allusion can illustrate both the dependent nature and independent function of a text, which marks a method that offers great potential for understanding Mormon scripture. This chapter draws upon textual theories from the field of

9. Benjamin D. Sommer, *A Prophet Reads Scripture: Allusion in Isaiah 40–66* (Stanford: Stanford University Press, 1998), 18. Michael Segal, a professor of Biblical Studies, adds:

> The dependence upon biblical compositions in the process of creating new works is a product of the author's desire to impute authority to his work; by associating his composition with the holiest of texts, the new work is also granted the same stamp of authority. The author's worldview and his interpretation of biblical passages are not presented as revolutionary ideas, created ex nihilo by the writer. The inclusion of this material within the framework of the biblical passages under interpretation transforms the ideas of the later writer into authoritative and accepted beliefs. They are no longer new ideas, but are found in ancient texts alongside accepted notions.

Michael Segal, "Between Bible and Rewritten Bible," in *Biblical Interpretation at Qumran*, ed. Matthias Henze (Grand Rapids, MI: William B. Eerdmans, 2005), 11.

10. John J. Collins, "Changing Scripture," in *Changes in Scripture: Rewriting and Interpreting Authoritative Traditions in the Second Temple Period*, ed. Hanne von Weissenberg, Juha Pakkala, and Marko Marttila (Berlin: De Gruyter, 2011), 34.

11. Sommer, *A Prophet Reads Scripture*, 19.

Pseudepigrapha studies and applies them to the "record of John" as incorporated in Joseph Smith's revelation of 6 May 1833.[12]

THE PRODUCTION OF PSEUDEPIGRAPHA

One text where scholars have seen the use of textual or authorial appropriation to support theological innovation is Deuteronomy. Bernard Levinson, in his study of Deuteronomy, argued that its authors "sought to implement a far-reaching transformation of religion, law, and social structure that was essentially without cultural precedent."[13] The solution to the challenges of innovation was to appropriate the language and authority of an already accepted text, in this case the Covenant code found in Exodus.[14] The author(s) of Deuteronomy "turned to the earlier code in order to anchor their departure from legal convention in the very textual heritage from which they cut themselves free in substantive terms. They deliberately presented their vision of the Judaean polity as continuous with the abrogated past and used the earlier textual material, carefully transformed, to sanction their own independent agenda."[15] The disassembly of an accepted, authoritative text and its subsequent reconstruction in a new context was crucial to the success of such an endeavor. According to Levinson: "The authors of Deuteronomy coopted those texts, accommodating them to their innovations, by citing selected key words and phrases (lemmas) from their source texts and giving them new contexts and meanings. In the process, authors camouflaged the radical and often subversive nature of their innovations, as the new textual content was often expressed, quite literally, using the terms of the older dispensation."[16] Thus, one fundamental feature of the production of pseudepigraphal or "rewritten" biblical texts was the *adoption* of an accepted text that was then *adapted* for a new audience.[17]

12. Small portions of this chapter (with a few minor changes) are reproduced from the author's book *The Bible, Mormon Scripture, and the Rhetoric of Allusivity,* primarily from pages xiii-xv and xx-xxi. My thanks to The Rowman and Littlefield Publishing Group for allowing the use of that content here. One of the issues explored in my book was how the May 1833 revelation represented an inversion of Johannine theology. The purpose in writing this chapter is to examine more closely the rhetorical techniques applied by Joseph Smith as a means of appropriating the literary authority behind that theological inversion.

13. Bernard Levinson, *Deuteronomy and the Hermeneutics of Legal Innovation* (Oxford and New York: Oxford University Press, 1997), 3.

14. Exodus 20:22–23:33.

15. Levinson, *Deuteronomy and the Hermeneutics of Legal Innovation,* 3–4.

16. Ibid., 5–6.

17. For a study of how Joseph Smith may have used pseudepigraphical methods in some of his other textual productions, such as the Book of Mormon or the Book of Moses, see David Bokovoy, *Authoring the Old Testament: Genesis–Deuteronomy* (Salt Lake City: Greg Kofford Books, 2014).

A second fundamental feature of the production of pseudepigraphal texts was the need for contemporary interpretation. Biblical and nonbiblical authors recognized that certain texts had outlived some of their usefulness and needed to be reinterpreted or rewritten to serve the needs of contemporary believers. As James Charlesworth observes:

> The Pseudepigrapha were often produced within the crucible of biblical interpretation.... But to speak to the curiosities and needs of a later time the stories needed to be retold and completed with details. All the evidence seems to suggest that what we call additional facts and details were considered by the early Jews who revered these Pseudepigrapha to be part of the true story. Now they were revealed to serve the curiosities and needs of later generations.[18]

Charlesworth prefers the phrase "pneumatic exegesis" as a means of describing the manner and method of pseudepigraphic composition: "Like the Dead Sea Scrolls and the documents collected into the New Testament, the Pseudepigrapha tend to treat the Tanach in ways that are shockingly cavalier to modern biblical critics. It seems obvious that the text was considered divine, but the spirit of interpretation allowed the Jewish exegete to alter, ignore, expand, and even rewrite the sacred Scripture."[19] When the author of Deutero-Isaiah appropriated content from Jeremiah and First Isaiah, he "formulated single lines and whole sections from the works of his predecessors" in order to help the Jews make sense of the Babylonian captivity.[20] As noted above, Deuteronomy is likely the product of a radical reworking of the covenant code. The work resulted from, as Sommer put it, a "deliberate attempt to rework prestigious texts in light of the innovation of centralization."[21]

Part of the reasoning behind this reworking of scripture likely stemmed from a belief that inspiration had not ceased. According to Shemaryahu Talmon, the covenanters at Qumran "considered biblical literature a living matter, and participated in the ongoing process of its creation"—which can be

18. James E. Charlesworth, "In the Crucible: The Pseudepigrapha as Biblical Interpretation," in *The Pseudepigrapha and Early Biblical Interpretation,* ed. James H. Charlesworth and Craig A. Evans, *Journal for the Study of the Pseudepigrapha* Supplement Series 14 (New York: Continuum International Publishing, 1993), 39.

19. Charlesworth, "In the Crucible," 39.

20. Sommer, *A Prophet Reads Scripture,* 3.

21. Levinson, *Deuteronomy and the Hermeneutics of Legal Innovation,* 6.

seen from works such as the Temple Scroll.[22] For those who sought to provide correct biblical understanding through contemporary texts, the use of both the *identity* of the author and the *language* of his text became very potent literary devices. Significantly, as Michael Segal has noted, "The rewritten texts ask the reader to accept the authority of their sources, but to understand those sources according to the rewritten text's interpretation."[23]

Deuteronomy again provides a fascinating example of this temporal recontextualization. In her own study of Deuteronomy, Hindy Najman takes issue with some of Levinson's conclusions, in particular his claims that one of the purposes of Deuteronomy was to replace the Covenant code and that the work itself represents fraudulence.[24] Najman agrees that some authors who rewrote the Bible did so as a way of claiming authority for their work.[25] However, she also sees a primary function of such works as advancing the claim for correct hermeneutical authority as well.[26] Using Jubilees and the Temple Scroll from Qumran as interlocutors, Najman homes in on the circumstances that may have led to the composition of these texts: "Texts that 'rewrote the Bible,' like *Jubilees* and the Temple Scroll, responded to both the demand for interpretation and the demand for a demonstration of authority." As a means of responding to these demands, "works like Deuteronomy, *Jubilees*, and the Temple Scroll acquire authority through their intermingling with the well-known words of traditions whose authority is already acknowledged . . . we can speak to the goal of *Jubilees* and the Temple Scroll as trying to provide an interpretive context for received revealed literature, a context whose absence might engender dangerous misinterpretations."[27] Najman rejects subversive or insidious motivations on the part of such authors, believing that the circumstances that arose during

22. Shemaryahu Talmon, "The Textual Study of the Bible—A New Outlook," in *Qumran and the History of the Biblical Text,* ed. F. M. Cross and S. Talmon (Cambridge, MA: Harvard University Press, 1975), 379. Regarding the Temple Scroll's usage of the Hebrew Bible, Old Testament scholar John Collins remarks: "The fact that it uses language familiar from traditional Torah would probably make it easier to accept as authentic revelation on Sinai" (Collins, "Changing Scripture," 39).

23. Segal, "Between Bible and Rewritten Bible," 12.

24. Najman writes sympathetically for authors who rewrote the Bible, stating at one point that such rewriting can function as "an act of reverence." Hindy Najman, *Seconding Sinai: The Development of Mosaic Discourse in Second Temple Judaism* (Leiden: Brill, 2003), 47.

25. Ibid., 16. "By reworking and expanding older traditions through interpretation, a new text claims for itself the authority that already attaches to those traditions."

26. Ibid., 17. "The new text is said to be associated with, or produced by, the founding figure, Moses. This claim serves to authorize the new interpretation as divine revelation or dictation and as prophecy or inspired interpretation. The new text can then be seen as an extension of earlier ancestral discourse."

27. Ibid., 46. Najman also writes: "In such a climate, it was entirely possible to aspire, not to replace, but rather to *accompany* traditions already regarded as authoritative, and thus to provide those traditions with their proper authoritative context" (46).

the second-temple period demanded a tethering of texts past and present: "But even the most innovative material could not present itself as innovative . . . The only passable roads to textual authority led through the past."[28]

HINDY NAJMAN'S THEORY OF CONFERRING AUTHORITY AND JOSEPH SMITH'S RECORD OF JOHN

In her study of Jubilees, Najman isolated four strategies employed by the author of the work as a means of conferring authority upon the text:

1. "*Jubilees* repeatedly claims that it reproduces material that has been written long before on the 'heavenly tablets,' a great corpus of divine teachings kept in heaven." As a means of conferring authority, a text may claim to incorporate material considered ancient and sacred.
2. "The entire content of the book of *Jubilees* was dictated by the angel of the presence at God's own command. Hence, it is itself the product of divine revelation." As a means of conferring authority, a text may claim that it has been dictated by a divine figure at the command of God.
3. "*Jubilees* was dictated to Moses, the same Moses to whom the Torah had been given on Mount Sinai. Thus the book of *Jubilees* is the co-equal accompaniment of the Torah; both were transmitted by the same true prophet." As a means of conferring authority, a text may claim that it was written by the author of another authoritative work, thereby placing it on par with that work.
4. "*Jubilees* claims that its teachings are the true interpretation of the Torah. Thus, its teachings also derive their authority from that of the Torah; that its interpretations match the Torah's words and resolve all interpretive problems further substantiates its veracity."[29] As a means of conferring authority, a text may claim that it provides the correct lens through which to view an authoritative work—if readers want to truly understand that work, they need to read the new text. In the process, the innovative ideas presented by the new text become valid.

28. Ibid., 15.

29. Hindy Najman, "Interpretation as Primordial Writing: Jubilees and its Authority Conferring Strategies," *Journal for the Studies of Judaism* 30, no. 4 (1999): 380. Najman's work builds upon that of Florentino Garcia-Martinez, "The Heavenly Tablets in the Book of Jubilees," in *Studies in the Book of Jubilees*, ed. Matthias Albani, Jörg Frey, Armin Lange (Tübingen: Mohr Siebeck, 1997), 243–60.

Najman's four claims provide a useful lens through which to interrogate the use of the Record of John embedded in the May 1833 revelation.

Using Najman's categories as a model, the following claims are applicable to Joseph Smith's reproduction of an excerpt from the Record of John with respect to the strategies of conveying authority:

1. It claims to be a translation of an ancient record.
2. It claims to be part of a divine revelation dictated to Joseph Smith.
3. It (implicitly) claims to be the product of John the Evangelist, the author of a significant New Testament text,[30] and reinforces this complementary status (or "co-equal accompaniment," as Najman puts it) through an appropriation of Johannine language and imagery.
4. It presents itself as the valid lens through which biblical theology should be understood and thus opens up theological space for hermeneutic innovation.

Through these four strategies, the Record of John positions itself as a more accurate documentary text from John and subsequently asserts hermeneutical authority—the theology and Christology presented in the Record of John

30. For Latter-day Saints who view Joseph Smith as a prophet and his revelations as divine, there is little doubt that the Record of John is authentic and that the translation provided by Smith divinely revealed. There is, however, a fair amount of disagreement over whether the John mentioned in the 6 May 1833 revelation was intended to be John the Evangelist or John the Baptist. In the revelation's excerpt from the Record of John, the narrator claims, "I John bear reccord and lo the heavens were opened and the holy ghost decended upon him in the form of a dove and set upon him and there came a voice out of heaven saying this is my beloved son." This event, which matches the gospel accounts of the divine approval manifested at the baptism of Jesus by John the Baptist, seems to identify the author of the Record of John as John the Baptist—although the revelation may be implying that John the Evangelist had been present at the baptism of Jesus and witnessed the manifestations of divine approval (Matthew 3:13–17; Mark 1:9–11; Luke 3:21–22; John 1:29–34). The author was identified as John the Baptist by prominent church authorities Orson Pratt, John Taylor, and Bruce R. McConkie (Orson Pratt, Discourse, 18 May 1873, in *Journal of Discourses*, 26 vols. [Liverpool: Joseph F. Smith; London: Latter-day Saints' Book Depot, 1854–1886], 16:58; John Taylor, *The Mediation and Atonement* [Salt Lake City: Deseret News, 1882], 55; Bruce R. McConkie, *Doctrinal New Testament Commentary*, 3 vols. [Salt Lake City: Bookcraft, 1966], 1:70–71). However, as historian Steven C. Harper has noted, "all editions of the Doctrine and Covenants since 1921 imply that these were the writings of John the Apostle." Steven C. Harper, *Making Sense of the Doctrine and Covenants* (Salt Lake City: Deseret Book, 2008), 560; compare Lyndon W. Cook, *The Revelations of the Prophet Joseph Smith* (Salt Lake City: Deseret Book, 1981), 194–95. Others who argue for John the Evangelist as author of the Record of John include Charles W. Penrose of the First Presidency. See "Prest. Charles W. Penrose," *Eighty-Sixth Annual Conference of the Church of Jesus Christ of Latter-day Saints: Held in the Tabernacle and Assembly Hall, Salt Lake City, Utah, April 6, 7 and 9, 1916, with a Full Report of the Discourses* (Salt Lake City: Deseret News, 1916, 19–20. Another possibility is that, given the parallel language from John 1 in the Record of John, the revelation implied that John the Baptist was John the Evangelist (though the Baptist was soon murdered). This chapter takes John the Evangelist as the implied author of the Record of John as presented in the May 1833 revelation.

should be taken as the correct interpretation of John's Prologue, thus resolving any interpretive problems stemming from the Gospel of John while buttressing the theological claims of the May 1833 revelation.

Strategies 1 and 2: Translation and Revelation

By the time he revealed the translation of John's record, sometime in early May 1833, Smith had dictated approximately one hundred revelations. These revelations conferred authority upon his teachings and imperatives. As historian Steven C. Harper has written: "By their nature as well as their tone, Smith's revelations assumed authority. The voice of God repeatedly declares His prerogative to make and execute the law and bring offenders to judgment. The revelations therefore created hostility to acceptable modes of discourse and challenged assumed wisdom. Simply put, for Smith and his followers, the undemocratic voice of God they heard 'so distinctly' trumped the voice of the people."[31]

So, what are we to make of the presence of a translated text in the May 1833 revelation? On one hand, Smith's prophetic career had begun in 1828–1829 with the production of the Book of Mormon, a text that claimed an ancient American provenance. Records attributed to Moses and Enoch had followed in 1830–1831, and Abraham would follow in 1835. Smith viewed his "restoration" project as an attempt to bring into the present that which had been forgotten in the past, and it is likely that the production (or reproduction) of translated texts went to the heart of his self-perception as a "seer" and "prophet."[32]

There may, however, be a different explanation for the presence of John's record in the May 1833 revelation. While the revelation contains the promise that the complete Record of John is "hereafter to be revealed"—a curious merging of translation with revelation—some early Mormons understood revelation as being a contemporaneous event occurring when God spoke to his people at a specific time and place. According to an early Mormon periodical, "we believe, from the Scriptures of truth, that to every church in the past ages, which the Lord recognized to be his, he gave revelations wisely calculated to govern them *in the peculiar situation and circumstances under which they were placed*, and to enable them by authority to do the peculiar work which they

31. Steven C. Harper, "'Dictated by Christ': Joseph Smith and the Politics of Revelation," *Journal of the Early Republic* 26, no. 2 (Summer 2006): 276–77.

32. These titles were ascribed to Joseph Smith in a revelation he dictated at the founding of the Church of Christ. Revelation, 6 April 1830, in *JSP*-D1:129 [D&C 21:1].

were to perform."[33] Conversely, translation is an event that merges past with present, providing God's former prophets the opportunity to have a voice in a future setting. Why would the May 1833 revelation explicitly produce both revelation and translation?

One possible solution can be found by examining the journey of the translation text from its stated origins to its final form. As mentioned above, Jubilees is an ancient Jewish text in which Moses received the record of what is essentially the stories of Genesis and Exodus with a hypersensitivity to the Law of Moses. What is remarkable about Jubilees is the manner of reception on the part of Moses. Not only does Moses receive the text of Jubilees from a divine figure, the "angel of the presence"; what the angel recites to Moses is a record written upon "heavenly tablets," producing a dual appropriation of both oral and written sources. In her discussion of Jubilees, Najman writes: "It speaks volumes about these Second Temple authors that they must have considered it insufficient to ground their interpretations and laws in a contemporaneous activity of interpretation or experience of prophecy. Clearly, they thought they had to ground their interpretation and laws in the pre-exilic past: in the Mosaic origins of the nation or, better yet, in the divine origins of history itself."[34] James C. VanderKam calls the process of Moses receiving the words of the angel who is reciting from the text of the heavenly tablets "unimpeachable transmission" and concludes that: "It is difficult to imagine a more secure way in which to transmit information. . . . There is no danger of contamination in this line of transmission, no worry about corruptions, text-critical problems and the like. The message of *Jubilees* is verbally inerrant."[35]

One can sense a similar motivation within the May 1833 revelation. Perhaps believing that the revelatory would not be enough to adequately support its innovative theology, Smith introduced a second line of transmission by incorporating a translated text into the revelation. To have these ideas originating from the abstract "voice of the Lord" and proceeding forth from the mouth of Joseph Smith was not substantial evidence for his post-enlightenment audience. But a text, especially a translated text, carried empirical weight—even if the text were lost and beyond corroboration. The presence of a record of John

33. "The Elders in the Land of Zion to the Church of Christ Scattered Abroad," *Evening and the Morning Star,* July 1832, 5 (emphasis added).

34. Najman, "Interpretation as Primordial Writing," 405–6.

35. James C. VanderKam, "Moses Trumping Moses: Making the Book of Jubilees," in *The Dead Sea Scrolls: Transmission of Traditions and Production of Texts,* ed. S. Metso, H. Najman, and E. Schurer, Studies on the Texts of the Desert of Judah 92 (Leiden: Brill, 2010), 33.

grounded the doctrine laid out in the revelation in a historical setting, with a human author—one who was revered due to his connection with the New Testament. To put it another way, the translated text signified authority, a weighty witness that granted validity to ideas that lacked historical verifiability. It was not just the *content* of the translation, but also the *claim* of translation, that was pivotal to the text. Through this merging of revelation and translation, the May 1833 revelation skillfully combined the priority of the past with the relevance of the present.

Strategy 3(a): Johannine Attribution

As potent as revelation and translation can be as tools of appropriation, Smith also relied upon the personality and reputation of John in the composition of the May 1833 revelation. The revelation begins with a short statement, rendered in the voice of "the Lord," before introducing John and his record: "And John saw and bear record of the fulness of my glory and the fulness of Johns reccord is hereafter to be reveiled and he bore record saying I saw his glory that he was in the begining before the world was." It is not known why the revelation chose John the Evangelist as the figure around whom to construct an alternate record.[36] Perhaps Joseph Smith felt more familiar with the Fourth Gospel,[37] or perhaps he sensed a superior authority in John's witness and gospel.

John possesses two distinct advantages over the other three gospel writers. First, John's apostolic career was closely linked with the ministry of Jesus Christ. John witnessed several important events, including the theophany upon the Mount of Transfiguration (although this event is not mentioned in the gospel bearing his name). Along with Peter and James, he appears to have been Jesus's most trusted associate. The same cannot be said for the Synoptic authors. While Matthew was designated as one of Jesus's twelve followers, he plays little role in the narrative itself. Mark's and Luke's entrance into the Christian narrative comes only after the resurrection, leaving them to rely

36. Earlier, the Book of Mormon apparently implied that the author of the Gospel of John and the author of the book of Revelation were identical. Nephi, a prophet in the Book of Mormon, has a vision similar to that found in the book of Revelation and subsequently learns that the person who will write down this vision is "the apostle of the Lamb [known as] John" (1 Nephi 14:27).

37. That Joseph Smith was familiar with John and his writings at an early point in his career is clear from two instances. First, Smith discussed John 21:23 with Oliver Cowdery in April 1829. Account of John—April 1829, in *JSP*-D1:47 [D&C 7]; see also David W. Grua and William V. Smith, "The Tarrying of the Beloved Disciple: The Textual Formation of the Account of John," Chapter 10 herein. Second, it was a reading of John 5:29 that prompted the revelation in February 1832. Vision, 16 February 1832, in *JSP*-D2:179 [D&C 76].

upon the accounts of others in crafting their gospels. Adam Clarke, Joseph Smith's contemporary and author of a massive series of commentaries on the Bible, wrote the following in his preface to John's gospel:

> It is evident that John was present at most of the things related by him in his Gospel; and that he was an *eye* and *ear witness* of our Lord's labours, journeyings, discourses, miracles, passion, crucifixion, resurrection, and ascension. After the ascension he returned with the other apostles from mount Olivet to Jerusalem, and took part in all transactions previous to the day of Pentecost: on which time, he with the rest, partook of the mighty outpourings of the Holy Spirit, by which he was eminently qualified, for the place he afterwards held in the Christian church.[38]

Clarke's comments reflect how John was primarily viewed by nineteenth-century Christians. As a witness to Jesus and his ministry, John's associated textual witness was to be considered authoritative. The May 1833 revelation, by placing its teachings in the mouth of John the Evangelist, conferred an authority upon itself that far outstripped the authority Joseph Smith could have conferred on his own. In this respect, Joseph Smith may have been simply following a literary practice popular in the early centuries of the Christian church. As explained by Lewis R. Donelson: "When doctrinal disputes began to trouble the church, both sides looked to apostolic times for guidance and vindication of their own views. You wrote in the name of an apostle simply because the apostle had greater credence than you or any contemporary did and by so doing your own ideas or the ideas of your sect were given greater credibility."[39] By associating this revelation with an apostolic figure such as John, Joseph Smith was attempting something similar.

A second advantage John's gospel held over the writings of the other three evangelists was a recognizable verbiage and a pregnant theology. This is especially true of the "Prologue" of John's gospel. As far as language goes, the Prologue contains a number of phrases that are recognizable as Johannine. If readers of the May 1833 revelation had encountered phrases such as "the power of God" or "the remission of sins," they may have recognized them as generally biblical, but would likely have been unable to identify them as the product of

38. Adam Clarke, *The New Testament of our Lord and Saviour Jesus Christ* (New York: J. Emory and B. Waugh, 1831), 479 (emphasis in original).

39. Lewis R. Donelson, *Pseudepigraphy and Ethical Argument in the Pastoral Epistles* (Tübingen: Mohr Siebeck, 1986), 20.

a specific author. However, phrases such as "born of God," "only begotten of the Father," "full of grace and truth," "grace for grace," "bosom of the Father," "sons of God," and "believe on his name" are phrases specific to the Johannine Prologue—as are longer constructions such as "the light shineth in the darkness" and "he came unto his own."

Furthermore, if Joseph Smith were seeking a text from which he could craft a unique theology, the Prologue of John's gospel provided a very viable opportunity. In the Prologue, much of the Christology of the primitive church is revealed, including the preexistent nature of the λόγος (KJV: "word"), the creative capacity of the λόγος, Jesus Christ as a divine yet incarnate figure, and the possibility of divine filiation. The unique vocabulary of John's gospel—familiar terms such as "life" and "light" from John 1:4 and "glory" and "truth" from John 1:14—appear frequently throughout these opening verses as well. The Prologue is, in the words of Raymond Brown, "a description of the history of salvation."[40] "The rest of the book," in the opinion of D. A. Carson, "is nothing other than an expansion of that theme."[41] Carson elaborates: the Prologue summarizes how the "Word" that was with God in the very beginning came into the sphere of time, history, tangibility—in other words, how the Son of God was sent into the world to become the Jesus of history, so that the glory and grace of God might be uniquely and perfectly disclosed.[42] By introducing new theology through the medium of a text written by an esteemed author, one who himself used distinct vocabulary and innovative theology, Smith was able to bestow upon this theology a viability that went beyond the "revelation" that dominated so many of his earlier prophetic statements. The use of an embedded translation ascribed to John may indicate just how important (or perhaps controversial) the revelation's innovative doctrine would be in its own reception environment.

Strategy 3(b): Complementary Status

As stated above, the Prologue of John contains a unique vocabulary. Much of that vocabulary, understandably, is carried directly into the May 1833 revelation, Joseph Smith's version of the Johannine Prologue. Thus, readers of the revelation encounter familiar phrases such as "in the beginning the Word was" and "full of grace and truth," as well as uniquely Johannine titles for Jesus such

40. Raymond E. Brown, *The Gospel According to John I–XII* (Garden City: Doubleday, 1966), 1:23–24. However, it would be a disservice to the Prologue to imply that it can be easily interpreted.

41. D. A. Carson, *The Gospel According to John* (Grand Rapids, MI: William B. Eerdmans, 1991), 111.

42. Ibid., 111.

as "the Only Begotten of the Father." In this regard, Smith may have only done what other American authors had done, namely to produce "pseudobiblical" literature that helped Americans situate themselves historically through application and exegesis of the biblical text. Eran Shalev has studied the Book of Mormon and other examples of pseudobiblical literature produced during the eighteenth and nineteenth centuries and concluded that, while the language of the King James Bible "was as strange and foreign to late eighteenth-century and nineteenth-century Anglophones as it is to twenty-first-century English-speakers," the Bible and especially the language of the King James version provided a medium for self-contextualization.[43] According to Shalev: "Generations of Americans reverted to that language and its accompanying structures and forms to discuss their difficulties and represent their achievements, past and present . . . American authors and commentators used this ontologically privileged language as a means to establish their claims for truth, as well as their authority and legitimacy in public discourse."[44] For those writers seeking to put forward an authoritative voice making sense of contemporaneous circumstances, the language of the Bible became an ideal vehicle.

Perhaps no American author understood this principle better than Joseph Smith. A few months before he produced the May 1833 revelation, Smith unabashedly proclaimed that it was "high time for a christian world to awake out of sleep and cry mightely to that God day and night whose anger we have Justly incurred."[45] Transferring the language of the Bible into the nineteenth century and finding application with his contemporary audience provided one means of staving off God's anger, restoring to the text an importance and luster that had dimmed with the passing of the centuries. Shalev notes that "Through pseudo-biblicism the Bible became a living text, an ongoing scriptural venture which complemented and fortified notions of national chosenness and mission."[46] The brilliance of the reconstruction of the Johannine Prologue in Smith's revelation is that it presents itself as an "ongoing scriptural venture" between Joseph Smith and John the Evangelist. For instead of just copying the

43. Eran Shalev, "Written in the Style of Antiquity: Pseudo-Biblicism and the Early American Republic, 1770–1830," *Church History* 79, no. 4 (December 2010): 801.

44. Ibid.

45. Letter to Noah C. Saxton, 4 January 1833, in *JSP*-D2:351.

46. Shalev, "Written in the Style of Antiquity," 812. One result of the contemporalization of the Bible through the Book of Mormon has been noted by Timothy L. Smith: "The Book of Mormon also helped bring to fruition the movement, rooted in puritan, pietist, Quaker, and Wesleyan experience, to restore to prominence the doctrine of the presence of the Holy Spirit in the lives of God's people and in the testimony of his witnesses. That the prophecy in Isaiah and Acts were so central to the Book of Mormon encouraged this result." Timothy L. Smith, "The Book of Mormon in a Biblical Culture," *Journal of Mormon History* 7 (1980): 18.

first few verses from John 1, the revelation carefully weaves together language that is both Johannine and pseudo-Johannine, with the result that it becomes a "living text" linking authors past and present.

This weaving of Johannine with pseudo-Johannine can be seen in two key statements from Joseph Smith's Record of John. The first is "therefore, in the beginning the word was for he was the word even the messenger of salvation the light and the redeemer of the world the spirit of truth." The presence of titles for Jesus such as "word" and "light" are to be expected in a Johannine text—both are significant titles for Jesus in John's gospel. However, the titles "messenger of salvation," "redeemer of the world," and "spirit of truth" are not Johannine titles for Jesus, with only "spirit of truth" even being found in the Gospel of John. The presence of "messenger of salvation" could be viewed as Joseph Smith extending the meaning of the term "word," a notoriously difficult term to interpret.[47] If Jesus is the "word," he could also be a "messenger." As far as Jesus being the "Redeemer of the world," the words "redeem" and "redemption" do appear in the New Testament, but never in a Johannine text. Additionally, the title "redeemer" is completely absent from the New Testament. However, the title "redeemer of the world" appears in both the Book of Mormon[48] and Smith's other revelations.[49] Its presence in the May 1833 revelation likely derives from Joseph Smith's

47. The Greek word translated into English as "word" in John 1:1 is λόγος. This figure of the λόγος, while new to the gospel writings, was by no means new to the ancient world. Heraclitus had first defined the intelligible unity of being or the determinate structure of thought and gave this concept the somewhat ambiguous name λόγος. By this he seemed to mean that every person had the capacity to understand the creative order of the universe, although not everyone would take advantage of this knowledge. Heraclitus Fragments 1 and 2, discussed in G. S. Kirk and J. E. Raven, *The Presocratic Philosophers: A Critical History with a Selection of Texts* (Cambridge and New York: Cambridge University Press, 1984), 181–213. With the advent of Stoicism, λόγος came to mean something more akin to the rationality and order of the universe. Because Stoicism was largely concerned with a rational explanation of the nature of the universe and humanity's role within it, λόγος was applied to humankind as well as a description or encapsulation of their proper moral attitudes. Thus, λόγος could be understood as "the intelligence behind an idea, the idea itself, or the expression of the idea." W. Robert Cook, *The Theology of John* (Chicago: Moody Press, 1979), 48. Significantly, the Stoic λόγος was not an emanation or aspect of God, but rather was God itself. T. W. Manson, a professor of biblical criticism and exegesis, noted: "The Stoic does not have a God, one of whose attributes is *logos*. He has one God who can be called indifferently . . . many other names including *logos*." T. W. Manson, "The Johannine Jesus as Logos," in *A Companion to John: Readings in Johannine Theology*, ed. Michael J. Taylor (New York: Alba House, 1977), 6. During the Middle Platonic period, λόγος began to be used as a mediating figure (likely building upon the idea of the "demiurge" in Plato's *Timaeus*) who bridges the gulf between the transcendent, spiritual God and the mortal realm. This view of the λόγος became particularly well-developed in the writings of the Jewish exegete Philo, who saw a need to combine his ancestral Jewish faith with the Hellenistic world in which he lived. It is Philo's concept of the λόγος that likely would have been familiar to the Fourth Gospel's contemporaneous audience. See Thomas Tobin, "The Prologue of John and Hellenistic Jewish Speculation," *Catholic Biblical Quarterly* 52, no. 2 (April 1990): 252–69.

48. 1 Nephi 10:5; 1 Nephi 11:27.

49. The title is also found in the opening lines of the 6 May 1833 revelation. Revelation, 6 May 1833, in *JSP*-D3:86 [D&C 93:9].

influence more than John's. Finally, the phrase "spirit of truth" is notable for different reasons. "Spirit of truth" is a Johannine title, one that appears only in Johannine texts.[50] In the Johannine context, the "spirit of truth" referred to the Holy Spirit who would act as a successor of sorts once Jesus had departed. All three passages from the Fourth Gospel clearly delineate between Jesus and the Holy Spirit; while Jesus may be the παράκλητος (KJV: "comforter"), the Holy Spirit will function as ἄλλον παράκλητον (KJV: "another comforter"). Thus while "spirit of truth" may apply to the Holy Spirit, it is unlikely that John would have applied it to Jesus.[51] The revealed Record of John, therefore, inserted two pseudo-Johannine Christological titles among two verifiably Johannine Christological titles, while recontextualizing a third Johannine title, "spirit of truth," to apply to Jesus rather than the Holy Spirit—making it Johannine with respect to language but pseudo-Johannine with respect to meaning.

A second important statement from Joseph Smith's Record of John, and one that will be crucial for the next section of this chapter, is: "And I John saw that he received not of the fulness at the first but received grace for grace and he received not of the fulness at first but continued from grace to grace until he received a fullness." In a remarkable theological statement, the Record of John describes how Jesus not only "received grace for grace" but "continued from grace to grace." As with the earlier use of Johannine vocabulary and phraseology, this statement presents readers with a merging of Johannine and pseudo-Johannine language through a subtle replacement of prepositions. The phrase "grace for grace" is found in the Bible only in John 1:17. The phrase "grace to grace" is completely absent from the Bible. However, like "redeemer of the world," the phrase "grace to grace" was part of the theological vocabulary of the eighteenth and nineteenth centuries. John Wesley used "grace to grace" to explicate his doctrine of sanctification, writing that "We go on from grace to grace, while we are careful to 'abstain from all appearance of evil,' and are 'zealous of good works,' as we have opportunity, doing good to all men; while we walk in all His ordinances blameless, therein worshipping Him in spirit and in truth; while we take up our cross, and deny ourselves every pleasure that does not lead us to God."[52] The presence of this phrase in the Record of John is

50. Compare John 14:17, 15:26, 16:13; 1 John 4:6. The title "spirit of truth" is found outside the Bible in Jubilees 25:14; Community Rule 4.21; Joseph and Asenath 19:11; and Shepherd of Hermas (Mand. 3.4). The use of "spirit of truth" in 1 John 4:6 is slightly more ambiguous than the usages in the Fourth Gospel, but still likely refers to the Holy Spirit. See Raymond E. Brown, *The Epistles of John* (Garden City, NY: Doubleday, 1982), 501.

51. See Herman Ridderbos, *The Gospel of John* (Grand Rapids, MI: William B. Eerdmans, 1997), 502–4.

52. John Wesley, *The Works of the Rev. John Wesley, A. M.* (London: John Mason, 1829), 6:46.

again most likely attributable to Joseph Smith, who wrote that he was inclined toward the Methodists early in his life. This exposure to Methodism may have led to the incorporation of the phrase into his later work.[53] Regardless, through a weaving of Johannine and pseudo-Johannine language, the Record of John presented in the May 1833 revelation by Joseph Smith correlates with Shalev's concept of a "living text." Through this close collaboration, one that extends to the phrasal level, the revelation tethers itself with John's own Prologue, conferring upon the Record of John the authority that history and tradition had bestowed upon the Gospel of John.

Strategy 4: Valid Interpretation and Hermeneutic Innovation

The three previous strategies—revelation, translation, and Johannine attribution/coequal accompaniment—lay the groundwork for the fourth strategy, namely positioning the Record of John as the hermeneutic lens through which Johannine theology ought to be interpreted. One of the major purposes of the May 1833 revelation is to explicate how humanity can become exalted. Smith's solution was to claim that human beings existed in a premortal state, and that they progress toward exaltation through the accumulation of intelligence. Following the translated Record of John, the "Lord" states the following:

> I give unto you these sayings that you may understand and know how to worship and know what you worship that you may come unto the father in my name and in due time receive of his fulness for if you keep my commandments you shall receive of his fulness and be glorified in me as I am in the father, therefore, I say unto you you shall receive grace for grace.

The model for this progression, according to the revelation, is Jesus Christ, who also existed in a premortal state and progressed until he reached his exalted state. The purpose of the revelation, and especially the inclusion of the Record of John, is to relay this information to humanity.

The Record of John thus plays a crucial role in constructing this theological argument. The Christian roots of American religious thought are predominantly Calvinist, and thus Trinitarian. As E. Brooks Holifield observes:

53. On Joseph Smith and Methodism, see Joseph Smith, History, 1838–1856, in *JSP*-H1:210; *JSP*-H1:8. On the interaction between incipient Mormonism and Methodism, see Christopher C. Jones, "Mormonism in the Methodist Marketplace: James Covel and the Historical Background of Doctrine and Covenants 39–40," *BYU Studies Quarterly* 51, no. 1 (2012): 67–98.

"The first-generation ministers spoke of Christ with the standard concepts of Reformed Christology. To them Christ was the incarnation of the second Person of the Trinitarian God. They understood him in accord with the way they understood the Trinity as the inner life of a God whom they described as 'increated being,' 'a Being that is not from any Being,' infinite, eternal, unchanging."[54] Significantly, this brand of Christology "seemed a natural inference from the texts of the New Testament."[55] By the early nineteenth century, the seeds of anti-Trinitarian thought sown by Michael Servetus and Faustus Socinus had begun to bear fruit in the form of Unitarianism and later by the Transcendentalism of Ralph Waldo Emerson and others. In his famous 1819 Baltimore sermon, William Ellery Channing summarized the Unitarians' anti-Trinitarian position:

> If we examine the passages in which Jesus is distinguished from God, we shall see, that they not only speak of him as another being, but seem to labor to express his inferiority. He is continually spoken of as the Son of God, sent of God, receiving all his power from God, working miracles because God was with him, judging justly because God taught him, having claims on our belief, because he was anointed and sealed by God, and was able of himself to do nothing.[56]

Fiery transcendentalist Theodore Parker fashioned a Jesus that further obliterated the lines between Christology and anthropology:

> In him the Godlike and the Human met and embraced, and a divine Life was born. Measure him by the world's greatest sons;—how poor they are. Try him by the best of men,—how little and low they appear. Exalt him as much as we may, we shall yet, perhaps, come short of the mark. But still was he not our brother; the son of man, as we are; the Son of God, like ourselves?[57]

The early decades of the nineteenth century found the relationships between God, his son, and humanity being radically redefined.

54. E. Brooks Holifield, *Theology in America: Christian Thought from the Age of the Puritans to the Civil War* (New Haven: Yale University Press, 2003), 35–36.

55. Ibid., 36.

56. William Ellery Channing, "Unitarian Christianity," in *The Complete Works of W. E. Channing, with an Introduction* (London: Routledge and Sons, 1884), 373.

57. Theodore Parker, "The Transient and Permanent in Christianity," in *The Transcendentalists: An Anthology*, ed. Perry Miller (Cambridge, MA: Harvard University Press, 1950), 274–75.

Like Channing and Parker, Joseph Smith "did not hesitate to assert the utter distinctness of the three members of the Godhead."[58] However, Smith did hesitate to move beyond the boundaries of scripture, recognizing, as did his contemporary Thomas Campbell, the value of speaking only "where the Bible speaks."[59] Perhaps due to this tension, rather than engage in a theological speculation that employed (or even acknowledged) the language of early church fathers such as Athanasius or Augustine, Smith simply returned to the literary wellspring of Christian theology, the New Testament, and rewrote it. Two key phrases from John's Prologue—one present in the Record of John and one conspicuously absent—illustrate how the revelation used the Johannine Prologue to construct an exaltation paradigm resulting in a remarkably non-Johannine Jesus. The first is the phrase treated in the previous section, "grace to grace," a nonbiblical expression that appears to be a variation on the Johannine "grace for grace." According to the excerpted Record of John, Jesus "received not of the fulness at the first." Instead, in a sort of heavenly *cursus honorum*, Jesus "continued from grace to grace until he received a fulness." As opposed to the Gospel of John, where Jesus is called the "Son of God" because of his unique, close relationship with the Father, in the May 1833 revelation Jesus is called the "Son of God" *because* he lacked the "fulness"—just as all humankind does prior to arriving at their exalted state. The significance of these statements, according to Mormon intellectual Terryl L. Givens, is that they "might be construed to indicate—in contradiction to the council of Chalcedon's pronouncement that Jesus was fully human and fully divine at birth, and 'perfect in his divinity'—a process of total divinization, or Christ's receipt of the Father's fullness, finally achieved through the experience of mortality."[60]

The second phrase is one that is present in John's Prologue but silently omitted from the revelation's Record of John. This is the crucial phrase from John 1:1, καὶ θεὸς ἦν ὁ λόγος, rendered in the King James translation as "and the Word was God." The revelation included another phrase from John 1:1, "in the beginning the Word was," as well as phrases from John 1:3, "because the world was made by him," and 1:4 "and in him was the life of men and the light of men." Yet the phrase "and the Word was God" is omitted. This statement is crucial for understanding the Johannine conceptions of Jesus. As J. Ramsey Michaels writes: "The placement of 'God,' or *theos,* first in its clause, before the verb, gives

58. Givens, *Wrestling the Angel*, 120.

59. William R. Baker, "Evangelicalism and the Stone-Campbell Movement," in *Evangelicalism and the Stone-Campbell Movement*, ed. William R. Baker (Downers Grove: InterVarsity Press, 2002), 24.

60. Givens, *Wrestling the Angel*, 120.

it a certain definiteness, warning against reducing it to a mere adjective. At the same time, the absence of the article alerts the reader that 'the Word' and 'God,' despite their close and intimate relationship, are not interchangeable."[61] Readers of the Gospel of John find the somewhat opaque relationship between Father and Son to be a prominent theme throughout the work.[62]

The absence of this phrase from the Record of John may be due to the Christology the revelation is constructing. By describing the progression of Jesus as one who "received not of the fulness at first" and then highlighting the baptism as the event at which (presumably) Jesus "received a fulness," the Record of John appears to be hinting at an "adoptionist" Christology.[63] According to this Christological view, which has recently been renamed "exaltation" Christology by popular New Testament scholar Bart D. Ehrman, "the man Jesus is showered with divine favors beyond anyone's wildest dreams, honored by God to an unbelievable extent, elevated to a divine status on a level with God himself, sitting at his right hand."[64] However, this adoptionist view of Jesus would eventually lose out to the Trinitarian position held by the dominant faction at the Council of Nicaea—for whom, ironically enough, John 1:1 provided a major plank in their argument. In order for Joseph Smith's exaltation paradigm to work, the May 1833 revelation needed to present a Christology that was coequal to its ambitious anthropology. Using the progression of Jesus as a model for humanity to follow if they are ultimately going to reach an exalted state themselves would fail if Jesus was a being disconnected from humanity, a figure whose emulation stood far removed from humanity's own potential. Yet the Christology needed to be grounded in a scriptural source, to have the backing of canonical authority. The result is a text perhaps best described as a collision between Johannine language and Smithine theology. Smith's revelation could borrow or even fully appropriate the language of John, as in the first part of the revelation, even if the theology it was attempting to construct differed from the theology in the Fourth Gospel.

61. J. Ramsey Michaels, *The Gospel of John* (Grand Rapids, MI: William B. Eerdmans, 2010), 47–48.

62. See Jesus's statements that "I and my Father are one" (John 10:30), and "I go unto the Father, for my Father is greater than I" (John 14:28).

63. Bart Ehrman offers one description of the Adoptionist movement: "Other Christians, however, rejected this claim and argued that Christ was a flesh and blood human being without remainder, a man who had been adopted by God to be his Son and to bring about the salvation of the world . . . by the second century, most believed that it had occurred at his baptism, when the Spirit of God descended upon him and a voice called out from heaven, 'You are my son, today I have begotten you.'" Bart D. Ehrman, *The Orthodox Corruption of Scripture: The Effect of Early Christological Controversies on the Text of the New Testament* (Oxford and New York: Oxford University Press, 1993), 47.

64. Bart D. Ehrman, *How Jesus Became God* (New York, NY: HarperCollins, 2014), 232.

In presenting a new scheme of exaltation, one that would be viewed as authoritative by its audience, the revelation constructed an innovative paradigm derived from an allegedly ancient record appearing at the beginning of the May 1833 revelation. As a result, textual authority was conferred on the broader text of the revelation in a variety of ways. The authority of a revered biblical figure and witness of Jesus's ministry was bestowed by positioning John the Evangelist as the author of the record. A divine authority was granted through the claim that the record was received by revelation from Jesus Christ. This intricately linked the Record of John not only to the biblical *text* but to the biblical *time*. The merging of Johannine verbiage with pseudo-Johannine phrases accentuated the link to the biblical Gospel of John, tethering the documents closely together in such a manner that to reject one would be to reject both. The result was a text that employed elements of the past to speak to men and women in the present, rooting new ideas in the very ground from which they sprung.

CONCLUSION

Understanding the May 1833 revelation from the perspective of rhetorical strategies designed to grant textual validity may lead to a better understanding of the nature of Smith's larger scriptural corpus. While the revelation built around the translation of John's record acutely demonstrated Smith's ability to construct new scripture out of old, it was by no means the only work produced along these lines. Significantly, many of Smith's other translation projects appear aimed at resolving the same tension present in the "Record of John," namely how to promote innovative theology while still maintaining a link with the biblical text. Smith's first composition, the Book of Mormon, carefully integrated passages and phrases from the Old and New Testament in the course of constructing a translation of a record left by a group dwelling in the Americas nearly two millennia ago. Smith's new translation of the Bible, a project begun in 1830, resulted in a biblical text that had been rewritten to speak more effectively and, Smith likely believed, more accurately, to a nineteenth-century audience.[65] A lengthy vision attributed to Moses, revealed to Smith in 1830, also employed several of the rhetorical strategies examined above in conjunction

65. For example, Joseph Smith changed the language of 1 Thessalonians 5:26 from "Greet all the brethren with an holy kiss" to "Greet all the brethren with a holy salutation." Joseph Smith, *Joseph Smith's New Translation of the Bible: Original Manuscripts*, ed. Scott H. Faulring, Kent P. Jackson, and Robert J. Matthews (Provo, UT: Religious Studies Center, Brigham Young University, 2004), 526–27. The purpose of such a

with the May 1833 revelation—including that of using biblical language and situating the text as the proper hermeneutical lens through which to interpret events recorded in the early chapters of Genesis. Smith would later attempt something similar with his Book of Abraham. Finally, while none of Smith's other canonized revelations employed translation as creatively as the May 1833 revelation, the attribution of the revelations to a contemporary and modern "voice of the Lord" and the careful weaving of biblical phrases into lengthier engagements with nineteenth-century concerns positions many of them as a kind of modernized or renovated Bible.[66] It is perhaps the desire to reconcile this tension between the traditional and the innovative that best explains Joseph Smith's role as translator.

---

change may have been to accommodate the sensibilities of his audience rather than to present what Paul actually wrote or meant.

66. In addition to the 6 May 1833 revelation, see Revelation, September 1830-A, in *JSP*-D1:177–82 [D&C 29]; Revelation, circa 7 March 1831, in *JSP*-D1:274–80 [D&C 45]; Vision, 16 February 1832, in *JSP*-D2:179–92 [D&C 76]; Revelation, 22–23 September 1832, in *JSP*-D2:289–304 [D&C 84]; Revelation, 27–28 December 1832, in *JSP*-D2:334–46 [D&C 88:1–126].

PART IV

Pure Language, the Book of Abraham, and the Kinderhook Plates

14

"Eternal Wisdom Engraven upon the Heavens"

Joseph Smith's Pure Language Project

DAVID GOLDING

About eight months after publishing the Book of Mormon, Joseph Smith expanded the Genesis account to describe a primordial "book of rememb[r] ance" of Adam and Eve's family written in a "pure & undefiled" language.[1] Though the Book of Mormon had narrated a Babel-era confounding of an original human language, this November 1830 Bible revision represents the first mention of "pure language" in Smith's extant record. He did not, however, leave the concept dangling: evidence points to Smith endeavoring to divine pure language. On the surface, his process appears cryptic, his output scarce. Unlike the voluminous Book of Mormon that Smith produced through similar revelatory and "translation" methods, the essential content of his pure language specimens can be contained in this chapter. Beyond an 1832 "sample" and an 1835 "specimen," only traces of pure language appear elsewhere in Smith's other works. Nevertheless, these limited sources attest to more than a passing curiosity; they manifest an effort (what this chapter will call Smith's "pure language project") to address and overcome fundamental problems of the human condition. But questions remain: What exactly did Joseph Smith attempt in acting on a concept of pure language? How did the mechanics of his pure language project correspond to his overall theory of translation? What could pure language accomplish in Smith's theology?

To answer these questions, this chapter examines the pure language project in its esoteric context. Western esotericism presented a worldview enjoying wide interest among Joseph Smith's contemporaries while he and his associates

1. Old Testament Revision 1, 10–11, in Joseph Smith, *Joseph Smith's New Translation of the Bible: Original Manuscripts*, ed. Scott H. Faulring, Kent P. Jackson, and Robert J. Matthews (Provo, UT: Religious Studies Center, Brigham Young University, 2004), 57 [Moses 6:6].

negotiated their own preoccupations with language. While Smith often left his specimens of pure language unexplained, he propounded a creative linguistic infused with Western esoteric terms and concepts. The method for divining pure words relied on a philosophical concern for language decay and a historical concern for primordial forms. Power resided in perfect language, and apparently names and other words carried potential energy. Such preoccupation with words as a medium for divine power appeared in many religious settings long before Smith's era.[2]

The term *esotericism* is used here to refer to a philosophy and worldview of intellectuals and pseudoscientists throughout Europe and colonial North America that treated absolute reality as elusive and hidden without intervention, be it divine revelation or some other mystical action. Ancient wisdom characterized a great deal of esoteric thought, since many concluded from biblical texts that the distant past included God; time was space, and the farther into the past a source went, the closer to God that source must have been. Figures like Moses, Abraham, and Adam loomed large as authorities on the deeper truths known to God and once known to mortals close to God. Searching out deeper truths through a combination of intellectual and mystical means placed one squarely within the Western esoteric tradition.[3]

Esoteric structure appears in one of Joseph Smith's most articulate descriptions of the problems of language. An 1832 letter addressed to William W. Phelps is particularly esoteric in how it treats the mundane as cosmic and renders the cosmic immediately powerful. Smith's followers had struggled to realize his vision for a holy society while gathering to Missouri that year. The system for managing "consecrations" (donated money and goods) and

2. See Bret E. Carroll, *Spiritualism in Antebellum America* (Bloomington: Indiana University Press, 1997); Jon Butler, "Magic, Astrology, and the Early American Religious Heritage, 1600–1760," *American Historical Review* 84, no. 2 (April 1979): 317–46; John L. Brooke, *The Refiner's Fire: The Making of Mormon Cosmology, 1644–1844* (Cambridge: Cambridge University Press, 1994); April D. DeConick, *The Gnostic New Age: How a Countercultural Spirituality Revolutionized Religion from Antiquity to Today* (New York: Columbia University Press, 2016), 187–92, 247–49. Recognizing the availability of esoteric traditions in Joseph Smith's cultural environment is not to run a genealogy of Smith's translation methods through European esoterica, but rather to posit the routine aspect of the philosophical preoccupation with language in Smith's time. See Mark Ashurst-McGee, "A Pathway to Prophethood: Joseph Smith Junior as Rodsman, Village Seer, and Judeo-Christian Prophet" (master's thesis, Utah State University, 2000), 48.

3. Like Wouter J. Hanegraaff's definition and use of *esotericism*, this description of the esoteric is not theoretically universal or "an entirely satisfactory label," but it remains true that scholars have not yet proffered superior terminology. Wouter J. Hanegraaff, *Western Esotericism: A Guide for the Perplexed* (New York: Bloomsbury Academic, 2013), vi; see also Egil Asprem and Kennet Granholm, eds., *Contemporary Esotericism* (London: Routledge, 2014), 22–24. For an overview of Western esotericism, see also Wouter J. Hanegraaff, *Esotericism and the Academy: Rejected Knowledge in Western Culture* (Cambridge: Cambridge University Press, 2012); Wouter J. Hanegraaff, "Textbooks and Introductions to Western Esotericism," *Religion* 43, no. 2 (2013): 178–200.

"inheritances" (stewardships of property) had seemed to falter, with some who had already received inheritances of land neglecting their pledge to assist in common welfare.[4] Smith's letter replied to other church leaders who had raised the issue. Rather than a typical administrative reply, Smith waxed apocalyptic and theological. He instructed the leaders to keep careful records—not only for sound accounting purposes, but because such records should one day constitute the "Book of the Law of God," a judgment-day ledger the Almighty would consult in declaring *eternal* inheritances. Such vehemence over something so temporal as donation records signaled an esoteric logic: the very act of setting "in order the house of God" relied on God's pronouncement, God's word. Concentrating on the mechanics of God's power, Smith found language at work. Uttering "Eternal words" to "arrange the inheritances of the saints" amounted to a kind of singularity, the very moment in which God actualized salvation.[5]

Smith and his associates wanted to exercise such power and believed their limited language, however feeble, could nevertheless call down blessings and pronounce inheritances. But Smith's ambitions did not stop there. If one could attain a fullness of heavenly power, one would be calling forth the language of God Himself—a language capable of every possible and perfectly precise declaration. Smith pursued this pure language while also recognizing his inherent limitations. Near the conclusion of his 1832 letter, he broke into prayer: "Oh Lord God deliver us in thy due time from the little narrow prison almost as it were totel darkness of paper pen and ink and a crooked broken scattered and imperfect language."[6]

This letter exemplifies Western esoteric thought in how Smith assumed there existed a pristine heavenly language. Though Smith never used the term "esoteric" to describe his methods—and though critics and scholars have relied on vocabularies of magic, occultism, hermeticism, and Freemasonry to describe Smith's translation milieu and frame of mind—the broader category of esotericism expands the palette of analytical tools and allows for the unique deviations Smith took.[7] Masonry, hermeticism, and other philosophies corresponded with Smith's thought for their shared esotericism. Critical perspectives treating Euro-American esotericism as a subculture within various

4. For one of Smith's foundational "Zion" revelations, see Revelation, 20 July 1831, in *JSP*-D2:343 [D&C 57].

5. Letter to William W. Phelps, 27 November 1832, in *JSP*-D2:315–21.

6. Ibid., 320.

7. For an assessment of Mormon history research into hermeticism and categories here organized under the heading "esoteric," see the roundtable on John L. Brooke, *The Refiner's Fire* (1994) in *Journal of Mormon History* 41, no. 4 (October 2015): 177–237.

religious, philosophical, and intellectual settings more precisely identify the innovations of Smith's translation work.

The esoteric background of Smith's creative linguistics informed his approach to the pure language project and surfaces strikingly in his 1832 letter to Phelps. He anticipated a day, he said, when he might stand and "gase upon Eternal wisdom engraven upon the hevens." Engraved wisdom—divine writing in a perfect language—had eluded humanity, as Smith explained, for "God holdeth up the dark curtain." But Smith hoped to part the curtain and "read the round of Eternity to the fullness and satisfaction" of his and Phelps's "immortal souls." As his translations of Egyptian would eventually manifest, the "round of Eternity" included a completeness of language, something capable of being read out loud and heard. Hidden knowledge, the kind held behind the curtain of God's mystery, could only come to light by those possessing the keys of the kingdom, keys Smith later endeavored to commit to others in esoteric ceremonies.[8] The pure language project proved a crucial step in Smith rendering the exoteric (the apparent and obvious reality), esoteric; the mundane, eternal.

In the sections that follow, this chapter further considers the esoteric context for Smith's religious philosophy and supernatural practice of translation, outlines the primary sources of his pure language project, and briefly considers its meager results. As Smith struggled against the "narrow prison" of "confounded" language in attempting to access the pure language of God, he relied on classic esoteric resources: the Hebrew and Egyptian languages, the Bible, direct revelation, and mystical secrets or "keys." Relative to pure language content, Smith ironically regressed, starting with larger explanations, text, and morphemes, and ending with quixotic pursuits of grammar study.

ESOTERIC CONTEXT

The 1830s witnessed an upswing in popularity of alternative religious ideas in Europe and North America. Awakenings and revivals had recently surged

8. Joseph Smith invoked an esoteric tone during the first meetings of the Female Relief Society of Nauvoo in 1844. He admonished the women of the society to "move according to the ancient Priesthood" and indicated his desire to make them "a kingdom of priests as in Enoch's day." The "keys of the kingdom [were] about to be given to them, that they [might] be able to detect every thing false—as well as to the Elders." The Masonic context was not lost on Eliza R. Snow, who wrote "So mote it be" as part of the frontispiece to the Relief Society's minute book. Nauvoo Relief Society Minute Book, 4, 22, 37–38, in *The First Fifty Years of Relief Society: Key Documents in Latter-day Saint Women's History*, ed. Jill Mulvay Derr et al. (Salt Lake City: Church Historian's Press, 2016), 28, 28n94, 43, 56–57; see also Kathleen Flake, "Ordering Antinomy: An Analysis of Early Mormonism's Priestly Offices, Councils, and Kinship," *Religion and American Culture: A Journal of Interpretation* 26, no. 2 (Summer 2016): 159–63.

throughout denominational Protestantism in the United States, but also many formerly heterodox religiosities gained enough currency for cultural media to reproduce esoteric philosophies for the masses. The rise of the British Empire in the world occasioned foreign correspondence that American editors curated into newspaper and magazine reports. New pseudoscientific movements spread apace with fringe Christian theologies, and with momentum growing into the twentieth century, a broader New Age spirituality movement eventually attracted a global audience.[9] While mainline preachers of the 1820s and 1830s railed against heterodoxies, ordinary parishioners entertained diverse perspectives, among them an undercurrent philosophy that something profoundly real lay beneath the visible universe.[10] A metaphysical orientation informed a number of nondenominational and other religious communities, which taught that a higher or complete nature of reality had been obscured and required special knowledge to access. A hybrid pseudobiblical and pseudoscientific theology encouraged a worldview of the secret and a willingness to explore ancient wisdom for supernatural clues.[11]

Incantation lent a palatable bridge for some Protestant Christians between the orthoprax rituals of prayer and the mystical uncovering of spirit and nature. Invoking the name of Jesus Christ rendered prayer effectual, and while the vast majority of American Protestants hardly spoke of Christian prayer as a form of incantation, they still subscribed to the same principle of interpellation—speaking a name for effect—that esoteric thinkers followed in treating prayer, spells, omens, and oaths as media for channeling hidden or spiritual power. Many Protestants well versed in prayer traditions found blessing, cursing,

9. J. Jeffrey Franklin, *Spirit Matters: Occult Beliefs, Alternative Religions, and the Crisis of Faith in Victorian Britain* (Ithaca, NY: Cornell University Press, 2018), xii–xvii.

10. Historians have commonly applied terms such as "folk magic," "hermeticism," "occultism," "witchcraft," and sometimes even "astrology" and "alchemy" to folk traditions and activities bearing this philosophy of a hidden, higher reality. Such terms arose in scholarly and clerical repudiations of each brand of esoteric activity, and usually so under the umbrella term "superstition," which has carried a polemical and sometimes elitist agenda. Hanegraaff, *Esotericism and the Academy*, 156–91. Thus "esotericism" is favored here as a technical term that, in addition to its descriptive potential, should not invoke normative judgments toward the practices to which it refers.

11. Carroll, *Spiritualism in Antebellum America*, 2–3; Lee Irwin, *Reincarnation in America: An Esoteric History* (Lanham, MD: Lexington Books, 2017), 128, 156. Historians have long argued that colonial North America imported a number of spiritualist practices from European esoteric traditions. See Herbert Leventhal, *In the Shadow of the Enlightenment: Occultism and Renaissance Science in Eighteenth-Century America* (New York: New York University Press, 1976); Butler, "Magic, Astrology, and the Early American Religious Heritage," 317–46; Arthur Versluis, *The Esoteric Origins of the American Renaissance* (New York: Oxford University Press, 2001); Jane Williams-Hogan, "Emanuel Swedenborg's Aesthetic Philosophy and Its Impact on Nineteenth-Century American Art," *Toronto Journal of Theology* 28, no. 1 (Spring 2012): 105–24.

spellcasting, séance, and other settings for interpellation and incantation agreeable and accessible within a Christian idiom.[12]

With interpellation as a mechanical premise of esoteric activity, language naturally attracted the attention of esoteric intellectuals. Renaissance Europeans speculated that Moses and God conversed in a perfect language, which had direct application to religious practice. Moses performed the grandest miracles of the Bible in speaking forth plagues on Egypt, parting the sea, and bringing God's holy presence to the tabernacle; believers could exercise that same power if they possessed Moses's knowledge.[13] Intellectuals figured that Hebrew and Egyptian carried divine vocabulary and therefore studied Afroasiatic word forms, grammar, and symbols for signs of pre-Hebraic linguistics. Kabbalism especially cultivated speculation in pristine languages, but some thought the system of expression hindered higher knowledge from being elegantly encoded—Hebrew lacked pictographic precision. Egyptian and Chinese characters teased language hunters for their obvious complexity, and a few determined only philosophical inference and deduction could lead one logically toward a perfect mode of writing. John Wilkins (1614–1672) and Gottfried Wilhelm Leibniz (1646–1716) both began constructing hypothetical improved languages of their own, Wilkins with a hypertext of open classification and Leibniz with an encyclopedia and alphabet of thought itself.[14]

Similar mechanics informed eighteenth- and nineteenth-century attempts to translate Egyptian hieroglyphs. Scholars of the age approached Egyptian with assumptions of ancient and hidden wisdom and the mystique of veiled secrets. The Bible persuaded these translators that the hieroglyph packed degrees of meaning intended to confound the unrighteous, and the more anciently one searched, the closer one approximated the primordial, hence the closest to the divine in human prehistory.[15] Without having yet discovered cuneiform artifacts of ancient Sumeria, they assumed that Egyptian epitomized the ancient language. It was Egyptian that appeared pictographic, verbose, and biblically validated. The hieroglyph carried the potential for a richer history that God intended only the intellectually and spiritually prepared, like Moses and Elijah, to learn. A process for deciphering the symbols that anyone could follow

12. Carroll, *Spiritualism in Antebellum America*, 73.

13. Hanegraaff, *Esotericism and the Academy*, 18–22, 61–68.

14. Umberto Eco, *The Search for the Perfect Language*, trans. James Fentress (Malden, MA: Blackwell, 1995), 25–33, 258–60, 269–92; David Parry, "Umberto Eco and the Echoes of Adamic Language," *Zagadnienia Rodzajów Literackich [The Problems of Literary Genres]* 58, no. 2 (2015): 20–25.

15. Samuel Brown, "Joseph (Smith) in Egypt: Babel, Hieroglyphs, and the Pure Language of Eden," *Church History* 78, no. 1 (March 2009): 40–51.

would not suffice—a more opaque and adventurous process forced translators to prove their righteous intentions and protected the truth from the ungodly.[16]

Joseph Smith displayed a deep concern for hidden knowledge and personal holiness at the same time he launched into pure language speculation. One of the earliest documents in Smith's handwriting (not including signatures) introduced his circa summer 1832 autobiography by mentioning "the Kees of the Kingdom of God" being "confered upon him [Smith] and the continuation of the blessings of God to him." Smith then narrated his discovery of God and described his initial distress at watching the Christian world depart from "a holy walk and Godly conversation" and at noticing the "darkness which pervaded [the] minds of mankind." Smith supposed that humankind, made in God's image, must possess "strength of beauty" and "power and intiligence in governing the things which are so exceding great and marvilous." And God, Smith continued, had decreed laws and bound all things. Concepts of the human condition, law, and divinity combined into a classic esoteric worldview: language was linked to binding all things and holding the universe together because law in this instance represented something decreed, a medium for God's power.[17] Smith could not fathom decoupling language from action, and the biblical phrase "keys of the kingdom" explained how some of the observable universe eluded human understanding.[18]

Later that year, Smith advanced a metaphysical scheme bringing this autobiographical prospectus into even deeper elaboration. A revelation Smith dictated in December 1832, which he called the "Olive Leaf," laid out his most detailed metaphysics, positing an opaque universe invisible to human comprehension. The revelation assured church members who worried about the impending calamities of the last days that they could trust in God's protection because God oversaw the destiny of numberless worlds. But the message went deeper, situating God's power not in raw force, but in his omnipresent *knowledge*. All action and reaction, even reality itself, relied on light emanating from

16. Richard Lyman Bushman, "Joseph Smith's Place in the Study of Antiquity in Antebellum America," in *Approaching Antiquity: Joseph Smith and the Ancient World*, ed. Lincoln H. Blumell, Matthew J. Grey, and Andrew H. Hedges (Provo, UT: Religious Studies Center, Brigham Young University; Salt Lake City: Deseret Book, 2015), 3–22; Jan Assman, *Moses the Egyptian: The Memory of Egypt in Western Monotheism* (Cambridge, MA: Harvard University Press, 1997), 107–15; Eco, *Search for the Perfect Language*, 124, 135, 154; *JSP*-R4:xvi–xvii.

17. Mie Inouye, "The Kingdom of God in Early Mormon Thought: Divine Governance in Heaven and on Earth," (working paper, Summer Seminar on Mormon Culture, Neal A. Maxwell Institute for Religious Scholarship, Brigham Young University, 2013).

18. History, circa Summer 1832, in *JSP*-D2:279–82. See also Kathleen Flake, "'Not to Be Riten': The Mormon Temple Rite as Oral Canon," *Journal of Ritual Studies* 9, no. 2 (Summer 1995): 1–21.

God's presence and filling the immensity of space. An excursus on the nature of reality and the laws of resurrection rank as among the most esoteric of Smith's writings. In a few paragraphs, the Olive Leaf revelation cast all human knowledge as materially connected to light, and that light connected to God; God existed physically in plain view yet remained incomprehensible to mortal minds, only apparent through enlightenment.[19]

To comprehend the higher order of knowledge required having one's inhibited nature changed, and within the context of the Olive Leaf revelation, this meant transformation by laws of nature into higher orders of existence. Smith's terminology from his vision of the resurrection, experienced ten months prior,[20] described these orders: people moved upward through states of "telestial," "terrestrial," and "celestial" glory as they adhered to telestial, terrestrial, and celestial laws ordained by God. Light that "quickeneth" human understanding originated with God and had the power to work a change, to make one come alive as a higher order of being, so long as the person welcomed and observed God's word. Such a progressive concept pointed toward an eternal future blinding in its abundance of light and knowledge. The Olive Leaf revelation presented reality as materially luminous. But to unenlightened minds as yet incapable of comprehending the ultimate truth around them, the fullness of reality was invisible.[21]

Opaque symbolism presented tantalizing evidence of both an obfuscated reality and decrypted knowledge. One only needed to decipher the embedded meanings in a symbol to reach the hidden knowledge below. Smith treated all language as opaque and capable of decryption and glyphs as fundamental units of symbolic compression. A single glyph could pack immense quantities of knowledge, history, or narrative. And, ancient languages made liberal use of such symbolism, ostensibly to communicate on a level closer to God's infinite store of knowledge.

Glyphs evidently grounded both Egyptian and pure language. The finger of God had traced pure language for Enoch's fathers, and as suggested in a specimen of such language produced by Smith's close associate William W. Phelps in 1835, Smith may have sought such divine shapes. Presumably via a prophetic or revelatory method, Smith ascertained some of the ancient glyphs, and only keys could unlock their embedded meanings. The keys functioned in an entirely esoteric way: translations themselves represented primers, not complete texts,

19. Revelation, 27–28 December 1832, in *JSP*-D2:336–38 [D&C 88:1–126, see especially 6–13, 45–50].
20. Vision, 16 February 1832, in *JSP*-D2:179–92 [D&C 76].
21. Revelation, 27–28 December 1832, in *JSP*-D2:337–39 [D&C 88:11–50].

and these led Smith and his associates toward keys.[22] With the keys, they could approach God directly to receive unadulterated illumination from the Source. The mind was quickened, the body changed; one endured the presence of God where all things might be opened to the mind.[23] On a mechanical level, the pure language project would show Smith taking one glyph at a time and unpacking it, exploring its depth of expression and what lay behind the symbol.

For Smith, the task of decoding Hebrew, Egyptian, "reformed Egyptian," or the pure language amounted ultimately to enlightening his fellows with saving knowledge of God—direct access to the one redeeming humankind and to the words of grace bringing initiates through the "veil" or "curtain" into celestial glory.[24] The keys of the kingdom could "not be riten [written]," Smith's associates discovered; they could only be performed in sacred ceremonies so guarded by religious codes, their details remain private and closed.[25] Smith mystified the world, an inexorable outcome of seeking the glory of a grander one.

SOURCES OF JOSEPH SMITH'S PURE LANGUAGE PROJECT

Joseph Smith's references to pure language almost entirely surface within larger translation and revelation projects. The Book of Mormon translation in 1829, the Bible revision in 1830, preparations to compile and publish revelations between 1832 and 1835, and the Book of Abraham and Egyptian project in 1835 offer the settings for the most explicit pure language material in Smith's

22. This dynamic had played out shortly after Oliver Cowdery followed up on the promise that he could "translate even as my servant Joseph." Revelation, April 1829-A, in *JSP*-D1:36 [D&C 6:25]. After attempting to translate and shortly abandoning the effort, Cowdery appealed for God to explain what had failed. Joseph Smith's ensuing revelation explained that translation depended on carefully studying the characters, putting forward a possible translation, and sensing a spiritual confirmation. The "keys" of the gift—the special knowledge of how to "apply unto it"—were now revealed to Cowdery. "Now if you had known this," he was told, "you could have translated." The revelation directed him to use this information to "assist" Smith, not to render any further translation of his own. Revelation, April 1829-D, in *JSP*-D1:48–50 [D&C 9].

23. Account of Meeting and Discourses, circa 9 March 1841, in *JSP*-D8:65; Jason Lindquist, "'Unlocking the Door of the Gospel': The Concept of 'Keys' in Mormonism and Early American Culture," in *Archive of Restoration Culture: Summer Fellows' Papers, 1997–1999* (Provo, UT: Joseph Fielding Smith Institute for Latter-day Saint History, 2000), 31–32.

24. Devery S. Anderson and Gary James Bergera, eds., *Joseph Smith's Quorum of the Anointed, 1842–1845: A Documentary History* (Salt Lake City: Signature Books, 2005), 1–49; Christopher James Blythe, "The Upper-Room Work: Esotericism in the Church of Jesus Christ (Cutlerite), 1853–1912," *Journal of Mormon History* 40, no. 3 (Summer 2014): 46–54; Fiona Givens, "'The Perfect Union of Man and Woman': Reclamation and Collaboration in Joseph Smith's Theology Making," *Dialogue: A Journal of Mormon Thought* 49, no. 1 (Spring 2016): 1–26.

25. Heber C. Kimball to Parley and Mary Ann Pratt, 17 June 1842, Parley P. Pratt Correspondence, 1842–1855, Church History Library, The Church of Jesus Christ of Latter-day Saints, Salt Lake City (hereafter Church History Library); see also Flake, "'Not to Be Riten,'" 1–2; Stanley B. Kimball, *Heber C. Kimball: Mormon Patriarch and Pioneer* (Urbana and Chicago: University of Illinois Press, 1981), 83–86.

extant corpus. Beyond these, other relevant sources in the historical record usually mention "Adamic" language in general without presenting examples.[26] The following sections examine the sources that most thoroughly manifest Smith's developing concept of an undefiled language or that identify words or characters as specifically pure, Adamic, Edenic, or divine.

Original and Confounded Languages in the Book of Mormon, 1829

Joseph Smith's first revelations directed him in the "knowledge concerning the engraveings of old Records which are ancient" and though his neighbors could not name the messenger bearing golden plates, they recognized Smith had purported to translate a record.[27] The resulting narrative wrestled with the shortcomings of corrupted languages.[28] In the book's opening pages, the young prophet Nephi risks his life to retrieve a record written on brass plates to "preserve unto our children the language of our fathers."[29] His family's journey from the Old World to the New World attested to more than a didactic concern on Nephi's part: without resisting a natural change to their language in a new land, their language would devolve and their people would lose knowledge of God as a result. Followers of Mulek, the narrative continued, departed Jerusalem for the Americas around the same time as Nephi's family, but brought no records. They therefore lost their original language, and with it, knowledge of God. Samuel Brown has emphasized how the Book of Mormon on the whole contends against such linguistic disaster: "The concluding author Moroni compiled but did not need to translate the writings of the first author Nephi, despite ten centuries separating them, because the prophets taught the people in 'all the language of [their] fathers.' [The] emphasis on the intrinsic importance of comprehensible, unadulterated language is striking."[30]

26. Brigham Young remembered a meeting in 1832 in which he offered a prayer in tongues that Smith identified as "pure Adamic language," but neither Young nor Smith expounded on what Young had said in his prayer. J. Spencer Fluhman, "The Joseph Smith Revelations and the Crisis of Early American Spirituality," in *The Doctrine and Covenants: Revelations in Context*, ed. Andrew H. Hedges, J. Spencer Fluhman, and Alonzo A. Gaskill (Provo, UT: Religious Studies Center, Brigham Young University, 2008), 86n23. See also Joseph Smith, Blessing to Joseph Smith Sr. and Lucy Mack Smith, between circa 15 and 28 September 1835, in *JSP*-D4:488.

27. Joseph Smith, Revelation, April 1829-B, *JSP*-D1:44–47 [D&C 8]; *The Wayne Sentinel*, 26 June 1829, 3.

28. See Brown, "Joseph (Smith) in Egypt," 32–34, for a careful review of Book of Mormon discussions of language. Key passages in the Book of Mormon treating "weakness in writing" and the confounding of languages include 2 Nephi 33:1, 11; Omni 1:17; Mosiah 1:2–4; 3 Nephi 5:18; Ether 1:33–37, and 12:23–40.

29. Printer's Manuscript of the Book of Mormon, circa August 1829–circa January 1830, in *JSP*-R3, part 1:29 [1 Nephi 3:19].

30. Brown, "Joseph (Smith) in Egypt," 34.

According to the Book of Mormon, its writers had engraved characters on the plates in a combination of Egyptian and Hebrew, using characters in "reformed Egyptian" to express Hebrew language.[31] This linguistic premise departed from the educational norm of Smith's time. Universities broadly required training in the classical languages of Greek and Latin, and cosmopolitan literature on ancient history often favored a Hellenistic over Hebraic concentration. Notwithstanding his apparent study of Bible commentaries and their presentation of Greek translations, Smith showed little interest in Greek, and conscientiously drew a shared Hebrew language, culture, and history between the Bible and Book of Mormon.[32] Hebrew and Egyptian conveyed sacred history, and Smith sought not just ancient wisdom, but spiritual enlightenment. He could value the expertise of a classically trained philologist like Charles Anthon, and even seek out such expertise to lend validity to his own translation abilities, but ultimately the "sealed" and effectively encrypted nature of the reformed Egyptian on the plates—which an exasperated Anthon dismissed—solidified the sacredness of Smith's methods for both himself and his followers.[33]

Sacred history allowed Smith to peer past known languages and speculate on even more ancient systems than Hebrew and Egyptian. The Book of Mormon also hinted at a pristine language before the time of Babel. The history of the Nephites included a nested history of an earlier people, the Jaredites, who spoke an older language than the Lehite clan's Hebrew.[34] According to Nephite chroniclers, the record of the Jaredites was engraved on twenty-four metal plates and was discovered among ruins.[35] The Nephite king Mosiah, possessed of "a gift from God, whereby he could interpret such engravings," translated the twenty-four plates and found that they contained "an account of the people who were destroyed, from the time that they were destroyed back to the building of the great tower, at the time the Lord confounded the language of the people."[36] The Jaredite language evinced in names and a few words, such as

31. Mormon 9:32–33.

32. Bushman, "Joseph Smith's Place in the Study of Antiquity in Antebellum America," 4–9; Seth Perry, "The Many Bibles of Joseph Smith: Textual, Prophetic, and Scholarly Authority in Early-National Bible Culture," *Journal of the American Academy of Religion* 84, no. 3 (September 2016): 750–75; Thomas A. Wayment and Haley Wilson-Lemmon, "A Recovered Resource: The Use of Adam Clarke's Bible Commentary in Joseph Smith's Bible Translation," Chapter 11 herein.

33. Bushman, "Joseph Smith's Place in the Study of Antiquity in Antebellum America," 4–5, 8; Introduction to Copies of Book of Mormon Characters, in *JSP*-D1:355–57. See also Michael Hubbard MacKay, "Performing the Translation: Character Transcripts and Joseph Smith's Earliest Translating Practices," Chapter 4 herein.

34. The Book of Mormon denominates this group of people "Jaredites" in Moroni 9:23.

35. Mosiah 8:8–9.

36. Mosiah 21:25–28, 28:17; compare Omni 1:22.

"deseret," gave the Book of Mormon specimens of an unconfounded language. Nephite writers, however, never equated the Jaredite language with the pure language of God.[37]

Old Testament Revisions, 1830

Within a few months of publishing the Book of Mormon, Joseph Smith and Oliver Cowdery applied their esoteric translation method to the Bible and composed revelatory revisions throughout the year. The new biblical accounts presented further allusions to a pre-Babel language. Details remained inchoate; only sounds and no appearance of letterforms or pictographs appear in a couple of references to a primordial language existing in Adam's time.[38] Throughout the second half of 1830, Smith expanded the Genesis text, producing previously unattested visions of Moses and a new account of the antediluvian prophet Enoch. Where Genesis 5 refers to a "record of the generations of Adam," Smith expounded: "A book of rememberance was kept in the which was recorded in the Language of Adam for it was given unto as many as called upon God to write with the finger of inspiration & by them their children were taught to read & write having a languag[e] which was pure & undefiled."[39]

The Bible presented the cue, some kind of Adamic genealogy, and Smith shifted the context, recasting a mundane Genesis 5 as itself a translation of the first "book of rememberance," written in what was originally pure language. "Adam spake as he was mooved upon," Smith added, and "a genealogy was kept . . . & this was the Book of the generations of Adam Saying . . ." (followed by the contents of Genesis 5 with some minor expansions and slight emendations). The text that follows in Smith's revision of Genesis offers no clear syntactical end to the translated Adamic book of remembrance. An "amen" appears where Smith likely left off a revision session on 30 November 1830, but this is followed immediately with further recording of the Adamic generations (particularly mentioning Cainan and Mahalaleel). The "amen" here may have functioned as a signal Smith commonly gave when dictating his other revelations, the word notifying the scribe that the revelation had closed.[40] If Smith

37. Ether 1:33–37.

38. Old Testament Revision 1, 11, 13, in *Joseph Smith's New Translation of the Bible*, 97, 100 [Moses 6:5–6, 46–47].

39. Old Testament Revision 1, 11, in *Joseph Smith's New Translation of the Bible*, 97 [Moses 6:5–6].

40. William E. McLellin, "Revelations," *The Ensign of Liberty*, August 1849, 98–99. Compare uses of the terminal "Amen" in the earliest manuscript versions of revelations as listed in "Correlation of Current

had conceived of the Book of Remembrance as strictly a genealogy, then the translation may have ended with the last of the genealogical sequence—where the revision manuscript gives "this is the genealogy of the Sons of God which was the sons of Adam with whom God himself conversed."[41] However, the narrative continues directly in describing the ministry of Enoch, with some scattered genealogical details thereafter.[42] Enough contextual information exists to posit that the Bible revision harked back to an Adamic urtext and presented a translation in some form. Still, the revision left out linguistic traces of the pure language, portraying no morphology, pictograph, or grammar.[43]

The ensuing account, a rich elaboration on the mysterious Enoch, augments pure language beyond a hypothetical primordial tongue. The revision associated pure language with a divine writing system, "given by the finger of God," and capable of capturing words powerful enough when uttered to shake people to the ground. Again, the revision supposes an Edenic-Adamic urtext, as the pattern "given by the finger of God . . . is given in our own language," Enoch declares, which the narrative follows with a "speech" given by Enoch. Editorial parentheses turn up throughout Enoch's preaching, most importantly in a brief aside on the name of God: "For no unclean thing can dwell there or dwell in his presence for in the language of Adam man of holyness is his name & the name of his only begotten is the Son of man even Jesus Christ."[44] In context, the scenario of Enoch explaining the meaning of words in pure language while speaking the same seems less likely than either the redactions of the Genesis narrator Smith was translating or Smith himself inserting a short exposition on word meanings. In any case, Smith's earliest definitions of pure words emerge in the account of Enoch.

Doctrine and Covenants with Earliest Sources on the Joseph Smith Papers Website" (accessible in the online edition of *The Joseph Smith Papers*).

41. Old Testament Revision 1, 12, in *Joseph Smith's New Translation of the Bible*, 98 [Moses 6:22].

42. Ibid., 98–113 [Moses 6:23–8:30].

43. In 1834, Joseph Smith and Oliver Cowdery associated genealogical knowledge with the keys of the kingdom. Cowdery reported that Smith ordered the councils of the priesthood according to a pattern Smith had learned in a vision. "The apostle, Peter, was the president of the council in ancient days and held the Keys of the Kingdom of God, <on the earth>," Smith taught. Cowdery later associated the keys of the kingdom with Smith's 1834 vision: the "governing principles of the prophets" flowed from the "keys of the mysteries [of] heaven"—principles and rules of government so dense that knowing such might as well have required "search[ing] the archives of the generations of the world." Minutes, 12 February 1834, in *JSP*-D3:427–31; Minutes, 17 February 1834, in *JSP*-D3:435–39; Minutes, 19 February 1834, in *JSP*-D3:444–48; Oliver Cowdery to W. W. Phelps, undated, published as "Letter IV," *Latter Day Saints' Messenger and Advocate*, February 1835, 78–79; History, 1834–1836, 5 December 1834, in *JSP*-H1:17–19.

44. Old Testament Revision 1, 13–14, in *Joseph Smith's New Translation of the Bible*, 100–102 [Moses 6:57].

Especially important for Smith's later samples of pure language, the account provides definitions, but not word forms, and the definitions correspond with the first words listed in the samples. The samples begin with questions about the name of God and the name of the Son of God in the pure language and proffer not only word forms for each, but also transliterations and original symbols. Smith continued his Bible revisions into 1832, at one point skipping the bulk of the Old Testament to start revising the New Testament. His forays into pure language were again spurred by Bible passages, though exactly which ones remains conjectural.

Sample of Pure Language, 1832

Sometime after April 1832, church clerk John Whitmer copied a "Sample of pure Language" into the book used for compiling Smith's revelations. Whitmer wrote in a headnote that the document came from "Joseph the Seer" and that it had been copied by "Br Johnson"—probably John Johnson Sr. (with whom Smith lived at the time).[45] A series of questions and answers followed, giving no additional detail about the circumstances surrounding the text's production.[46] A loose leaf in the handwriting of Frederick G. Williams, another scribe, contains another version of the text (as transcribed below), but with no contextual detail or account of provenance.[47]

First Question What is the name of God as taught in the pure Language[?]

Answer—	A-man—
2^d. Q.s. "	What is the meaning of the word—A-man[?]
Answer—	it is the being who made all things in his parts
3^d Q. "	What is the name of the son of God[?]
Answer	son- Aman
4 Q "	What does the son Aman—mean[?]
Ans—"	it means the greatest of all the parts of Aman——which is the Godhead—the first born
5th Q—	Men[?]

45. Joseph Smith was living in the home of John and Alice (Elsa) Johnson in March 1832 when this revelation was most likely received. See *JSP*-D2:214.

46. Sample of Pure Language, between circa 4 and circa 20 March 1832, in *JSP*-D2:213–15.

47. Questions and Answers, circa 1832, handwriting of Frederick G. Williams, in "Historical Memoranda, Minutes, and Journal Entries," Thomas Bullock Collection 1830–1939, Church History Library.

Ans	this word signifies sons Aman; the human family—the children of men—the greatest parts of A man save the son A-man
6 Q "	What are angels called in the pure Language[?]
Ans. "	A man—Anglo-men
7 Q "	~~the~~ What are the meaning of these words[?]
Ans "	Aman~~s~~ ministring servants sanctified who are sent from heaven to minester ~~to~~ for or to sons Aman the greatest parts of A man save sons Aman son~~s~~- Aman Aman

The Williams version spells words of the pure language differently, appearing closer to a dictation transcript than a fair copy. For instance, the name of God "as taught in the pure language" is spelled "A-man" and "Aman," whereas in the Whitmer version it is spelled "Awmen." For Williams to have copied from either Whitmer as a source or Whitmer's source, he would have had to subtract a letter and replace another letter to arrive at "A-man."

The versions of the Sample of Pure Language demonstrate composite word forms, with some parts of the words seemingly derived from English and the other parts ostensibly from pure language. The name of the Son of God, as both Whitmer and Williams have it, is "son A[h]man," and the angels are called "Anglo[-]men." That Williams employed the hyphen, unlike Whitmer and other sources, suggests he may have consciously noted the syntactical separation of English and pure language derivatives.[48]

Orson Pratt remarked in 1855 that earlier Latter-day Saints had not known of an unpublished revelation giving the name of God in pure language. His description followed the sample words of pure language, mentioning the names "Ahman," "Son Ahman," "Sons Ahman," and "Anglo-man."[49] A notebook kept by Pratt in 1835 and 1836 contains yet another version of the Sample of Pure Language.[50] Pratt's sample closely resembles Whitmer's 1832 text, preserving "Awman" where a couple of insertions in Whitmer's sample replace "Awmen" with "Awman." Pratt very likely produced his copy from Whitmer or from Whitmer's source.

48. Ibid.; compare with Sample of Pure Language, D2:215.

49. Orson Pratt, Discourse, 18 February 1855, in *Journal of Discourses*, 26 vols. (Liverpool and London: LDS Booksellers Depot, 1854–1886), 2:342–43.

50. This source was located by Brent Metcalfe, see Brent Metcalfe, "Newly Discovered Copies of JS's Adamic Q&A," http://www.mormonstudiespodcast.org/newly-discovered-copies-of-jss-adamic-qa (archived at: https://perma.cc/MJ2Q-BPE5); Orson Pratt, Notebook, 1835–1836, Church History Library.

However they ultimately relate to each other, the versions of the Sample of Pure Language correspond enough to give evidence of Smith exploring pure language questions in 1832, probably during his Bible revision sessions. In the revelation book he was keeping, Whitmer's version of the sample immediately follows another set of questions and answers, a text he titled "Revelation Explained," in reference to the book of Revelation in the New Testament.[51] These questions align with the timeline of the Bible revision, leading some scholars to infer that Smith's inquiries into pure language arose as a result of his work on the Apocalypse.[52] The first question listed in the Sample of Pure Language asks, "What is the name of God in pure Language[?]" Several passages in Revelation refer to God's name, any of which may have prompted the question. Or, Smith may have wondered at the reference to the pure names of God and the Son of God in the account of Enoch.[53]

The catechistic format to both Whitmer's sample of pure language and the text immediately preceding it in Whitmer's revelation book offers another possibility not only for what may have prompted Smith's inquiry into pure language, but also for the mechanics of how Smith divined the pure name of God. Catechisms presented a series of questions and answers arranged in a progression from basic to advanced concepts, and had gained popularity in the colonial period among clergy searching for improved preaching methods.[54] American Protestants in the 1820s and 1830s recognized that published catechisms enabled Sabbath Schools and missionaries to instruct children and foreign proselytes in the Bible and the English language.[55] The strategy aimed to render arcane biblical passages intelligible, deliver the word of God to illiterate students, help them commit the word to memory, and lead them to a complete understanding of scripture.[56] Missionaries especially wanted to

51. Revelation Book 1, in *JSP*-R1:258–59. This was Answers to Questions, between circa 4 March and circa 20 March 1832, in *JSP*-D2:208–13 [D&C 77].

52. See Historical Introduction to Sample of Pure Language, between circa 4 March and circa 20 March 1832, in *JSP*-D2:214.

53. Joseph Smith's New Testament revision manuscript covering the book of Revelation contains changes to Revelation 3:12, "and ~~I will write upon him~~ <this is> my new name." Other references in Revelation to God's name or a God-given new name were left unrevised (2:17, 14:1, 19:12).

54. Kenneth L. Alford, "A History of Mormon Catechisms," in *A Firm Foundation: Church Organization and Administration*, ed. David J. Whittaker and Arnold K. Garr (Provo, UT: Religious Studies Center, Brigham Young University, 2011), 224–28.

55. Use of catechisms in Sabbath Schools and missions is widely attested in American missionary reports and periodicals of the 1830s. See "Missionary Periodicals of the Antebellum United States," Open Source History, https://opensourcehistory.github.io/missionary-periodicals (archived at: https://doi.org/10.5281/zenodo.2575068).

56. See James Hastie, "Madagascar," *Religious Intelligencer*, 1 July 1826, 68; "Thirtieth Report of the Religious Tract Society," *The Missionary Herald*, February 1830, 54–55; "Bombay: Review of a Year,"

reach those who had not heard of God or Christ before with catechisms, often when their presses had yet to translate the Bible into the local language. The contest against "pagan darkness" and "heathen ignorance" of God persuaded several prominent missionaries that catechistic pedagogy outclassed all other preaching methods. Catechism made sense to missionary editors as an apparatus of published Bibles.[57]

Curiously, Smith's own catechistically formatted texts surface in his Bible revision and scripture publication efforts. If Smith shared the pedagogical concern with his evangelist contemporaries, then preparing his "new translation" of the Bible, his revelations, and his lectures on theology for publication as *scriptural* texts and resources could have easily prompted an interest in a first-principle question on which to build a progression of questions and answers. The domain of the fundamental coincided with prime knowledge, the end and the beginning of esoteric solutions to abstruse knowledge.

Independently of format, the content at hand fell within classic esoterica. The antediluvian setting of Genesis combined with the apocryphal books of Enoch, the use of Enoch as an exemplar of faith in Hebrews 11:5, the enigmatic reference to Enoch in Jude 1:14, the cryptic book of Revelation, and secret names known only by revelation fascinated esoteric commentators. Few mysteries sparked esoteric interest as much as the real name of God.[58] Smith interpreted scripture with an esoteric apparatus. Between his revision sessions of 1 and 8 December 1830—sessions ending and beginning respectively with discussions of pure language—Smith dictated a revelation describing the Bible translation for a new acquaintance, Sidney Rigdon, given in the voice of God and with words dripping with esoteric import: "I have sent forth the fullness of [my] Gospel by the hand of my servent Joseph . . . & I have given unto him the Keys of the mystery of those things which have been sealed even things which was from the foundation of the world." The revelation told Rigdon to scribe for Smith, promising "the scriptures shall be given even as they are in mine

The Missionary Herald, December 1830, 378–80; Thomas Simons, "Mr. Simons's Journal of His Return from Kyouk Phyoo to Maulmein," *The Baptist Missionary Magazine*, October 1836, 243–44; and Carla Gardina Pestana, *Protestant Empire: Religion and the Making of the British Atlantic World* (Philadelphia: University of Pennsylvania Press, 2009), 61.

57. See "Sunday School Catechism," *Religious Intelligencer*, 27 June 1818, 64; Pliny Fisk, "Palestine Mission: Extracts from Mr. Fisk's Communications," *Religious Intelligencer*, 17 May 1823, 802; and "Bombay," 378–80.

58. Haim Hillel Ben-Sasson, "'The Name of God and the Linguistic Theory of the Kabbalah' Revisited," *Journal of Religion* 98, no. 1 (January 2018): 1–28; Guy G. Stroumsa, *The Scriptural Universe of Ancient Christianity* (Cambridge, MA: Harvard University Press, 2016), 115–20; Robert J. Wilkinson, *Tetragrammaton: Western Christians and the Hebrew Name of God from the Beginnings to the Seventeenth Century* (Leiden: Brill, 2016), esp. 483.

own bosom." By "the keys which [would be] given" would a latter-day Zion and Israel "be led & no more be confounded at all."[59] Ancient wisdom sealed up as mysteries waited to be unlocked through inspired, seer-like translation. The Sample of Pure Language, arranged as questions and answers with foreign sounds, offered compelling tokens of the reality outside of human reach.

"Adam-ondi-Ahman" Toponym, 1835

Joseph Smith reached peak activity in pure language study in 1835. Between March and August, he revealed his most well-known pure name, "Adam-ondi-Ahman"; cast code names in a pure veneer; presumably supplied a specimen of pure language characters to William W. Phelps; and developed an Egyptian alphabet, grammar, and translation carrying further specimens of potentially pure content. Two forces sparked this burst of interest: the revelation of the name "Adam-ondi-Ahman" and the arrival in Kirtland of Phelps, Smith's closest compatriot in language study.

Exactly how William W. Phelps influenced and may have written pure language material remains blurry and only circumstantially supported by the historical record. Joining Smith's church in 1831, Phelps lent his talents in editing and publishing materials for the church in Missouri, corresponding with Smith over the printing of revelations, and occasionally discussing a favorite topic—languages. Phelps admitted he had no formal training in linguistics, but prided himself a polyglot. After a mob ransacked the church press in Missouri, Phelps relocated to Kirtland in May 1835 and quickly gained Smith's trust in joining esoteric projects.[60] Smith wrote to Phelps's wife Sally that her husband would teach "hid[d]en things of old times" and "treasures hid in the sand."[61] Immediately upon purchasing Egyptian mummies and papyri from a touring exhibitor in July, Smith employed Phelps to assist him in translating their contents. Phelps came prepared for the job, having written the year before how ancient Egyptians had concealed "their arts in mystical characters or hieroglyphics."[62] Later, in 1843, Smith enlisted Phelps to counter public criticisms of the Book of Mormon translation. Phelps ghostwrote for Smith in describing an etymology

59. Revelation, 7 December 1830, in *JSP*-D1:219–23 [D&C 35].

60. Samuel Brown, "The Translator and the Ghostwriter: Joseph Smith and W. W. Phelps," *Journal of Mormon History* 34, no. 1 (Winter 2008): 31–35.

61. Letter to Sally Waterman Phelps, 20 July 1835, in *JSP*-D4:368–71.

62. Editor of the Star [Oliver Cowdery], "Reflections for the Fourth of July, 1834," *Evening and the Morning Star*, July 1834, 173.

of the word "Mormon." In this and other responses, Phelps attempted a rarefied rhetoric, exhibiting linguistic prowess in a wide mix of languages that ranged from Egyptian, Hebrew, Greek, and Latin; through European standards like German and French; to the impressively exotic Chaldean, Samaritan, and Lenape. Regardless of his overt excesses, Phelps shared Smith's vision for overcoming the confounding of languages and for comprehending, if possible, a fullness of language. His touch on Smith's Egyptian alphabet and grammar seems to scholars rather undeniable.[63]

Shortly before Phelps arrived in Kirtland, Smith instructed the Quorum of the Twelve Apostles on priesthood and church organization to prepare the group for regulating smaller congregations in the eastern United States. In the instruction, Smith described "Adam-ondi-Ahman," a valley where Adam gathered "the residue of his posterity" to bestow a final blessing. The name made a clear reference to the 1832 sample of pure language with "Ahman," but the instruction merely mentioned the name as part of a toponym and without delving into language themes. The earliest text for the instruction on priesthood appears as Section 3 in Part 2 of the first edition of the Doctrine and Covenants, and by its publication in 1835, Smith had merged it with previous revelations, associating it with a revelatory production. Brigham Young recalled that Smith spent two hours composing a "Revelation on Priesthood"—likely the 1835 instruction.[64] Sources challenge a tight dating of the instruction, however, leaving open the possibility that the instruction underwent revision between its initial delivery to the apostles and its publication in the Doctrine and Covenants. Regardless of the likelihood of revision, the proximity of this source to Phelps's arrival in May, the last preparations for the Doctrine and Covenants in April and May, Phelps's publication of his poem "Adam-ondi-Ahman" in June, and the exhibiting and purchase of Egyptian artifacts in July point to the instruction on priesthood as a key catalyst for renewed interest in pure language.[65]

But what triggered the sudden use of "Adam-ondi-Ahman" in the instruction on priesthood? Smith may have divined "Adam-ondi-Ahman" while in

63. See Brown, "The Translator and the Ghostwriter," 41–46, 61–62; Historical Introduction to Grammar and Alphabet of the Egyptian Language, circa July–circa November 1835, in *JSP*-R4:112–13.

64. Historical Introduction to Instruction on Priesthood, between circa 1 March and circa 4 May 1835, in *JSP*-D4:308–9 [D&C 107].

65. W. W. Phelps, "Adam-ondi-Ahman," *Latter Day Saints' Messenger and Advocate*, June 1835, 144. The final preparations on the text for the first edition of the Doctrine and Covenants—in which Joseph Smith introduced major emendations to several revelations and also added lectures on theology given in meetings of the Kirtland School of the Elders—likely occurred in April and/or May because of the production timeline evident in church periodical announcements about the book. See Historical Introduction to Doctrine and Covenants, 1835, in *JSP*-R2:304–7.

in his prophetic role, composing the instruction as a revelation; he may have arrived at the name while formulating a catechistic progression of priesthood doctrines based on the lineage of the ancient patriarchs in Genesis or the Book of Remembrance (or both); or he may have been influenced by Phelps while they were working out the final revisions for the text of the Doctrine and Covenants. Owing to a lack of direct information in primary sources, each of these scenarios relies on circumstantial evidence for plausibility. Perhaps true to style, it appears that Adam-ondi-Ahman—however it came to Smith—ignited the pure language content that followed, which holds significance for Smith's methodology. The difference between a creative collaboration with Phelps, a direct revelation, a pedagogical approach to sacred history, or a combination of methods depends on the activities surrounding the emergence of the place-name "Adam-ondi-Ahman."

The simplest scenario is a direct revelation of the instruction on priesthood, with Adam-ondi-Ahman emerging in the same way as other revelations composed in Smith's direct style. This requires placing Smith in the context of integrating his prior November 1831 revelation on "Church business" with charging the Twelve Apostles to regulate the eastern branches of the church.[66] The setting of apostles gathering as early as March 1835 for their charge would suggest that Smith recognized priesthood as a feature of ordering loose congregations, and expected priesthood organization to involve a restoration of ancient covenants and orders (as in the first priesthood conferences in Kirtland).[67] In this reconstruction, Adam-ondi-Ahman would connote a linking of last days and the Ancient of Days via priesthood order, a concern Smith announced at the outset when declaring that the original name of priesthood included the "Order of the Son of God."[68] Apostles needed to view their work as validating the church order by aligning theirs with that of the patriarchs. It is conceivable that the new toponym "Adam-ondi-Ahman," which tied priesthood lineage to Adam and the true God (Ahman), could engender sufficient interest to spark Smith's and Phelps's creative energies.

For Phelps to have inspired or influenced the rendition of Adam-ondi-Ahman would seem to require his arrival before Smith's instruction to the Twelve. Barring the discovery of a new source showing Phelps conveying the term "Adam-ondi-Ahman" from Missouri, this scenario would also require

66. Revelation, 11 November 1831-B, in *JSP*, D2:132–36 [D&C 107 (partial)].

67. Mark Lyman Staker, *Hearken, O Ye People: The Historical Setting of Joseph Smith's Ohio Revelations* (Salt Lake City: Greg Kofford Books, 2009), 147–74.

68. Instruction on Priesthood, between circa 1 March and circa 4 May 1835, in *JSP*-D4:312 [D&C 107:3].

Smith to have prepared the original instruction in or after May. Since the apostles departed on 4 May and Phelps arrived in Kirtland on 16 May, Phelps could not have been present for the instruction, but could have learned about it sometime after its composition and before its publication.[69] Phelps could only have collaborated on the name "Adam-ondi-Ahman" if Smith had introduced the name in between giving the original instruction and preparing the instruction for publication in the Doctrine and Covenants. Given Phelps's involvement in printing the Doctrine and Covenants in May and June, this scenario is plausible.

That the instruction on priesthood shares strong structural similarities with the second of the lectures on theology lends support to another scenario. Within weeks of each other in early 1835, Smith prepared the lectures for publication and held meetings with the Twelve.[70] While the original lectures were delivered in sessions of the School of the Elders between 25 November and 1 December 1834, additional sections—catechisms designed to make the lectures accessible to the whole church—were likely composed in January 1835.[71] Several studies have called into question Smith's authorship of the lectures, which may have been largely the work of Sidney Rigdon,[72] but the second lecture stands out as the strongest candidate of the group for being Smith's. It is this lecture that takes the theme of faith, relates faith to knowledge, and argues for an accurate knowledge of God predicated on being able to trace an intellectual genealogy through the patriarchs back to God.[73] The lecture waxes tedious in explaining the lifespans and relations of the patriarchs, taking the patriarchal lineage in Genesis and the Book of Remembrance to a minute extreme. Catechizing this dense outline of patriarchal lineage served readers with an intelligible sequence of the abstract argument. In the instruction on priesthood, the same logic and abstraction of patriarchal lineage informs the doctrine of priesthood order, and instead of arranging the patriarchs by age, the instruction builds a sequence of ordination. Within this sequence, in the culminating moment of finally reaching the first patriarch, Adam, the

69. Historical Department Journal History of the Church, 16 May 1835, Church History Library.

70. Historical Introduction to First Theological Lecture on Faith, circa January–May 1835, in *JSP*-D4:457–60.

71. Editorial, *Latter Day Saints' Messenger and Advocate*, May 1835, 122; Historical Introduction to First Theological Lecture on Faith, circa January–May 1835, in *JSP*-D4:459.

72. Historical Introduction to First Theological Lecture on Faith, circa January–May 1835, in *JSP*-D4:458–59.

73. Larry E. Dahl, "Authorship and History of the Lectures on Faith," in *The Lectures on Faith in Historical Perspective*, ed. Larry E. Dahl and Charles D. Tate Jr. (Provo, UT: Religious Studies Center, Brigham Young University, 1990), 8.

genealogy stops, and Adam is placed in Adam-ondi-Ahman, there to bless his righteous posterity.[74]

Preparing this new work of scripture for publication, which included the lectures ("Doctrine") and revelations ("Covenants"), could have elicited a pedagogical concern, not unlike the pedagogical concern Smith exhibited in training the Twelve Apostles in their duties.[75] The use of catechistic formats suggests a pedagogical context as well, which corresponds with the circa March 1832 sample of pure language. In breaking down lofty concepts such as priesthood, faith, knowledge, and primordial language, Smith may have proceeded from a design, still reliant on a revelatory query, but nevertheless answering instructional objectives. The impetus for pure language, in the sense of Smith's translation mechanics, probably arose from scriptural hermeneutics, not (as in the case of the golden plates) from an artifact inviting the translation gifts of a seer.

Code Names, 1835

After the instruction on priesthood and as part of Smith's emendations to the 1835 Doctrine and Covenants, he and fellow committee members replaced names in five revelations with pseudonyms. These code names were intended to obscure the identities of the members of a joint business enterprise among church leaders, the United Firm, against litigation or public knowledge of the firm's debts. The publication committee had debated previously whether to publish these five revelations at all. The pseudonyms satisfied their concerns, but an unintended consequence emerged in later editions, as the code names persisted and later church members took the names as belonging to the original texts of the revelations.[76]

At first glance, the code names resemble biblical names and sounds, and Phelps later associated a Hebrew origin for them.[77] However, Phelps's meanings betray a novice knowledge of Hebrew and nearly all the names match or strongly share phonemes with the anglicized Hebrew names of the King James Version of the Bible. Despite reports from Orson Pratt and Phelps, no principal

74. Lecture Second, in *JSP*-R2:322–45.

75. Historical Introduction to Doctrine and Covenants, 1835, in *JSP*-R2:304–7.

76. Christopher C. Smith, "The Inspired Fictionalization of the 1835 United Firm Revelations," *Claremont Journal of Mormon Studies* 1, no. 1 (April 2011): 15–31.

77. William W. Phelps to Brigham Young, 12 October 1863, Brigham Young Office Files, General Correspondence, Incoming, 1840–1877, Letters from Church Leaders and Others, 1840–1877, W. W. Phelps, 1860–1866, Church History Library.

observer mentioned pure language when explaining the pseudonyms. Christopher Smith has postulated that "Olihah," "Zombre," "Gazelam," and "Shule" bore enough similarity to other pure language specimens that the substituting of code names in the United Firm revelations amounted to an "inspired fictionalization," or another rendering of pure language.[78] "Olihah" did not likely correspond to "olach" in the specimen of pure language (produced around the same time as the United Firm pseudonyms). But a later 1838 revelation referenced the "mountains of Adam Ondi Awmen" and the "plains of Olaha Shinehah" as together "the land where Adam dwelt." This lent a retrojected connection of "Olihah" to one of two toponyms associated with the Adamic era, the other (Adam-ondi-Ahman) already solidly asserted as a pure name.[79] As Christopher Smith has observed, "Gazelam" maps onto "Gazelem" in Alma 37:23 and "Shule" maps onto "Shule" in Ether 1:30, both names that the Book of Mormon placed in the pre-Babel context of Jaredite language. "Zombre" bears some resemblance to the pure language word "Zomar," which Smith developed in his Egyptian Grammar, but *Zambres/Jambre* from the New Testament and apocryphal texts offer a stronger (and evidently esoteric) candidate match.[80]

In 2 Timothy 3:8, Paul identifies two who had contended against Moses: "Jannes and Jambres." Christian readers most commonly considered Jannes and Jambres the unnamed magicians in Exodus who replicated Moses's miracles in the court of Pharaoh, but Paul's reference did not expound on the two names. The mystery of the two magicians fascinated esoteric thinkers and frustrated some Protestant theologians. Classic esoteric sources made Jannes and Jambres into famous magicians who had acquired deeper occult knowledge and, in some accounts, assisted rather than withstood Moses.[81] Lore and commentaries transliterated "Jambres" into various forms, including "Zambres," which chaplain Thomas Godwyn used in his widely read *Moses and Aaron*. Godwyn's treatise intended to outline the civil organization and ecclesiastical rites of the ancient Hebrews, but attracted esoteric readers for its deep analysis of Hebrew lore.[82]

78. Smith, "The Inspired Fictionalization of the 1835 United Firm Revelations," 23.

79. Revelation, 8 July 1838-E, in Smith, Journal, in *JSP*-J1:289 [D&C 117:8].

80. Smith, "The Inspired Fictionalization of the 1835 United Firm Revelations," 23.

81. Adam Clarke, *The Holy Bible, Containing the Old and New Testaments* (London: Joseph Butterworth and Son, 1825), 1:348–47 [Exodus 7:25].

82. Thomas Godwyn, *Moses and Aaron: Civil and Ecclesiastical Rites, Used by the Ancient Hebrews* [. . .], 12th ed. (London: R. Scot et al., 1685); William Britten, *Art Magic; or, Mundane, Sub-Mundane and Super-Mundane Spiritism* (New York: William Britten, 1876), 277, 280. Godwyn (circa 1587–1642) was sometimes confused with an earlier Thomas Godwin (1517–1590) who was bishop of Bath and Wells, England, from 1584 to 1590.

The full tale of Jambres was alleged to be in the book of Jasher, an apocryphal text that captured Smith's curiosity for its status as a "lost book" of the Bible. An English translation of Jasher circulated in Europe and North America, but Smith apparently had not obtained a copy until 1840.[83] In a letter to church leaders in 1833, Smith mentioned how their combined search for the book of Jasher had turned up empty, and despite their excitement over what this lost book might contain, they maintained some caution owing to a revelation directing Smith not to translate apocryphal writings.[84] The original 1833 letter mentioned the names of some United Firm members. These included John Johnson, for whom the code name "Zombre" was applied. Later, when the letter was reprinted in the church newspaper as part of the serialized "History of Joseph Smith," the pseudonym "Zombre" was used—the most proximate between Jasher and Jambres/Zambres in Smith's corpus.[85] In any event, the frequency of Jambres/Zambres in the contemporaneous soundscape of mystical apocryphal names and mainstream biblical commentaries lends as much support to a pseudobiblical etymology for the code name "Zombre" as do alternatives (like *Zomar*). The code names as a whole thus lean toward a biblical phonetic, and presented no new pure language specimens except for possibly "Olihah."[86]

Specimen of Pure Language, 1835

Joseph Smith's next surviving reference to pure language indicates that he moved from a concept of undefiled language to the sounds of words and a writing system itself. A letter by William W. Phelps dated 26 May 1835 contains a "specimen of some of the 'pure language,'" a table listing six characters in rows with corresponding material in three adjoining columns.[87] This "specimen" is reproduced

83. Edward J. Brandt, "The Book of Jasher and the Latter-day Saints," chap. 15 in *Apocryphal Writings and the Latter-day Saints*, ed. C. Wilfred Griggs (Provo, UT: Religious Studies Center, Brigham Young University, 1986).

84. Letter to Church Leaders in Jackson County, Missouri, 25 June 1833, in *JSP*-D3:147–58. See also Gerrit Dirkmaat, "Lost Scripture and 'the Interpolations of Men': Joseph Smith's Revelation on the Apocrypha," Chapter 12 herein.

85. "History of Joseph Smith," *Times and Seasons*, 15 February 1845, 800.

86. "Zombre" and "Zambre" appear more frequently in eighteenth-century literature as the name of a lake or river in the deep interior of Africa that fed the Nile. Notwithstanding the esoteric import of the Zombre—its hidden location and its being the source of water for Egypt—this etymology unlikely influenced Smith's composition of code names. Henry Curson, *A New Description of the World: Delineating Europe-Africa and Asia-America*, 2nd ed. (London: Benjamin Barker, 1715), 338.

87. William W. Phelps to Sally Waterman Phelps, 26–27 May 1835, William Wines Phelps Papers, L. Tom Perry Special Collections, Harold B. Lee Library, Brigham Young University.

as a photographic facsimile in Figure 14.1 and as a typographical facsimile in Table 14.1. The words match those given in the Sample of Pure Language, but with alternate spellings and two exceptions: Phelps distinguishes between "saunsahman" and "Sons ahman," the one representing "sons of God" and the other "children of Men," and the characters for each having the same simple form of right angles turned at opposite directions. The specimen's characters iterate from a base symbol, the horizontal bar representing "olach"/"the Earth," and work upward with extensions playing on the previous motif. The "olach" bar extends into a right angle for "Sons ahman"; then flips upward for "saunsahman" and "anglo"; then progresses with an ornament on "sonahman," until finally terminating with a composite of the "anglo"/"angels," "saunsahman"/"sons of God," and "sonahman"/"Son of God," all blending into the symbol for "ahman"/"God."

Lacking any additional information, the specimen remains a puzzle. The characters receive no provenance from Phelps; the phonetic representations likewise appear without citation. Phelps lived in Missouri at the time Williams and Whitmer (re)produced their copies of the Sample of Pure Language.[88] Therefore, Phelps likely obtained words like "ahman," "sonahman," "Sons ahman," and "anglo" from Smith.

The "Egyptian Alphabet" text produced some months later by Smith (and Cowdery) lists the same character forms (morphemes), among many others (mainly from the papyri), but with different interpretations than in the Sample or Specimen. Phelps's symbol for "aine"/"anglo" is described in the alphabet by Smith as "Alchobeth ministers not ordained of God Sinful." The Phelps specimen shares little correspondence with the alphabet, making an Egyptian context less likely. Smith or Phelps seem to have participated in a kind of constructive linguistics rather than developing word forms out of any other languages, modern or ancient.

Egyptian Alphabet and Grammar, 1835

In early July 1835—within a few months of Phelps sharing the Specimen of Pure Language with his wife—Michael Chandler visited Kirtland, Ohio, with his travelling mummy show, and sold Egyptian mummies and papyri to Smith and others.[89] Smith's 1838–1856 history noted that soon after the purchase,

88. Brown, "The Translator and the Ghostwriter," 31–32.

89. Oliver Cowdery, "Egyptian Mummies—Ancient Records," *Latter Day Saints' Messenger and Advocate*, December 1835, 235; see also Smith, History, 1838–1856, vol. B-1, 596, 6 July 1835 (accessible in the Histories series of the online edition of *The Joseph Smith Papers*).

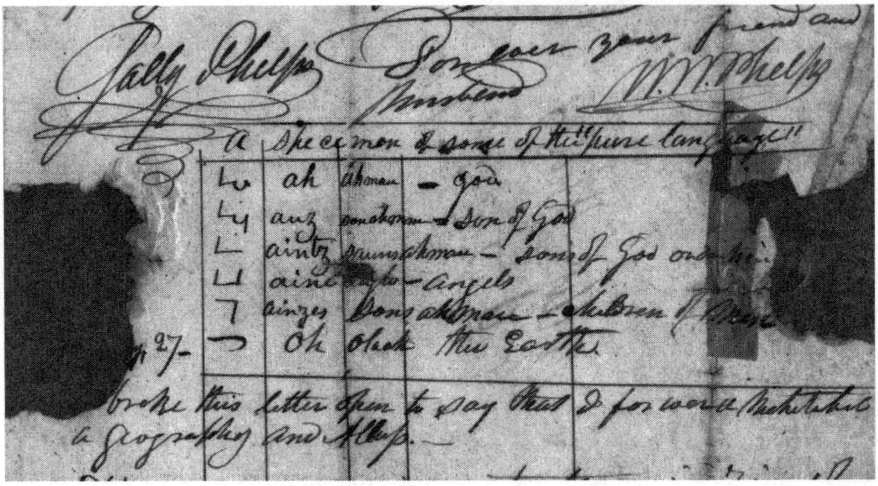

FIGURE 14.1. Specimen of Pure Language. Joseph Smith's close associate, William W. Phelps, appended this "Specimen of some of the 'pure language'" at the end of a letter to his wife, Sally Waterman Phelps, 26–27 May 1835. Joseph Smith, William Phelps, and other early Latter-day Saints believed that Adam and Eve and their posterity had spoken a pure language that was later confounded at the Tower of Babel. Smith and Phelps apparently hoped to acquire this language through revelation, linguistic reconstruction, or some combination thereof. William Wines Phelps Papers, L. Tom Perry Special Collections, Harold B. Lee Library, Brigham Young University, Provo, UT.

TABLE 14.1. Phelps, Specimen of Pure Language, 1835

	ah	ahman	—God
	auz	sonahman	—Son of God
	aintz	saunsahman	—sons of God [*illegible*]
	aine	anglo	—angels
	ainges	Sons ahman	—children of Men
	oh	olach	the Earth

A specimen of some of the "pure language"

Smith "commenced . . . the translation of some of the characters or hieroglyphics."[90] After 19 July he spent the remainder of the month "continually engaged in translating an alphabet [and] arrangeing a grammar of the Egyptian language."[91] Two handmade notebooks containing hieratic characters and three loose copies of other hieratic characters likely predate the alphabet and grammar documents to which the history refers, since the alphabet and grammar draw from the copies in some places.[92]

Beginning in July 1835, Smith worked with Cowdery and Phelps in building a lexicon of Egyptian characters. The first draft, the only manuscript of Smith's Egyptian project papers containing his own handwriting, lists dozens of hieratic characters in sections labeled as "parts" of the "first degree." Smith and Cowdery apparently copied characters before rendering translations, as the list of characters runs out of translations on the second of five pages and the majority of copied characters never received any corresponding definition or explanation. The other two versions of the Egyptian alphabet text, in the handwriting of Oliver Cowdery and William Phelps, are based on the first. Smith's alphabet manuscript also contains the most text of the three.[93]

Phelps's version of the Egyptian alphabet makes the tabular data explicit, lending each column a title.[94] Smith constructed his alphabet character by character, providing a "letter," a "sound," and an "explanation" for each. In only a couple of instances is a "letter" supplied, and Smith apparently worked out the sounds before writing a translation, as the column of character explanations did not get as far as the column of character sounds.[95]

In his "Grammar & A[l]phabet of the Egyptian Language," a bound volume based in part of the preceding Egyptian alphabet text, Smith employed Phelps and Warren Parrish, and anticipated a more elaborate system than what Smith and his scribes ultimately recorded: the grammar and alphabet book works from the "first degree" to the "fifth degree" but is inscribed in reverse order,

90. Joseph Smith, History, 1838–1856, vol. B-1, 596, 1 September 1834–2 November 1838.

91. Ibid., 597.

92. Ibid.; *JSP*-R4:3–4. Three loose pages of Egyptian characters in unknown handwriting comprise the remaining copy sheets. The papers were manufactured in the nineteenth century, ruling out an ancient author for the inscriptions. No translations appear on the copies, though in some instances the ink changes to red, perhaps preserving changes in the papyri. Smith had announced the papyri contained writings of the patriarchs Abraham and Joseph, and Cowdery once mentioned the writings in red being those of Joseph. H. Michael Marquardt, "Joseph Smith's Egyptian Papers: A History," in *The Joseph Smith Egyptian Papyri: A Complete Edition*, Robert K. Ritner, with contributions by Marc Coenen, H. Michael Marquardt, and Christopher Woods (Salt Lake City: Signature Books, 2013), 17.

93. Egyptian Alphabet Documents, circa early July–circa November 1835, in *JSP*-R4:53–93.

94. Egyptian Alphabet, circa early July–circa November 1835-C, in *JSP*-R4:85–93.

95. Egyptian Alphabet, circa early July–circa November 1835-A, in *JSP*-R4:55–71.

interspersing blank pages between blocks of text.[96] Smith may have derived portions of the Book of Abraham narrative from the grammar book and earlier versions of the alphabet text. For instance, the explanations associated with "Ah-broam" in the first through fifth degrees describe "The father of the faithful, the first right"; "A follower of [righteousness]"; "One who possesses great Knowledge"; "A follower of righteousness, a possessor of greater knowledge"; "The father of many nations, a prince of peace, one who keeps the commandments of God, a patriarch, a rightful heir, a high priest." The Book of Abraham opens with Abraham recounting how he had "been a follower of righteousness; desiring ~~one~~ <to be> one who possessed great Knowledge; a greater follower of righteousness; <a possessor of greater Knowledge;> a father of many nations; a prince of peace; one who keeps the commandments of God; a rightful heir; a high priest, holding the right belonging to the fathers." The passage in the earliest extant manuscript is keyed to an Egyptian character matching the character in the Egyptian alphabet with an explanation similar to the content of the passage.[97]

Sequentially, the primary sources by this point in 1835 only progressed as far as a basic lexicography with characters projected onto ancient Egypt and primordial Eden, and a translation agenda indicating a simple yet broad scheme. Smith's interest in translating the writings of Abraham pulled him from overtly Edenic-Adamic language study and drove him toward mastering actual Egyptian and Hebrew. Language study widened Smith's linguistic repertoire, and he soon incorporated grammatical conventions into his translations of Egyptian.

The Egyptian project stalled in August and September of 1835, but Smith, Cowdery, and Phelps resumed expanding the alphabet on 1 October, unfolding the "System of astronomy."[98] The following week, Smith translated Egyptian and made irregular progress for the next month.[99] In November, Cowdery returned from New York with books about Hebrew, including a Hebrew Bible,

96. Grammar and Alphabet of the Egyptian Language, circa July–circa November 1835, 1–2, in *JSP*-R4:111–90. Smith had hired Parrish as a scribe in October 1835, see Smith, Journal, 29 October 1835, in *JSP*-J1:76.

97. Book of Abraham Manuscript, circa July–circa November 1835-C, in *JSP*-R4:219 [Abraham 1:1–2:18]; Egyptian Alphabet, circa early July–circa November 1835-A, 5, in *JSP*-R4:70–71; Marquardt, "Joseph Smith's Egyptian Papers," 33–35; Christopher C. Smith, "The Dependence of Abraham 1:1–3 on the Egyptian Alphabet and Grammar," *John Whitmer Historical Association Journal* 29 (2009): 38–54. See also Brian M. Hauglid, "'Translating an Alphabet to the Book of Abraham': Joseph Smith's Study of the Egyptian Language and His Translation of the Book of Abraham," Chapter 15 herein.

98. Smith, Journal, 1 October 1835, in *JSP*-J1:67.

99. Smith, Journal, 7 October 1835, in *JSP*-J1:71; Hauglid, "'Translating an Alphabet to the Book of Abraham.'"

TABLE 14.2. Example of Character Degrees

No		
5		When this character has a horizontal line under it, it reduces it into the fourth degree, consequently it has but four connecting parts of speech.
6		When it has two horizontal lines, it is reduced into the third degree and has but three connecting parts of speech,
7		and when it has three horizontal lines, it is reduced into the second degree and has but two connecting parts of speech.

lexicon, and grammar.[100] The materials further stoked Smith's fascination with Hebrew, and he enlisted church leaders to solicit instruction from Jewish experts.[101] For several days throughout November and December, Smith studied his Hebrew grammar from which he likely derived new approaches to his Egyptian alphabet. The largest of the Egyptian papers, aside from his Book of Abraham, expands the title to include *grammar*, something readily available to Smith when Cowdery delivered the Hebrew grammar purchased in New York.

By "grammar," Smith meant morphology, the task of building from the simplest conceptual morphemes and transforming them into compound ideograms. The first line of the grammar introduces a character that functions "independent and arbitrary," but by "inserting a straight mark over it" the "signification" of the character increases, and by inserting a straight mark below it the signification decreases.[102] The presentation of this rule of grammar is reconstructed in Table 14.2. "By counting the numbers of st[r]aight lines," the grammar book continues, "or considering them as qualifying adjectives we have the degrees of comparison." Each character could be morphed by this system of degrees and connections. Because the base character already had the "five connecting parts of speech"—what the Grammar identifies as verbs, participles, prepositions, conjunctions, and adverbs—increasing, dissecting, and decreasing the character with these additional markings made possible some 5^4 (625) significations.[103] This grammatical rule compares with the esoteric idea

100. Smith, Journal, 20 November 1835, in *JSP*-J1:107.

101. Matthew J. Grey, "'The Word of the Lord in the Original': Joseph Smith's Study of Hebrew in Kirtland," in *Approaching Antiquity: Joseph Smith and the Ancient World*, ed. Lincoln H. Blumell, Matthew J. Grey, and Andrew H. Hedges (Provo, UT: Religious Studies Center, Brigham Young University; Salt Lake City: Deseret Book, 2015), 249–302; Matthew J. Grey, "Approaching Egyptian Papyri through Biblical Language: Joseph Smith's Use of Hebrew in His Translation of the Book of Abraham," Chapter 16 herein.

102. Grammar and Alphabet of the Egyptian Language, circa July–circa November 1835, 1–2, in *JSP*-R4:116–17.

103. Ibid., 2, in *JSP*-R4:118–19.

of Egyptian hieroglyphs as mystic symbols packed with meaning, and the idea in the Book of Mormon that Egyptian was more compact than Hebrew.[104]

The grammar book proceeds with morphemes grouped by degree and ventures a definition for each, usually about a paragraph in length. The character called "Ho-e-oop," for instance, is defined as a "prince of the royal blood a true descendant from Ham, the son of Noah, and inheritor of the Kingly blessings from under the hand of Noah, but not according to the priestly blessing, because of the trangrissions of Ham, which blessing fell upon Shem from under the hand of Noah."[105] In some cases, Smith apparently treated morphemes as pictographs, symbols reflecting things in nature or behaviors of people and animals, which maintained the more common approach than the growing scholarly consensus of his time that treated Egyptian characters as phonetic symbols.[106]

The grammar book exhibits a baroque sensibility to Egyptian—Smith or Phelps (or both of them) projected a carefully ordered system of expression with compounding layers of meaning. Though vastly incomplete relative to its proposed scope, the grammar book amplified the mechanics of translation apparent in Smith's version of the Egyptian alphabet and in the Sample of Pure Language before it. Because Smith regarded pure language as inherently capable of all possible expression, the more elaborate grammar book (as built upon the simpler Egyptian alphabet) still attempted a comparatively limited range. Smith, however, here realized a close study at the root level of written language—the morpheme—that further expanded his repertoire for esoteric thought.

In the grammar book, the strongest candidate for a word in the pure language appears under the definition for "Beth." To uncover the hidden meaning of the symbol labeled "Beth," Smith tapped into pure language: "The place appointed of God for the residence of Adam; Adam ondi= Ahman a ~~fruit~~ garden made to be fruitful, by blessing or promise; great valley or plain given by promise, fitted with fruit trees and precious flowers, made for the healing of Man. Good to the task pleasing to the eye; sweet and ~~precious~~ <deligh[t]ful> to the smell; place of happiness—purity, holiness, and rest: even Zomar—Zion."[107]

104. Mormon 9:32–33.

105. Grammar and Alphabet of the Egyptian Language, circa July–circa November 1835, 4, in *JSP*-R4:122–23.

106. Brown, "Joseph (Smith) in Egypt," 45; Bushman, "Joseph Smith's Place in the Study of Antiquity in Antebellum America," 17–19; Samuel Morris Brown, *In Heaven as It Is on Earth: Joseph Smith and the Early Mormon Conquest of Death* (New York: Oxford University Press, 2012), 134–38.

107. Comparison of Characters, in *JSP*-R4:360.

Ezra Booth had reported in 1831 that Joseph Smith marked the site for a temple in the land of Zion with "ZOM" for "Zomar," which Smith had said was "the original word for Zion."[108] Smith apparently arrived at this more developed definition of "Beth" similar to the Specimen of Pure Language. "Beth" had undergone a progression of inflections, through "an arbitrary sound or signification" to dozens of forms, like "Baethchu" and "Ebethchuaintrieth." As with symbols in the specimen of pure language, the symbol "Beth" followed a progression of previous symbols to arrive at this more developed definition.[109]

Smith maintained the separation between Egyptian and pure language in his explanations of "Beth" and for other symbols as well. The sound "Ah" sharing the first syllable and definition of "Ahman" was expanded in the grammar book into "Ahlish" instead of being expanded into "Ahman."[110] Smith here evoked the confounding influences on pure language with a root form common to a pure word, yet devolved with sounds somewhat dissimilar to pure names. By working meanings along layers of degrees, Smith practiced in his creative linguistics what his concept of pure language had intimated: the further one delved into the etymology—the past history of a word form or symbol—the closer one arrived at a pure expression. Relics of post-Adamic languages ornamented the Egyptian and ostensibly the Hebrew and all that followed, requiring Smith to strip away morphological accretions to arrive at a divine sound.

CONCLUSION

Even in the scant, pointillistic sources for Joseph Smith's pure language project, an image of a demanding exercise emerges. A seriousness appears, an earnest interest in approximating the first principles of language. Though the classical and Hellenistic school of ancient linguistics was certainly available for his study, especially its methodologies of translation and interpretation, it held little sway over Smith's more creative approach. Smith prioritized ancient languages in a typical esoteric direction, working back through biblical Hebrew to a more distant Egyptian through a pre-Babel Jaredite tongue and the primordial language of Adam and Eve. Basing all language, confounded or not, on the premise of a grand first principle—the very name of God in its purest

108. Ezra Booth to Ira Eddy, 14 November 1831, in "Mormonism—No. VI," *Ohio Star* (Ravenna, OH), 17 November 1831, 1.

109. Comparison of Characters, in *JSP*-R4:358–62.

110. Ibid., 351.

form—demonstrated Smith's theological concern, not just toward language, but toward the fundamental order all human activity derived from language. Smith aspired to be a kind of philosophical linguist, a proto-structuralist who could discern the relationships between language and the world.

Proffering pure language as a celestial solution to the discordance in humanity at once called out language as a singular problem and proved the complexity of the theory. Smith's method of accessing pure language through a synthesis of revelation, language study, and creative linguistics—what ideally should overcome the dark barriers to hidden knowledge—had the effect of further confronting him with the manifold constraints of language. The narrow prison of paper, pen, and ink emerges in the pure language sources; despite some brief moments of enlightenment, pure language remained elusive. The pure language sources diminished over time as the task proved more difficult.

And yet, Smith soldiered on, rallying the Latter-day Saints toward a "victory" of their dispensation, culminating in a "fullness of times."[111] With a revelation of the names, signs, and tokens of priesthood associated with the ritual of the temple under construction in Nauvoo, Smith could finally render everything esoteric, the whole life project trapped within a veneer of mortality and the true nature always hidden from the world. All was spiritual to God, nothing temporal, and by invoking what little pure language one knew, an order of prayer could summon the angels.[112] When learned, pure language sounds like "Ahman" and "Son Ahman" invited the righteous initiated hearer further into the realm of the hidden sacred. In Joseph Smith's final calculation, pure language could translate confounded people into joint heirs with Jesus Christ and members of the general assembly and Church of the Firstborn.

111. Joseph Smith to "The Church of Jesus Christ of Latter Day Saints," 6 September 1842, 7–8, [D&C 128] (accessible in the Documents series of the online edition of *The Joseph Smith Papers*).

112. D&C 29:34; William Clayton, Daily Account of Joseph Smith's Activities, 15 June 1844, in *JSP*-J3:334.

15

"Translating an Alphabet to the Book of Abraham"

Joseph Smith's Study of the Egyptian Language and His Translation of the Book of Abraham

BRIAN M. HAUGLID

Joseph Smith's "translation" of the "Book of Abraham" has emerged as the most problematic and controversial issue in the Mormon canon of scripture, especially as it relates to his capabilities as a translator of ancient texts. Smith derived his translation of the Book of Abraham from Egyptian papyri he acquired in 1835 and presented it as the autobiographical writings of the biblical patriarch. Whereas the golden plates of the Book of Mormon and the parchment of John and "record of John" referenced in Smith's revelations are not available for public scrutiny, significant documents from the Book of Abraham translation project are extant. Most notably, in addition to fragments from the original Egyptian papyri Smith acquired, there is a corpus of his own Egyptian "Alphabet" and "Grammar" documents and manuscripts containing parts of the Book of Abraham.[1]

While the Egyptian papyri and the English Book of Abraham manuscripts are fairly straightforward, the alphabet and grammar manuscripts have remained enigmatic, leaving scholars with little certainty of what Smith and others were thinking when they created them. Despite their lack of context, these documents do attest to the fact that Smith launched a serious, heuristic effort—after acquiring four mummies and several fragments of papyri in 1835—to understand the Egyptian language. Smith pursued this linguistic project with help from Oliver Cowdery, William Wines Phelps, and others. During the same period, Smith began his translation of the Book of Abraham. Over the second half of 1835, these men produced not only the original Book of Abraham manuscripts, but copies of Egyptian characters and

1. See *JSP*-R4.

illustrations, an Egyptian alphabet, and the beginnings of a grammar manual. Later, in 1842, Smith produced the rest of the Book of Abraham and published it, along with three illustrations from the papyri and his interpretations of their meaning.[2] Whereas the Egyptian papyri and the Book of Abraham are fairly easy to understand, the alphabet and grammar documents—which do not accord with modern Egyptology[3]—and their relationship to the Book of Abraham have posed a serious challenge to historians. One purpose of this chapter will be to propose that Smith's approach to translating the Book of Abraham included both intellectual investigation and reliance on a spiritual "gift of translation"—whether real, imagined, or pretended.[4]

This concept of a cognitive component in Smith's prophetic translation process can be found in one of the revelations he dictated in 1829. The revelation was directed to Oliver Cowdery, his scribe, when they were beginning their work on the translation of the Book of Mormon. In the revelation, Cowdery was told that he had received divine approval to translate like Smith.[5] Cowdery, however, faltered in his attempt. Then Smith dictated another revelation in which Cowdery was told that he had misunderstood the translation process by supposing his role was to be a passive receiver: "Behold you have not understood, you have supposed that I would give it unto you, when you took no thought, save it was to ask me." The revelation made clear that much more was required of him: "You must study it out in your mind; then you must ask me if it be right, and if it is right, I will cause that your bosom shall burn within you."[6]

2. "A Translation of Some Ancient Records that Have Fallen into Our Hands, from the Catecombs of Egypt, Purporting to Be the Writings of Abraham, while He Was in Egypt, Called the Book of Abraham, Written by His Own Hand, upon Papyrus: The Book of Abraham," *Times and Seasons*, 1 March 1842, 703–6; 15 March 1842, 719–22 (including unpaginated insert); 16 May 1842, 783–84. The three installments of the Book of Abraham were compiled and republished in 1851 by church apostle Franklin D. Richards as part of a collection of the religious writings of Joseph Smith titled *The Pearl of Great Price* [...] (Liverpool: F. D. Richards, 1851), 18–29. The Pearl of Great Price was canonized by the Church of Jesus Christ of Latter-day Saints in 1880. See introduction to The Pearl of Great Price (Salt Lake City: The Church of Jesus Christ of Latter-day Saints, 2013). The three installments of the Book of Abraham in the *Times and Seasons* are reproduced with transcripts and with textual and contextual annotation as Book of Abraham and Facsimiles, 1 March–16 May 1842, in *JSP*-R4:303–27 (hereafter BoA).

3. That the creators of these documents could not actually read the hieroglyphs and hieratic characters on the papyri is abundantly clear. From the perspective of modern Egyptology, the Egyptian alphabet and grammar documents produced by Smith and his assistants in 1835 bear no evidence of an accurate understanding of the Egyptian language. Kerry Muhlestein, "Assessing the Joseph Smith Papyri: An Introduction to the Historiography of their Acquisitions, Translations, and Interpretations," *Interpreter: A Journal of Mormon Scripture* 22 (2016): 34.

4. See Christopher James Blythe, "'By the Gift and Power of God': Translation among the Gifts of the Spirit," Chapter 2 herein.

5. Revelation, April 1829-A, in *JSP*-D1:36–37 [D&C 6:25–28].

6. Revelation, April 1829-D, in *JSP*-D1:50 [D&C 9:7–9].

This process of intellectual study and inquiry followed by spiritual confirmation may characterize Smith's approach to translation generally. In fact, Smith likely viewed the intellectual and the supernatural as inseparable elements of the translation process.[7]

To demonstrate the inseparable nature of these elements with regard to the translation of the Book of Abraham, this chapter establishes the chronology of the concurrent production of the Book of Abraham translation documents and the Egyptian language study documents. The chapter also explores the intertextual relationship between the two sets of documents. Finally, it provides an analysis of this textual relationship suggesting that at least part of the Book of Abraham was derived from the Egyptian language documents.

HISTORICAL DATA: ESTABLISHING THE PRODUCTION CHRONOLOGY

Joseph Smith's interest in the Egyptian language was certainly piqued in mid-1835 when Michael Chandler and his traveling mummy show stopped in Kirtland. By early July, Smith and a few others had pooled their resources and purchased four mummies. Oliver Cowdery wrote that the purchase also included "two rolls of papyrus" and "two or three other small pieces of papyrus, with astronomical calculations, epitaphs, &c."[8] From July to November 1835, there were at least ten days in which Smith was engaged in either the translation of the Book of Abraham text or the production of the Egyptian language documents or both.

1835

According to the personal history that Smith initiated in 1838, it was most likely sometime between 6 and 8 July 1835 that he, "with W. W. Phelps and O. Cowdery, as scribes, commenced . . . the translation of some of the characters or hieroglyphics." The men "found that one of the rolls contained the

7. Warren Parrish to the Editor, 5 February 1838, *Painesville Republican* (Painesville, OH), 15 February 1838, 3. In this hostile letter, Parrish wrote that he had sat by "his [Smith's] side and penned down the translation of the Egyptian Hieroglyphicks as he [Smith] claimed to receive it by direct inspiration from Heaven." Though Parrish no longer believed that Smith indeed received inspiration, he may have believed that Smith believed it.

8. Oliver Cowdery to William Frye, 22 December 1835, in *Latter Day Saints' Messenger and Advocate*, December 1835, 236.

writings of Abraham; another the writings of Joseph of Egypt. . . . the Lord is beginning to reveal the abundance of peace and truth."[9] According to this retrospective entry, recorded by Willard Richards in 1843,[10] Smith's initial translation of the papyri had led him to believe that the papyri contained the writings of Abraham and his great-grandson Joseph, both of whom had spent time in Egypt according to the book of Genesis in the Old Testament.[11] Notably, this entry in Smith's history explicitly states that he translated directly from some of "the characters or hieroglyphics"—indicating that Smith believed the papyri contained the text of Abraham's record. Jean-François Champollion, the brilliant French linguist, had only recently deciphered Egyptian when Smith acquired his papyri and it would still be many years before Champollion's findings were published in English, so there were no translation manuals for Egyptian that Smith and his scribes could have used when they were working with the papyri.[12] Smith presumably performed his translation of the Book of Abraham in the same or a similar manner to which he had translated the Book of Mormon—by the "gift and power of God."[13]

An entry in Smith's history for late July states that for "the remainder of this month" he "was continually engaged in translating an alphabet to the Book of Abraham, and arrangeing a grammar of the Egyptian language as practiced by the ancients."[14] This brief notation was recorded by Willard Richards in 1843.[15] Though retrospective, this recounting of continual engagement in late July 1835 indicates that more than one day, at the very least two days, were

9. Joseph Smith, History, 1838–1856, 6 July 1835, vol. B-1, 596 (accessible in the Histories series of the online edition of *The Joseph Smith Papers*).

10. Dean C. Jessee, "The Writing of Joseph Smith's History," *BYU Studies* 11, no. 4 (Summer 1971): 441.

11. Smith, History, 1838–1856, 6 July 1835, vol. B-1, 596. Historian Dan Vogel notes that Willard Richards inserted this entry into the history and that he likely did so in 1843 with the help of William Phelps. Dan Vogel, ed., *History of Joseph Smith and The Church of Jesus Christ of Latter-day Saints: A Source and Text-Critical Edition* (Salt Lake City: Smith-Pettit Foundation, 2015), 2:240n22, also 1:lxxxix. Although this entry was recorded eight years after the fact, the general accuracy of what was recorded is plausible since Smith was still alive and may have been consulted regarding it.

12. John Gee, "Joseph Smith and Ancient Egypt," in *Approaching Antiquity: Joseph Smith and the Ancient World*, ed. Lincoln H. Blumell, Matthew J. Grey, and Andrew H. Hedges (Provo, UT: Religious Studies Center, Brigham Young University; Salt Lake City: Deseret Book, 2015), 427–48.

13. The Book of Mormon: An Account Written by the Hand of Mormon, upon Plates Taken from the Plates of Nephi, trans. Joseph Smith, Junior (Palmyra, NY: E. B. Grandin, 1830), iii; Smith, History, 1838–1856, 7 September 1843, vol. E-1, Addenda, 8.

14. This notation in Smith's history follows an entry for 19 July. See Smith, History, 1838–1856, vol. B-1, 597. Like the entry for 6 (6–8) July 1835, this entry likely relies on the reminiscences that William W. Phelps provided on 16 September 1843. *History of Joseph Smith and The Church of Jesus Christ of Latter-day Saints*, 2:244. The general timeframe (late July) seems a reasonable estimate for something that had occurred several years earlier.

15. Jessee, "The Writing of Joseph Smith's History," 441.

spent on these endeavors. Moreover, the entry suggests that translating the Book of Abraham and studying the Egyptian language were understood as two aspects of the same project. Or, if they were understood as two projects, they were somehow closely related.[16] It may be that "translating an alphabet" and "arrangeing a grammar" of ancient Egyptian functioned as preliminary steps to producing the Book of Abraham, with Smith operating on the assumption that before one could proficiently translate an unknown language, an alphabet and grammar should be created.

Smith seems to have followed the same initial approach he had taken to translating the Book of Mormon. His mother, Lucy Mack Smith, reportedly stated that Joseph had received divine instructions "to take off [from the golden plates] a fac simile of the characters composing the alphabet which were called reformed egyptian Alphabetically and send them to all the learned men."[17] Joseph Smith's friend Joseph Knight recounted that Smith "now Began to be anxious to git them [the golden plates] translated" and "therefore with his wife Drew of[f] the Caricters exactley like the ancient and sent Martin Harris to see if he Could git them Translated."[18] And Smith himself recounted that in addition to transcribing "a considerable number of them" he also "*translated* some of them."[19] So Smith apparently attempted to begin his translation of the Book of Mormon with a list of characters, like an alphabet, some of which were translated.[20] He also approached his study of Hebrew, beginning in late November 1835, in a similar fashion. His journal entry for 21 November 1835 notes: "Spent the day in examining my books and studying <the> ~~my~~ Hebrew alphabet."[21] While there are significant differences among these three situations, in all three Smith's initial approach was to study (or to attempt to study) the source language's alphabet.

Finally, the retrospective entry in Smith's history for late July 1835 also implies—in its use of the phrase "as practiced by the ancients"—that Smith and

16. There is a clear correspondence between the opening lines of the Book of Abraham and content in the grammar book. Christopher C. Smith, "The Dependence of Abraham 1:1–3 on the Egyptian Alphabet and Grammar," *John Whitmer Historical Association Journal* 29 (2009): 38–54.

17. Lucy Mack Smith, *Lucy's Book: A Critical Edition of Lucy Mack Smith's Family Memoir*, ed. Lavina Fielding Anderson (Salt Lake City: Signature Books, 2001), 393. See also Richard Lyman Bushman, *Joseph Smith: Rough Stone Rolling* (New York: Alfred A. Knopf, 2005), 64.

18. Dean C. Jessee, "Joseph Knight's Recollection of Early Mormon History," *BYU Studies* 17, no. 1 (1977): 34.

19. Smith, History, 1838–1856, vol. A-1, 9, in *JSP*-H1:240 (emphasis added).

20. See Michael Hubbard MacKay, "Performing the Translation: Character Transcripts and Joseph Smith's Earliest Translating Practices," Chapter 4 herein.

21. Joseph Smith, Journal, 21 November 1835, in *JSP*-J1:107.

his scribes viewed their study of the Egyptian language as a genuine attempt at understanding how the Egyptian language actually worked. The late July entry's statement that the men were "translating an alphabet to the Book of Abraham, and arrangeing a grammar of the Egyptian language" suggests that Smith took certain characters from the papyri, translated them, and then arranged them in such a way that they resembled an alphabet. This may be when Smith, Cowdery, and Phelps created three versions of a text they each labeled "Egyptian Alphabet."[22] These Egyptian alphabet manuscripts do not follow the traditional notion of an alphabet in which an array of letters primarily represents the fundamental sounds of a language. Instead, their alphabet apparently operated on the idea that a character represented both a sound and a concept. For instance, the first character in Smith's version of the "Egyptian Alphabet" document represents the pronunciation "ah" and also conveys the concept of "the first being who exercises Supreme power."[23] A manuscript book was begun soon thereafter. Its first page bears the title "Grammar & A[l]phabet of the Egyptian Language" and, at some point in time, the label "Egyptian Alphabet" was inscribed and affixed to the spine. This grammar and alphabet book incorporates and elaborates on the Egyptian alphabet text by explaining and implementing a system of five "degrees" or levels of layered meaning progressively ranging from the first degree, which was the least and most basic, to the fifth degree, which was the greatest and most elaborate.[24]

On 11 September 1835, William W. Phelps wrote to his wife, Sally Waterman Phelps, and mentioned his work with Joseph Smith on the papyri (or rather the lack of work): "Nothing has been doing in the translation of the Egyptian Record for a long time, and probably will not for some time to come."[25] The letter from Phelps provides contemporaneous confirmation of the earlier translation

22. Egyptian Alphabet, circa early July–circa November 1835-A; Egyptian Alphabet, circa early July–circa November 1835-B; Egyptian Alphabet, circa early July–circa November 1835-C (all in *JSP*-R4:53–93). The first version (A), in the handwriting of Joseph Smith with some handwriting by Oliver Cowdery also, bears the title "Egyptian alphabet first degree." The third version (C), in the handwriting of William Phelps and also Warren Parrish, bears the title "Egyptian Alphabet first degree." The second version (B), in the handwriting of Oliver Cowdery, apparently bore a similar title, though most of the inscription has now broken off from the brittle head of the page. The descender loops for the "gyp" of "Egypt" and for the "p" in "Alphabet" are still intact, as are smaller parts of other letters.

23. Egyptian Alphabet, circa early July–circa November 1835-A, 1, in *JSP*-R4:56–57.

24. Grammar and Alphabet of the Egyptian Language, circa July–circa November 1835, in *JSP*-R4:111–90 (hereafter GAEL). See also Brian M. Hauglid, "The Book of Abraham and the Egyptian Project: 'A Knowledge of Hidden Languages,'" in *Approaching Antiquity*, 492–501.

25. Bruce Van Orden, "Writing to Zion: The William W. Phelps Kirtland Letters (1835–1836)," *BYU Studies* 33, no. 3 (1993): 15. See also Brian M. Hauglid, *A Textual History of the Book of Abraham* (Provo, UT: Neal A. Maxwell Institute for Religious Scholarship, 2010), 214.

activity and at the same time indicates that by this time their translation work had ceased. Combining the notation in Smith's history regarding the translation activity of late July with the statement from Phelps on 11 September that no translation work had been done "for a long time," it appears that the work of translation had ceased at the end of July or sometime in August. However, the letter from Phelps also conveyed his expectation that their work would eventually resume.

By October they had recommenced their efforts.[26] Smith's journal entry for 1 October includes a peculiar notation: "This after noon labored on the Egyptian alphabet, in company with brsr O[liver] Cowdery and W[illiam] W. Phelps: The system of astronomy was unfolded."[27] Here again, the historical record mentions the Egyptian alphabet but this time in connection with the word "unfolded," a word often associated with Smith's revelations.[28]

Toward the end of the month, on 29 October, Joseph Smith hired Warren Parrish as his personal scribe.[29] Parrish would serve as the principal scribe for Smith's journal for the rest of the year and into the early months of 1836.[30] In Smith's journal entry for 16 December 1835, Parrish noted that Smith "exibited and explaind the Egyptian Records" to William E. McLellin, Brigham Young, and Jared Carter, and also "explained many things to them concerning the dealings of God with the ancient<s> and the formation of the planetary System."[31] When Parrish repurposed this journal entry for Smith's 1834–1836 history, which he was also producing for Smith, he followed the language nearly verbatim except for the final words. Parrish revised "and the formation of the planetary System" to "especially the system of astronomy as taught by Abraham, which is contained upon these manuscripts."[32]

26. The translation effort had arguably resumed by late September 1835, since Oliver Cowdery used clear phraseology from the opening lines of the Book of Abraham when he revised an 18 December 1833 patriarchal blessing on 22 September 1835: "We diligently sought for the right of the fathers and the authority of the Holy Priesthood, and the power to administer the same; for we desired to be followers of righteousness and the possessors of greater knowledge, even the knowledge of the mysteries of the Kingdom of God." Patriarchal Blessings, 1:15, Church History Library, The Church of Jesus Christ of Latter-day Saints, Salt Lake City (hereafter Church History Library); compare Book of Abraham Manuscript, circa July–circa November 1835-C, 1, in *JSP*-R4:219 [Abraham 1:2]. See also Smith, Journal, 22 September 1835, in *JSP*-J1:61–62.

27. Smith, Journal, 1 October 1835, in *JSP*-J1:67.

28. See 1 Nephi 10:19; Mosiah 8:19; Ether 4:7, 16; Revelation, April 1829-A, in *JSP*-D1:35 [D&C 6:7]; Revelation, May 1829-A, in *JSP*-D1:53–54 [D&C 11:7]; Revelation, 27–28 December 1832, in *JSP*-D2:343 [D&C 88:95]; Revelation, 8 March 1833, in *JSP*-D3:29 [D&C 90:14].

29. Smith, Journal, 29 October 1835, in *JSP*-J1:76.

30. See *JSP*-J1:53–56.

31. Smith, Journal, 16 December 1835, in *JSP*-J1:123–24.

32. Joseph Smith, History, 1834–1836, 16 December 1835, in *JSP*-H1:147.

Parrish stated that the Abrahamic system of astronomy was contained "upon these manuscripts" but did not specify what he meant by "these manuscripts." It may have been a reference to manuscripts created on 1 October when Smith "labored on the Egyptian alphabet, in company with brsr O[liver] Cowdery and W[illiam] W. Phelps." The explanations Smith reportedly gave on 16 December regarding "the system of astronomy as taught by Abraham" may have been based on the Egyptian alphabet work of 1 October when "the system of astronomy was unfolded." The three versions of the alphabet text, which was inscribed by the three men,[33] includes some astronomical content. Alternatively, "these manuscripts" could refer to the astronomical content as incorporated in the grammar book. Historian Dan Vogel asserts that "these manuscripts" refers to "the bound 'Grammar and Alphabet' where on page 24 the subject matter suddenly shifts from Abraham, Egypt, and the patriarchal priesthood to astronomy."[34] The bound grammar and alphabet book, however, only constitutes a single manuscript. But "these manuscripts" (plural) could refer to the grammar book and one or more other manuscripts, like the three manuscript copies of the alphabet text. One last possibility is that "these manuscripts" refers to the papyrus fragments since the phrase "Egyptian records" immediately follows.

In terms of chronology, it seems *unlikely* that "these manuscripts" has reference to the astronomical content found in Abraham's cosmic vision in the middle of the Book of Abraham (now Abraham 3) or to the explanation of the second illustration published with the Book of Abraham, as there is little indication that either emerged before March 1842.[35] As argued below, some of the astronomical material in the 1835 grammar book—found between pages 23 and 33—was likely revised in 1842 when it was incorporated into the explanations found in a manuscript titled "Cut 2."[36] This manuscript is in the handwriting of Willard Richards, who served as a scribe for Joseph Smith beginning in

33. Egyptian Alphabet, circa early July–circa November 1835-A; Egyptian Alphabet, circa early July–circa November 1835-B; Egyptian Alphabet, circa early July–circa November 1835-C (all in *JSP*-R4:53–93), see note 22 above.

34. *History of Joseph Smith and the Church of Jesus Christ of Latter-day Saints*, 1:cxxxvi.

35. The term "shinehah," which appears in the middle of the Book of Abraham (BoA, in *JSP*-R4:314–15 [Abraham 3:13]), also appears in the first edition of the Doctrine and Covenants. See *The Doctrine and Covenants of the Church of the Latter Day Saints* [. . .] (Kirtland, OH: F. G. Williams, 1835), 86:4 (220); 96: section heading (234). The Doctrine and Covenants was evidently printed by August 1835 (Doctrine and Covenants, 1835, in *JSP*-R2:306–8). The author has previously argued that the appearance of the term "shinehah" in 1835 suggests that the "translation was at least up to Abraham 3:13 by this time" (Hauglid, *A Textual History of the Book of Abraham*, 2). However, it is likewise plausible that Smith divined the term in 1835 (or earlier) and imported it into the text of the Book of Abraham in 1842. Thus the 1835 attestation of the word "shinehah" is weak evidence for a translation chronology (and therefore not used here as such).

36. Explanation of Facsimile 2, circa 15 March 1842, in *JSP*-R4:276–83.

December 1841.[37] The manuscript titled "Cut 2" was quite clearly created in preparation for the printing of the second illustration published along with the Book of Abraham translation text. The illustration and the explanations of its various parts appeared in the church newspaper in March 1842 (as discussed further below).[38]

Smith's journal entry for 7 October 1835 notes that he "recommenced translating the ancient records."[39] The phrase "the ancient records" seems to be a direct reference to the papyri. It is unclear whether this implicitly referenced back to the entry of 1 October—when Smith, Cowdery, and Phelps "labored on the Egyptian alphabet" and the "system of astronomy was unfolded"—or to previous work that was more narrowly considered as translation.

Smith conducted further translation in late November, as noted in his journal. The journal entry for 19 November notes that he "spent the day in translating the Egyptian records." The entry for 20 November includes a similar notation, this time including at least one other person: "We spent the day in translating, and made rapid progress." Cowdery would not return from a trip to New York until later that day, so Smith was likely referring to work with William Phelps or Warren Parrish. The entry for 24 November includes a similar notation: "We translated some of the Egyptian, records." The entry for 25 November notes that at least Smith, and perhaps the others, "spent the day in Translating." A final relevant entry, for 26 November includes this note: "We spent the day in transcribing Egyptian characters from the papyrus."[40] This "transcribing" of characters could refer to copying characters from the Egyptian papyri onto the alphabet or grammar documents, although this seems unlikely considering the retrospective entries for July and 1 October found in Smith's history. More likely, the 26 November entry refers to work on the three manuscripts of the Book of Abraham text, which include Egyptian characters transcribed from the papyri in the left margin adjacent to passages of the Book of Abraham.[41]

37. Smith, Journal, 13 December 1841, in *JSP*-J2:11.

38. Almost the entire explanation for the first numbered figure of the second illustration can be found in the handwriting of Warren Parrish in the 1835 grammar book (GAEL, 26, in *JSP*-R4:166–67). Moreover, many of the strange terms in the explanation for the second illustration—such as Kolob, Jah-oh-eh, Oliblish, Enish-go-on-dosh, Kae-e-vanrash, and Kli-flos-is-es—can also be found in the grammar book (GAEL, 24–25, in *JSP*-R4:162–65). However, as argued below, there is no evidence that these 1835 terms were incorporated into the explanations for the second illustration before 1842.

39. Smith, Journal, 7 October 1835, in *JSP*-J1:71.

40. Smith, Journal, 19–26 November 1835, in *JSP*-J1:107–111.

41. Book of Abraham Manuscript, circa July–circa November 1835-A [Abraham 1:4–2:6]; Book of Abraham Manuscript, circa July–circa November 1835-B [Abraham 1:4–2:2]; Book of Abraham Manuscript, circa July–circa November 1835-C [Abraham 1:1–2:18], all in *JSP*-R4:191–242.

These entries for 1835 suggest the possibility that the translation of the papyri and the creation of the Egyptian study manuscripts somehow worked hand in hand with each other within the broadly numinous context of Smith's providential worldview, his personal sense of spiritual mission, and his efforts to fulfill the role of a prophetic translator. It may have been that Smith and his associates viewed the definitions and explanations in their 1835 Egyptian alphabet and grammar documents as part of God's providential workings or even as divinely inspired information that became at least somewhat influential in the translation of the Book of Abraham.

Apparently, there was no further translation of the Book of Abraham after late November 1835. Although his journal continued, with almost daily entries into early April 1836, nothing more is mentioned there.[42] In a December 1835 letter to William Frye, Oliver Cowdery wrote about the translation project's uncertain timetable: "When the translation of these valuable documents will be completed, I am unable to say; neither can I give you a probable idea how large volumes they will make."[43] Cowdery did not indicate whether any more translating had occurred since November, but seemed to anticipate that much more of the Book of Abraham would eventually be produced—apparently a text so extensive that he thought it would comprise a multi-volume work. In December 1835, Smith apparently put further work on the grammar construction and the Abraham translation on hold in order to study Hebrew—possibly with the hope that a knowledge of Hebrew would help him to better understand Egyptian.[44] Smith completed his formal study of Hebrew in late March 1836.[45] Although he intended to do more translating, other important church matters consumed his time, apparently preventing him from making any further progress on the Book of Abraham for the next six years.[46]

42. Smith, Journal, September 1835–April 1836, in *JSP*-J1:52–223.

43. Cowdery to Frye, 22 December 1835.

44. Smith's interest in learning Hebrew may have derived, at least in part, from an early nineteenth-century understanding that Egyptian and Hebrew were closely related to each other and to the original human language. See J. G. H. Greppo, *Essay on the Hieroglyphic System of M. Champollion, Jun. And the Advantages Which it Offers to Sacred Criticism*, trans. Isaac Stuart (Boston: Perkins and Marvin, 1830). See also Matthew J. Grey, "Approaching Egyptian Papyri through Biblical Language: Joseph Smith's Use of Hebrew in His Translation of the Book of Abraham," 396–98 herein.

45. Smith, Journal, 29 March 1836, in *JSP*-J1:211–12; Certificate from Joshua Seixas, 30 March 1836, in *JSP*-D5:214–16. See also D. Kelly Ogden, "The Kirtland Hebrew School (1835–36)," in *Regional Studies in Latter-day Saint Church History: Ohio*, ed. Milton V. Backman Jr. (Provo, UT: Department of Church History and Doctrine, Brigham Young University, 1990), 63–87, 155–66.

46. In 1840 Smith hoped to "engage, more particularly, in the spiritual welfare of the Saints & also, to the translating of the Egyptian Records." Minutes, 20 June 1840, in *JSP*-D7:299. About a year later, Smith still desired to "attend to the business of translating," but was unable to do so. "Conference Minutes," *Times and Seasons*, 1 September 1841, 521–22. See also *JSP*-R4:xxvii.

1842

The impetus to resume translation finally came when Joseph Smith became the editor of the *Times and Seasons*—the church newspaper published in Nauvoo, Illinois—and began publishing the Book of Abraham.[47] The issue of the *Times and Seasons* dated 1 March 1842 included the beginning of the Book of Abraham, as well as the first illustration and its accompanying explanation.[48] The text was presented as "A Translation Of some ancient Records that have fallen into our hands, from the Catecombs of Egypt, purporting to be the writings of Abraham, while he was in Egypt, called the Book of Abraham, written by his own hand, upon papyrus."[49] Some have taken this to mean that Abraham's original text was copied many times, like many ancient texts, and that Joseph Smith acquired a much later copy.[50] However, the more significant takeaway from this title-headnote seems to be that Smith believed the papyri he acquired had been personally inscribed by the father of the faithful.[51] The 1 March 1842 issue was the ninth issue of volume 3 of the *Times and Seasons*. The entry for 8 March 1842 in Joseph Smith's journal, which was being kept for him by Willard Richards, notes that Smith "Commenced Translating from the Book of Abraham, for the 10 No of the Times and seasons"—the tenth issue of volume 3. This was the forthcoming issue dated 15 March 1842. In a journal entry for 9 March, Richards noted that Smith "continued translation of the Book of Abraham," attended a meeting, and then "continued translating & revising."[52] The phrase "Translating from the Book of Abraham" in the 8 March entry seems to suggest that Smith was translating the Book of Abraham from the papyri, thus further reinforcing the evidence that Smith believed the papyri to contain the original Book of Abraham.

In spite of these 1842 journal entries, some have argued that Smith had completed the entire Book of Abraham in 1835—at least all that was ever

47. Joseph Smith, "To Subscribers," *Times and Seasons*, 1 March 1842, 703–6.

48. BoA, in *JSP*-R4:306–13 [Abraham 1:1–2:18].

49. BoA, in *JSP*-R4:308–9 [Abraham headnote].

50. John Gee, *An Introduction to the Book of Abraham* (Provo, UT: Religious Studies Center, Brigham Young University, 2017), 180. See also Kerry Muhlestein, "Egyptian Papyri and the Book of Abraham: Some Questions and Answers," *Religious Educator* 11, no. 1 (2010): 95.

51. BoA, in *JSP*-R4:308–9 [Abraham headnote]. In 1840, it was reported that Smith once pointed to a certain character on the papyri and declared it was the signature of Abraham. See "From the Alexandria Gazette: A Glance at the Mormons," *Supplement to the Courant* (Hartford, CT), 29 August 1840, 140. The papyri date to the second century BCE, see Robert K. Ritner, with contributions by Marc Coenen, H. Michael Marquardt, and Christopher Woods, *The Joseph Smith Egyptian Papyri: A Complete Edition* (Salt Lake City: Smith-Pettit Foundation, 2011), 62–65; Gee, *An Introduction to the Book of Abraham*, chap. 5.

52. Smith, Journal, 8–9 March 1842, in *JSP*-J2:42.

published of it and maybe even more material that never was published and is no longer extant. The underlying motivation for this argument seems to focus on the notion that if Smith's translation occurred before the creation of the Abraham/Egyptian papers, then these documents could not have been a part of Smith's translation efforts. This thinking led the iconic Hugh Nibley to reason that these papers (which he called the Kirtland Egyptian Papers [KEP]) were entirely derivative from the already translated Book of Abraham.

John Gee, in his book *An Introduction to the Book of Abraham*, follows this same line of reasoning. He writes that "Joseph *revised* the translation preparatory to its publication in 1842, but other than that, no evidence has survived that he worked on the translation of the existing Book of Abraham after 1835."[53] Kerry Muhlestein and Megan Hansen have gone so far as to say that if Smith had spent 8–9 March 1842 in translating the Book of Abraham he would have had to be "frantically" translating in order to complete the production. Muhlestein and Hansen therefore posit that "it is reasonable to suppose that when Joseph said he was 'translating' between the first and second installments of publication, he was actually revising."[54] Dating Smith's Abraham translation to 1835 allows for Smith to be distanced from the Abraham/Egyptian papers and supports Nibley's hypothesis that they were created by Smith's scribes *after* his translation in some kind of lexicographical reverse-engineering project.[55] However, an 1835 date for the entire translation goes against the stronger evidence since Smith's journal entries for 8 and 9 March employ the terms "translating" and "translation" respectively. Moreover, the 9 March entry states that he was both "translating and revising"—apparently cognizant of the difference between these two kinds of work. It seems most likely that Smith and Richards would have understood the difference in meaning between the words

53. Gee, *An Introduction to the Book of Abraham*, 15 (emphasis added).

54. Kerry Muhlestein and Megan Hansen, "'The Work of Translating': The Book of Abraham's Translation Chronology," in *Let Us Reason Together: Essays in Honor of the Life's Work of Robert L. Millet*, ed. J. Spencer Fluhman and Brent L. Top (Provo, UT: Religious Studies Center and Neal A. Maxwell Institute for Religious Scholarship, Brigham Young University, 2016), 142, 149. Conversely, apologists for the Book of Mormon often write about the impressive speed with which Smith translated the Book of Mormon. See John W. Welch, "The Miraculous Timing of the Translation of the Book of Mormon," in *Opening the Heavens: Accounts of Divine Manifestations, 1820–1844*, ed. John W. Welch, 2nd ed. (Provo, UT: Brigham Young University Press; Salt Lake City: Deseret Book, 2017), 78–125.

55. Hugh W. Nibley, *An Approach to the Book of Abraham*, vol. 18 in the Collected Works of Hugh Nibley (Salt Lake City: Deseret Book; Provo, UT: Foundation for Ancient Research and Mormon Studies and The Neal A. Maxwell Institute for Religious Scholarship, Brigham Young University, 2009), 502–68. See especially the assignment of an 1836/1837 date to most of the Abraham/Egyptian papers by Nibley in the tables on pages 504–5 (as opposed to the more recent assignment of 1835 dates by the Joseph Smith Papers Project (*JSP*-R4:25–242).

"translating" and "revising" and would have used them with the straightforward meaning they readily convey.

More evidence related to the resumption of translating in 1842 is found in a draft for an editorial that was apparently intended for the 1 March 1842 issue of the *Times and Seasons*, though never published. The draft is written in Joseph Smith's voice but is in the handwriting of his principal scribe, Willard Richards. Smith may have dictated the text to Richards or Richards may have written it by assignment on Smith's behalf. The draft stated: "In the penst [present] no. will be found the Commencmet of the Records discoverd in Egypt. some time since. as penend by the hand. of Father Abraham. which I shall contin[u]e to translate & publish as fast as possible till the whole is completed."[56] It appears from this draft editorial that as of 1 March Smith had not yet translated the complete Abraham text nor even the content for the second installment, which would appear in the 15 March issue.[57] Furthermore, on 9 March, Smith dictated a letter to Willard Richards for early Mormon Edward Hunter of Pennsylvania that corresponds with what is written in Smith's journal entry for the same day. The letter states: "I am now very busily engaged in Translating, and therefore cannot give as much time to Public matters as I could wish."[58] Thus, this documentary evidence strongly affirms that Smith translated the material for the second installment of the Book of Abraham in 1842 and not in 1835.

One other important consideration is Smith's use of Hebrew words and phrasing in the second half of the Book of Abraham. Matthew J. Grey, in his analysis of Smith's study of Hebrew, concludes that "it is not likely a coincidence that the portions of the translation attested in 1835 (Abraham 1:1–2:18) contain no traces of Hebraic influences beyond what is found in the biblical (KJV) Abraham story, whereas the material first attested in 1842 (Abraham 3–5 and the facsimile explanations) is infused with Hebrew words, concepts, phraseology, and other Hebrew-inspired enhancements Joseph Smith learned in 1836."[59] Thus, it seems most likely that Smith translated the material published

56. Editorial, circa 1 March 1842, Draft, 1, *JSP*-D9:206–7.

57. BoA, in *JSP*-R4:314–23 [Abraham 2:19–5:21].

58. The letter to Hunter was written on both 9 and 11 March. The passage regarding Smith being "very busily engaged in Translating" is in the part of the letter written on 9 March. Letter to Edward Hunter, 9 and 11 March 1842, 2, in *JSP*-D9:231.

59. See Grey, "Approaching Egyptian Papyri through Biblical Language," Chapter 16 herein. Grey also responds to the argument made by Muhlestein and Hansen that the 1842 Hebrew represents only glosses. He explains that "their analysis does not consider the full range of Hebrew evidence in the Book of Abraham, nor does it sufficiently weigh the extent to which Smith's Hebrew studies influenced his later work on the text—especially in the text's creation account" (394–95n9).

in the first installment (now Abraham 1:1–2:18) in 1835 and then translated the material for the second installment (now Abraham 2:19–5:21) in 1842.

An examination of the 1835 material and its production as documented in the journals and histories of Joseph Smith, the letters of William Phelps and Oliver Cowdery, and other documents indicates an interweaving of Egyptian language study and Book of Abraham translation during the same period. The documents produced during this period include several unusual and previously unattested terms, such as Enish-go-on-dosh and Kae-E-vanrash.[60] Then, in 1842, Smith incorporated attested Hebrew terms such as Kokob (star), Kokaubeam (stars), and (the Sephardic) gnolaum (eternal). In early 1836, after a brief period of personal study in late 1835, Joseph Smith formally studied the Hebrew language with Joshua Seixas, and Smith owned and studied from the Hebrew manual Seixas had published.[61] The Hebrew terms incorporated in the Book of Abraham are spelled according to the transliteration scheme found in the manual produced by Seixas, a Jew from the Sephardic (Iberian) tradition (and dialect). Similarly, the Hebrew words appearing in the explanations for the first two illustrations indicate that these explanations were produced in 1842. This suggests that the explanation for the third illustration originated in 1842 as well. To better ascertain the nature and methodology of Smith's translation work, these emphases on Egyptian and Hebrew language interest and the implications regarding periodization should be paramount. Hence, in what follows, the history of Smith's language study will be treated as an essential part in developing a translation hypothesis.

INTERTEXTUAL DATA: ESTABLISHING THE RELATIONSHIPS

That the Egyptian language and Abraham translation projects occurred concurrently means that a clear chronological direction of influence cannot be argued in any certain or obvious manner. The textual relationship is also complex. The Egyptian language documents contain some vocabulary and concepts that are found in the Book of Abraham as well as some that are not. The converse is also true: The Book of Abraham contains some vocabulary and concepts that can be found in the Egyptian language documents and some that cannot. Thus,

60. Explanation of Facsimile 2, circa 15 March 1842, 2, in *JSP*-R4:280–81 [Abraham, Fac. 2, Fig. 5].

61. Grey argues that Smith was following Seixas's transliteration scheme in his use of "au" to transliterate the Hebrew vowel qametz. Grey, "Approaching Egyptian Papyri through Biblical Language," 410 herein.

while it is clear that the language documents and the translation documents are textually related, there is no clear direction of textual dependency. However, it *is* clear that there are several substantive textual relationships.

To begin, the acquisition of the papyri marks the crucial point where Joseph Smith fused the intellectual with the numinous in his efforts to translate the Book of Abraham. And surely, the Egyptian alphabet and grammar documents represent an intellectual and testable endeavor, but this alone cannot account for the entire translation process. Smith and others may have viewed these materials as only part of the overall process. And yet, it was apparently an *intricate* part of the translation experience. Furthermore, apologetic efforts to artificially separate the intellectual work of the language documents from the spiritual effort of translating the Book of Abraham violates the admonition found in Smith's April 1829 revelation to Cowdery to first "study it out in your mind" and *then* seek divine affirmation.[62] Whereas Smith's prophetic gift may fall outside the realm of testable inquiry, the intellectual work in the Egyptian language documents can be scrutinized and compared to the Book of Abraham, possibly offering a glimpse into the method Smith employed in translating the papyri to produce all or part of the Book of Abraham.

The Book of Abraham Narrative and the Abraham/Egyptian Papers

One of the extant papyri fragments includes the vignette that was used for the first illustration of the Book of Abraham.[63] In the published facsimile of this vignette, the columns of hieroglyphs to the left and right of the vignette have been omitted. However, many of the hieroglyphs on this fragment were copied into the 1835 alphabet text (in all three versions), starting at the right of the vignette and going down the columns from top to bottom and moving through the columns from right to left. The bottom of the left-most extant column of the fragment may have included two more glyphs in 1835, as there are two additional glyphs that appear in the left margin of one of the 1835 Abraham manuscripts.[64] The rest of the Egyptian characters on the three 1835 Abraham manuscripts derive from the first three lines of another papyrus fragment, taken one by one, sequentially, from right to left.[65] Notably, before

62. Revelation, April 1829-D, in *JSP*-D1:50 [D&C 9:8–9].

63. Fragment of Book of Breathing for Horos-A, between 238 and circa 153 BC, in *JSP*-R4:8–9.

64. These lines are in the handwriting of William W. Phelps (Book of Abraham Manuscript, circa July–circa November 1835-C, 1, in *JSP*-R4:218–19 [Abraham 1:1–3]).

65. Fragment of Book of Breathing for Horos-A, between 238 and circa 153 BC, in *JSP*-R4:8–9.

this fragment was separated, it had originally followed the vignette.[66] Two of the 1835 Abraham manuscripts begin with an inscription linking them to the five-degree system of definition found in the alphabet and grammar documents: "Sign of the fifth degree of the ~~first~~ second part." This statement seems to indicate that Smith and/or one of his assistants, Frederick Williams and Warren Parrish, believed the Abraham text included in these manuscripts was derived from or somehow connected with the highest degree of meaning in the five-degree system.

Of the three versions of the 1835 Egyptian alphabet text—produced by Smith, Cowdery, and Phelps—Smith's seems to be the primary version upon which Cowdery and Phelps drew and provided minor elaboration.[67] Furthermore, of the three versions, only Smith's introduces the linguistic system in which a word's definition increases through five "degrees" or levels of meaning from the most basic to the most elaborate. This takes place at the end of the Smith version in an inscription that was added by Cowdery:

> In the *first degree* Ah-broam—signifies The father of the faithful, the first right, the elders[.] *second degree*—same sound—A follower of rightiousness—*Third degree*—same sound—One who possesses great Knowledge—*Fourth degree*—same sound—A follower of righteousness, a possessor of greater of Knowledge. *Fifth degree*—Ah-bra-oam. The father of many nations, a prince of peace, one who keeps the commandments of God, a patriarch, a rightful heir, a high priest.[68]

This five-degree text in Smith's alphabet manuscript was incorporated in the bound grammar book and then apparently reworked in the opening lines of the Book of Abraham: "I sought for the blessings of the fathers, and the right whereunto I should be ordained to administer the same: Having been a follower of righteousness; desiring to be one who possessed great Knowledge; a greater follower of righteousness; a possessor of greater Knowledge; a father of many nations; a prince of peace; one who keeps the commandments of God;

66. Michael D. Rhodes, *The Hor Book of Breathings: A Translation and Commentary*, Studies in the Book of Abraham (Provo, UT: Foundation for Ancient Research and Mormon Studies, Brigham Young University, 2002), 4, fig. 1.

67. For a technical analysis of Smith's version of the alphabet document as the primary version of the three, see Hauglid, "The Book of Abraham and the Egyptian Project," 487–94.

68. Egyptian Alphabet, circa early July–circa November 1835-A, 5, in *JSP*-R4:70–71 (emphasis added).

TABLE 15.1. "Iota toues Zip-Zi" through Five Degrees of Definition

Degree	Definition
1st	The land of Egypt
2nd	The land which was discovered under water by a woman
3rd	The woman sought to settle her sons in that land. she being the daughter of Ham
4th	The land of Egypt discovered by a woman, who afterwards settled persons in it
5th	The land of Egypt which was first discovered by a woman while underwater, and afterwards settled by her Sons she being a daughter of Ham

a rightful heir; a high priest."[69] Here, it can be seen that the text of the Book of Abraham closely resembles the meaning of Ah-broam/Ah-bra-oam in the fifth degree.

Another passage from early in the Book of Abraham with corresponding material in the Egyptian language documents concerns the origins of Egypt. In Table 15.1, for the character called "Iota toues Zip-Zi," it can be seen that the meaning of the character generally increases through the five degrees.[70] These definitions can be compared with a passage in the Book of Abraham: "The land of Egypt being first discovered, by a woman, who was the daughter of Ham, and the daughter of Zeptah, which in the chaldea, signifies Egypt, which signifies that which is forbidden. When this woman discovered the land. it was under water, who after settled her sons in it, and thus from Ham, sprang that race, which preserved, the curse in the land."[71] This passage in the Book of Abraham corresponds with the meanings of the character named "Iota toues Zip-Zi" and it most closely corresponds with this character in its fifth degree of meaning.

In addition to these two characters—which can be seen to develop through the five degrees in the alphabet and grammar documents into a fuller narrative form—there are other definitions in the grammar book, including phrases that resonate with phrases appearing early in the Book of Abraham. The Egyptian grammar book and the Book of Abraham clearly share concepts regarding Ham, the son of Noah. According to a fifth-degree definition from the grammar book, Ham was an "inheritor of the Kingly blessings from under the hand

69. Book of Abraham Manuscript, circa July–circa November 1835-C, 1, in *JSP*-R4:218–19 [Abraham 1:2]. For an in-depth study of the textual relationship between the Egyptian language documents and the opening lines of the Book of Abraham, see Smith, "The Dependence of Abraham 1:1–3 on the Egyptian Alphabet and Grammar," 38–54.

70. GAEL, 5 (fifth degree), 10 (fourth degree), 14 (third degree), 18 (second degree), 21 (first degree), in *JSP*-R4:124–25, 134–35, 142–43, 150–51, 156–57 (spelling standardized).

71. Book of Abraham Manuscript, circa July–circa November 1835-C, 5, in *JSP*-R4:226–27 [Abraham 1:23–24].

of Noah, but not according to the priestly blessing, because of the transgrissions of Ham, which blessing fell upon Shem."[72] The following passages from the Book of Abraham include similar concepts regarding Ham and the priesthood (with the words, phrases, and concepts that also appear in the grammar book italicized):

> which *Pharaoh signifies king* by *royal blood.* Now this *king* of *Egypt* was a *descendant from the loins of Ham*, and was a partaker of the *blood* of the *Canaanites* by birth. From this descent sprang all the *Egyptians*, and thus the blood of the *Canaanites* was *preserved in the land.* . . . Now the *first government* of Egypt was established by *Pharaoh* . . . and it was after the manner of the government of Ham, *which was patriarchal. Pharaoh, being a righteous man*, established his *kingdom* . . . seeking earnestly to imitate that *order* established by the *fathers* in the *first generations*, in the days of the *first patriarchal reign*, even in the *reign of Adam*, and also *Noah, his father, who blessed him* with the *blessings* of the earth, and with the *blessings* of wisdom, but *cursed him as pertaining to the priesthood.* Now, *Pharaoh being of that lineage by which he could not have right of priesthood.*[73]

The number and nature of these correspondences attest to the intricate relationship between the content of the grammar book and the Book of Abraham text.

Other words or phrases in the language documents have a conceptual relationship to passages appearing early in the Book of Abraham. The grammar book includes the idea of a "Patriarchal right by appointment" and "a change by appointment."[74] Similarly, in the beginning of the Book of Abraham, the future father of nations seeks for his "appointment unto the priesthood according to the appointment of God."[75] Also, the grammar book includes information about the familial lineage of a royal figure named Onitas, while the Book of Abraham includes an early reference to virgins of royal descent from Ham, called "the daughters of Onitah."[76] The grammar book also includes informa-

72. GAEL, 4, in *JSP*-R4:122–23.

73. Book of Abraham Manuscript, circa July–circa November 1835-C, 4–5, in *JSP*-R4:224–27 (spelling, capitalization, and punctuation standardized) [Abraham 1:20–22, 25–27].

74. GAEL, 3, 20, in *JSP*-R4:120–21, 154–55.

75. Book of Abraham Manuscript, circa July–circa November 1835-C, 1, in *JSP*-R4:218–19 [Abraham 1:4].

76. GAEL, 5, in *JSP*-R4:124–25; Book of Abraham Manuscript, circa July–circa November 1835-C, 2, in *JSP*-R4:220–21 [Abraham 1:11].

tion regarding "a record of the fathers" and early on in the Book of Abraham the protagonist refers to "the records of the fathers."[77]

The Book of Abraham Illustration Explanations and the Abraham/Egyptian Papers

About half of the Egyptian grammar book contains astronomical information that corresponds with the explanations of various parts of the second illustration published as part of the Book of Abraham. This illustration, presented under the title "A Fac-simile from the Book of Abraham, No. 2," was likely a disk-shaped piece of papyri that included several subsections or registers, each of which included characters or illustrations (or both). As published, the "figures" in these subsections were numbered and keyed to accompanying explanations (see Figure 15.1). Smith and Cowdery may have begun associating the original papyri source for the second illustration with astronomy even before they purchased it from Michael Chandler. In December 1835, Oliver Cowdery recounted that when Chandler came to Kirtland that summer he related that he had already sold seven mummies and "a small quantity of papyrus, similar, (as he says), to the astronomical representation, contained with the present two rolls."[78] One of the Egyptian characters copied into the grammar book is named "Kolob" and is defined in all five degrees. In the fifth degree, it is defined as "the first creation nearer to the celestial, or the residence of Lord, first in government, the last pertaining to the measurement of time, the measurement according to celestial time which signifies, one day to a cubit which day is equal to a thousand years according to the measurement of this Eearth or Jah=oh=eh."[79] In the second illustration, the explanation for figure 1 matches the fifth-degree definition for "Kolob" almost verbatim.[80]

The definitions for other characters in the grammar book correspond to explanations for other figures in the second illustration. For instance, the explanation for figure 2 can be conceptually associated with the explanation for Oliblish and the associated power of other planets named in the grammar

77. GAEL, 4, in *JSP*-R4:122–23; Book of Abraham Manuscript, circa July–circa November 1835-C, 6, in *JSP*-R4:228–29 [Abraham 1:31].

78. Cowdery to Frye, 22 December 1835. Christopher C. Smith and Don Bradley, "'The Reckoning of Time': Toward a Production Chronology for the Joseph Smith Egyptian Papers" (unpublished typescript, n.d.), 3 (copy in author's possession). The author expresses appreciation to Smith and Bradley for sharing their unpublished article.

79. GAEL, 26, in *JSP*-R4:166–67.

80. Explanation of Facsimile 2, circa 15 March 1842, 1, in *JSP*-R4:278–79 [Abraham, Fac. 2, Fig. 1].

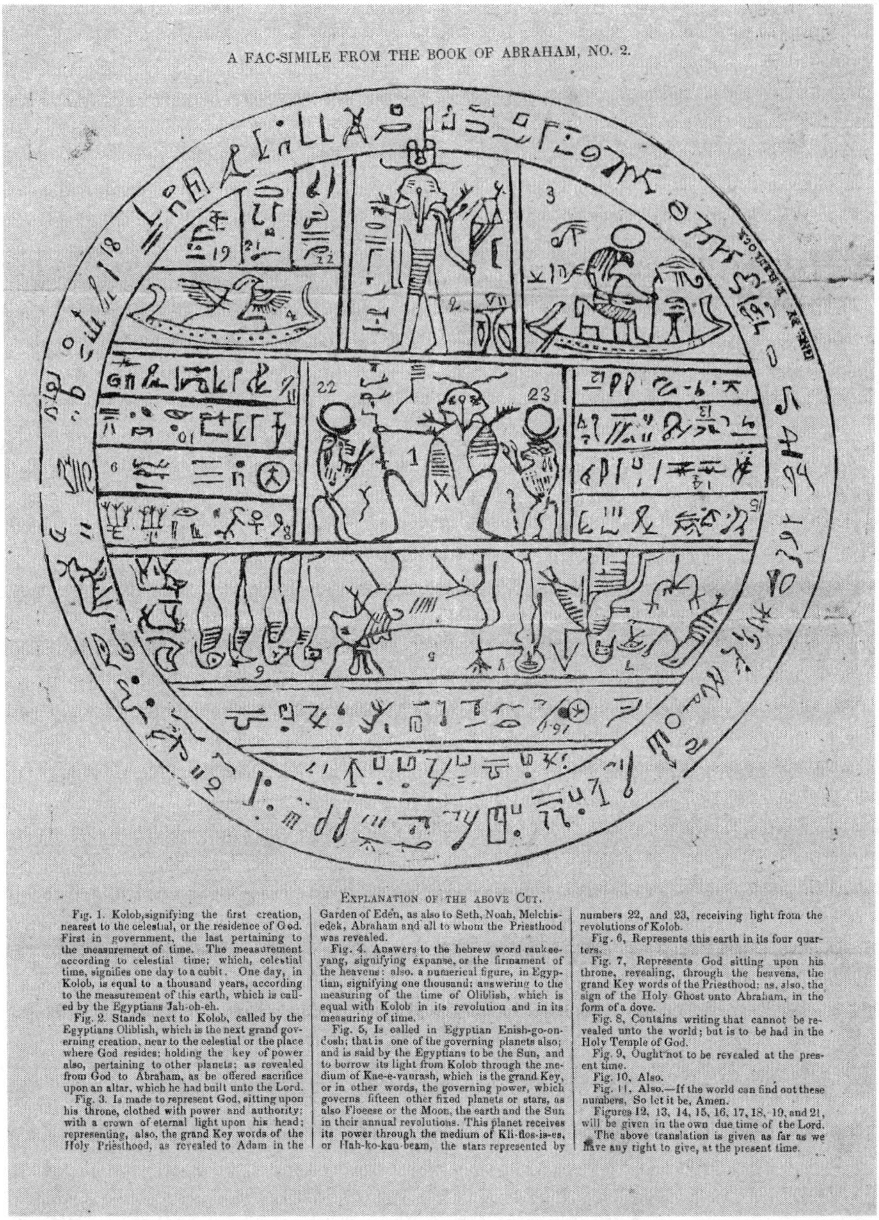

A FAC-SIMILE FROM THE BOOK OF ABRAHAM, NO. 2.

EXPLANATION OF THE ABOVE CUT.

Fig. 1. Kolob, signifying the first creation, nearest to the celestial, or the residence of God. First in government, the last pertaining to the measurement of time. The measurement according to celestial time; which, celestial time, signifies one day to a cubit. One day, in Kolob, is equal to a thousand years, according to the measurement of this earth, which is called by the Egyptians Jah-oh-eh.

Fig. 2. Stands next to Kolob, called by the Egyptians Oliblish, which is the next grand governing creation, near to the celestial or the place where God resides; holding the key of power also, pertaining to other planets; as revealed from God to Abraham, as he offered sacrifice upon an altar, which he had built unto the Lord.

Fig. 3. Is made to represent God, sitting upon his throne, clothed with power and authority; with a crown of eternal light upon his head; representing, also, the grand Key words of the Holy Priesthood, as revealed to Adam in the Garden of Edén, as also to Seth, Noah, Melchisedek, Abraham and all to whom the Priesthood was revealed.

Fig. 4. Answers to the hebrew word raukeeyang, signifying expanse, or the firmament of the heavens: also, a numerical figure, in Egyptian, signifying one thousand; answering to the measuring of the time of Oliblish, which is equal with Kolob in its revolution and in its measuring of time.

Fig. 5, Is called in Egyptian Enish-go-ondosh; that is one of the governing planets also; and is said by the Egyptians to be the Sun, and to borrow its light from Kolob through the medium of Kae-e-vanrash, which is the grand Key, or in other words, the governing power, which governs fifteen other fixed planets or stars, as also Floeese or the Moon, the earth and the Sun in their annual revolutions. This planet receives its power through the medium of Kli-flos-is-es, or Hah-ko-kau-beam, the stars represented by numbers 22, and 23, receiving light from the revolutions of Kolob.

Fig. 6, Represents this earth in its four quarters.

Fig. 7, Represents God sitting upon his throne, revealing, through the heavens, the grand Key words of the Priesthood: as, also, the sign of the Holy Ghost unto Abraham, in the form of a dove.

Fig. 8, Contains writing that cannot be revealed unto the world; but is to be had in the Holy Temple of God.

Fig. 9, Ought not to be revealed at the present time.

Fig. 10, Also.

Fig. 11, Also.—If the world can find out these numbers, So let it be, Amen.

Figures 12, 13, 14, 15, 16, 17, 18, 19, and 21, will be given in the own due time of the Lord.

The above translation is given as far as we have any right to give, at the present time.

FIGURE 15.1. Egyptian Funerary Charm with Explanations. Illustration from the Book of Abraham. The Egyptian papyri that Joseph Smith and others acquired in 1835 included a hypocephalus. Hypocephali were cosmic diagrams used as funerary charms placed "under (or beside) the head" of the deceased. Joseph Smith used material from his Egyptian study documents to explain some of the figures found in this hypocephalus. As editor of his church's newspaper, Joseph Smith published a print facsimile of the hypocephalus, along with an "Explanation" thereof. The facsimile was reprinted in a broadside edition, a copy of which is featured here. Church History Library, Salt Lake City.

book.[81] The explanations for figures 2 and 4, which reference Oliblish, likely appeared for the first time in 1842—especially in that the explanation for figure 4 invokes the Hebrew word *Raukeeyang* and its meaning (expanse).[82]

The explanation for figure 5 includes more of the 1835 astronomical vocabulary of the grammar book than any of the other figures, with words such as Enish-go-on-dosh, Kae-e-van-rash, Floeese, and Kli-flos-is-es. In the grammar book, the fifth-degree definition for the word Jah-oh-eh is "The earth under the governing powers of oliblish, Enish go on dosh, and Kae-e van rash, which are the grand key or in other words, the governing power, which governs the fifteen fixed stars."[83] Flo=ees in the fifth degree means "the moon, the earth and the sun in their annual revolutions" and Kli flosisis in the fifth degree "signifies Kolob in its motion, which is swifter than the rest of the twelve fixed stars; going before, being first in motion, being delegated to have power over others."[84] One can see that the explanations for the figures in the second illustration, particularly figures 1 and 5, include words and concepts from the 1835 grammar book.

Some of the 1835 terms were revised in 1842. Kli flosisis was defined in 1835 as the star "Kolob in its motion" but redefined in 1842 as one of two stars "reciving light from the revolutions of Kolob."[85] Similarly, the 1835 definition for Jah-oh-eh in the grammar book identifies Oliblish, Enish-go-on-dosh, and Kae-e van rash as governing twelve fixed stars, whereas the explanation to figure 5 in the second illustration has Kae-e-vanrash as a governing power over fifteen other planets, as well as the sun, moon, and earth.[86] Thus, one can see in 1835 the beginnings of some of the explanations, conceptually and terminologically, that underwent a development of thought by 1842.

It is unclear whether Smith's understanding of these parts of the Book of Abraham had developed gradually over the previous six years or was changed suddenly as he prepared it for publication in 1842. While most of it likely came from his known work on the Book of Abraham in March 1842, some of

81. Explanation of Facsimile 2, circa 15 March 1842, 1, in *JSP*-R4:278–79 [Abraham, Fac. 2, Fig. 2]; GAEL, 24, 31, in *JSP*-R4:162–63, 176–77.

82. Explanation of Facsimile 2, circa 15 March 1842, 2, in *JSP*-R4:278–81 [Abraham, Fac. 2, Figs. 3 and 4].

83. GAEL, 24, in *JSP*-R4:162–63.

84. GAEL, 25, in *JSP*-R4:164–65.

85. GAEL, 25, in *JSP*-R4:164–165; Explanation of Facsimile 2, circa 15 March 1842, 2, in *JSP*-R4:280–81 [Abraham Fac. 2: Fig. 5].

86. GAEL, 24, in *JSP*-R4:162–63; Explanation of Facsimile 2, circa 15 March 1842, 2, in *JSP*-R4:280–81 [Abraham, Fac. 2, Fig. 5]. Similarly, the definition for *Flos isis* states that "He [God] hath set a cloud round about in the heavens, and the light of the grand govering of 15 fixed stars centre there" (GAEL, 25, in *JSP*-R4:164–65). Fifteen "moving planets"—apparently of our Sun's own solar system—have place in the grammar book and have even been given specific (albeit previously unattested) names (GAEL, 24–25, in *JSP*-R4:162–65).

it may also have developed over time. Smith's journal for mid-1838 notes that on one occasion he "instructed the Church in the mistories of the Kingdom of God; giving them a history of the plannets &c. and of Abraham's writings upon the Plannettary Systems &c."[87] This manifests Smith's continued interest in a heavenly astronomy and perhaps a further development of ideas. A note given below the explanations to the figures of the second illustration states that "the above translation is given as far as we have any right to give, at the present time."[88] This suggests that his translation process for the Book of Abraham included an incremental aspect that could theoretically go on for years.

The content of the middle of Book of Abraham (in what now constitutes chapter 3) does not bear as much conceptual resemblance to the Egyptian language documents of 1835, except in employing certain words such as "Urim and Thummim," "Kolob," "planet," and "order."[89] However, Smith had spoken on subjects related to concepts in Abraham 3 on various occasions between 1835 and 1842, such as astronomy,[90] the plurality of gods,[91] and the eternal nature of humankind.[92] Also, the rest of the Book of Abraham includes several Hebrew words reflecting his study of Hebrew in early 1836.[93]

From this examination of the Book of Abraham content and the Egyptian alphabet and grammar documents, there are several strong correspondences between words, short phrases, and even passages of the Abraham documents and the language documents—especially in the fifth degree of meaning. As noted above, the relationships are complex and there is no definitive direction of overall textual dependency. Nevertheless, the manuscripts taken as a whole contain enough interrelated material that a working theory of direction and an evolutionary translation process can be hypothesized.

87. Smith, Journal, 6 May 1838, in *JSP*-J1:266.

88. Explanation of Facsimile 2, circa 15 March 1842, 3, in *JSP*-R4:282–83 [Abraham, Fac. 2].

89. See BoA, in *JSP*-R4:314–15 [Abraham 3:1, 3, 5, 9].

90. In 1900, early Mormon George Woodward reminisced that in December 1839 Smith had spoken "upon astronomy and told where God resides." St. George Temple Minute Book, 11 January 1900, 45, Church History Library. Compare Joseph Smith, Discourse, between circa 26 June and circa 4 August 1839-A, in *JSP*-D6:543–44; BoA, in *JSP*-R4:314–15 [Abraham 3:2–3].

91. Joseph Smith, Discourse, 16 June 1844, in Joseph Smith, *The Words of Joseph Smith: The Contemporary Accounts of the Nauvoo Discourses of the Prophet Joseph*, comp. and ed. Andrew F. Ehat and Lyndon Cook (Provo, UT: Religious Studies Center, Brigham Young University, 1980; Orem, UT: Grandin Book, 1991), 378–83.

92. In 1840, Smith reportedly stated his belief "that God is Eternal. That he had no beginning and can have no End. Eternity means that which is without beginning or End. . . . the Soul is Eternal. It had no beginning; it can have no End." Smith, Discourse, 5 February 1840, in *JSP*, D7:178. Compare BoA, in *JSP*-R4:318–19 [Abraham 3:18]. It is possible that these ideas originated as early as 1833, see Revelation, 6 May 1833, in *JSP*-D3:88–89 [D&C 93:23, 29, 33].

93. See Grey, "Approaching Egyptian Papyri through Biblical Language," 431–45 herein.

STEMMATOLOGICAL OBSERVATIONS: HYPOTHESIZING THE DIRECTION OF TEXTUAL DEPENDENCY

The Egyptian language documents and the beginning of the Book of Abraham were produced during the same period and share several close textual correspondences. They are clearly related. However, the nature of this relationship has been contentiously debated for several decades. Evangelical anti-Mormons, Egyptologists, skeptical scholars, and others have argued that Joseph Smith derived the Book of Abraham from a rather common extant Egyptian funerary document. In evidence of this, three 1835 Abraham manuscripts contain hieratic characters from this document in the left margin opposite Abraham text, denoting a translation effort. These critics, especially Egyptologists, have correctly determined that the hieratic characters do not translate to the Abraham text and have thereby rejected or dismissed the authenticity of the Book of Abraham. Conversely, Mormon apologists have argued that the translation of the Book of Abraham was accomplished in 1835 by Joseph Smith alone, from papyri we no longer have, acting under pure revelation from God, after which he and his scribes compared the papyri characters with the translated Book of Abraham in an attempt to reverse engineer the Egyptian alphabet and grammar[94]—similar to the way Champollion used parallel Egyptian and Coptic texts to understand the Egyptian language.[95]

Whereas the textual relationships between the Egyptian language documents and the Book of Abraham are obvious, a definitive direction of influence is not. As noted above, not all of the content in the Book of Abraham can be derived from the language documents and not all of the content in the language documents can be derived from the Book of Abraham. The relationship is complex. However, based on the chronological and textual analysis given above, there are a few clues suggesting a general direction of textual dependency. The five-degree system of definition explicated in the grammar book provides some traction in the investigation of textual dependency. Among the many passages in the Book of Abraham with matching material in the language documents, the closest matches are to character definitions in their fifth degree of meaning. As demonstrated, this is especially true for the beginning of the Book of Abraham and for the explanations of the second illustration.

94. See Gee, *Introduction to the Book of Abraham*, 9.

95. Brian M. Fagan, *The Rape of the Nile: Tomb Robbers, Tourists, and Archaeologists in Egypt* (Boulder, CO: Westview Press, 2004), 153–67.

This finding adds further specificity to the two major historiographical interpretations of the textual correspondences. In the critical perspective, the correspondences with fifth-degree definitions would determine the following reconstruction: Smith and his assistants translated a basic definition of the Egyptian characters, expanded that definition through the five levels of meaning, and then used the expanded content of the fifth-degree definitions to construct certain passages of the Book of Abraham. In the apologetic perspective, the correspondences with fifth-degree definitions would determine the opposite reconstruction: Smith and his assistants translated the Book of Abraham, reverse engineered the fifth-degree definitions of the grammar, and then diminished those definitions down through the five-degree system to produce the other four degrees of definition; completing the process by determining the most basic definitions found in the first degree of meaning.

The five-degree system is most clearly explicated in the beginning of the grammar book, which begins with fifth-degree definitions and steadily progresses downward through the five degrees until it reaches the first-degree definitions. However, the grammar book was not inscribed continuously from front to back. Instead, it is divided by degree into different sections of the book that are separated from each other by several blank pages. Therefore, while from a cursory glance it appears to have been written from fifth-degree definitions to first-degree definitions, this is far from clear. Moreover, the first-degree definitions are textually dependent on the alphabet text, which consists almost entirely of first-degree definitions.[96]

The one clear exception to this in the Alphabet document is the definition for Ah-broam/Ahbra-oam. This definition, which *was* written continuously from beginning to end, starts with the first degree and ascends through the five-degree system ending with the fifth degree. It is plausible that this text is the result of some reverse engineering accomplished on a different document that is no longer extant. But from the evidence that is available for scrutiny, it appears that Smith and his assistants started with the first degree and worked from there toward the fifth degree. The retrospective entry in Smith's history for late July 1835, which recounts that Smith spent time "translating an alphabet to the Book of Abraham,"[97] seems to affirm that Smith began by translating

96. On direction of dependency, see also Smith, "The Dependence of Abraham 1:1–3 on the Egyptian Alphabet and Grammar," 40–41, esp. 41n18.

97. The relevant notation in Smith's history follows an entry for 19 July. See Smith, History, 1838–1856, vol. B-1, 597. Like the entry for 6 (actually 6–8) July 1835, this entry likely relies on the reminiscences that

characters, as in the alphabet text, and that he and his assistants then used the elaborative process of the five-degree system to produce certain parts of what are now chapters 1 and 3 of the Book of Abraham.

Differing levels of correspondence between content in the grammar book and content in the Book of Abraham also suggest a pattern of direction. The 1835 grammar book corresponds more closely to the 1835 Abraham text than to the 1842 Abraham text. The Abraham text translated in 1842 was obviously produced after the content of the 1835 grammar book that it corresponds to and therefore was likely drawn from it. This, in turn, suggests that the text of the Book of Abraham translated in 1835 that corresponds to content in the grammar book was also drawn from that source. Furthermore, the passage of time between 1835 and 1842 provides a good explanation for the 1835 Abraham content drawing more closely from the grammar book, and the 1842 Abraham content drawing more loosely from it.

The use of Hebrew in the Book of Abraham seems to confirm this pattern of direction. As one would expect, Hebrew words and concepts from the Hebrew grammar book that Smith studied in 1836 do not appear in the manuscripts of the early Book of Abraham translation that are in the handwriting of the Kirtland-era scribes, William Phelps and Warren Parrish, who worked with Smith on the Egyptian material in 1835.[98] Conversely, as one might also expect, Hebrew words and concepts from the Hebrew grammar book that Smith studied in 1836 *do* appear in the Abraham manuscripts that are in the handwriting of Smith's principal Nauvoo-era scribe, Willard Richards, as well as in the Book of Abraham text as it was published in 1842. This is especially true for the middle and the end of the Book of Abraham (now Abraham 3–5)[99] and the explanations of the first and second illustrations (now Abraham, Facsimile 1, and Abraham, Facsimile 2). That the 1842 Abraham text drew on the Hebrew grammar book suggests that the 1835 Abraham text similarly drew on the Egyptian grammar book.

William W. Phelps provided on 16 September 1843. *History of Joseph Smith and The Church of Jesus Christ of Latter-day Saints*, 2:244. Here too, the general timeframe (late July) seems a reasonable reconstruction for something that had occurred several years earlier.

98. Frederick G. Williams also wrote one of these manuscripts of the early Book of Abraham text. Book of Abraham Manuscript, circa July–circa November 1835-A [Abraham 1:4–2:6]; Book of Abraham Manuscript, circa July–circa November 1835-B [Abraham 1:4–2:2]; and Book of Abraham Manuscript, circa July–circa November 1835-C [Abraham 1:1–2:18], all in *JSP*-R4:191–242.

99. For a comprehensive comparison of words and phrases in the Egyptian alphabet and grammar documents with the entire text of the Book of Abraham (now Abraham 1–5), see Hauglid, *A Textual History of the Book of Abraham*, 225–31.

PRELIMINARY CONCLUSIONS

The foregoing analysis of the chronological and textual relationships among the papyri, the Egyptian language documents, and the Book of Abraham leads to a few preliminary conclusions regarding Joseph Smith's approach to the translation of the Book of Abraham.

1. Smith and his assistants viewed some of the papyri—such as the fragment and its once-attached vignette used for the first illustration—as containing the Book of Abraham.
2. Smith and his assistants apparently believed that the Old Testament patriarch Abraham had written his autobiographical account "by his own hand, upon papyrus" and that this very papyrus, personally inscribed by Abraham, was among the papyri they had purchased.
3. Smith and his assistants apparently believed that the translation of the Book of Abraham included and involved grammatical groundwork—perhaps along the lines of a process with an initial period of study and intellectual inquiry followed by revelatory confirmation. This would be in keeping with the revelation regarding Oliver Cowdery's failed translation effort that Smith had dictated six years earlier.
4. Smith translated what became the beginning of the Book of Abraham (now constituting Abraham 1:1–2:18) between July and November 1835, and during the same time he was engaged with William Phelps and Oliver Cowdery in an intellectual study of the Egyptian language.
5. Based on the surviving manuscripts, these interlaced activities appear to have developed a rather intricate if misguided linguistic theory of a "grammar" system in which a character conveyed more significance as it ascended from its first level of meaning to its fifth level of meaning.
6. This five-degree system explains why two of the 1835 Abraham documents (covering Abraham 1:4–2:18) have the phrase "sign of the fifth degree of the second part" written at the top of the first page and why certain parts of what now constitutes Abraham 1 bear close resemblance to content in the Egyptian alphabet and grammar documents—especially those from fifth-degree definitions.
7. In 1842, when Smith translated what now constitutes Abraham 2:19–5:21 and the three illustrations, he incorporated content from both the Egyptian grammar book he had produced with William Phelps and

Oliver Cowdery in 1835 and the Hebrew grammar book he had studied under Joshua Seixas in 1836.

These preliminary conclusions suggest that Smith's approach to translating the Book of Abraham (including the illustrations) incorporated words that were translated from the characters on the Egyptian papyrus through the five levels of layered meaning as well as words and concepts from his Hebrew studies. These preliminary conclusions also suggest that Smith, Phelps, Cowdery, and perhaps others viewed the translation process within a framework in which the intellectual aspect of the process represented a significant part of the whole and went well beyond mere speculation and conjecture.

This inclusive view leads to the idea that the curious Egyptian language documents of 1835 should be considered as contributing to the overall process of translation, although some of the Egyptian language text does not appear in the Book of Abraham translation text and some Abraham translation text cannot be derived from the Egyptian language documents. Perhaps even the supposedly nonessential content in the Egyptian alphabet and grammar documents (the content that was not used in the Book of Abraham) should not be thought of as superfluous, but as an intricate part of the translation process as a whole. In this holistic view, the papyri, the hieroglyph transcripts and illustration copies, the versions of the alphabet document, the grammar book (with its five-degree system), and the Book of Abraham manuscripts could all be considered revered relics of the sacred work of translating the Book of Abraham.

16

Approaching Egyptian Papyri through Biblical Language

Joseph Smith's Use of Hebrew in His Translation of the Book of Abraham

MATTHEW J. GREY

Among the various translation projects undertaken by Joseph Smith, some of the most unique opportunities to examine his interrelated work as a "seer, translator, [and] prophet" derive from his production of the Book of Abraham, an expansion of the biblical account of the patriarch Abraham that was initially inspired by Smith's acquisition of and engagement with Egyptian papyri in the summer of 1835.[1] In this instance, a variety of extant source material—including manuscript evidence showing the development of the text, contemporaneous descriptions of Smith's translation activities, and some of the resources he consulted during the project—provide valuable insights into the book's production and rare glimpses into the mechanics of his approach to scriptural translation. This confluence of sources suggests that Smith's translation of the Book of Abraham was a dynamic and complex process involving a creative synthesis of his academic efforts and prophetic voice, which included his examination of characters and vignettes on the Egyptian papyri, attempts to create an Egyptian lexicon, interaction with the King James Version of the Bible, and claims to divine inspiration. In addition, the published text of the Book of Abraham shows that Joseph Smith incorporated into the translation process his knowledge of Biblical Hebrew—which he concurrently acquired through textbooks and formal study with a Hebrew instructor—thus marking the first (and perhaps only) time Smith conscientiously used a conventional ancient language in his production of scripture.

Because the Hebrew verbiage that appears in the book is clearly discernable and the Hebrew resources Joseph Smith had at his disposal are becoming

1. For the related roles of prophet and translator ascribed to Joseph Smith in one of his early revelations, see Revelation, 6 April 1830, in *JSP*-D1:129 [D&C 21:1].

increasingly accessible, the Hebrew elements in the Book of Abraham have the potential to shed significant light on how Smith viewed and carried out his scriptural translation activities. Despite this potential, however, the influence of Smith's Hebrew studies upon the text and the role those studies played in his translation process have received only minimal attention in Book of Abraham scholarship. Since its publication, most of the research and polemics surrounding the Book of Abraham have naturally focused on the relationship between Smith's interpretation of the papyri and the views of modern Egyptologists. Nevertheless, since the late nineteenth and early twentieth centuries there has been a small number of scholars who have briefly noted and questioned the origins of the text's recognizable (though unusually spelled) Hebrew words, as well as the subtler Hebraisms that appear in Smith's translation.

The earliest scholars to notice Hebrew terms in the Book of Abraham were not aware of Smith's formal study of Hebrew or the impact it had on his translation process and, as a result, simply dismissed the presence of these words in an ostensibly Egyptian document as historically anachronistic. Moreover, being unaware that the unconventional spelling of these words derived from the transliteration system taught to Joseph Smith by his Hebrew teacher, Joshua Seixas, early scholars viewed their orthography as evidence of Smith's fanciful efforts as a translator.[2] By the mid-twentieth century, though, the connection between Smith's studies with Seixas and the Hebrew elements in the Book of Abraham had been rediscovered, and it became clear that the former had to some degree influenced the latter.[3] Subsequent research regarding Joshua

2. The first scholar to make these observations was Théodule Devéria, who in 1856 encountered a copy of the Book of Abraham in the Louvre and briefly commentated on its "badly transcribed" Hebrew words. See Jules Remy and Julius Brenchley, *Journey to Great Salt Lake City* (London: W. Jeffs, 1861), 2:540–46. Similar (though more extensive) criticisms of the Hebrew elements in the Book of Abraham were offered by Samuel Mercer, who dismissed Smith's unusual spellings of Hebrew words as "pure imagination." F. S. Spalding, *Joseph Smith, Jr., as a Translator: An Inquiry Conducted* (Salt Lake City, UT: Arrow Press, 1912), 29; and Samuel Mercer, "Joseph Smith as an Interpreter and Translator of Egyptian," *The Utah Survey* 1, no. 1 (September 1913): 4–36, esp. 19–24, 34–35. Like Devéria and Mercer, Mormon respondents also seemed unaware of the connection between these words and the transliteration system taught to Joseph Smith by Joshua Seixas, and were thus unable to address the criticisms over their spelling. See George Reynolds, *The Book of Abraham: Its Authenticity Established as a Divine and Ancient Record* (Salt Lake City: Deseret News, 1879), 44–49; B. H. Roberts, "A Plea in Bar of Final Conclusions," *Improvement Era*, February 1913, 309–25; and J. M. Sjodahl, "The Book of Abraham," *Improvement Era*, February 1913, 326–33.

3. John Peters from the University of Pennsylvania may have been the first scholar to recognize that Joseph Smith's unusual Hebrew spelling reflected Sephardic transliterations, while the non-Mormon defender of the Book of Abraham, James E. Homans (under the pseudonym R. C. Webb), was the first to suggest that Smith learned this form of spelling from Joshua Seixas, who came from a Sephardic Jewish family. See R. C. Webb, "Truth Seekers," *Improvement Era*, May 1913, 1075–91; and Webb, "Have Joseph Smith's Interpretations Been Discredited?," *Deseret News*, 15 November 1913, vi–vii. In addition to making this case in print, Homans privately shared his insights into the Seixas connection with church apostle James E. Talmage.

Seixas, his teaching methods (including his spelling system), and his instruction of Joseph Smith increasingly illuminated the ways in which Smith incorporated his knowledge of Hebrew into his Book of Abraham translation,[4] including his insertion of Hebrew terminology into the text and his reworking of the biblical creation account based on insights he acquired in his study of Hebrew.[5] Yet, despite the important implications of these observations for both the development of the Book of Abraham text and the work of its translator, relatively few scholars have closely examined the relationship between Smith's Hebrew studies and his translation of the Book of Abraham, with the result that the topic has not been well integrated into Book of Abraham research.[6]

One reason for this lack of treatment may be that assessing Joseph Smith's use of Hebrew in the Book of Abraham requires a working knowledge of both Biblical Hebrew and a wide range of nineteenth-century sources. However, these disparate fields do not often converge in Book of Abraham scholarship, which may explain why no one has heretofore undertaken a systematic and properly contextualized study of the Hebrew elements in Smith's translation. In addition, the limited work that has so far been done on this topic was conducted prior to the more recent discoveries and clarifications related to the relevant source materials,[7] with the result that confusion and problematic

---

See the letters between Homans and Talmage, 14 December 1920–26 February 1921, James E. Talmage Collection, General Correspondence, Church History Library, The Church of Jesus Christ of Latter-day Saints, Salt Lake City (hereafter Church History Library). Curiously, however, detailed research on Seixas and his relationship with Smith would not be published for over two decades after Homans made his initial suggestion. LeRoi C. Snow, "Who Was Professor Joshua Seixas?," *Improvement Era*, February 1936, 67–71.

4. The first proper study of this topic, which remained the classic treatment for over four decades, was Louis Zucker, "Joseph Smith as a Student of Hebrew," *Dialogue: A Journal of Mormon Thought* 3, no. 2 (Summer 1968): 41–55.

5. See Michael T. Walton, "Professor Seixas, the Hebrew Bible, and the Book of Abraham," *Sunstone* 6, vol. 2 (March–April 1981): 41–43; Anthony Hutchinson, "A Mormon Midrash?: LDS Creation Narratives Reconsidered," *Dialogue: A Journal of Mormon Thought* 21, no. 4 (Winter 1988): 11–74; Karl C. Sandberg, "Knowing Brother Joseph Again: The Book of Abraham and Joseph Smith as a Translator," *Dialogue: A Journal of Mormon Thought* 22, no. 4 (Winter 1989): 17–38; and H. Michael Marquardt, "Joseph Smith's Egyptian Papers: A History," in *The Joseph Smith Egyptian Papyri: A Complete Edition*, Robert K. Ritner, with Contributions by Marc Coenen, H. Michael Marquardt, and Christopher Woods (Salt Lake City: Smith-Pettit Foundation, 2011), 11–56.

6. Beyond the relatively few treatments noted above, most commentaries, studies, and histories of the Book of Abraham ranging from the mid-twentieth century to the early twenty-first century do not make any serious mention of the book's Hebrew elements or the impact of Seixas's teachings on Smith's translation process. See, for example, Milton R. Hunter, *Pearl of Great Price Commentary* (Salt Lake City: Bookcraft, 1951); H. Donl Peterson, *The Story of the Book of Abraham: Mummies, Manuscripts, and Mormonism* (Salt Lake City: Deseret Book, 1995); and Richard D. Draper, S. Kent Brown, and Michael D. Rhodes, *The Pearl of Great Price: A Verse by Verse Commentary* (Salt Lake City: Deseret Book, 2005).

7. Recent groundbreaking work includes the official publication of the Joseph Smith journals and histories spanning the period of Smith's translation activities (*JSP*-J1; *JSP*-J2; *JSP*-H1); scholarly editions of the extant manuscripts of the Book of Abraham (Brian M. Hauglid, *A Textual History of the Book of Abraham:*

assumptions frequently circulate regarding the interrelationship between Smith's Egyptian project, Hebrew study, and translation effort. Such confusion includes the precise sequence of Smith's translation activities (was the Book of Abraham translation completed prior to or after his study of Hebrew?), the degree to which Smith intended to integrate his work with the Egyptian papyri and his Hebrew studies (was the relationship deliberate or merely coincidental?), and the method by which Smith translated the Book of Abraham (was it a supernatural process, an intellectual exercise, or both?). All of these aspects of the translation affect the way Smith's efforts should be viewed. To clarify these issues and highlight their significance for understanding Smith's work as a translator, this chapter will provide a systematic examination of his use of Hebrew in the translation of the Book of Abraham in light of earlier research, recent developments in scholarship, and previously unexamined source materials.

In order to properly evaluate the Hebrew elements within the Book of Abraham, the first two sections of this chapter will consider the context, chronology, and relationships among Joseph Smith's work with the Egyptian papyri, his study of the Hebrew language, and his production of the Abraham text. This survey of evidence will demonstrate that from an early stage Smith's Egyptian project and Hebrew studies appear to have been intentionally intertwined, as he evidently believed that a knowledge of Hebrew would assist his decipherment of the Egyptian characters and thus facilitate his translation of the Book of Abraham. This survey will also show that while Smith's translation of the Book of Abraham began in the summer of 1835 (*before* his study of Hebrew in the winter of 1835–1836) it was not completed until the spring of 1842 (several years *after* his formal study of Hebrew), with the presence of Seixas-inspired Hebrew elements helping to clarify the chronology of the book's textual development. The third section of this chapter will analyze the Hebrew words, concepts, and other influences in the text of the Book of Abraham, including the ways in which Smith's Hebrew studies, grammar books, and lexicons informed his translation process. The chapter will conclude by

Manuscripts and Editions [Provo, UT: Neal A. Maxwell Institute for Religious Scholarship, Brigham Young University, 2010]; *JSP*-R4]); advances in the study of Smith's Egyptian papers (Brian M. Hauglid, "The Book of Abraham and the Egyptian Project," chap. 17 in *Approaching Antiquity: Joseph Smith and the Ancient World*, ed. Lincoln H. Blumell, Matthew J. Grey, and Andrew H. Hedges [Provo, UT: Religious Studies Center, Brigham Young University; Salt Lake City: Deseret Book, 2015]); and a detailed reconstruction of Smith's Hebrew studies with Seixas (Matthew J. Grey, "'The Word of the Lord in the Original': Joseph Smith's Study of Hebrew in Kirtland," chap. 10 in *Approaching Antiquity*), all of which shed important light on Smith's use of Hebrew in the Book of Abraham.

considering the implications of this evidence for Joseph Smith's views and mechanics of scriptural translation (which included a dynamic blend of academic and prophetic activity), as well as the impact this process had on the development of Smith's most innovative theological teachings.

JOSEPH SMITH'S EGYPTIAN PROJECT AND HIS MOTIVATIONS FOR LEARNING HEBREW

Before Joseph Smith's use of Hebrew in the Book of Abraham can be properly assessed, it is first necessary to understand the relationships among Smith's work on the Egyptian papyri, his study of the Hebrew language, and his production of the Abraham text, as well as the chronology of these overlapping activities. Often, scholarly literature either does not mention these efforts in conjunction with one another or describes them as unrelated projects that, as a mere coincidence, produced minor glosses to the Abraham translation.[8] These oversights may stem from the frequent but problematic claims that Smith had mostly completed his translation of the Book of Abraham in 1835 (*before* his study of Hebrew in 1836) and that his Hebrew study was a separate endeavor that brought an abrupt end to the Egyptian project.[9] However, a confluence

8. Karl C. Sandberg asserted that the brief overlap of the work by Smith and others on the Egyptian papers and their study of Hebrew was only a "powerful coincidence." Sandberg, "Knowing Brother Joseph Again," 31; compare Walton, "Professor Seixas, the Hebrew Bible, and the Book of Abraham," 41). Part of the confusion on this issue may be related to the inaccurate assumptions that—despite working with the papyri since July 1835—Smith had not considered studying Hebrew until the following November when he encountered the local Jewish scholar Daniel Peixotto, and that it was not until December 1835 that he first saw a potential relevance between his study of Hebrew and the (then mostly complete) Book of Abraham. For examples of these assumptions, see Zucker, "Joseph Smith as a Student of Hebrew," 44; and Donna Hill, *Joseph Smith: The First Mormon* (New York: Doubleday, 1977), 190–91.

9. Such claims (or variations of them) can be seen in Zucker, "Joseph Smith as a Student of Hebrew," 50; Walton, "Professor Seixas, the Hebrew Bible, and the Book of Abraham," 41–42; Hugh W. Nibley, "A New Look at the Pearl of Great Price: Part 7; The Unknown Abraham," *Improvement Era*, January 1969, 27–28; John Gee, "Eyewitnesses, Hearsay, and Physical Evidence of the Joseph Smith Papyri," chap. 7 in *The Disciple as Witness: Essays on Latter-day Saint History and Doctrine in Honor of Richard Lloyd Anderson*, ed. Stephen D. Ricks, Donald W. Parry, and Andrew H. Hedges (Provo, UT: Foundation for Ancient Research and Mormon Studies at Brigham Young University, 2000); and John Gee, *An Introduction to the Book of Abraham* (Provo, UT: Religious Studies Center, Brigham Young University; Salt Lake City: Deseret Book, 2017), 14–15, 21, 42. Kerry Muhlestein and Megan Hansen also claim that the translation was mostly complete in 1835, although they do briefly consider the Hebrew elements of the book, which they see as only minor glosses made in 1842. Muhlestein and Hansen, "'The Work of Translating': The Book of Abraham's Translation Chronology," in *Let Us Reason Together: Essays in Honor of the Life's Work of Robert L. Millet*, ed. J. Spencer Fluhman and Brent L. Top (Provo, UT: Religious Studies Center, Brigham Young University, 2016), 139–62. However, their analysis does not consider the full range of Hebrew evidence in the Book of Abraham, nor does it sufficiently weigh the extent to which Smith's Hebrew studies influenced his later work on the text—especially in the text's creation account. Book of Abraham and Facsimiles, 1 March–16 May 1842, in *JSP*-R4:318–21 (hereafter BoA) [Abraham 4–5]).

of evidence indicates that Smith's Egyptian and Hebrew interests were closely related from the beginning, and that his translation of the Book of Abraham was a gradual process that he *began* in the summer of 1835, continued after his Hebrew studies in the winter of 1835–1836, and *completed* in early 1842 after he had methodically incorporated Hebrew verbiage into the text.

To begin this survey of evidence, it is important to consider the timing and logic of Smith's efforts to commence studying Hebrew in late 1835, only a few months after his acquisition of the Egyptian papyri. Smith may have had a variety of compelling motivations for learning Hebrew that predated his work with the papyri, including his earlier revelations on the need for language study,[10] a desire to enhance his prophetic calling by reading "the word of the Lord in the original,"[11] and his ongoing efforts to reconstruct the "pure language" of Adam from disparate ancient sources.[12] However, it is unlikely a mere coincidence that he first made arrangements to study Hebrew shortly after he began his efforts to interpret the Egyptian characters on the papyri and to translate the Book of Abraham. Although these activities might not seem mutually relevant to modern scholars, the intellectual climate and religious worldviews of the early nineteenth century help explain Smith's attempt to integrate Hebrew study and the translation of Egyptian documents into a single enterprise.

Since the earliest days of Mormonism, Joseph Smith and his close associates had sought to recover scripture and language from the ancient past as a part of their larger restoration project.[13] Over time, this pursuit drew heavily upon widespread antebellum beliefs—based on the opening chapters of Genesis—that humanity originally shared a common "Adamic" language that contained

10. In 1832 and 1833, Smith had dictated revelations commanding the Saints to pursue language studies, leading to the establishment of an ecclesiastical school system in Kirtland, see Revelation, 27–28 December 1832, in *JSP*-D2:341–42, 345 [D&C 88:77–80, 118–19]; Revelation, 8 March 1833, in *JSP*-D3:29 [D&C 90:14–15]; Revelation, 6 May 1833, in *JSP*-D3:91 [D&C 93:53]. However, these revelations did not specify Hebrew as a course of study and the Kirtland school did not offer a Hebrew curriculum until January 1836. Grey, "'The Word of the Lord in the Original,'" 253–72.

11. Smith, Journal, 17 February 1836, in *JSP*-J1:186. See similar statements in Smith's journal entries for 19 January and 4 February 1836 (*JSP*-J1:164, 180); and in the preface to the abbreviated Hebrew grammar published for the Kirtland Hebrew school. *Supplement to J. Seixas' Manual Hebrew Grammar for the Kirtland, Ohio, Theological Institution* (New York: West & Trow, 1836), 8.

12. See Samuel Morris Brown, "Joseph (Smith) in Egypt: Babel, Hieroglyphics, and the Pure Language of Eden," *Church History* 78, no. 1 (March 2009): 26–65; Brown, *In Heaven as It Is on Earth: Joseph Smith and the Early Mormon Conquest of Death* (New York and Oxford: Oxford University Press, 2012), 129–41; and David Golding, "'Eternal Wisdom Engraven upon the Heavens': Joseph Smith's Pure Language Project," Chapter 14 herein. For more on Smith's various motivations for learning Hebrew, see Grey, "'The Word of the Lord in the Original,'" 255–61.

13. See Samuel Brown, "Mormonism as Restoration," in *Mormonism: A Historical Encyclopedia*, ed. Paul Reeve and Ardis Parshall (Santa Barbara, CA: ABC-CLIO, 2010), 365–71.

pristine insights into the divine mysteries, but that this pure language was confounded, lost, or fractured at the Tower of Babel.[14] As a result of this view, many scholars and theologians contemporary with Smith believed that Hebrew and Egyptian were among the surviving ancient linguistic systems that most closely resembled the primitive language of Adam, and were therefore related in their origins as well as in their ability to reveal, or at least partially access, the earliest divine truths known to humanity.[15]

However, while Hebrew had been known by western scholars and clergymen since the Reformation in the sixteenth century, Egyptian hieroglyphs had not yet been fully deciphered.[16] Therefore, in the early nineteenth century there existed a wide variety of approaches to the interpretation and significance of Egyptian characters. These included popular beliefs that hieroglyphs possessed deeply symbolic meanings from the sacred past that, according to mystical thinkers such as the Swedenborgians, could only be understood through divine means.[17] Although this metaphysical approach remained widespread in the early nineteenth century, by the 1830s it began to be challenged by the emerging view—encouraged by the work of French philologist Jean-François Champollion—that Egyptian hieroglyphs were not mystical symbols, but were made up of phonetic characters mixed with ideograms and thus reflected a spoken language.[18] Despite

14. See Genesis 11:1–9.

15. For a survey of these views ranging from seventeenth-century British theologian Theophilus Gale to eighteenth-century American clergymen Jonathan Edwards and Ezra Stiles, see Shalom Goldman, *God's Sacred Tongue: Hebrew and the American Imagination* (Chapel Hill, NC: University of North Carolina Press, 2004), 2, 23–26, 80–82; compare Brown, *In Heaven as It Is on Earth*, 129–31. Related claims can also be found in popular publications from the early nineteenth century such as the writings of Elias Boudinot and Josiah Priest. Elias Boudinot, *The Second Advent, or Coming of the Messiah in Glory* (Trenton, NJ: D. Fenton & S. Hutchinson, 1815), 168–72; and Josiah Priest, *American Antiquities, and Discoveries in the West* (Albany: Hoffman and White, 1835), 17, 25, 65, 123, 126, 208.

16. Thomas Young and Jean-François Champollion, who were pivotal scholars in the ultimate decipherment of Egyptian, had been publishing some of their initial findings in European venues since the 1820s, and some of those findings had made their way into print in English and were available in America by the early 1830s. However, as noted below, during the time of Joseph Smith's translation activities their work was only in limited circulation and was not yet widely understood or accepted by American scholars.

17. This approach was popular as early as the seventeenth century, as reflected in the writing of Athanasius Kircher, *Oedipus Aegyptiacus*, 3 vols. (Rome: V. Mascardi, 1652–1654), and as continued in several variations well into the nineteenth century (see Emanuel Swedenborg, *The Hieroglyphical Key to Natural and Spiritual Mysteries* [London: n.p., 1784]; Sampson Reed, *New Jerusalem Magazine*, October 1830, 69–71; and J. D., "Egyptian Hieroglyphs," *New Jerusalem Magazine*, February 1831, 233–36). For more on these views, see Richard Lyman Bushman, "Joseph Smith and the Study of Antiquity," *Approaching Antiquity*, 13–19; and John T. Irwin, *American Hieroglyphics: The Symbol of the Egyptian Hieroglyphics in the American Renaissance* (New Haven: Yale University Press, 1980), 3–14.

18. For early academic approaches and attempts to highlight for American readers the work of Champollion with the Rosetta Stone, see Henry Wheaton, "Egyptian Antiquities," *The North American Review* 29, no. 65 (October 1829): 361–88; and Edward Everett, "Hieroglyphics," *The North American Review* 32, no. 70 (January 1831): 95–127. John Gee provides a helpful overview of Champollion's work and the nebulous state of

these competing views, adherents to both approaches believed that Egyptian and Hebrew were closely related. For instance, Stephen Sewall—a professor of Hebrew and Oriental languages at Harvard—claimed in the late eighteenth century that Hebrew was the "original language" of humanity and that it eventually influenced the development of Egyptian.[19] Similarly, though with slight variation, the classicist J. G. H. Greppo claimed in 1830 that both languages contained "traces of the primitive [pre-Babel] language from which they are both derived," and that one could be used in the process of deciphering the other.[20]

This belief can be seen in contemporaneous efforts to use Biblical Hebrew as a key resource in the interpretation of Egyptian characters. Such efforts included attempts by prominent scholars to translate Egyptian coffin texts using Hebrew language,[21] to use Hebrew scripture to understand Egyptian temple inscriptions,[22] to argue that Egyptian hieroglyphs contained embedded Hebrew words,[23] to demonstrate through the biblical creation account that Hebrew letter forms developed out of Egyptian characters,[24] and to compare Egyptian and Hebrew with other forms of ancient hieroglyphs (including Chinese and Mayan characters) as a way of considering their shared origins and developments.[25] Other scholars were more circumspect, but still attempted to demon-

American Egyptology as the context for Smith's work with the papyri. John Gee, "Joseph Smith and Ancient Egypt," in *Approaching Antiquity*, 427–48.

19. Goldman, *God's Sacred Tongue*, 45–51; Thomas Siegel, "Professor Stephen Sewall and the Transformation of Hebrew at Harvard," in *Hebrew and the Bible in America: The First Two Centuries*, ed. Shalom Goldman (Hanover, NH: University Press of New England, 1993), 228–45.

20. See J. G. H. Greppo, *Essay on the Hieroglyphic System of M. Champollion*, trans. Isaac Stuart (Boston: Perkins and Marvin, 1830). In this lengthy treatise, Greppo drew heavily upon the work of Champollion to support his claims that Egyptian and Hebrew were linked both historically and philologically, and therefore "should be studied together" (3–5, 66–82).

21. French scholar Court de Gebelin attempted to use Hebrew, Greek, Arabic, and Phoenician to translate an Egyptian coffin inscription. See M. de la Sauvagère, *Recueil d' antiquitès* (Paris: Herrisant, 1770), 361–77. Compare Greppo, *Essay on the Hieroglyphic System of M. Champollion*, 14.

22. One early nineteenth-century scholar drew upon Psalm 110 in an attempt to interpret the Dendera zodiac. See *De l' Étude des hiéroglyphiques* (Paris: n.p., 1822). Compare Greppo, *Essay on the Hieroglyphic System of M. Champollion*, 14; and Irwin, *American Hieroglyphics*, 4–5.

23. Believing that Hebrew letter forms could be seen in Egyptian characters, Pierre Lacour attempted to create a "hieroglyphic dictionary of Hebrew, for ease of interpretation of Egyptian hieroglyphics." Lacour, *Essai sur les hiéroglyphiques Égyptiens* (Bordeaux: Impr. Brossier, 1821). Compare Greppo, *Essay on the Hieroglyphic System of M. Champollion*, 14.

24. For example, Cambridge professor John Lamb creatively charted what he saw as the development from Egyptian hieroglyphs to Hebrew letter forms and examined their original meanings in light of Genesis 1–3. John Lamb, *Hebrew Characters Derived from Hieroglyphics* (London: John William Parker, 1835).

25. See Greppo, *Essay on the Hieroglyphic System of M. Champollion*, 206–15; and Michael Russell, *View of Ancient and Modern Egypt* (Edinburgh: Oliver and Boyd, 1831), 181–215. For other efforts to compare writing systems from the old and new worlds (apparently motivated by the belief that all ancient languages derived from a common source), see Michael Hubbard MacKay and Gerrit J. Dirkmaat, *From Darkness unto Light: Joseph Smith's Translation and Publication of the Book of Mormon* (Provo, UT: Religious Studies Center, Brigham Young University, 2015), 44–49.

strate the parallel developments of Egyptian and Hebrew by comparing their respective pictorial forms, phonetic pronunciations, and original meanings.[26] This included Champollion as well as Moses Stuart, the eminent American Hebraist whose textbook would be studied by Joseph Smith. Both scholars saw similarities in the ways Hebrew letters and Egyptian hieroglyphs were named after the objects they resembled—such as the original form of *aleph* (א) resembling an "ox head" or *beth* (ב) resembling a "house"—and believed that further research would prove the close relationship between the two writing systems.[27] Although many of these views gradually faded or were significantly refined over later generations, in the intellectual climate of the early nineteenth century it is not surprising that Smith and his associates worked under the assumption that Egyptian and Hebrew shared common origins in an Edenic language, and that both could be used in tandem to recover the sacred past.[28]

Views of the interconnectedness of Egyptian and Hebrew were present in Mormon thought from the beginning with Joseph Smith's first scriptural translation, the Book of Mormon. Throughout that project, Smith claimed that the gold plates were written by Hebrew-speaking Israelites in a language called "reformed Egyptian."[29] This language was understood within the Book of Mormon as some kind of amalgam of Hebrew and Egyptian, consisting of "the learning of the Jews and the language of the Egyptians."[30] This view of the relationship between Hebrew knowledge and the Reformed Egyptian characters on the plates may have been encouraged early in the translation process by statements attributed to Columbia classics professor Charles Anthon. Joseph Smith had supplied his scribe, Martin Harris, with a transcript of some of the characters from the gold plates that Harris took with him when he traveled to New York City to consult with Anthon. Reports vary regarding Anthon's

26. See Jean-François Champollion, *Précis du système hiéroglyphique des anciens Égyptiens* (Paris: Imprimerie Royale, 1828), 73–75, 109–17; compare Greppo, *Essay on the Hieroglyphic System of M. Champollion*, 73; and Everett, "Hieroglyphics," 122.

27. See Moses Stuart's excursus on the "Similarity of Egyptian and Hebrew Writing and Language," in Greppo, *Essay on the Hieroglyphic System of M. Champollion*, 267–70.

28. For more on the perceived relationships between Egyptian, Hebrew, and the "pure language of Adam," see Brown, "Joseph (Smith) in Egypt," 26–65; and Brown, *In Heaven as It Is on Earth*, 129–41. See also Terryl L. Givens with Brian M. Hauglid, *The Pearl of Greatest Price: Mormonism's Most Controversial Scripture* (New York and Oxford: Oxford University Press, 2019), 113–18 and 185–88.

29. The book's final narrator states that the language written on the gold plates consists of "characters which are called among us the reformed Egyptian, being handed down and altered by us, according to our manner of speech," and explains, "if our plates had been sufficiently large we should have written in Hebrew; but the Hebrew hath been altered by us also; and if we could have written in Hebrew, behold, ye would have had no imperfection in our record" (Mormon 9:32–33).

30. 1 Nephi 1:2; compare Mosiah 1:4.

assessment of the transcript, but several of the reports claim the professor identified both Egyptian and Hebrew characters in the transcript. Smith recorded Harris's report that Anthon declared the Book of Mormon characters to be a mixture of "Egyptian, Chaldaic [Aramaic], Assyriac, and Arabic,"[31] whereas Anthon himself wrote that the transcript contained "a most singular medley . . . [of] Greek, Hebrew, and all sorts of letters, more or less distorted."[32] According to another account, Anthon "pronounced the characters to be ancient Hebrew corrupted, and the language to be degenerate Hebrew with a mixture of Egyptian."[33]

Though exactly what Anthon said on that occasion remains uncertain, the sentiments ascribed to him consistently reflect (and to some degree may have informed) the common early Mormon understanding of the composite nature of the characters on the plates as being a combination of "Hebrew [and] reformed Egyptian."[34] This belief is seen in a creative attempt by Oliver Cowdery—Smith's primary scribe in the Book of Mormon translation—to reproduce some of the book's original "Hebrew" text. In this attempt, Cowdery wrote out the English translations of Jacob 5:13 ("for it grieveth me that I should lose this tree & the fruit thereof") and of Jacob 7:27 ("brethren I bid you adieu"), and then somehow transliterated their original "Hebrew" text as "fin Zemin ezmon E. Zer Oms. Ifs veris exzer ens. vonis vinesis" and "ifs E. Zamtri" respectively.[35] While Cowdery's transliterations do not contain any recognizable Hebrew words and do not represent Hebrew in any traditional sense, they do reflect the conviction that the Reformed Egyptian of the Book

31. History drafts, 1838–circa 1841, in *JSP*-H1: 239–45 [JS-H1:63–65].

32. "Communications," *Times and Seasons*, 15 September 1841, 545; John A. Clark, *Gleanings by the Way* (New York: Robert Carter, 1842), 233. Despite a lack of formal training in these nonclassical languages, Anthon was aware of the work of Champollion and inserted several Egyptian words and definitions into his revision of J. Lempriere's *Classical Dictionary* (Bushman, "Joseph Smith and the Study of Antiquity," 17). Since the extant documents containing transcripts of Book of Mormon characters contain no obvious Hebrew or Egyptian writing, it is not clear what might have prompted Anthon's assessment of their origins. See images of the original documents in Appendix 2: Copies of Book of Mormon Characters, in *JSP*-D1:353–67. See also Michael Hubbard MacKay, Gerrit J. Dirkmaat, and Robin Scott Jensen, "The 'Caracters' Document: New Light on an Early Transcription of the Book of Mormon Characters," *Mormon Historical Studies* 14, no. 1 (Spring 2013): 131–52.

33. This statement comes from an 1841 remembrance of Joseph Smith's younger brother William Smith. James Murdock, "The Mormons and Their Prophet," *Congregational Observer*, 3 July 1841, 1. William Smith was sixteen at the time of the Anthon episode (Smith, History, 1834–1836, in *JSP*-H1:31). For more on Anthon and on Smith's evolving understanding of the Reformed Egyptian characters on the plates, see MacKay and Dirkmaat, *From Darkness unto Light*, 41–44.

34. "The Book of Mormon," *Evening and the Morning Star*, January 1833, 2. Although Smith himself never explicitly described the characters on the gold plates as being Hebrew, he did compare their ordering to "Hebrew writing in general." "History of Joseph Smith," *Times and Seasons*, 1 October 1842, 943.

35. Characters Copied by Oliver Cowdery, circa 1835–1836, in *JSP*-D1:361–65.

of Mormon was somehow associated with Hebrew and that one language could be used to illuminate or even reconstruct the other.[36]

Therefore, in July 1835 when the Egyptian papyri arrived in Kirtland, Ohio, and Smith declared that they contained the writings of biblical patriarchs, he and his associates naturally would have considered Hebrew a helpful resource in their efforts to decipher the Egyptian characters and restore the writings of Abraham. At that time, however, no one in the Mormon community knew much about either language with the possible exception of W. W. Phelps, an amateur linguist who occasionally dabbled with Hebrew words in his newspaper editorials,[37] and who since 1832 had been periodically involved with Smith in reconstructing the "pure language" of Adam[38] (a linguistic system he believed was closely related to Hebrew).[39] Nevertheless, when Smith and his associates first examined the papyri, they immediately compared them with the Hebraic Reformed Egyptian characters, "which were previously copied from the [Book of Mormon] plates," and thought they saw a resemblance between the two scripts.[40] They also thought (perhaps at Phelps's suggestion) that some

36. Although editors for the *Joseph Smith Papers* dated this document to sometime between 1835 and 1836 (*JSP*-D1:361–65), it was most likely produced relatively early within that date range, *before* Cowdery had received any Hebrew training (see below).

37. See "Hosea Chapter III," *Evening and the Morning Star*, July 1832, 6; "The Ten Tribes," *Evening and the Morning Star*, October 1832, 1–2; and "The Book of Mormon," *Evening and the Morning Star*, January 1833, 1–3. The *Evening and the Morning Star* was edited by W. W. Phelps & Co., as named on the last page of every issue. The unsigned articles cited above were likely written by Phelps, although it is unclear when and where he would have acquired his (limited) knowledge of Hebrew. For a consideration of his broader linguistic interests, see Samuel Brown, "The Translator and the Ghostwriter: Joseph Smith and W. W. Phelps," *Journal of Mormon History* 34, no. 1 (Winter 2008): 26–62, esp. 31–32.

38. For examples of efforts by Smith and Phelps to reconstruct the Adamic language, see the circa March 1832 document, "A Sample of pure Language given by Joseph the Seer." Sample of Pure Language, in *JSP*-D2:213–15; Revelation, 1 June 1833, in D3:108 [D&C 95:17]; and "A Specimen of some of the 'pure language'" that William W. Phelps appended to a letter to his wife (William Wines Phelps, Kirtland, OH, to Sally Waterman Phelps, Liberty, MO, 26 May 1835, in William W. Phelps Papers, Nineteenth-Century Western & Mormon Manuscripts, L. Tom Perry Special Collections, Harold B. Lee Library, Brigham Young University, Provo, UT). Some Latter-day Saints believed that this was the "pure language" mentioned in Zephaniah 3:9 and that it would be restored in its fullness during the Millennium. See Oliver Cowdery, "The Prophecy of Zephaniah," *Evening and the Morning Star*, March 1834, 281–82. Earlier Mormon references to a pure, pre-Babel "Language of Adam" can be found in the Book of Mormon (Ether 1:33–37) and in Smith's 1830 revisions of the Bible, see Old Testament Manuscript 1, 11–13, in Joseph Smith, *Joseph Smith's New Translation of the Bible: Original Manuscripts*, ed. Scott H. Faulring, Kent P. Jackson, and Robert J. Matthews (Provo, UT: Religious Studies Center, Brigham Young University, 2004), 97, 100 [Moses 6:5–6, 46]. See also Golding, "'Eternal Wisdom Engraven upon the Heavens,'" Chapter 14 herein.

39. An article in the church newspaper stated that "Hebrew . . . was nearer the pure language, with which Adam gave names, than any other since used by man." "Sacred Poetry," *Evening and the Morning Star*, November 1832, 5. This article was likely written by Phelps (see note 37 above).

40. Oliver Cowdery to William Frye, 22 December 1835, copy in Oliver Cowdery Letterbook, 72, photocopy at Church History Library; Cowdery, "Egyptian Mummies—Ancient Records," *Latter Day Saints' Messenger and Advocate*, December 1835, 235.

of the hieroglyphic characters on the papyri looked "exactly like the present, (though probably not quite so square,) form of the Hebrew without points,"[41] and in subsequent years reportedly stated that the papyri were written "chiefly in the Egyptian language, with the exception of a little Hebrew."[42] These observations inferred that, similar to the gold plates, the papyri were written in some combination of Hebrew and Egyptian.

In retrospect, the language of the surviving papyri is considered by modern Egyptologists to be a form of hieratic Egyptian (abridged hieroglyphs) and devoid of any Hebrew writing. However, in light of nineteenth-century theories regarding the pre-Babel relationship between Egyptian and Hebrew, their own experiences with the Hebraic Reformed Egyptian of the Book of Mormon, and their belief that the Egyptian characters on the papyri resembled Hebrew letters, it was reasonable for Joseph Smith and his associates to presume that they could gain valuable insights into the Egyptian language and the contents of the Abraham text by studying Hebrew. This assumption almost certainly led to their desire and efforts to organize a Hebrew class within about three months of acquiring the papyri.[43] However, the school term would not start until later in the fall, and Smith and his scribes were anxious to start immediately on the Egyptian project and the Book of Abraham translation.

Based on journal entries and other extant documents, it appears that their earliest efforts began in July 1835 as they attempted to copy, transliterate, and define the Egyptian characters they saw on the papyri, perhaps with the intention of creating a type of primer to facilitate the translation of the Book of

41. Cowdery, "Egyptian Mummies—Ancient Records," 234. In evaluating this statement by Oliver Cowdery, it is important to note that he did not know Hebrew at the time he gave this description of the papyri. He later acknowledged that he was "unacquainted" with Hebrew before classes began in January 1836 (*Latter Day Saints' Messenger and Advocate*, January 1836, 252), which was several weeks after he recalled his initial impression that the characters on the papyri resembled Hebrew letters. Still, in their initial approach to understanding the papyri, Smith and Cowdery paralleled similar attempts by contemporaneous scholars to view Egyptian materials through the lens of Hebrew scripture. Cowdery, for example, interpreted the Egyptian vignettes on the papyri as stories from the book of Genesis, such as the creation and the beguilement of Eve in Eden, see Cowdery, "Egyptian Mummies—Ancient Records," 236.

42. This statement is from William Appleby, who in 1841 recorded Joseph Smith's description of the papyri and their connection to biblical history. William I. Appleby, Journal, 5 May 1841, Church History Library. Similarly, according to Charlotte Haven (a young woman visiting Nauvoo), Smith's mother, Lucy Mack Smith, claimed during her presentation of the mummies and papyri to visitors in 1843 that the papyri were "written in Hebrew and Sanscrit." Charlotte Haven to "My dear Mother," 19 February 1843, in "A Girl's Letters from Nauvoo," *Overland Monthly*, December 1890, 624. For contemporaneous thinking that connected Hebrew and Egyptian with Sanskrit, see Priest, *American Antiquities and Discoveries in the West*, 123.

43. For the appointment of a committee to organize the Hebrew class in early October 1835, see note 65 below.

Abraham.[44] These activities produced three versions of an "Egyptian Alphabet" text—written by Smith, Phelps, and Cowdery—which transcribed the papyri's Egyptian characters, gave them names and pronunciations, and provided interpretations that connected the hieroglyphs to themes from the early chapters of Genesis and a developing Abrahamic narrative.[45] In addition, the alphabet documents reflect a creative linguistic system in which various characters were broken down into their composite parts and assigned deeper meanings by degrees. The results of this project apparently informed what is now the first chapter of the Book of Abraham,[46] the beginning of which seems to have developed concurrently with the creation of the Egyptian Alphabet (circa July 1835).[47]

Conceptually, the Egyptian Alphabet text produced by Smith and his scribes is not unlike the charts created by contemporary linguists showing the characters, sounds, and original meanings of various alphabets—such as tables juxtaposing Egyptian hieroglyphs and other phonetic scripts (including Hebrew and Coptic), comparing old world and new world hieroglyphs,

44. The entries in the manuscript History of Joseph Smith for 6–8 and 17–31 July 1835, which were apparently inserted in 1843 by William W. Phelps and Willard Richards, state that in early July 1835, Smith "commenced the translation of some of the characters or hieroglyphics," and that he spent the remainder of the month "continually engaged in translating an alphabet to the Book of Abraham, and arranging a grammar of the Egyptian language as practiced by the ancients." Joseph Smith, History, 1838–1856, vol. B-1, 597, Church History Library (accessible in the Histories series of the online edition of *The Joseph Smith Papers*). For fuller treatment of the Egyptian Alphabet and related documents, see Brian M. Hauglid, "'Translating an Alphabet to the Book of Abraham': Joseph Smith's Study of the Egyptian Language and His Translation of the Book of Abraham," Chapter 15 herein.

45. The extant versions of the Egyptian Alphabet text—in the handwriting of Smith, Phelps, and Cowdery—were most likely produced in July 1835, thus representing their earliest attempts to work with the Egyptian papyri. Egyptian Alphabet, circa early July–circa November 1835-A (hereafter EA-A), in *JSP*-R4:55; Egyptian Alphabet, circa early July–circa November 1835-B (hereafter EA-B), in *JSP*-R4:73; Egyptian Alphabet, circa early July–circa November 1835-C (hereafter EA-C), in *JSP*-R4:85.

46. Compare the Egyptian Alphabet definitions for *Ah-broam, Bethka*, and *Iota-Tou-es Zip-zi* with the content of the Book of Abraham (BoA, in *JSP*-R4:308–11 [Abraham 1:1–3, 23–24]), describing the origins of Abraham "in the land of the Chaldeans" and his need to obtain "another place of residence" (308–9 [1:1]); his desire to "possess great knowledge," be a "follower of righteousness," and become a "rightful . . . high priest" (308–9 [1:2]); and a woman's discovery of Egypt while it was under water (310–11 [1:23–24]). For closer analysis of these and other passages, see Marquardt, "Joseph Smith's Egyptian Papers," 29–32; Hauglid, *A Textual History of the Book of Abraham*, 226–27; and Christopher C. Smith, "The Dependence of Abraham 1:1–3 on the Egyptian Alphabet and Grammar," *John Whitmer Historical Association Journal* 29 (2009): 38–54.

47. The manuscript copy of the Book of Abraham in the handwriting of Warren Parrish and William W. Phelps contains the translated text of the opening lines of the Book of Abraham, with Egyptian characters in the margins matching characters found on the Smith papyri and defined with similar content in the Egyptian Alphabet. Book of Abraham Manuscript, circa July–circa November 1835-C, in *JSP*-R4:218–19 [Abraham 1:1–3]. This evidence suggests that the manuscript was produced around the same time as the production of the Egyptian Alphabet. Hauglid, *A Textual History of the Book of Abraham*, 58–61.

and showing the development of Hebrew and related Semitic alphabets[48]—although most of the pronunciations and definitions of the Egyptian characters Smith and his associates provided are completely unattested and unrelated to any known language. Instead, while they adopted a *format* similar to scholarly linguistic charts, Smith and his associates were methodologically closer in their interpretations to the metaphysical approaches of contemporaneous mystical thinkers, who maintained that the hidden meanings of Egyptian hieroglyphs could only be manifested through divine inspiration or revelation (a spiritual gift claimed by Smith for his translation of the Book of Mormon and perhaps for the Egyptian characters in the alphabet text as well).[49]

In addition to assigning unique names, pronunciations, and definitions to the Egyptian characters, the Egyptian Alphabet text incorporated traces of other ancient languages into the list of characters and their explanations—including a few characters from Greek, from an earlier reconstruction of the "pure language," and perhaps even from one or more masonic ciphers—likely reflecting a belief that these languages also shared common origins with Egyptian.[50] Among these were a few Hebrew letters and variations of their lexical

48. See Champollion, *Précis du système hiéroglyphique des anciens Égyptiens*, 106, plate 3; Samuel Rafinesque, "Tabular View of the Compared Atlantic Alphabets & Glyphs of Africa and America," *Atlantic Journal* (1832), as shown in MacKay and Dirkmaat, *From Darkness unto Light*, 46; and Moses Stuart, *A Grammar of the Hebrew Language*, 5th ed. (Andover, MA: Gould and Newman, 1835), 9–10, charts 1–3.

49. The year before the arrival of the papyri in Kirtland, Oliver Cowdery had published an article in the church newspaper expressing the belief that the Egyptians "could astonish the universe for centuries with their knowledge . . . of concealing their arts in mystical characters or hieroglyphics." [Oliver Cowdery], "Reflections for the Fourth of July, 1834," *Evening and the Morning Star*, July 1834, 173. For references to Joseph Smith's claim to divine revelation in deciphering the hieroglyphs, see John Whitmer, History, 1831–circa 1847, in *JSP*-H2:86; William S. West, *A Few Interesting Facts Respecting the Rise, Progress and Pretensions of the Mormons* ([Warren, OH?]: n.p., 1837), 5–6; and Warren Parrish, "Letter to the Editor, Feb. 5, 1838," *Painesville Republican* (Painesville, OH), 15 February 1838, 3. For the earliest mention of Smith's use of seer stones in the process, see "Another Humbug," *Cleveland Whig*, 31 July 1835.

50. Greek elements in the Egyptian Alphabet include a dot-shaped character named *Iota* and defined as an "eye" or "sight." EA-A, 1, in *JSP*-R4:56–57; EA-B, 1, in *JSP*-R4:74–75; EA-C, 1, in *JSP*-R4:86–87). There are also two characters associated with *Hah-dees* (EA-A, 2, in *JSP*-R4:58; EA-B, 2, in *JSP*-R4:76; and EA-C, 2, in *JSP*-R4:88–89), later defined in the "Grammar and Alphabet of the Egyptian Language" as "~~Hell~~ . . . [a] domin[ion] of darkness . . . governed by him who is an enemy to God"—an oblique reference to the Greek *Hades*. Grammar and Alphabet of the Egyptian Language, circa July–circa November 1835, 31, 33, in *JSP*-R4:176–77, 180–81 (hereafter GAEL). The inclusion of these Greek elements in the Egyptian documents may have prompted Smith to acquire and briefly consult a Greek lexicon in late 1835. Smith, Journal, 20 November and 23 December 1835, in *JSP*-J1:107 and 135. For other attempts to connect Greek with Egyptian during this period, see de Gebelin, *Recueil d' antiquitès*, 361–77; and Ethan Smith, *Key to the Figurative Language Found in the Sacred Scriptures in the Form of Questions and Answers* (New Hampshire: C. Norris, 1814), 20. For Smith's later attempts to work with Greek, see John W. Welch, "Joseph Smith's Awareness of Greek and Latin," chap. 11 in *Approaching Antiquity*. For examples of pure language symbols being incorporated into versions of the Egyptian Alphabet text, see EA-A, 1, in *JSP*-R4:56–57; EA-B, 1, in *JSP*-R4:74–75; EA-C, 1, in *JSP*-R4:86–87; and Hauglid, "The Book of Abraham and the Egyptian Project," 481–82. The possibility

definitions, including characters designated as *Aleph* and *Beth* (compare א [*aleph*] and ב [*beth*], the first two letters of the Hebrew alphabet).[51] The characters given these designations bear little or no orthographic resemblance to their Hebrew counterparts, but the definitions given to them by Smith and his scribes clearly reflect their presumed Hebrew origin.[52] To illustrate, *Aleph* is defined in these documents as "In the beginning with God the Son or first born," which likely derives from the position of א as the first letter in the Hebrew alphabet.[53] Similarly, *Beth* is defined as "man's first residence a fruitful garden," which is likely a variation on the original meaning of the Hebrew ב as a "house."[54] How these elements came to be incorporated into the documents is uncertain, though it is again possible that Phelps prompted their inclusion.[55] In

---

of one or more masonic ciphers being incorporated into versions of the Egyptian Alphabet text has also been argued (Will Schryver, "The Meaning of the Kirtland Egyptian Papers," FairMormon Conference, 5–6 August 2010, Sandy, UT), but more research is necessary to confirm and clarify this suggestion.

51. For these characters, their designations, and their definitions, see EA-A, 1–2, in *JSP*-R4:56–58; EA-B, 1–2, in *JSP*-R4:74–76; and EA-C, 1–2, in *JSP*-R4:86–89. See also Brown, *In Heaven as It Is on Earth*, 137–39. It is possible that the Hebrew letter *gimel* (ג) is represented in the Egyptian Alphabet as well, but the "Gah-nel" or "Gahmel" character of those documents bears little resemblance to a ג in form (unless it was seen as the base of the letter, without its upward vertical stoke) and its definition in the later GAEL as "landscape . . . a place or country" (GAEL, 33, in *JSP*-R4:180–81) shares no similarity to the standard lexical definition of the Hebrew *gimel* as a "camel" (Stuart, *A Grammar of the Hebrew Language*, 9). Therefore, this letter is less likely to be Hebrew in origin than *Aleph* and *Beth*. For contemporaneous academic attempts to compare Hebrew letters (including א and ב) to Egyptian hieroglyphs, see Champollion, *Précis du système hiéroglyphique des anciens Égyptiens*, 109–17; Greppo, *Essay on the Hieroglyphic System of M. Champollion*, 73; and Lamb, *Hebrew Characters derived from Hieroglyphics*.

52. It is possible that the *Aleph* character was seen by Smith and his associates as an א without the left downward stroke. Samuel Morris Brown has argued, based on the later GAEL, that Smith or his associates viewed the vertical stem identified as *Beth* (GAEL, 23, in *JSP*-R4:160–61) as a wall of the Hebrew pictographic letter meaning "house" and that they perceived a mirror image of the Hebrew ב in the character identified as *Hi* (GAEL, 2, in *JSP*-R4:118–19). See Brown, *In Heaven as It Is on Earth*, 137n129. However, these claims are difficult to substantiate.

53. EA-A, 1, in *JSP*-R4:56–57; EA-B, 1, in *JSP*-R4:74–75; and EA-C, 1, in *JSP*-R4:86–87. It is possible that this character and definition were incorporated into the beginning of the Abraham translation, which mentions "the beginning of time . . . before the foundation of the earth." BoA, in *JSP*-R4:308–9 [Abraham 1:3].

54. EA-A, 2, in *JSP*-R4:58–59; compare EA-B, 2, in *JSP*-R4:76–77; and EA-C, 2, in *JSP*-R4:88–89. Derivatives such as *Beth Ka*, *Beth Ki*, and *Beth Ku* have related definitions, see *JSP*-R4:359–62. For the standard lexical definition for the Hebrew letter ב (*beth*), see Stuart, *A Grammar of the Hebrew Language*, 9. This character and its definition may have formed the basis for the translation of the opening lines of the Book of Abraham, which describe Abraham's desire "to obtain another place of residence." BoA, in *JSP*-R4:308–9 [Abraham 1:1].

55. The spelling of these Hebrew letters in the Egyptian Alphabet represents a standard transliteration system that is noticeably different from the distinct pronunciation taught to Smith and other Latter-day Saints by Joshua Seixas in early 1836, thus providing additional evidence that these documents (and the derivative GAEL) were produced in 1835 before Smith's formal study of Hebrew had begun. Since Phelps is the only known member of the Mormon community who had been exposed to some Hebrew before 1836, it seems likely that he was responsible for incorporating Hebrew elements into Smith's Egyptian alphabet and grammar documents. John Gee has asserted that the GAEL *does* use the transliteration system taught by Seixas (which would thus date the GAEL to 1836 or later), but the only evidence he offers for this assertion is his observation that the GAEL includes words with long final vowels ending in an "h." Gee, "Joseph

any case, the presence of Hebrew letters and concepts in the Egyptian Alphabet text confirms that from the beginning of the project Smith and his associates believed Hebrew was to some degree either represented on the papyri or somehow embedded within the Egyptian characters.[56]

Following the initial work in July 1835 with the papyri, the Egyptian Alphabet, and at least the beginning of the Book of Abraham, it appears that the entire project stalled during the months of August and September.[57] It was reignited in early October as Smith revisited the papyri and in the process received an epiphany on "the system of astronomy."[58] This presumably led to an anticipation that further translation of the Book of Abraham would reveal deeper insights into the creation and cosmos as understood by the biblical patriarchs.[59] Translation activities then resumed on 7 October and continued through 26 November.[60] It is likely that during this time Smith produced the first part of what is now chapter two in the Book of Abraham—a first person expansion of the King James Version (hereafter KJV) of Genesis 11:28–12:6 (Abraham's

Smith and Egypt," 440–41. Gee's observation, however, is not documented and, as far as can be determined, is not clearly attested in the GAEL.

56. For contemporaneous attempts to read Hebrew letters into Egyptian hieroglyphs and to use Hebrew to create an Egyptian lexicon, see notes 21–27 above.

57. William W. Phelps wrote in an 11 September 1835 letter to his wife that "nothing has been doing in the translation of the Egyptian Record for a long time, and probably will not for some time to come." Bruce Van Orden, "Writing to Zion: The William W. Phelps Kirtland Letters (1835–1836)," *BYU Studies* 33, no. 3 (1993): 15.

58. Smith, Journal, 1 October 1835, in *JSP*-J1:67; compare Cowdery, "Egyptian Mummies—Ancient Records," 234. A few terms and brief explanations related to astronomy appeared in the earlier Egyptian Alphabet text—such as *Jah-oh-eh* (earth), *Flo-ees* (moon), *Flos-isis* (sun), and a later interpolation of *Kolob* (with no definition) (EA-C, 2, in *JSP*-R4:88–89)—but nothing like the expansive system of astronomy found after the 1 October 1835 epiphany in the GAEL, the cosmological portions of the Book of Abraham (BoA, in *JSP*-R4:314–15, 318–23 [Abraham 3–5]), or the explanations accompanying the second illustration published with the text (BoA, in *JSP*-R4:316–17 [Abraham Fac. 2]). See Marquardt, "Joseph Smith's Egyptian Papers," 20–22; and Hauglid, "The Book of Abraham and the Egyptian Project," 485.

59. See Cowdery, "Egyptian Mummies—Ancient Records," 234, 236; Smith, Journal, 16 December 1835, in *JSP*-J1:123–24. See also the passages toward the end of what is now the first chapter of the Book of Abraham in which Abraham declares that his record preserves "a knowledge of the creation, and also of the planets, and of the stars, as they were made known unto the fathers." BoA, in *JSP*-R4:310–11 [Abraham 1:28, 31]. Although these passages may have been translated earlier (circa July 1835), the earliest extant manuscript containing this reference (Book of Abraham Manuscript, circa July–circa November 1835-A, in *JSP*-R4:192–201) was in the handwriting of Frederick G. Williams—Smith's scribe in early October (Smith, Journal, 3–8 October 1835, in *JSP*-J1:67–71, esp. 67n49 and 71n55)—suggesting that this part of the Book of Abraham (now Abraham 1:4–2:6) was produced sometime between 1 October, when the epiphany occurred, and 29 October, when Warren Parrish became Smith's journal scribe and presumably his main scribe on the Egyptian project. See Hauglid, *A Textual History of the Book of Abraham*, 64–65.

60. Smith's journal indicates that he "recommenced translating the ancient records" on 7 October 1835, and subsequent translation activities (including his displaying and explaining the Egyptian records to interested observers) are attested in Smith's journal through 26 November, which is the final entry describing his translation work on the Book of Abraham until early 1842. Smith, Journal, 7 October–26 November 1835, in *JSP*-J1:71–112.

journey to Canaan)[61]—along with a development of the Egyptian Alphabet text into the more complex "Grammar and A[l]phabet of the Egyptian Language" (hereafter GAEL).[62] This latter document reflected Smith's expanding view of Abrahamic astronomy and elaborated upon the basic Hebrew elements of the Egyptian Alphabet.[63] It also provided some of the conceptual content for his eventual translation of a revelation on astronomy in the middle of the Book of Abraham (what is now Abraham 3) and the explanation that accompanied the second illustration published with the text (what is now Abraham Fac. 2), neither of which would be finalized until 1842 (see below).[64] Significantly, it was during this renewal of the Egyptian project in October and November 1835 that Smith and his associates began making arrangements for a formal study of Hebrew—an effort that, as shown by the evidence surveyed in this section, was almost certainly motivated by their belief that a knowledge of Hebrew would help facilitate their ongoing work on the Book of Abraham.

61. The earliest extant manuscript evidence for this material is in the handwriting of Warren Parrish. Book of Abraham Manuscript, circa July–circa November 1835-B, in *JSP*-R4:203–15 [Abraham 1:4–2:2]; Book of Abraham Manuscript, circa July–circa November 1835-C, in *JSP*-R4:217–37 [Abraham 1:1–2:18]. As noted above, Smith hired Parrish as a scribe on 29 October 1835 (Smith, Journal, 29 October 1835, in *JSP*-J:176). Parrish served as the primary scribe for Smith's journal from then until early April 1836 (Historical Introduction to Smith, Journal, 1835–1836, in *JSP*-J1:55–56), and presumably became the primary scribe on the Egyptian project as well. Therefore, the manuscripts and their content were likely produced sometime in November. Hauglid, *A Textual History of the Book of Abraham*, 84–85, 110–11. For a synoptic comparison of KJV Genesis 11:28–12:6 and what is now Abraham 2:1–18, see Marquardt, "Joseph Smith's Egyptian Papers," 32–35. It is also interesting to note that the early manuscript copies of this portion of the Book of Abraham all contain copies of hieratic characters in their left margins, showing the ways in which Smith and his scribes connected this part of the Abraham text with the papyri, see Book of Abraham Manuscripts, circa July–circa November 1835, in *JSP*-R4:191–242). These characters also suggest that the complex degree system of the GAEL informed Smith's translation of this portion of the Abraham text. BoA, in *JSP*-R4:306–13 [Abraham 1:4–2:18].

62. The GAEL contains the handwriting of William W. Phelps and Warren Parrish, indicating a date for its composition between 29 October 1835 (the day Parrish was employed as Smith's scribe) and 26 November 1835 (Smith's last recorded day of translation until 1842). See Hauglid, "The Book of Abraham and the Egyptian Project," 494–503.

63. The Hebrew elements in the GAEL preserve the pre-Seixas spelling system found in the Egyptian Alphabet, which provides additional support for its composition in late 1835 rather than in 1836 (thus challenging the claim made in Gee, "Joseph Smith and Egypt," 440–41). With regard to these Hebrew elements, the GAEL omits the *Aleph* character in all the "degrees" except for the second part of the second degree (GAEL, 31, in *JSP*-R4:176–77), but it greatly expands the significance of the *Beth* character and its variants (GAEL, 2, 9, 12–23, 27, 31, 33, in *JSP*-R4:118–19, 132–33, 138–61, 168–69, 176–77, 180–81). This expansion of the significance of *Beth* includes connecting it to *Adam-ondi-Ahman*, "the place appointed of God for the residence of Adam." GAEL, 23, in *JSP*-R4: 160–61.

64. The GAEL includes significant expansions of cosmological concepts such as *Jah-oh-eh*, *Oliblish*, *Enish go-on-dosh*, *Kae-ee-van-rash*, *Kli flos-isis*, and *Kolob* (GAEL, 24–34, in *JSP*-R4:162–83), that closely resemble the astronomical content in the middle of the Book of Abraham (BoA, in *JSP*-R4:314–15, 318–19 [Abraham 3:1–16]) and the explanation accompanying the second illustration (BoA, in *JSP*-R4:316–17 [Abraham Fac. 2: Figs. 1–5]). For a fuller comparison, see Hauglid, *A Textual History of the Book of Abraham*, 227–31.

Joseph Smith's Study of Hebrew and the Translation of the Book of Abraham

Efforts by Joseph Smith and his associates to arrange a formal study of Hebrew had begun by early October 1835 with the formation of a committee to organize a class, find an instructor, and acquire the best resources to assist with Hebrew study.[65] Having difficulty locating a teacher, Smith travelled in early November to nearby Willoughby Medical College to hear a lecture by a Jewish scholar, Daniel Peixotto, and approached him with the prospect of instructing the Latter-day Saints in Hebrew. Peixotto agreed and gave recommendations on the necessary Hebrew course materials. Although the arrangement for Peixotto to teach the class eventually fell through, his textbook recommendations prompted Smith to send Oliver Cowdery on a trip to New York City to acquire the needed Hebrew resources.[66]

On 20 November, after two days of Smith "translating the Egyptian records," Cowdery returned to Kirtland with "a quantity of Hebrew book's for the benefit of the school . . . a Hebrew bible, lexicon & Grammar, [and] also a Greek Lexicon."[67] Cowdery's acquisitions included copies of an edition of the *Biblia Hebraica* (Hebrew Bible),[68] Moses Stuart's *Grammar of the Hebrew Language*,[69] and Josiah Gibbs's *A Manual Hebrew and English Lexicon*[70]—all some of the highest quality Hebrew resources available at that time.[71] The fol-

65. The earliest surviving reference to the effort to organize a Hebrew class is in a 28 October 1835 letter written by Oliver Cowdery to Lucius Parker—a cousin of Brigham Young who knew the basics of biblical Hebrew. In inquiring after a potential teacher, Cowdery noted that a committee had been formed to organize the class earlier that month and that they sought "an accomplished scholar" to teach them the language. Oliver Cowdery to Lucius Parker, 28 October 1835, in Oliver Cowdery Letter Book, 57. It is clear from this letter that previous correspondence on the matter had been exchanged, but this earlier correspondence is apparently no longer extant. See Grey, "'The Word of the Lord in the Original,'" 261–62.

66. For further information on the coordinated efforts of Daniel Peixotto and Oliver Cowdery to acquire Hebrew textbooks and on Cowdery's trip to New York City, see Grey, "'The Word of the Lord in the Original,'" 259–61.

67. Smith, Journal, 19–20 November 1835, in *JSP*-J1:107; see also Smith, History, 1834–1836, 19–20 November 1835, in *JSP*-H1:131. As noted previously, the acquisition of a Greek lexicon along with the Hebrew reference works may have been motivated by the presence of a few Greek elements (such as *Iota* and *Hah-dees*) in the Egyptian Alphabet text and the GAEL (see note 50 above). For Smith's brief study of his Greek lexicon, see Smith, Journal, 23 December 1835, in *JSP*-J1:135.

68. Augustus Hahn, ed., *Biblia Hebraica*, 2nd ed. (Leipzig: Caroli Tauchnitz, 1833). See also *JSP*-J1:107n159.

69. Stuart, *A Grammar of the Hebrew Language.*

70. Josiah W. Gibbs, *A Manual Hebrew and English Lexicon*, 2nd ed. (New Haven: Hezekiah Howe, 1832).

71. For a list and description of the extant copies of these volumes, see Grey, "'The Word of the Lord in the Original,'" 262n57–59. In addition to these resources, it is possible that at some point between 1835 and 1836 Smith acquired other volumes as listed in a document associated with Brigham Young labelled

lowing day, 21 November, Smith began "examining [his] books and studying the Hebrew alphabet," and for the next week alternated between studying Hebrew, translating the Egyptian records, and displaying the Egyptian artifacts to interested visitors.[72] Throughout the month of December, Smith continued to rotate between reading his Hebrew books and expounding upon the meaning of the Egyptian papyri, although no specific translation activities are attested during this period.[73] Nevertheless, Smith and his scribes saw their Egyptian and Hebrew interests as mutually illuminating.[74] As manifestations of these interests, Smith wrote in his journal on 21 December that he spent the morning at home "indeavering to treasure up know[l]edge"—apparently studying Hebrew—and that this was, as he wrote, "for the be[n]ifit of my Calling."[75] The next day Smith wrote that he "continued [his] studies" and added a written prayer: "O may God give me learning, even Language and indo [endue] me with qualifycations to magnify his name"—presumably through his prophetic ministry and its consequent responsibilities, which included his continuous efforts to recover ancient scripture.[76]

Further indication that Smith closely associated his Hebrew study with his ongoing Egyptian project was his dedication on 4 January 1836 of the "translation room" in the Kirtland temple, which he intended to use for

---

"List of works in Hebrew Greek Latin Syraic Arabic Chaldaee & English." List of works in Hebrew, Greek, and Latin, circa 1836, Church History Library. This document lists over forty lexicons, grammars, and textbooks in various languages either purchased or desired by the Kirtland school. Among those listed are Hebrew resources such as the *Biblia Hebraica*, the Gibbs *Lexicon*, and grammars by Moses Stuart and Joshua Seixas, as well as lexicons by Wilhelm Gesenius. An edition of the Gesenius lexicon, translated into English by Josiah Gibbs and Edward Robinson, may have been the lexicon that Smith and his associates hoped to obtain from Seixas as shown in their correspondence with his wife. See Joseph Smith, Sidney Rigdon, F. G. Williams, and Oliver Cowdery to Henrietta Raphael Seixas, 13 February 1836, Oliver Cowdery Letter Book, 77–78. Although it has not yet been determined whether Smith or his associates actually acquired a copy of a Gesenius lexicon, evidence from the Book of Abraham strongly suggests that Smith had consulted entries from it in his translation (see below).

72. According to his journal, Smith spent 21, 23, and 27 November 1835 reading his new Hebrew books; 24, 25, and 26 November translating or transcribing the Egyptian records; and 23 and 30 November exhibiting the Egyptian artifacts. Smith, Journal, 21–30 November 1835, in *JSP*-J1:107–12.

73. Smith's journal indicates that he read his Hebrew books on 4, 5, 7, 8, 14, 21, 22, 26, 30, and 31 December (with a serious effort to learn the language beginning the day after Christmas), and that he displayed or explained the Egyptian materials on 7, 10, 12, 14, 15, 16, 20, and 23 December. Smith, Journal, 4–31 December 1835, in *JSP*-J1:115–40.

74. It was during December 1835 that Oliver Cowdery noted that the Egyptian characters on the papyri looked "exactly like the present, (though probably not quite so square,) form of the Hebrew without points." Cowdery, "Egyptian Mummies—Ancient Records," 234. Cowdery may have drawn this language from the Moses Stuart textbook, which described "the present square form of the Hebrew letters." Stuart, *A Grammar of the Hebrew Language*, 12.

75. Smith, Journal, 21 December 1835, in *JSP*-J1:135.

76. Ibid.

both conducting Hebrew classes and working on the Egyptian materials.[77] In that setting, though still lacking a proper teacher, Smith and his associates attempted to work through their Hebrew books as a class with Smith guiding the study sessions through most of January.[78] However, the highly technical materials they had at their disposal—which included Moses Stuart's Semitic alphabet charts, complex philological discussions, and dense introduction to Hebrew grammar—were not intended for beginning students, causing the class members to struggle in their learning.[79] Still, Smith believed that their efforts to read their Hebrew Bibles (presumably starting with Genesis 1) were ultimately successful, even if it is unclear how accurate they were in their readings or what connections they may have begun making with the papyri.[80]

By late January, the Latter-day Saints had succeeded in hiring a qualified instructor for the Hebrew class. This "highly celebrated" teacher was Joshua Seixas, a respected Jewish scholar from a prominent Sephardic family in New York. In recent years Seixas had been earning a reputation for his skills with ancient languages (including Hebrew, Aramaic, Syriac, and Arabic), had taught Hebrew as an adjunct professor at various academic institutions in the northeast (including Oberlin and Western Reserve), and had collaborated on the edition of Moses Stuart's Hebrew textbook that Smith had been reading since late November.[81] Upon his arrival in Kirtland, Seixas organized over a hundred Mormon students into four concurrent classes that met daily for an intensive seven-week course on Biblical Hebrew grammar and translation. For the time period, this amount of coursework was roughly equivalent to one or two semesters at a Protestant seminary.[82] Joseph Smith, William W. Phelps, Oliver Cowdery, and Warren Parrish—the primary participants in the Egyptian

77. This was also a room in which Smith and others participated in anointing rituals in late January 1836 that were modelled after the Hebrew anointing practices mentioned in the Old Testament. Smith, Journal, 31 December 1835, 4, 21, and 28 January 1836, in *JSP*-J1:140, 143, 166–71, 174; also Smith, History, 1834–1836, 31 December 1835 and 4 January 1836, in *JSP*-H1:163, 167; Jay M. Todd, *The Saga of the Book of Abraham* (Salt Lake City: Deseret Book, 1969), 196–201.

78. These self-guided study sessions occurred on 4, 5, 6, 8, 9, 14, 18, 19, 20, and 21 January, Smith, Journal, 4–21 January 1836, in *JSP*-J1:143–66.

79. For a detailed description of the advanced nature of the Moses Stuart textbook and the learning struggles experienced by Smith's group of students, see Grey, "'The Word of the Lord in the Original,'" 263n66–68.

80. Smith's journal entry for 19 January 1836 notes: "This day we commenced reading in our hebrew bibles with much success, it seems as if the Lord opens our minds, in a marvelous manner to understand his word in the original language." Smith, Journal, 19 January 1836, in *JSP*-J1:164. Stuart's grammar manual included reading exercises for Genesis 1, see Stuart, *A Grammar of the Hebrew Language*, 44–45 (§91).

81. For more on Seixas's background and qualifications as a Hebrew scholar, see Grey, "'The Word of the Lord in the Original,'" 262–66.

82. For a more complete reconstruction of Seixas's Hebrew classes and coursework, see Ibid., 266–72.

project—were assigned to Seixas's "first class" of ten students, which received additional instruction beyond the basics of the course.[83]

The course was designed by Seixas to work through his own textbook, *Manual Hebrew Grammar for the Use of Beginners*,[84] along with an abbreviated supplement to the Seixas grammar published by the church for wider use among the Mormon students.[85] These materials contained an introduction to Hebrew vocabulary and grammar, and had the advantage over Moses Stuart's textbook in their utility for beginning students.[86] The distinctive aspect of Seixas's textbook, however, was its presentation of ancient Hebrew with a Sephardic (Iberian Jewish) transliteration system that differed from the Ashkenazic (Germanic Jewish) pronunciation of Biblical Hebrew that was becoming the standard in European universities. As seen in Seixas's pronunciation guide, his transliterations were most distinct in the vowels and gutturals, using "au" to represent the vowel *qametz*, "oo" to represent the vowel *sureq*, "ee" to represent the vowel *hireq* and the consonant *yod*, "gn" to represent the consonant *ayin* at the beginning of a word, and "ng" to represent an *ayin* at the end of a word.[87] This system would not necessarily have lessened the quality of Hebrew instruction received by the Latter-day Saints in Kirtland. However, as demonstrated below, the Sephardic transliterations would leave their distinct mark on Smith's subsequent use of the language, including in the Book of Abraham.

A comparison of the Seixas textbook and student journal entries indicates that during the first week of class students learned the Hebrew alphabet and Seixas's spelling methods,[88] and that during the second week they began grammar lessons with large units on nouns and verbs.[89] Following this introduction, the remainder of the course focused on translation from the Hebrew Bible,

83. Smith, Journal, 19 February 1836, in *JSP*-J1:187.

84. Some students used the 1833 edition of the textbook, while others had access to copies of the revised 1834 edition. J. Seixas, *Manual Hebrew Grammar for the Use of Beginners* (Andover, MA: Flagg, Gould, and Newman, 1833); Seixas, *Manual Hebrew Grammar for the Use of Beginners*, 2nd ed. (Andover, MA: Gould and Newman, 1834). For a list of the extant Seixas grammar books used by members of the class, see Grey, "'The Word of the Lord in the Original,'" 293n100. Unless otherwise specified, all subsequent references to the Seixas textbook are to the second edition.

85. *Supplement to J. Seixas' Manual Hebrew Grammar for the Kirtland, Ohio, Theological Institution.*

86. See Seixas, *Manual Hebrew Grammar for the Use of Beginners*, iii. A review of Seixas's grammar in the *Christian Examiner* celebrated its accessibility compared to the more technical textbook of Moses Stuart. Unsigned review of *A Manual Hebrew Grammar for the Use of Beginners*, by J. Seixas, *The Christian Examiner and General Review*, September 1833, 67.

87. Seixas, *Manual Hebrew Grammar for the Use of Beginners*, 5–6.

88. The second edition of the Seixas grammar contains the spelling exercises conducted by the class. Ibid., 5–18).

89. Ibid., 20–52.

including portions of Genesis, Exodus, and the Psalms.[90] Throughout their studies, Smith and his associates maintained their interest in the Egyptian project (although their translation of the papyri had come to a temporary halt),[91] and they likely paid careful attention to potential points of contact between their newly acquired knowledge of Hebrew and the developing Book of Abraham. This included material relating to creation and astronomy—concepts they may have anticipated to appear in the translation since the October 1835 epiphany—as they read and analyzed the Hebrew of Genesis 1 (one of the biblical creation accounts);[92] translated parts of the Abraham story from Genesis 17 and 22 (the Abrahamic covenant and binding of Isaac);[93] and learned Hebrew vocabulary that would eventually be incorporated into the Book of Abraham (see below).

Throughout the Hebrew course Smith was earnest and diligent in his studies, and seems to have acquired a competent (if rudimentary) understanding of the language. Upon completion of the course, Seixas gave Smith a certificate that complimented him for his "indefatigable" study of the language, stated that he had "accomplished a knowledge of it," and declared that he was "able to translate to [Seixas's] entire satisfaction."[94] In addition to demonstrating success with a traditional study of Hebrew, however, Smith also began developing his own distinct ideas about the language and its theological applications—at times even in disagreement with the instruction given by his teacher or textbooks. As examined further below, this included his interest in intriguing but unconventional interpretations of various Hebrew words and concepts

90. See Smith's journal for this period, Smith, Journal, 15 February–8 March 1836, in *JSP*-J1:186–95. For the class's exercises in translation, vocabulary lists, and biblical passages, see Seixas, *A Manual Hebrew Grammar for the Use of Beginners*, 83–100.

91. No Egyptian translation activities were recorded during this time, but over the course of the Hebrew class Smith continued to exhibit and explain the Egyptian artifacts to interested visitors, including Joshua Seixas, who "examined them with deep interest & pronouncd them to be original beyound all doubt." After this conversation, Smith declared Seixas to be "a man of excellent understanding [who] has a knowledge of many languages which were spoken by the Antints [ancients]." Smith, Journal, 30 January 1836, in *JSP*-J1:178. For other instances of Smith displaying and expounding upon the Egyptian documents during this period, see Smith, Journal, 3, 11, and 16 February 1836, in *JSP*-J1:180–86.

92. The Hebrew text of the creation account in Genesis 1, along with a vocabulary list and commentary, can be found in the Seixas grammar and its supplement. Seixas, *Manual Hebrew Grammar for the Use of Beginners*, 83–86; and *Supplement to J. Seixas' Manual Hebrew Grammar*, 28–32. An extant 1833 edition of the Seixas grammar owned by Kirtland Latter-day Saint Newel K. Whitney shows that students marked key words relating to the creation account (including בָּרָא ["he created"], עָשָׂה ["he made"], and יום ["day"]), and wrote additional vocabulary words in the margins that were omitted from Seixas's list (including בָּדַל ["he divided"] and רָקִיעַ ["an expanse"]). See the Whitney copy of Seixas, *Manual Hebrew Grammar for the Use of Beginners* (1833), 44, Church History Library.

93. Smith, Journal, 7–8 March 1836, in *JSP*-J1:195.

94. Certificate from Joshua Seixas, 30 March 1836, in *JSP*-D5:214–16.

that caught his attention during his studies. It was likely during his reading of Genesis 1 that he noticed the potential implications of Hebrew vocabulary related to creation. Examples may have included his reading of the word בָּרָא (traditionally translated "to create") as an "organization" of preexisting matter and his reading of the word אֱלֹהִים (traditionally translated "God") in the plural as "gods." Both readings would come to have a significant impact on his Abraham translation and, by extension, Mormon cosmology.

Smith concluded his formal study of Hebrew in late March 1836, but his Egyptian project and translation activities remained largely if not almost completely suspended—this time for almost six years. During this period, Smith often expressed a hope to return to the project, but other concerns hindered him from revisiting and completing the translation of the Book of Abraham until early 1842.[95] Yet despite the apparent absence of formal translation activity, it is clear that during this period he continued to contemplate and ponder upon aspects of the Abraham translation that he anticipated would be forthcoming, and apparently even considered ways in which his Hebrew studies could inform that translation. His letters and sermons between 1836 and 1841 show a developing interest in concepts that were either directly inspired or enhanced by his Hebrew studies—including the plurality of gods,[96] Abrahamic astronomy (such as the planetary system and the residence of God),[97] and

95. In late 1837, Smith was still hopeful that church members in Kirtland would raise sufficient funds to support future translation work. See Joseph Smith, History, 1838–1856, 5 November 1837, vol. B-1, 775. In mid-1838, church members in Far West, Missouri, began preparing to build a house in which Smith could continue translating the Egyptian records. See Smith, Journal, 12 May 1838, in *JSP*-J1:269; and William Swartzell, *Mormonism Exposed* [. . .] (Pekin, O[H]: n.p., 1840), 25. But Smith spent early 1839 incarcerated in Missouri and the rest of the year managing a refugee crisis and resettlement effort in western Illinois. Richard Lyman Bushman, *Joseph Smith: Rough Stone Rolling* (New York: Alfred A. Knopf, 2005), chaps. 21–22. In 1840–1841, Smith occasionally requested assistance from church leaders and members in Nauvoo, Illinois, to allow him to continue his translation activities. Smith, History, 1838–1856, vol. C-1, 18 June 1840, 1062–63; and "Conference Minutes," *Times and Seasons*, 1 September 1841, 522.

96. The earliest direct statement on developing teachings regarding the plurality of gods—a concept inspired or informed by the plural Hebrew word for God—is found in an 1839 letter that Smith wrote from the Clay County jailhouse in Liberty, Missouri. The letter promises forthcoming information on "whether there be one God or many gods" and regarding the "Council of the Eternal God of all other gods before this world was." Letter to the Church and Edward Partridge, 20 March 1839, in *JSP*-D6:370 [D&C 121:28–32]. These statements are clear references to material that would appear in the Book of Abraham in 1842, see BoA, in *JSP*-R4:318–23 [Abraham 4:1–5:21]. For similar statements made by Smith in 1841 discourses, see Discourse, circa 16 February 1841, in *JSP*-D8:47–48; see also Joseph Smith, *The Words of Joseph Smith*, ed. Andrew F. Ehat and Lyndon W. Cook (Provo, UT: Religious Studies Center, Brigham Young University, 1980), 87–88n5.

97. Statements by Smith on astronomy and the planetary system contained in the Book of Abraham can be found in a May 1838 journal entry (Smith, Journal, 6 May 1838, in *JSP*-J1:266), the March 1839 letter from the Liberty jail (Letter to the Church and Edward Partridge, 20 March 1839, in *JSP*-D6:369–70 [D&C 121:28–32]), and in sermons given in late 1839 and early 1841 (Joseph Smith, Discourse, 1 January 1840, in Smith, *Words of Joseph Smith*, 45n1; Account of Meeting and Discourses, 9 March 1841, in *JSP*-D8:66; also Hauglid, *A Textual*

the eternal nature of spirit and matter[98]—all of which he would eventually incorporate into those portions of the Book of Abraham that had not yet been translated (or completely translated).[99]

According to contemporaneous documentary evidence, it was not until early 1842—after he had moved from Ohio to Missouri and from Missouri to Illinois—that Smith revisited the Book of Abraham translation project and began publishing his translation in the church newspaper, the *Times and Seasons*, printed in Nauvoo, Illinois. Entries in Smith's journal note that in February of that year he proofread the Abraham material that had been fully translated in 1835 (what is now known as Abraham 1:1–2:18) and finalized his editorial explanations for the Egyptian scene depicted in the first illustration published with the text (now known as Abraham Fac. 1), with the latter containing his first application of Hebrew terminology (see below). He approved the publication of those items on 1 March 1842,[100] and a few days later they were published in the issue of the *Times and Seasons* bearing this date.[101] Then, during the first two weeks of March, he proceeded to "translate & revise" the next installment of the Book of Abraham (what is now known as Abraham 2:19–5:21) and to provide explanations of the Egyptian figures in the published text's second illustration (now known as Abraham Fac. 2), all of which would be published in the issue of the *Times and Seasons* dated 15 March 1842.[102] This later material incorporated the astronomical insights Smith had begun unfolding in October 1835 through his work with Cowdery and Phelps on the GAEL (contained in what is now known as Abraham 3 and Abraham Fac. 2) and the anticipated expansion of the biblical creation story (in what is now

History of the Book of Abraham, 218). These statements clearly resemble the astronomical material in the middle of the Book of Abraham and in the explanations to the book's second illustration, though without the Hebrew glosses of the 1842 Abraham material. See BoA, in R4:314–19 [Abraham 3; Fac. 2: Figs. 4–5].

98. Statements on the eternal nature of spirit and matter—concepts inspired by Hebrew terminology—can be seen in discourses Smith delivered in 1840 and 1841. See Discourse, 5 February 1840, in *JSP*-D7:175–79; Discourse, 5 January 1841, in *JSP*-D7:490–95; Discourse, circa 28 March 1841, in *JSP*-D8:86–87.

99. According to William Appleby, in early 1841 Joseph Smith was still interested in the Hebrew writing he believed was found on the papyri and was still formulating his ideas about the papyri's biblical connections—such as their depiction of a woman facing a serpent standing upright on legs as a representation of Eve being beguiled by Satan (compare Cowdery, "Egyptian Mummies—Ancient Records," 236)—as well as the general meaning of the three illustrations for which facsimiles were published. William I. Appleby, Journal, 5 May 1841, Church History Library.

100. See Smith's journal entries for 23 February and 1–2 March 1842, in *JSP*-J2:36, 39–40.

101. "A Translation of Some Ancient Records that Have Fallen into Our Hands [. . .]," *Times and Seasons*, 1 March 1842, 704–6 [Abraham 1:1–2:18]; "A Fac-simile from the Book of Abraham, No. 1," *Times and Seasons*, 1 March 1842, 703 [Abraham Fac. 1].

102. See Smith, Journal, 4, 8, and 9 March 1836, in *JSP*-J2:40–42; "Book of Abraham," *Times and Seasons*, 15 March 1842, 719–22 [Abraham 2:19–5:21]; "A Fac-simile from the Book of Abraham, No. 2," *Times and Seasons*, 15 March 1842, insert between pages 720 and 721 [Abraham Fac. 2].

Abraham 4–5).[103] A third and final installment belatedly appeared in the issue of the *Times and Seasons* dated 16 May 1842, but this installment consisted only of a third illustration and its explanation (now known as Abraham Fac. 3).[104]

Significantly, as demonstrated below, these later portions of the Book of Abraham that were translated or finalized in 1842 are also the parts of the text that contain transliterated Hebrew words (spelled using the system taught by Seixas) and that incorporate Smith's theological reflections on the ways in which Hebrew insights illuminate biblical cosmology. In these instances, it appears that Smith had some conceptual grasp of the text's contents in the fall of 1835 (such as its inclusion of new astronomical and creation material) and that he studied Hebrew in early 1836 with those anticipated contents in mind, pondered the implications of his Hebrew studies for this material from 1836 to 1841, and completed his translation of the material with Hebrew glosses and Hebrew-inspired enhancements just prior to the book's publication in early 1842. Thus, Smith's initial hopes that his Egyptian project and Hebrew study would be mutually elucidating came to fruition in the final text of the Book of Abraham.

In the years following the book's publication, Smith did not attempt to conceal the fact that he had incorporated his knowledge of Hebrew into the text of the Book of Abraham. Rather, he openly acknowledged it and continued to express an interest in the close connections among his Hebrew studies, the Book of Abraham, and the larger Egyptian project. This was reflected in public sermons he later gave in Nauvoo, in which he expounded upon the Hebrew-inspired portions of the Book of Abraham relating to the plurality of gods, the eternal duration of spirit and matter, and views of the afterlife.[105] Smith also incorporated many of these concepts into the ritual drama of his "quorum of anointing" (the precursor to the Mormon temple endowment),[106] the ceremonies of which often occurred in the same upper-level room of Smith's Nauvoo store where he kept his Hebrew books and finished translating the Book of Abraham.[107] In addition, when Smith entertained visitors in Nauvoo he often

103. BoA, in *JSP*-R4:314–23 [Abraham 3–5; Fac. 2].

104. See BoA, in *JSP*-R4:324–27 [Abraham Fac. 3]; "A Fac-simile from the Book of Abraham, No. 3," *Times and Seasons*, 16 May 1842, 783–84. The explanation for the third illustration did not include any obvious Hebrew elements.

105. See the discourse on the doctrine of exaltation that Smith delivered on 7 April 1844 in honor of his recently deceased friend King Follett and the discourse on the plurality of Gods Smith delivered on 16 June 1844. Smith, *Words of Joseph Smith*, 340–62, 379–83.

106. See *JSP*-J3:xx–xxi, especially xxin33.

107. See Smith, History, 1838–1856, vol. C-1, 1328; Devery S. Anderson and Gary James Bergera, eds., *Joseph Smith's Quorum of the Anointed, 1842–1845: A Documentary History* (Salt Lake City: Signature Books, 2005), 5, 25–26; and Smith, Journal, 7 May 1843, in *JSP*-J3:13.

showed them the Egyptian materials, the Book of Abraham, and his Hebrew books in the same conversation, attempting to convince his guests that all three worked together to reveal insights into the biblical past.[108]

Finally, Smith's conviction that Hebrew and Egyptian were related can be seen a year after publishing the Book of Abraham in the episode surrounding the fraudulent Kinderhook plates. In early 1843, when the inscribed plates of brass arrived in Nauvoo, Smith and his associates immediately compared them to characters copied from the gold plates of the Book of Mormon, the characters copied from the Egyptian papyri into the GAEL, or both.[109] Remarkably, they believed that they saw a close resemblance between some of these characters. Apparently thinking that the Kinderhook plates might also be related to the Hebraic Reformed Egyptian, they sent for a Hebrew grammar and Hebrew Bible from Smith's office to help facilitate the translation. Unlike previous translation projects, this effort was abandoned quickly, but the episode shows that their assumptions about the interrelationship of Hebrew and Egyptian continued well after the translation and publication of the Book of Abraham.[110]

This survey of the main developments in Joseph Smith's translation activities provides an important context for understanding the Hebrew elements in the Book of Abraham. In conjunction with the previous section—which considered the belief of Smith and his associates that Hebrew would elucidate his larger Egyptian project—it has shown that his translation of the Book of Abraham and his Hebrew studies were deliberately interconnected endeavors. This is evident from the chronological overlapping of his translation activities with his personal study of Hebrew books in late 1835, his intensive Hebrew

108. One visitor to Nauvoo in 1840 met with Smith in his home, where Smith showed him a copy of the Seixas Hebrew grammar along with the Egyptian papyri as he explained how the Book of Abraham would "throw great light on the subject of Christianity." "A Glance at the Mormons," *Alexandria Gazette*, as reprinted in *Quincy Whig*, 17 October 1840, 1. A similar episode occurred in 1844 with the visit of Josiah Quincy and Charles Francis Adams, during which Smith both translated Hebrew for his guests and showed them the Egyptian papyri. Josiah Quincy, *Figures of the Past from the Leaves of Old Journals* (Boston: Roberts Brothers, 1883), 385–86.

109. A Nauvoo resident who wrote regarding the Kinderhook plates to a New York City newspaper, stated: "The plates . . . are covered on both sides with hieroglyphics. They were brought up and shown to Joseph Smith. He compared, in my presence, with his Egyptian Alphabet, which he took from the plates from which the Book of Mormon was translated, and they are evidently the same characters. He therefore will be able to decipher them." "A Gentile," "Late and Interesting from the Mormon Empire on the Upper Mississippi," *New York Herald*, 30 May 1843, 2. For more on this episode, see Don Bradley and Mark Ashurst-McGee, "'President Joseph Has Translated a Portion': Joseph Smith and the Mistranslation of the Kinderhook Plates," 499–517 herein.

110. See Smith, Journal, 7 May 1843, in *JSP*-J3:13. Bradley and Ashurst-McGee have argued that, by remarkable coincidence, a character at the top of one of the Kinderhook plates resembles the character designated as "Ho e oop hah" in the GAEL. Bradley and Ashurst-McGee, "'President Joseph Has Translated a Portion,'" 507–11 and 521–22 herein.

coursework with Joshua Seixas in early 1836 (during which he apparently sought connections with his work on the papyri), and his subsequent incorporation of Hebrew insights into his unfolding translation of the Book of Abraham prior to its publication in early 1842.

HEBREW IN THE TEXT AND TRANSLATION OF THE BOOK OF ABRAHAM

With the survey in the previous sections of the intellectual climate of the early nineteenth century, the interrelationship of Joseph Smith's Egyptian project and Hebrew studies, and the chronology of events related to those activities, it is now possible to more closely examine and better understand Smith's use of Hebrew in the text of the Book of Abraham and to discern some of the mechanics of his translation process. As already mentioned, scholars have long noted the presence of Hebrew words in Smith's translation, even if the origins and full extent of the language's influence has not always been clearly understood. While previous treatments of the topic have made valuable observations, most have been limited by a lack of information regarding the cultural context, chronological precision regarding the book's textual development, and careful analysis of the multifaceted ways in which Smith incorporated Hebrew into the translation project. In some cases, there has also been a lack of clarity as to which elements in the text were inspired by Smith's Hebrew studies and which were not. Some authors have speculated on words that might derive from Hebrew—such as *Jah-oh-eh*,[111] *Kolob*,[112] and the names of Egyptian

111. From the beginning, several scholars have assumed that *Jah-oh-eh* (the ostensible Egyptian term for "the measurement of this earth"), in the explanation for the second illustration (BoA, in R4:316–17 [Abraham Fac. 2: Fig. 1]), was not Egyptian, but was "a faulty transliteration of the Hebrew יהוה [*Jehovah*]." Remy and Brenchley, *Journey to Great Salt Lake City*, 2:542; see also Spalding, *Joseph Smith as Translator*, 29; and Mercer, "Joseph Smith as an Interpreter," 21–23. Louis Zucker connected this term to Smith's Hebrew studies by speculating that it was based on the divine name as Joshua Seixas spelled it—"Ye-ho-vau" (Seixas, *Manual Hebrew Grammar for the Use of Beginners*, 12 [no. 4], 15)—which Smith then inverted. Zucker, "Joseph Smith as a Student of Hebrew," 51. However, the appearance of this term in the 1835 Egyptian alphabet documents indicates that the name *Jah-oh-eh* had entered Smith's vocabulary several months before he began studying Hebrew. See EA-A, 2, in *JSP*-R4:60; EA-B, 2 , in *JSP*-R4:78; EA-C, 2, in *JSP*-R4:88–89; GAEL, 24, 29, 31, 33, in *JSP*-R4:162–63, 172–73, 176–77, 180–81. Furthermore, Smith's identification of the word as "the measurement of this earth" rather than the name of God weakens its possible connection to Hebrew. An alternative possibility is that *Jah-oh-eh* was originally inspired by the triune names of God (based on יהוה) as uttered in the era's Freemasonry rituals (such as "Jah-buh-lun" and "Je-ho-vah"), which Smith or his associates adapted for use in the Book of Abraham. For the possible Masonic origins of the word, see Brown, *In Heaven as It Is on Earth*, 182n60; compare Avery Allyn, *A Ritual of Freemasonry* (New York: William Gowans, 1853), 123–24.

112. Some scholars have argued that *Kolob*, the book's term for the residence of God, was a variation of the Hebrew verb קָרַב (*QRB*), meaning "to draw near"—with the transition from *QRB* to *KLB [Kolob]* reflecting the interchange between *R* and *L* common in ancient Semitic languages. R. C. Webb [James E.

gods[113]—but that have no convincing connection to Smith's study of the language. Therefore, a systematic examination of the text's Hebrew features is necessary to properly integrate this topic into Book of Abraham scholarship.

In light of the deficiencies just listed, a few criteria will help refine the analysis of this material. First, it is necessary to correctly identify those elements within the Book of Abraham that were demonstrably influenced by Smith's Hebrew studies. This can be done most methodically by recognizing Smith's use of Seixas's distinct transliteration system in his spelling of Hebrew words and by identifying features that derive from the Hebrew resources in his possession.[114]

Second, it is necessary to consider the chronological development of the text in light of its Hebrew elements. As mentioned in the first section, all of these elements appear in material that was finalized in early 1842 (now

---

Homans], *Joseph Smith as a Translator* [...] (Salt Lake City: Deseret News, 1936), 102–5; Charles Edward Haggerty, "A Study of the Book of Abraham" (master's thesis, Brigham Young University, 1946), 46–49; D. Kelly Ogden, "The Kirtland Hebrew School (1835–36)," in *Regional Studies in Latter-day Saint Church History*, ed. Milton V. Backman Jr. (Provo, UT: Brigham Young University, 1990), 165; and Draper, Brown, and Rhodes, *Pearl of Great Price*, 289–90. This claim is an intriguing one, especially in light of Smith's consistent rendering of *Kolob* as being "nearest unto the throne of God," "near unto me [God]," "nigh unto the throne of God," "near unto the throne of God," "nearest unto me," and "nearest to the celestial, or the residence of God." See BoA, in *JSP*-R4:314–19 [Abraham 3:2–3, 9–10, 16; Fac. 2: Fig. 1]. However, while קָרַב and its variants appear in Smith's Hebrew textbooks (see Gibbs, *Manual Hebrew and English Lexicon*, 195), the rules of consonantal interchangeability do not—thus making it unlikely that Smith would have learned about this technicality in his studies (unless he had heard it verbally from Seixas during class or in private discussion). Furthermore, the word *Kolob* was inserted by Warren Parrish into the versions of the Egyptian Alphabet text (EA-A, 2, in *JSP*-R4:60; EA-C, 2, in *JSP*-R4:88–89; Scrap, circa July–circa November 1835, in *JSP*-R4:102–3) and the GAEL (26, 28, 30, 32, 34, in R4:166–67, 170–71, 174–75, 178–79, and 182–83), indicating that it may have been part of Smith's vocabulary as early as October 1835, in which case it would predate Smith's study of Hebrew.

113. Several scholars have claimed that *Libnah*—the name of one of the Egyptian gods in the Book of Abraham (BoA, in *JSP*-R4:306–9 [Abraham 1:6, 13, 17; Fac. 1: Figs. 4, 6)—is related to the Hebrew words לָבָן (*laban*) or לְבָנָה (*l'banah*), meaning "white" or "moon" respectively. See Webb, *Joseph Smith as a Translator*, 143; Zucker, "Joseph Smith as a Student of Hebrew," 51; Walton, "Professor Seixas, the Hebrew Bible, and the Book of Abraham," 42–43; Ogden, "Kirtland Hebrew School," 165; and Draper, Brown, and Rhodes, *Pearl of Great Price*, 286. These terms do appear in Smith's Hebrew textbooks, see Gibbs, *Manual Hebrew and English Lexicon*, 106. However, the earliest manuscript evidence for the Book of Abraham indicates that the word was originally translated as *Zibnah* (Book of Abraham Manuscript, circa July–circa November 1835-A, 2, in *JSP*-R4:196–97; Book of Abraham Manuscript, circa July–circa November 1835-B, 3, in *JSP*-R4:208–9; Book of Abraham Manuscript, circa July–circa November 1835-C, 4, in *JSP*-R4:224–25) and was not changed to *Libnah* until the 1842 revisions made just prior to the book's publication (Book of Abraham Manuscript and Explanation of Facsimile 1, circa February 1842, in *JSP*-R4:250–59; BoA, in *JSP*-R4:306–9 [Abraham 1:6, 13, 17; Fac. 1: Figs. 4, 6]; and Hauglid, *A Textual History of the Book of Abraham*, 11, 26–28). It is possible that this change was inspired by Smith's study of Hebrew, but there is nothing in the way Smith spells, defines, or uses the word in the final version of the Abraham text that would confirm this.

114. In this section, Hebrew terms drawn from the Book of Abraham and Joseph Smith's writings will often be spelled using the transliteration system from the Seixas manual, rather than using standard academic transliterations, so as to highlight the connections between Smith's primary academic resources and his translation work.

Abraham 3–5 and the facsimile explanations), six years after Smith's formal study of Hebrew. It is also important to note, however, that Smith's references to Hebrew in the intervening years (1836–1841) can provide valuable insights into how some concepts evolved in his thinking and were eventually incorporated into the translation. This may suggest that Smith performed some of the conceptual but undocumented work of "translation" during this period.

Third, since Smith's use of Hebrew in the Book of Abraham was not homogeneous, it is important to consider the multifaceted ways in which he integrated Hebrew into the translation process. A close reading of the text shows that Hebrew influences on the Book of Abraham fall into three major categories: (1) the transliterated Hebrew words and definitions Smith used in his editorial explanations for the first two illustrations (Abraham Fac. 1; Fac. 2); (2) the transliterated Hebrew words and definitions Smith incorporated into Abraham's celestial vision in the middle of the text (Abraham 3); and (3) the implicit but profound ways in which Smith's Hebrew studies influenced his translation of the creation account given at the end of the text (Abraham 4–5). These categories demonstrate the complexities of the text's production and show that Smith's translation process involved a range of activities, all of which suggest a dynamic blending of his academic resources and methods with his prophetic inspiration. This section will examine each of these three categories in light of the above criteria.

Hebrew Terms in the Illustration Explanations

The first category to examine is Joseph Smith's use of Hebrew words and definitions in his explanations of the illustrations accompanying the text of the Book of Abraham, especially of certain figures found in the first illustration (which was taken from a vignette in the Egyptian papyri) and second illustration (which represents a funerary charm found among Smith's Egyptian artifacts).[115] These explanations were apparently completed in 1842 just prior to being published along with the Book of Abraham translation.[116] Although the

115. This funerary charm is a *hypocephalus*: a charm that was sometimes placed "under (or beside) the head" of the deceased. Hypocephali were cosmic diagrams, typically round, that included scenes of the afterlife. For helpful surveys of hypocephali and their significance in ancient Egypt, see John Gee, "Towards an Interpretation of Hypocephali," in *"Le lotus qui sort du terre": Mélanges offerts à Edith Varga*, ed. Hedvig Győry (Budapest: Musée Hongrois des Beaux-Arts, 2001), 325–34; and Gee, "Non-Round Hypocephali," in *Aegyptus et Pannonia III*, ed. Hedvig Győry (Budapest: MEBT-ÓEB Comité de l'Égypte Ancienne de l'Association Amicale Hongroise-Égyptienne, 2006), 41–58.

116. See notes 100–103 above.

illustrations were presented as facsimile images "from the book of Abraham,"[117] they are qualitatively different from the narrative text and the precise relationship between the two is not always clear. Moreover, Smith's explanations of the figures in the illustrations represent a unique aspect of the book's production since he did not necessarily present all of his explanations as direct translations of Egyptian script. (The explanation for the second illustration bills itself as a "translation,"[118] but the other two do not.) Instead, Smith may have presented his interpretations of the illustrations—and many if not all of their component figures—as editorial elucidations.[119] As such, Smith apparently felt free to draw upon Hebrew insights he had gleaned from his studies to help explain the Egyptian images. In some instances, Smith used Hebrew verbiage to clarify astronomical ideas he had initially presented in the 1835 Egyptian alphabet and grammar documents, and in some cases he drew attention to these inter-linguistic connections—occasionally even using the phrases "answering to the Hebrew" and "answers to the Hebrew."[120] Conceptually, this approach resembles nineteenth-century scholarly efforts to use Hebrew language and scripture to interpret other Egyptian discoveries—such as the coffin texts or temple iconography mentioned previously—although naturally Smith's specific interpretations were unique to the Abraham illustrations.[121]

The earliest example of Smith using Hebrew terminology in this way is in his explanation accompanying the first illustration, a funerary image found on the papyri.[122] This image depicts an Osiris figure (identified by Smith as

117. BoA, in *JSP*-R4:306–7, 316–17, 324–27 [Abraham Fac. 1; Fac. 2; Fac. 3].

118. BoA, in *JSP*-R4:316–17 [Abraham Fac. 2].

119. The list of explanations for the keyed figures in the second illustration concluded with a general statement: "The above translation is given as far as we have any right to give at the present time." However, the expository wording of Smith's descriptions—and their appearance under the heading "*Explanation* of the above Cut [woodcut-based print facsimile]"—suggest that in this instance he used the word "translation" broadly to include his editorial explanations. The earliest manuscripts of the explanations for the figures in the illustrations are in the handwriting of Willard Richards. BoA, in *JSP*-R4:250–51; Explanation of Facsimile 2, circa 15 March 1842, in *JSP*-R4:276–83 [Abraham Fac. 2] (emphasis added). Based on this, John Gee has attempted to distance Smith from the explanations given for the illustrations (Gee, in "Joseph Smith and Ancient Egypt," 437–38). However, with Smith's frequent use of scribes and his oversight of the editing and publication of this material, there is no compelling reason to think that he was not involved in their creation. Furthermore, the vignette explanations contain Seixas-inspired Hebrew, and Richards had not been a student in the Kirtland Hebrew class. This indicates that someone who knew Seixas's transliteration system, such as Smith or Phelps, had produced the content of the explanations just as they corrected the spelling of some Hebrew words as inscribed by Richards (as seen below).

120. BoA, in *JSP*-R4:306–7, 316–17 [Abraham Fac. 1: Fig. 12; Fac. 2: Fig. 4].

121. For contemporaneous examples of attempts to interpret Egyptian images through the lens of Hebrew language and scripture, see notes 21–27 above.

122. Fragment of Book of Breathing for Horos-A, between 238 and circa 153 BC, in *JSP*-R4:8–9; BoA, in *JSP*-R4:306–7 [Abraham Fac. 1].

Abraham) lying on a lion couch (identified as an altar) accompanied by Anubis (interpreted as a priest attempting to sacrifice Abraham).[123] Smith had associated this image with the Abraham narrative in 1835, early in his work with the papyri, but his formal explanation of it was not completed until its publication in 1842.[124] In that explanation, Smith identified the hatched lines (the waters of the Nile) below the lion couch as "Raukeeyang, signifying expanse, or the firmament over our heads; but in this case, in relation to this subject, the Egyptians meant it to signify Shaumau, to be high, or the heavens, answering to the Hebrew word, Shaumahyeem." Below this is a series of vertical lines (niched brick) that Smith interpreted as representing "the pillars of heaven, as understood by the Egyptians."[125] It is unclear how Smith meant this interpretation of the heavenly expanse and its supporting pillars to be understood as appearing *beneath* the altar of sacrifice, or even within the larger schema of the sacrificial scene. Nevertheless, his explanations explicitly drew upon Hebrew words, definitions, and concepts that he had learned during his studies in 1836.

The first recognizable Hebrew word in these explanations is *raukeeyang* (רָקִיעַ), the term in the biblical creation account traditionally translated into English as "firmament."[126] Smith would have encountered this word during his first week of Hebrew class with Joshua Seixas, when it was used to illustrate Seixas's spelling rules,[127] and later in the course while translating Genesis 1.[128]

123. For a modern Egyptological view of this vignette, see Ritner, *The Joseph Smith Egyptian Papyri*, 90–94.

124. The vignette is referenced early in the text of the Book of Abraham, in the part that had been produced in 1835. See Book of Abraham Manuscript, circa July–circa November 1835-A, in *JSP*-R4:194–95; Book of Abraham Manuscript, circa July–circa November 1835-B, in *JSP*-R4:206–7; Book of Abraham Manuscript, circa July–circa November 1835-C, in *JSP*-R4:220–23 [Abraham 1:12]. However, Smith's journal entries show that he wrote (or at least finalized) his explanations for the illustration in February 1842 (see notes 100–101 above).

125. Fragment of Book of Breathing for Horos-A, between 238 and circa 153 BC, in *JSP*-R4:8–9; compare BoA, in *JSP*-R4:306–7 [Abraham Fac. 1: Fig. 11 and 12].

126. See KJV Genesis 1:6–8, 14–20. Incidentally, Smith had retained this traditional translation of the word in his 1830 revision of Genesis. Old Testament Manuscript 1, 3–4, in Smith, *Joseph Smith's New Translation of the Bible*, 86–87 [Moses 2:6–8, 14–20].

127. The Seixas grammar, *Manual Hebrew Grammar for the Use of Beginners*, uses "*bir-kee-ang*" (בִּרְקִיעַ) to illustrate the pronunciation of a silent shewa (8 [§7]), and "*rau-kee-ang*" (רָקִיעַ) to illustrate the pronunciation of a final *ayin* (12 [no. 5]). A worksheet Seixas produced for students to practice the "Hebrew Alphabet" also contains the word in Hebrew and transliterates it as "*rau-kee-ang*." Hebrew worksheet owned by Peter Whitmer [possibly Peter Whitmer Jr.], Community of Christ Library and Archives, Community of Christ, Independence, MO.

128. See note 92 above. For a list of nouns used in Genesis 1 (including רָקִיעַ), see Seixas, *Manual Hebrew Grammar for the Use of Beginners*, 78 (§103). The 1833 edition of the Seixas grammar omitted this word in the vocabulary list (Seixas, *Manual Hebrew Grammar for the Use of Beginners* [1833], 44), but an extant copy of Newel K. Whitney's 1833 edition indicates that students were instructed to write it into the margins to make their vocabulary list reflect the more complete 1834 edition (Whitney copy at Church History Library). The full Hebrew text of Genesis 1 was included in the grammar supplement published for the use of the class. *Supplement to J. Seixas' Manual Hebrew Grammar*, 28–32.

In his spelling of *raukeeyang*, Smith closely followed Seixas's transliteration for vowels and gutturals, writing "au" for the *qametz*, "ee" for the *hireq*, and "ng" for the final *ayin*.[129] In his explanation, Smith retained the word's traditional definition of "firmament," but he followed his textbooks—in this case the Joshua Seixas grammar and the Josiah Gibbs lexicon—by prioritizing its less conventional definition as "expanse."[130] Smith followed a similar pattern in his explanation of the hawk depicted in the second illustration, which he said also "Answers to the Hebrew word Raukeeyang, signifying expanse, or the firmament of the heavens."[131]

The choice by Gibbs and Seixas to emphasize "expanse" over "firmament" likely relates to attempts by some early nineteenth-century commentators on Genesis 1 to replace the Latin Vulgate's use of *firmamentum* (suggesting a physical vault of heaven) with terminology that better reflects the Hebrew רָקִיעַ, for which the verbal root רָקַע means "to spread out" (like a curtain).[132] Such scholars, trying to harmonize the Bible with modern scientific views, argued that this word did not refer to a hard dome (as implied by "firmament") but was either a reference to an atmospheric "expanse" or to the entire planetary system that surrounded the earth.[133] Smith appears to have been intrigued by

129. For Seixas's spelling rules, see Seixas, *Manual Hebrew Grammar for the Use of Beginners*, 5–12. In the earliest extant manuscript copy of the explanations for the first illustration, Willard Richards initially spelled this word as *Raukeeyagn*. Book of Abraham Manuscript and Explanation of Facsimile 1, circa February 1842, 2 verso, in *JSP*-R4:250–51. This was incorrect, as Richards was following the spelling for *ayin* (gn) when it is *not* the final syllable, a common error that the Seixas grammar warned against. See Seixas, *Manual Hebrew Grammar for the Use of Beginners*, 12 (no. 5). However, another scribe—presumably Smith but possibly Phelps or someone else—corrected this spelling (in the same manuscript) by revising "gn" to "ng." Hauglid, *A Textual History of the Book of Abraham*, 156–57.

130. For the definition of רָקִיעַ as "an expanse," see Seixas, *Manual Hebrew Grammar for the Use of Beginners*, 21, 32 (§21), 78 (§103). Similarly, the Gibbs Lexicon defined רָקִיעַ as "the expanse, arch, or vault of heaven." Gibbs, *A Manual Hebrew and English Lexicon*, 207.

131. BoA, in *JSP*-R4:316–17 [Abraham Fac. 2: Fig. 4].

132. For commentary on the verbal root of רָקִיעַ, see Gibbs, *A Manual Hebrew and English Lexicon*, 207; and Seixas, *Manual Hebrew Grammar for the Use of Beginners*, 21. Apparently, Smith viewed the outstretched wings of the hawk in the second illustration as a reflection of this "spreading out" of the *raukeeyang*. BoA, in *JSP*-R4:316–17 [Abraham Fac. 2: Fig. 4].

133. Consider the explanation of Genesis 1:6 in Adam Clarke's Bible Commentary:

> Our translators, by following the firmamentum of the Vulgate, which is a translation of the στερεωμα of the Septuagint, have deprived this passage of all sense and meaning. The Hebrew word רקיע rakia, from רקע raka, to spread out as the curtains of a tent or pavilion, simply signifies an expanse or space, and consequently that circumambient space or expansion separating the clouds, which are in the higher regions of it, from the seas, etc., which are below it. This we call the atmosphere, the orb of atoms or inconceivably small particles; but the word appears to have been used by Moses in a more extensive sense, and to include the whole of the planetary vortex, or the space which is occupied by the whole solar system.

Adam Clarke, *The Holy Bible Containing the Old and New Testaments* (1815; repr., Nashville: Abingdon, 1977), 1:33. Subsequent translators of Genesis 1 have generally returned to "firmament" (or heavenly dome) as a more authentic reflection of ancient Near Eastern cosmology. See the treatment of this concept in

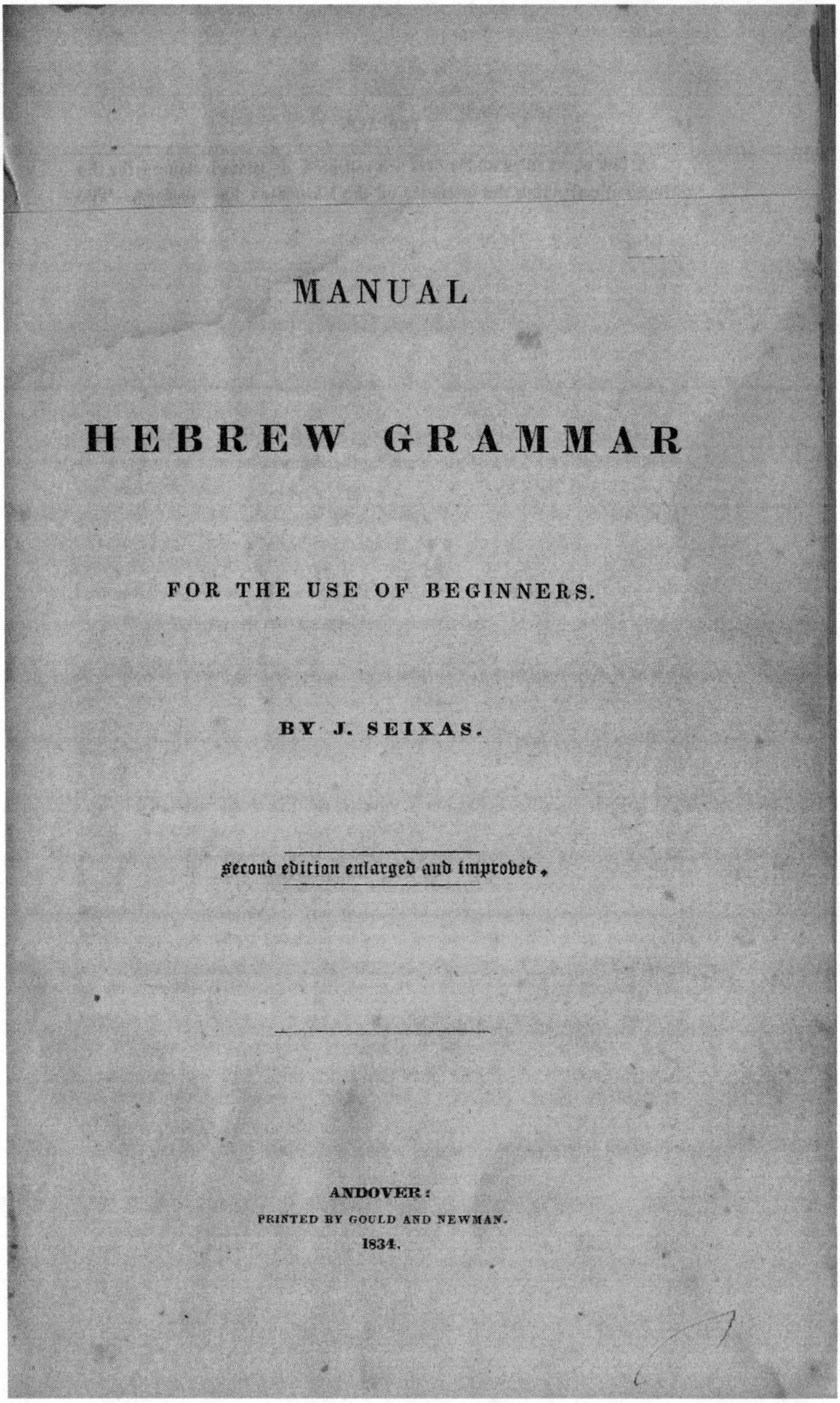

MANUAL

HEBREW GRAMMAR

FOR THE USE OF BEGINNERS.

BY J. SEIXAS.

Second edition enlarged and improved.

ANDOVER:
PRINTED BY GOULD AND NEWMAN.
1834.

FIGURE 16.1. Hebrew manual by Joshua Seixas. The instructor of the Kirtland Hebrew School, Joshua Seixas, assigned the beginner's manual he had written for use in his classes. Joseph Smith likely had an 1834 edition like that pictured here. Copy attributed to Persis Goodall Young by descendant. Church History Library, Salt Lake City.

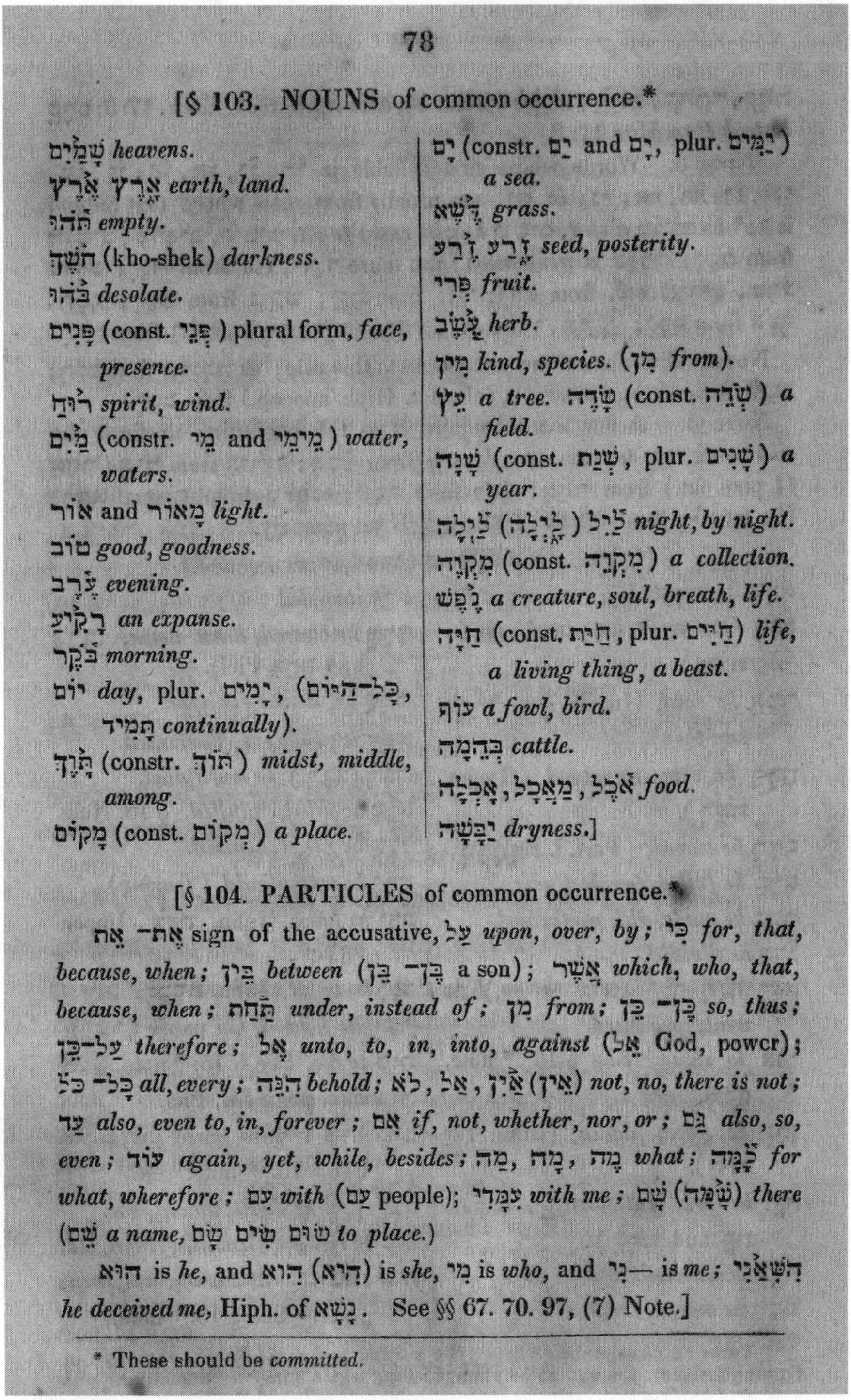

78

[§ 103. NOUNS of common occurrence.*

שָׁמַיִם *heavens.*

אֶרֶץ אָרֶץ *earth, land.*

תֹּהוּ *empty.*

חֹשֶׁךְ (kho-shek) *darkness.*

בֹּהוּ *desolate.*

פָּנִים (const. פְּנֵי) plural form, *face, presence.*

רוּחַ *spirit, wind.*

מַיִם (constr. מֵי and מֵימֵי) *water, waters.*

אוֹר and מָאוֹר *light.*

טוֹב *good, goodness.*

עֶרֶב *evening.*

רָקִיעַ *an expanse.*

בֹּקֶר *morning.*

יוֹם *day*, plur. יָמִים, (כָּל־הַיּוֹם, תָּמִיד *continually*).

תָּוֶךְ (constr. תּוֹךְ) *midst, middle, among.*

מָקוֹם (const. מְקוֹם) *a place.*

יָם (constr. יַם and יָם, plur. יַמִּים) *a sea.*

דֶּשֶׁא *grass.*

זֶרַע זָרַע *seed, posterity.*

פְּרִי *fruit.*

עֵשֶׂב *herb.*

מִין *kind, species.* (מִן *from*).

עֵץ *a tree.* שָׂדֶה (const. שְׂדֵה) *a field.*

שָׁנָה (const. שְׁנַת, plur. שָׁנִים) *a year.*

לַיִל (לַיְלָה) לַיְלָה *night, by night.*

מִקְוֶה (const. מִקְוֵה) *a collection.*

נֶפֶשׁ *a creature, soul, breath, life.*

חַיָּה (const. חַיַּת, plur. חַיִּים) *life, a living thing, a beast.*

עוֹף *a fowl, bird.*

בְּהֵמָה *cattle.*

אֹכֶל, מַאֲכָל, אָכְלָה *food.*

יַבָּשָׁה *dryness.*]

[§ 104. PARTICLES of common occurrence.*

אֵת אֶת־ sign of the accusative, עַל *upon, over, by;* כִּי *for, that, because, when;* בֵּין *between* (בֵּן בֶּן־ a son); אֲשֶׁר *which, who, that, because, when;* תַּחַת *under, instead of;* מִן *from;* כֵּן כֶּן־ *so, thus;* עַל־כֵּן *therefore;* אֶל *unto, to, in, into, against* (אֵל God, power); כֹּל כָּל־ *all, every;* הִנֵּה *behold;* לֹא, אַל, אַיִן (אֵין) *not, no, there is not;* עַד *also, even to, in, forever;* אִם *if, not, whether, nor, or;* גַּם *also, so, even;* עוֹד *again, yet, while, besides;* מַה, מָה, מֶה *what;* לָמָּה *for what, wherefore;* עִם *with* (עַם people); עִמָּדִי *with me;* שָׁם (שָׁמָּה) *there* (שֵׁם *a name,* שָׂם שִׂים שׂוּם *to place.*)

הוּא is *he*, and הִוא (הִיא) is *she*, מִי is *who*, and נִי— is *me;* הִשִּׁאַנִי *he deceived me*, Hiph. of נָשָׁא. See §§ 67. 70. 97, (7) Note.]

* These should be *committed.*

FIGURE 16.2. *Raukeeyang* translated as "expanse." The textbook used by Joseph Smith in his Hebrew coursework included a list of "nouns of common occurrence"—which were drawn from the creation account in Genesis 1 and were to be "committed" (committed to memory). This list included the Hebrew word *raukeeyang*, translated as "an expanse" (as opposed to "firmament"), along with other terms and definitions Smith incorporated into his translation of the Book of Abraham. Copy attributed to Persis Goodall Young by descendant. Church History Library, Salt Lake City.

these contemporaneous views of the "expanse," and in his post-1836 translation activities tended to defer to his Hebrew manuals in highlighting that translation of רָקִיעַ, including in his explanations of the illustrations and his other work with the Abraham text (see below). At the same time, however, he apparently remained open to the more traditional concept of a "firmament" as indicated by his ongoing, if occasional, use of that word and his description of the "pillars" upholding the heavens. Smith thus seems to have blended the two views in his translation efforts.[134]

The second recognizable Hebrew word Smith used in his explanation for the first illustration is *shaumahyeem* (שָׁמַיִם), a plural Hebrew word for the "heavens" (typically translated in the KJV of Genesis 1 as the singular "heaven").[135] Smith had also encountered this word in his studies. As with *raukeeyang*, Smith's spelling and translation of *shaumahyeem* closely follows the Seixas grammar, particularly in his emphasis of the word's plural form.[136] Throughout his earlier revelations and translation projects, including the Book of Mormon and the "new translation" of the Bible (hereafter New Translation), Smith used the singular "heaven" and the plural "heavens" interchangeably, usually without distinguishing between their meanings.[137] However, after learning from

---

J. H. Walton, "Creation," in *Dictionary of the Old Testament Pentateuch*, ed. T. Desmond Alexander and David W. Baker (Downers Grove, IL: InterVarsity Press, 2003), 158–59; and compare Hutchinson, "A Mormon Midrash," 21n7.

134. As mentioned previously, Smith used both "expanse" and "firmament" together (though giving priority to the former) in his explanations for the first two illustrations published with the Book of Abraham. BoA, in *JSP*-R4:306–7, 316–17 [Abraham Fac. 1: Fig. 12; Fac. 2: Fig. 4]. In his translation of the creation account in the Book of Abraham, he would use "expanse" nine times on its own (BoA, in *JSP*-R4:318–21 [Abraham 4:6, 7, 8, 14, 15, 17, 20]), while he used "firmament" without any additional elaboration only once (BoA, in *JSP*-R4: 318–19 [Abraham 3:13]). In addition to the definitions of רָקִיעַ available in his Hebrew resources, Smith may also have read Adam Clarke's description of the word as "the curtains of a tent or pavilion" (Clarke, *The Holy Bible Containing the Old and New Testaments*, 1:33) and used similar language in his own writings, such as the phrase "the pavilion that covereth [God's] hiding place" (Letter to the Church and Edward Partridge, 20 March 1839, in *JSP*-D6:362 [D&C 121:1]). Use of this language among Smith's associates can be seen in a poem by William W. Phelps that draws extensively from the cosmology of the Book of Abraham and describes "the outside curtains" that covered the bounds of creation, including the heavens. Phelps, "There Is No End," *Deseret News*, 19 November 1856, 2 (now "If You Could Hie to Kolob," in *Hymns of the Church of Jesus Christ of Latter-day Saints* [Salt Lake City: Church of Jesus Christ of Latter-day Saints, 1985], hymn 284).

135. See KJV Genesis 1:1, 8–9, 14–17, 20.

136. Students in the Kirtland Hebrew school would have encountered שָׁמַיִם several times while working through their textbook. See Seixas, *Manual Hebrew Grammar for the Use of Beginners*. Specifically, they would have encountered the word, its variants, and its definition in their study of dual noun forms (22 [no. 8]), the locative ה (23 [§13]), definite articles (53 [§59]), prefixes (54 [§61]), verbs (69 [§91]), common nouns (78 [§103]), vocabulary for Genesis 1:1 (85), and practice sentences (88).

137. See the many entries for both terms—as they appear in the Book of Mormon, Smith's revelations, and other writings—in Eldin Ricks, *Eldin Ricks's Thorough Concordance of the LDS Standard Works: Book of Mormon, Doctrine and Covenants, Pearl of Great Price* (Provo, UT: Foundation for Ancient Research and Mormon Studies, 1995), 329–31. One rare commentary on the differences between the two terms can

Seixas or through his personal studies that in Hebrew the ִים– (–yeem) ending technically rendered the word for heaven in its plural form,[138] Smith seems to have become intrigued by the theological implications of this technicality and tended to favor the plural "heavens" throughout his subsequent treatment of Abrahamic cosmology—both in his explanations of the illustrations and in his translation of the Abraham creation account.[139] This tendency may have been motivated by his earlier visions of three levels of heavenly glory,[140] although his occasional use of the singular "heaven" in subsequent writings shows that he was not insistent on an exclusive interpretation of the word.[141]

In his figure explanations for the hatched lines (waters of the Nile) and the vertical lines (niched brick) at the bottom of the first illustration, Smith used this Hebrew terminology to help elucidate the Egyptian understanding of *raukeeyang*.[142] In the case of the hatched lines, he wrote that "the Egyptians meant ... to signify Shaumau, to be high, or the heavens, answering to the Hebrew word, Shaumahyeem." Several observers have noted that the term *shaumau* is not an attested Egyptian word, as might be implied by an initial reading of Smith's explanation.[143] Others, attempting to identify the origins of

---

be seen in Smith's 1830 revision of Genesis, in which he highlighted the notion that "the Heavens ... are many & they cannot be numbered unto man." Old Testament Manuscript 1, 2–3, in Smith, *Joseph Smith's New Translation of the Bible*, 85–86 [Moses 1:36–38]. Following that statement, Smith proceeded to translate the entire Genesis creation account using the singular "heaven" in reference to "*this* Heaven & this Earth." See Old Testament Manuscript 1, 3, in Smith, *Joseph Smith's New Translation of the Bible*, 86 [Moses 2:1] (emphasis added). Smith even changed the few instances the KJV translated שָׁמַיִם as "heavens" from its plural to its singular form, such as KJV Genesis 2:1–4. See Old Testament Manuscript 1, 5, in Smith, *Joseph Smith's New Translation of the Bible*, 88 [Moses 3:1–4]. The intentional nature of this decision is demonstrated by the manuscript evidence for Smith's revision of KJV Genesis 2:1, in which Smith's scribe originally wrote "heavens" but later crossed out the "s." Old Testament Manuscript 2, 6, in Smith, *Joseph Smith's New Translation of the Bible*, 597 [Moses 3:1–4].

138. The Seixas textbook states that "the dual form שָׁמַיִם *heavens* ... [is] plural." Seixas, *Manual Hebrew Grammar for the Use of Beginners*, 22 (no. 8). Similarly, the Gibbs lexicon identifies שָׁמַיִם as a "pl. m. const. שְׁמֵי," which can be translated either as "heaven" or "heavens." Gibbs, *A Manual Hebrew and English Lexicon*, 222.

139. In the Abraham material that Smith finalized in 1842, six years after his formal study of Hebrew in 1836, he used the singular "heaven" eight times (BoA, in *JSP*-R4:306–7, 318–21 [Abraham 3:13, 4:8, 9, 14, 15, 20; Fac. 1: Fig. 11; Fac. 3: Fig. 1]) and the plural "heavens" ten times (BoA, in *JSP*-R4:306–7, 316–23 [Abraham 3:21, 4:1, 17, 5:1, 3, 4; Fac. 1: Fig. 12; Fac. 2: Figs. 4, 7]).

140. Vision, 16 February 1832, in *JSP*-D2:179–92 [D&C 76]; Visions, 21 January 1836, in *JSP*-D5:157–60 [D&C 137]. See also Smith, History, 1838–1856, 16–17 May 1843, vol. D-1, 1551–52 [D&C 131:1–4].

141. For a listing of both terms as they appear in Smith's post-1836 revelations, see Ricks, *Eldin Ricks's Thorough Concordance of the LDS Standard Works*, 330–31. See also Grant Underwood, "'Saved or Damned': Tracing a Persistent Protestantism in Early Mormon Thought," *BYU Studies* 25, no. 3 (Summer 1985): 85–103.

142. BoA, in *JSP*-R4:306–7 [Abraham Fac. 1: Figs. 11–12].

143. Samuel Mercer wrote: "The Prophet refers to 'shaumau' as if it were an Egyptian word. There is no such word known to the Egyptian language meaning 'to be high or the heavens;' neither does it mean 'to be high or the heavens' in Hebrew." Mercer, "Joseph Smith as an Interpreter," 19–20. Compare Remy and Brenchley, *Journey to Great Salt Lake City*, 2:541; Ritner, *The Joseph Smith Egyptian Papyri*, 93.

this word in Smith's thinking, have speculated that it is a creative reconstruction of an unattested Hebrew verbal root (*shomah*), meaning "to be high," or is an invented singular form of the noun *shaumahyeem* that is not present in the Bible.[144] These speculations can now be refined in light of the Hebrew resources Smith had at his disposal. Smith seems to have become intrigued by the instruction in the Seixas grammar regarding a class of nouns and verbs that are related by the meaning of their shared roots.[145] Although Seixas did not list *shaumahyeem* and *shaumau* in his manual as examples of this phenomenon, Smith may have inferred—or Seixas may have taught in his class—that the latter was the hypothetical verbal counterpart of the former (that is, that the noun "heavens" derived its meaning from a theoretical verb "to be high"). Since many examples of similar counterparts listed by Seixas show the verbal form being vowelled with a double *qametz* (au . . . au),[146] Smith's claim that *shaumau* (to be high) was a verb related to the noun *shaumahyeem* (heavens) would make sense in light of the Seixas curriculum.

In fact, some Hebrew lexicons in circulation at that time, to which Smith seems to have had access, make this very argument.[147] Examples of this can be found in the work of the German scholar Wilhelm Gesenius, which had been available in English translations by Josiah Gibbs and Edward Robinson since the 1820s. These sources list שָׁמָה—which would have been transliterated with Seixas's spelling rules as *shaumau*—as an "obsol[ete] root" related to the Arabic verb "to be high" and as the origin of the word שָׁמַיִם (heavens).[148] Moreover, the entire entry for שָׁמַיִם in the Gesenius lexicon translated by Gibbs closely resembles the language in Smith's explanation for the first illustration, with its description of the heavens, the expanse (רָקִיעַ), the pillars supporting the heavens, and the hypothetical verbal root "to be high":

> שָׁמַיִם masc. plur. const. שְׁמֵי, *the heaven* or *heavens*. (The singular is found in the Arab. سَمَاءٌ, from سما *to be high*. The corresponding form of the

144. See Webb, *Joseph Smith as a Translator*, 191; and Zucker, "Joseph Smith as a Student of Hebrew," 51; compare Draper, Brown, and Rhodes, *Pearl of Great Price*, 286.

145. For a list of these "Heemantive Nouns," including the noun רָקִיעַ (an expanse) and related verb רָקַע (he spread out), see Seixas, *Manual Hebrew Grammar for the Use of Beginners*, 21.

146. Ibid.

147. See note 71 above for a document listing books either purchased or desired by the Kirtland school, including "Gesenius Lex. translated by Robins[on] or Gibbs," indicating that Smith may have consulted either or both of the Gesenius lexicons mentioned in this section.

148. See Wilhelm Gesenius, *A Hebrew and English Lexicon of the Old Testament, including the Biblical Chaldee*, trans. Edward Robinson (Boston: Crocker and Brewster, 1836), 1025. Some modern lexicons base a similar claim on Gesenius, as can be seen in the entry for שמה in F. Brown, S. Driver, and C. Briggs, *The Brown-Driver-Briggs Hebrew and English Lexicon* (Peabody, MA: Hendrickson, 1996), 1029.

> singular may in Hebrew have been שָׁמַי, whence the plural שָׁמַיִם ... The Hebrews conceived of heaven as a solid arch, (see רָקִיעַ) as resting on pillars, (Job 26:11.) as having foundations, (2 Sam. 22:8.) and a gate, (Gen. 28:17) and as sending down rain from its open doors or sluices, (Ps. 78:23. 2 K 7:2, 19.).[149]

If Smith indeed had access to this definition, which seems to be the case based on such closely related wording, it appears that in his explanation he did not intend for *shaumau* to be understood as an Egyptian term. Instead, he seems to have seen it as a Hebrew verb that—along with the nouns *raukeeyang* and *shaumahyeem*—helped describe the Egyptian view of the heavens.[150]

Other uses of Hebrew terminology are found in Smith's explanation for the second illustration, the rendering of a funerary charm (hypocephalus) that Smith viewed as a diagram of the cosmos as understood by Abraham. In addition to his second use of *raukeeyang*, Smith identified the Hathor cow in the lower half of the hypocephalus as "Enish-go-on-dosh"—"one of the governing planets," which received power "through the medium of Kli-flos-is-es, or Hah-ko-kau-beam" (a pair of stars).[151] The first two terms—*Enish-go-on-dosh* and *Kli-flos-is-es*—are astronomical terms found in the Egyptian Alphabet text and the GAEL (both produced in 1835).[152] However, the third term, *Hah-ko-kau-beam* (הַכּוֹכָבִים), is the plural form of the Hebrew word for star (כּוֹכָב)—with the definite article (-הַ) added as a prefix (thus "*the* stars")—spelled using Seixas's transliteration rules.[153] Smith editorially inserted this word to elucidate *Kli-*

149. Wilhelm Gesenius, *Hebrew and English Lexicon of the Old Testament including the Biblical Chaldee*, trans. Josiah W. Gibbs (Andover, MA: Flagg and Gould, 1824), 671. Compare the entry on רָקִיעַ, which also defines it as "expanse of heaven" (616). The entry for שָׁמַיִם in the Gesenius lexicon as translated by Robinson similarly lists the plural "heavens," the hypothetical singular שָׁמַי, the רָקִיעַ being "spread out ... above the earth," and its supporting columns. Gesenius, *A Hebrew and English Lexicon of the Old Testament* (1836), 1026.

150. Additional evidence that Smith did not consider *shaumau* to be an Egyptian word is its absence in the versions of the Egyptian Alphabet text and in the GAEL. Instead, this term and its definition were first added to Smith's illustration explanations in 1842 as seen in its secondary insertion into the manuscript copy of the explanations accompanying the first illustration. BoA, in *JSP*-R4:250–51.

151. BoA, in *JSP*-R4:316–17 [Abraham Fac. 2: Fig. 4 and 5].

152. *Kli-flos-isis* appears undefined in the three versions of the Egyptian Alphabet text (EA-A, 2, in *JSP*-R4:60; EA-B, 2, in *JSP*-R4:78; and EA-C, 2, in *JSP*-R4:88–89), and defined in association with various concepts of planetary motion and time in the grammar book (GAEL, 25, 32, 34, in *JSP*-R4:164–65, 178–79, 182–83). *Enish-go-an=dosh* appears in the grammar book as the second governing planet. GAEL, 29–30, in *JSP*-R4:172–75. In every instance, these terms appear in Smith's Egyptian documents without accompanying Hebrew vocabulary, further supporting an 1835 date for the production of these documents (prior to Smith's study of Hebrew in 1836).

153. As far as can be determined, הַכּוֹכָבִים does not appear in the Seixas grammar, but the singular כּוֹכָב is listed in the Gibbs lexicon as "*a star*; metaph. *a mighty prince*." Gibbs, *A Manual Hebrew and English*

flos-is-es, the ostensible Egyptian term associated with the power emanating from the stars, which he understood as represented by the lunar discs in the central frame of the hypocephalus.[154] In this instance, Smith did not use the accompanying phrase, "answers to the Hebrew," but his definition of *Hah-ko-kau-beam* as "the stars" clearly shows that, once again, he freely used Hebrew terminology in his interpretation of Egyptian vignettes and in his explanation of Egyptian cosmology.

These editorial explanations demonstrate that, along with his other possible sources of inspiration, Smith was comfortable drawing upon and applying his academic studies to his prophetic elucidation of the sacred past. Although his motivations for openly using Hebrew terminology to help describe Egyptian imagery are uncertain, they might have included a desire to provide biblical verisimilitude for his Abrahamic record, display his erudition, or help his fellow students of Hebrew make connections between their studies and the papyri.[155] In any case, Smith's editorial activity reflected common attitudes toward the potential of Hebrew language to interpret Egyptian iconography. As noted earlier, while some of the astronomical content found in Smith's explanations for the illustrations had been present in his thinking, at least in conceptual form, since late 1835—being initially inspired by his examination of the papyri and work on the GAEL—his Hebrew studies in 1836 provided additional vocabulary with which he could elaborate upon and articulate these concepts.

Hebrew Terminology in the Revelation on Astronomy

Another use of Hebrew in the Book of Abraham is seen in a series of words and concepts Joseph Smith integrated into a portion of its narrative text in which Abraham recounts a revelation regarding astronomy given by God through "the Urim and Thummim" (what is now Abraham 3:1–28).[156] This astronomical

---

Lexicon, 97; compare Gesenius, *Hebrew and English Lexicon of the Old Testament* (1824), 297. In the only extant manuscript for the explanations accompanying the second illustration, "the" is partially underlined in the English translation of *Hah-ko-kau-beam* as "the stars," apparently to emphasize the addition of the definite article *Hah* (–הַ) in the Hebrew term. Hauglid, *A Textual History of the Book of Abraham*, 188–89; Explanation of Facsimile 2, circa 15 March 1842, in *JSP*-R4:281 [Abraham Fac. 2: Fig. 5].

154. BoA, in *JSP*-R4:316–17 [Abraham Fac. 2: Figs. 22 and 23]. For modern Egyptological interpretations of these images, see Ritner, *The Joseph Smith Egyptian Papers*, 215–26.

155. Michael T. Walton asserted that Smith was simply "showing off." Walton, "Professor Seixas, the Hebrew Bible, and the Book of Abraham," 42.

156. Although what is now Abraham 2 largely followed and expanded upon the biblical narrative of Genesis 11–12 (Abraham's journeys from Ur, through Canaan, and into Egypt), what is now Abraham 3 inserts a vision that Abraham has of the stars and an accompanying promise of endless posterity. BoA, in *JSP*-R4:314–15, 318–19 [Abraham 3:1–2, 14]. This insertion may signal a recontextualized expansion of

revelation contains a number of peculiar terms in its description of the cosmos, including many concepts that first appeared in the GAEL in 1835, such as teachings on the sun, the moon, the stars, and the star *Kolob* (the "nearest unto the throne of God").[157] In the course of the revelation, God shows these celestial luminaries to Abraham and in describing them uses a cluster of ancient words (including Hebrew terms) with their definitions: "And he said unto me this is Shinehah, (which is the sun.) And he said unto me, Kokob, which is star. And he said unto me, Olea, which is the moon. And he said unto me, Kokaubeam, which signifies stars, or all the great lights, which were in the firmament of heaven."[158] In this passage, which represents God's words to Abraham, the terminology used for the sun (*shinehah*) and moon (*olea*) appears to derive from Smith's previous work on the "pure language of Adam."[159] The terminology used to describe the stars, however, is drawn from Hebrew vocabulary.

Similar to the occurrence of *Hah-ko-kau-beam* in the second illustration,[160] these terms are transliterated Hebrew words spelled and defined following Smith's textbooks: *Kokob* (כּוֹכָב) is the singular Hebrew word for "star" and *Kokaubeam* (כּוֹכָבִים) is its indefinite plural form (stars).[161] The latter is repeated, though without its accompanying definition, when God explains to Abraham that "Kolob is the greatest of all the Kokaubeam that thou hast seen."[162] One of the functions of this terminology in the text is to highlight the stars that

---

KJV Genesis 15:5 ("And he [the Lord] brought him [Abraham] forth abroad, and said, Look now toward heaven, and tell the stars, if thou be able to number them . . . So shall thy seed be").

157. See GAEL, 25–30, in *JSP*-R4:164–75; BoA, in *JSP*-R4:314–15 [Abraham 3:2].

158. BoA, in *JSP*-R4:314–15, 318–19 [Abraham 3:13].

159. The Hebrew word for *sun* is *shemesh* (שֶׁמֶשׁ), which bears little resemblance to *Shinehah*. Gibbs, *A Manual Hebrew and English Lexicon*, 223. For unconvincing attempts to connect *Shinehah* with Hebrew terminology, see Webb, *Joseph Smith as a Translator*, 104–5; and Draper, Brown, and Rhodes, *Pearl of Great Price*, 273. Based on the Semitic interchange between *L* and *R* discussed previously in the context of *Kolob* (see note 112 above), some scholars have suggested that *Olea* is a variation of the Hebrew word for moon, יָרֵחַ (*yareah*). See Webb, *Joseph Smith as a Translator*, 103, 105; Haggerty, "Study of the Book of Abraham," 46–49; and Draper, Brown, and Rhodes, *Pearl of Great Price*, 273. This seems unlikely, though, since Seixas's transliteration of that Hebrew word would have been *Yau-ra-akh* (Zucker, "Joseph Smith as a Student of Hebrew," 51), which bears little or no resemblance to *Olea*. Unfortunately, neither term appears in the Egyptian alphabet or grammar documents for further clarification. However, one of Smith's 1838 revelations identifies "the land where Adam dwelt" as the "mountains of Adam-ondi-Ahman, and . . . the plains of Olea Shinihah." Revelation, 8 July 1838-E, in *JSP*-D6:193 [D&C 117:8]. In another version, "Olea Shinihah" is rendered "Olaha Shinehah." Smith, Journal, 8 July 1838, in *JSP*-J1:289. The wording of this passage suggests that the terms "Olea" and "Shinehah" were, like the term "Adam-ondi-Ahman," understood as being related to the "pure language" of Adam. *Olea Shinihah* seems to be a combination of *Olea* (the word in Abraham's astronomical vision for the moon) and Shinehah (the word in the same vision for the sun) (BoA, in *JSP*-R4:314–15, 318–19 [Abraham 3:13]), but any possible Hebrew connections are extremely tenuous.

160. BoA, in *JSP*-R4:316–17 [Abraham Fac. 2: Fig. 5].

161. See note 153 above.

162. BoA, in *JSP*-R4:318–19 [Abraham 3:16].

represent Abraham's numberless future posterity.[163] However, while at first glance God seems to be speaking the Hebrew words in direct discourse, the precise identity of the voice defining them is uncertain. It may be that the definitions were meant to be understood as given by God to clarify the terms to Abraham, as inserted by Abraham into God's speech to clarify the terms for the readers of his writings, or as inserted by Smith as editorial expansions to clarify the terms of the translated text. In any case, it seems that this linguistic blending of words from the Hebrew language and the pure language of Adam—all within an Egyptian text—fit comfortably within Smith's beliefs regarding the ancient relationship of these languages.

A final Hebrew word that appears in the translated text of the astronomy revelation is a reference to the duration of intelligences as "Gnolaum, or Eternal."[164] This word is recognizable as the Hebrew עוֹלָם (eternity), using Seixas's rules of transliterating an *ayin* at the beginning of a word with "gn" and a *qametz* with "au." Although Smith followed the general meaning of this word as found in his textbooks, he transformed the noun (eternity) into an adjective (eternal).[165] The only extant manuscript for this passage of text, which was inscribed by Willard Richards in early 1842, sheds important light on Smith's use of the word in the translation process. It indicates that the word Smith first translated to describe the intelligences was "immortal." However, Richards then cancelled that word by striking through it and—presumably under Smith's direction—replaced it with the pairing of the Hebrew word with its English definition: "Gnolaum, or eternal."[166]

This emendation shows not only that the text was still in flux just prior to the book's publication in 1842, but that as a translator Smith ultimately decided a Hebrew term and its definition—which he had learned either in class or in his textbooks—were preferable to the English word he had initially used to

163. BoA, in *JSP*-R4:318–19 [Abraham 3:14]; compare Genesis 15:5.

164. BoA, in *JSP*-R4:318–19 [Abraham 3:18].

165. Gibbs primarily defined עוֹלָם and עָלַם as "*eternity*; also *a long period*," and noted that their plural form (עוֹלָמִים) could also be used as an adverb (eternally). Gibbs, *A Manual Hebrew and English Lexicon*, 160, 165; compare Gesenius, *Hebrew and English Lexicon of the Old Testament* (1824), 482, 497. For the appearance of לְעוֹלָם (forever) in a practice sentence, see Seixas, *Manual Hebrew Grammar for the Use of Beginners*, 91. Although *gnolaum* does not appear again in the Book of Abraham, Smith must have considered the word significant as he continued to use it following his publication of the Book of Abraham. He used it with a negative meaning in an 1844 sermon in which he declared that "those who commit the unpardonable sin are doomed to Gnaolom. without end." Smith, Discourse, 7 April 1844, in Smith, *Words of Joseph Smith*, 343. Smith also used this term in casual conversation, as attested by an account of a non-Mormon visitor to Nauvoo who was amused by Smith's unusual Sephardic pronunciation of the word, humorously remembered by the visitor as *Gneou-law-umph*. W. S. B., "A Visit to Nauvoo," *Universalist Union* (New York), 4 May 1844, 392.

166. Book of Abraham Manuscript, 8–circa 15 March 1842, in *JSP*-R4:286–87 [Abraham 3:18].

express his translation from the papyri. As noted previously, a similar development occurred with the secondary insertion of "Shaumau, to be high" in the 1842 manuscript of the explanation for the first illustration.[167] Based on these two examples, it is possible that Smith made similar emendations to the other instances of astronomical vocabulary by secondarily inserting *Kolob*, *Shinehah*, *Olea*, *Kokob*, and *Kokaubeam* into his initial translation of the astronomy revelation. Unfortunately, though, the absence of any further manuscript evidence for these passages makes this suggestion impossible to verify or disconfirm.[168]

Unlike the explanations for the illustrations, which were apparently presented at least in part as editorial clarifications, the narrative text of the astronomy revelation (Abraham 3) represents Smith's direct translation from the papyri. In both cases Smith followed a similar pattern by providing transliterated Hebrew words followed by their definitions. However, in the text of the astronomy revelation—which does not contain the phrase "answering/answers to the Hebrew"—the use of Hebrew terminology is presented as less of an editorial gloss and more as a formal part of the translation. This suggests once again that Smith felt free as a translator to incorporate words he learned from his academic studies into the translated content he derived from the papyri. In these instances, the Hebrew does not greatly alter the substance of the text; Smith easily could have conveyed the same ideas by simply translating the words as "star," "stars," or "eternal." Instead, his choice to articulate these concepts with Hebrew vocabulary seems to reflect his convictions that the Hebrew language was somehow represented on the papyri and that Hebrew vocabulary could be efficaciously used to illuminate the Egyptian text.

Hebrew Influence on the Abrahamic Creation Account

The third part of the Book of Abraham that contains clear Hebrew influences is the translation of the creation account found at the end of the book (Abraham 4–5), an account that expands upon the biblical narrative in Genesis 1–2.[169]

167. BoA, in *JSP*-R4:250–51 [Abraham Fac. 1: Fig. 12]. Also, see note 150 above and compare Hauglid, *A Textual History of the Book of Abraham*, 156–57.

168. The lone surviving manuscript for the revelation on astronomy contains what is now Abraham 3:18b–26a, whereas the sequence of astronomical terms only appears in the published version of preceding passages (what is now Abraham 3:13–16). See Hauglid, *A Textual History of the Book of Abraham*, 196–99; and Book of Abraham Manuscript, 8–circa 15 March 1842, in *JSP*-R4:285–89.

169. Various perspectives on the close relationship between the creation accounts in KJV Genesis (1–2) and the Book of Abraham (BoA, in *JSP*-R4:318–23 [Abraham 4–5]) can be found in Mercer, "Joseph Smith as an Interpreter," 34–35; Fawn Brodie, *No Man Knows My History: The Life of Joseph Smith* (New York: Knopf, 1945), 171; Philip L. Barlow, *Mormons and the Bible: The Place of the Latter-day Saints in American Religion*,

This category of influences is different from the other two in that the Abraham creation account does not explicitly contain any transliterated Hebrew words, glosses, or explanatory phrases such as "answers to the Hebrew." Nevertheless, it demonstrates additional, if subtler, ways in which Joseph Smith incorporated Hebrew concepts and phraseology into his translation activities. The Abraham creation narrative does not represent the first time Smith worked through and altered the biblical creation account; in 1830, relying on a King James Bible and divine inspiration, he offered an expansive revision of Genesis 1–2 as part of his New Translation of the Old Testament.[170] However, the Book of Abraham does represent the first time Smith interacted with the creation account after he had studied Hebrew, and as such the Abraham narrative provides valuable insights into his approach to scriptural translation.

As mentioned previously, Smith may have come to believe that the Egyptian papyri contained an account of the creation as early as October 1835. Shortly thereafter, Smith began studying Hebrew, first through his own reading of textbooks and the Hebrew Bible, and eventually through formal coursework with Joshua Seixas. As he progressed through his studies, it is reasonable that he would have sought for Hebraic insights into the creation story that could illuminate his work with the forthcoming Abrahamic account. This may have started in December 1835 or early January 1836 with his personal study of Moses Stuart's textbook and a self-guided reading of Genesis 1 in his *Biblia Hebraica*, but it certainly would have occurred (or intensified) in February 1836 when he read through the Hebrew text of Genesis 1 under Seixas's tutelage during the third week of the class. During that part of the course, Smith and his fellow students were examined on the translation of that chapter's vocabulary, the parsing of its verbs, and the nuances of its syntax—all of which would have required

---

rev. ed. (New York and Oxford: Oxford University Press, 2013), 75–77; Draper, Brown, and Rhodes, *Pearl of Great Price*, 177–235; and David Bokovoy, *Authoring the Old Testament: Genesis–Deuteronomy* (Salt Lake City: Greg Kofford Books, 2014), 165–69. Bokovoy analyzes Abraham 4–5 in light of modern historical criticism of the Pentateuch (the P [Priestly] and J [Yahwist] sources represented in Genesis 1–2), though without considering the influence of Smith's Hebrew studies on the production of the Abraham text. For previous attempts to examine Smith's incorporation of Hebrew into the Book of Abraham creation account, see Walton, "Professor Seixas, the Hebrew Bible, and the Book of Abraham," 41–42; Hutchinson, "A Mormon Midrash," 11–74, esp. 19–30; and Marquardt, "Joseph Smith's Egyptian Papers," 35–44. For a recent consideration of the Abraham creation material within an ancient Near Eastern context, see Gee, *An Introduction to the Book of Abraham*, 132–36, 140–42.

170. In a careful analysis of the relationship between KJV Genesis 1–2 and Smith's revision of those chapters in his New Translation (Old Testament Manuscript 2, 3–6, in Smith, *Joseph Smith's New Translation of the Bible*, 86–90 [Moses 2–3]), Anthony Hutchinson has highlighted the ways in which the latter translation often interacted with the italicized words in the KJV of the Genesis text. Hutchinson, "A Mormon Midrash," 30–37, 41–45.

a careful and analytical reading of the Genesis material.[171] Apparently, Smith obtained several insights during these exercises that he felt could benefit his translation of the creation account he believed was represented on the papyri.

The text of the Abraham creation account is not attested in manuscript form prior to its publication in 1842, but Smith's other writings suggest that its contents developed conceptually over the years following Seixas's Hebrew class. A close reading of the text indicates that, whenever it formally began, Smith's translation of this material was a complex process involving various sources of inspiration. Internal textual evidence suggests that after Smith became convinced that the papyri contained a creation narrative, he turned to Genesis 1–2 in his King James Bible in order to use it as the base text for his translation. He then altered or expanded the biblical account in light of his Hebrew knowledge and resources, and added his own unique expansions to it, which presumably derived from his examination of the papyri and his experience of prophetic revelation. Unfortunately, the papyri that inspired this process either did not survive or are not clearly identifiable. However, a synoptic comparison of the other resources Smith used in this endeavor—the English text of Genesis 1–2 in his KJV and the Hebrew text of Genesis 1–2 in his *Biblia Hebraica*—with his translation of the Abraham creation account greatly illuminates his work as a translator and his thought process during this part of the Book of Abraham translation.

An exhaustive analysis of these sources is beyond the spatial limitations of this chapter, but a preliminary comparison highlights the major trends of Smith's approach to the project (Table 16.1 offers a few representative passages that show Smith's interaction with his source materials).[172] Such a comparison shows that in the Abraham creation account, Smith retained the structural outline and approximately 75 percent of the wording from the King James Version of Genesis 1–2. It also shows that at significant junctures he either directly or indirectly based alterations of that text on his reading of Genesis in Hebrew.[173]

171. For Smith's possible self-guided interaction with the Hebrew of Genesis 1 prior to the beginning of the Seixas course, see note 80 above. For his close reading and analysis of the text as part of his formal coursework, see note 92 above.

172. For a fuller synoptic comparison of the creation accounts in KJV Genesis (1–2) and the Book of Abraham (BoA, in *JSP*-R4:318–23 [Abraham 4–5]), see Marquardt, "Joseph Smith's Egyptian Papers," 37–44. Marquardt's synopsis is a helpful resource for understanding Smith's interaction with the KJV, but it does not include the *Biblia Hebraica*, which provides important insights into the role of the Hebrew text of Genesis in Smith's translation process.

173. Michael T. Walton hesitates to view the KJV as being heavily involved in this process, but instead suggests that the similarities with the Book of Abraham stem from both the KJV translators and Smith sharing a reliance on the Hebrew text of Genesis, see Walton, "Professor Seixas, the Hebrew Bible, and the Book of Abraham," 43n8. However, a synoptic comparison between the creation accounts in KJV Genesis (1–2) and the Book of Abraham (BoA, in *JSP*-R4:318–23 [Abraham 4–5])—with their extensive word-for-word

Some of these alterations reflected the Hebrew nuances already seen in his translation of the astronomy revelation (Abraham 3) and in his facsimile explanations (Abraham Fac. 1; Fac. 2). Others involved minor grammatical issues that were likely based on insights Smith had drawn from his Hebrew resources, but that do not affect the essential meaning of the text. Still other Hebrew-inspired alterations introduced profound theological changes to the creation account and would come to influence Mormon cosmology in significant ways.

Examples of the first type of alteration can be seen in Smith's revisions to the opening passages of the creation account, in which he followed the tendencies of his illustration explanations by consistently replacing the KJV's use of "firmament" with the word "expanse"—the primary definition of רָקִיעַ (*raukeeyang*) as found in his Hebrew textbooks[174]—and by occasionally changing the singular "heaven" in the KJV to the pluralized "heavens" to reflect the plural Hebrew word שָׁמַיִם (*shaumahyeem*).[175] He also made other subtle Hebrew-inspired changes to the KJV creation account that were not represented elsewhere in the Abraham text. In reworking Genesis 1:2 Smith changed the KJV's translation of "the Spirit of God *moved* upon the *face* of the waters" to "the Spirit . . . *was brooding* upon the *faces* of the water."[176] These alterations follow Seixas and other biblical commentators in rendering the Hebrew participle מְרַחֶפֶת as "brooding,"[177] and reflect the morphologically plural form of the Hebrew construct פְּנֵי (faces of).[178]

---

agreements—leaves little room to dispute the KJV's role in serving as Smith's base text for his translation of the Abraham creation narrative.

174. See the nine instances of this change between KJV Genesis (1:6–8, 14–20) and the Book of Abraham (BoA, in *JSP*-R4:318–21 [Abraham 4:6–8, 14–20]). For other uses of "expanse" and "firmament" in the middle of the Book of Abraham (BoA, in R4:314–15, 318–19 [Abraham 3]) and in Smith's explanations for the published illustrations (BoA, in R4:306–7, 316–17, 324–27 [Abraham Facs. 1–3]), see note 134 above.

175. In the Book of Abraham creation account, which is based on, but occasionally revises the KJV translation of Genesis 1–2, Smith changed the singular "heaven" to the plural "heavens" in two instances (BoA, in *JSP*-R4:318–21 [Abraham 4:1, 17]; compare Genesis 1:1, 17), retained the singular "heaven" in five instances (BoA, in *JSP*-R4:318–21 [Abraham 4:8, 9, 14, 15, 20]; compare Genesis 1:8, 9, 14, 15, 20), retained the plural "heavens" in three instances (BoA, in *JSP*-R4:322–23 [Abraham 5:1, 4]; compare Genesis 2:1, 4), and introduced one new instance of the plural "heavens" (BoA, in *JSP*-R4:322–23 [Abraham 5:3]; compare Genesis 2:3). These revisions show that, following his study of Hebrew, Smith was not insistent on a single interpretation of the word in his Abraham translation, whereas in his earlier 1830 revision of the Old Testament he consistently and deliberately chose the singular "heaven" (see note 137 above).

176. BoA, in *JSP*-R4:318–19 [Abraham 4:2] (emphasis added).

177. For the translation of מְרַחֶפֶת as "brooding" rather than the traditional "moving," see Seixas, *Manual Hebrew Grammar for the Use of Beginners*, 31 (§18), 77 (§102); compare Gibbs, *A Manual Hebrew and English Lexicon*, 202 (רָחַף). Contemporaneous arguments in favor of "brooding" can also be found in Adam Clarke's commentary on Genesis 1:2. Clarke, *The Holy Bible Containing the Old and New Testaments*, 1:32. For more on Smith's use of this word in the Book of Abraham, see Walton, "Professor Seixas, the Hebrew Bible, and the Book of Abraham," 42; and Hutchinson, "A Mormon Midrash," 53.

178. At the end of Genesis 1:2, Smith followed the Seixas manual, which translates פְּנֵי (a plural masculine construct) as "faces of" (Seixas, *Manual Hebrew Grammar for the Use of Beginners*, 21 [§11], 32 [§21], 78

TABLE 16.1. Creation Accounts in the *Biblia Hebraica*, King James Bible, and Book of Abraham
This table provides a synoptic comparison through representative passages from the Hebrew text of Genesis 1–2 as found in Joseph Smith's *Biblia Hebraica*, the English translation of Genesis 1–2 in the King James Bible, and the creation account in the Book of Abraham (with versification from the original *Times and Seasons* publication [and the current LDS edition of the text in brackets]). Smith's changes to the KJV are **bolded**. Changes that were either directly or indirectly inspired by Smith's reading of Genesis in Hebrew are also **underlined**.

Genesis 1–2 (*Biblia Hebraica*)	**Genesis 1–2** **(King James Version)**	**Book of Abraham** (*Times and Seasons*)
		23 [4:1] **And then the Lord said,**
		Let us go down; and they went
1 בְּרֵאשִׁית	1:1 In the beginning	**down at** the beginning, **and**
בָּרָא אֱלֹהִים	God created	**they organized and formed,**
אֵת הַשָּׁמַיִם וְאֵת הָאָרֶץ	the heaven and the earth.	**(that is, the Gods,)** the heav-
		ens and the earth.
2 וְהָאָרֶץ הָיְתָה	2 And the earth was	[4:2] And the earth, **after it**
תֹהוּ וָבֹהוּ	without form, and void;	**was formed**, was **empty and**
		desolate; because they had not
		formed anything but the earth:
וְחֹשֶׁךְ עַל־	and darkness *was* upon	and darkness **reigned** upon the
פְּנֵי תְהוֹם	the face of the deep.	face of the deep,
וְרוּחַ	And the Spirit of	and the spirit of
אֱלֹהִים מְרַחֶפֶת	God moved	**the Gods was brooding**
עַל־פְּנֵי הַמָּיִם	upon the face of the waters.	upon the faces of the **water**.
3 וַיֹּאמֶר אֱלֹהִים	3 And God said,	24 [4:3] And **they said, the Gods,**
יְהִי אוֹר	Let there be light:	let there be light,
וַיְהִי־אוֹר	and there was light.	and there was light.
4 וַיַּרְא אֱלֹהִים	4 And God saw	[4:4] And **they, the Gods,**
אֶת־הָאוֹר	the light, that *it was* good:	**comprehended**
כִּי־טוֹב		the light, **for it was bright**;
וַיַּבְדֵּל אֱלֹהִים בֵּין הָאוֹר	and God divided the light	and **they** divided the light,
		or caused it to be divided
וּבֵין הַחֹשֶׁךְ	from the darkness.	from the darkness,
6 וַיֹּאמֶר אֱלֹהִים	6 And God said,	25 [4:6] And **the Gods also** said
יְהִי רָקִיעַ	Let there be a firmament	let there be **an expanse**
בְּתוֹךְ הַמָּיִם	in the midst of the waters,	in the midst of the waters,
וִיהִי מַבְדִּיל בֵּין מַיִם	and let it divide the waters	and **it shall** divide the waters
לָמָיִם	from the waters.	from the waters.
7 וַיַּעַשׂ אֱלֹהִים	7 And God made	[4:7] And **the Gods ordered the**
אֶת־הָרָקִיעַ	the firmament,	**expanse, so that it**
וַיַּבְדֵּל בֵּין	and divided	divided
הַמַּיִם אֲשֶׁר	the waters which	the waters which
מִתַּחַת לָרָקִיעַ	*were* under the firmament	were under the **expanse,**
וּבֵין הַמַּיִם	from the waters	from the waters
אֲשֶׁר מֵעַל	which *were* above	which were above
לָרָקִיעַ וַיְהִי־כֵן	the firmament: and it was so.	**the expanse**: and it was so, **even**
		as they ordered.

Other alterations to the KJV were more grammatical in nature, showing that in some instances Smith desired technical accuracy in his translation of the Hebrew even when there was no apparent theological significance to the changes. For example, he seems to have been interested in the causative nature of the Hiphil verb הִבְדִּיל, which is present in the Hebrew text of Genesis 1 but is not overtly expressed in the King James translation. Whereas the KJV states that "God *divided* [וַיַּבְדֵּל] the light from the darkness,"[179] Smith ensured that the Hiphil verb was represented by writing that Deity "divided the light, *or caused it to be divided*, from the darkness."[180] Throughout the remainder of the narrative, Smith consistently changed "divided" to reflect its literal Hiphil form ("caused to be divided") and in some instances even added causative verbiage to verses that did not contain Hiphil verbs.[181] On several occasions, Smith also inserted the phrase "and it came to pass" into the Abraham narrative. In these insertions he was apparently taking his cue from occurrences of וַיְהִי in the Hebrew text of Genesis 1–2—which are not directly represented in the KJV—and echoing his propensity to use the phrase in other translation projects.[182]

[§103]; compare BoA, in *JSP*-R4:318–19 [Abraham 4:2]), although this was redacted to the singular "face" in subsequent editions (Hauglid, *A Textual History of the Book of Abraham*, 39). Curiously, however, elsewhere in Genesis 1:2—and in 1:29 and 2:6—Smith retained the KJV's singular "face of." BoA, in *JSP*-R4:318–19 [Abraham 4:2, 29, and 5:6]. Also anomalous is Smith's use of the singular "water" in the original text of the passage paralleling Genesis 1:2 (BoA, in *JSP*-R4:318–19 [Abraham 4:2]), as he retained the plural "waters" elsewhere in his translation and inserted the plural "waters" or "great waters" (a replacement for "seas") into the text of Genesis 1 in verses 6–10 and 20–22 (BoA, in *JSP*-R4:318–21 [Abraham 4:6–10, 20–22]). In either case, Smith could find justification in his copy of the Seixas grammar, which translated the dual form מַיִם in some instances as the plural "waters" (Seixas, *Manual Hebrew Grammar for the Use of Beginners*, 22 [no. 8], 32 [§21], 53 [§59], 78 [§103], 99) and in other instances as the singular "water" (78 [§103], 93). For Smith's deliberate use of the singular "water" in his 1830 revision of Genesis, see Hutchinson, "A Mormon Midrash," 48, 50, 53.

179. Genesis 1:4.

180. BoA, in *JSP*-R4:318–19 [Abraham 4:4] (emphasis added). The Seixas grammar teaches that Hiphil verbs are causative and are created by adding ה and י into a Qal root. Seixas, *Manual Hebrew Grammar for the Use of Beginners*, 28 (no. 3c). It also teaches that הִבְדִּיל (to cause to divide) is the Hiphil form of the Qal בָּדַל (he divided) (31 [§18] and 39 [§31]; also 8 [§7, no. 1], 20, 25 [§15], 33 [§23], 77 [§102]). Smith therefore would have believed that he was being technically correct by translating הִבְדִּיל as a causative throughout his creation account, see especially BoA, in *JSP*-R4:318–21 [Abraham 4:4, 14, 17]; compare Genesis 1:4, 14, 18. However, while Hiphil verbs are typically translated this way, in the case of this word there is no attested Qal form, leaving its Hiphil form to function as a Qal (and therefore not as a causative). Thus, Smith's causative translation of הִבְדִּיל reflects a unique interpretation of Hebrew grammar, as it was taught by Seixas, that was based on the idea of a hypothetical Qal root. In Smith's translation of this word, there is only one instance—perhaps an outlier—in which he retained the noncausative "divided." See BoA, in *JSP*-R4:318–19 [Abraham 4:6–7]; compare Genesis 1:6–7. For more on Smith's treatment of הִבְדִּיל, see Walton, "Professor Seixas, the Hebrew Bible, and the Book of Abraham," 42; and Hutchinson, "A Mormon Midrash," 62.

181. Compare Genesis 1:22, 28 with the Book of Abraham translation of "cause them to be fruitful and multiply" (BoA, in *JSP*-R4:320–21 [Abraham 4:22, 28]).

182. See BoA, in *JSP*-R4:318–23 [Abraham 4:5, 8, 13, 19, 23, 31]; compare Genesis 1:5, 8, 13, 19, 23, 31. In other instances, however, Smith chose not to translate וַיְהִי as "and it came to pass," but rather followed the KJV and left it as simply "and it was" (BoA, in *JSP*-R4:320–21 [Abraham 4:9, 11, 15, 24]; compare Genesis 1:9,

While most of these examples have no obvious theological significance, they show once again that Smith often deferred to his academic resources in his translation, using them to enhance his work, refine the narrative flow of the account, and present a more literal rendering of the Hebrew text.[183]

Beyond these subtle alterations, however, Smith's Hebrew studies influenced his translation of the Abraham creation account in at least two profound and theologically significant ways, both of which may have been initially informed by his earlier revelations and both of which gave further shape and substance to his subsequent doctrinal teachings. The first and most prominent of these was Smith's infusing into the narrative the existence of a plurality of gods acting as a divine council orchestrating the creation. This was done through his consistent rendering of the Hebrew אֱלֹהִים (*elohim*) and יְהוָה אֱלֹהִים (*Yahweh-elohim*)—typically translated throughout the Hebrew Bible as the singular "God" and "Lord God"—as the plural "they . . . (that is, the Gods)," "they, the Gods," or simply "the Gods," along with a pluralization of all accompanying pronouns and verbs.[184] This innovation was almost certainly prompted by the morphologically plural form of the word for "God" (אֱלֹהִים [*elohim*]) in the Hebrew text of Genesis 1–2.

The full development of Smith's view of the nature of God lies beyond the scope of this chapter, but it seems that by the mid-1830s he was already thinking of the Godhead in ways that challenged traditional notions.[185] This

---

11, 15, 24). The Seixas grammar consistently translates וַיְהִי as "and it was" rather than "and it came to pass," showing that Smith frequently departed from his textbook in his translation of this phrase. Seixas, *Manual Hebrew Grammar for the Use of Beginners*, 33 (§23, no. 1), 37, 86.

183. Another way in which Smith attempted to refine his narrative was by continuing his practice—seen in other translation projects—of replacing or omitting italicized words in the KJV (compare the italicized words in KJV Genesis 1–2 with the parallel passages in BoA, in *JSP*-R4:318–23 [Abraham 4–5]). He also occasionally retranslated the Hebrew prefix -בְּ (meaning "in," "into," and so forth) according to one of its many other possibilities (such as "at") in places where such a change would smooth out his revised narrative. See BoA, in *JSP*-R4:318–23 [Abraham 4:1, 5:11]; compare Genesis 1:1, 2:15. See also Smith's related comments on the multifaceted meanings of -בְּ. Smith, Discourse, 7 April 1844, in Smith, *Words of Joseph Smith*, 350, 358; compare Seixas, *Manual Hebrew Grammar for the Use of Beginners*, 19 (§9). In addition, Michael T. Walton argues that Smith's replacement of the phrase "let it divide" (KJV Genesis 4:6) with "and it shall divide" (BoA, in *JSP*-R4:318–19 [Abraham 4:6]) may also be an attempt to literalize the Hebrew (וִיהִי מַבְדִּיל)—albeit in a way that is grammatically incorrect. Walton, "Professor Seixas, the Hebrew Bible, and the Book of Abraham," 42.

184. Among the plural nouns, pronouns, and verbs inserted into the creation account at the end of the Book of Abraham, there are over a hundred references to a plurality of gods acting in concert as the agents of creation. BoA, in *JSP*-R4:318–23 [Abraham 4–5].

185. See the church's teachings (possibly Smith's) on the persons of the Godhead as given in an 1834 lecture on the doctrine of faith (Doctrine and Covenants of the Church of the Latter Day Saints, Part 1, 5:1–3 [52–54]), Smith's 1835 account of two beings appearing in his first vision (Smith, Journal, 9–11 November 1835, in *JSP*-J1:88), or his earlier revelations hinting at the potential of human apotheosis (Vision, 16 February 1832, in *JSP*-D2:188 [D&C 76:58]; and Revelation, 27 December 1832, in *JSP*-D2:344 [D&C 88:107]). For more detailed and contextualized discussions of Smith's developing ideas on the nature of God, see Brown,

theological trajectory seems to have been further encouraged with the arrival of the Egyptian papyri in 1835. When Smith and his associates came into possession of the papyri, one of the vignettes that apparently first caught their attention depicted a row of three Egyptian deities. Cowdery wrote that they represented "the god-head—three, yet in one," and thereby provided "more or less of the correct ideas of notions of the Deity."[186] Possibly anticipating that the forthcoming Abraham translation would shed important light on the topic, Smith and his scribes likely went into their Hebrew studies looking for potential insights into the nature of God. As he would later state publicly, Smith found such insights when he learned that the (ים– [*-im*]) ending of the Hebrew word for God (אֱלֹהִים [*elohim*]) was plural in form and thus implied a plurality of divine beings. It is not clear whether Smith first noticed this technicality during his personal reading of Stuart's textbook in December 1835, his self-guided translation of Genesis 1 in early January 1836, or his coursework with Seixas in February and March of 1836, but Smith later recounted a debate he had with a "learned Jew" on this very topic. This "learned Jew" was almost certainly Joshua Seixas, and the recounted incident most likely occurred while Smith's class of the Hebrew school was translating Genesis 1.[187]

In Heaven as It Is on Earth, 271–72; and Terryl L. Givens, *Wrestling the Angel: The Foundations of Mormon Thought* (New York and Oxford: Oxford University Press, 2015), 69–74.

186. Cowdery, "Egyptian Mummies—Ancient Records," 236. In his subsequent teachings on the plurality of gods, Smith's description of God in terms of three "heads" may have been related to the three heads depicted on the figure in the Egyptian vignette. For example, in 1841 Smith reportedly taught that the God-head "was Not as many imagined—three Heads & but one body . . . the three were separate bodys—God the first & Jesus the Mediator the 2d & the Holy Ghost & these three agree in one." Discourse, circa 16 February 1841, in *JSP*-D8:47–48. In his later sermons, Smith focused on the Hebrew word ראש (*rosh*)—defined in his Hebrew manuals as "head" (Gibbs, *A Manual Hebrew and English Lexicon*, 198; Seixas, *Manual Hebrew Grammar for the Use of Beginners*, 84)—in his description of "The Head one of the Gods" and "the heads of the Gods [who] appointed one God for us." Smith, Discourse, 7 April 1844, in Smith, *Words of Joseph Smith*, 341, 345, 350–51, 358, 379–80, 383. He went on to state that he learned these concepts "by translating the papyrus now in my house." Smith, Discourse, 16 June 1844, in Smith, *Words of Joseph Smith*, 341, 345, 350–51, 358, 379–80, 383. Another oblique reference to such imagery on the papyri may be found in Smith's explanation of the crown of Osiris (flanked by two feather plumes) as "emblematical of the grand Presidency in Heaven." BoA, in *JSP*-R4:324–27 [Abraham Fac. 3: Fig. 1]. For a modern Egyptological assessment of the vignette that likely inspired the commentary by Cowdery and Smith, see Ritner, *The Joseph Smith Egyptian Papyri*, 155, 192–93.

187. According to notes taken from one of Smith's 1844 discourses, he said that he "once asked a learned Jew . . . if the Heb. language compels us to render all words ending in heam in the plural–why not render the first plural–he replied it would ruin the Bible–he acknowledged I was right." Smith, Discourse, 16 June 1844, in Smith, *Words of Joseph Smith*, 379. Although this "learned Jew" (almost certainly Joshua Seixas) believed otherwise, following Smith's insistence on translating אֱלֹהִים (*elohim*) as a plural noun he reportedly acquiesced. Smith would have learned about plural nouns in either the Stuart or Seixas grammars (Stuart, *A Grammar of the Hebrew Language*, 140 [§325]; Seixas, *Manual Hebrew Grammar for the Use of Beginners*, 21 [§11]), and would have encountered references to אֱלֹהִים (*elohim*) in his Seixas grammar (Seixas, *Manual Hebrew Grammar for the Use of Beginners*, 8 [§6], 15, 34 [§25, no. 4], 55 [§63], 85, 88, 90, 94).

For his part, Seixas acknowledged that the word אֱלֹהִים (*elohim*) was technically plural but, following his colleague Moses Stuart, he preferred its singular translation (God). Like other scholars, Stuart and Seixas considered the word to be a *pluralis excellentiae*, which "for the sake of emphasis" was rendered "in the plur. form but with the sense of the singular."[188] To some extent, this view may have been a reaction against popular attempts to see in אֱלֹהִים a reference to the Christian trinity, a claim made by some Hebrew grammar books and biblical commentaries at the time.[189] In any case, the plural form of *elohim* captured Smith's imagination and he insisted, despite Seixas's reluctance, on translating it literally as "Gods" until his teacher grudgingly conceded. Smith may have found further support and inspiration for his developing position in some of his other Hebrew resources, including a Gesenius lexicon that notes that אֱלֹהִים could indeed be translated "in a plural sense" as "*gods* [or] *deities*" and "may perhaps be . . . understood of the higher powers or intelligences."[190]

After these encounters, Smith continued to reflect on the implications of *elohim*. This may be seen in a letter he wrote in early 1839—three years after his Hebrew class—wherein he stated that revelations concerning the plurality of gods would soon be forthcoming to the Latter-day Saints.[191] His translation of the Abrahamic creation account, completed in early 1842, appears to have been

188. Stuart, *A Grammar of the Hebrew Language*, 180 (§437, no. 2). A similar description of the plural form but singular meaning of אֱלֹהִים (*elohim*) can be found in the Gibbs lexicon. See Gibbs, *A Manual Hebrew and English Lexicon*, 12 (אֱלוֹהַּ). The Seixas grammar also includes several examples of the author translating the word as the singular "God." Seixas, *Manual Hebrew Grammar for the Use of Beginners*, 32 (§21), 34 (§25, no. 4), 85, 88, 94.

189. Adam Clarke argued that in Genesis 1:1, "The original word אלהים Elohim, God, is certainly the plural form of אל El . . . and has long been supposed, by the most eminently learned and pious men, to imply a plurality of Persons in the Divine nature . . . this plurality appears in so many parts of the sacred writings to be confined to three Persons, hence the doctrine of the Trinity." Clarke, *The Holy Bible Containing the Old and New Testaments*, 1:27; compare Clarke on Genesis 1:26 in *The Holy Bible Containing the Old and New Testaments*, 1:38. Similarly, an early nineteenth-century Hebrew textbook written by John Smith (a professor of ancient languages at Dartmouth) states that "The masculine noun plural Elohim, when meaning the true God (the adorable Trinity), is frequently joined with verbs singular to express the unity of essence and operation, as in 'God Created' (Genesis 1:1)." John Smith, *A Hebrew Grammar, without Points* (Boston: John West, 1803), 20, no. 20.

190. Gesenius, *A Hebrew and English Lexicon of the Old Testament* (1836), 60. In his secondary entry for אֱלֹהִים, Gesenius notes that it could also be read as a singular "*Pluralis majestatis* [or] *excellentiae*" and accompanied by a singular verb, as in Genesis 1:1 (60).

191. Smith wrote this letter from the Clay County Jail in Liberty, Missouri. For this and other references to Smith's developing (Hebrew-inspired) teachings on the plurality of gods between 1839 and 1841, see note 96 above. Kerry Muhlestein and Megan Hansen view the reference to the plurality of gods in the 1839 letter as evidence that the creation narrative at the end of the Book of Abraham had been fully translated by that point. Muhlestein and Hansen, "'The Work of Translating,'" 146–47. However, it may be that this reference is only evidence for the conceptual development of the book's forthcoming contents. Indeed, with such meager additional evidence that the Book of Abraham yet existed in its final form, this latter possibility is the more likely scenario.

that revelation. It includes over a hundred references to a divine council inserted into the narrative (all of which were either directly or indirectly based on the plural form of אֱלֹהִים or יְהוָה אֱלֹהִים in Genesis 1–2),[192] and the close association of Deity with the premortal "intelligences" (similar to the description of אֱלֹהִים in the Gesenius lexicon).[193] Curiously, Smith did not explicitly use the term *elohim* in the Abraham creation account; he merely translated it as "the Gods." However, following the publication of the Book of Abraham in 1842, he often used the term in public sermons and in the ritual drama of his "quorum of anointing."[194]

A second theological alteration of the biblical creation account is Smith's insertion of language that replaced the traditional reading of God's *ex nihilo* creation of the earth with the divine council's organization of preexisting materials. This was done as Smith consistently rendered the Hebrew verbs בָּרָא (typically translated as "to create") and עָשָׂה (typically translated as "to make") in Genesis 1–2 as "to organize" and "to form."[195] He also added verbiage of "organization" and "formation" into verses of Genesis that do not contain any Hebrew precedent.[196] Furthermore, he retained the KJV's translation of God "forming" human bodies—based on the Hebrew יָצַר—in which the premortal spirits of Adam and Eve would be placed.[197] For בָּרָא and עָשָׂה, as with *elohim*, Smith departed from

192. See the many plural nouns, pronouns, and verbs that Smith inserted throughout the Abraham creation account, BoA, in *JSP*-R4:318–23 [Abraham 4–5]; compare Genesis 1–2.

193. BoA, in *JSP*-R4:318–19 [Abraham 3:18–23]; compare Gesenius, *A Hebrew and English Lexicon of the Old Testament* (1836), 60. For the theological connections Smith made between God and self-existent "intelligences" (an association that may have been partially influenced by the listing of "higher powers or intelligences" in Gesenius's lexical entry for *elohim*), see Smith, Discourse, 7 April 1844, in Smith, *Words of Joseph Smith*, 341, 346, 351, 359–60.

194. See the reports of discourses Smith delivered on 30 June 1843 (Smith, *Words of Joseph Smith*, 221); 9 July 1843 (Ibid., 229–31); 7 April 1844 (Ibid., 341–62); and 16 June 1844 (Ibid., 378–83). For the contemporaneous use of the name "quorum of anointing" to describe Smith's inner circle who received temple rituals prior to the completion of the temple, see *JSP*-J3:xxin33. For the use of the word *elohim* in the ritual drama of the quorum of anointing, see Anderson and Bergera, *Joseph Smith's Quorum of the Anointed*, 5–6 (4 May 1842), 201 (10 December 1845), and 205–9 (11 December 1845). Shortly after the publication of the Book of Abraham, the book's references to the plurality of gods were defended in an unattributed editorial in the church's British newspaper, which noted that "in the beginning of Genesis, and throughout the bible, the Hebrew word *Elohim* (Gods), is actually in the plural, though the translators have rendered it (God) in the singular." *Latter-Day Saints' Millennial Star*, 1 August 1842, 71. This editorial was likely written by Parley P. Pratt, who was one of the newspaper's two editors and had studied Hebrew in Kirtland in 1836, see Terryl L. Givens and Matthew J. Grow, *Parley P. Pratt: the Apostle Paul of Mormonism* (New York and Oxford: Oxford University Press, 2011), 81–82. The statement, which manifests a deference to Hebrew, likely reflects the way Smith explained to his associates his use of the plural "Gods" in the Abraham text.

195. For instances of Smith changing בָּרָא (create) to "organize" or "form," see BoA, in *JSP*-R4:318–23 [Abraham 4:1, 27, 5:3, 4]; compare Genesis 1:1, 27, 2:3, 4. For instances of Smith changing עָשָׂה (make) to "organize" or "form," see BoA, in *JSP*-R4:320–23 [Abraham 4:16, 25, 26, 31, 5:3, 4, 14, 16]; compare Genesis 1:16, 25, 26, 31, 2:3, 4, 18, 22.

196. See BoA, in *JSP*-R4:318–23 [Abraham 4:2, 12, 14, 15, 30, 5:5]; compare Genesis 1:2, 12, 14, 15, 30, 2:5.

197. See BoA, in *JSP*-R4:322–23 [Abraham 5:7, 8, 20]; compare Genesis 2:7, 8, 19. For the lexical definition of יָצַר as "to form," see Gibbs, *A Manual Hebrew and English Lexicon*, 91.

his teacher. Seixas preferred the traditional translations of these words ("create" and "make"), which have been understood in the orthodox tradition of classical Christian theology to imply God's creation of the cosmos out of nothing.[198] In this view, Seixas may have followed Moses Stuart, who specifically argued against the claim that those words could imply God's "organization" of preexisting materials.[199]

In contrast, Smith—who by the early 1830s had been considering the possibilities of premortal existence[200]—apparently became interested in alternative Hebrew definitions that could accommodate or inform his own developing theology. He may have found such possibilities in the Gibbs lexicon, which lists "to form" (rather than "to create") as the primary definitions of both בָּרָא and עָשָׂה, thus implying the giving of shape to something already in existence.[201] This entry may have inspired Smith to retranslate these words ("create" and "make" in the KJV) as "organize" or "form" in the Book of Abraham. The concept of organization from preexisting materials is also reflected in Smith's translation of the phrase תֹהוּ וָבֹהוּ, describing the state of the primordial earth in Genesis 1:2. Instead of following the traditional KJV translation of "without form and void," the Book of Abraham has "empty and desolate."[202] In the case of תֹהוּ וָבֹהוּ, however, Smith returned to the definitions provided by Seixas since they implied

198. Occurrences of בָּרָא and its definition as "to create" can be found in Seixas, *Manual Hebrew Grammar for the Use of Beginners*, 8 (§6), 9 (§8), 15, 85, 90. Occurrences of עָשָׂה and its definition of "to do" or "to make" can also be found in the Seixas grammar, see 31 (§20), 34–35 (§26, nos. 1 and 3), 37, 68 (§88), 70 (§95), 77 (§102), 88.

199. Stuart wrote:

> Some have supposed that בָּרָא in [Genesis 1:1] means only *to dispose of, to arrange, to form*, viz. out of materials already existing. . . . but v. 2 shows that no mere arrangement or disposition of matter can be intended by בָּרָא; for after the action implied by בָּרָא had been performed, the *earth* still remained in a chaotic state. . . . The *original act* of creation, as understood by the sacred writers, appears plainly to have been, *the calling of matter into being, the causing of it to exist.*

Moses Stuart, *A Hebrew Chrestomathy*, 2nd ed. (Andover, MA: Flagg and Gould, 1832), 79–80. Unfortunately, Stuart did not indicate who at that time had been arguing that בָּרָא referred to an organization of preexisting materials.

200. Smith's thinking on these matters was complex, with hints of preexistence appearing as early as 1828 in the translation of the Book of Mormon and continuing through the 1830s, as indicated by sermons, letters, and editorials by close associates William W. Phelps and Parley P. Pratt. Givens, *Wrestling the Angel*, 51–56, 147–56. In addition, a revelation that Smith dictated in 1833 states that "intelligence . . . was not created or made, neither indeed can it be" and that "the elements are eternal." Revelation, 6 May 1833, in *JSP*-D3:89 [D&C 93:29, 33].

201. The Gibbs lexicon defines בָּרָא as "*to form, make, or create*," and the Gesenius lexicon offers several similar possibilities: "1. strictly *to hew, to hew out*. . . . 2. *to form, make, or produce*." Gibbs, *A Manual Hebrew and English Lexicon*, 36; Gesenius, *Hebrew and English Lexicon of the Old Testament* (1824), 100. For עָשָׂה, the Gibbs lexicon offered the definition of "*to form, make*," whereas the Gesenius lexicon listed: "1. *to make, do, act*. . . . [and] 4. *to prepare, to get ready*"—any one of which could have influenced Smith's translation. Gibbs, *A Manual Hebrew and English Lexicon*, 172; Gesenius, *Hebrew and English Lexicon of the Old Testament* (1824), 516.

202. BoA, in *JSP*-R4:318–19 [Abraham 4:2].

that the earth already existed in an "empty" state, which was consistent with and implicitly buttressed Smith's evolving cosmology.[203] After being inspired by or finding clarity in these Hebrew interpretations of a divine organization, Smith's thinking on their relevance for the creation story can be seen in the sermons he delivered following his Hebrew studies (1840–1844),[204] his translation of the Abraham creation account (1842), and in the ritual drama of his quorum of anointing (1842–1844).[205]

These last themes—the plurality of Gods and divine creation through the organization of preexisting materials—are an important reminder that, in his post-1836 translations, Smith did not slavishly adhere to the teachings of Joshua Seixas,[206] but felt free to adapt his academic learning to his prophetic thinking in innovative ways. While Smith clearly deferred to his various textbooks on several points—sometimes preferring one resource over another—there were other instances in which his own examination of the papyri, developing theology, and revelations merged with his creative use of less conventional Hebrew definitions or technicalities, thus allowing him to tease out unique theological concepts and produce a distinctively expansive translation. Additional evidence for this dynamic process can be found in those passages of the Abraham

203. The Seixas grammar contains occurrences of תֹהוּ וָבֹהוּ and their transliterations (Seixas, *Manual Hebrew Grammar for the Use of Beginners*, 8 [§6], 12 [no. 4], and 15), and also defines them as "empty" and "desolate" (78 [§103])—as do the Stuart grammar and the Gibbs and Gesenius lexicons (Stuart, *A Grammar of the Hebrew Language*, 182 [§441], 224 [§571a]; Gibbs, *A Manual Hebrew and English Lexicon*, 27, 229; and Gesenius, *Hebrew and English Lexicon of the Old Testament* [1824], 73, 693–94).

204. In 1841 Smith preached on the eternal nature of matter and spirits, drawing upon the Hebrew terms בָּרָא and תֹהוּ וָבֹהוּ—as well as his preferred definitions of them. He reportedly stated that "in the translation [of Genesis 1:2], 'without form and void' . . . should read 'empty and desolate' [and] the word 'created' should be formed and organized." Accounts of Meeting and Discourse, 5 January 1841, in *JSP*-D7:494. As shown above, this was just as he would translate the same two words in the Book of Abraham one year later. Smith had delivered similar teachings in 1840 (Smith, Discourse, 5 February 1840, in *JSP*-D7:175–79); and would do so again in 1843 and 1844 (Smith, Discourse, 17 May 1843, in Smith, *Words of Joseph Smith*, 203; Smith, Discourse, 7 April 1844, in Ibid., 341, 345, 352, 361; and Smith, Discourse, 16 June 1844, in Ibid., 379, 383). Smith's associates also used these Hebrew terms and definitions in their teachings on creation. See Parley P. Pratt, *An Appeal to the Inhabitants of the State of New York, Letter to Queen Victoria* [. . .] (Nauvoo, IL: John Taylor, 1844), 22–24.

205. See Hutchinson, "A Mormon Midrash," 63–69; Anderson and Bergera, *Joseph Smith's Quorum of the Anointed*, xxi; and Glen M. Leonard, *Nauvoo: A Place of Peace, A People of Promise* (Salt Lake City: Deseret Book; Provo, UT: Brigham Young University Press, 2002), 258–59.

206. A few less theological examples of Smith deviating from the Seixas grammar in his translation can be given. Smith regularly inserted "and it came to pass" for וַיְהִי rather than "and it was," as it is translated in the Seixas grammar (see note 182 above). In the passage of the Book of Abraham paralleling Genesis 1:21, Smith retained "great whales" for תַּנִּינִם (BoA, in *JSP*-R4:320–21 [Abraham 4:21]), as in the KJV, rather than translate the word as "sea monsters," as in the Seixas grammar (Seixas, *Manual Hebrew Grammar for the Use of Beginners*, 21 [§11]). Similarly, in the passage of the Book of Abraham paralleling Genesis 1:5, Smith retained "called the light day, and the darkness . . . night" for לָאוֹר יוֹם וְלַחֹשֶׁךְ קָרָא לָיְלָה (BoA, in *JSP*-R4:318–19 [Abraham 4:5]), as in the KJV, rather than using "as to the light" and "as to the darkness," as in the Seixas grammar (Seixas, *Manual Hebrew Grammar for the Use of Beginners*, 85–86).

creation account that go beyond the KJV or *Biblia Hebraica* texts of Genesis 1–2 and that incorporate original concepts into the creation story. These include that the darkness "reigned" upon the deep,[207] and that then the Gods "comprehended" the light,[208] "counseled" together (in first person dialogue),[209] "pronounced" the earth dry,[210] "prepared" the earth and waters to bring forth living things,[211] and saw that their orders for creation were "obeyed."[212] The text also records the existence of seven creative "times" (in contrast to "days"),[213] removes the names of Eden's rivers,[214] configures time in Eden "after the time of

207. In the Book of Abraham, Smith inserted this word in place of the italicized "*was*" in KJV Genesis 1:2. BoA, in *JSP*-R4:318–19 [Abraham 4:2].

208. In the Book of Abraham, Smith inserted this word in place of "seeing" in KJV Genesis 1:4. BoA, in *JSP*-R4:318–19 [Abraham 4:4].

209. In the Book of Abraham, the discussion and cooperation among the Gods replaces the solitary speaking and making by God in KJV Genesis 4:26, 5:1–3, 5. BoA, in *JSP*-R4:321–23 [Abraham 4:26, 5:1–3, 5].

210. Smith generally retained the traditional KJV translation of קָרָא as "called" in various parts of his narrative. See BoA, in *JSP*-R4:318–23 [Abraham 4:5, 8, 5:17, 20]; compare KJV Genesis 1:5, 8, 2:19, 23. However, in the passage paralleling Genesis 1:10, Smith twice translated קָרָא as "pronounced," see BoA, in *JSP*-R4:320–21 [Abraham 4:10]. The Seixas grammar generally follows the traditional translation of קָרָא as "called" (Seixas, *Manual Hebrew Grammar for the Use of Beginners*, 25 [§15], 38 [§30], 40 [§33], 70 [§96], 71 [§97, no. 4], 77 [§102], 85, 97, 99), but in one instance does add the possibility of "proclaim" (68 [§89]). The Gibbs and Gesenius lexicons also add "*to announce, proclaim* . . . [and] *to name*." Gibbs, *A Manual Hebrew and English Lexicon*, 195; and Gesenius, *Hebrew and English Lexicon of the Old Testament* (1824), 597. Smith's use of the word "pronounced" may have been related to the words "proclaim" and "announce" offered in one of these lexicons.

211. In the Book of Abraham, active preparation replaces creation by fiat in KJV Genesis 1:11, 20, 21, 24. BoA, in *JSP*-R4:320–21 [Abraham 4:11, 20, 21, 24].

212. As noted by Anthony Hutchinson, Smith's translation of the creation account in the Book of Abraham highlights the Gods' concern with order and obedience to their commands. Hutchinson, "A Mormon Midrash," 45–48. This is seen in instances in which Smith replaced God declaring that the creation "was good" in the KJV with the Gods being "obeyed" by the elements in the Book of Abraham. See BoA, in *JSP*-R4:320–23 [Abraham 4:10, 12, 18, 21]; compare Genesis 1:10, 12, 18, 21. See also BoA, in *JSP* R4:320–23 [Abraham 4:25, 31]; compare Genesis 1: 25, 31. Smith also repeatedly expanded "and it was so" (וַיְהִי־כֵן) to include the phrase "as they [the Gods] ordered." BoA, in *JSP*-R4:318–21 [Abraham 4:7, 9, 11]; compare Genesis 1:7, 9, 11. See also BoA, in *JSP*-R4:320–21 [Abraham 4:18, 24]; compare Genesis 1:18, 24.

213. When referring to a twenty-four-hour period, Smith retained the traditional translation of יוֹם as "day." BoA, in *JSP*-R4:318–23 [Abraham 4:5, 14, 16, 17, 5:4]; compare Genesis 1:5, 14, 16, 18, 2:4. However, when referring to a period of creation, he consistently translated it as "time." BoA, in *JSP*-R4:321–23 [Abraham 4:8, 13, 19, 23, 31, 5:2, 3]; compare Genesis 1:8, 13, 19, 23, 31, 2:2, 3. He similarly translated יוֹם as "time" instead of "day" for the period after which Adam and Eve partake of the fruit and die. BoA, in *JSP*-R4:322–23 [Abraham 5:13]; compare Genesis 2:17. Smith departed from his teacher in this broader rendering of the term, as the Seixas grammar consistently translated יוֹם as "day," see Seixas, *Manual Hebrew Grammar for the Use of Beginners*, 20 (§9), 22 (no. 7), 78 (§103), 85, 93, 95, 96, 99. The Gibbs lexicon also lists "day" as the primary meaning of יוֹם, but also includes "*time* generally; *some* or *several days*; [and] *some* or *a considerable time*" as alternative possibilities for the term. Gibbs, *A Manual Hebrew and English Lexicon*, 86; compare Gesenius, *Hebrew and English Lexicon of the Old Testament* (1824), 263–64. Therefore, it may be that in this instance Smith's translation of the Book of Abraham was informed by his lexicons. In addition, Hutchinson points out that Smith also inverted the evening-morning sequence of the Hebrew day in order to provide the narrative with a more modern (though non-Jewish) meaning. Hutchinson, "A Mormon Midrash," 45–48.

214. The four rivers flowing out of Eden are named and geographically located in the Bible: Pison, "which compasseth the whole land of Havilah"; Gihon, "that compasseth the whole land of Ethiopia";

Kolob,"[215] and reorders the sequence of creation pertaining to the woman and the animals.[216] Each of these examples shows Smith's ability to expand upon or otherwise revise his source texts in theologically creative ways.

One final issue to be considered is Smith's reasoning for using the KJV text of Genesis 1–2 as the structural basis of his Abraham creation account, which ostensibly derived from the Egyptian papyri. In such a biblically literate culture as nineteenth-century America, it would seem curious for Smith to claim to possess a new version of the story, only to turn to such a well-known biblical source as a starting point for his translation of it. While the surviving evidence does not allow for complete clarity on this matter, a few sources close to Smith may provide some insight into his logic. There are indications that Smith believed the creation account on the papyri actually predated the book of Genesis and represented the primary source used by Moses to compile the biblical narrative. This is seen in the claims of Smith's associates that the Abraham creation story was "of greater antiquity than the Bible,"[217] and

Hiddekel, "which goeth toward the east of Assyria"; and Euphrates, which was apparently familiar enough that no geographical location was required (Genesis 2:11–14). While Smith retained these rivers in his revision of the Bible in 1830 (Old Testament Manuscript 1, 5, in Smith, *Joseph Smith's New Translation*, 89 [Moses 3:11–14]), they were removed in his translation of the Book of Abraham in 1842. BoA, in *JSP*-R4:322–23 [Abraham 5:10–11]. In 1838, Smith had apparently had a revelation locating the postlapsarian residence of Adam and Eve in Daviess County, Missouri. This implicitly relocated the site of Eden from the Middle East—in the vicinity of Assyria and the Euphrates River—to somewhere in or near western Missouri. See Smith, Journal, 18 May–1 June 1838, in *JSP*-J1:271 [D&C 117:8]; John Corrill, *A Brief History of the Church of Jesus Christ of Latter Day Saints* [...] (St. Louis: self-pub., 1839), 28, in *JSP*-H2:163; Reynolds Cahoon, Far West, MO, to Newel K. Whitney, Kirtland, OH, 23 July 1838, Church History Library; Letter to Stephen Post, 17 September 1838, in *JSP*-D6:242; also Max H Parkin, *Missouri*, vol. 4 of *Sacred Places: A Comprehensive Guide to Early LDS Historical Sites*, ed. LaMar C. Berrett (Salt Lake City: Deseret Book, 2004), 377–97. Some scholars have suggested that this removal of the four rivers between Smith's first and second renditions of the Eden story was due to the intervening revelation that relocated Eden from the Old World to the New World. See Hutchinson, "A Mormon Midrash," 53–56; and Marquardt, "Joseph Smith's Egyptian Papers," 42.

215. See BoA, in *JSP*-R4:322–23 [Abraham 5:13]; compare note 112 above. In his explanation for the second illustration published with the Book of Abraham, Smith described one day on *Kolob* as being "equal to a thousand years according to the measurement of this earth" (BoA, in *JSP*-R4:316–17 [Abraham Fac. 2: Fig. 1]), thus incorporating a literal reading of Psalm 90:4 and 2 Peter 3:8 into the Book of Abraham.

216. The account in Genesis 2 has the animals being created after Adam but before the woman, whereas the parallel material in the Book of Abraham relocates the two verses dealing with the animals (Genesis 2:19–20) to the end of the narrative, with the result that the woman was created after Adam but before the animals. See BoA, in *JSP*-R4:322–23 [Abraham 5:14–21]; compare Genesis 2:18–25 (the woman is named Eve in Genesis 3:20 and 4:1).

217. See "Ed.," "Notices," *The Latter-Day Saints' Millennial Star*, June 1842, 32; and [no author], editorial, *The Latter-Day Saints' Millennial Star*, July 1842, 46. Both articles were likely written by Parley P. Pratt, who was one of the two editors of the newspaper and had studied Hebrew in Kirtland in 1836, see Givens and Grow, *Parley P. Pratt*, 81–82. Similarly, William I. Appleby noted in his journal entry for 5 May 1841 that there was "a vivid description given on the Papyrus, of the creation, far more accurately or minutely, than the account given in the Bible." William I. Appleby, Autobiography and Journal, 1848–1856, 72, Church History Library.

in a later recollection by Josiah Quincy that Smith had described the Book of Abraham as containing "the earliest accounts of the Creation, from which Moses composed the first Book of Genesis."[218] If this reminiscence is accurate, it may explain why Smith so openly used the KJV of Genesis 1–2 as the base text for his Abraham translation. In short, if Smith and his associates believed that the papyri contained the urtext of Genesis, they may have felt that rather than laboring over the papyri to translate that original source, it was more convenient to start with the surviving derivative source (Genesis 1–2) and work backward to recover the original account. In this process of reverse engineering, Smith may have drawn upon his study of Hebrew to help restore the text to what he felt was its pristine version.[219]

Whatever the exact motivation for Smith's methodology, the final result of his translation was a creation account that—even if initially inspired by the papyri—was largely based on the KJV text of Genesis 1–2 and adjusted or expanded at key points to reflect various Hebrew nuances, many of which derived from his personal studies and coursework with Joshua Seixas. These resources and his other sources of inspiration all converged and were animated by Smith's prophetic genius to produce a distinct narrative of a divine council of Gods planning the creation of the world, organizing preexisting materials into a terrestrial form, and providing human bodies to house premortal intelligences so as to provide them with an opportunity for eternal progression.[220] Thus in the process of translating the Book of Abraham, the blending of Joseph Smith's academic endeavors and his prophetic creativity led to some of the most innovative aspects of subsequent Mormon theology.

218. This statement by Smith was recorded by Quincy as being given during Quincy's tour of the Smith's residence in Nauvoo on 15 May 1844, during which Smith showed him the papyri, explained the significance of the Book of Abraham, and read Hebrew from a polyglot Bible. Quincy, *Figures of the Past*, 386.

219. In this case, Smith would not have viewed the creation narrative in KJV Genesis 1–2 as the source for the creation narrative in the Book of Abraham, but instead would have viewed the creation account possessed by Abraham as the original source behind Moses's writing of Genesis 1–2. The Book of Abraham even suggests that Abraham's creation account was itself based on records from earlier biblical patriarchs (BoA, in *JSP*-R4:310–11 [Abraham 1:28, 31])—presumably Noah and his forefathers—thus Smith may have believed he was recovering material dating back to the origins of humanity. For use of this logic in modern LDS apologetics, see Draper, Brown, and Rhodes, *Pearl of Great Price*, 237–38. For a historical-critical treatment of the creation narratives in Genesis and the Book of Abraham in light of the Pentateuchal sources (P and J), see Bokovoy, *Authoring the Old Testament*, 165–69.

220. See BoA, in *JSP*-R4:318–19 [Abraham 3:21–28]. Even though the creation narrative in the Book of Abraham can be seen as Smith's second revision of KJV Genesis 1–2, there is no indication that Smith intended for it to replace his 1830 revision (Old Testament Manuscript 2, 3–6, in Smith, *Joseph Smith's New Translation*, 86–90 [Moses 2–3]), with its emphasis on a dual spiritual/physical creation and its highly Christological expansions. Rather, Smith seems to have allowed both versions to coexist in his scriptural corpus. For a careful comparison of the similarities, differences, and theological implications of both accounts, see Hutchinson, "A Mormon Midrash," 30–41, 48–53.

CONCLUDING OBSERVATIONS AND HISTORICAL IMPLICATIONS

Unsurprisingly, the evidence highlighted in this chapter does not provide an exhaustive understanding of the Book of Abraham or its translation process. By all accounts, the Book of Abraham is an enigmatic text with a complex history, and a significant amount of research remains to be done regarding its relationship to modern Egyptology, the full range of approaches and resources used in its production, its contributions to Mormon cosmology and ritual practices, and several other issues. However, the evidence surveyed in this chapter does provide a few important observations regarding the relationship between Joseph Smith's larger Egyptian project and his Hebrew studies, the historical development of the Abraham text, the mechanics of Smith's translation process, and the impact of this process on subsequent Mormon thought. These observations and their historical implications can be briefly summarized as follows.

First, it is clear that Joseph Smith's Egyptian project—which began in the summer of 1835 and included his work with the papyri, his attempt to create an Egyptian lexicon, and his translation of the Book of Abraham—deliberately coincided with his efforts to study biblical Hebrew in late 1835 and early 1836. Not only did the era's intellectual climate foster widespread assumptions about the shared origins and mutually illuminating relationship between Hebrew and Egyptian hieroglyphs, but the previous experience of Smith and his associates with the Hebraic Reformed Egyptian script of the Book of Mormon and their belief that the Egyptian papyri included some Hebrew writing contributed to Smith's conviction that a knowledge of Hebrew would help facilitate his Egyptian translation efforts. Therefore, shortly after beginning his work with the papyri and his translation of the Book of Abraham, he made arrangements to study Hebrew formally, first through his own reading of Hebrew reference works and eventually through intensive coursework with Joshua Seixas. Over time, these studies fulfilled their intended purpose as Smith was able to incorporate Hebrew words, definitions, and concepts into his translation of the Abraham text and into his explanations of figures in the Egyptian illustrations

Second, a comparative examination of the extant Book of Abraham manuscripts, contemporaneous accounts of Joseph Smith's translation activities, and an identification of the Hebrew elements incorporated into the book's contents provides valuable insights into the chronology of its textual development. Although some scholars have claimed that Smith had almost completely translated the Book of Abraham by 1835, it is becoming increasingly clear that the text developed incrementally over a period of several years. Other scholars have argued based on early manuscript evidence, the Egyptian Alphabet text, and the GAEL that the translation of the first published installment of the Book of Abraham (now Abraham 1:1–2:18) was completed by the fall of 1835, but the translation of the second installment (now Abraham 2:19–5:21) and the explanations of the illustrations (Abraham Fac. 1; Fac. 2; Fac. 3) were not produced until early 1842.[221] The presence of discernable Hebrew elements in the Book of Abraham supports and further clarifies this later chronology.

As shown in this chapter, it is unlikely a mere coincidence that the portions of the translation attested in 1835 (Abraham 1–2) contain no traces of Hebraic influences beyond what is found in the biblical Abraham story, whereas the material first attested in 1842 (Abraham 3–5 and the facsimile explanations) is infused with Hebrew words, concepts, phraseology, and other Hebrew-inspired enhancements that Smith would have learned in 1836. Since most of these Hebrew words, transliterations, and definitions derived from Smith's academic resources—the Seixas textbook and his other manuals—the Hebrew elements in the text provide an 1836 *terminus post quem* for Smith's translation of the second installment of the Book of Abraham and his explanations for the illustrations published along with the book. There is evidence that some of the astronomical concepts found within those portions existed in conceptual form by late 1835 and that, following his Hebrew studies in 1836, Smith continued to develop these concepts through 1841. However, the manuscript evidence (including textual emendations), accounts of translation activities, and the presence of Hebrew in the text show that Smith did not translate (or at least did not finalize) those portions of the Book of Abraham until the spring of 1842, six years after he had studied Hebrew with Seixas and just prior to the book's publication.

Third, the evidence surveyed in this chapter provides important insights into Joseph Smith's views on the mechanics of his prophetic translations. Traditionally, many critical scholars have argued that Smith's translation of the Book of Abraham was simply a matter of him cobbling together various outside sources—such as the writings of Josephus, Thomas Dick, and the King James Bible—to invent the text's narrative and theology separate from a prophetic interaction with the papyri.[222] In contrast, most Mormon commentators have

221. See Marquardt, "Joseph Smith's Egyptian Papers," 13–50; Hauglid, *A Textual History of the Book of Abraham*, 2–11; and Hauglid, "The Book of Abraham and the Egyptian Project," 474–511.

222. See Brodie, *No Man Knows My History*, 170–75; Hutchinson, "A Mormon Midrash," 50–53; and Sandberg, "Knowing Brother Joseph Again," 30–33.

been content with the claim that Smith simply translated the Book of Abraham directly from the papyri through divine inspiration. The latter sentiments can be found in statements by Smith's associates that they witnessed him in the role of a "Seer" translating the papyri "by the revelation of Jesus Christ,"[223] "by direct inspiration from heaven,"[224] or even through the "Urim and Thummim."[225] However, the full scope of evidence indicates that these two options present a false dichotomy and that neither approach can account for the range of complexity that attended Smith's translation efforts. In short, it seems that Smith's production of the Book of Abraham resulted from a dynamic blending of his interaction with the papyri, his prophetic gifts, and his incorporation of academic training, scholarly resources, and personal intellectual effort.

In fact, current research on his other translation projects shows that this observation reflects a larger pattern in Smith's approach to scriptural translation. It is becoming clear that Smith's translations typically began with an artifact that served as the primary object of inspiration, and proceeded with a unique fusion of academic and prophetic endeavor. Smith's approach to translation therefore adhered in a meaningful way to his revelations, which included commandments to "study it out in your mind," to "study and learn, and become acquainted with all good books, and with languages," and to "obtain a knowledge of history."[226] The Book of Mormon translation (1827–1829) saw a dynamic interplay between the gold plates, documents of transcribed Reformed Egyptian characters, consultation with scholars of ancient scripts and cultures, the use of seer stones, and extensive textual interactions with the King James Bible.[227] Smith's New Translation, or revision, of the Bible (1830–1833) saw sim-

223. John Whitmer, History, 1831–circa 1847, in *JSP*-H2:86.

224. See Parrish, "Letter to the Editor, Feb. 5, 1838"; and West, *A Few Interesting Facts*, 5–6.

225. References to Smith using the Urim and Thummim (likely a seer stone) in the Book of Abraham translation can be found in "Another Humbug," *Cleveland Whig*, 31 July 1835; Wilford Woodruff, Journal, 27 December 1841, 19 February 1842, Church History Library; [Probably Parley P. Pratt], editorial, *Millennial Star*, July 1842, 46–47. See also a reported reminiscence of Lucy Mack Smith in "Correspondence of Friends' Weekly Intelligencer," *Friends' Weekly Intelligencer*, 3 October 1846, 211; and a late sermon by Orson Pratt, Discourse, 25 August 1878, in *Journal of Discourses*, 26 vols. (Liverpool, UK: William Budge; London: Latter-Day Saints' Book Depot, 1880), 20:65.

226. See Revelation, April 1829-D, in *JSP*-D1:50 [D&C 9:8]; Revelation, 8 March 1833, in *JSP*-D3:29 [D&C 90:13–15]; and Revelation, 6 May 1833, in *JSP*-D3:91 [D&C 93:53].

227. On the gold plates as an object of inspiration, attempts to transcribe and decipher Reformed Egyptian characters, and interaction with local scholars, see MacKay and Dirkmaat, *From Darkness unto Light*, 1–139; Michael Hubbard MacKay, "'Git Them Translated': Translating the Characters on the Gold Plates," in *Approaching Antiquity*, 83–116; and Michael Hubbard MacKay, "Performing the Translation: Character Transcripts and Joseph Smith's Earliest Translating Practices," Chapter 4 herein. On the textual interaction between the Book of Mormon and the King James Bible, see David P. Wright, "'In Plain Terms that We May Understand': Joseph Smith's Transformation of Hebrews in Alma 12–13," in *New Approaches to the Book of Mormon: Explorations in Critical Methodology*, ed. Brent Lee Metcalfe (Salt Lake City: Signature

ilar interplay between an 1828 King James Bible, prophetic elucidation, and at least one popular biblical commentary.[228] Similarly, the Book of Abraham (1835–1842) appears to have been initiated with the examination of Egyptian papyri and eventually unfolded through an attempt to create an Egyptian lexicon, a formal study of the Hebrew language, the experience of prophetic inspiration, the consulting of Hebrew reference works, and a complex interaction with a King James Bible.[229]

Thus, as a translator Joseph Smith drew upon several sources of inspiration in his production of scriptural texts, including ancient artifacts (a set of metal plates, a King James Version of the Holy Bible, and a collection of Egyptian papyri) and supernatural gifts (visions, prophetic inspiration, and other forms of revelation), along with insights and verbiage derived from the surrounding intellectual climate, culture, and circumstances (consultation with New York scholars, a Bible commentary, and Hebrew coursework) and complemented by his personal studies, ideas, and insights. The results of this dynamic blend of resources and methods were not traditional or static translations of source documents, but rather prophetically expansive and fluid elucidations of the sacred past, in which Smith felt free to incorporate his own editorial glosses, explanations, and enhancements.[230] In this process, his use of external resources

---

Books, 1993), 165–229; Wright, "Isaiah in the Book of Mormon: Or Joseph Smith in Isaiah," in *American Apocrypha: Essays on the Book of Mormon*, ed. Dan Vogel and Brent Lee Metcalfe (Salt Lake City: Signature Books, 2002), 157–234; Nicholas J. Frederick, "What Has Moroni to Do with John?," *Religious Educator* 14, no. 3 (2013): 93–109; and Frederick, "Evaluating the Interaction between the New Testament and the Book of Mormon: A Proposed Methodology," *Journal of Book of Mormon Studies* 24, no. 1 (2015): 1–30.

228. For an introduction to Smith's revision of the Bible, including its translation process and multifaceted interaction with the text of the KJV, see Scott H. Faulring, Kent P. Jackson, and Robert J. Matthews, "Joseph Smith's New Translation of the Bible," in Smith, *Joseph Smith's New Translation of the Bible*, 3–54. For Smith's apparent use of contemporaneous biblical reference works in the translation process—most evidently Adam Clarke's influential Bible commentary—see Thomas A. Wayment and Haley Wilson-Lemmon, "A Recovered Resource: The Use of Adam Clarke's Bible Commentary in Joseph Smith's Bible Translation," Chapter 11 herein. For a late reminiscence of Smith claiming to have received visions through the Urim and Thummim (or a seer stone) as part of his revision of the Bible, see Lorenzo Brown, statement, quoted in Robert J. Matthews, *"A Plainer Translation": Joseph Smith's Translation of the Bible; A History and Commentary* (Provo, UT: Brigham Young University, 1975), 25.

229. The main historical challenge in arguing that Smith's translation projects incorporated outside source material is that, with the exception of his Bible revision, there are no eyewitness accounts of Smith using other resources during his translation activities. Rather, the compelling evidence for his use of external sources is found almost exclusively within the texts of his various scriptural productions. This conflict between the eyewitness accounts and internal textual evidence is difficult to reconcile. In the case of the Book of Abraham, the strongest nontextual evidence that Smith used various resources in his translation may be the several examples of Smith showing guests in Nauvoo the Egyptian mummies and papyri, his Hebrew textbooks and a polyglot Bible, and the Book of Abraham translation as a way to explain his restoration of ancient texts (see note 108 above).

230. It is also interesting to note that Smith apparently did not feel bound to a single translation of a scriptural text, as seen in his different versions of the Sermon on the Mount in the Book of Mormon (3 Nephi

defies simplistic categorizations of scriptural plagiarism, but instead has been described by some scholars as more closely resembling biblically attested models of inspired targums or midrash.[231] Whether or not these categories serve as precise analogies for the Book of Abraham, Smith's fusion of his religious genius and academic efforts resulted in scriptural texts that ostensibly merged a restoration of ancient history with modern prophetic relevance.[232] For Smith, this seems to have been the essence of revelatory translation.[233]

Finally, the dynamic process of translation seen in the Book of Abraham not only produced new Mormon scripture, but it also strongly influenced subsequent Mormon theology and ritual practice. In addition to expanding the biblical Abraham narrative and teachings on priesthood (in the first installment), the Book of Abraham provided Mormon cosmology with unique views of the cosmos, the location of God within space and time, the premortal nature of the human spirit, and the creation (in the second installment). Throughout the process of translating this latter material, Joseph Smith's Hebrew studies enhanced these concepts in unique ways as his interest in linguistic technicalities, alternative definitions, and other aspects of the language planted the

12–14) and in his Bible revision (New Testament Manuscript 2, 6–12, in Smith, *Joseph Smith's New Translation of the Bible*, 242–49), as well as in his willingness to allow his 1830 inspired translation of Genesis 1–2 (Old Testament Manuscript 2, 3–6, in Smith, *Joseph Smith's New Translation of the Bible*, 86–90 [Moses 2–3]), his revised creation narrative in the Book of Abraham (BoA, in *JSP*-R4:318–23 [Abraham 4–5]), and even later translations of the Genesis creation account—such as in the funeral sermon given for King Follett (Smith, Discourse, 7 April 1844, in Smith, *Words of Joseph Smith*, 340–62)—to coexist as providing theologically varied insights into the same material. It seems, therefore, that the nature of Smith's translations, and perhaps even the translation process, were at least somewhat fluid even in his own mind. Smith was not interested in continually supporting his previous versions, but rather felt free to expand and otherwise revise the text based on his experience of ongoing scholarly studies and prophetic insights.

231. For attempts to analyze Smith's translations within ancient categories of scriptural expansion such as pseudepigrapha, targums, or midrash, see Wright, "'In Plain Terms that We May Understand,'" 207–10; Hutchinson, "A Mormon Midrash?"; Barlow, *Mormons and the Bible*, 57–61; and Bokovoy, *Authoring the Old Testament*, 169–73.

232. Smith's approach of inserting his own prophetic and intellectual insights into an ostensibly ancient document may have been inspired by (or at least reflected in) the model given in the Book of Mormon, in which an ancient prophet (Mormon) compiled earlier source materials and, in his narration of the sacred past, consistently interjected his own inspired commentary as informed by the world around him. For literary analysis of Mormon's combined prophetic roles as a compiler of ancient sources, commentator, and producer of scripture, see Grant Hardy, *Understanding the Book of Mormon: A Reader's Guide* (New York and Oxford: Oxford University Press, 2010), 89–120. For discussion on Smith's multifaceted efforts in his Bible revision to restore ancient material, edit the biblical text for modern readers, update the Bible to comport with his own revelations, and provide his own prophetic commentary on the text, see Faulring, Jackson, and Matthews, "Joseph Smith's New Translation of the Bible," in Smith, *Joseph Smith's New Translation of the Bible*, 8–11.

233. For a more theoretical treatment of Smith's expansive view of translation, which included his prophetic prerogative to interpret a source document, see Kathleen Flake, "Translating Time: The Nature and Function of Joseph Smith's Narrative Canon," *The Journal of Religion* 87, no. 4 (October 2007): 497–527, esp. 505–8.

seeds for blossoming theologies of the plurality of Gods, their organization of preexisting materials during seven creative periods, and their plan for the eternal progression of humankind.

These concepts appear to have been inspired or at least buttressed by Smith's study and knowledge of Hebrew. They also came to be articulated in Smith's translation of the Abraham text and were the catalyst for his most theologically innovative sermons between the publication of the Book of Abraham in 1842 and his death in 1844. Although early Mormon temple rituals are not well documented, it is also clear that these Hebrew-inspired aspects of the Book of Abraham helped shape the theological framework for the ritual drama performed in Smith's quorum of anointing, which would subsequently inform the ceremonies of the Nauvoo Temple with its cosmological teachings, creation narrative, and promises of heavenly exaltation in the afterlife. In this way, Joseph Smith's production of the Book of Abraham with its Hebrew elements proved to be a significant source of inspiration in his efforts to restore "the Ancient order of things,"[234] to bring the Latter-day Saints into communion with the sacred past, and to help the faithful obtain the blessings of the patriarchs that came down "from the beginning of time … or before the foundation of the earth."[235]

234. History Draft [for 1 January–30 June 1842], 11, 4 May 1842, History Drafts, 1844–1856, Church History Library (accessible in the Histories series of the online edition of *The Joseph Smith Papers*).

235. BoA, in *JSP*-R4:308–9 [Abraham 1:3].

17

"President Joseph Has Translated a Portion"

Joseph Smith and the Mistranslation of the Kinderhook Plates

DON BRADLEY AND MARK ASHURST-MCGEE

It was in early 1843 that Joseph Smith, the founding prophet of Mormon Christianity, translated a portion of the Kinderhook plates. These six small plates of brass—each covered on both sides with mysterious inscriptions—have become known as the "Kinderhook plates" because they were extracted from an Indian burial mound near the small village of Kinderhook in western Illinois. Kinderhook was about seventy miles downriver from Nauvoo, then the center of the Mormon "gathering." Over the years since the publication of the Book of Mormon in 1830, Joseph Smith had become widely known for his claim to have been led by a heavenly messenger to an ancient record inscribed on a set of gold plates, buried in a hill in western New York, and to have translated the record by means of a spiritual gift from God. Given the obvious similarity between the gold plates of the Book of Mormon and the brass plates from Kinderhook, the Kinderhook plates were brought to Smith. He kept the plates at his house for about a week and "translated" at least part of them.[1]

According to William Clayton, Joseph Smith's private clerk, Smith had "translated a portion" of the plates and said that they contained "the history of the person with whom they were found . . . a descendant of Ham through the loins of Pharaoh king of Egypt."[2] About a week later, church apostle Parley Parker Pratt wrote about the Kinderhook plates in a letter to a cousin.

1. The authors express appreciation to student interns Madison Porter, Nicholas Shrum, Michael Duvall, Ami Chopine, Jessica Wright, Brian Passantino, and Garrett Elkins, who helped with various aspects of the research for this chapter.

2. William Clayton, Journal, 1 May 1843, Church History Library, The Church of Jesus Christ of Latter-day Saints, Salt Lake City (hereafter Church History Library).

FIGURE 17.1. Kinderhook plate. Sole surviving Kinderhook plate, one of six brass plates fabricated in 1843, planted in a Native American burial mound, and then unearthed as part of an archaeological hoax modelled on the gold plates of the Book of Mormon. Left: Front. Right: Back. Chicago History Museum, Chicago, Illinois.

According to Pratt, the plates contained "the genealogy of one of the ancient Jaredites back to Ham the son of Noah."[3] While also associating the plates with the Jaredites, one of the peoples in the Book of Mormon,[4] Pratt basically agreed with what Clayton had written about the plates being associated with a descendant of Ham.

Decades later, one of the men who was present when the plates were disinterred revealed that the plates and their "discovery" were a hoax. Wilburn Fugate claimed that he and Robert Wiley had made the plates with some help from local blacksmith Bridge Whitton and then planted them in the burial mound the night before they were unearthed. In 1980, scientific testing confirmed the modern manufacture of the plates.

This chapter presents and analyzes the various sources that attest to Smith's involvement with the Kinderhook plates. These sources strongly indicate that Smith did indeed attempt to translate a portion of their fraudulent inscriptions. At the same time, these sources indicate that Smith attempted to translate the plates by ordinary methods of traditional translation—not by revelation.

3. Brian M. Hauglid, "'Come & Help Build the Temple & City': Parley P. and Orson Pratt's May 1843 Letter to John Van Cott," *Mormon Historical Studies* 12, no. 1 (Spring 2011): 155.

4. See Title Page; Ether; Moroni 9:23.

According to one of Wilburn Fugate's sons, his father was a Freemason, "and one of the first of that order in the state."[5] If Fugate had belonged to the fraternity that early, he may have been less than enthused with the installation of the Nauvoo lodge in 1842, and even less so with the surge of Mormon initiations and advancements that soon followed (at a speed that other Freemasons in Illinois considered "irregular" and improper).[6] Another of Fugate's sons explained that his father was also "a free thinker and essentially opposed to the Mormons, thousands of whom had colonized in Illinois."[7] Wilburn Fugate's co-conspirators, Robert Wiley and Bridge Whitton, may well have shared his sentiments. Bridge Whitton, who established the village of Kinderhook with Chester Churchill in 1836,[8] owned and sold several of the municipal lots and helped found the new settlement in Pike County as the village postmaster and blacksmith;[9] Wiley was known as "a respectable merchant" in the village;[10] and Fugate himself operated a farm in the nearby countryside.[11] Time and again, wherever the Latter-day Saints had gathered in settlements, they had garnered the resentment of the earlier settlers in the area—especially when their swelling numbers began posing a threat at the ballot box.[12] Mormon missionaries had begun gaining converts in Pike County shortly after the Latter-day Saints were expelled as a group from Missouri and resettled in Illinois. Mormontown, a settlement near Pittsfield, the seat of Pike County, had three hundred voters by 1845.[13] There was also a congregation of about a hundred Saints near Pleasant Vale, just a few miles to the south of Kinderhook.[14]

5. "Second Book of Mormon," *Colchester Independent* (Colchester, IL), 2 February 1888, 2. See also W. P. Harris to Willard C. Flagg, 25 April 1855, reproduced in "A Hoax," *Journal of the Illinois State Historical Society* 5, no. 2 (July 1912): 272–73.

6. Michael W. Homer, *Joseph's Temples: The Dynamic Relationship between Freemasonry and Mormonism* (Salt Lake City, UT: University of Utah Press, 2014), 158–64.

7. "Book of Mormon Plates 'Planted' by Illinois Man," *St. Louis Times* (St. Louis, MO), 23 September 1913, 1.

8. Jason Frederick Peters, "The Kinderhook Plates: Examining a Nineteenth-Century Hoax," *Journal of the Illinois State Historical Society* 96, no. 2 (Summer 2003): 133.

9. Peters, "The Kinderhook Plates," 134.

10. W. P. Harris to the Editor of the Times & Seasons [John Taylor], [undated], in "Ancient Records," *Times and Seasons*, 1 May 1843, 186.

11. Peters, "The Kinderhook Plates," 134.

12. For a general overview of early Mormon history in the context of party politics and political culture, see Marvin S. Hill, *Quest for Refuge: The Mormon Flight from American Pluralism* (Salt Lake City, UT: Signature Books, 1989); Kenneth H. Winn, *Exiles in a Land of Liberty: Mormons in America, 1830–1846*, Studies in Religion, edited by Charles H. Long (Chapel Hill, NC: University of North Carolina Press, 1989).

13. *History of Pike County, Illinois* [. . .] (Chicago: Chas. C. Chapman, 1880), 239.

14. M. D. Massie, *Past and Present of Pike County, Illinois* (Chicago: S. J. Clarke, 1906), 87.

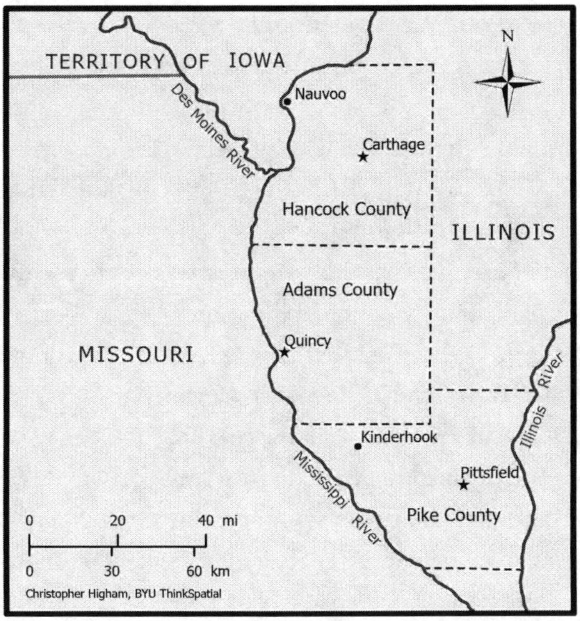

FIGURE 17.2. Western Illinois. Map of Nauvoo, Hancock County; Quincy, Adams County; and Kinderhook, Pike County—Mississippi River towns in western Illinois.

Mormon missionaries proselytizing in Illinois and throughout the Anglo-Atlantic world commonly used apostle Parley Pratt's *A Voice of Warning* as a conversion tool.[15] Terryl L. Givens and Matthew J. Grow, Pratt's biographers, explain that *A Voice of Warning* was "a work that served the church as its most powerful proselytizing tool—after the Book of Mormon."[16] The book had sold over five thousand copies in the previous five years.[17]

In the spring of 1843, Fugate and Wiley were perusing the ubiquitous missionary tract. According to Fugate, they "read in Pratt's prophecy that 'Truth would spring up out of the earth'" and "concluded to prove the prophecy by way of a joke."[18] In a chapter on the Book of Mormon, Pratt wrote: "The 85th Psalm is very plain on the subject: speaking of the restoration of Israel to their own land, it says, 'Mercy and Truth are met together; Righteousness and Peace have kissed each other. *Truth shall spring out of the earth:* and Righteousness

15. P[arley]. P. Pratt, *A Voice of Warning, and Instruction to All People* [. . .], 3rd ed., rev. (New York: J. W. Harrison, 1842).

16. Terryl L. Givens and Matthew J. Grow, *Parley P. Pratt: The Apostle Paul of Mormonism* (New York and Oxford: Oxford University Press, 2011), 90. See also Peter Crawley, *A Descriptive Bibliography of the Mormon Church*, vol. 1, *1830–1847* (Provo, UT: Religious Studies Center, Brigham Young University, 1997), 71.

17. The three thousand copies of the first edition (published in 1837) sold in two years and the twenty-five hundred copies of the second edition (published in 1839) sold in about two years. "Voice of Warning," *Times and Seasons*, 1 January 1842, 647.

18. Wilburn Fugate to James Cobb, 30 June 1879, in W. Wyl, *Mormon Portraits: Or, the Truth about the Mormon Leaders from 1830 to 1886* [. . .] (Salt Lake City: Tribune Printing, 1886), 207.

shall look down from heaven.'" Pratt next quoted John 17:17: "Sanctify them through thy *truth*—thy *word* is *truth*." As emphasized by Pratt's use of italics, he was here establishing an equivalence between God's "word" and the "truth." Pratt next applied this equivalence to the statement in Psalm 85:11 that "truth shall spring out of the earth." Thus, in a syllogistic move, Pratt concluded that "from these passages, we learn that his [God's] word is to spring out of the earth."[19] Pratt, however, was not arguing that this prophecy was yet to be fulfilled. Rather, this was part of a larger argument that these and other scriptures had already been fulfilled by Smith's discovery of the prophetic record on the buried plates of gold and by the translation of the Book of Mormon.

Although Fugate and Wiley had misread this passage from Pratt's *A Voice of Warning*, they were nevertheless inspired by it—just not in the way Pratt had intended. They decided to make their own set of inscribed metal plates, like the gold plates of the Book of Mormon. Archaeologist Stephen Williams writes that the nineteenth century was a golden age of archaeological hoaxes in America.[20] Fugate later made a statement in which he provided the essential details of the forgery:

> Bridge Whitton cut them (the plates) out of some pieces of copper; Wiley and I made the hieroglyphics by making impressions on beeswax and filling them with acid and putting it on the plates. When they were finished we put them together with rust made of nitric acid, old iron and lead, and bound them with a piece of hoop iron, covering them completely with the rust. Our plans worked admirably. A certain Sunday was appointed for digging. The night before, Wiley went to the Mound where he had previously dug to the depth of about eight feet, there being a flat rock that sounded hollow beneath, and put them under it.[21]

The Indian burial mound, near Kinderhook, was relatively large, at least a dozen feet high.[22] On Sunday, 23 April 1843, Wiley gathered several others with him at the mound to remove the stone and see what lay beneath.[23]

19. Pratt, *A Voice of Warning*, 102.

20. Stephen Williams, *Fantastic Archaeology: The Wild Side of North American Prehistory* (Philadelphia: University of Pennsylvania Press, 1991), 7, 78–80.

21. Fugate to Cobb, 207–8.

22. "Singular Discovery—Material for Another Mormon Book," *Quincy Whig* (Quincy, IL), 3 May 1843, 2; Harris to the Editor of the Times & Seasons, 186.

23. Harris to the Editor of the Times & Seasons, 186; Rob't Wiley et al., certificate and declaration, [undated], in "Ancient Records," 186.

When the stone was removed, the group found some human skeletal remains and the set of six brass plates, each bell shaped and nearly three inches long. There was a hole near the top of each plate for a metal ring that connected them together. The plates were also held together with two metal clasps. The ring was broken open and the clasps were removed from the plates. It was found that the plates were covered with inscriptions—unknown characters that appeared to be some ancient language.[24] According to Fugate, there were two "*Mormon elders* present"—surnamed Marsh and Sharp.[25] These two Latter-day Saints may have been invited along as the prank's primary targets, or in any case were its most immediate victims. It was reported that one of the Mormon men "leaped for joy at the discovery, and remarked that it would go to prove the authenticity of the Book of Mormon."[26] This may have been just the kind of reaction that Wiley and Fugate were hoping for when they made the plates and planted them. In a general study of hoaxes, sociologist Curtis D. MacDougall found that "the potential hoaxer's task is made easy by the predisposition of his intended victims to give credence to whatever fortifies them in their beliefs concerning a cherished cause."[27] In Fugate's own assessment, the forgery of the plates and the ruse of digging had worked "admirably."[28]

Fugate's statement was published in an anti-Mormon book by W. Wyl (a pen name used by Wilhelm Ritter Von Wymetal), titled *Joseph Smith the Prophet, His Family and His Friends: A Study Based on Facts and Documents.* Wyl showcased the letter in a chapter on the Kinderhook plates, framing the hoax as a trap. He began the chapter by telling his readers that "the day came when the seer and translator [Joseph Smith] was caught in a trap."[29] Then, after introducing the plates generally, Wyl introduced Fugate's statement within this entrapment framework: "But let us look at the trap with the translator's leg in it. Here it is, in the shape of a letter from Mr. Wilbur Fugate."[30] Finally, after reproducing Fugate's statement and spelling out its implications as he saw them, Wyl closed the chapter with an interrogatory to the reader: "Don't you see it now in the trap, the *peeper's leg?*"[31]

24. Harris to the Editor of the Times & Seasons, 186.
25. Fugate to Cobb, 207–8.
26. "Singular Discovery," 2. See also Fugate to Cobb, 208.
27. Curtis D. MacDougall, *Hoaxes* (New York: Dover, 1958), 102.
28. Fugate to Cobb, 207–8.
29. Wyl, *Mormon Portraits*, 205.
30. Ibid., 207.
31. Ibid., 211.

Although Wyl framed the episode as a trap in which Smith was caught, he never specified whether the trap had been intentionally laid *for Smith.* In fact, Fugate himself presented the hoax as having worked well on the day of discovery. Also, while Fugate proudly admitted to being involved in the forging and planting of the plates, he did not boast of any ruse to get the plates delivered to Smith. Instead he recounted that "the Mormons wanted to take the plates to Joe Smith, but we refused to let them go."[32] For whatever reason, it seems that Fugate and Wiley did not want the plates taken to Nauvoo. Perhaps they were worried that if the plates were taken there they would be subjected to serious scrutiny and the forgery would be detected.

One of Fugate's sons, who related that the joke was well-known within his family, described the Kinderhook hoax not as an elaborate trap meant to ensnare the Mormon prophet upriver in Nauvoo, but rather "a little plan by which to startle the natives."[33] Similarly, in a late recollection by "an old resident" of Kinderhook who claimed that he "remembered the incident well," the aim of the hoax had been "to bolster up the visionary plans of Joseph Smith, and to lead the unsuspecting public to follow him."[34] The hoax was apparently only a community affair, not the well-laid trap for Joseph Smith that almost all historians, producers of anti-Mormon literature, Mormon apologists, and other writers have assumed.[35] As Fugate explained, "the plates were made simply for a joke"—a little prank on the neighbors.[36]

The news of the discovery was published in nearby Quincy, Illinois, in the pages of the *Quincy Whig*,[37] and was soon reprinted in several other newspapers in the region.[38] The story was also picked up and reprinted in Nauvoo in the *Times and Seasons* (the church newspaper) and the *Nauvoo Neighbor* (the city newspaper)—both published by John Taylor and Wilford Woodruff,

32. Fugate to Cobb, 208.

33. "Second Book of Mormon," *The Daily Inter Ocean* (Chicago, IL), 31 January 1888, 1.

34. Quoted in "A Hoax," 271.

35. See John E. Hallwas, *Western Illinois Heritage* (Macomb, IL: Illinois Heritage Press, 1983), 77–79; Richard Lyman Bushman *Joseph Smith: Rough Stone Rolling* (New York: Alfred A. Knopf, 2005), 489–90; Martha Bradley-Evans, *Glorious in Persecution: Joseph Smith, American Prophet, 1839–1844* (Salt Lake City, UT: Smith-Pettit Foundation, 2016), 420–24; Jerald and Sandra Tanner, *Mormonism—Shadow or Reality?*, 5th ed. (Salt Lake City, UT: Utah Lighthouse Ministry, 1987), 112; Brian M. Hauglid, "Did Joseph Smith Translate the Kinderhook Plates?," in *No Weapon Shall Prosper: New Light on Sensitive Issues*, ed. Robert L. Millet (Provo, UT: Religious Studies Center, Brigham Young University; Salt Lake City, UT: Deseret Book, 2011), 94–96, 101–2.

36. Wilburn Fugate to James Cobb, 8 April 1878, Theodore Albert Schroeder Papers, 1845–1901, Wisconsin Historical Society, Madison, WI (hereafter Schroeder Papers).

37. "Singular Discovery," 2.

38. See, for example, "Singular Discovery—Material for Another Mormon Book," *Sangamo Journal* (Springfield, IL), 11 May 1843, 3.

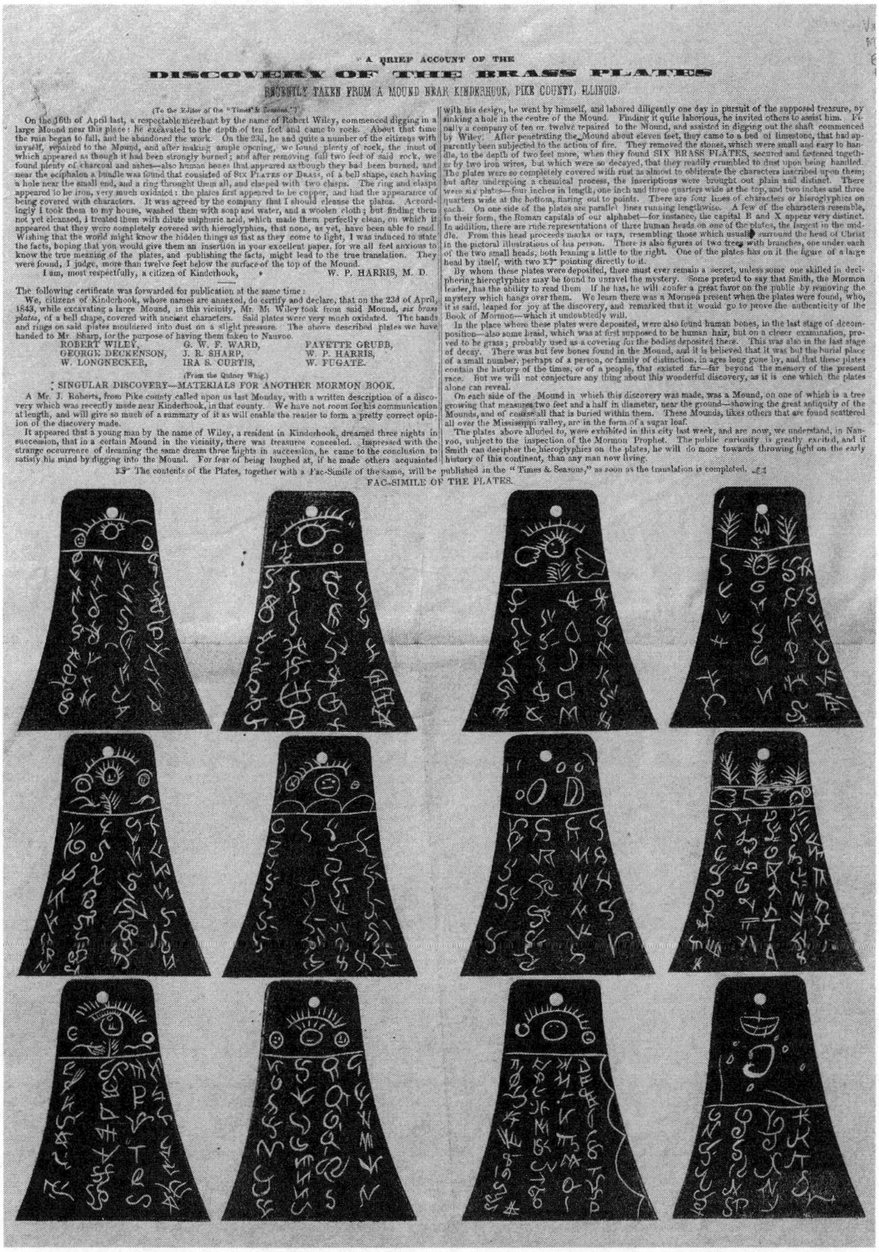

A BRIEF ACCOUNT OF THE

DISCOVERY OF THE BRASS PLATES

RECENTLY TAKEN FROM A MOUND NEAR KINDERHOOK, PIKE COUNTY, ILLINOIS.

(To the Editor of the "Times & Seasons.")

On the 16th of April last, a respectable merchant by the name of Robert Wiley, commenced digging in a large Mound near this place: he excavated to the depth of ten feet and came to rock. About that time the rain began to fall, and he abandoned the work. On the 23d, he and quite a number of the citizens with myself, repaired to the Mound, and after making ample opening, we found plenty of rock, the most of which appeared as though it had been strongly burned; and after removing full two feet of said rock, we found plenty of charcoal and ashes—also human bones that appeared as though they had been burned, and near the eciphalon a bundle was found that consisted of SIX PLATES OF BRASS, of a bell shape, each having a hole near the small end, and a ring throught them all, and clasped with two clasps. The ring and clasps appeared to be iron, very much oxidated: the plates first appeared to be copper, and had the appearance of being covered with characters. It was agreed by the company that I should cleanse the plates. Accordingly I took them to my house, washed them with soap and water, and a woolen cloth; but finding them not yet cleansed, I treated them with dilute sulphuric acid, which made them perfectly clean, on which it appeared that they were completely covered with hieroglyphics, that none, as yet, have been able to read. Wishing that the world might know the hidden things as fast as they come to light, I was induced to state the facts, hoping that you would give them an insertion in your excellent paper, for we all feel anxious to know the true meaning of the plates, and publishing the facts, might lead to the true translation. They were found, I judge, more than twelve feet below the surface of the top of the Mound.

I am, most respectfully, a citizen of Kinderhook, W. P. HARRIS, M. D.

The following certificate was forwarded for publication at the same time:

We, citizens of Kinderhook, whose names are annexed, do certify and declare, that on the 23d of April, 1843, while excavating a large Mound, in this vicinity, Mr. M: Wiley took from said Mound, *six brass plates*, of a bell shape, covered with ancient characters. Said plates were very much oxidated. The bands and rings on said plates mouldered into dust on a slight pressure. The above described plates we have handed to Mr. Sharp, for the purpose of having them taken to Nauvoo.

ROBERT WILEY,	G. W. F. WARD,	FAYETTE GRUBB,
GEORGE DECKENSON,	J. R. SHARP,	W. P. HARRIS,
W. LONGNECKER,	IRA S. CURTIS,	W. FUGATE.

(From the Quincy Whig.)

SINGULAR DISCOVERY—MATERIALS FOR ANOTHER MORMON BOOK.

A Mr. J. Roberts, from Pike county called upon us last Monday, with a written description of a discovery which was recently made near Kinderhook, in that county. We have not room for his communication at length, and will give so much of a summary of it as will enable the reader to form a pretty correct opinion of the discovery made.

It appeared that a young man by the name of Wiley, a resident in Kinderhook, dreamed three nights in succession, that in a certain Mound in the vicinity, there was treasures concealed. Impressed with the strange occurrence of dreaming the same dream three nights in succession, he came to the conclusion to satisfy his mind by digging into the Mound. For fear of being laughed at, if he made others acquainted with his design, he went by himself, and labored diligently one day in pursuit of the supposed treasure, by sinking a hole in the centre of the Mound. Finding it quite laborious, he invited others to assist him. Finally a company of ten or twelve repaired to the Mound, and assisted in digging out the shaft commenced by Wiley. After penetrating the Mound about eleven feet, they came to a bed of limestone, that had apparently been subjected to the action of fire. They removed the stones, which were small and easy to handle, to the depth of two feet more, when they found SIX BRASS PLATES, secured and fastened together by two iron wires, but which were so decayed, that they readily crumbled to dust upon being handled. The plates were so completely covered with rust as almost to obliterate the characters inscribed upon them; but after undergoing a chemical process, the inscriptions were brought out plain and distinct. There were six plates—four inches in length, one inch and three quarters wide at the top, and two inches and three quarters wide at the bottom, flaring out to points. There are four lines of characters or hieroglyphics on each. On one side of the plates are parallel lines running lengthwise. A few of the characters resemble, in their form, the Roman capitals of our alphabet—for instance, the capital B and X appear very distinct. In addition, there are rude representations of three human heads on one of the plates, the largest in the middle. From this head proceeds marks or rays, resembling those which usually surround the head of Christ in the pictoral illustrations of his person. There is also figures of two trees with branches, one under each of the two small heads, both leaning a little to the right. One of the plates has on it the figure of a large head by itself, with two ☞ pointing directly to it.

By whom these plates were deposited, there must ever remain a secret, unless some one skilled in deciphering hieroglyphics may be found to unravel the mystery. Some pretend to say that Smith, the Mormon leader, has the ability to read them. If he has, he will confer a great favor on the public by removing the mystery which hangs over them. We learn there was a Mormon present when the plates were found, who, it is said, leaped for joy at the discovery, and remarked that it would go to prove the authenticity of the Book of Mormon—which it undoubtedly will.

In the place where these plates were deposited, were also found human bones, in the last stage of decomposition—also some braid, which was at first supposed to be human hair, but on a closer examination, proved to be grass; probably used as a covering for the bodies deposited there. This was also in the last stage of decay. There was but few bones found in the Mound, and it is believed that it was but the burial place of a small number, perhaps of a person, or family of distinction, in ages long gone by, and that these plates contain the history of the times, or of a people, that existed far—far beyond the memory of the present race. But we will not conjecture any thing about this wonderful discovery, as it is one which the plates alone can reveal.

On each side of the Mound in which this discovery was made, was a Mound, on one of which is a tree growing that measures two feet and a half in diameter, near the ground—showing the great antiquity of the Mounds, and of course all that is buried within them. These Mounds, likes others that are found scattered all over the Mississippi valley, are in the form of a sugar loaf.

The plates above alluded to, were exhibited in this city last week, and are now, we understand, in Nauvoo, subject to the inspection of the Mormon Prophet. The public curiosity is greatly excited, and if Smith can decipher the hieroglyphics on the plates, he will do more towards throwing light on the early history of this continent, than any man now living.

☞ The contents of the Plates, together with a Fac-Simile of the same, will be published in the "Times & Seasons," as soon as the translation is completed. ☜

FAC-SIMILE OF THE PLATES.

FIGURE 17.3. Broadside of the Kinderhook plates. Mormon apostles John Taylor and Wilford Woodruff, the Nauvoo publishers of the *Times and Seasons* (church newspaper) and *Nauvoo Neighbor* (city newspaper), published a broadside of print facsimiles of all twelve sides of the six Kinderhook plates on 24 June 1843. Church History Library, Salt Lake City.

members of the church's Quorum of the Twelve Apostles.[39] It was likely Taylor, who was also the editor of the *Times and Seasons*, who introduced the story with an editorial noting that "circumstances are daily transpiring which give additional testimony to the authenticity of the Book of Mormon."[40] The *Times and Seasons* also reported that the man who had brought the plates to Nauvoo had already taken them away, "or we should have given a fac similie of the plates and characters in this number." However, the editor added, it was expected that the plates would soon be brought back to Nauvoo again "for translation."[41] That the plates were returned to Nauvoo is evident from the fact that Taylor and Woodruff published facsimiles of them in a broadside in June. The broadside also announced: "☞ The contents of the Plates, together with a Fac-Simile of the same, will be published in the 'Times & Seasons,' as soon as the translation is completed. ☜"[42] This could easily give the impression that Smith's translation was well underway and would soon be completed.

When the widely circulated broadside reached Fugate and Wiley, they would have realized that their little joke had played out beyond their wildest dreams. At this point, a financial motive may have entered their continued promotion of the plates. In November Wiley sent copies of the broadside to congressman John J. Hardin, one of the Illinois representatives in the nation's capital, asking Hardin to help him sell the plates to the National Institution for the Promotion of Science.[43] The institution was interested in the plates, and expressed no suspicion of their authenticity, but expressed no interest in purchasing them either (hoping that Wiley would eventually donate them).[44] So perhaps the hoax was a letdown in the end.

If Smith ever came to suspect the authenticity of the Kinderhook plates, he apparently never voiced any concern to his inner circle of friends. Church leaders, historians, and publicists continued to consider the plates genuine through the remainder of Smith's lifetime and far beyond, reprinting the facsimiles of the plates and the story of their discovery in various church publications. The most influential of these was the biography of Joseph Smith that was

39. "Ancient Records," 186; "Ancient Records," *Nauvoo Neighbor*, 10 May 1843, 2.

40. "Ancient Records," *Times and Seasons*, 1 May 1843, 185. (All subsequent references, unless otherwise noted, are to the original version of the article published in the *Times and Seasons*.)

41. Ibid., 186.

42. Some copies of the broadside are dated 24 June 1843. *A Brief Account of the Discovery of the Brass Plates Previously Taken from a Mound near Kinderhook, Pike County, Illinois* (Nauvoo, IL: Taylor & Woodruff, 1843).

43. Robert Wiley to John Hardin, 15 November 1843, Hardin Family Collection, Chicago History Museum, Chicago (hereafter Hardin Collection).

44. Francis Markoe to John Hardin, 9 December 1843, Hardin Collection.

serialized in early church newspapers and later compiled as the official history of the church. Thomas Bullock, a clerk working in the Historian's Office of the Church of Jesus Christ of Latter-day Saints,[45] used the journal of William Clayton—who, after all, was Joseph Smith's private clerk—to compile the content for the 1 May 1843 entry of Smith's personal history. In doing so, he followed the general practice of those working on Smith's history of converting not only his journal entries but other primary documents into first-person narrative voice, as if they had all been written by Smith himself.[46] Therefore Clayton's statement "Pres[t.] J. has translated a portion" was revised to "I have translated a portion."[47] Leo Hawkins, another clerk working in the Historian's Office,[48] then copied this content from the rough draft notes into the manuscript history.[49] The text was later published as part of the serialized "History of Joseph Smith"—the entry on the Kinderhook plates appearing in 1856.[50] A half century later, the complete series of installments was compiled and edited by Brigham H. Roberts, a high-ranking authority in the church,[51] and published as *History of the Church*.[52] The complex process of composition behind the history easily gave way to the polished presentation in print.

Historiographically, the Kinderhook plates episode has most often been approached within a dichotomous and polarized defender/detractor framework that has proved highly polemical on both sides. This tradition began with Latter-day Saints using the story of the discovery of the plates as supportive evidence for the gold plates of the Book of Mormon. For many years, the authenticity of the plates was accepted generally, and not just by the Latter-day Saints. Dan Jones, a Latter-day Saint who himself "saw those plates," wrote that "the case was publicized through the newspapers, and I did not hear that anyone disbelieved it; but if the one who found them were to utter a word that angels had anything to do with the matter, we do not think that he would be

45. Dean C. Jessee, "The Writing of Joseph Smith's History," *BYU Studies* 11, no. 4 (Summer 1971): 456–58.

46. Ibid.

47. Joseph Smith, History Draft, 1 March–31 December 1843, 28, 1 May 1843, in Joseph Smith, History Drafts, 1844–1856, Church History Library (accessible in the Histories series of the online edition of *The Joseph Smith Papers*).

48. Jessee, "The Writing of Joseph Smith's History," 460.

49. Smith, History, 1838–1856, vol. D-1, 1542, 1 May 1843.

50. "History of Joseph Smith," *Deseret News*, 3 September 1856, 201–2. When apostles Wilford Woodruff and George A. Smith finished publishing the serialized history, they stated that it had been inspected and approved by church president Brigham Young. "History of Joseph Smith," *Deseret News*, 20 January 1858, 363.

51. *Deseret News 2009 Church Almanac* (Salt Lake City, UT: Deseret News, n.d.), 100.

52. Joseph Smith Jr. *History of the Church of Jesus Christ of Latter-day Saints: Period I*, with introduction and notes by B. H. Roberts (Salt Lake City: Deseret News, 1909), 5:372–78.

believed about this."[53] Even authors of anti-Mormon literature accepted the plates as genuine.[54] All of this changed when Fugate's 1879 statement about the hoax was published in Wyl's 1886 exposé of Mormonism.[55]

The publication of Fugate's letter framed the historiography for the next century. Producers of anti-Mormon literature promulgated this evidence that the plates were a hoax and argued that because Smith had translated them—as published in the official *History of the Church*—he had fallen for the hoax and inadvertently exposed himself as a fraudulent translator. By the second half of the twentieth century, many anti-Mormon publications had adopted the pithy aphorism that "only a bogus prophet translates bogus plates."[56] Mormon apologists, on the other hand, held that Fugate was lying in order to injure Smith's reputation and thus defended Smith's translation and prophethood. In 1962, an article on the Kinderhook plates in the official magazine of the Church of Jesus Christ of Latter-day Saints affirmed the authenticity of the plates, stood by the content of Smith's translation (as it appears in the *History of the Church*), and stated that the existence of the plates reaffirmed "his prophetic calling."[57]

Clearly, what was needed was modern scientific testing to determine the authenticity of the plates. Although five of the six plates have been lost, a sole surviving plate is housed at the Chicago History Museum.[58] In 1980, Mormon historian Stanley B. Kimball received permission to have it tested by D. Lynn Johnson, a professor of materials science and engineering at Northwestern University. Fugate had written that he and Wiley made the inscriptions "by making impressions on beeswax and filling them with acid and putting it on the plates."[59] If the Kinderhook plates had been made in the Americas before

53. [Dan Jones], "Description of the Plates," *Prophet of the Jubilee* (Rhydybont, Wales), August 1846, 38, in *Prophet of the Jubilee*, trans. and ed. Ronald D. Dennis (Provo, UT: Religious Studies Center, Brigham Young University, 1997), 38.

54. See, for example, John Hyde Jr., *Mormonism: Its Leaders and Designs* (New York: W. P. Fetridge, 1857), 266–69.

55. Fugate to Cobb, 207–8. See also Fugate to Cobb, 8 April 1878. John Hodgen, who grew up in Pike County, claimed that he "knew the man who made the plates." John Hodgen, St. Louis, MO, to James Cobb, 28 November 1879, Schroeder Papers. In 1912, the Illinois State Historical Society published an earlier letter written by W. P. Harris, who was also present when the plates were unearthed, confirming what Fugate had written. In his 1855 letter, Harris admitted that he had initially believed in the discovery, but that blacksmith Bridge Whitton later told him he had made the plates for Fugate and Wiley. See Harris to Flagg.

56. Charles A. Shook to James D. Bales, quoted in James D. Bales, *Book of Mormon?* (Rosemead, CA: Old Paths Book Club, 1958), 98. See Ed Decker and Dave Hunt, *The God Makers* (Eugene, OR: Harvest House, 1984), 99–100; [Jerald Tanner], *Joseph Smith and the Kinderhook Plates* [tract] (Salt Lake City, UT: Utah Lighthouse Ministry, n.d.); MormonThink, http://www.mormonthink.com/kinderhookweb.htm.

57. Welby W. Ricks, "The Kinderhook Plates," *Improvement Era*, September 1962, 637.

58. The plate was acquired by the Chicago Historical Society (now Chicago History Museum) in 1920. Accession Number 1920.487, Decorative and Industrial Arts Department, Chicago History Museum, Chicago.

59. Fugate to Cobb, 207.

European contact, they would most likely have been engraved with a stylus of some sort, rather than being acid etched. Testing with a scanning electron microscope showed that the characters on the plates were etched with acid, not engraved with a tool, and testing with a scanning auger microprobe found traces of etching acid in the character grooves. Most important, destructive testing showed that the metal was a fine alloy, consistent with nineteenth-century manufacturing techniques and unlike the crude alloys of antiquity. These results determined conclusively that the Kinderhook plates were of modern manufacture.[60] In 1981, Kimball presented the test results in an article on the Kinderhook plates published in the church's magazine.[61]

In the article, Kimball also noted that the characters on the plates were similarly spurious. They bear little resemblance to any known language. In fact, they do not resemble language at all, because they have almost none of the character permutation frequencies found in genuine script.[62] When Wiley and Fugate drew the characters, they apparently just made them up on the spot. The characters were clearly intended to imitate genuine linguistic script, but bear no actual intellectual content to be translated. No legitimate translation is even possible.

Coincidentally, around the time of the scientific testing, it was discovered that William Clayton's Nauvoo journal was the source behind the 1 May 1843 entry in Smith's history. This created an opening on a new line of apologetic defense. Whereas it had been assumed for decades that Smith himself had written about translating the plates, Kimball could now show that these words had been written by Clayton and could bring Clayton's accuracy into question. Categorizing what Clayton wrote as "hearsay," Kimball argued that Smith never actually translated from the plates.[63]

Kimball's article, especially the conclusive evidence of forgery, was a milepost in the historiography of the plates. Prior to the publication, the major debate was whether the plates were authentic or fake. Afterward, the issue of authenticity was essentially settled and the debate shifted to whether or not Smith had actually translated from the plates. The new evidence for forgery—presented by Kimball—invigorated those producing anti-Mormon literature,

60. D. Lynn Johnson, "Analysis of the Kinderhook Plate Owned by the Chicago Historical Society," November 1980, Stanley H. Buchholz Kimball Collection of Historical Documents, Church History Library.

61. Stanley B. Kimball, "Kinderhook Plates Brought to Joseph Smith Appear to Be a Nineteenth-Century Hoax," *Ensign*, August 1981, 66–74.

62. As explained by Kimball: "The arrangement of the characters and the paucity of repeated signs and sign clusters does not suggest any real language." Kimball, "Kinderhook Plates Brought to Joseph Smith Appear to Be a Nineteenth-Century Hoax," 74n17.

63. Ibid., 67–68, 73–74.

who trumpeted this evidence while insisting that Smith *did* translate from the false plates and was therefore a false prophet. The episode has thus endured as a favorite subject in anti-Mormon literature produced by evangelical detractors, disaffected Mormons, and others.[64] On the other hand, Mormon historians and apologists have generally followed Kimball in questioning whether Smith had really translated from the plates.[65] The historiographical framework, however, has begun to shift again. In the mid-1990s, the authors of this chapter began collaborating on an argument that Smith had indeed translated at least a portion of the Kinderhook plates, though not by revelation.[66]

LANGUAGE AND TRANSLATION

As noted above, the Kinderhook plates were brought to Joseph Smith because of their obvious similarity to the gold plates from which Smith claimed to have translated the Book of Mormon. After completing his translation of the Book of Mormon, Smith engaged in other translation projects. Along with his more renowned interest in supernatural translation, he acquired a deep interest in natural translation. His translation of the Kinderhook plates must therefore be considered within the context of both his natural and supernatural translation practices. This section introduces Smith's experience with languages and translation, focusing on aspects of Smith's prior translation projects that are relevant to his translation of the Kinderhook plates.

64. See Decker and Hunt, *The God Makers*, 99–101; *Joseph Smith and the Kinderhook Plates* [tract]; Grant H. Palmer, *An Insider's View of Mormon Origins* (Salt Lake City, UT: Signature Books, 2002), 30–34; Jeremy T. Runnells, *CES Letter: My Search for Answers to My Mormon Doubts* (n.p.: n.p., 2013, October 2017 edition), 70–73; and the MormonThink website, http://www.mormonthink.com/kinderhookweb.htm.

65. See James B. Allen, *No Toil nor Labor Fear: The Story of William Clayton* (Provo, UT: Brigham Young University Press, 2002), 112–13; Richard E. Turley Jr., *Victims: The LDS Church and the Mark Hofmann Case* (Urbana and Chicago: University of Illinois Press, 1992), 10–11; William J. Hamblin, review of *Archaeology and the Book of Mormon*, by Jerald and Sandra Tanner, *Review of Books on the Book of Mormon* 5 (1993): 269–70.

66. Mark Ashurst-McGee, "Joseph Smith, the Kinderhook Plates, and the Question of Revelation" (paper presented at the Annual Meeting of the Mormon History Association, Snowbird, UT, 18 May 1996); Mark Ashurst-McGee, "A One-Sided View of Mormon Origins," review essay of *An Insider's View of Mormon Origins*, by Grant H. Palmer, *FARMS Review* 15, no. 2 (2003): 320–22; Don Bradley, "'President Joseph Has Translated a Portion': Solving the Mystery of the Kinderhook Plates" (paper presented at the Thirteenth Annual FairMormon Conference, Sandy, UT, 5 August 2011); Don Bradley and Mark Ashurst-McGee, "Joseph Smith and the Kinderhook Plates," in *A Reason for Faith: Navigating LDS Doctrine & Church History*, ed. Laura Harris Hales (Provo, UT: Religious Studies Center, Brigham Young University; Salt Lake City: Deseret Book Company, 2016), 93–115. Our research has also been published with permission in Hauglid, "Did Joseph Smith Translate the Kinderhook Plates?," 102n16, 103n17; Hauglid, "'Come & Help Build the Temple & City,'" 157n3; and Mark Alan Wright, "Joseph Smith and Native American Artifacts," in *Approaching Antiquity: Joseph Smith and the Ancient World*, ed. Lincoln H. Blumell, Matthew J. Grey, and Andrew H. Hedges (Provo, UT: Religious Studies Center, Brigham Young University; Salt Lake City, UT: Deseret Book, 2015), 133.

Early Translation Projects

Smith produced his translation of the Book of Mormon in 1828 and 1829.[67] One of the ancient prophets given voice in the resulting text explained that the gold plates were written using an unusual script, "which consists of the learning of the Jews and the language of the Egyptians" and was called "reformed Egyptian."[68] That Hebrew and Egyptian were related was a common belief of the great philologists of the day, including Jean-François Champollion, the French savant who first successfully deciphered Egyptian, and Moses Stuart, one of the most eminent American Hebraists.[69]

Soon after the Book of Mormon was published, Smith organized a church and began what he sometimes called a "New Translation" of the Bible.[70] From 1830 to 1833, Smith and his scribes worked on this Bible revision.[71] Starting with the King James Version, they made a few major expansions, many smaller expansions and substantial revisions, and hundreds of minor revisions to the text. Some of the revisions, such as the significant expansions of text, were certainly meant to be understood as resulting from revelation. Others, such as small grammatical changes, may well have been considered the result of human reason rather than revelation.[72] Some of the changes followed the relatively minor textual revisions put forward in the well-known Bible commentary by Methodist theologian Adam Clarke.[73] Smith could read neither Hebrew nor Greek, but working his way through the Bible—and consulting Clarke's commentary along the way—he would have been heavily exposed to both

67. John W. Welch, "The Miraculous Translation of the Book of Mormon," in *Opening the Heavens: Accounts of Divine Manifestations, 1820–1844*, ed. John W. Welch with Eric Carlson (Provo, UT: BYU Studies, 2005), 77–213; Larry E. Morris, *A Documentary History of the Book of Mormon* (New York, NY: Oxford University Press, 2019), chaps. 4–8; Samuel Morris Brown, "Seeing the Voice of God: The Book of Mormon on Its Own Translation," Chapter 6 herein. During the same period, Smith translated a brief text purportedly written by the first-century apostle John. See David W. Grua and William V. Smith, "The Tarrying of the Beloved Disciple: The Textual Formation of the Account of John," Chapter 10 herein.

68. 1 Nephi 1:2; Mormon 9:32–33. See also "History of Joseph Smith," *Times and Seasons*, 1 October 1842, 943.

69. See Matthew J. Grey, "Approaching Egyptian Papyri through Biblical Language: Joseph Smith's Use of Hebrew in His Translation of the Book of Abraham," Chapter 16 herein, see esp. 396–98.

70. Letter to Church Leaders in Jackson County, Missouri, 21 April 1833, in *JSP*-D3:68; Letter to Church Leaders in Jackson County, Missouri, 25 June 1833, in *JSP*-D3:154; Letter to Church Leaders in Jackson County, Missouri, 2 July 1833, in *JSP*-D3:167; Letter to Church Leaders in Jackson County, Missouri, 6 August 1833; in *JSP*-D3:233.

71. Robert J. Matthews, *"A Plainer Translation": Joseph Smith's Translation of the Bible; A History and Commentary* (Provo, UT: Brigham Young University Press, 1975), chaps. 1–3.

72. Matthews, *"A Plainer Translation,"* 252–53.

73. Thomas A. Wayment and Haley Wilson-Lemmon, "A Recovered Resource: The Use of Adam Clarke's Bible Commentary in Joseph Smith's Bible Translation," Chapter 11 herein.

scripts. In a March 1833 revelation, which Smith dictated just a few months before the conclusion of the Bible revision, the voice of God commanded Smith that he and other church officers "study and Learn and become acquainted with all good books and with Languages tongues and people."[74]

It was about two years later that Michael Chandler rolled into Kirtland, Ohio—where Smith was then living—with his traveling mummy show and a collection of Egyptian papyri.[75] Oliver Cowdery, one of Smith's scribes, wrote that when Chandler "first presented his papyrus to bro.—Smith, he [Chandler] was shown a number of characters like those upon the writings of Mr. C. which were previously copied from the plates, containing the history of the Nephites, or book of Mormon."[76] Thus the first thing Smith did when he encountered the Egyptian papyri was to retrieve a transcript of characters from the gold plates. He approached these new artifacts by drawing upon prior experience, comparing the inscriptions on the papyri with those he had previously encountered on the plates. And, according to Cowdery, Smith apparently found the Egyptian of the papyri comparable to the "reformed Egyptian" of the plates. The characters on the papyri were also compared to Hebrew characters. As Cowdery wrote: "The characters are such as you find upon the coffins of mummies, hieroglyphics, &c. with many characters or letters exactly like the present, (though probably not quite so square,) form of the Hebrew without points."[77] Later, following a conversation with Joseph Smith about the Egyptian papyri, church member William Appleby wrote in his journal that Smith said the papyri were written "chiefly in the Egyptian language, with the exception of a little Hebrew."[78] Like the characters on the gold plates, the characters on the papyri were seen as mainly Egyptian but also involving the Hebrew language.

In early July 1835, Smith and others in Kirtland purchased the mummies and the accompanying papyri.[79] Later that month, William Wines Phelps, one of his scribes, explained that "as no one could translate these writings they were presented to President Smith. He soon knew what they were and said

74. Revelation, 8 March 1833, in *JSP*-D3:29 [D&C 90:15].

75. Chandler reportedly arrived in Kirtland on either 30 June or 1 July 1835. Oliver Cowdery to William Frye, 22 December 1835, in "Egyptian Mummies—Ancient Records," *Latter Day Saints' Messenger and Advocate*, December 1835, 235.

76. Cowdery to Frye, 235.

77. Ibid., 234. See also Grey, "Approaching Egyptian Papyri through Biblical Language," 400–401 herein.

78. William I. Appleby, Journal, 5 May 1841, Church History Library.

79. See William W. Phelps to Sally Phelps, 20 July 1835, in Historical Department, Journal History of the Church, 20 July 1835, Church History Library; Cowdery to Frye, 235; Smith, History, vol. B-1, 596, 6 July 1835.

that the rolls of papyrus contained a sacred record kept by Joseph in Pharoah's court in Egypt and the teachings of Father Abraham."[80] Smith's later history stated the same: "I, with W[illiam] W. Phelps and O[liver] Cowdery, as scribes, commenced the translation of some of the characters or hieroglyphics, and much to our joy found that one of the rolls contained the writings of Abraham; another the writings of Joseph of Egypt."[81] This was when Smith "*commenced* the translation of *some* of the characters"—prior to beginning his translation of the one roll associated with Abraham (resulting in what is now the Book of Abraham). This preliminary translation was presumably by the same spiritual gift that he had claimed for his translation of the Book of Mormon. Smith then began his translation of the Book of Abraham, in the role of a "Seer."[82]

In addition to the Egyptian papyri and the Book of Abraham translation manuscripts, there are several other manuscripts from this period that are clearly related to both. This curious collection of documents—commonly referred to in secondary literature as the "Kirtland Egyptian Papers"[83]—are in the handwriting of Smith and others who were assisting him at the time.[84] A text titled "Egyptian Alphabet" exists in three versions.[85] Another document, derived from the "Egyptian Alphabet" text, is a bound volume with the expanded title "Grammar & A[l]phabet of the Egyptian Language."[86] Going beyond the initial "Egyptian Alphabet" text, the book also included a few rules of grammar.[87] The interest in an "alphabet" and "grammar" of the Egyptian language, as well as the designing of these documents in a tabular format and lexicographical style, indicate an approach to understanding the papyri that was at least partly academic in intent and style. The running heads on the pages of the "Grammar and Alphabet of the Egyptian Language" bear the shortened title "Egyptian Alphabet."[88] At some point in time—perhaps a

80. Phelps to Phelps, 1.

81. Smith, History, vol. B-1, 596, 6 July 1835.

82. John Whitmer, History, 1831–circa 1847, in *JSP*-H2:86. See also H. Donl Peterson, *The Story of the Book of Abraham: Mummies, Manuscripts, and Mormonism* (Salt Lake City: Deseret Book, 1995), 119–24.

83. For an early example, see Hugh Nibley, "The Meaning of the Kirtland Egyptian Papers," *BYU Studies* 11, no. 4 (Summer 1971): 350–99.

84. For transcripts and introductions to these documents, see *JSP*-R4:53–190.

85. Egyptian Alphabet, circa early July–circa November 1835-A, in *JSP*-R4:55–71; Egyptian Alphabet, circa early July–circa November 1835-B, in *JSP*-R4:73–83; Egyptian Alphabet, circa early July–circa November 1835-C, in *JSP*-R4:85–93.

86. Grammar and Alphabet of the Egyptian Language, circa July–circa November 1835, 1, in *JSP*-R4:116–17.

87. Grammar and Alphabet of the Egyptian Language, circa July–circa November 1835, 1–2, 3, 10, 17, 20–21, in *JSP*-R4:116–19, 120–21, 134–35, 148–49, 154–57.

88. Grammar and Alphabet of the Egyptian Language, circa July–circa November 1835, 9, 13, 15, 20, in *JSP*-R4:132–33, 140–41, 144–45, and 154–55. See also 33, in *JSP*-R4:180–81.

decade or more later in territorial Utah—a label was placed on the spine with the same shortened title.[89] Like the loose leaf copies of the "Egyptian Alphabet" text that preceded it, the "Egyptian Alphabet" book is really more of a lexical text—a sort of dual-language dictionary with Egyptian characters and corresponding definitions or interpretations in English.[90] The inscriptions in the book, with several blank pages between sections, indicate that the project fell far short of initial expectations. Though the book is evidently unfinished, it appears that Smith drew on at least some of this enigmatic material in his translation of the Book of Abraham.[91]

Language Study and Extemporaneous Translation

Difficulty with the Egyptian alphabet seems to have driven Smith to the study of Hebrew, a language that he believed was related to Egyptian. Since Hebrew *was* well understood, and could be profitably studied like other known languages, he apparently hoped that a knowledge of Hebrew could be utilized to help interpret the Egyptian.[92] Smith's journal notes that he began his studies in November 1835 with "a Hebrew bible, lexicon & Grammar, also a Greek Lexicon and Webster's English Lexicon."[93] In early 1836, he and others began an intensive Hebrew course with a Jewish instructor, meeting almost daily for eight weeks.[94] Smith's journal notes that on 19 January the class began reading: "We commenced reading in our hebrew bibles with much success, it seems as if the Lord opens our minds, in a marvelous manner to understand this word in the original language, and my prayer is that God will speedily indue [endue] us with a knowledge of all languages and toungs [tongues]."[95] Among other exercises, the students also practiced translating passages of the Hebrew

89. Grammar and Alphabet of the Egyptian Language, circa July–circa November 1835, in *JSP*-R4:111. See also Figure 17.7.

90. The English definitions offered for the characters do not reflect a modern understanding of the Egyptian language. Kerry Muhlestein, "Assessing the Joseph Smith Papyri: An Introduction to the Historiography of their Acquisitions, Translations, and Interpretations," *Interpreter: A Journal of Mormon Scripture* 22 (2016): 34.

91. Christopher C. Smith, "The Dependence of Abraham 1:1–3 on the Egyptian Alphabet and Grammar," *John Whitmer Historical Association Journal* 29 (2009): 38–54; Brian M. Hauglid, "'Translating an Alphabet to the Book of Abraham': Joseph Smith's Study of the Egyptian Language and His Translation of the Book of Abraham," Chapter 15 herein.

92. Grey, "Approaching Egyptian Papyri through Biblical Language," 394–406 herein.

93. Joseph Smith, Journal, 2 November 1835, in *JSP*-J1:82.

94. See Matthew J. Grey, "'The Word of the Lord in the Original': Joseph Smith's Study of Hebrew in Kirtland," chap. 10 in *Approaching Antiquity*.

95. Smith, Journal, 19 January 1836, in *JSP*-J1:164.

Bible into English. Smith enthusiastically applied himself to his studies and to practicing natural translation. On 17 February 1836 he wrote in his journal: "[I] attend[ed] the school and read and translated with my class as usual, and my soul delights in reading the word of the Lord in the original, and I am determined to persue the study of languages untill I shall become master of them, if I am permitted to live long enough, at any rate so long as I do live I am determined to make this my object."[96] Smith never mastered Hebrew, but he studied in earnest and did gain some rudimentary proficiency with the language.[97]

Smith maintained an interest in languages through the remainder of his busy life, and engaged in intermittent study as occasion would permit. In 1842, he resumed his translation of the Book of Abraham. Smith's journal reports that he was "translating" the Book of Abraham on 8 March 1842, and then "translating and revising" on 9 March—shortly before he published the second installment of the Book of Abraham and little more than a year before he attempted to translate from the Kinderhook plates.[98] Although he never completed the Book of Abraham, he published three installments of the translation in the church newspaper. The first installment consisted of thirteen paragraphs of text, numbered like verses in the Bible. It also included an illustration, reproduced from the papyri, along with explanations for various figures in the illustration. The second installment consisted of nineteen more numbered paragraphs and included another illustration with explanations. The third installment was an illustration only, with explanations.[99]

Some of the explanations for the figures in the illustrations used Hebrew words, reflecting the belief that the papyri were primarily Egyptian but with some Hebrew. Part of the first Egyptian illustration was explained with reference to the Hebrew word "Raukeeyang, signifying expanse, or the firmament over our heads." The explanation added that "in this case, in relation to this subject, the Egyptians meant it to signify Shaumau, to be high, or the heavens, answering to the Hebrew word, Shaumahyeem."[100] A figure in the second Egyptian illustration was given a similar explanation: "Answers to the Hebrew

96. Smith, Journal, 17 February 1836, in *JSP*-J1:186.

97. Certificate from Joshua Seixas, 30 March 1836, in *JSP*-D5:214–16. See also Grey, "'The Word of the Lord in the Original.'"

98. Smith, Journal, 8–9 March 1842, in *JSP*-J2:42.

99. Book of Abraham and Facsimiles, 1 March–16 May 1842, in *JSP*-R4:303–27 (hereafter BoA).

100. BoA, in *JSP*-R4:306–7 [Abraham Fac. 1: Fig. 12].

word Raukeeyang."[101] Thus the Book of Abraham, like the Book of Mormon, drew an explicit connection between the Hebrew and Egyptian languages.[102]

In early 1843, Smith took up an interest in German, studying both Hebrew and German with Alexander Neibaur, a German Jew who had converted to Mormon Christianity in Europe and gathered to Nauvoo.[103] In addition to Hebrew and German, Smith apparently studied a little Greek and in Nauvoo occasionally quoted from the Greek New Testament in his sermons.[104] He also sprinkled his sermons and letters with Latinisms.[105] In an April 1844 sermon, about a year after the Kinderhook plates episode, Smith drew from Hebrew, Greek, Latin, and German translations of the Bible—and especially his knowledge of Hebrew—to give an interpretive translation of Genesis 1:1.[106]

Restorationist Prophet and Amateur Linguist

In April 1843, when the Kinderhook plates were brought to Smith, he was still intent on resuming and completing the Book of Abraham, which he would presumably continue translating in the role of a prophet.[107] However, Smith did not always see himself acting in the prophetic role. Three months prior to the Kinderhook plates episode, he explained the limits of his prophetic claim to a group of his followers. He reportedly stated that "'A Prophet is not always a Prophet' only when he is acting as such."[108] In a sermon Smith delivered about a month after encountering the Kinderhook plates, he introduced his treatment of a few Greek words by declaring, "I will turn linguist."[109] Although Smith was

101. BoA, in *JSP*-R4:316–17 [Abraham Fac. 2: Fig. 4].

102. Smith also used a few Hebrew words in the translation of the narrative text of the Book of Abraham and drew upon his knowledge of Hebrew in the creation account appearing at the end of the Book of Abraham. Grey, "Approaching Egyptian Papyri through Biblical Language," Chapter 16 herein.

103. Joseph Smith, Journal, 1 January 1843, 3, 5, 13, 14, 20, 23 February 1843, 1, 6 March 1843, 8 April 1843, 18, 20, 22 March 1844, 23 May 1844, 3 June 1844, in *JSP*-J2:208, 254, 255, 263, 264, 267, 276, 279, 297–99, 349; *JSP*-J3:205, 206, 207, 257, 271; biographical note on Neibaur in *JSP*, J3:431; also Alexander Neibaur, Journal, 24 May 1844, Church History Library.

104. Andrew F. Ehat and Lyndon W. Cook, comps. and eds., *The Words of Joseph Smith: The Contemporary Accounts of the Nauvoo Discourses of the Prophet Joseph* (Orem, UT: Grandin Book Company, 1991), 244, 351, 354, 358, 366, 380. See also John W. Welch, "Joseph Smith's Awareness of Greek and Latin," in *Approaching Antiquity*, 314.

105. See Joseph Smith, "Journeying," letter to The Church of Jesus Christ of Latter Day Saints, 6 September 1842 [D&C 128:11], Revelations Collection, Church History Library. See also Welch, "Joseph Smith's Awareness of Greek and Latin."

106. See Ehat and Cook, *The Words of Joseph Smith*, 340–62. See also Stan Larson, "The King Follett Discourse: A Newly Amalgamated Text," *BYU Studies* 18, no. 2 (Winter 1978): 202–3, 207.

107. BoA, in *JSP*-R4:304.

108. Smith, Journal, 8 February 1843, in *JSP*-J2:256.

109. Smith, Journal, 11 June 1843, in *JSP*-J3:33.

very much an amateur—and as church prophet and president had little time to fulfill his desire "to pursue the study of languages [and] become master of them"—he nevertheless saw himself in the role of a linguist on this occasion and others. Smith's understanding of his different roles requires a consideration of what role he saw himself in when he "translated a portion" of the Kinderhook plates. Did he see himself "acting as" a prophet or had he decided to "turn linguist"? Considering the full range of Smith's natural and supernatural translation interests, efforts, and practices, it could have been either (or both).

The fact that the characters on the Kinderhook plates did not match any known language was not necessarily a deterrent to attempting a traditional translation. In a history of archaeology in America, archaeologists Gordon R. Willey and Jeremy A. Sabloff write that the period in which Smith lived was characterized by "rampant speculation."[110] In a history of amateur archaeology, archaeologist Stephen Williams explains that because there was no professional field of archaeology in Smith's era, "archaeology was open to anyone . . . the data could be interpreted almost any way and . . . usually was."[111] Enthusiastic amateurs were eager to try to decipher ancient script.[112] Even in the modern age of professional archaeology, examples can be given of scholars producing mistranslations, mistaking nonlinguistic patterns for actual language, and translating forgeries—all in good faith.[113]

As investigated in this chapter, there is strong evidence that Joseph Smith translated at least a small part of the Kinderhook plates. As noted above, William Clayton wrote that Smith had "translated a portion" and said "they contain the history of the person with whom they were found & he was a descendant of Ham," while Parley Pratt wrote that the plates contained "the genealogy of one of the ancient Jaredites back to Ham." This and other documentary evidence will be examined below in detail.

110. Gordon R. Willey and Jeremy A. Sabloff, *A History of American Archaeology* (London: Thames and Hudson, 1974; San Francisco: W. H. Freeman, n.d.), 22.

111. Williams, *Fantastic Archaeology*, 78–79.

112. Ibid., 12, 13.

113. Archaeologists are unsure whether some cylinder seal patterns are lingual, see Dominique Collon, *First Impressions: Cylinder Seals in the Ancient Near East* (Chicago: University of Chicago Press, 1987), 105–6. Noted biblical scholar James Charlesworth claimed to have translated a newly discovered ancient text into prose, but it was later shown to be a basically meaningless writing exercise including some miscellaneous letters, words, and names (Joseph Naveh, "A Medical Document or a Writing Exercise? The So-called 4Q Therapeia," *Israel Exploration Journal* 36, no. 1–2 [1986]: 52–55)—an error that Charlesworth later admitted, see J. H. Charlesworth, "A Misunderstood Recently Published Dead Sea Scroll (4QM 130)," *Explorations* 1, no. 2 (1987): 2. Cyrus Gordon, a professor of Near Eastern Studies, translated part of the inscription on the Bat Creek Stone, which was later shown to be a forgery. Robert C. Mainfort Jr. and Mary L. Kwas, "The Bat Creek Stone Revisited: A Fraud Exposed," *American Antiquity* 69, no. 4 (October 2004): 761–69.

JOSEPH SMITH'S PLAN TO TRANSLATE ACCORDING TO CHARLOTTE HAVEN

Charlotte Ann Haven, a young woman who had recently moved from Quincy to Nauvoo,[114] saw and wrote about the Kinderhook plates in early May of 1843. Haven was a Unitarian from Portsmouth, New Hampshire.[115] Her letter about the Kinderhook plates was later published along with several other letters she wrote as "A Girl's Letters from Nauvoo."[116] While the letters are attributed to "A Girl," Haven was actually a grown woman in her early or middle twenties.[117]

Haven wrote that she and Joseph Smith had been shown the Kinderhook plates in Nauvoo by a "Mr. Joshua Moore." As later recounted by Wilburn Fugate, "a man assuming the name of Savage, of Quincy, borrowed the plates of Wiley to show to his literary friends there, and took them to Joe Smith."[118] Quincy was located along the Mississippi River between Kinderhook and Nauvoo (as seen in Figure 17.2). The 3 May 1843 issue of a Quincy newspaper, the *Quincy Whig*, reported that the plates "were exhibited in this city last week."[119] Another Quincy newspaper, the *Quincy Herald*, reported that the plates were "in the possession of Mr. J. J. Moore, and can be seen at the Quincy House."[120] This "Mr. J. J. Moore," in Quincy, was apparently the man who had presented himself to Wiley as "Savage, of Quincy." The Quincy House was a boarding

114. Haven apparently arrived in Quincy, Illinois, in October 1842 and spent two months there before moving to Nauvoo, where she arrived by the end of the year. Charlotte Haven, Letter, 3 January 1843, in "A Girl's Letters from Nauvoo," *Overland Monthly* (San Francisco), December 1890, 616 (all subsequent Haven letters are from this article).

115. Haven occasionally referenced her Unitarianism in her letters home. See Haven to "My dear friends at home," 26 March and 2 April 1843, 628; compare Haven to "My dear friends at home," 8 September 1843, 635. Her letters frequently indicate that she was from a municipality named Portsmouth in New England (616–38). The probate records of Charlotte Ann Haven's father, as well as a Haven family history, indicate that she was from Portsmouth, New Hampshire. New Hampshire, Wills and Probate Records, 1643–1982, for William Haven; Rockingham Estate Papers, 15013–15064, 1845–1846; William Haven, comp., *William Haven and His Descendants* [. . .] (Tulsa, OK: 1927), 46.

116. "A Girl's Letters from Nauvoo," 616–38.

117. Genealogical sources vary slightly on Charlotte Ann Haven's birth year, but two sources state that she was born in early September 1819, which would make her twenty-three years old when she was shown the Kinderhook plates in April 1843 and through most of the months when she was writing her letters from Nauvoo. Haven, *William Haven and His Descendants*, 46; Charlotte Ann Mason Record of Death, 6 March 1900, California, Death and Burial Records from Select Counties, 1873–1987.

118. Fugate to Cobb, 207–8. See also Fugate to Cobb, 8 April 1878; Wiley to Hardin.

119. "Singular Discovery," 2.

120. This issue of the *Quincy Herald* is apparently not extant, but its article on the Kinderhook plates was reprinted by both the *Southport Telegraph* and the *Mississippi Free Trader and Natchez Daily Gazette*. The comparison of reprinted articles is nearly verbatim and the quotation given above is verbatim. "Great Curiosities—Relics of Antiquity," *Southport Telegraph* (Southport, WI), 16 May 1843, 1; "Great Curiosities—Relics of Antiquity," *Mississippi Free Trader and Natchez Daily Gazette* (Natchez, MS), 8 June 1843, 2.

house known for its "size and elegance."[121] Moore was presumably a boarder there. As the *Whig* also reported, "the plates ... are now, we understand, in Nauvoo, subject to the inspection of the Mormon Prophet."[122] Whoever had taken the plates from Quincy had, before leaving, apparently communicated their intention of taking them to Nauvoo and showing them to Smith.

Haven wrote that she and Smith had been shown the Kinderhook plates by Moore when he was passing through on one of "his monthly zigzag tours through the State."[123] Hancock County records show that a Joshua J. Moore owned land in the county. Six months after the Kinderhook plates episode, he appears in circuit court records as the plaintiff in a trespassing case showing that he owned land in Hancock by 1838, if not earlier.[124] County deed books record that in July 1843, within a few months of the Kinderhook plates episode, a Joshua J. Moore of Philadelphia "sold" 160 acres of land a few miles east of Nauvoo to Joseph Smith, acting as Trustee in Trust for the Church of Jesus Christ of Latter-day Saints, for the sum of one dollar—and that he did so "for and in consideration of the love and good will he bears to the Church of Jesus Christ of Latter Day Saints."[125] This was a legal form often taken when giving gifts in real estate. To build the temple in Nauvoo, the church solicited donations from both church members and neighboring residents, and several nonmembers did make gifts in money, in kind, and in real estate.[126]

Joshua Moore's "monthly zigzag tours through the State" mentioned by Haven may have been in his role as an eastern speculator in western lands. This would explain him being from Philadelphia, owning land near Nauvoo in Hancock County, and boarding at the Quincy House in Adams County. The Quincy House was built by the land agency in charge of the Military Tract of 1812 in western Illinois in connection with the Government Land Office in Quincy. The founders of the agency, including Francis C. Moore (a relative?), were easterners and known for "their frequent periodical trips into all the

121. William H. Collins and Cicero F. Perry, *Past and Present of the City of Quincy and Adams County, Illinois* (Chicago: S. J. Clark, 1905), 49–52.

122. "Singular Discovery," 2.

123. Haven to "My dear home friends," 630.

124. Joshua J. Moore vs. Baldwin L. Samuel, Hancock County Circuit Court Case Files, 1830–1846, October 1843.

125. Hancock County Deeds, Book M, 9–10 (entry 5776).

126. Smith wrote that "even strangers, who were not in the church, united with an unprecedented liberality in the accomplishment of this great work. . . . We feel at this time to tender to all, old and young, both in the church and out of it, our unfeigned thanks for their unprecedented liberality." Ed[itor] [Joseph Smith], "The Temple," *Times and Seasons*, 2 May 1842, 775.

counties of the tract."[127] This "Joshua J. Moore" who gave land near Nauvoo to Joseph Smith was probably the same "Mr. J. J. Moore" who was showing the Kinderhook plates to interested residents in Quincy and the "Mr. Joshua Moore" who showed the plates to Smith and Haven in Nauvoo.

Joshua Moore may have been a close relative of or otherwise familiar with George Moore, the Unitarian minister in Quincy.[128] George Moore was himself a boarder in the Quincy House,[129] where "everybody knew everybody."[130] The reverend wrote in his diary the previous June that, while visiting Nauvoo, Joseph Smith had shown him a transcript of characters from the gold plates of the Book of Mormon.[131] Charlotte Haven was friends with both George Moore and Joshua Moore, who both gave her news of "Quincy friends" when they visited her in Nauvoo.[132] Haven, on another occasion, wrote of her old "Quincy House friends."[133] She had likely boarded there herself prior to her move from Quincy to Nauvoo. George Moore's previous visit with Joseph Smith, in which Smith reportedly showed him characters from the gold plates, may have given Joshua Moore the idea of visiting Smith in Nauvoo to show him the Kinderhook plates.

Source

On 2 May 1843, Haven wrote a letter to friends back home in New Hampshire in which she shared that Moore had shown both her and Smith the Kinderhook plates:

> We hear very frequently from our Quincy friends through Mr. Joshua Moore, who passes through that place and this in his monthly zigzag tours through the State, traveling horseback. His last call on us was last

127. Collins and Perry, *Past and Present of the City of Quincy and Adams County, Illinois*, 49–52.

128. David F. Wilcox, "Second Congregational Unitarian Church," in *Quincy and Adams County History and Representative Men* (Chicago and New York: Lewis, 1919), 1:551.

129. George Moore, Diary, 2, 10, and 11 December 1840, 20 November 1845, transcribed in Kenneth Walter Cameron, ed., *Transcendental Epilogue: Primary Materials for Research in Emerson, Thoreau, Literary New England, the Influence of German Theology, and Higher Biblical Criticism* (Hartford, CT: Transcendental Books, 1965, 1982), 1:318, 320, 2:451.

130. Collins and Perry, *Past and Present of the City of Quincy and Adams County, Illinois*, 51.

131. George Moore wrote in his diary for 3 June 1842 that he had called on Joseph Smith, who invited Moore into his home. As noted by Moore, they "conversed about the gold plates" and Smith "showed . . . some specimens of the hieroglyphics, such as, he says, were on the gold plates." Moore, Diary, 3 June 1842, transcribed in Cameron, ed., *Transcendental Epilogue*, 1:356.

132. Haven to "My dear friends at home," 628; Haven to "My dear friends at home," 630.

133. Haven, Letter, 3 January 1843, 616.

> Saturday and he brought with him half a dozen thin pieces of brass, apparently very old, in the form of a bell about five or six inches long. They had on them scratches that looked like writing, and strange figures like symbolic characters. They were recently found, he said, in a mound a few miles below Quincy. When he showed them to Joseph, the latter said that the figures or writing on them was similar to that in which the Book of Mormon was written, and if Mr. Moore could leave them, he thought that by the help of revelation he would be able to translate them. So a sequel to that holy book may soon be expected.[134]

Haven's account is routinely quoted in almost anything written about the Kinderhook plates, especially her claim that Smith thought he might be able to translate the plates "by the help of revelation."

Source Criticism and Analysis

Haven wrote that Moore had visited her "last Saturday." She was writing on 2 May, a Tuesday, so the previous Saturday would have been 29 April—three days earlier. Her description of the Kinderhook plates was largely accurate. In fact, she was entirely accurate in that there were six plates, that they were thin pieces of brass, that they were "apparently" very old (as they had been made to appear), that they had a bell shape, and that they bore inscriptions resembling characters and other figures. Her description of the size of the plates, however, is larger than accurate. The one extant plate, as well as tracings of plates in the journals of Latter-day Saints William Clayton and Brigham Young, show that the plates were only 2 7/8 inches long—about half of the "five or six inches" Haven remembered.[135] Over the intervening days between seeing the plates and writing about them, their size had grown in her memory.

Haven's accuracy in reporting on the Kinderhook plates can also be approximated by considering the somewhat parallel case of her reporting on the Egyptian mummies and papyri associated with the Book of Abraham. In her

134. Haven to "My dear home friends," 630.

135. The extant plate measures 2 7/8" in height with a width of 2 1/4" at the bottom (Bridge Whitton, Kinderhook plate, 1843, Chicago History Museum, Chicago, IL). The tracing in Clayton's journal measures 2 13/16" in height with a width of 2 1/4" at the bottom (William Clayton, journal, 1 May 1843). The tracing in Young's journal measures 2 7/8" in height with a width of 2 1/4" at the bottom (Brigham Young, Journal, 3 May 1843, Brigham Young Office Files, Church History Library).

letter of 19 February 1843, written about two months before she saw the Kinderhook plates, Haven related that she had gone to the home of Lucy Mack Smith to see the antiquities and saw "half a dozen mummies."[136] It is well-attested that Smith only had four mummies.[137] For whatever reason, Haven reported the wrong number of mummies.

Haven also recounted that Lucy Mack Smith "read several minutes" from a papyrus text "as if it were English," adding that "it sounded very much like passages from the Old Testament—and it might have been for anything we knew—but she said she read it through the inspiration of her son Joseph, in whom she seemed to have perfect confidence."[138] There are no other known accounts of Lucy Mack Smith reading from the papyri "through the inspiration of her son" (whatever that means). Another visitor to Smith reported that she exhibited "half a dozen sheets of papyri, and, from a large octavo, of which her prophet's son is author, read an interpretation, so called, of the mysterious hieroglyphics, which those ancient records are declared to contain."[139] This and other accounts in which Lucy Mack Smith relayed things her son had translated or said appear to be more accurate reports of how she made her presentation of the papyri.[140] Haven, in her letters, never made any mention of the Book of Abraham, and seems to have had no knowledge of its translation or publication. Rather than hearing Lucy Mack Smith read directly from the papyri "through the inspiration of her son," Haven more likely heard her reading, reciting, or paraphrasing passages from the Book of Abraham in connection with her display of the papyri.

Historical Implications

In fairness to Haven, it should be noted that her recollections were largely accurate in their basic content: Lucy Mack Smith *did* have a few Egyptian mummies and there *was* an English translation of the papyri with passages that sounded very much like passages from the Old Testament. Haven's letters in

136. Haven to "My dear Mother," 19 February 1843, 623.

137. Cowdery to Frye, 234–36. See also Peterson, *The Story of the Book of Abraham*, 97, 111, 116–18, 196, 197, 203.

138. Haven to "My dear Mother," 624.

139. Letter to the Editor, 25 April 1844, in *Buffalo Daily Courier and Economist* (Buffalo, NY), 15 June 1844.

140. M to *Friends' Weekly Intelligencer*, October 1846, in "Correspondence of Friends' Weekly Intelligencer," *Friends' Weekly Intelligencer*, 3 October 1846, 3; Eudocia Baldwin Marsh, "Mormons in Hancock County: A Reminiscence," ed. Douglas L. Wilson and Rodney O. Davis, *Journal of the Illinois State Historical Society* 64, no. 1 (Spring 1971): 38.

general provide a vivid and invaluable view of Mormon Nauvoo. Yet when it comes to some of the specific details she related, there are significant problems. Her memory of extra mummies is inaccurate and her uncorroborated claim of Lucy Mack Smith reading from a papyrus text "through the inspiration of her son Joseph" is likely mistaken. The remarks Haven made about the mummies and papyri and what Lucy Mack Smith said about them show that there is sufficient reason to question what she wrote about the Kinderhook plates and what Joshua Moore said about them. This is not to impugn in any way Haven's intellectual capacity or character in maintaining a lively correspondence with family members and dear friends, but merely to demonstrate an ordinary and understandable lack of accuracy when she was reporting details on things with which she was by and large unfamiliar.

Joshua Moore's Second Visit with Joseph Smith

Moore had the plates with him when he visited Haven on 29 April, so he (or someone else) must have taken them back to Smith, who had them at his home by 1 May when William Clayton saw them there. It is possible that there is a scrap of information from Moore's second visit with Smith reported in one of Moore's hometown newspapers. A brief and anonymous, yet remarkable, notice in Philadelphia's *North American and Daily Advertiser* reported that "Jo Smith, the Mormon prophet has examined some brass plates lately found in Illonois [Illinois], and translated a portion of the figures or characters on them. He pronounces them of Egyptian origin."[141] The statement "he pronounces them" sounds as if it were actually based on having heard the same. The "Egyptian origin" of the characters could have been a reference to the "reformed Egyptian" of the Book of Mormon, as in Haven's account. An even closer match would be a reference to the hieratic characters of the papyri, which Smith and others referred to simply as "Egyptian."[142] Most noteworthy, the brief notice stated that Smith had "translated a portion" of the Kinderhook plates—using the same words that William Clayton used in his journal.[143]

141. "Important," *The North American and Daily Advertiser* (Philadelphia, PA), 29 May 1843, 2.

142. The papyri were written in Egyptian, which was well-known by Joseph Smith, the Latter-day Saints generally, and others who viewed the Egyptiana and wrote about it. Peterson, *The Story of the Book of Abraham*.

143. "Important," 2.

JOSEPH SMITH'S TRANSLATION ACCORDING TO WILLIAM CLAYTON

According to church member William Clayton, Joseph Smith had translated a part of the Kinderhook plates by 1 May 1843. Clayton, age twenty-eight, had converted to Mormonism in England in 1837.[144] By profession, he was a factory clerk.[145] James B. Allen, Clayton's biographer, writes that he was "of a meticulous, methodical nature." In addition to having excellent penmanship, "he was a gifted musician (he played the violin, drum, and French horn), a lover of fine craftsmanship, and a devoted husband and father."[146] He reportedly "refused to carry a watch that would not run accurately," which "may have been one manifestation of the meticulous, methodical nature that he revealed throughout his adult life."[147] Within a few months of joining the church, Clayton was made a counselor in the British mission presidency.[148]

Clayton emigrated to Nauvoo in 1840, where his clerical skills were soon put to good use in various capacities in the church and in Nauvoo's city government. In September 1842 he was appointed Nauvoo city treasurer.[149] In October 1842 Joseph Smith appointed him to serve as the church's temple recorder, keeping track of financial donations. And, on the same occasion, Smith also made Clayton his private clerk. Clayton wrote that when he received these appointments, Smith also stated: "When I have any revelations to write, you are the one to write them."[150] Clayton would later serve as the clerk of Smith's confidential Council of Fifty—the general officers of the political kingdom of God on the earth.[151] He also kept a journal for Smith during the last month of Smith's life, presumably at Smith's request.[152] When the Nauvoo temple was completed, Clayton helped keep the temple records.[153] He thus served as the scribe and recorder for the church's most important documents. According

144. Allen, *No Toil nor Labor Fear*, 7.

145. Ibid., 9.

146. James B. Allen, "William Clayton and the Records of Church History," *Preserving the History of the Latter-day Saints*, ed. Richard E. Turley Jr. and Steven C. Harper (Provo, UT: Religious Studies Center, Brigham Young University; Salt Lake City, UT: Deseret Book, 2010), 85, 107.

147. Allen, *No Toil nor Labor Fear*, 1.

148. Allen, "William Clayton and the Records of Church History," 85.

149. Nauvoo City Council Minute Book, 9 September 1842, 101, Church History Library. Clayton also served as secretary of Nauvoo's Freemasonry lodge. Nauvoo Masonic Lodge Minute Book, 10 November 1842, Church History Library.

150. William Clayton, "History of the Nauvoo Temple," 1845, 31, Church History Library.

151. Council of Fifty, "Record," 10 March 1844, in *JSP*-A1:39, also 2–14.

152. William Clayton, Daily Account of Joseph Smith's Activities, 14–22 June 1844, Appendix 2 in *JSP*-J3.

153. Allen, "William Clayton and the Records of Church History," 101–2.

to Allen, Clayton "thought of these [church papers], including his journals, as sacred records that would help preserve for all time the workings and activities of the kingdom of God."[154] In early 1845, apostles Brigham Young and Heber Kimball gave Clayton a blessing, telling him that "he should be a scribe for this church in the resurrection."[155]

While carrying out his duties, Clayton often worked closely with Smith. As Allen explained: "Beginning in early 1842, William Clayton found himself involved in nearly every important activity of Nauvoo, but especially the private concerns of Joseph Smith.... until Joseph's death in 1844, they were in each other's company almost daily."[156] Over time, they became very close friends. In October 1842 Smith sent Clayton a brief note in which he referred to himself and Clayton as David and Jonathan, evoking the devoted friendship of the ages as portrayed in the chronicles of ancient Israel.[157] Clayton was fiercely loyal to Smith.[158] When Smith was in hiding, Clayton was one of the small circle of trusted friends who knew his location and visited him often.[159]

Clayton's Nauvoo journal, in three volumes, covers the period of November 1842 to January 1846. Because Clayton was so close to Smith, his journal contains valuable information about the things Smith said and did. It includes detailed information on Smith's leadership as church president, including his revelations and teachings; his financial operations as the church's sole trustee-in-trust, including his handling of church and personal debts; his confidential councils with other church leaders, including matters of church discipline; his legal difficulties, including his evasions from officers of the law; and aspects of his family life, including several polygamous marriages and the resulting anguish these unions caused Emma Smith (his first and only publicly recognized wife).[160]

Church leaders trusted the information in Clayton's journal enough to convert several of its entries, which describe Smith in third-person narrative, into

154. Ibid., 90.

155. Ibid., 85.

156. Allen, *No Toil nor Labor Fear*, 73. Benjamin F. Johnson, another friend of Joseph Smith's, reminisced decades later that in the spring of 1843, when the Kinderhook episode took place, Clayton "always acompanied" Smith. Benjamin F. Johnson to George F. Gibbs, circa 1903, in *I Knew the Prophets: An Analysis of the Letter of Benjamin F. Johnson to George F. Gibbs, Reporting Doctrinal Views of Joseph Smith and Brigham Young*, ed. Dean R. Zimmerman (Bountiful, UT: Horizon Publishers, 1976), 43.

157. Joseph Smith to William Clayton, 7 October 1842, International Society Daughters of Utah Pioneers Pioneer Memorial Museum, Salt Lake City, UT (accessible in the Documents series of the online edition of *The Joseph Smith Papers*). On the friendship, love, and covenant between David and Jonathan, see 1 Samuel 18:1–4; 2 Samuel 1:26.

158. Allen, "William Clayton and the Records of Church History," 109–11.

159. See Smith, Journal, 11–16 August 1842, in *JSP*-J2:83–96.

160. Allen, "William Clayton and the Records of Church History," 92–98.

entries in the "History of Joseph Smith," which are rendered in first-person narrative as if written by Smith himself.[161] They also utilized Clayton's journal notes of Smith's sermons. This includes the reports in Clayton's journal of the instructions Smith gave on 2 April and 16–17 May 1843—just before and after the Kinderhook plates episode—now canonized in Mormon scripture as Sections 130 and 131 of the Doctrine and Covenants. Clayton also served as the scribe for Smith's lengthy, detailed, and consequential revelation on the doctrines of polygamy, eternal marriage, and exaltation—now canonized as Section 132 of the Doctrine and Covenants.[162] Modern historians also consider Clayton as one of the most accurate and important sources on Nauvoo history generally and on Joseph Smith in particular. Allen wrote that Clayton "delighted in the specific and the concrete, which helps account for his success as a scribe and a clerk. . . . as a diarist and historian he described what he saw around him, usually with skill and great descriptive power but seldom with any interpretive imagination."[163]

Clayton's journal keeping, however, has been brought into question in the special case of the Kinderhook plates. Stanley B. Kimball, in his article on the Kinderhook plates, stated that it was uncertain "whether or not he [Clayton] was present when Joseph Smith saw the plates."[164] And therefore, Kimball adds: "Where the ideas written by William Clayton originated is unknown."[165] Even James B. Allen—who has emphasized Clayton's meticulous, methodical, skillful, specific, concrete, and even unimaginative "descriptive power"—has followed Kimball's argument: "It must be noted," Allen writes, "that in his diary Clayton did not quote Joseph directly—he only reported what he thought was happening. Whether Joseph actually told Clayton that he had translated the plates, or whether Clayton was simply reporting what he heard from a variety of sources, is not clear. The latter appears to be the case, especially when one realizes that Clayton's account contains several inaccuracies."[166] The "several inaccuracies" alleged by Allen, following Kimball, refer to perceived discrepancies

161. Jessee, "The Writing of Joseph Smith's History," 439–73.

162. Revelation, 12 July 1843 (accessible in the Documents series of the online edition of *The Joseph Smith Papers*).

163. Allen, *No Toil nor Labor Fear*, 62. James B. Allen was also an editor of the journal Clayton kept in England before emigrating to Illinois, see William Clayton, *Manchester Mormons: The Journal of William Clayton, 1840 to 1842*, ed. James B. Allen and Thomas G. Alexander (Santa Barbara, CA, and Salt Lake City, UT: Peregrine Smith, 1974), i. See also George D. Smith, "Introduction," in William Clayton, *An Intimate Chronicle: The Journals of William Clayton*, ed. George D. Smith (Salt Lake City, UT: Signature Books, in association with Smith Research Associates, 1991), xxii–xxiii.

164. Kimball, "Kinderhook Plates Brought to Joseph Smith Appear to Be a Nineteenth-Century Hoax," 71.

165. Ibid., 67.

166. Allen, "William Clayton and the Records of Church History," 96.

between what Clayton and others wrote about the Kinderhook plates (analyzed below). In order to assess Kimball's arguments, it is best to begin by placing Clayton's comments regarding the Kinderhook plates into the context of the full journal entry and its recorded events of the day. These details were not investigated in Kimball's analysis. In fairness to Kimball, the full journal entry may not have been made available to him. The complete entry is published here for the first time (both in photographic facsimile and diplomatic transcript).

Source

William Clayton's journal entry for 1 May 1843 regarding the Kinderhook plates, is in his "Journal No 1" on pages [8]–[9]. As seen in Figure 17.4, Clayton placed one of the plates on one of the pages of his small journal and traced its outline, after which he wrote his journal entry around the tracing.

> May 1st. A.M at the Temple—at 10—m J to L. W. P.M at prest. Josephs—he is gone out with Woodworth he borrowed £20—of Wm. Allen
>
> I took supper with him.
>
> Prest. paid £20.—to Woodworth for Nauvoo House
>
> I have seen 6 brass plates which were found in Adams County by some persons who were digging in a mound[.] They found a skeleton about 6 feet from the surface of the earth which [end of page [8]] [*traced outline of one of the Kinderhook plates*] was 9 foot high[.] The plates were on the breast of the skeleton—This diagram shows the size of the plates being drawn on the edge of one of them. They are covered with ancient characters of language containing from 30 to 40 on each side of the plates. Prest. J. has translated a portion and says they contain the history of the person with whom they were found & he was a descendant of Ham through the loins of Pharaoh king of Egypt, and that he received his kingdom from the ruler of heaven & earth[.][167]

The journal entry shows that Clayton spent time that day with Smith, that he spent time at Smith's residence, and that he saw and handled the Kinderhook plates while there. According to Clayton, Smith had "translated a portion" of the plates and told him about the content of the translation.

167. William Clayton, Journal, 1 May 1843. See also Alex D. Smith, "The Book of the Law of the Lord," *Journal of Mormon History* 38, no. 4 (Fall 2012): 131–63.

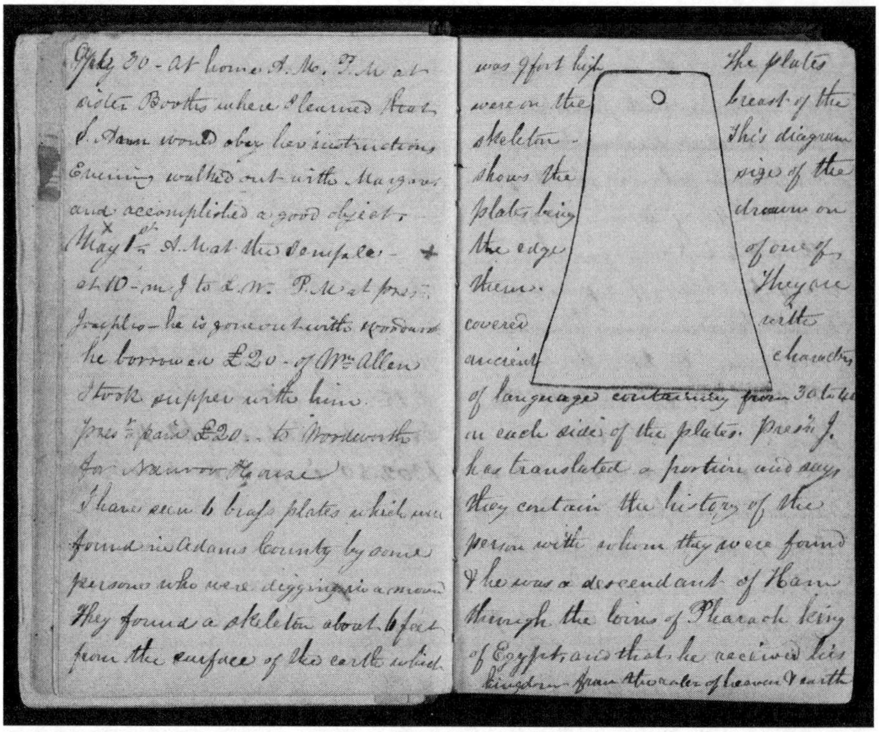

FIGURE 17.4. William Clayton journal entry for 1 May 1843. William Clayton saw and handled the Kinderhook plates in Joseph Smith's home on 1 May 1843. He traced the outline of one of the plates in his journal and wrote his journal entry for the day around the tracing. Church History Library, Salt Lake City.

Source Criticism and Analysis

Clayton began his entry with the note "A.M at the Temple." His small brick office near the building site for the temple was where he fulfilled his office of temple recorder. It was there that he kept a record of the donations to the temple in the Book of the Law of the Lord.[168]

Next, Clayton wrote "at 10—m J to L. W." Alex D. Smith, one of the editors of Clayton's Nauvoo journal, has noted that Clayton, in his journal, usually referred to Joseph Smith, the church's president, as "Prest. J." or even just "J."[169] Clayton's abbreviated note "at 10—m J to L. W." should most likely be expanded as "at 10 [AM]—[I] m[arried] J[oseph Smith] to L[ucy] W[alker]." Later in

168. Alex D. Smith and Andrew H. Hedges, "Joseph Smith's Nauvoo Journals," in *Foundational Texts of Mormonism: Examining Major Early Sources*, ed. Mark Ashurst-McGee, Robin Scott Jensen, and Sharalyn D. Howcroft (New York and Oxford: Oxford University Press, 2018), 248–49.

169. Ibid., 258.

life, Lucy Walker made several statements regarding her marriage to Joseph Smith as one of his polygamous wives and their 1 May 1843 wedding solemnized by William Clayton.[170] Clayton also made a statement to this effect.[171] Furthermore, both Walker and Clayton specified that the wedding took place in Smith's home.[172] Thus, on the morning of 1 May, Clayton was with Smith in Smith's home.

Clayton's next subentry for the day was "P.M at pres^t. Josephs—he is gone out with Woodworth he borrowed £20—of W^m. Allen." There were several early church members surnamed Woodworth.[173] One possibility is that this was Flora Woodworth. Clayton later attested that Joseph Smith married Flora Woodworth about 1843.[174] However, "Woodworth" may also be a reference to her father, Lucien Woodworth, the architect of the Nauvoo House.[175] Two weeks earlier, Smith had instructed the Quorum of the Twelve Apostles to direct Woodworth to resume the construction of the Nauvoo House.[176] Smith may have been out with Woodworth at the construction site or elsewhere discussing the building's construction or funding.[177] Clayton's journal entry for the next day, 2 May 1843, notes that he received "$50 of H.C. Kimball for [the] Nauvoo House & paid it to Woodworth" and also that "Joseph rode out to day with Flora W."[178] That Smith rode out with Flora Woodworth on 2 May suggests the possibility that when Smith was "gone out with Woodworth" on 1 May he had gone out for a ride with Flora. On the other hand, in Clayton's 2 May entry he referred to Flora Woodworth as "Flora W." and referred to Lucien Woodworth as "Woodworth," suggesting the possibility that when Smith was "gone out with Woodworth" he was out with Lucien. In either case, Clayton was minding Smith's home and still minding Smith's business.

170. See Lucy W[alker] [Smith] Kimball, Affidavit (copied signature), 9 August 1869, copied at an unknown date, Andrew Jenson Collection, 25, Church History Library; Lucy W[alker] [Smith] Kimball, Statement, undated, printed in Andrew Jenson, "Plural Marriage," *Historical Record*, May 1887, 229–30. See also "Proxy Wife: Lucy Walker (Smith Kimball)," in *In Sacred Loneliness: The Plural Wives of Joseph Smith*, ed. Todd Compton (Salt Lake City, UT: Signature Books, 2001), 463–65.

171. William Clayton, Affidavit, 16 February 1874, published in Andrew Jenson, "Plural Marriage," 225.

172. Lucy Walker Kimball Smith, "A Brief Biographical Sketch of the Life and Labors of Lucy Walker Kimball Smith," undated, 12, Church History Library; Clayton, Affidavit, 225.

173. Susan Ward Easton Black, comp., *Membership of the Church of Jesus Christ of Latter-day Saints from 1830 to 1848* (Provo, UT: Religious Studies Center, Brigham Young University, 1984–1988), 47:563–71.

174. William Clayton, Affidavit, 16 February 1874, Affidavits about Celestial Marriage, Church History Library. See also Compton, *In Sacred Loneliness*, 389–91.

175. Alex D. Smith, "Symbol of Mormonism: The Nauvoo Boarding House," *John Whitmer Historical Association Journal* 35, no. 2 (Fall/Winter 2015): 118–20.

176. Smith, Journal, 19 April 1843, in *JSP*-J2:365.

177. See Smith, Journal, 1 May 1843, in *JSP*-J3:8n12.

178. Clayton, Journal, 2 May 1843.

After Smith returned home and the two shared supper, Clayton noted the same and added that "Pres[t.] paid £20.—to Woodworth for Nauvoo House." This second mention of "Woodworth" certainly refers to Lucien Woodworth and suggests that the first mention does as well. Apparently, Clayton knew that Smith was going out to meet with Woodworth earlier in the day, with £20 he had borrowed from William Allen to give to Woodworth, and that when Smith returned, he informed Clayton that he had paid the £20 borrowed of Allen to Woodworth. This may have been discussed over the supper they shared.

Clayton then wrote concerning the Kinderhook plates—a subject that may also have been discussed over supper. Clayton's statement that he had "seen 6 brass plates" affirms that Smith was in possession of the full set of plates. The tracing Clayton made in his journal demonstrates that he not only saw the plates but personally handled at least one of them. The tracing further affirms that he saw and handled the plates at Smith's home because Smith had them there over several days. Brigham Young, president of the church's Quorum of the Twelve Apostles,[179] handled the Kinderhook plates two days later and like Clayton made a tracing of one of the plates in his journal. Inside of the tracing, Young wrote that he made it "at Joseph Smith's," as can be seen in Figure 17.5. On 7 May 1843, Smith would be "visited by several gentlemen"—presumably at his home—and would examine the Kinderhook plates with them (as analyzed below). Thus, it is quite clear that when Clayton saw and handled the plates it was in Smith's home.

In writing about what he heard regarding the circumstances of their "discovery," Clayton stated that the plates had been "found in Adams County," whereas they had actually been disinterred near Kinderhook, in Pike County. Based on this factual error, Stanley B. Kimball questioned the accuracy of what Clayton wrote about Smith's translation.[180] Though Clayton's location of the site of disinterment was inaccurate, it makes some sense that Clayton would have associated the Kinderhook plates with Adams, the county between Hancock (including Nauvoo) and Pike (including Kinderhook). The seat of Adams County was Quincy, an important river town in western Illinois.[181]

179. Heber C. Kimball, Clitheroe, England, to Vilate Kimball, Commerce, IL, 2 May 1840, 1, Church History Library.

180. Kimball, "Kinderhook Plates Brought to Joseph Smith Appear to Be a Nineteenth-Century Hoax," 73.

181. Saul B. Cohen, ed., *The Columbia Gazetteer of North America* (New York: Columbia University Press, 2000), 831; *Illinois: A Descriptive and Historical Guide*, compiled and written by the Federal Writers' Project of the Work Projects Administration for the State of Illinois, American Guide Series (Chicago: A. C. McClurg, 1939), 580–82.

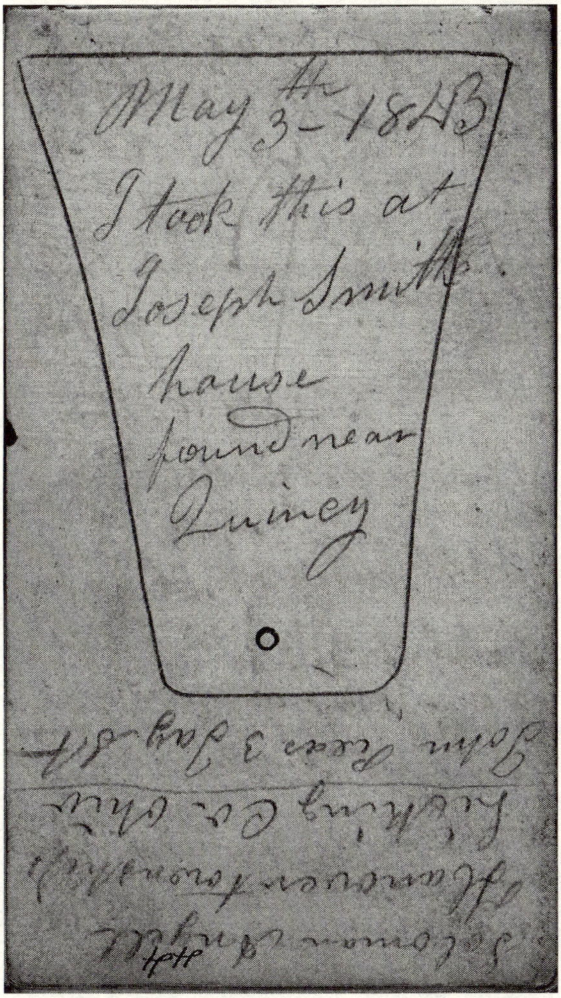

FIGURE 17.5. Brigham Young journal entry for 3 May 1843. Brigham Young, president of the Quorum of the Twelve Apostles, saw and handled the Kinderhook plates in Joseph Smith's home on 3 May 1843. He traced the outline of one of the plates in his journal. Church History Library, Salt Lake City.

Quincy was about fifty miles downriver from Nauvoo, in the southern half of Adams County, and Kinderhook was a much smaller town that was located just a few miles beyond the southern border of Adams into Pike.[182] The plates had been originally shown to Joseph Smith by Joshua Moore, who was apparently boarding in Quincy. While in Nauvoo, Moore also showed the plates to Charlotte Haven, who wrote that "they were recently found, *he said*, in a

182. See U.S. Department of State, "Aggregate Amount of Each Description of Persons within the District of Illinois," in *Sixth Census or Enumeration of the Inhabitants of the United States as Corrected at the Department of State in 1840* (Washington, D.C.: Blair and Rives, 1841), 376–77; J. D. B. DeBow, Superintendent of the United States Census, "Population of States, Counties, Etc.," in *The Seventh Census of the United States: 1850* (Washington, D.C.: Robert Armstrong, 1853), cxxvii.

mound *a few miles below Quincy*."[183] If Moore indeed told Haven that the plates were found a few miles below Quincy, he most likely said the same thing to Smith, understandably locating the find in terms of Quincy—a much larger municipality and a better known geographical reference point.

When Smith visited with others about the Kinderhook plates, he likely passed on information he received from Moore, including where the plates had been found and the location of the discovery with reference to Quincy. As seen in Figure 17.5, when Brigham Young observed the plates at Joseph Smith's home on 3 May—two days after William Clayton had seen them there—he wrote that the plates had been "found near Quincy."[184] Apostle Willard Richards, who was keeping Smith's journal at the time, would write in Smith's journal entry for 7 May 1843 that the plates were "dug out of a mound near quncy [Quincy]."[185] Thus apostles Young and Richards both wrote that the plates were found "near Quincy" while examining the plates at Smith's home, which seemingly points to Smith as the common source of their information. Smith probably told Clayton the same thing, which would explain why Clayton located the discovery of the plates in Adams County (instead of Pike County). In terms of what Clayton wrote about Smith translating from the plates, the precise location of their discovery is not really the relevant issue, but rather *what Smith had communicated to Clayton*. That Clayton's error in locating the site of disinterment likely came from Smith actually *increases* the compelling force of what he wrote about Smith having "translated a portion" of the plates.

Finally, Clayton wrote that "Pres$^{t.}$ J. . . . *says* they contain the history of the person with whom they were found."[186] While it is *possible*, as Kimball and others maintain, that Clayton did not hear this directly from Smith, it seems nearly certain that he did. In other entries, Clayton names those with whom he interacted.[187] While Smith is mentioned repeatedly in the journal entry for 1 May, no one else in Smith's household is. Clayton could not have heard this information from Emma Smith as she was on a trip to St. Louis (which is why he was able to marry Joseph Smith to Lucy Walker in the Smith home).[188]

183. Haven to "My dear home friends," 630 (emphasis added).

184. Young, Journal, 3 May 1843.

185. Smith, Journal, 7 May 1843, in *JSP*-J3:13. When this journal entry was utilized in the text of Smith's history, it was revised to "dug out near Kinderhook." Smith, History, vol. D-1, 1547.

186. Emphasis added.

187. For example, a few days earlier Clayton "took supper at President Joseph's with B. Young." Clayton, Journal, 25 April 1843.

188. Emma Smith returned from St. Louis to Nauvoo the next day. Smith, Journal, 2 May 1843, in *JSP*-J3:8; Clayton, Journal, 2 May 1843.

Historical Implications

Clayton's journal entry—including his tracing of one of the plates—shows that Clayton was with Smith on 1 May in Smith's home, personally saw all of the plates there, handled at least one of the plates, and had his pocket-sized journal with him. When the things Clayton wrote about the Kinderhook plates are placed within the full context of the entire journal entry, it can be seen that his ideas about the Kinderhook plates almost certainly originated directly from Joseph Smith. Furthermore, given Clayton's meticulous and unimaginative clerical habits, his entry about Smith's translation and the things Smith said are likely accurate.

As noted above, toward the end of the month a Philadelphia newspaper included a brief notice stating that Smith had examined the Kinderhook plates, had pronounced them "of Egyptian origin," and had "translated a portion of the figures or characters on them." As suggested, this information may have come from Joshua Moore. The only connection, however, is that Moore was from Philadelphia. Whoever provided this information used the identical words found in Clayton's journal—"translated a portion." It is highly unlikely, however, that this information came from Clayton. It is possible that the identical use of this short phrase was mere coincidence. Alternatively, if the identical language in the two sources was not mere coincidence, it may be that the language was being echoed from a common source (and that the common source was Joseph Smith).

Martha Bradley-Evans, in her biography of Smith during his Nauvoo years, states that what Clayton wrote "leaves unanswered what [he] meant when he said Joseph 'translated' the plates or, more fundamentally, what he understood by the word 'translation.'"[189] However, there are further historical sources that shed light on what Clayton meant by his use of the word. Three of these sources were produced on the same day, Sunday, 7 May 1843.

7 May 1843 According to Willard Richards

The distance from Quincy to Nauvoo is was approximately fifty miles, whether overland or up the river.[190] It is doubtful, therefore, that the 3 May 1843 issue of the *Quincy Whig* would have reached Nauvoo before 4 or even 5 May. It likely

189. Bradley-Evans, *Glorious in Persecution*, 422n23.

190. Measured in Google Earth using the path function available in the Ruler tool (https://www.google.com/earth/). See also Letter from Heber C. Kimball, 9 July 1840, in *JSP*-D7:317.

arrived on 5 or 6 May. The story reported in the paper, with its concluding claim that the plates were "now . . . in Nauvoo, subject to the inspection of the Mormon Prophet," may have been what led a group of men to visit Smith at his home on the morning of Sunday, 7 May 1843. He and this group of visitors examined the Kinderhook plates together. Three sources dated 7 May 1843 corroborate each other and, in some respects, corroborate Clayton's journal entry from a few days earlier. A close examination of these sources confirms that Smith did indeed attempt to translate from the Kinderhook plates and that he did so by traditional linguistic methods.

The first of these three sources from 7 May 1843 is Joseph Smith's own journal, which was kept for him at the time by Willard Richards, his private secretary. Richards, age thirty-eight, had been baptized into the church in 1836 and ordained a member of the Quorum of the Twelve Apostles in 1840.[191] In 1841, he was appointed as the recorder for the Nauvoo temple and "the Scribe for the private office of the President."[192] In December 1842, a few months prior to the Kinderhook plates episode, Smith appointed Richards to be his "private se[c]retary & historian."[193] One of his primary duties was to keep Smith's journal. By this point in his life, Smith was no longer writing entries in his journal or even dictating them to scribes.[194] The entries for Smith's final Nauvoo journal are almost entirely based on the observations of Richards, acting as Smith's private secretary and historian.[195] Moreover, Smith apparently exercised very little supervision over the journal-keeping endeavor. As explained by historians Alex D. Smith and Andrew H. Hedges, experts on Smith's Nauvoo journals, he seems to have left Richards "virtually autonomous in deciding what to include."[196]

Source

As explained above, Joseph Smith's journal entry for 7 May 1843 is in the handwriting of Willard Richards, who likely decided what to write for that day. The full entry is reproduced here both in photographic facsimile (Figure 17.6) and diplomatic transcript:

191. "History of Willard Richards," *Deseret News*, 23 June 1858, 73; Willard Richards, Journal, November 1837–May 1838, 1; Richards, Journal, 14 April 1840.

192. Smith, Journal, 13 December 1841, in *JSP*-J2:11.

193. Smith, Journal, 21 December 1842, in *JSP*-J2:191.

194. Historical Introduction to Journal, December 1842–June 1844, in *JSP*-J2:186.

195. Historical Introduction to Journal, December 1842–June 1844, in *JSP*-J2:186–88.

196. Smith and Hedges, "Joseph Smith's Nauvoo Journals," 233. Smith and Hedges were the primary historical editors for the Nauvoo journals of Joseph Smith in the Journals series of *The Joseph Smith Papers* (*JSP*-J2; *JSP*-J3).

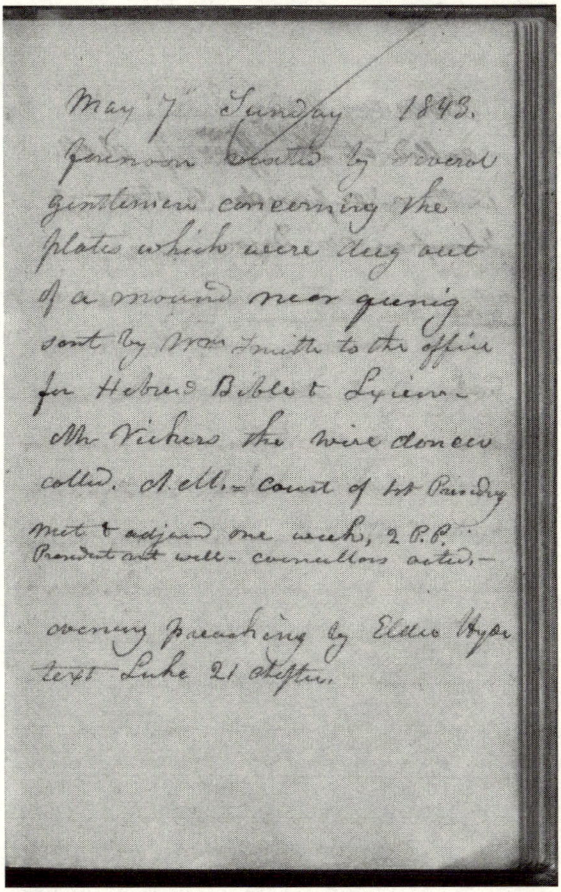
May 7 Sunday 1843.
forenoon visited by several
gentlemen concerning the
plates which were dug out
of a mound near quncy
sent by Wm Smith to the office
for Hebrew Bible & Lexicon—
Mr Vickers the wire dancer
called. A.M.—court of 1st Presidncy
met & adjond one week, 2 P.P.
President not well— councellors acted.—
evening preaching by Elder Hyde
text Luke 21 chapter.

FIGURE 17.6. Joseph Smith journal entry for 7 May 1843. Joseph Smith had his journal kept by apostle Willard Richards, who served as Smith's private secretary. Richards wrote the entry for 7 May 1843 in Smith's journal, noting that Smith was visited by several gentlemen about the Kinderhook plates. Church History Library, Salt Lake City.

> May 7[th] Sunday 1843.
>
> forenoon visited by several gentlemen concerning the plates which were dug out of a mound near quncy [Quincy] sent by W$^{\underline{m}}$ Smith to the office for Hebrew Bible & Lexicon—
>
> Mr Vickers the wire dancer called. A.M.—court of 1st Preside[n]cy met & adjond [adjourned] one week, 2 P.P. [p.m.] President not well—councellors [counselors] acted.—
>
> evening preaching by Elder [Orson] Hyde text Luke 21 chapter.[197]

In this entry, "the plates which were dug out of a mound near quncy [Quincy]" is a fairly obvious reference to the Kinderhook plates.

197. Transcript based on Smith, Journal, 7 May 1843, in *JSP*-J3:13, with format adapted based on image of original (accessible in the Journals series of the online edition of *The Joseph Smith Papers*).

Source Criticism and Analysis

The paragraph on the Kinderhook plates—set off by Richards with slight indention—follows immediately after the dateline. This paragraph is essentially composed of two sentences, each with an implied subject. As Richards was keeping this journal for and on behalf of Smith, the implied subject in the entries is usually Smith. Therefore, it was presumably Smith who was visited by the gentlemen concerning the plates. In the manuscript for the "History of Joseph Smith" that was serially published in church newspapers, the sentence was expanded: "In the forenoon I was visited by several Gentlemen, concerning the plates, which were dug out near Kinderhook"[198]—affirming that Smith was the implied subject and that the plates found "near Quincy" were the Kinderhook plates. Presumably the meeting had not been previously arranged by Smith, but rather he was "visited by" the men who came to discuss the plates with him.

The group of "several gentlemen" may have included church members, as William Smith and Willard Richards were apparently present during the visit. These two, however, may have already been with Smith when he received a visit from the "gentlemen."[199] In England, this English word's homeland, the word *gentleman* most precisely referred to a man holding "a middle rank between the nobility and yeomanry." Webster's early American dictionary explained that in the United States, where there were no noblemen, the term was "applied to men of education and of good breeding."[200] This was especially so with those who had received a classical education, including some training in Latin and Greek—an association that gave rise to the common compound "gentleman-scholar."[201] Richards, in the journal he was keeping for Smith, generally referred to men who were church members by their priesthood offices or as "Brethren."[202] Conversely, the terms "gentlemen" and "gentleman" were

198. Smith, History, vol. D-1, 1547. See also "History of Joseph Smith," *Deseret News*, 17 September 1856, 1.

199. Four weeks earlier, on Sunday, 9 April 1843, Richards had also "called at Joseph[']s." Richards, Journal, 9 April 1843.

200. Noah Webster, *An American Dictionary of the English Language* (New York: Harper & Brothers, 1845), s.v. "gentleman." See also R. S. Jameson, *A Dictionary of the English Language* [...] (London: W. Pickering, 1828), s.v. "gentleman"; and *Oxford English Dictionary* (Oxford and New York: Oxford University Press, online edition), s.v. "gentleman."

201. *Oxford English Dictionary*, s.v. "gentleman."

202. For contemporaneous examples of "brethren" and "brother" (or abbreviated forms thereof), see Smith, Journal, 16, 18, 19, 30 April 1843, 15, 17, 19, 20, 21 May, in *JSP*-J2:358, 363, 368–69, 374, *JSP*-J3:17, 18, 18, 19, 20.

usually used in Smith's journal and other Smith documents to refer to nonmembers and mainly for nonmembers possessed of gentility, education, and a profession. Richards applied the term especially to non-Mormon attorneys, who belonged to the legal profession and would have had some Latin.[203]

In the second sentence—"sent by W$^{\underline{m}}$ Smith to the office for Hebrew Bible & Lexicon"—the implied subject is much less clear. This sentence was dropped in the manuscript for the "History of Joseph Smith," so the text was never expanded or reconstructed by those more familiar with Smith's life. The expanded version of the first sentence—"I was visited by several Gentlemen"—suggests that the second sentence should be expanded in a similar manner: "[I was] sent by Wm Smith to the office for Hebrew Bible & Lexicon." However, it is difficult to imagine that Joseph Smith, in his own home, was "sent by" his younger brother William Smith to fetch the books. Moreover, given Joseph Smith's preeminence in the community as their prophet and church president, and as their mayor and the general of their city militia, it is difficult to imagine Smith being "sent by" anyone other than perhaps his mother, to whom he showed parental deference. But there is no indication of his mother being present.[204] Retaining Smith as the implied subject, perhaps the sentence should be expanded as "[I] sent . . . for [my] Hebrew Bible & Lexicon [to be retrieved by my younger brother]."

More likely, Richards had shifted into his own first-person narration of the event. In this case, the sentence would be expanded as "[I, Willard Richards, was] sent by W[illia]m Smith to the office for [a] Hebrew Bible & Lexicon." Both Willard Richards and William Smith belonged to the Quorum of the Twelve Apostles. Richards was a few years older than Smith,[205] but Smith held seniority over Richards according to tenure within the quorum. Smith had been a charter member of the quorum, ordained in 1835.[206] Richards was ordained half a

203. Richards used the term "gentleman" in Smith's journals to refer to attorneys Josiah Lamborn and Jesse Thomas. Smith, Journal, 4 January 1843, in *JSP*-J2:222–23; Smith, Journal, 27 May 1844, in *JSP*-J3:264. See also Smith, Journal, 1 January 1843, in *JSP*-J2:206; Richards, Journal, 25 June 1844, in *JSP*-J3:310. Smith and his associates occasionally used the term "gentleman" when referring to church members as well. However, this was usually in the context of their interactions with government officials and other eminent nonmembers, as with a letter of introduction. See letters of introduction that Smith wrote for apostles Orson Pratt and Orson Hyde. Authorization for Orson Pratt, 12 March 1844; Authorization for Orson Hyde, 30 March 1844 (both available in the Documents series of the online edition of *The Joseph Smith Papers*).

204. Lucy Mack Smith was living in a separate home at the time. Haven to "My dear Mother," 623.

205. At the time, Willard Richards was thirty-eight and William Smith was thirty-two. "History of Willard Richards," *Deseret News*, 23 June 1858, 73; Joseph Smith, History, 1834–1836, in *JSP*-H1:31.

206. Minutes, Discourse, and Blessings, 14–15 February 1835, in *JSP*-D4:219–34. Smith had been temporarily suspended from the quorum in early May 1839 (Minutes, 4–5 May 1839, in *JSP*-D6:446), but the suspension was lifted later that month (Wilford Woodruff, Journal, 25 May 1839, Church History Library).

decade later, in 1840.[207] Both before and after the Kinderhook plates episode, documents listing the members of the quorum name William Smith ahead of Richards.[208] It made some sense to send Willard Richards, Joseph Smith's private secretary who worked near Smith in his store, to obtain the Hebrew books from Smith's office in the store. William Smith apparently felt he could send Willard Richards to do so, and Richards apparently obliged him.

These Hebrew books were allegedly sent for in connection with the visit regarding the Kinderhook plates, the subject in the previous and only other sentence of the same paragraph. In 1835, when Michael Chandler had shown Joseph Smith the Egyptian papyri he was selling, Smith compared the characters on the papyri with characters copied from the gold plates. Thus, when given the opportunity to inspect the Kinderhook plates, it might be expected that Smith would compare their characters with other ancient scripts available to him: the "reformed Egyptian" characters from the gold plates, Egyptian characters from the papyri, or Hebrew characters found in materials he used to study Hebrew. According to Charlotte Haven, when the plates were first brought to Joseph Smith by Joshua Moore, Smith "said that the figures or writing on them was similar to that in which the Book of Mormon was written," which was known as "reformed Egyptian." Clayton wrote that Smith said the Kinderhook plates contained the history of a descendant of "Pharaoh king of Egypt"—again associating the plates with Egypt. As noted above, it was believed that the characters on both the gold plates of the Book of Mormon and the papyri of the Book of Abraham were primarily Egyptian scripts but also associated with Hebrew. The association of the Kinderhook characters with Egyptian script would thus suggest the propriety of consulting Hebrew script as well. Also, as noted above, Smith had earlier conceived of his study of Hebrew as a kind of gateway to attaining "a knowledge of all languages." Hebrew was widely considered one of the most ancient of languages, and some philologists considered it a surviving remnant of the original human tongue.[209] A comparison of the Kinderhook characters with Hebrew characters might thus prove profitable.

The edition of Smith's journal published by the *Joseph Smith Papers* annotates this passage, noting that the "Hebrew Bible & Lexicon" were possibly the

207. Richards was ordained 14 April 1840. Woodruff, Journal, 14 April 1840, Church History Library; see also Heber C. Kimball to Vilate Kimball 2 May 1840, 1.

208. See "Notice," 11 May 1842, in *Times and Seasons*, 15 June 1842, 830; "October Conference Minutes," 7 October 1844, in *Times and Seasons*, 1 November 1844, 692.

209. Richard Lyman Bushman, "Joseph Smith and the Study of Antiquity," in *Approaching Antiquity*, 13–19. See also Grey, "Approaching Egyptian Papyri through Biblical Language," 396–98 herein.

"books purchased in New York by Oliver Cowdery in November 1835."[210] The entry for 20 November 1835 in Smith's journal notes that "President [Oliver] Cowdery returned from New York, bringing with him a quantity of Hebrew book's for the benefit of the school, he presented me with a Hebrew bible, lexicon & Grammar."[211] Here, for this passage of Smith's journal, the *Joseph Smith Papers* supplies annotation providing plausible identifications for the books:

> The Hebrew Bible referred to here is probably Augustus Hahn, ed., *Biblia Hebraica*, 2nd ed. (Leipzig: Caroli Tauchnitz, 1833). The copy housed at the Community of Christ Library-Archives has an "FWC" endorsement inside the back cover, indicating that it was the property of F. G. Williams & Co. That repository also has evidence that this copy was previously in the possession of JS's descendants. The grammar is probably Moses Stuart, *A Grammar of the Hebrew Language*, 5th ed. (Andover, MA: Gould and Newman, 1835), as JS owned this manual. His copy is housed in the Community of Christ Library-Archives. The lexicon is probably Josiah M. Gibbs, *A Manual Hebrew and English Lexicon Including the Biblical Chaldee. Designed Particularly for Beginners*, 2nd ed. (New Haven, CT: Hezekiah Howe, 1832). The copy owned by the Community of Christ Library-Archives has a binding that matches the Stuart grammar and an "FWC" endorsement inside the back cover.[212]

Based on content in the Book of Abraham and in Smith's sermons, Hebraist Matthew J. Grey argues that Smith also owned one or both of the English translations of the Hebrew-to-German lexicon by eminent Hebraist Wilhelm Gesenius.[213]

These linguistic resources included reference tools for potential use in translating. Smith's Hebrew Bible concludes with an index, where words in Hebrew are referenced to the Old Testament.[214] His Hebrew grammar begins with a table of the "Ancient Hebrew Alphabet," followed by comparative columns for Arabic, Syriac, and Samarian alphabets and by "Remarks on the Alphabet." The main body of the grammar that follows includes sections on vowels and consonants, diacritical points and various other marks, word

210. Smith, Journal, 7 May 1843, in *JSP*-J3:13n29.
211. Smith, Journal, 20 November 1835, in *JSP*-J1:107.
212. Smith, Journal, 20 November 1835, in *JSP*-J1:107n159.
213. Grey, "Approaching Egyptian Papyri through Biblical Language," 426–27, 439, 440, 441n201 herein.
214. Augustus Hahn, ed., *Biblia Hebraica*, 2nd ed. (Leipzig: Caroli Tauchnitz, 1833).

structure, parts of speech, syntax, orthography, and "Rules for Reading Hebrew."[215] The Gibbs lexicon is an ordinary lexicon, with Hebrew words in Hebrew script followed by definitions in English.[216] The Gesenius lexicon is also an ordinary lexicon.[217] Smith's Hebrew books thus included several reference tools that might be used in attempting a scholarly translation.

Historical Implications

That one of the apostles was dispatched to obtain a Hebrew Bible and lexicon suggests that the group wanted to compare the characters on the Kinderhook plates with Hebrew characters. This in turn suggests that Smith and the others were taking a traditional linguistic approach to translation. Richards did not write anything further about the visiting gentlemen, possibly because he had been sent to fetch the books. Alex D. Smith and Andrew H. Hedges observe that Smith's activities are often "more thoroughly illuminated in other people's journals than they are in his own."[218] In this case, Smith's activities are more thoroughly illuminated in letters that were written the same day by Parley Pratt and Sylvester Emmons.

7 MAY 1843 ACCORDING TO PARLEY PRATT

The second of the three sources from 7 May 1843 is a letter written by Parley Parker Pratt, a member of the Quorum of the Twelve Apostles, who may have also been among the group of men who discussed the Kinderhook plates that morning, along with fellow apostles William Smith and Willard Richards. Pratt, age thirty-six, had been baptized into the church in 1830 and ordained an apostle in 1835.[219] He wrote on 7 May 1843 to a cousin, John Van Cott, reporting the discovery of the plates and their arrival in Nauvoo.

215. Moses Stuart, *A Grammar of the Hebrew Language*, 5th ed. (Andover, MA: Gould and Newman, 1835).

216. Josiah W. Gibbs, *A Manual Hebrew and English Lexicon including the Biblical Chaldee* (New Haven: Hezekiah Howe, 1832).

217. Wilhelm Gesenius, *Hebrew and English Lexicon of the Old Testament including the Biblical Chaldee*, trans. Josiah W. Gibbs (Andover, MA: Flagg and Gould, 1824); Wilhelm Gesenius, *A Hebrew and English Lexicon of the Old Testament, including the Biblical Chaldee*, trans. Edward Robinson (Boston: Crocker and Brewster, 1836).

218. Smith and Hedges, "Joseph Smith's Nauvoo Journals," 265.

219. Parley Parker Pratt, *The Autobiography of Parley Parker Pratt* [...], ed. Parley P. Pratt [Jr.] (New York: Russell Brothers, 1874), 17, 43, 127; Minutes and Blessings, 21 February 1835, in *JSP*-D4:239–42.

Source

Parley Pratt began his letter to John Van Cott by conveying recent news and reporting on the health and well-being of his own family. Pratt then apparently responded to questions about the church that Van Cott had posed in a previous letter. He closed his communication by encouraging his cousin to come to Nauvoo and join with the Saints in building the city and its temple—the main thrust of the letter. Parley Pratt's younger brother Orson Pratt followed with a short missive of his own, sort of a postscript added on the second leaf of Parley Pratt's bifolium letter. The information on the Kinderhook plates was among the Nauvoo news in the beginning of the letter:

> I have no further news except that six plates having the appearance of Brass have lately been dug out of a mound by a gentleman in Pike Co. Illinois, they are small and filled with engravings in Egyptian language and contain the genealogy of one of the ancient Jaredites back to Ham the son of Noah his bones were found in the same vase (made of Cement) part of the bones had crumbled to dust & the other part were part preserved the bones were 15 ft. under ground. The gentlemen who found them were unconnected with this church but have brought them to Joseph Smith for examination & translation a large number of Citizens here have seen them and compared the characters with those on the Egyptian papyrus which is now in this city. I have no time for particulars but you will hear more soon on this subject.[220]

Pratt emphasized to Van Cott, who had not yet joined the Church of Jesus Christ of Latter-day Saints, that the men who unearthed the plates "were unconnected with this church." He was hoping that the verified discovery of plates like the gold plates would help convert his cousin.

Source Criticism and Analysis

By his own admission, Pratt had written a "short and imperfect communication."[221] Most importantly, he did not give the source of his information about

220. Parley Parker Pratt, Nauvoo, IL, to John Van Cott, Canaan, NY, 7 May 1843, Church History Library. For an annotated transcript, see Hauglid, "'Come & Help Build the Temple & City,'" 155.

221. Hauglid, "'Come & Help Build the Temple & City,'" 155.

the Kinderhook plates. If Pratt obtained this information from the morning visit at Smith's home, the letter is especially significant for its contemporaneity. It was completed before the afternoon had turned to evening, as is evident from Pratt's closing: "It is sunday [Sunday] afternoon & my house has been several times filled & emtied [emptied] of old acquaintance and others who call to see us, & it is now full again and what with how do ye dos, goodbys, & shaking hands & conversation, I have made but a blundering business & must now close."[222] Pratt made no mention of the morning visit at Joseph Smith's home, and his mention of several rounds of social visiting in his own home suggest the possibility that he had been there all day. At the same time, Pratt's aside regarding his various visitors manifests the appropriateness, and even popularity, of Sunday visiting among the Saints in Nauvoo. Perhaps Pratt had made one or more visits of his own, as had William Smith, Willard Richards, Mr. Vickers, and the "several gentlemen" who had called on Smith in the morning. Furthermore, Pratt's earlier comment about the Kinderhook plates—that "a large number of Citizens here have seen them and compared the characters with those on the Egyptian papyrus which is now in this city"—may be a reference to the morning visit at Smith's home. His choice of the word "Citizens," as opposed to "brethren," may connote the gentile component of the gentlemen visitors.

Pratt's statement that several citizens had compared the characters on the plates "with those on the Egyptian papyrus" is interesting in terms of Charlotte Haven's report that Joseph Smith had said "that the figures or writing on them was similar to that in which the Book of Mormon was written." The Book of Mormon, according to the text, was written in "reformed Egyptian," so this would naturally suggest the propriety of also comparing the Kinderhook characters to the Egyptian characters of the papyri. As Pratt wrote, "I have no time for particulars[,] but you will hear more soon on this subject."[223] This implies that Pratt had more information that he *could* have shared—possibly from his presence with Joseph Smith and his fellow apostles that morning when Smith was visited by the group of gentlemen.

Stanley B. Kimball discounted what was written about the Kinderhook plates by both William Clayton and Parley Pratt by pitting the two against each other:

> It seems, then, that there was considerable talk about the plates in Nauvoo—and apparently as much misinformation and hearsay was current

222. Ibid., 156.
223. Ibid., 155.

> among people as there was fact. Pratt heard of a discovery in Pike County, Clayton said Adams County. Clayton said that the find was made six feet underground; Pratt, fifteen. Elder Pratt spoke of a cement vase—an item mentioned in no other account. Clayton mentioned a skeleton nine feet tall—also unmentioned in any other account. Clayton said that the plates gave a history of an Egyptian; Pratt mentioned a Jaredite.[224]

This drawing of contrasts allowed Kimball to conclude that what both had written was based on "hearsay" and "speculation."[225]

Kimball's argument has been uncritically adopted by many, and even overstated. James B. Allen writes:

> William Clayton's account is not consistent with a similar account by Parley P. Pratt, which was also probably obtained by hearsay rather than from the Prophet himself. There is no evidence of any direct statement by Joseph Smith about the authenticity of the plates and no evidence that he ever attempted a translation. As historian Stanley B. Kimball has demonstrated, all kinds of stories about the plates were circulating, but Joseph Smith did not get involved with the plates at all.[226]

Aside from strong evidence in Clayton's journal that Smith *did* attempt a translation, most of Kimball's inconsistencies break down or become largely irrelevant upon closer scrutiny.

Kimball's first comparison, that "Pratt heard of a discovery in Pike County, Clayton said Adams County," is easily explained by historical developments. As mentioned earlier, the story had come to Joseph Smith from Joshua Moore of Quincy, who apparently told him that the plates had been found near Quincy (which is in Adams County). However, the article published in the 3 May 1843 issue of the *Quincy Whig*, which would have easily reached Nauvoo by 7 May 1843, explicitly stated that the plates had been discovered in Pike County near Kinderhook.[227] Thus Pratt likely had access to this updated information.

Kimball's second comparison, that "Clayton said that the find was made six feet underground; Pratt, fifteen," also has to do with the story of discovery.

224. Kimball, "Kinderhook Plates Brought to Joseph Smith Appear to Be a Nineteenth-Century Hoax," 73.

225. Ibid.

226. Allen, "William Clayton and the Records of Church History," 97.

227. "Singular Discovery," 2.

According to the report in the *Quincy Whig*, the bones and plates were found after "penetrating the mound *about* 11 feet."[228] Wilburn Fugate later remembered that Wiley had "dug to the depth of *about* eight feet" before planting the plates.[229] The use of the word "about" in both the *Whig* article and Fugate's letter indicates that the precise measurement was relatively insignificant.

Kimball also drew out unique details in each account. First, "Elder Pratt spoke of a cement vase—an item mentioned in no other account." While no other account mentions a cement vase, Fugate wrote that Wiley had dug down to a "flat rock," and that "under this rock was *dome-like* in appearance, about three feet in *diameter*."[230] This rounded cavity described decades later by Fugate may have been the same configuration that Pratt described as a cement vase. Second, "Clayton mentioned a skeleton nine feet tall—also unmentioned in any other account." As shown in the next section of this chapter, a skeleton of about the same height actually *is* mentioned in another account—a recently discovered source of which Kimball was unaware. Even so, all of these comparisons concern the unearthing of the plates. Neither Smith, nor Clayton, nor Pratt was present for the occasion.

The real issue is not what Smith had heard from others but what others had heard from him—especially whether Smith told others he had translated from the plates and anything he had to say about the translation. The only really significant contrast that Kimball draws is thus the final one: "Clayton said that the plates gave a history of an Egyptian; Pratt mentioned a Jaredite." However, Clayton never actually called the individual in question an "Egyptian." Rather, he wrote that the man was "a descendant of Ham through the loins of Pharaoh, king of Egypt." Similarly, Pratt wrote that the plates contained "the genealogy of one of the ancient Jaredites back to Ham the son of Noah." Pratt therefore actually *corroborates* Clayton on the most essential detail of the translation content, that the person with whom the plates were buried had been identified as a descendant of Ham.

The Book of Abraham, which was published about a year earlier, narrates that "the land of Egypt" was first discovered and settled by a daughter of Ham named Egyptus. One of her sons, named Pharaoh, became the first king (pharaoh) of Egypt.[231] The Book of Abraham also teaches that Egyptus and Pharaoh

228. Ibid (emphasis added). More precisely, after digging down about eleven feet they dug through an additional two feet of rock and then found the plates.

229. Fugate to Cobb, 208 (emphasis added).

230. Ibid.

231. BoA, in *JSP*-R4:310–11 [Abraham 1:21–25].

were the founders of Egypt and that "from this descent sprang all the Egyptians."[232] That Pratt said the plates were written "in Egyptian language" suggests that they were written by someone who was an Egyptian or of Egyptian descent and therefore a descendant of Pharaoh and Egyptus, the founders of Egypt. Therefore, Pratt probably held that the person in question was not only a descendant of Ham, but of Pharaoh as well. Pratt's "Jaredite" is thus about as Egyptian as was Clayton's "descendant . . . of Pharaoh, king of Egypt." The real difference is that for Pratt, the individual was also a Jaredite, associated with the people in the Book of Mormon whom God had brought to the Americas after the confusion of tongues at the Tower of Babel.[233]

Historical Implications

Upon closer consideration, it can be seen that there is not as much contradiction between Clayton's journal entry and Pratt's letter as Kimball portrayed. The information Pratt provided in his letter actually corroborates, more than it contradicts, what Clayton had written in his journal a few days earlier. Together, these sources aver that the plates were inscribed in Egyptian, that the inscriptions gave a history or genealogy of the person with whom they were buried, and that the person was a descendant of Ham through Pharaoh. Pratt closed his description of the Kinderhook plates by stating that he had "no time for particulars but you will hear more soon on this subject." Further particulars on this subject are found in another letter that was written the same day.

7 MAY 1843 ACCORDING TO SYLVESTER EMMONS

The third of the three sources from 7 May 1843 is a letter that was apparently written by one of the group of gentlemen visitors. With a little tongue in cheek, this correspondent wrote from Nauvoo to the editor of the *New York Herald* under the pseudonym "A Gentile." A possibility that must be considered is that this letter was written by a Mormon correspondent surreptitiously claiming "Gentile" status in order to receive a more sympathetic hearing from the *Herald's* non-Mormon editor and his readership. There is at least one case in which a contemporary Latter-day Saint wrote to the "Gentile" press posing as a non-Mormon. In early March of 1843, about two months before the 7 May

232. BoA, in *JSP*-R4:310–11 [Abraham 1:23–26].
233. Title Page; Omni 1:22; Mosiah 28:17; Ether 1:1–6, 33–43.

visit, Willard Richards began writing a series of letters from Nauvoo to the *Boston Daily Bee*. Richards signed all these letters with the pseudonym "Viator," Latin for traveler, and presented himself as a non-Mormon traveler who visited Nauvoo to observe the Saints and their prophet.[234]

In contrast, "A Gentile" was just who he claimed to be. The author was Nauvoo non-Mormon Sylvester Emmons. Earlier, before moving to Nauvoo, Emmons had studied law in Philadelphia,[235] and somewhere along the way had served as not only an attorney but a judge.[236] Emmons had moved to Illinois in 1840, eager to take advantage of prospects for advancement in the young and rapidly growing state.[237] He had not yet married; in December 1842, when Charlotte Haven (in her early or mid-twenties) met Emmons (in his mid-thirties), she described him as "a forlorn bachelor."[238]

In January 1843, the ambitious attorney considered running for mayor. However, before declaring his candidacy, he wrote to Joseph Smith of his intentions and asked whether Smith planned to run for reelection. If Smith were planning to run for mayor, Emmons pledged his support. Conversely, if Smith had no such plans, Emmons requested Smith's support for a mayoral campaign of his own. Emmons assured the Mormon prophet that he was bound to the citizens of Nauvoo with "the strongest ties of friendship and love," though "still not in Church communion."[239] No further correspondence on the matter is extant, but the two men may well have communicated—either by letter or in person—prior to the election. Smith did run for mayor and was elected on 6 February, presumably with the Gentile attorney's pledged support. And Emmons, although not in the church, was elected to the Nauvoo city council the same day, perhaps with Smith's support.[240] A few days later, he was appointed to two standing committees in the city council, including the Committee of

234. See Smith, Journal, 6 and 17 March 1843, in *JSP*-J2:297, 312, see also 297–298n571 and 312n644.

235. John W. Savage, *Illustrated Atlas Map of Cass County, Illinois* (n.p.: W. R. Brink, 1874), 40; William Henry Perrin, ed., *History of Cass County, Illinois* (Chicago: O. L. Baskin, 1882), 239.

236. Emmons was frequently referred to as "Judge Emmons" in Nauvoo documents. Nauvoo City Council Rough Minute Book, February–December 1841, 1 November 1841, 33; Nauvoo City Council Rough Minute Book, January–November 1842, 1 January 1842, 5; Transcript of Proceedings, 10 March 1842, City of Nauvoo v. Davis for Slander of JS, Nauvoo, IL, Records, 3; docket entries for circa 29 November 1842 and circa 4 February 1843, in Nauvoo Municipal Court, docket book, 9, 18 (all held at Church History Library and all accessed at www.josephsmithpapers.org). See also Smith, History, vol. D-1, 31 May 1843, 1566 (accessible in the Histories series of the online edition of *The Joseph Smith Papers*). Charlotte Haven referred to him throughout her letters to friends and family as "the Judge." "A Girl's Letters from Nauvoo."

237. Savage, *Illustrated Atlas Map of Cass County, Illinois*, 40; Perrin, *History of Cass County, Illinois*, 239.

238. Haven, letter, 618. At the time, Emmons was thirty-five years old. Perrin, *History of Cass County, Illinois*, 239.

239. Letter from Sylvester Emmons, 29 January 1843, accessed at www.josephsmithpapers.org.

240. "City Election," *The Wasp* (Nauvoo, IL), 8 February 1843, 2.

Municipal Laws.[241] Emmons had become a prominent non-Mormon gentleman of Nauvoo. He continued serving on the city council until mid-June of 1844, when his relationship with Smith took a turn for the worse.[242]

Earlier that month, Emmons served as the newspaper editor for the one and only issue of the infamous *Nauvoo Expositor*, which exposed Smith's still secretive practice of polygamy and denounced some of his recent teachings, especially his doctrine of a plurality of gods.[243] Several years later, when Emmons recounted how he had become the editor of the *Expositor*, he revealed his identity as the *Herald*'s Nauvoo correspondent: "None of us knew anything about journalism [but] I had written a few letters that were published in the *New York Herald*, so in organizing the forces, I was elected as editor."[244] A search through the issues of the *Herald* for 1838–1846 turns up only one unnamed Nauvoo correspondent—the pseudonymous author of five letters written between 5 September 1842 and 3 July 1843. All five letters were written in the same style and about many of the same topics of interest. All five were signed with precisely the same pseudonym: "A Gentile."[245] Sylvester Emmons was not only a "Gentile" living among the Saints of Nauvoo, but "A Gentile"—the person who wrote about the Kinderhook plates on 7 May 1843.[246]

His friend Charlotte Haven wrote in her letters about several aspects of Mormon social custom. For instance, she had written the previous year of hearing "it is etiquette for new comers [to Nauvoo] to make the first call on old residents." She soon learned that Emma Smith "wished to become acquainted" and had been expecting Haven to "honor her with a call." Sylvester Emmons, who called frequently on Haven, "volunteered to accompany and introduce"

241. Nauvoo City Council Minute Book, 11 February 1843, in *The Nauvoo City and High Council Minutes*, ed. John S. Dinger (Salt Lake City: Signature Books, 2011), 156–57.

242. Sylvester Emmons, Oath of Office as City Councilor, Nauvoo, Illinois, 11 February 1843, Nauvoo, IL, Records, 1841–1845, Church History Library; City Council of the City of Nauvoo, "A Record of the Proceedings of the City Council of the City of Nauvoo Handcock [Hancock] County, State of Illinois, Commencing A.D. 1841," February 1841–February 1845, 11 February 1843, 160, 11 June 1844, 212, and 21 June 1844, 212; City Council Proceedings, Minutes (rough book), 11 May 1844, 14, and 11 June 1844, 31, 32, Nauvoo Records 1841–1845; Sylvester Emmons, Letter of Resignation as City Councilor, received 21 June 1844, Nauvoo, IL, Records, 1841–1845, Church History Library.

243. Perrin, *History of Cass County, Illinois*, 239; *Nauvoo Expositor* (Nauvoo, IL), 7 June 1844.

244. Sylvester Emmons, "Nauvoo in 1843–4," *Carthage Republican*, 14 May 1875, 2.

245. "A Gentile" to James Gordon Bennett, 5 September 1842, transcribed in "Late and Important from Nauvoo," *New York Herald*, 25 September 1842, 2; "A Gentile" to Bennett, 22 October 1842, transcribed in "Nauvoo," *New York Herald*, 5 November 1842, 1; "A Gentile" to Bennett, 6 March 1843, transcribed in "Nauvoo," *New York Herald* 23 April 1843, 2; "A Gentile" to Bennett, 7 May 1843, published in "Late and Interesting from the Mormon Empire on the Upper Mississippi," *New York Herald*, 30 May 1843, 2; "A Gentile" to Bennett, 3 July 1843, transcribed in "Highly Important from Nauvoo," *New York Herald*, 23 July 1843, 2.

246. For a more detailed view of Sylvester Emmons, see the letters cited in the previous footnote.

her to the Smiths.[247] As an attorney and former judge, Emmons would have been familiar with genteel customs generally. As someone who had lived in Nauvoo for almost a year, he would have been somewhat familiar with the customs of the city's Latter-day Saints.[248] And, as a prominent member of the Nauvoo city council, he probably had some idea of how to arrange calling on the city's mayor and his lady. Emmons introduced Haven to the Smiths at their home on or shortly before 19 February 1843.[249]

Emmons apparently called on Joseph Smith again on 7 May 1843. As a member of a learned profession, especially the law, he probably knew some Latin, and may even have had an interest in classical and other ancient languages. As a prominent and professional non-Mormon, he fit well into the group of men that Willard Richards described as "gentlemen" in the 7 May 1843 entry for Joseph Smith's journal.[250]

Source

After a visit with Smith, Emmons wrote to the *New York Herald*. He vaunted Nauvoo's growing population and urban improvements, including the temple; mentioned the recent parade of the Nauvoo Legion, and the esprit de corps on display; urged the investment of eastern capital, which was sure to be rewarding; and included other subjects typical of western boosterism. His letter also included news of the recently discovered Kinderhook plates:

> Another set of plates have been found in Pike county, in this State; they were dug out of a large mound, fifteen feet from the summit, by a company of persons, fifteen in number, who all affirm to the fact of their situation when found. There were six in number, about three inches in length, and two and a half broad at one end, and one inch broad at the other, being something of the form of a bell, about the sixteenth of an inch thick, with a hole in the small end of each, fastened together with a ring, apparantly of iron or steel, but which was so oxidised as to crumble to pieces when handled. The plates are evidently brass, and are

247. Haven to "My dear Mother," 622–23.

248. In his 5 September 1842 letter from Nauvoo, "A Gentile" indicated that he had spent "a residence here of six months," thereby placing his arrival in Nauvoo around March 1842. "A Gentile" to Bennett, 5 September 1842, 2.

249. Haven to "My dear Mother," 623.

250. Regarding another visit with Emmons, see Smith, Journal, 31 May 1843, in *JSP*-J3:28, 28n98; Smith, History, vol. D-1, 31 May 1843, 1566.

> covered on both sides with hyerogliphics. They were brought up and shown to Joseph Smith. He compared them in my presence with his Egyptian alphabet, which he took from the plates from which the Book of Mormon was translated, and they are evidently the same characters. He therefore will be able to decipher them. There can be no doubt but they are a record of some kind, buried with an individual, centuries ago; a skeleton was found with them—some of the bones in such a state of preservation as to show the size of the individual, whose height must have been eight and a half feet. You may expect something very remarkably pretty soon.[251]

Emmons did not state *when* he had seen the plates. While this could have occurred as much as a week earlier, when the plates were brought to Nauvoo, it was most likely that very morning, during the visit Smith received from "several gentlemen."

Source Criticism and Analysis

It seems that Emmons, like everyone else, believed the plates were genuine archaeological artifacts. In writing to the editor (and readers) of the *New York Herald*, Emmons backed up his remarkable report by citing the testimony of the men present during the disinterment: "All affirm to the fact of their situation when found." This suggests that the signed statement that would soon be published in the *Times and Seasons* had already arrived in town,[252] though the issue would not be printed for at least a few more days.[253]

Some of the things written by Emmons, likely based on a morning visit with Smith, suggest that Parley Pratt had been there as well. Emmons, like Pratt, stated that the plates had been found in Pike County (while neither

251. "A Gentile," to [James Gordon] Bennett, 7 May 1843, published in "Late and Interesting from the Mormon Empire on the Upper Mississippi," *New York Herald*, 30 May 1843, 2.

252. One historical wrinkle here is that Emmons mentioned fifteen men in the company who unearthed the plates, all affirming to the events. The statement published in the *Times and Seasons* was only signed by nine men. Certificate signed by Rob't Wiley, G. W. F. Ward, Fayette Grubb, Geo. Deckenson, J. R. Sharp, W. P. Harris, W. Longnecker, Ira S. Curtis, and W. Fugate, published in "Ancient Records," 186.

253. The issue of the *Times and Seasons* dated 1 May 1843, includes a notice dated 8 May 1843, see "Notice," *Times and Seasons*, 1 May 1843, 185. Given the time it took for editing, typesetting, imposing, making margin, locking up the forms, pulling proofs, correcting, making ready, making register, inking, printing, drying, folding, stacking, and distributing, it is unlikely that this issue was available before 9 or even 10 May. On the printing process, see Richard-Gabriel Rummonds, *Nineteenth-Century Printing Practices and the Iron Handpress, with Selected Readings* (New Castle, DE, and London, U.K.: Oak Knoll Press and the British Library, in association with Five Roses Press, 2004).

specifically mentioned the tiny village of Kinderhook). Emmons explained that the plates "were dug out of a large mound, fifteen feet from the summit," while Pratt wrote that "the bones were 15 ft. under ground." Emmons related that the bones were in a partial "state of preservation," while Pratt noted that "part were part preserved." Emmons wrote that the plates were "evidently brass," while Pratt remarked that they had the "appearance of Brass." Emmons described the plates as "covered on both sides with hyerogliphics," while Pratt wrote that they were "filled with engravings in Egyptian language." Emmons stated that they "were brought up and shown to Joseph Smith," while Pratt related that they were "brought . . . to Joseph Smith for examination." Most remarkably, Emmons declared that the characters on the plates were "compared" in his presence with the Egyptian characters in Smith's "Egyptian alphabet," while Pratt held that "a large number of Citizens" in Nauvoo had seen the plates and had "compared the characters with those on the Egyptian papyrus." Both closed the subject anticipating further information: Emmons predicted "you may expect something very remarkably pretty soon," while Pratt promised "you will hear more soon on this subject."

Some of the elements related by Emmons also echo things mentioned by William Clayton. Earlier, Clayton wrote that the plates were found with a skeleton "which was 9 foot high"—an astounding height—while Emmons wrote that "a skeleton was found with them" and that "some of the bones [were] in such a state of preservation as to show the size of the individual, whose height must have been eight and a half feet." In 1834, during the "Camp of Israel" expedition of Mormon men from Ohio to Missouri, some of the men in the camp had dug into an Indian burial mound along the Illinois River (about thirty miles west of Kinderhook) and extracted some bones. Moses Martin, one of the men present, wrote in his diary that the group disinterred "the bones of an extraordinar[il]y large person or human being the thigh bones being 2 inches longer from one socket to the other than of the prophet who is upwards of 6 feete high which would have cons[ti]tuted some 8 or 9 feete high."[254] The human bones found in the mound near Kinderhook were apparently used to make a similar calculation of the person's height. Thus, both Clayton and Emmons had been given to believe that the person buried in the mound had in life stood between eight and nine feet. Emmons was most likely informed of the person's height by the person who had supplied the same information to Clayton, Joseph Smith.

254. Quoted in Kenneth W. Godfrey, "The Zelph Story," *BYU Studies* 29, no. 2 (Spring 1989): 35.

FIGURE 17.7. Joseph Smith's "Egyptian Alphabet" book. In 1835, Joseph Smith and others produced a collection of papers related to the recently purchased Egyptian papyri and the "Book of Abraham" that Smith translated from the papyri. The title page of the pictured volume bears the title "Grammar and A[l]phabet of the Egyptian Language." Running heads on interior pages include a shorter title: "Egyptian Alphabet." At some point in time this short version of the title was added as a label on the spine of the volume. Joseph Smith apparently used this book to translate one of the characters from the Kinderhook plates. Church History Library, Salt Lake City.

According to Emmons, when Smith was examining the plates, he had "his Egyptian alphabet" with him. This "Egyptian alphabet" is apparently the same "Egyptian Alphabet" book that was related to Smith's translation of the Book of Abraham. Emmons, however, wrote that the characters in the "Egyptian alphabet" had been taken from the Book of Mormon plates. Knowing that "A Gentile" really was a "Gentile" has bearing on how the things Emmons wrote should be evaluated. He likely made the mistake of associating the Egyptian Alphabet with the Book of Mormon instead of the Book of Abraham due to the fact that Smith was so much better known for the Book of Mormon. His conflation of the various volumes of Mormon scripture can be easily understood as the simple mistake of an outsider to the faith. What Emmons called Smith's "Egyptian alphabet, which he took from the plates from which the Book of Mormon was translated" was more likely the document titled "Egyptian Alphabet" that included Egyptian characters taken from the Egyptian papyri associated with the Book of Abraham.

As noted above, Smith had displayed a transcript of Book of Mormon characters to Unitarian minister George Moore several months earlier. It is thus plausible that Smith exhibited this transcript again on 7 May, along with the Egyptian Alphabet book, when visitors came to see the Kinderhook plates. In that case, the juxtaposition of Egyptian characters from both the Book of

Mormon and the Book of Abraham could have easily added to this Gentile visitor's confusion over which volume of Mormon scripture the characters in the Egyptian Alphabet had come from.

It was not the first time Smith had used or displayed the Egyptian Alphabet book. In November 1835, shortly after its creation, Smith had "exibited [exhibited] the Alphabet of the ancient records" to a group of visitors.[255] Then, in March 1842, he apparently drew upon the book in composing some of his explanations of the second illustration published along with the Book of Abraham.[256] In November 1843, six months after his encounter with the Kinderhook plates, Smith had the book at his home when William Phelps called on him to borrow it for use in a writing assignment. Two days later, when conversing with Willard Richards and perhaps others in his office, Smith "Suggested the Idea of preparing a grammar of the Egyptian Language."[257] The April–May 1843 Kinderhook plates episode fits within this longer context of interest in and use of the book. In November, when Phelps asked to borrow the book, Smith evidently had it at his home and lent it because Phelps used it in drafting Smith's letter to James Arlington Bennet.[258] Similarly, Smith apparently had the book at his residence on 7 May when he was "visited by several gentlemen."

Emmons made no mention of papyri being used for comparison, as might be expected had any been present. He only mentioned the Egyptian Alphabet. It may be noteworthy that Pratt does not actually mention the papyri itself, but more specifically states that "a large number of Citizens here have seen them [the Kinderhook plates] and compared the characters [on the plates] with those [characters] on the Egyptian papyrus." The *characters* on the papyri existed not only on the papyri but in the documents such as the Egyptian Alphabet book into which they had been copied.

Whether the characters on the plates had ever been *directly* compared with the characters on the papyri, it is quite clear that they were compared with the papyri characters copied in the Egyptian Alphabet book. As Emmons stated, Smith "compared them in my presence." Not only had Smith compared the characters, but they had been compared favorably. Moreover, Emmons himself seems to have accepted the correspondence, reporting that "they are evidently

255. Smith, Journal, 17 November 1835, in *JSP*-J1:105.

256. Hauglid, "'Translating an Alphabet to the Book of Abraham,'" 381–83 and 387 herein.

257. Smith, Journal, 15 November 1843, in *JSP*-J3:130.

258. Joseph Smith to James Arlington Bennet, 13 November 1843 (accessible in the Documents series of the online edition of *The Joseph Smith Papers*). See also *JSP*-J3:128–30n574.

the same characters." Emmons further added: "He therefore will be able to decipher them."

This final comment from Emmons, however, sounds at least slightly suspicious. While Emmons apparently believed that the plates were genuine, it seems unlikely that he would consider Smith's Egyptian Alphabet book a legitimate translation tool. However, the conclusion stated by Emmons does fit within his larger project of Nauvoo boosterism. The discovery of the Kinderhook plates appeared to give credence to the Book of Mormon. More converts to Mormonism meant more immigrants to Nauvoo. And for Emmons, more immigrants to Nauvoo meant more customers for his legal practice.

Historical Implications

Nauvoo non-Mormon Sylvester Emmons was personally present to witness Joseph Smith comparing characters from the Kinderhook plates to characters in the Egyptian Alphabet lexicon, which shows that Smith was openly engaged in this typical method of traditional translation. Furthermore, that one of the apostles was dispatched to retrieve a Hebrew lexicon suggests that Smith and other men examining the plates wanted to compare the characters not only with Egyptian but with Hebrew—languages connected by both the Book of Mormon and the Book of Abraham. This comparison of the inscriptions on the plates with different scripts indicates that the group was taking a pragmatic and traditional linguistic approach to deciphering the plates. While the 7 May 1843 letter of Parley Pratt seems to indicate that Smith had shared with his visitors the content of the translation that he had earlier communicated to Clayton, the 7 May 1843 letter of Sylvester Emmons indicates that Joseph Smith had also shared with his visitors the *method* he had used for the translation.

THE KINDERHOOK PLATES AND THE EGYPTIAN ALPHABET BOOK

That Joseph Smith found matching characters in the Egyptian Alphabet book naturally leads to the question of which characters were found to match. William Clayton's journal entry for 1 May 1843, written a few days earlier, indicates one such character. Clayton wrote that Smith had translated a portion of the plates and had said they contained "the history of the person with whom they were found, and he was a descendant of Ham through the loins of Pharaoh, king of Egypt, and that he received his kingdom from the Ruler of heaven and

TABLE 17.1. Comparison of Joseph Smith's Translation to "Egyptian Alphabet" Character

Clayton on Smith's translation	The character *ho-e-oop-hah* defined
he was *a descendant of* Ham **through the loins of Pharaoh** king of Egypt, and that he *received his kingdom* from the **ruler of heaven & earth**	honor *by birth*, kingly power **by the line of Pharaoh**. possession *by birth* one who *riegns upon his throne* universally— **possessor of heaven and earth**, and of the blessings of the earth

earth." This identification bears remarkable resemblance to one of the character definitions found in the Egyptian Alphabet book. The character named "Ho e oop hah" (hereafter *ho-e-oop-hah*) was given this definition: "honor by birth, kingly power by the line of Pharoah. possession by birth one who riegns [reigns] upon his throne universally—possessor of heaven and earth, and of the blessings of the earth."[259] A careful comparison of this definition with the content of the translation as reported in Clayton's journal reveals their parallel content. Above, in Table 17.1, the parallels are represented with corresponding styles of emphasis: The character in the Egyptian Alphabet book named *ho-e-oop-hah*—with a definition corresponding with the translation content—has the shape of a closed half circle or the outline of a half disk. As seen in Table 17.2, this character bears some resemblance to one of the characters on the Kinderhook plates.

There are also some obvious differences between these two characters. The character on the Kinderhook plates has a basic outline of a half disk but with four additional lines. To assess this configuration in historical context, it must be noted that the Egyptian Alphabet book includes a rule of "grammar" explaining that characters can be "dissected" into parts that have meaningful definitions of their own. In fact, the book *begins* with this linguistic theory, which appears less than three pages before the *ho-e-oop-hah* character is defined.[260] If the extraneous lines are "dissected" from the semi-disk character on the Kinderhook plates it bears a close resemblance to the *ho-e-oop-hah* character in the Egyptian Alphabet book (as seen in Table 17.3).[261]

259. Grammar and Alphabet of the Egyptian Language, circa July–circa November 1835, 4–5, in *JSP*-R4:122–25.

260. Grammar and Alphabet of the Egyptian Language, circa July–circa November 1835, 1–2, in *JSP*-R4:116–19.

261. As explained in connection with the first character on the first page of the Egyptian Alphabet book: "In Translating this chara[c]ter, this subject must be continued until there are as many of these connecting parts of speech used as there are connections or connecting parts found in the character." Grammar and Alphabet of the Egyptian Language, circa July–circa November 1835, 1, in *JSP*-R4:117. The Egyptian Alphabet

TABLE 17.2. Comparison of Characters

Character from Kinderhook plates	Character from "Egyptian Alphabet" book
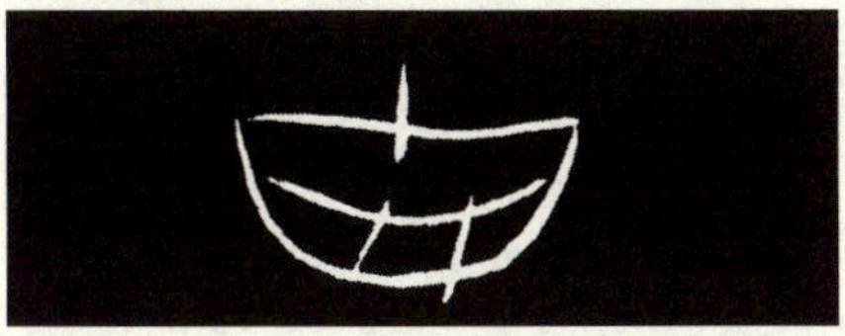	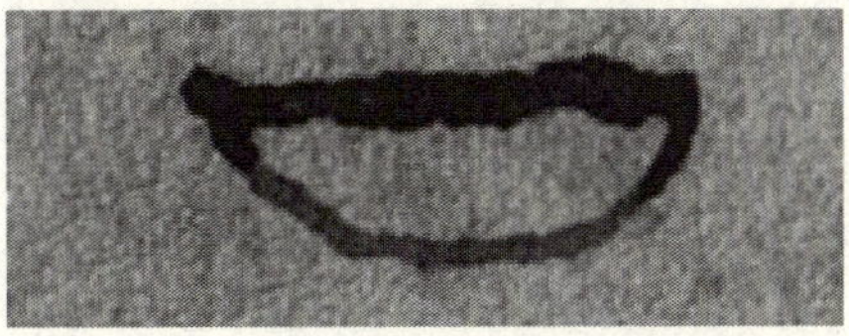

TABLE 17.3. Comparison with Dissected Character

Character from Kinderhook Plates Dissected	Character from "Egyptian Alphabet" book
	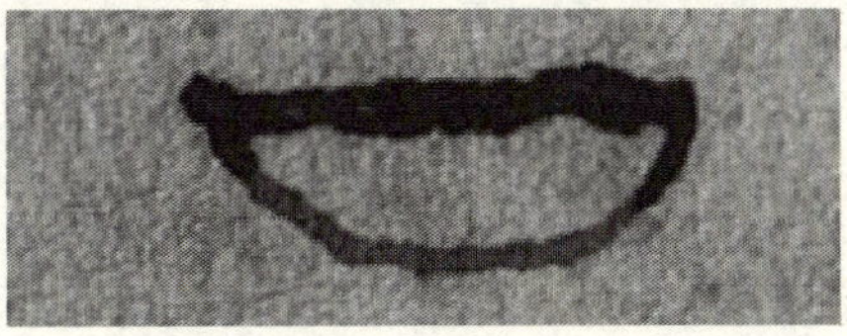

Approaching Translation

On the Kinderhook plates, the semi-disk character is relatively large and prominently placed at the top of one of the plates. The plates had originally been held together by a ring through the holes in the tops of the plates and also by two clasps, possibly maintaining an intended order. However, within moments of the plates being unearthed, the ring and clasps were broken off. While it is doubtful that there had ever been any intentional order among the fraudulent plates, it is more unlikely that any sense of order was maintained after the plates were broken free of the ring and clasps, and it is even more improbable that any sense of order was conveyed to Smith when the plates were presented to him in Nauvoo. Smith could have begun a translation attempt at any character on any side of any plate, but would most likely have attempted to begin at any possibly perceived beginning—as he had with the Book of Mormon and the Book of Abraham.[262]

book provides two examples of characters that are shown "dissected" into their connecting parts. In both cases, the characters are mostly broken down into their individual strokes, bars, and dots, but not entirely so. In both dissections, there are sub-characters consisting of two connecting parts. See character 5.27, in *JSP*-R4:116–119; and character 3.11a, in *JSP*-R4:120–21.

262. On the sense of order regarding the gold plates and the Book of Mormon, see "History of Joseph Smith," *Times and Seasons*, 1 October 1842, 943. On the sense of order regarding the papyri and the Book of

But where, if anywhere, might Smith have perceived the beginning of the inscriptions? Although the plates are covered with meaningless pseudo-characters, there are some possible hints and clues by which an enthusiastic would-be translator might approach the task. First, the plates are oriented by some of their inscriptions. In addition to random characters, the inscriptions include several illustrative figures. The extant plate includes a few faces—each with two eyes and a mouth—as do some of the other plates depicted in the print facsimiles. As seen in Figure 17.1 and Figure 17.3, these facial configurations orient the plates with the smallest side of each plate upward and the opposite end downward. Smith's native language of English and the foreign languages he is known to have studied—German, Latin, Greek, Hebrew, and hieratic Egyptian—all read from top to bottom.[263] From whichever side of whichever plate Smith began attempting to translate, he likely began at the top of the plate.

On the surfaces of the plates, there is a general pattern of inscription design. From the printed facsimiles, it can be seen that on all twelve sides of the six plates the characters and illustrations are divided top from bottom by an inscribed horizontal line—with a generally more illustrative section at the head of the plate (above the line) and characters inscribed on the main body of the plate (below the line). As noted in the description published in the *Quincy Whig*, most plates have "four lines [columns] of characters."[264] Smith's only other experience with buried metal plates inscribed with characters was the gold plates of the Book of Mormon (on which the Kinderhook plates had been conceptually modeled). The Book of Mormon, like the Bible, is a collection of several smaller books. Most of these books within the Book of Mormon have their own headings. The Book of Mormon also has a title page that functions as a heading of sorts for the entire collection. The first words of the title page of the Book of Mormon are the book's title, which also identifies the book's principal author, Mormon. Similarly, in the first sentence of the Book of Abraham, the Father of the Faithful identifies himself as the author of the text. This concept and pattern of introductory text in the Book of Mormon and the Book of Abraham may have influenced Smith to search for introductory script on the

---

Abraham, see Charles M. Larson, *By His Own Hand upon Papyrus: A New Look at the Joseph Smith Papyri*, 2nd ed. (Grand Rapids, MI: Institute for Religious Research, 1992), 49.

263. In fact, inscription from top to bottom is nearly universal among known languages. Jared Diamond, *Guns, Germs, and Steel: The Fates of Human Societies* (New York and London: W. W. Norton, 1997), 218; David Diringer, *The Alphabet: A Key to the History of Mankind* (London: Hutchinson of London, 1968), 1:359, 2:ii.

264. "Singular Discovery," 2.

Kinderhook plates. He may have taken the inscriptions above the lines as headings of some sort—or a place where such a heading might have been placed.

Whereas most of the headings on the plates consist of illustrative figures—most prominently suns with faces—there is some variation within this general pattern. The last facsimile among the printed facsimiles of the broadside has a heading area that is significantly larger than any of the others. Moreover, this heading seems to feature characters rather than illustrative figures. Furthermore, the characters are in larger script than the characters in the main bodies of the plates. The relatively large size of the heading, the character content of the heading, and the relatively large size of the characters make this side of this plate arguably the most distinctive, and perhaps an intuitive place to begin translating.

There are only two characters in this heading—one on top of the other (presumably following the general columnar arrangement of the other characters on the plates). If Smith were to begin translating on this side of this plate, he would presumably commence at the top of the heading with the first character. This is the character on the Kinderhook plates that resembles the semi-disk character in the Egyptian Alphabet book (with a definition paralleling the content of Smith's translation).

If Smith began his translation effort by searching the Egyptian Alphabet book for a character with a shape similar to the character at the top of the largest heading, it would not have taken him long to find a decent match. A semi-disk-shaped character is the twenty-second character listed. It appears on the fourth page of the book.[265]

To summarize, the character named *ho-e-oop-hah* in Smith's Egyptian Alphabet book is similar in shape to a character featured prominently at the top of one of the Kinderhook plates, and the reported content of Smith's translation from the plates can be substantially drawn from that character's definition in the Egyptian Alphabet book. It may be that the "portion" of the Kinderhook plates that Smith translated on or before 1 May 1843 was no more than this single character from the top of one of the plates.

The Translation

This evidence from within the text of the Egyptian Alphabet book, supplying the content of the translation, combined with the other relevant historical

265. The definition of the character runs from the bottom of the fourth page to the top of the fifth page. Grammar and Alphabet of the Egyptian Language, circa July–circa November 1835, 1–5, in *JSP*-R4:116–25.

FIGURE 17.8. Kinderhook plate with larger heading. One of the sides of one of the Kinderhook plates had a heading that was significantly larger than the others and consisted of characters (rather than illustrative figures). The characters are also relatively large in comparison to the characters in the columns below. Compare facsimiles in Figure 17.3. Church History Library, Salt Lake City.

sources—the Clayton and Smith journal entries and the Pratt and Emmons letters—indicates that Smith was attempting to translate the Kinderhook plates through character matching and lexical equivalence. Instead of being a supernatural effort, like his translations of the Book of Mormon and the Book of Abraham, it was apparently a natural effort by ordinary methods of traditional translation.

Though Smith's translation from the Kinderhook plates fell short of what modern professional translators would consider a rigorous method, it was nevertheless considered a translation by those involved at the time. Clayton stated that Smith had "translated" from the plates and Emmons wrote that Smith was able to "decipher" the characters. There is every indication that Smith would have been comfortable with these descriptions of his interpretive efforts.

Furthermore, the sources indicate that Smith replicated his translation technique openly, in the company of a group of church members (William Smith, Willard Richards, and perhaps Pratt and others) and nonmembers (Sylvester Emmons and other "gentlemen"). In contrast, there is no mention in any of the sources close to the event of Joseph Smith using a Urim and Thummim, a seer stone, or divine revelation of any kind. William Clayton, in his earlier journal entry (written closer to the time of Smith's translation), mentioned nothing about any particular kind of revelation or of revelation in general.

Accounts of Charlotte Haven and Sylvester Emmons Compared

The foregoing analysis regarding Smith's use of the Egyptian Alphabet book suggests that Charlotte Haven's account be reconsidered—especially with respect to the account of Sylvester Emmons, the "forlorn bachelor" with whom she spent so much of her time in Nauvoo.[266] As Emmons observed, Smith had found what were considered matching characters in the Egyptian Alphabet book, which included characters copied from the papyri of the Book of Abraham (rather than the characters allegedly copied from the gold plates of the Book of Mormon). Haven may have made the same mistake that Emmons made in associating the compared characters with the Book of Mormon. In Haven's account of seeing the mummies and some of the papyri associated with the Book of Abraham she made no mention of the Book of Abraham and to all appearances was unaware of its translation and publication.[267] She could have easily mistaken things relayed to her by Moore about the Book of Abraham or the Egyptian Alphabet book for the Book of Mormon. It is also possible that she accurately conveyed what she had heard from Moore but that Moore himself had conflated the volumes of Mormon scripture (as would Emmons).

266. In her letters, Haven frequently mentioned Emmons calling on her, spending time as a guest in her home, and escorting her on outings in the city. "A Girl's Letters from Nauvoo."

267. Haven to "My dear Mother," 623–24.

TABLE 17.4. Comparison of Charlotte Haven and Sylvester Emmons

Charlotte Haven	Sylvester Emmons
When he [Joshua Moore] showed them to Joseph [Smith],	He [Joseph Smith] compared them in my presence
the latter said that the figures or writing on them was similar to that in which the Book of Mormon was written,	with his Egyptian alphabet, which he took from the plates from which the Book of Mormon was translated, and they are evidently the same characters.
and if Mr. Moore could leave them, he thought that by the help of revelation he would be able to translate them.	He therefore will be able to decipher them.

The accounts left by Haven and Emmons are actually quite similar in structure, as seen in Table 17.4. The most significant difference is that in Haven's account Smith planned to translate the plates with "the help of revelation." However, the logic of Haven's account jars with Smith's own view of his spiritual gift of translation. In Haven's account, the conjunction "and" apparently serves a causative function, implying that it was *because* of the similarity between the characters from the Kinderhook plates and the gold plates that Smith would be able to translate the Kinderhook characters by revelation. Yet Smith never limited or conditioned his gift of revelatory translation in relation to any source text. He translated the Book of Mormon with instruments that the book itself portrays as capable of translating any origination language to any destination language.

The book's exemplar of seership and translation is the Nephite king Mosiah, who translated a record of the Jaredites into the language of the Nephites. Mosiah was described in the Book of Mormon as "a man that can translate the records; for he has wherewith that he can look, and translate all records that are of ancient date; and it is a gift from God. And the things are called interpreters. . . . And whosoever is commanded to look in them, the same is called seer."[268] Mosiah could translate the recently discovered record of the Jaredites not because he had previously seen Jaredite script or because he thought Jaredite script was comparable to Nephite script, but because he had the "interpreters" and was a "seer." He was therefore able to "translate *all* records"—the only possibly limiting factor being that the records be "of ancient date."[269]

268. Mosiah 8:13.

269. For a consideration of Smith's gift of translation within the Christian tradition of spiritual gifts and early Mormon charismatic practice, see Christopher James Blythe, "'By the Gift and Power of God': Translation among the Gifts of the Spirit," Chapter 2 herein.

Following this logic, perhaps Smith was saying that the characters on the Kinderhook plates were similar to those of the gold plates, apparently of ancient date, and that he would therefore be able to translate them by revelation. But it seems more plausible that Smith had said something to Joshua Moore that was comparable to what was understood by Sylvester Emmons—that based on the similarities between the characters on the plates and the characters in which the Book of Abraham was written (as copied in the Egyptian Alphabet book) the plates could be deciphered (using said book). The Emmons account is not only more compatible with Smith's pneumatology, but more contemporaneous. It evidently constitutes a first-hand account of what Smith had said in Emmons's presence earlier that day, as opposed to Haven's report of what Joshua Moore had told her three days earlier about what Smith had said to him sometime before that.

As stated earlier, Haven recounted that when she visited caretaker Lucy Mack Smith to see the Egyptian mummies and papyri, Smith purportedly read her passages from the papyri "through the inspiration of her son Joseph." The accounts of others to whom Smith showed the mummies and papyri strongly suggest that Smith was actually reading, reciting, or paraphrasing from the Book of Abraham. Just as she was apparently reading revelation into Lucy Mack Smith's sharing of information from the Book of Abraham, Haven may have been reading revelation into Joseph Smith's plans to translate from the Kinderhook plates.

However, it is possible that Haven accurately conveyed what she had heard from Moore. Furthermore, it is possible that Moore had accurately conveyed to Haven what he had heard from Smith. If so, and Smith *had* initially planned to translate the Kinderhook plates by revelation, he apparently changed his mind sometime before 1 May when he conveyed to Clayton the translation content that accords with the content of the *ho-e-oop-hah* definition in the Egyptian Alphabet book and with the translation method of character matching described by Emmons.[270]

One final possibility to consider is that Smith understood his translation from the Kinderhook plates as a mixture of natural study and supernatural revelation. There are precedents for such a possibility in Smith's background. Some of the revisions he made in his New Translation of the Bible (such as the significant expansions of text) were certainly meant to be understood as resulting from revelation, while others (such as slight grammatical changes)

270. Hauglid, "Did Joseph Smith Translate the Kinderhook Plates?," 101.

may well have been considered the result of human reason.[271] In the Book of Abraham, there are a few passages that seem to have been derived from the Egyptian Alphabet book, while the rest of the text was presumably understood as the result of revelation that was attributed to the translation process.[272]

The "Zelph" episode from the 1834 Camp of Israel expedition of Mormon men from Ohio to Missouri offers another comparison. Digging into an Indian burial mound, the men exhumed a skeleton and an arrowhead. Finding the arrowhead near the skeleton's spine, they adduced that it was the head of the arrow that had killed him in battle. Comparing the length of the skeleton's femur to the length of Smith's upper leg, the men calculated the deceased person's height (the same or similar process as that used to calculate the height of the person buried with the Kinderhook plates). Later that day, Smith claimed to have a vision regarding the man and revealed that his name was Zelph, a "white Lamanite" warrior who had served under a Nephite prophet named Onandagus.[273] The interpretation of the skeleton and arrowhead was thus a mixture of reasoning and revelation.

However, if Smith had translated the Kinderhook plates through a mixture of natural and supernatural methods, it might then be expected that he would have *named* the deceased with whom the plates were found. While the definition in the Egyptian Alphabet book for the *ho-e-oop-hah* character provided some identification for the person whose remains were disrupted at Kinderhook—identifying him as a royal descendant of Pharaoh—it did not provide him with a personal name. Unlike Smith's translation of the gold plates of the Book of Mormon, there was no associated name given like Mormon or Moroni. Unlike his translation from the rolls of Egyptian papyri, there was no Abraham or Joseph. Unlike his interpretation of the bones dug from the mound on the Illinois River, no Zelph or Onandagus. Instead, there was only an adjusted version of the *ho-e-oop-hah* definition. All of the evidence having to do with Smith's actual engagement with the plates points only to an attempt at natural linguistic translation based on character matching from Egyptian (and perhaps Hebrew) characters and a consideration of lexical equivalents—done openly among both Mormons and non-Mormons.

271. Matthews, *"A Plainer Translation,"* 252–53. Some of the changes followed the relatively minor textual revisions put forward in the well-known Bible commentary by Methodist theologian Adam Clarke. Wayment and Wilson-Lemmon, "A Recovered Resource," Chapter 11 herein.

272. Smith, "The Dependence of Abraham 1:1–3 on the Egyptian Alphabet and Grammar," 38–54; Hauglid, "'Translating an Alphabet to the Book of Abraham,'" 376–87 herein.

273. Godfrey, "The Zelph Story."

Smith's Use of the Egyptian Alphabet Book

Whereas Joseph Smith's open use of the Egyptian Alphabet book indicates that he saw himself acting in this case as a linguist, not a prophet, his possession and use of the book has implications for how his relationship with the book should be understood. Many, if not most, Mormon scholars have been skeptical about Smith's involvement in the production of the curious Egyptian Alphabet documents, which do not reflect modern Egyptological understanding.[274] Some have outright dismissed the relevance of these documents in understanding Smith's translation of the Book of Abraham.[275]

Samuel Brown, in an article on the relationship between Joseph Smith and William Phelps, argues that while Smith had been interested and involved in the production of the Egyptian Alphabet documents in 1835, he had then laid them aside, only to have Phelps revive them when Smith assigned Phelps to write a letter for him in November 1843. Brown writes: "Phelps appears to have made use of the Kirtland Egyptian Papers fairly autonomously in 1843, bringing the documents back to Smith's attention after a long hiatus. . . . Smith does not seem to have been concerned with the Egyptian Grammar documents until Phelps came calling with his letter to James Arlington Bennet in hand."[276]

However, Smith's autonomous use of the Egyptian Alphabet book six months earlier in the translation of the Kinderhook plates shows that he considered it a legitimate translation tool. Perhaps it was Smith who brought the document back to Phelps's attention. Smith's reliance on the book to translate a portion of the Kinderhook plates thus calls for a reconsideration of Smith's relationship with this and the other Egyptian study documents.

FURTHER CONSIDERATIONS

There are at least two questions that merit further consideration. One is whether Smith considered the translated "portion" as a sort of preliminary translation to identify the author or basic content of the text on the plates. Another is whether Smith ever pursued any further translation after 7 May 1843.

274. Muhlestein, "Assessing the Joseph Smith Papyri," 34.

275. See John Gee, *An Introduction to the Book of Abraham* (Provo, UT: Religious Studies Center, Brigham Young University; Salt Lake City, UT: Deseret Book Company, 2017), 32–39.

276. Samuel Brown, "The Translator and the Ghostwriter: Joseph Smith and W. W. Phelps," *Journal of Mormon History* 34, no. 1 (Winter 2008): esp. 59–62. In a sequel article, Brown provides insightful analysis of the alphabet texts with implications for understanding Smith's religious sensibilities. Samuel Brown, "Joseph [Smith] in Egypt: Babel, Hieroglyphs, and the Pure Language of Eden," *Church History* 78, no. 1 (March 2009): 26–65.

The Translated Portion as a Preliminary Identification

When Smith acquired the Egyptian papyri in 1835, he conducted a preliminary translation, identifying Abraham and Joseph as the authors of the two papyrus rolls. Similarly, the translated portion of the Kinderhook plates to which Clayton referred may have been intended as a preliminary translation effort to determine who had authored the record inscribed on the plates or the general nature of the record's content (or both). Alternatively, a preliminary translation may not have been Smith's original intent, but the random results of having found the *ho-e-oop-hah* definition as a translation may have satisfied Smith in terms of providing an effective identification that would suffice for the time being.

In their comments concerning the content of the translation, both Clayton and Pratt focused on the authorship of the plates and the general nature of the contents, as if the "portion" that Smith had translated were really more of a preliminary identification. Also, the comment by Sylvester Emmons, that with the result of successful character matching Smith would "therefore . . . be able to decipher them" sounds as if the real decipherment, or translation, had not yet begun. Similarly, the author of the article on the Kinderhook plates in the *Times and Seasons*—likely John Taylor—claimed that the plates would soon be returned to Smith "for translation," again suggesting that the process of translation had not yet begun.

Finally, for whatever it is worth, Wilburn Fugate later wrote that when the plates were returned to Kinderhook he and Robert Wiley were given to understand that Smith had not translated them: "He would not agree to translate them until they were sent to the Antiquarian society at Philadelphia[,] France, and England. they were sent and the answer was that there were no such Hyeroglyphics known and if there ever had been. they had long since passed away. Then Smith began his translation."[277] Thus Fugate also seems to have understood that Smith had not yet begun a formal translation.

The Possibility and Prospects of Further Translation

It is possible, however, that Smith performed some translation beyond the preliminary identification. Emmons wrote that Smith had found matching "characters" (plural)—implying that more than a single match was found. Perhaps Smith had conducted some further translation sometime between 1 May,

277. Fugate to Cobb, 8 April 1878, 3–4.

when he spoke with Clayton about the content that can be derived from a single character, and 7 May, when he demonstrated matching characters to his visitors. The June 1843 broadside, declaring that the translation would be published as soon as it was completed, seemed to imply that Smith had begun a translation. However, in contrast to Smith's previous translation projects, there were no appointed scribes, no records of translation work, and no translation manuscripts.

Smith had appointed scribes for his previous translation projects. When Smith was translating the Book of Mormon, he was assisted by Martin Harris, Emma Smith, Oliver Cowdery, and others.[278] When Smith was working on his New Translation of the Bible, he was assisted by Oliver Cowdery, John Whitmer, Sidney Rigdon, Frederick Williams, and others.[279] When Smith was working on the Book of Abraham, he was assisted by Frederick Williams, Warren Parrish, William Phelps, Willard Richards, and others.[280] In contrast, there is no indication of Smith appointing Richards or Clayton or Phelps, or any other member of his 1843–1844 clerical staff, or anyone else to serve as a scribe for the translation of the Kinderhook plates.

Smith's journal, when being kept, included entries that recorded the production of previous translation projects. Because Smith did not begin keeping a journal until 1832, there are no journal entries regarding his 1828–1829 translation of the Book of Mormon.[281] Though Smith's 1832–1834 journal is very spotty, it includes an entry recording his work on the New Translation of the Bible.[282] The translation of the Book of Abraham, which was conducted in part during periods when Smith's journal was being kept daily, accordingly appears in several journal entries.[283] The most successful run of journal keeping in Smith's entire life was between late 1842 and mid-1844 when Richards managed to keep a daily record of Smith's activities.[284] Yet there is no record of any translating sessions for the Kinderhook plates.[285]

278. See *JSP*-R3 and *JSP*-R5.

279. See "Time Sequence of the New Translation," in Joseph Smith, *Joseph Smith's New Translation of the Bible: Original Manuscripts*, ed. Scott H. Faulring, Kent P. Jackson, and Robert J. Matthews (Provo, UT: Religious Studies Center, Brigham Young University, 2004), 55–59.

280. *JSP*-R4:191–293.

281. While it is possible that Smith had kept a journal earlier, his first extant journal is to all appearances his first. *JSP*-J1:xliii, 4–9.

282. Smith, Journal, 5 December 1832, in *JSP*-J1:11.

283. Smith, Journal, 7 October, 19, 20, 24, 25 November 1835, in *JSP*-J1:71, 107, 109–10; 8–9 March 1842, in *JSP*-J2:42.

284. "Joseph Smith's Journals," in *JSP*-J1:xlv–xlvi.

285. See Hauglid, "Did Joseph Smith Translate the Kinderhook Plates?," 92–103.

Finally, Smith's previous translation projects have known manuscripts. While Smith's initial work on the Book of Mormon was lost or stolen and most of the remaining translation manuscript was destroyed by water damage, all of this material is attested in historical sources and some has survived.[286] All of Smith's translation papers for his New Translation of the Bible have apparently survived.[287] Though it is evident that not all of Smith's translation manuscripts for the Book of Abraham have survived, several have.[288] In contrast, there are no extant translation manuscripts for the Kinderhook plates and no historical indications of any such documents. Ed Decker and Dave Hunt, former Latter-day Saints, wrote in their exposé of Mormonism that Smith's full translation of the Kinderhook plates was "probably locked in the Church archives in Salt Lake City"[289]—a suspicion that was more reasonable in the twentieth century.

It is highly doubtful that a translation manuscript of any length ever existed, despite the manifest anticipation, dating all the way back to the breaking news story published in the *Quincy Whig*. The article in the *Whig* ran under the title "Singular Discovery—Material for Another Mormon Book." When John Taylor ran the Kinderhook plates story in the *Times and Seasons* and the *Nauvoo Neighbor*, he included the article from the *Whig* and reproduced its full title.[290] The broadside followed suit.[291] Taylor's inclusion of the *Whig* title may have been an implicit acknowledgment that he believed the plates could indeed provide material for another sacred book. After all, the broadside also declared that the translation would be published in the *Times and Seasons* as soon as it was completed. In 1850, however, when Taylor printed a version of the broadside in the back of a proselytizing tract, he included only half of the original title from the Quincy *Whig*: "Singular Discovery." Presumably, Taylor reproduced the facsimiles because he still considered them evidence of the Book of Mormon but dropped the second half of the title—"Material for Another Mormon Book"—because Smith had died without ever producing a translation.[292]

If Smith ever did translate any more than the first character on the plates, he would have presumably continued as he had started. As Emmons explained

286. *JSP*-R5. See also *JSP*-R3.

287. Smith, *Joseph Smith's New Translation of the Bible*.

288. *JSP*-R4:191–293.

289. Decker and Hunt, *The God Makers*, 99.

290. "Ancient Records," *Times and Seasons*, 1 May 1843, 186; "Ancient Records," *Nauvoo Neighbor*, 10 May 1843, 2.

291. *A Brief Account of the Discovery of the Brass Plates*.

292. *Three Nights' Public Discussion between the Revds. C. W. Cleeve, James Robertson, and Philip Cater, and Elder John Taylor, of the Church of Jesus Christ of Latter-Day Saints, at Boulogne-Sur-Mer, France* (Liverpool: John Taylor, 1850), foldout following page 50.

it, Smith had "compared" the characters on the Kinderhook plates with those in "his Egyptian alphabet," had found them to be "the same characters," and would "therefore" be "able to decipher them." The implication was that any further decipherment would be done by the same method of ordinary translation.

CONCLUSION

When Joseph Smith began studying Hebrew, he had intended to become a "master" of languages, and in later years would occasionally "turn linguist" in the pulpit. He had in fact gained some rudimentary proficiency with Hebrew—as well as a smattering of German, Greek, and Latin. Nevertheless, he was still very much an amateur linguist in 1843 when he encountered the Kinderhook plates.

The foregoing analysis suggests a reconstruction of Joseph Smith's translation (and its aftermath) as follows: Examining the Kinderhook plates and their characters, Smith believed he saw similarities to the gold plates characters of the Book of Mormon or the papyri characters of the Book of Abraham (or both). Smith apparently believed that the Kinderhook plates were inscribed in Egyptian, or some form of Egyptian, or some closely related language for which it would be profitable to compare the characters on the plates with the characters in the Egyptian Alphabet book. Smith may also have sought to compare the Kinderhook characters with Hebrew characters. As when he approached his translation of the Book of Abraham—with a preliminary translation to determine the authorship of the papyri—Smith may have intended to attempt a preliminary translation of the Kinderhook plates to determine their authorship or basic content (or both). Surveying the plates, he searched for clues as to what might constitute the beginning of the record and noticed that one side of one of the plates had a heading that was significantly larger than the others, was comprised of characters instead of illustrative figures, and featured characters that were comparatively large.

Concentrating on the first character—apparently understood as a hieroglyphic character representing an entire word—Smith began searching through the Egyptian Alphabet book for a comparable character. A few pages into the book, Smith found a character similar in shape. The corresponding definition did not supply a personal name, but did apply well to an individual, providing information regarding the person's lineage, royal status, and divine blessings. The definition effectively situated the deceased person with whom the plates were found within Smith's scriptural cosmos. He concluded that he had arrived

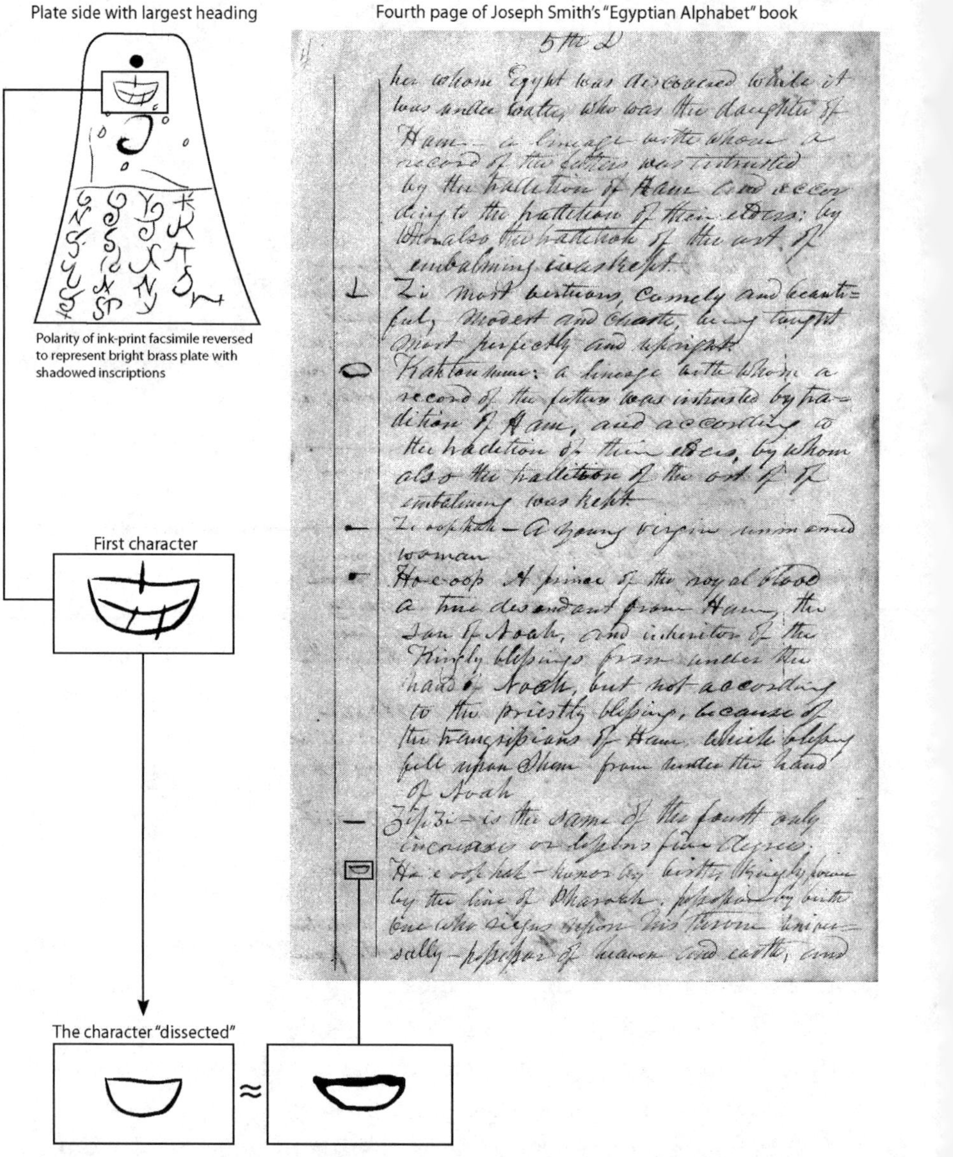

FIGURE 17.9. Comparison of characters from the Kinderhook plates and Joseph Smith's "Egyptian Alphabet." As shown in this diagram, Joseph Smith apparently identified a character in his "Egyptian Alphabet" book that was comparable to a prominent character from one of the Kinderhook plates. The definition for this character in the "Egyptian Alphabet" matches what Smith said about his translation of "a portion" of the plates. Don Bradley and Mark Ashurst-McGee.

at an adequate identification of the author of the plates and therefore deemed the definition valid and usable for translation. Smith slightly adapted the raw content of the provided definition to produce a sensible translation of the character (see Figure 17.9).

On 1 May 1843, William Clayton saw the Kinderhook plates at Smith's home and spoke with him about them. Smith informed Clayton that he had translated a portion of the plates and related the content of the translation. On 7 May, Sylvester Emmons and other men visited Smith at his home. Apostles William Smith and Willard Richards were probably already there and apostle Parley Pratt may have been there as well. When discussing the plates with the group of Mormons and non-Mormons, Smith showed them the plates, pointed out characters in the Egyptian Alphabet book comparable to those on the plates, and shared his preliminary translation of a character. Soon thereafter, John Taylor published news of the discovery of the plates in the Nauvoo newspapers, declaring that they would help "prove the authenticity of the Book of Mormon" and expressing his confidence in Smith's ability to translate them. The following month, he indicated in the broadside of print facsimiles that Smith would provide such a translation. Presumably this was motivated in part by the financial aim of increasing subscriptions to the church newspaper (as with the promises of further installments from the Book of Abraham), but must have also been based on some actual expectation. However, Smith was murdered before ever returning to either the Book of Abraham or the Kinderhook plates.

Thus, the Kinderhook plates neither prove the authenticity of the Book of Mormon (though they may have helped convert John Van Cott and others) nor provide a proof-text for exposing Joseph Smith as a false prophet (though they do reveal an amateur linguist). The Kinderhook plates episode, however, does provide a glimpse into the mental universe of Joseph Smith and other early Latter-day Saints. They inhabited a providential cosmos and continent that had been previously inhabited by peoples brought there by the Lord, with prophets and kings among them who had kept records and had buried them in the earth to come forth in the last days.

CONTRIBUTORS

Mark Ashurst-McGee is senior historian in the Church History Department of the Church of Jesus Christ of Latter-day Saints and the senior research and review editor for the Joseph Smith Papers Project. He is a coeditor of *Foundational Texts of Mormonism: Examining Major Early Sources* and five volumes of *The Joseph Smith Papers*. His writings have appeared in several scholarly journals, including *Mormon Studies Review* and *Journal of Mormon History*.

Christopher James Blythe is a research associate at Laura F. Willes Center for Book of Mormon Studies, Neal A. Maxwell Institute for Religious Scholarship, Brigham Young University. He is coeditor of two volumes of *The Joseph Smith Papers*. His writings have appeared in several scholarly journals, including the *Journal of Book of Mormon Studies*, the *Journal of Religion*, *Journal of the Bible and Its Reception*, and *Nova Religio*.

Don Bradley is an independent historian specializing in Latter-day Saint history and scripture. His writing has appeared in *Sunstone* magazine and he is the assistant author, with Brian C. Hales, of *Joseph Smith's Polygamy*.

Samuel Morris Brown is associate professor of critical care medicine and medical ethics and humanities at the University of Utah School of Medicine. His books include *In Heaven as It Is on Earth: Joseph Smith and the Early Mormon Conquest of Death* and *Joseph Smith's Translation: The Words and Worlds of Mormonism*. His historical writings have also appeared in *Church History*, *Journal of the Early Republic*, and *Journal of Mormon History*.

Richard Lyman Bushman is Gouverneur Morris Professor of History Emeritus at Columbia University, and more recently Howard W. Hunter Chair of Mormon Studies at Claremont Graduate University. His several books include *From Puritan to Yankee: Character and the Social Order in Connecticut, 1690–1765*; *The Refinement of America: Persons, Houses, Cities*; *Joseph Smith: Rough Stone Rolling*; and *The American Farmer in the Eighteenth Century: A Social and Cultural History*.

Rachel Cope is associate professor of church history and doctrine at Brigham Young University. She is the lead series editor of the Mormon Studies Series through Fairleigh Dickinson University Press and one of the founding editors of the Transcribing Early American Manuscript Sermons project. She is coeditor of *Family Life in England and America, 1690–1820*. Her writings have also appeared in several scholarly journals, including *New York History* and *Journal of Spirituality*.

Gerrit Dirkmaat is assistant professor of church history and doctrine at Brigham Young University. He also serves as editor of *Mormon Historical Studies*. He is the coauthor, with Michael Hubbard MacKay, of *From Darkness unto Light: Joseph Smith's Translation and Publication of the Book of Mormon* and is a coeditor for four volumes of *The Joseph Smith Papers*. His writings have also appeared in several scholarly journals, including *Brigham Young University Studies Quarterly*.

Amy Easton-Flake is assistant professor of ancient scripture at Brigham Young University. She is coeditor of *Mormon Women's History: Beyond Biography*. Her writings have appeared in several scholarly venues, including *New England Quarterly* and *Women's History Review*.

Nicholas J. Frederick is assistant professor of ancient scripture at Brigham Young University. His is the author of *The Bible, Mormon Scripture, and the Rhetoric of Allusivity* and the coauthor, with Michael Hubbard MacKay, of *Joseph Smith's Seer Stones*. His articles have been published in the *Journal of the Bible and its Reception* and the *Journal of Book of Mormon Studies*.

David Golding is a historian and writer in the Church History Department of the Church of Jesus Christ of Latter-day Saints. His work has been published in *World Religions and Their Missions*.

Matthew J. Grey is associate professor of ancient scripture at Brigham Young University. He is a coeditor of *Approaching Antiquity: Joseph Smith and the Ancient World*. His writings have appeared in the *Journal for the Study of Judaism in the Persian, Hellenistic, and Roman Period* and the *Journal of Roman Archaeology*.

David W. Grua is a historian and documentary editor for the Joseph Smith Papers in the Church History Department of the Church of Jesus Christ of

Latter-day Saints, where he specializes in the Mormon experience in Missouri, Joseph Smith's legal papers, and Mormon-Indian relations. He is the author of *Surviving Wounded Knee: The Lakotas and the Politics of Memory*. His writings have been published in several scholarly journals, including *The American Historical Review* and *Journal of Mormon History*.

Grant Hardy is professor of history and religious studies at the University of North Carolina at Asheville. He is the author of several books, including *Understanding the Book of Mormon: A Reader's Guide*. He is the editor of *The Book of Mormon: A Reader's Edition* and a study edition of the Book of Mormon, published by the Neal A. Maxwell Institute for Religious Scholarship and the Religious Studies Center at Brigham Young University. He is also coeditor of the first volume of the *Oxford History of Historical Writing*.

Brian M. Hauglid is associate professor and visiting fellow at the Neal A. Maxwell Institute for Religious Scholarship at Brigham Young University. His books include *A Textual History of the Book of Abraham: Manuscripts and Editions*. He is also a coeditor, with Robin Scott Jensen, of the *Book of Abraham and Related Manuscripts* volume of *The Joseph Smith Papers*. He has also contributed to the *Encyclopedia of the Bible and its Reception*. He has served as editor of the *Journal of Book of Mormon Studies* and *Studies in the Bible and Antiquity*, published by the Maxwell Institute.

Jared Hickman is associate professor of English at Johns Hopkins University. He is author of *Black Prometheus: Race and Radicalism in the Age of Atlantic Slavery* and a coeditor of *Abolitionist Places* and *Americanist Approaches to The Book of Mormon*. His work has also appeared in *American Literature*; *Early American Literature*; and *Nineteenth-Century Literature*, as well as several other scholarly venues.

Michael Hubbard MacKay is associate professor of church history and doctrine at Brigham Young University. His books include *Sacred Space: Exploring the Birthplace of Mormonism* and *Joseph Smith's Seer Stones*. He is a coeditor for volume 1 of the Documents series of *The Joseph Smith Papers* and has been published in several scholarly journals, including *Mormon Historical Studies*.

William V. Smith is emeritus professor of mathematics at Brigham Young University. He is the author of *Textual Studies of the Doctrine and Covenants:*

The Plural Marriage Revelation. His historical writings have appeared in *Foundational Texts of Mormonism: Examining Major Early Sources* and in several scholarly journals, including *Dialogue: A Journal of Mormon Thought*.

Ann Taves is professor of religious studies at University of California, Santa Barbara. Her books include *Fits, Trances, and Visions: Experiencing Religion and Explaining Experience from Wesley to James*; *Religious Experience Reconsidered: A Building-Block Approach to the Study of Religion and Other Special Things*; and *Revelatory Events: Three Case Studies of the Emergence of New Spiritual Paths*.

Thomas A. Wayment is professor of classics at Brigham Young University. He is the author, with Lincoln Blumell, of *Christian Oxyrhynchus: Texts, Documents, and Sources*. He has been published in several scholarly venues, including *Foundational Texts of Mormonism: Examining Major Early Sources* and *Approaching Antiquity: Joseph Smith and the Ancient World*.

Haley Wilson-Lemmon is a graduate student in early Christian studies at the University of Notre Dame. Her research focuses on understanding the development of early Christianity in its Greco-Roman context.

INDEX

Page numbers in *italics* indicate illustrations. Use of "Smith" without a first name or initial references Joseph Smith.